THE BOMBAY FLORA

THE BOMBAY FLORA

OR,

SHORT DESCRIPTIONS

OF ALL

THE INDIGENOUS PLANTS

HITHERTO DISCOVERED IN OR NEAR THE BOMBAY PRESIDENCY;

TOGETHER WITH

A SUPPLEMENT OF INTRODUCED AND NATURALISED SPECIES

NICHOLAS A. DALZELL, M. A.

AND

ALEXANDER GIBSON, F. L. S.

GYAN

Published by

Gyan Publishing House
5, Ansari Road
Daryaganj, New Delhi-110002
Phone: 011-47034999, 9811692060
E-mail: books@gyanbooks.com

Distribution Network
gyanbooks.com
India, USA, Canada, UK, Australia, France

ISBN: 978-81-212-8354-0 (PB)
First Published, 1861

2nd Impression 2023

Printed at: Gyan Press, Delhi.

THE BOMBAY FLORA
Authors: NICHOLAS A. DALZELL, ALEXANDER GIBSON

THE BOMBAY FLORA:

OR,

SHORT DESCRIPTIONS

OF ALL

THE INDIGENOUS PLANTS

HITHERTO DISCOVERED IN OR NEAR THE BOMBAY PRESIDENCY;

TOGETHER WITH

A SUPPLEMENT OF INTRODUCED AND NATURALISED SPECIES.

BY

NICHOLAS A. DALZELL, M.A.,

AND

ALEXANDER GIBSON, F.L.S.

Bombay:
PRINTED AT THE
EDUCATION SOCIETY'S PRESS, BYCULLA.

1861.

PREFACE.

In presenting to the Public the accompanying "Flora" of the Bombay Presidency, the Authors may be allowed to express the hope that it will be found to supply a want much felt by the increasing number of young Botanists, as well as others of an inquiring turn of mind.

Great have been the advances made in the knowledge of Indian Plants since the date of Mr. Graham's Catalogue, and it will be seen that researches throughout the Jungle Districts of our Presidency, for which the Authors have enjoyed the best opportunities, have tended to enrich our "Flora" in no ordinary degree.

Very many new species of Plants have been discovered, and, in addition to a greater degree of precision in the nomenclature, and a more accurate determination of species already known, an obvious improvement has been made in the separation of all Plants not truly indigenous.

Introduced, cultivated, and naturalised species seem to belong more properly to horticulture and rural economy, and such will be found in Part No. 2.

This has been framed, as in Mr. Graham's list—from which, indeed, many of the descriptions are taken—partly on the basis of the Linnæan system, as it was deemed probable, that as the students and alumni of our colleges can but seldom enjoy the opportunity of extending their researches beyond the limits of the public and other gardens in or near Bombay and Poona, it is to them of much importance to have every facility for the identification of Plants and Trees.

In conclusion, the Authors are far from supposing their work as free from errors, or that the lists are even complete; and they may mention, for the encouragement of the young and ardent explorers of nature anxious to make discoveries, that the field is not yet exhausted;—that new species of Plants have been found while the last sheets were passing through the Press. The Cryptogamic portion of the Catalogue has, in order to meet the present wants of our Readers, been literally transcribed from that of Mr. Graham; but we hope on a future opportunity to be able to present it to the Public in a more complete and enlarged form.

No. I.

CATALOGUE OF PLANTS INDIGENOUS TO WESTERN INDIA IN AND NEAR THE BOMBAY PRESIDENCY.

I. RANUNCULACEÆ.

1. NARAVELIA, DC.

1. N. ZEYLANICA, DC. *syst.* 1, 167. *Prod.* 1, 10.—Climbing; leaves broadly ovate, shortly acuminate, cordate or rounded at the base, pubescent or tomentose beneath, rarely glabrous, surmounted by tendrils; petals linear spathulate. Syn. Atragene Zeylanica, Linn. Rox. Cor. Pl *t.* 188, Flor Ind. ii, 670. Hab. Southern Ghauts only.

2. CLEMATIS, Linn.

1. C. SMILACIFOLIA, Wall. in As. Research. xiii, 414.—Climbing, quite smooth; leaves very large, simple or ternate partite, generally entire, purple beneath, 5 to 10 inches long; panicles elongated, many-flowered; sepals oblong, acute, spreading or reflexed. DC. *Prod.* 1, 10; Hook. Bot. Mag. *t.* 4259; Syn. C. munroiana, Wight. Illus. 1, 5; C. affinis. Wight Ill. 1, 5; C. subpeltata, Wall. Pl As. Rar. *t.* 20; C. smilacina Blume. Bijdr. i. Hab. Phoonda Ghaut.

2. C. TRILOBA, Heyne, in Roth. nov. sp. 251.—Climbing, all softly silky; leaves small, on longish petioles, simple or ternately divided, elliptic or ovate. Hab. Mawul districts; flowers in September; the flowers are large and white. Native name "Moriel" or "Ranjàe."

3. C. GOURIANA, Rox. Fl Ind. ii, 670.—Climbing; all over smooth, except the younger parts; leaves very various, pinnately or bi-pinnately divided; segments ovate or oblong acuminate, membranaceous, shining on the upper surface; panicles decompound, many-flowered; flowers small, appear in October. In thickets on the Ghauts; pretty common.

4. C. WIGHTIANA, Wall. Cat. 4674.—Pubescent; leaves pinnate, segments broadly ovate, 3-lobed, 2 to 3 inches long, sometimes 5-lobed, coarsely toothed, densely hairy beneath; panicles longer than the leaves, decompound; seeds ovate, compressed, very silky. W. and A. *Prod.* 1, 2; Wight. Ic. 935. On the highest Ghauts, Mahableshwur, &c.

3. THALICTRUM, Linn.

1. T. Dalzellii, Hook. Ic. Pl *t.* 856.—A rigid plant, one foot high; leaves ternately divided; leaflets large rounded, kidney-shaped, deeply cordate, crevato-lobate; panicle small, flowers in clusters; seeds oblong, furrowed. East side of Hurrychunder.

4. DELPHINIUM, Linn.

1. D. Dasycaulon, Fresen. Mus. Senkenb. ii, 272.—Stem branched, with few leaves; leaves radical, large, round reniform, broadly 5-lobed lobes again 3-lobed and deeply cut; stem leaves 5-divided; racemes lax elongated; flowers of a beautiful blue, very showy. Near Jooneer; found also in Abyssinia. Flowers in August and September.

II. DILLENIACEÆ.

1. Dillenia, Linn. Speciosa. Thunb. Linn. Trans. i, 200.—A middle-sized tree; leaves petioled, oblong or lanceolate acute, sharply serrated, 8 to 10 inches long; flowers large, 6 to 9 inches in diameter, solitary; fruit large, round, smooth, size of a cocoanut. S. Concan, at Banda, in the Warree country, Alibaug. Syn. D. elliptica Thunb. loc. cit.; DC. *Prod.* 1, 76; D. Indica, Linn. sp. 765; Syalita Rheede Mal. iii, *t.* 38, 39. Maratha name "Mota Kurmul." The leaves of the calyx have an agreeable acid flavour, and are eaten, Graham; when added to syrup, useful as a cough-mixture; the fruit has a disagreeable odour.

2. Pentagyna, Roxb. Cor. Pl 1, *t.* 20.—A middle-sized tree; leaves very large, 2 to 4 feet long, oblong lanceolate acute, narrowing towards the base, denticulate; when old, glabrous; flowers on the branches, when leafless, in clusters, yellow, small; appear in April; fruit size of a gooseberry, edible. Southern Maratha Country and thinly about the Ghauts, up to lat. 19°. Syn. D. Augusta and Pilosa Rox. Fl Ind. ii, 652; Colbertia Coromandeliana, DC. *Prod.* 1, 75. The leaves are used at Poona as a substratum for thatched roofs. These two species are remarkable for the grandeur of their foliage, and the showiness of their flowers.

III. ANONACEÆ.

1. SAGERAEA, Dalzell.

1. S. Laurina, Dalz. in Hook. Jour. Bot. iii, 307.—An elegant middle-sized laurel-looking tree; leaves 5 to 7 inches long, linear oblong; flowers white, about one inch in diameter; carpels globose, smooth, 6-seeded; flowers in October and November. Hab. Concans. Yields a valuable reddish timber. Syn. Guatteria laurifolia, Grah. Cat. Bomb. Pl p. 4. Native name "Sajeree."

2. UVARIA, Linn.

1. U. Lurida, Hook. F. and Thoms. Fl Ind. i, 101.—A climbing shrub; leaves 6 to 9 inches long, oblong lanceolate, shining above, paler beneath; flowers at the tops of the branchlets, solitary or twin, luridly purple, 2 inches in diameter; fruit unknown; flowers in November. Hab. Southern Ghauts.

2. U. Narum, Wall. Cat. 6473.—A climbing shrub; leaves oblong lanceolate, or linear oblong, smooth on both sides; flowers terminal, subsolitary, reddish or ferruginous, 1½ inch in diameter; carpels ovoid obtuse, on longish stalks, numerous, smooth. Wight. Illus. i, *t.* 6; Syn. U. Zeylanica, Lam.; Unona narum, Dunal. Hab. Parwar and neighbouring Ghauts.

3. UNONA, Linn.

1. U. Dunalii, Wall. Cat. 6435.—Climbing; leaves oblong or oblong lanceolate, somewhat membranaceous, smooth on both sides or slightly pubescent beneath; peduncles axillary and terminal; flowers pale-yellow; sepals broad ovate; petals lanceolate, with a broad base; carpels with 1 to 3 articulations. Concan, Dr. Stocks, Hook. and Thoms, Fl Ind. i, p 132.

2. U. Lawii, Hook. Fil. and Thoms. Fl Ind.—Leaves oblong lanceolate, thinly coriaceous, slightly puberulous or smooth above, glaucous and pubescent beneath; peduncles slender, about opposite to the leaves, outer petals 2¼ inches long, pubescent, linear; closely resembles the following, but distinguished by the narrow petals. Hab. Concan, Law.

3. U. Discolor, Vahl. Symb. ii, 63, *t.* 36.—A shrub; leaves oblong lanceolate, 2 to 8 inches long, shining above, glaucous, smooth or scarcely pubescent beneath; petals lanceolate, 2 inches long, a little silky; carpels with 1 to 6 articulations. Hab. Sivapore, in the Warree country; in fruit in February. Syn. Uvaria chinensis, DC. *syst.*; U. Amherstiana, A., DC. mem.; U. biglandulosa, Bulm. Bijdr.; U. undulata, Wall. Pl as. rar. *t.* 265; U. cordifolia, Rox. Fl Ind. ii, 662?

4. U. Farinosa, Dalz. in Hook. Jour. Bot. iii, 207.—A tree; leaves 2½ to 4 inches long, ovate, lanceolate, obtusely acuminate, pellucid dotted, coriaceous, sparingly pubescent beneath; flowers axillary subsessile; petals oblong lanceolate, villous, feeling like woollen-cloth; carpels 5 to 6, oval obtuse. Between Parwar Ghaut and Tullaware; flowers in March. Syn. Uvaria mollis, Wall. Cat. 6475.

4. GUATTERIA, Ruiz. and Pavon.

1. G. Cerasoides, Dunal. anon. 28.—A tree; leaves lanceolate, or oblong lanceolate, pubescent beneath; pedicles, 1 to 3, on the

apex of a tubercle, like peduncle; fruit size of a cherry, dark-red, slightly hairy, ⅓-inch long. Thull Ghaut, Jowar forests; flowers in February and March. Syn. Uvaria cerasoides, Roxb. Fl Cor. *t.* 32, Ind. ii, 666. Native name "Hoom."

2. G. Fragrans, Dalz. in Hook. Jour. Bot. iii, 206.—A tree; leaves oblong lanceolate, oval or ovate, sometimes obovate, 4 to 9 inches long, strongly nerved; peduncles short, stout, much-branched, many-flowered; petals narrow linear, yellow, very fragrant; carpels large, ovoid, hoary, ash-coloured, long-stalked. Jungles at Sivapore, Warree country.

5. SACCOPETALUM, Bennet.

1. S. Tomentosum, Hook. Fil. and Thoms. Flor. Ind. i, 152.—A tree; leaves oval or ovate oblong, acute, pubescent on both sides; pedicles slender, elongated, three exterior petals very minute, all covered on the inside with white tomentum; carpels subglobose, one inch long, fulvous, tomentose. Hab. Tulkut Ghaut. Syn. Uvaria tomentosa, Rox. Cor. Pl *t.* 35.; Flor. Ind. ii, 667.

IV. MYRISTICACEÆ.

1. MYRISTICA, Linn.

1. M. Attenuata. Wall. Cat. 6791, Hook. and Thoms. Fl Ind. i, p 157.—A tall tree; branches slightly scurfy; leaves oblong lanceolate, long attenuated, acute or rounded at the base, glaucous beneath; peduncles axillary, few-flowered, disc flat, 12-lobed; fruit oval or oblong, 1½ inch long, covered with tawny tomentum, aril very thin. The Ghauts. M. Amygdalina, Graham Cat. p 175; Wallich's specimens were received from Heyne.

2. M. Malabarica, Lam. Aet. Paris, 1788, p 162.—A tall tree; branchlets glabrous, with a smooth, reddish bark; leaves narrow oblong, or elliptic lanceolate, male inflorescence axillary, dichotomously cymose, many-flowered; flowers loosely umbellate; fruit oblong, with a tawny hoariness, 2½ to 3 inches long. Dense woods of the Ghauts. Flowers November to February. Blume. Rumph. i, 185; M. dactyloides, Wall. Cat. 6786; Rheed. Hort. Mal. iv, *t.* 5.

V. MENISPERMACEÆ.

1. ANAMIRTA, Colebrooke.

1. Cocculus, W. and A. *Prod.* 1, 466.—A twining shrub, with thick corky bark; leaves exactly cordate, glabrous, 4 to 8 inches long; petioles elongated; panicles pendulous from the thicker branches

above a foot long, many-flowered; flowers rather large; drupes glabrous. Concan; common. Syn. Menispermum cocculus, Linn. sp. 1468; M. heteroclitum, Rox. Fl Ind. iii, 817; Cocculus lacunosus, DC. *syst.* 1, 519; *Prod.* 1, 97.; C. suberosus, DC. *syst.* 1, 519; W. and A. *Prod.* 1, 11; C. populi folius, DC. *Prod.* 1, 97.

2. TINOSPORA, Miers.

1. Malabarica, Miers in Taylor's Annals, Ser. ii vii, 38.—Leaves cordate, ovate, slightly or densely pubescent beneath; a climbing shrub, with ash-coloured bark, young parts with whitish hairs; leaves 7-nerved, 3 to 6 inches long, and nearly as broad; racemes as long as the leaf; flowers green; ripe drupes red. The Concan. Menispermum malabaricum, Lam. Willd.; Cocculus Malabaricus, DC. *syst.* 1, 518., *Prod.* 1, 97; Rheed. Mal. vii, *t.* 19.

2. T. Cordifolia, Miers in Taylor's Annals, Ser. 2, vii 38.—A twining shrub, with scabrous corky bark, and broad cordate leaves on longish petioles; racemes axillary, solitary; flowers yellow, small; drupe size of a small cherry, red. Concan. Syn. Menispermum malabaricum, B. Lam. Dict. iv, 96; M. cordifolium, Willd. Roxb. Flor Ind. iii, 811; Cocculus cordifolius, DC. *syst.* 1, 518. *Prod.* 197. Stems sold in the bazars under the name of "Gulo," the Guluncha of Bengal, and is useful in fevers.

3. COCCULUS, DC.

1. Macrocarpus. W. and A. *Prod.* 1, 13.—Shrubby, climbing; bark ash-coloured, wrinkled; leaves rounded or reniform, cordate or truncate at the base, shining, 5-nerved, quite smooth, glaucous beneath; panicles long-branched, many-flowered; drupes obovate oblong, an inch long. Jungles in the Concan. Syn. Diploclisia macrocarpa, Miers in Ann. Nat. Hist., Ser. ii vii, 42.

2. C. Villosus, DC. *Prod.* 1, 98.—Leaves oval oblong, sub-deltoid, villous; male panicles abbreviated, female flowers 1 to 3 in the axils, small, yellow; drupes dark-purple when ripe, of which ink is made, according to Roxb., and a decoction of the roots a substitute for sarsaparilla. Very common in hedges. Syn. C. sepium, Coleb. in Linn. Trans. xiii, 58; C. hastatus, DC. *Prod.* 1, 98; Menispermum hirsatum, Linn. Roxb. Fl Ind. iii, 814; M. Myosotoides.

4. CISSAMPELOS, Linn.

1. Pareira, Linn. Spec. Pl 1473.—Climbing; leaves reniform or rounded or broadly cordate, more or less pubescent; male cymes long-peduncled, many-flowered, hairy; female racemes with large round bracts; drupes subglobose hirsute; flowers yellowish, very

small. Common in hedges; flowers in the rains. Syn. Caapeba, Linn. sp. 1473, Rox. Fl Ind. iii, 842; C. convolvulacea, Willd. DC. *Prod.* 1, 101; Roxb. Fl Ind. iii, 842, with 18 others.

5. CYCLEA, Arnott.

1. Burmanni, Miers in Taylor's Annals.—Leaves peltate elongatedeltoid acuminated, cordate at the base, shining above; panicles as long as or longer than the leaves, many-flowered, pubescent, male flowers twice as large as in the following specie; calyx inflated, subglobose, 6 to 8-lobed; corolla a half smaller, scarcely lobed. Hilly parts of the Concan and Ghauts; flowers in January. Syn. Cocculus burmanni, DC. *Prod.* 1, 96; Clypea burmanni, W. and A. *Prod.* 1, in part only.

2. Peltata, H. Fil. et T.—Leaves peltate deltoid, slightly cordate at the base; calyx companulate, 4-lobed; petals half the length, united into a 4-lobed cup. Concan. Syn. Menispermum pellatum, Lam.; Cocculus peltattus, DC. *Prod*, 1, 96; Clypea burmanni, W. and A. *Prod.* 1, 14, in part; Rheed. Mal. vii, *t.* 49.

6. STEPHANIA, Lourciro.

1. Hernandifolia, Walp. Rep. 1. 96.—Climbing shrub; branches striated, glabrous; leaves ovate or sub-deltoid, truncate or slightly cordate at the base, pale or glaucous beneath; peduncles axillary, umbelled at the apex; sepals obovate obtuse; petals a half smaller. Concan. Syn. Cissampelos hernandifolia, Willd; Clypea hernandifolia, W. and A. *Prod.* 1, 14; Wight. Ic. *t.* 939; Cissampelos discolor, DC. *Prod.* 1, 101; C. hexandra, Rox. Fl Ind. iii, 842.

VI. NYMPHAEACEÆ.

1. NYMPHAEA, Linn.

1. Lotus, Linn. sp. Pl 729.—Leaves sharply sinuate dentate, pubescent beneath; sepals oblong obtuse, 5 to 7-ribbed; petals linear or ovate oblong, filaments broadly dilated at the base; anthers without appendages; appendages of the stigma cylindric clavate; flowers large, red, rose-coloured, or white. Tanks in the Concan. Syn. N. rubra, Rox. Fl Ind. ii, 576; N. edulis, Rox. loc. cit. 578; N. pubescens, Willd. sp. Pl. ii, 1154.

2. Stellata, Willd. sp. Pl ii, 1153.—Leaves orbicular or elliptic-orbicular, obtusely sinuate dentate, or entire; sepals nerved, but not ribbed; petals linear oblong or lanceolate acute, or narrowed at the apex; anthers with long appendages; rays of the stigma with short horns without appendages; flowers blue, white, rose-coloured,

or purple. Very common. Syn. N. cyanea, Roxb. Fl Ind. iii, 577.; N. versi color, Roxb. Fl Ind. ii, 577.

VII. NELUMBIACEÆ.

1. NELUMBIUM.

1. N. SPECIOSUM, Willd. sp. Pl ii, 1288.—Leaves 1 to 2 feet in diameter, peltate, smooth, paler beneath, with prominent veins, margins slightly waved; flowers white or rose-coloured, half a foot in diameter; fruit turbinate, with a flat top, containing many edible nuts. Roxb. Fl Ind. 647; Syn. N. ascaticum, Rich. Ann. mus. xvii 249, *t.* 19, *fig* 2.; Nelumbo nucifera, Gaertn. *fr* i, 73, *t.* 19, *fig* 2. In tanks; pretty common; flowers in the rains. Native name "Kummul." Well described by Herodotus, who saw it in Egypt, where it no longer exists. The roots are a native vegetable in Sind. "Kummul" of the Marathas.

VIII. FUMARIACEÆ.

1. FUMARIA, Linn.

1. F. PARVIFLORA, Lam. Dict. ii, 567, variety Vaillantii.—From a span to two feet high; leaves much divided; flowers small, rose-coloured; fruit globose, smooth. W. and A. *Prod.* i, 18; Wight. Illus. *t.* 11, Roxb. Fl Ind. iii, 217. Deccan and Khandeish; pretty common, flowering in the cold weather.

IX. CRUCIFERÆ.

1. CARDAMINE, Linn.

1. C. HIRSUTA, Linn. sp. 915, variety Subumbellata.—Six inches high; leaves pinnately divided, leaflets, 5 to 7, coarsely toothed; flowers somewhat corymbose, few, yellow, minute; pods linear acute, about 1 inch long. On hills near Belgaum; flowers in July.

X. CAPPARIDEÆ.

1. GYNANDROPSIS, DC.

1. PENTAPHYLLA, DC.—An annual erect plant, covered with glandular pubescence; leaves 3 to 5 foliolate, leaflets obovate; flowers white. A common weed in waste places. Syn. G. affinis, Blume; Cleome pentaphylla, Linn.; Rumph Amt. v, *t.* 96, *fig* 3; Torr. and Gr. Fl N. Am. i, 121.

2. CLEOME, Linn.

1. MONOPHYLLA, Linn.—Herbaceous pubescent; leaves simple lanceolate; siliqua puberulous, round and striated; flowers pink. A common weed.

2. BURMANNI, W. and A. *Prod.* 1, 22.—Herbaceous, glabrous; leaves trifoliolate; leaflets obovate; siliqua terete glabrous. A weed. Syn. Polanisia dodecandra, DC. *Prod.* 1, p. 242; Burm. Zeyl. *t.* 100, *fig* 1.

3. POLANISIA, Rafin.

1. ICOSANDRA, W. and A.—Glandular viscid; leaves 3 to 5 foliolate; leaflets obovate pubescent; siliqua round striated, rough, with glandular hairs. A weed. Syn. P. viscosa B., DC. *Prod.*; Cleome icosandra, Linn; C. viscosa, Linn.; Rumph. Amb. v, *t.* 96, *fig* 2; Burm. Zeyl. *t.* 99.

2. P. SIMPLICIFOLIA, Camb. in Jacq. Voy. iv 20, *t.* 20.—Branches spreading, all rough, hairy; leaves simple obovate or oblong mucronulate; flowers axillary, solitary, purple; silique subcylindric, torulose glabrous, pointed with the style; seeds scabrous, brown. Common in the Poona Collectorate; flowers in July and August.

3. CHELIDONII, DC. *Prod.* 2, p 242.—Stem hispid; leaves, 7 to 9, foliolate; leaflets obovate or oblong hispid; flowers-rose coloured; siliqua glabrous, terete, sessile. Syn. P. Schraderi, DC. Fl Rar. Hort. Gen. fasc. 3, p 57.; P. Leschenaultii, DC. loc. cit.; Cleome chelidonii, Linn. Moist places in the Deccan, Bojapoor, on the road to Poona.

4. CRATAEVA, Linn.

1. ROXBURGHII, Br.—A small tree, with 3 foliolate leaves; leaflets obovate acuminate; fruit woody, globose, scurfy, like that of Feronia. Banks of the Nerbudda, near Chandode, Warree jungles. Syn. C. odora., Ham. in Linn. trans.; C. religioso, Ham. loc. cit.; Capparis 3 folia, Roxb. Fl Ind.

2. NURVALA, Ham.—Leaflets ovate lanceolate acuminate, in other respects much like the last, only the fruit is more oblong; flowers in February. Caranjah Hill, Warree country. This species is the true Varvunna.

5. NIEBHURIA, DC.

1. OBLONGIFOLIA, DC.—A climbing shrub; leaves simple, oval, oblong; fruit elongated and constricted between the seeds, resembling a necklace. Flowers and fruit in November. Syn. N. arenaria, DC. *Prod.*; Capparis hetero clita, Rox. Fl Ind.; Crataeva oblongifolia, Sprengel. In hedges in Gujerat and Deccan.

6. CADABA, Forsk.

C. Indica, Lam.—A small shrub, with small oblong glabrous leaves; flowers terminal, whitish; siliqua linear. Syn. Cleome fruticosa, Linn.; Strœmia tetrandra, Vahl.; Roxb. Fl Ind. ii, p 678. Guzerat and the Deccan.

7. CAPPARIS, Linn.

1. Brevispina, DC.—A thorny shrub, with linear lanceolate or oval leaves; pedicles axillary solitary, one-flowered; fruit globular, bright scarlet, 1½ inch in diameter. Western Deccan, banks of nullahs, &c., near Vingorla. Syn. C. acuminata, Roxb. Fl Ind. ii, p 566; C. Rheed. DC. *Prod.* 1, p 246; C. rotundifolia, Rottl. and Willd. DC. *Prod.* ii, p 245. "Wagutty" of the Marathas. Hook. Ic. Pl *t.* 126.

2. Roxburghii, DC.—A shrub; leaves elliptic oblong obtuse; racemes terminal corymbiform; flowers large, white, handsome; fruit bright scarlet, 3 inches in diameter. Syn. C. corymbosa, Roxb. Hort. Beng., p 93, Fl Ind. ii, 569; C. aguba, Roxb. in E. I. C. mus. *t.* 158. On the Ghauts. Maratha name "Poorwi." The unripe fruit when fresh cut smells like cresses.

3. Pedunculosa, Wall.—Leaves roundish ovate, cordate at the base, nearly sessile; stipules thorny, hooked; pedicles and calyx glabrous; umbels 2 to 5-flowered, sessile terminal; fruit globose, with several seeds. Vide Hook. Ic. 128. Mahableshwur, and in the thickest jungles generally.

4. Murrayana, I. Grah. Cat. Bom. Pl.—A diffuse prostrate shrub, with short recurved orange-coloured thorns; leaves small, roundish; flowers white, large and showy; anthers purple; berry oblong, many-seeded. Wight Ic. 379. At Mahableshwur, and in most nullas and rivers, but along the ghauts as far north as the Malsej.

5. Formosa, Dalz. in Hook. Jour. Bot. ii, p 41.—Shrubby, erect, unarmed; leaves ovate or oblong, acute at both ends, or lanceolate, younger ones covered with a stellate tomentum, easily wiped off, older ones coriaceous glabrous, reticulately veined, shining, 5 inches long; racemes corymbiform, few-flowered; flowers large, handsome, pale-blue, with a round yellow spot in the middle. Chorla ghaut; flowers in April. Syn. C. cœrulea, Heyne.

6. Tener, Dalz. in loc. cit.—Shrubby, branched, glabrous; stipules short, thorny, hooked; leaves short-petioled ovate lanceolate, glabrous, membranaceous, transparent; pedicles axillary, solitary filiform, one-flowered, shorter than the leaf; flowers small. On the Ghauts; rare, leaves 2 inches long.

7. Aphylla, Roxb.—A large straggling much-branched shrub or small tree; leaves on the young shoots only, linear subulate;

flowers red; fruit globular, size of a small cherry. Common in Guzerat and Deccan in waste places.

8. HORRIDA, Linn.—Thorns hooked; leaves elliptic oblong and ovate, with a long mucro, younger ones only densely pubescent; pedicles supra-axillary in a vertical line; flowers conspicuous by their long purple filaments; flowers in February. Syn. C. terniflora, DC. *Prod.* 1, p 274; C. quadriflora, DC. *Prod.*; C. zeylanica, Roxb. Fl Ind. 2, p 567. Very common in hedges.

9. SEPIARIA, Linn.—Shrubby; stipules thorny; leaves roundish ovate or broad-elliptical, corymbs many-flowered, sessile; flowers small, white; fruit black, size of a pea; very common.

10. C. STYLOSA, DC. *Prod.* 1, p 246.—A shrub or small tree; stipules thorny, short, nearly straight; leaves linear lanceolate, or elliptic mucronate; pedicles short, stout, axillary solitary, one-flowered; flowers rather large, green; ovarium smooth, oblong, furrowed; fruit size of a billiard-ball, scarlet, warted, with 6 ridges. Syn. C. divaricata, Wight. Ic. 889. Our plant agrees perfectly with Wight's figure and with W. and A.'s description of Stylosa, except in the globose ovary ascribed by them to Stylosa. Common all over the Deccan.

11. C. GRANDIS, Linn.—A small tree, covered all over with a grey or fulvous tomentum; stipules wart-like, or wanting; leaves rhomboid-ovate, sometimes smooth above; corymbs terminal, many-flowered, berry globose, 2-seeded, a little larger than a cherry. Sparingly found in the Ghants and Deccan; flowers in May. In the Forts of Sholapore and Meruj. Syn. We believe this to be identical with C. bisperma, Roxb., a fact suspected by Roxburgh himself. Syn. C. racemifera, DC. *Prod.* 1, p 248; C. maxima, Heyne in Roth. nov. sp., p 237; DC. *Prod.* 1, p 248. Native name "Puchownda."

XI. FLACOURTIANEÆ.

1. FLACOURTIA, Commerson.

1. RAMONTCHI, L'Her.—A tree; thorns few, naked; leaves roundish ovate or oblong; flowers diœcious; stigmas 5 to 9. F sapida, Roxb. Found wild on the Chorla ghaut; in fruit in April; racemes terminal. Wight Ic. *t.* 85.

2. CATAPHRACTA, Willd.—A tree, trunk armed with large multiple thorns; berry size of a small plum, purple, with very hard sharp-edged seed. Found in the Warree country on the banks of rivers. Native name "Juggum."

3. MONTANA, I. Graham.—A middle-sized tree with the trunk armed, young shoots with axillary thorns; leaves ovate oblong crenate; fruit scarlet, of the size of a cherry, agreeable and

slightly acid; in perfection in March. Found at Virdee and the ghaut districts generally. Native name "Attuck."

4. SEPIARIA, Roxb. Cor. *t.* 68.—A thorny small tree common in the Deccan, towards the Ghants; leaves obovate; fruit size of a pea; flowers in December. Native name "Tambat."

2. PHOBEROS, Lour.

1. CRENATUS, Wight, in Wight and Arn. *Prod.* 1, 29.—Thorny; leaves elliptic oblong lanceolate, acute at the base, with glands obtusely serrated. On the Ghauts to the south of the Ram Ghaut.

XII. PANGIACEÆ.

1. HYDNOCARPUS, Gaert.

1. H. WIGHTIANA, Blume Rumph. iv, 22.—A tree with elliptic oblong acutely serrated leaves; flowers axillary, subracemose; fruit large, woody, warted. Common in the South Concan. Syn. H. inebrians, Wight and Arnott; Wight Illust. i 38, *t.* 16.

XIII. SAMYDACEÆ.

1. CASEARIA, Jacq.

1. ANAVINGA, Rheed.,Ovata, Willd.—A tree; leaves oblique and subcordate at the base, ovate oblong, serrulate, downy underneath; fruit oblong, smooth and shining, larger than a nutmeg, and twice as large as that of the following species. Found on Caranjah hill and at Rajahpoor; flowers in November. C. tomentosa, Roxb. Appears to be the same species. *Vide* Flor Ind. ii, pp 420 & 411.

2. GRAVEOLENS, Dalz. in Hook. Jour. Bot. iv, 107.—Arboreous glabrous; leaves short-petioled broad elliptic, shortly acuminated, slightly and obtusely serrated, coriaceous and hard when old; stipules lanceolate acuminated, glabrous; flowers numerous, clustered in the axils; pedicles articulated above the base, very short; fruit oblong, almost round, smooth, shining, one inch long; flowers green. On open hills in the South Concan; flowers in the rains; odour disagreeable.

3. LAEVIGATA, Dalz. loc. cit.—Shrubby, 4 feet high, glabrous; leaves short-petioled oblong acuminated, obscurely serrated or nearly entire, half folded, coriaceous, shining on both sides; stipules acuminated; flowers numerous, clustered in the axils; pedicles articulated above the base; bark on the young branches white, highly polished.

4. RUBESCENS, Dalz. loc. cit.—Shrubby, 4 to 6 feet high, all glabrous; leaves petioled ovate oblong, quite entire, rounded at the base, suddenly and obtusely acuminated, coriaceous, with the

margins recurved; younger leaves with the midrib bright red; stipules minute ruform, scale-like; fruit oblong, glabrous, seated in a ring. On the Ghauts to the south; flowers in February.

XIV. VIOLACEÆ.

1. IONIDIUM, Vent.

1. Enneaspermum, Vent.—A small suffrutescent plant, spreading or half erect, with rather simple branches, and pink flowers and narrow leaves. Syn. I. suffruticosum, Ging.; I. heterophyllum, Vent.; I. Capensey, Burmanni, DC. *Prod.*; Viola 9 sperma, Linn; I. frutescens, Ging. in DC. *Prod.*; Viola suffruticosa, Linn.; Roxb. Fl Ind. i, 649; Roth. nov. sp. p 165; V. frutescens, Roth. loc. cit. Common in the Southern Concan.

2. Hexaspermum, Dalz. in Hook Jour. Bot. iv, p 342.—Half a foot high; stem simple, straight, pubescent; leaves linear, attenuated at both ends, glabrous, roughish, and remotely denticulate on the margin; stipules subulate ciliated; lateral petals ovate oblong, obtuse mucronate; capsule 6-seeded; leaves 20 to 22 lines long, 2 lines broad; flowers deep orange red. Hills near Belgaum. Syn. Viola erecta, Roth. nov. sp. p 165; Ionidium erectum, Ging. in DC. *Prod.* 1, 311.

XV. DROSERACEÆ.

1. DROSERA, Linn.

1. D. Burmanni, Vahl. DC. *Prod.* 1, p 318.—Stemless; leaves all radical obovate cuneate sessile, covered with gland-bearing hairs; scapes erect, 3 to 4 inches high; flowers white. Common in the South Concan; flowers in the rains.

2. D. Indica, Linn.—Stem branched; leaves narrow linear spathulate; racemes and calyx puberulous. This and the preceding are figured in Wight's Illust. *t.* 20. At Vingorla; common in pastures in the rains.

XVI. POLYGALEÆ.

1. POLYGALA, Linn.

1. Arvensis, Willd.—Herbaceous, branched from the base, procumbent, pubescent; leaves elliptic oblong or obovate petioled; racemes 4 to 8-flowered nearly opposite to the leaves, and half their length; flowers yellow; capsule roundish oblique ciliated, not margined. Guzerat and Deccan, at Surat; flowers in July and

August. Syn. P. procumbens and Roth. nov. sp. p 329. Rheed. Mal. ix, *t*. 61.

2. Campestris, Dalz. in Hook. Jour. ii, p 40.—Annual glaucous, 4 to 5 inches high; stem erect, round pubescent, sparingly branched below; leaves linear subsessile glabrous mucronulate, margins recurved, lower flowers 1 to 2, solitary outside of the axils, upper ones racemed numerous; racemes above the axil or opposite the leaf, and 3 to 4 times longer than the leaf, wings obliquely ovate mucronulate, longer than the capsule; capsule nearly round, obliquely emarginate, ciliated on the margin; flowers yellow.

3. Rothiana, W. and A.—Stems herbaceous, branched from the base, erect; leaves glabrous ciliated, narrow oblong, or linear obtuse mucronulate; racemes nearly capitate, 4 to 6-flowered; capsule glabrous ciliate margined. Island of Bombay. Syn. P. procumbens, B. Roth. nov. sp. p 329; P. glaucoides, Willd. sp. iii, p 896.

4. Triflora, Linn.—Stems nearly simple erect, with a roughish pubescence; leaves glabrous linear mucronulate; racemes about 3-flowered axillary or above the axils, half the length of the leaf; capsule oblong, scarcely margined, pubescent ciliated. Sholapore districts. Law. Syn. P. linarifolia, Roth. nov. sp. p 330. Common in Sind.

5. Elongata? Klein.—Branched from the base, pubescent, lateral branches procumbent; leaves oblong linear, tapering downwards; racemes above the axils, or opposite to the leaves, many-flowered at length, elongated 2 to 4 times longer than the leaves; flowers purple, alac oval obtuse, greenish-yellow, veined with purple; capsule glabrous, neither ciliate nor margined. Coast of Kattywar; in sandy soil.

6. P. Vahliana, DC.—Branches few, long, divaricating, younger ones pubescent terete; leaves linear oblong mucronate, very shortly petioled; peduncles lateral or leaf-opposed, shorter than the leaf, 4 to 8-flowered; pedicles distant, drooping; alac obovate or oval obtuse, pubescent, ciliated; ovary silky; fruit oblong emarginate, ciliated and puberulous, not margined; in light soil. Guzerat; flowers yellow.

7. P. Persicariæfolia, DC. *Prod.*—Stem erect, bipid at the apex; leaves oblong, acuminated at both ends, paler beneath; racemes 10 to 15-flowered, rising from the divisions of the stem; flowers of a beautiful rose-colour, wings obovate; capsule obcordate, ciliate, shorter than the wings. On the highest Ghauts east of Bombay; flowers in August. Syn. P. Wallichiana, Wight Illust. i, p 49, *t*. 22.

2. SALOMONIA, Lour.

S. Cordata, Arnott, in Wight. Illust. i, p 49, *t*. 22.—A diminutive plant 3 to 4 inches high, branched; leaves small sessile cordate, ovate, glabrous, ciliated on the margin; spikes of small red flowers, elongated; capsules crested pectinate. Vingorla; North Concan. Nimmo.

XVII. TAMARISCINEÆ.

1. TRICHAURUS, Arnott.

1. T. Ericoides, Arnott in W. and A. *Prod* 1, p 40.—A beautiful shrub, with foliage like the tamarisk, and rather large heath-like flowers. Common in the beds of the Concan and Deccan rivers. Syn. Tamarix ericoides, Rottl. and Willd., Roth. nov. sp. 184.

XVIII. ELATINEÆ.

1. BERGIA, Linn.

1. B. Verticillata, Willd. DC. *Prod.* 1, 390.—Glabrous; stem branched, rooting from the lower joints; leaves opposite lanceolate, attenuated into a longish petiole, serrated towards the point; flowers densely capitate sessile axillary. Syn. Elatine verticillata, W. and A. *Prod.* 41; E. luxurians, Delille; B. aquatica, Roxb. Cor. *t.* 142; B. Capensis, Linn. Margins of tanks.

2. B. Ammannoides, Roxb. Fl Ind. ii, 457.—Stems branched, erect or ascending; leaves oblong lanceolate acute, sharply serrated; flowers pedicelled several together in the axils of the leaves; stems usually rough, with short capitate hairs. Found with the preceding. Wight in Hook. Bot. misc. supp. *t.* 28.

2. ELATINE, Linn.

1. E. Odorata, Edgeworth in Hook. Jour. Bot. ii, p 283.—Pubescent; stem branched, branches decumbent; leaves oblong elliptic sessile serrated; cymes axillary, few-flowered; flowers pink, 5-divided, decandrous. Pretty common throughout Guzerat.

XIX. SESUVIACEÆ.

1. TRIANTHEMA, Sauv.

1. T. Crystallina, Vahl., W. and A. *Prod.* 1, 355.—Stems diffuse prostrate, dotted with crystalline specks; leaves oval or spathulate; flowers several together, protruded from the sheath of the leaves; stamens 5; capsule 2-seeded. Dehgaum, near Cambay. Syn. T. triquetra, Rottl.; Papularia crystallina, Forsk.

2. T. Obcordata, Roxb. Flor Ind. ii, 445.—Perennial; stems

diffuse prostrate; leaves one of each pair larger, obovate or obcordate, the other smaller and oblong; flowers solitary sessile, nearly concealed within the broad sheath of the petiole; stamens 15 to 20; style simple; capsule 6 to 8-seeded, lid concave, including 2 seeds; seeds black, muricated; leaves often with red margins. A common weed on rice-fields.

3. T. Decandra, Linn.—Stems diffuse prostrate; leaves elliptic obtuse or acute petioled, one of each pair a little larger; flowers several, pedicelled on a short peduncle; stamens 10 to 12; style bipartite; capsule 4-seeded. DC. *Prod.* iii, 352; Spr. *syst.* ii, 381; Roxb. Fl Ind. ii, 444; Syn. Zaleya decandra; Burm. Ind. *t.* 31 *f.* 3.

2. SESUVIUM, Linn.

1. Portulacastrum, Rottl.—A fleshy glabrous plant; stems prostrate, rooting at the joints; leaves opposite, oval spathulate or oblong linear; flowers axillary solitary pedicellate. A common weed, generally near the sea. Roxb. Fl Ind. ii, 509.; Syn. S. repens. Rottl.; Willd. enum. 521; DC. *Prod.* iii, 453; Spr. *syst.* ii, 504.

XX. PORTULACACEÆ.

1. PORTULACA, Lournef.

1. P. Oleracea, Linn.—A low herbaceous fleshy plant, annual diffuse; leaves cuneiform, their axils and the joints naked; flowers sessile, petals 5; stamens 10 to 12; style 5 partite. DC. *Prod.* iii, 353; Roxb. Fl Ind. ii, 463. The ανδραχνη of the Greeks, used as a pot-herb, being cooling and antiscorbutic.

2. P. Quadrifida, Linn. Maut. p 678.—Annual diffuse creeping, joints and axils hairy; leaves oblong, flat; flowers terminal, nearly sessile, yellow, surrounded by four leaves; petals 4; stamens 8 to 12; style 4-cleft at the apex. A common weed. DC. *Prod.* iii, p 354; Roxb. Fl Ind. ii, 464; Syn. P. meridiana, Linn. suppl. 248; Roxb. Fl Ind. ii, 463.

XXI. CARYOPHYLLACEÆ.

1. ARENARIA, Linn.

1. A. Neilgherrense, W. and A. *Prod.* 1, 43.—Stems elongated, much-branched, procumbent; leaves distant obovate-mucronulate glabrous, with minute whitish points, one-nerved, margins thickened; flowers axillary or in terminal panicles; pedicles viscidly pubescent, longish slender; sepals oblong acute; petals longer than the calyx; capsules ovate. Wight Ic. 940. Belgaum and Dharwar collectorates.

2. MOLLUGO, Linn.

1. M. Pentaphylla, Linn.—A weed, glabrous, stems decumbent, leafy, angled; leaves slightly glaucous obovate obtuse mucronulate, tapering at the base; panicles elongated, many-flowered; stamens usually three; seeds minutely tuberculated. DC. *Prod.* 1, p 391; Roxb. Fl Ind. i 359; Syn. Pharnaceum pentaphyllum; Spr. *syst.* i, 949; M. triphylla, Linn.

2. M. Stricta, Linn.—Glabrous; stems straightish, angled; leaves linear lanceolate-pointed; panicle elongated, many-flowered; stamens 3; petals none. DC. *Prod.* 1, 391. A common weed. Syn. Pharnaceum strictum, Spr. *syst.* i, 949.

3. GLINUS, Linn.

1. G. Lotoides, Linn.—A weed, hoary, with short stellate tomentum; leaves obovate, flat fascicled, unequal; pedicles one-flowered axillary; petals 5, deeply cloven. Linn. sp., p 663; Syn. G. dictamnoides, Lam.

XXII. PARONYCHIACEÆ.

1. POLYCARPAEA, Lam.

1. P. Corymbosa, Lam.—A rigidly erect plant, with few branches; leaves narrow linear or setaceous mucronate; cymes terminal, dichotomous; sepals entirely scariose, lanceolate acuminate, white shining, 2 to 3 times longer than the capsule. On the sea-shore, Southern Concan and Guzerat; also in the Deccan. Syn. Achyranthes corymbosa, Linn; Celosia corymbosa, Willd. sp. i, 1200.

XXIII. LINEÆ.

1. LINUM, Linn.

Mysorense, Heyne, Benth. in Bot. Reg. 1326.—A small plant, glabrous, erect; leaves small alternate oblong bluntish, tapering to the base; flowers paniculately corymbose; petals yellow, as long as or longer than the calyx (in Bombay specimens) double the length; capsule acutely mucronate. Island of Caranjah, Kandalla, Deccan, &c.; flowers in September. "Native name Woondree."

2. REINWARDLIA, Dumort.

1. R. Trigyna, Planchon, in Hook. Jour. Bot. vii, p 522. Shrubby, glabrous; leaves elliptical, pointed at both ends, minutely serrulated; flowers large, yellow, peduncled, solitary; capsule

globular obtuse. Parr Ghaut, Bassein, Bombay; planted, but certainly wild on the Meera hills, near Penn. Bot. Mag. *t.* 1100. Flowers in January. Syn. Linum trigynum, Roxb. Fl Ind. ii, 110.

XXIV. HUGONIACEÆ.

1. HUGONIA, Linn.

1. H MYSTAX, Linn.—A large much-branched shrub; leaves oval, glabrous, quite entire; peduncles axillary one-flowered, often transformed into curious circinate spines; flowers largish, yellow, rather showy; fruit a berry (enclosing 5 long carpels), size of a large pea; flowers and fruit in August; rare, found only between Malwan and Vingorla. DC. *Prod.* 1, 522; Rheed. Mal. ii, *t.* 29; Syn. H obovata, Ham. Linn. Trans. xiv, 205; Wight Illust. *t.* 32.

XXV. MALVACEÆ.

1. SIDA, Linn.

1. HUMILIS, Willd.—Slender, diffuse; leaves roundish, cordate, acute, serrated; pedicles jointed above the middle, slender; axillary solitary, shorter than the leaves; carpels 5, not beaked, obtuse or slightly bicuspidate. Common in sandy soil. DC. *Prod.* 1, p. 463; Syn. S pilosa, Ratz.; S multicaulis, Cav.

2. ALBA, Linn.—Shrubby, branches with 1 to 2 prickly tubercles below the leaves; leaves ovate or obovate, or oblong obtuse, hoary beneath; pedicles solitary, as long as the petioles; carpels 5, birostrate. At Surat. Syn. S alba, DC. *Prod.*; S spinosa, Linn.

3. ACUTA, Burm.—Shrubby; leaves narrow lanceolate, acuminate, glabrous, serrated; pedicles axillary, solitary, not longer than the stipules; carpels 5 to 9, birostrate. Syn. S lanceolata, Ratz.; S stauntoniana, DC.; S ocoparia, Lour. Bombay.

4. CORDIFOLIA, Linn.—Shrubby; leaves cordate, obtuse or scarcely acute, bluntly serrated, tomentose; carpels 9 to 10, with two setaceous downward pointing hairy beaks, as long as the carpel. Syn. S herbacea, Cav.; S rotundifolia, Cav.

5. RETUSA, Linn.—Shrubby; leaves obovate retuse, toothed towards the apex; carpels 7 to 10, birostrate. Very common; all the species have small yellow flowers.

2. ABUTILON, Dill.

1. POLYANDRUM, W. and A.—Leaves roundish cordate, with a sudden long acumination, distantly repand toothed, younger ones

velvetty; carpels 5, not twice as long as the calyx. Syn. Sida polyandra, Roxb. On the Ghauts. S pusica, Burm. Ind. *t.* 47, *f.* 1; DC. *Prod.* 1, 473.

2. INDICUM, G. Don.—Leaves cordate, somewhat lobed, soft, shortly tomentose, unequally toothed; capsule truncated, longer than the calyx; carpels 11 to 20, acute, not awned, hairy. Common; flowers entirely yellow, open in the evening. Syn. A asiaticum, G. Don; Sida indica, Linn; S populifolia, Lam.; S belocre, L'Her.; S eteromischos, Cav.; Sida asiatica, Linn; A graveolens? W. & A.

3. TOMENTOSUM, W. and A.—Leaves cordate, tomentose on both sides, toothed; capsule globose, depressed or concave, very tomentose; carpels reniform. At Surat. Syn. Sida tomentosa, Roxb. Hort., Bengal. All the species have yellow flowers.

4. A SIDOIDES, Dalz. Mss.—Fruticose erect, with white bark; leaves long-petioled, rounded cordate, acutely 3-lobed, coarsely crenate, membranaceous, green on both sides, smooth, ciliolated on the margin; peduncles axillary, solitary, or rarely twin, bearing twin pedicles articulated in the middle; calyx half divided, divisions suddenly acuminate; flowers very small, yellow; carpels with glutinous pubescence, 5 to 7, bicuspidate, twice the length of the calyx; 3-seeded; seeds dark-coloured, tubercled. Very rare; found only near Cambay.

3. URENA, Linn.

1. U LOBATA, Linn.—Herbaceous; leaves roundish, with three or more short, sometimes obsolete, acute or obtuse lobes, more or less velvetty; flowers rose-coloured. A common weed. DC. *Prod.* 1, p. 441, Rumph. Amb. vi, *t.* 25, *f.* 2A. St. Hil. Pl. as. *t.* 56; Bot. Mag. *t.* 3043.

2. U SCABRIUSCULA, DC. *Prod.* 1, p 441.—Herbaceous; leaves roundish, scarcely lobed, harshly pubescent on both sides, 5 to 7-nerved, with 1 to 3 glands beneath, segments of involucal 5, linear acuminated; flowers rose-coloured; carpels pubescent, echinated. Phoonda and Ram Ghauts; not common. W. and A. suspected this to be the same as the preceding, but they are very distinct.

3. U SINUATA, Linn.—Shrubby; leaves deeply 3 to 5-lobed, lobes dilated upwards, and the sinuses rounded; flowers rose-coloured and rather handsome. A common weed. Syn. U morifolia, DC. *Prod.* 1, p 441; U muricata, DC. loc. cit.; U lappago, Smith in DC. loc. cit.; U heterophylla; Smith in DC. *Prod.* 1, 442.

4. THESPESIA, Correa.

1. T POPULNEA.—Arboreous; leaves roundish, cordate acuminate, entire, smooth; flowers large, yellow, with a purple base;

capsule spherical, depressed, coriaceous, indehiscent. The common Bendy tree. Syn. Hibiscus populneus, Linn.; Malvaviscus populneus, Gaertn, *t.* 135. The wood is fine-grained and tough; makes good gun-stocks, wheels, and boat timbers.

2. T LAMPAS, Dalz. Mss.—Shrubby; leaves cordate 3-lobed, sub-glabrous, lobes spreading, acuminate; peduncles axillary, three-flowered; calyx truncated with five minute teeth; flower as in the preceding; capsule ovoid indehiscent. Common in the Concan and Ghauts; 3 to 4 feet high. Syn. Hibiscus lampas, Cav.; Paritium gangeticum, G. Don; Wight's Ic. without number. Native name "Ran Bendy."

5. PARITIUM, Adr. Juss.

1. P TITIACEUM, Adr. Juss. in. St. Hil. Flor Bras. 1, 198.—A tree; leaves roundish cordate, with a sudden acumination, crenulated or entire, underside hoary; flowers like the Bendy, involucel 10-lobed; capsule 5-celled 5-valved. At Rutnagherry and banks of the Tericol river, Warree country. Syn. Hibiscus tiliacens, Linn.; Wight Ic. *t.* 7.

6. ABELMOSCHUS, Med.

1. A TETRAPHYLLUS, Graham in Cat. Bomb. Pl, p 14.—A large, annual erect hairy plant; leaves long-petioled, palmate, variously lobed and toothed; flowers yellow, with a dark-purple bottom; involucel 4-leaved; capsule hairy. Island of Caranjah and the Meera hills; abundant. Syn. Hibiscus tetraphyllus, Roxb. Fl Ind. iii, p 211.

2. A WARREENSIS, Dalz. in Hook. Jour. Bot. iii, p. 123.—Stem rough, with erect bristles; leaves broadly cordate acuminate, coarsely crenate, sprinkled with stiff hairs on both sides; involucre as in the preceding, but not falling off as in that species; flowers fascicled terminal, or on short axillary branches. In the Warree country; flowers and fruit in January.

7. HIBISCUS, Linn.

1. H FURCATUS, Roxb.—Climbing, all rough with numerous recurved prickles; stipules oblong or lanceolate; leaves palmately 3 to 5-lobed, densely pubescent beneath, nerves beneath prickly; leaves of involucel about 10, linear incurved, with an oblong foliaceous appendage at their back about the middle. DC. *Prod.* 1, 449. Common on the Ghauts.

2. VESICARIUS, Cav.—Annual, with hairy stems, 5-cleft leaves, and inflated membranaceous calyx. Common during the rains, chiefly on black soils. Syn. H trionum ?

3. SURATTENSIS, Linn.—Herbaceous, erect, covered with small recurved prickles; stipules semicordate; flowers pale-yellow. Malabar Hill.

4. PANDURIFORMIS.—Herbaceous, 6 to 8 feet high, stem covered with rigid-spreading hairs; leaves cordate, unequally toothed, upper side hispidly tomentose, under with a soft dense tomentum; pedicles axillary, very short, one-flowered; involucel leaves 8, spathulate; capsule ovoid-pointed, very hairy. At Surat. Syn. H tubulosus, Cav.; H pilosus, Roxb. in E. I. C. Mus. *t.* 672; H. velutinus ? DC. *Prod.*

5. CANNABINUS, Linn.—Stem glabrous, prickly; leaves palmately 5-partite, glabrous; segments lanceolate acuminated serrated; fruit nearly globose, acuminated, very hairy. The common "Ambaree" cultivated for the flax, which its bark yields; the leaves are also eaten as a pot-herb.

6. VITIFOLIUS, Linn.—Leaves roundish cordate, toothed or crenated, with 5 lobes or angles, upper side nearly smooth or tomentose, under softly tomentose; leaves of involucel 12, subulate; carpels hairy, compressed at the back into a short wing. At Malwan. Syn. H obtusifolius, Willd.; H truncatus, Roxb. Hort., Beng.

7. H PUNCTATUS, Dalz.—Suffruticose 3 to 4 feet high, scarcely branched; leaves unequally 3-lobate (middle lobe very long), crenate dentate, with pellucid dots; pedicles solitary axillary, longer than the petiole; flowers pale rose-coloured, very small; calyx half divided, divisions acuminate, all the younger parts glutinous and pubescent; capsule ovoid apiculate, scarcely longer than the calyx; seeds black, muricated. Broach Collectorate; rare.

8. SCANDENS, Dalz. Mss.—Stems long, subscandent, unbranched slender; leaves palmately 7-lobed, lobes narrow acute, dentate, glabrous; flowers axillary, solitary, small, one inch, pale-yellow with a purple bottom. Coast of Kattywar.

9. HIRTUS, Linn.—Shrubby; leaves ovate acuminate or cordate, strongly serrated; pedicles axillary, longer than the leaf; involucel leaves 5 to 7, subulate, hairy, shorter than the calyx; flowers rather small, white, Common in the North Concan. Syn. H. phœnicens in Willd.; H rosa malabarica, Kœnig.

10. H MICRANTHUS, Linn.—Shrubby, rigidly erect; leaves ovate or roundish, acutely serrated, rough with bristly hairs; pedicles longer than the leaf; involucel leaves 7, setaceous; flowers small, seeds covered with long white, silky hairs. In the Deccan, Kattywar, and the Kaira district, in hedges. Syn. H. rigidus, Linn.

11. H HEPTAPHYLLUS, Dalz. and Gibs.—Herbaceous, erect, 4 to 5 feet high, covered over with scattered prickly hairs; leaves on longish petioles, palmately 5 to 7-divided; leaflets lanceolate serrate, attenuated at both ends; pedicles axillary solitary, as long

as or longer than the leaf; involucel leaves about 9, linear subulate, spreading bristly, rather longer than the acuminate calyx leaves; flowers large yellow, showy, with a purple bottom; capsules ovoid-pointed, covered with spreading bristles. Mountain valleys, eastern side of the Northern Ghauts.

8. LAGUNEA, Cav.

1. L Lobata, Willd.—Herbaceous, lower leaves cordate, upper palmate, uppermost tripid or lanceolate; pedicles arranged in a terminal lax, leafless raceme. Near Belgaum. Syn. Lolandra lobata, Murray; Triguera acerifolia, Cav.; Hibiscus solandra, L'Her.; Sida diversifolia, Spr. *syst.* iii, 116.

9. PAVONIA, Cav.

1. P Zeylanica, Cav.—Lower leaves roundish cordate crenated, upper deeply 3 to 5-lobed, coarsely toothed; pedicles axillary 1-flowered; leaves of involucel 10, ciliated; carpels unarmed. Near Gogo. Syn. Hibiscus zeylanicus, Linn.

10. DECASCHISTIA, W. and A.

1. D. Trilobata. Wight Ic. 88.—Herbaceous tomentose; leaves deeply 3-lobed, lobes narrow minutely dentate serrate on the margin; stipules subulate, longer than the petioles; capsules 10-valved; flowers in October. Common on the Ram Ghaut, also the Koombarli Ghaut.

11. MALVA, Linn.

1. M Rotundifolia, Linn.—Stems herbaceous, spreading; leaves cordate roundish, shortly and obtusely lobed, crenated, petioles elongated; pedicles several together, unequal; axillary one-flowered; flowers small, white or pale-pink; carpels wrinkled and reticulated on the back. Common about the Deccan villages.

12. GOSSYPIUM.

1. G Obtusifolium, Roxb. Fl Ind. iii, p 183.—Shrubby, branched, diffuse, straggling; leaves small with 3, rarely 5, obtuse ovate entire lobes; stipules falcate; exterior calyx with entire divisions; capsules ovate, cells 3-seeded, cotton on the seeds of a dirty greenish, grey colour. Drier parts of the Deccan; not common. Roxburgh says that it is a native of Ceylon, but this must be a mistake, as it is not in Thwaites' list. This is with good reason supposed to be the parent of the common cultivated cotton, and is found all over the limestone rocks of the Sind coast.

XXVI. STERCULIACEÆ.

1. SALMALIA, Schott. & Endl.

1. MALABARICA.—A large tree, trunk prickly; leaves palmate; leaflets 5 to 7, acuminated at both ends; flowers large bright red, appearing in February, when the tree is without leaves; fruit oblong obtuse, full of silky cotton. Very common. Syn. Bombax malabaricum, DC.; B heptaphyllum, Cav.; Roxb. Hort. Beng., Cor. *t.* 247; B ceiba, Burm. Fl Ind.; Gossampinus rubra, Ham. in Linn. Trans. Rheede Mal. iii, *t.* 52. The bark is said to be emetic, and the honey of the flowers purgative and emetic; but this is denied by Mr. O'Shaughnessy and others.

2. ERIODENDRON, DC.; GOSSYMPIUM, Schott. & Endl.

1. ANFRACTUOSUM, DC.—A tree something like the preceding, with prickly trunk and palmate leaves; flowers drooping, of a dingy white; fruit like Salmalia. Syn. Bombax pentandrum, Linn.; Roxb. Fl Ind. iii, 165; Ceiba, Gaertn. *t.* 133; Gossampium, Rumph. Amb. *t.* 80; Gossampinus alba, Ham. loc. cit. Grows in Khandeish. Native name "Shameula."

NOTE.—The glutinous sap is applied to parts effected by rheumatism, and the cottony seeds are used as a soporific pillow in the Philippines (Adams).

3. HELICTERES, Linn.

1. ISORA, Linn.—A shrub, with roundish toothed and acuminate leaves, and bright red flowers; carpels 5-twisted, like a screw. Common in the hilly parts of the Concan and Deccan. Syn. H Roxburghii, Don. in Mill. Dict. Native names "Kewun" and "Muradsing"; the fruit is used by the natives medicinally, but its qualities are fanciful, though safe.

4. HERITIERA, Art.

1. LITTORALIS DRYANDER, in Ait. Hort , Kew., iii, 546.—A tree with alternate oval entire leaves, and axillary panicles of small red flowers; said in Grah. Cat., fide Nimmo, to grow in the S. Concan, but we have failed to find it. Syn. Balanopteris tothila, Gaertn. fr. *t.* 99; Rheede Mal. vi, *t.* 21; Rumph. Amb. iii, *t.* 63.

5. STERCULIA, Linn.

1. VILLOSA, Roxb. Fl Ind. iii, 153.—A tree; leaves palmately 5 to 7-lobed, lobes acuminated tomentose and velvetty beneath;

racemes of flowers yellow, very long pendulous; aestivation of calyx in duplicate; carpels rough, with stellate pubescence; flowers in December. South Concan, Vingorla, Canara. Ropes and bags are made from the bark of this tree in Goa and Canara.

2. GUTTATA, Roxb.—Leaves broadly ovate and oblong, entire; flowers in simple axillary terminal racemes, velvetty yellow, spotted with purple; carpels large, of a reddish colour; seeds large, eatable. Roxb. Fl Ind. iii, 148; Wight Ic. *t.* 487; flowers in threes, subsessile; calyx tomentose outside, villous within. Common on the Ghauts. Cloth is manufactured from this tree in Malabar. Native names " Kookur," " Goldar."

3. COLORATA, Roxb. Cor. i, 28, *t.* 25.—Leaves palmately 5-lobed, glabrous; calyces cylindrical clavate, bright orange red, velvetty; carpels oblong glabrous, opening long before the seeds are ripe—a very rare peculiarity. Common on the Ghauts and jungles in the Deccan; flowers in March and April, when the young leaves make their appearance. Roxb. Cor. *t* 25. This is called now " Firmiana colorata," ex. Walp. Sect. erythropsis, Lindley. Native name " Khowsey" or " Bhaeekoee." Hook. Ic. Pl, *t.* 148; Firmiana (Marsili Aet. Patav. 1, 116, *t.* 1 and 2); Erythropsis Roxburghiana. Schott. and Endl. Meletem Bot. 33.

4. URENS, Roxb.—A large tree; leaves 5-lobed, soft and velvetty beneath; panicles terminal, short; carpels covered with bristly hairs which sting like those of the Cowitch (Mucuna); bark of the trunk white; the seeds are said to be cathartic, but has been used as coffee; flowers in December. Common in the Concan. This tree exudes a white gum like tragacanth.

XXVII. BYTTNERIACEÆ.

1. BYTTNERIA, Lœfl., Linn.

1. HERBACEA, Roxb.—A small plant with polymorphous serrate downy leaves, and red and yellow flowers from the axils of the leaves. Roxb. Cor. i, *t.* 29; Fl Ind. i, 619; Syn. Commersonia herbacea, Don. Pretty common about Bombay in the rains.

2. KLEINHOVIA, Linn.

1. HOSPITA, Linn.—A small tree with broad cordate leaves and small pink flowers in terminal panicles; capsule turbinate inflated. S. Concan, Nimmo; Rumph. Amb. iii, *t.* 113. A doubtful native.

3. WALTHERIA, Linn.

1. INDICA, Linn.—Herbaceous plant, with oblong softly tomentose leaves; head of flowers terminal and axillary sessile or pedunculated; flowers small, yellow. A very variable plant, hence burdened

with synonyms. Syn. W. americana, Linn; W. elliptica, Cav.; W. microphylla, Cav. At Raree, in South Concan; at Domus. Guill. and Perr. tent. Fl Senegambia i, 84.

4. RIEDLEIA, Vent.

1. Corchorifolia, DC.—A common herbaceous plant, with cordate ovate serrated leaves; flowers pink, in short dense spikes, which are terminal. Syn. Melochia corchorifolia, Rox. Fl Ind. iii, 139.

2. Tiliaefolia.—A small tree with long-petioled subcordate serrate leaves, young ones soft and velvetty; flowers small, pink, in axillary and terminal corymbiform panicles. Bassein, Kandalla, Belgaum. Native name "Methooree."

5. PTEROSPERMUM, Schreb.

1. Suberifolium, Lam. Illust. Gen. *t.* 576, *f.* 1.—A tree with cuneate oblong leaves shortly acuminated, obliquely cordate at the base, densely pubescent beneath; peduncles axillary, three-flowered; flowers very fragrant, 1¼ inch across; involucel leaves linear, entire. The Concans. Reich. Fl Exoti. *t.* 166. Wight in Hook. Bot. misc. *t.* 26; P. canescens, Roxb. Hort. Beng., 50; Pentapeter suberifolia, Linn. "*Muchucuda.*"

2. Lawianum, Nimmo in Grah. Cat.—Leaves 3-lobed cordate acuminate subpeltate, tomentose, involucel palmatifid. Dharwar, and the Southern Ghauts. Whole plant of a pale, tawny colour.

6. KYDIA, Roxb.

1. Calycina, Roxb.—A middle-sized tree with broad cordate angled leaves, and white flowers in terminal panicles. They appear in October and November; capsule hid in the calyx, size of a pea. Roxb. Cor. *t.* 215; Syn. K fraterna, Roxb. Common on the Ghauts. Native name "Warung."

7. ERIOLAENA, DC.

1. Candollii, Wall. Pl. as. rarior. i 57, *t.* 64.—Leaves ovate cordate, toothed, white beneath; flowers yellow, showy; capsule woody, cone-shaped, much pointed. Certainly the same as the Pegu plant. Ram Ghaut; common.

XXVIII. SILIACEÆ.

1. CORCHORUS, Linn.

1. Fascicularis, Linn.—Leaves oblong or lanceolate serrated; peduncles 3 to 5-flowered, opposite to the leaves; capsules linear oblong, nearly terete, rostrate, 3-celled. At Surat.

2. Trilocularis, Linn.—Leaves oblong, more or less obtuse; peduncles 1 to 2-flowered; capsules 3 to 4-angled, slender, rostrate, and entire at the point. Sholapore districts, Law; Guzerat, Dalz.

3. Olitorius, Linn.—Leaves ovate, acuminated; capsules nearly cylindrical, 10-ribbed, glabrous, rostrate, 5-celled. Common. Syn. C decemangularis, Roxb. Fl Ind. ii, p 582.

4. Acutangulus, Lam.—Leaves ovate; capsules prismatical, 6-angled, with 2 to 3 of the angles winged, truncate, with tifid horns. A common weed. Syn. C fuscus, Roxb. Fl Ind. ii, p 582; C aestuas, Gaertn. *t.* 64; Pluk. *t.* 44, *fig* i.

5. Capsularis.—Leaves oblong acuminated; capsules globose truncated, wrinkled, and muricated, 5-celled. This species furnishes the fibre called Jute, from which gunny-bags are made. Wight Ic. Pl i, *t.* 311. It grows to a much larger size in Bengal.

6. C Humilis, Munro. Wight Ic. 1,073.—Shrubby, prostrate, lying flat on the ground; leaves small, long-petioled, ovate crenate, peduncles two-flowered; capsules linear oblong, 6 to 8 times longer than broad, nearly glabrous, 4 to 5-celled, 4 to 5-valved. Munro hortus agrensis, p 35. Kattywar, Guzerat, and the Deccan; a member of the desert flora. Syn. Antichorus depressus, Linn.

2. TRUMPHETTA, Plum.

1. Pilosa, Roth.—Herbaceous plant, rough, hairy, upper leaves ovate acuminate, lower somewhat 3-lobed, all unequally serrated, hairy, underside tomentose; fruit 4-celled, size of a small cherry, hairy or rather prickly, prickles ciliated below. On a hill at Warree; rather rare. Roth. nov. sp. 223.

2. Angulata, Lam.—Uppermost leaves ovate acuminate, lower cuspidately 3 to 5-lobed, serrated; fruit pubescent, prickles glabrous. Very common everywhere. Syn. T bartramia, Linn.; Roxb. Fl Ind. ii, p 463; Lappago amboinica, Rumph. Amb. vi, *t* 25, *fig* 2.

3. Rotundifolia, Lam.—Leaves roundish unequally and deeply toothed, upperside glabrous, under tomentose; peduncles in an interrupted raceme; fruit small, densely pubescent. At Surat, Deccan. Syn. T. suborbiculata, DC. *Prod.* 1, p 506; Spr. *syst.* ii, p 451.

3. GREWIA, Juss.

1. G Villosa, Herb. Miss.—Leaves 5-nerved, roundish cordate wrinkled, toothed, upperside rough, under covered with short tomentum, young parts and inflorescence very villous; flowers rather small, white; drupes globose and hairy, crustaceous, having a sweet edible pulp within. Syn. G rotundifolia, Don in Mill. Dict. Sparingly over the Deccan, extending to Sind and Senegambia; supposed to be the same as G corylifolia of Guill. and Perr.

2. G PILOSA, Lam.—Shrubby; leaves 3-nerved, on very short petioles, cuneate or obovate oblong, rounded or slightly cordate at the base, unequally serrated, rough with stellate hairs; peduncles axillary, 1 to 3, as long as the petiole, 3-flowered; flowers yellow, largish; drupes 1 to 4-lobed, crustaceous covered with stellate hairs. The Deccan; flowers in July. Syn. G carpinifolia, Roxb. Fl Ind. ii, 587.

3. G ABUTILIFOLIA, Juss.—Arborescent; leaves 3-nerved, roundish cordate, irregularly and coarsely toothed, upperside rough, under harshly tomentose; peduncles several together, axillary, about half as long as the petiole, 3 to 4-flowered; sepals oblong, about thrice the length of the oblong entire petals; drupes 4-lobed, pubescent and hairy; nuts four or less, 1 to 2-celled. Juss. in Ann. Mus. 4, p 92; G aspera, Roxb. Fl Ind. ii, p 590. The Deccan; flowers in June; fruit in August.

4. G TILIAEFOLIA, Vahl.—Leaves 5-nerved, roundish cordate, bluntly toothed; stipules auricled on one side; drupes 2-lobed, smooth and shining. Common in Bombay. Syn. G arborea, Roth. nov. sp. p 247.

5. G ASIATICA, Linn.—Arborescent; leaves 5-nerved, roundish cordate, obtuse or acutish, sometimes unequal at the base, unequally serrated, upperside at length nearly glabrous, under glabrous, pubescent or hoary; stipules lanceolate subulate; peduncles axillary, 2 to 4, twice or thrice as long as the petiole, 3-flowered; flowers yellow; drupes globose, with 1 to 2 one-celled nuts. This is the common cultivated Phulsi, but which we have found truly wild in the Poona Collectorate.

6. G ORIENTALIS, Linn.—A scandent shrub; leaves 3-nerved, ovate or oblong lanceolate, shortly and bluntly acuminated, nearly quite glabrous; peduncles axillary, solitary, three-flowered; drupes nearly globose, slightly 4-lobed, covered with a short tomentum. On the Southern Ghauts. Syn. G rhamnifolia, Roth. nov. sp. p 244.

7. G COLUMNARIS, Sm.—Leaves 3-nerved, ovate, oblong or lanceolate, rigid crenated, scabrous on both sides; drupes turbinate, bristly hairy; flowers white. Syn. G pilosa, Lam. Encycl.; G orientalis, Vahl., Symb. Pluk. *t.* 50, *f.* 4; Wight. Ic. *t.* 44.

8. G MICROCOS, Linn.—Leaves ovate or obovate lanceolate, glabrous; flowers terminal panicled, very different in inflorescence from all the rest. Common in the hilly parts of the Concan. G ulimfolia, Roxb. Fl Ind. ii, p 591; Microcos paniculata, Linn; Rheed. Mal. i, *t.* 56. Native name "Sheerul."

9. G. POLYGAMA, Roxb. Fl Ind. ii, 588.—Shrubby; leaves lanceolate serrate hairy; peduncles axillary, longer than the petioles, 2 to 6-flowered; drupes 2, each 2-lobed, with a solitary

one-celled one-seeded nut in each; flowers white, polygamous. The Ghauts; common. Native name "Gowlee." This is the G lancæfolia of Graham's Catalogue.

4. ERINOCARPUS, Nimmo.

1. E Nimmonii, I. Grah. in Cat. Bomb. Pl, p 21.—A small tree; leaves on long petioles, roundish cordate, strongly nerved beneath; flowers rather large, yellow, in terminal panicles, appear in September and October; fruit triangular, bristly, angles winged. Common on the Concan hills; allied to Clappertonia of Meisner. Native name "Chowra" or "Jungle Bendy"; bark used for making ropes.

XXIX. ELAEOCARPEÆ.

1. ELAEOCARPUS, Linn.

1. Oblongus, Gaertn.—A small tree; leaves elliptic oblong-pointed, with blunt serratures; racemes simple, short; nut oblong, very hard, indehiscent; prominently tubercled; petals white, beautifully fringed. Rare; on the higher Ghauts to the south, Syn.

2. Ganitrus, Roxb. Fl Ind. ii, p 592.—Leaves lanceolate serrulate, glabrous; racemes simple, drooping; drupe spherical, smooth, purple; nut 5-grooved, and elegantly tubercled. These are generally imported from Singapore for necklaces for faqueers. On the higher Ghauts. Syn. Ganitrus sphærica, Gaertn. *t.* 139. Maratha name "Roodraksh."

2. MONOCERA, Jack.

1. Tuberculata, W. and A.—Leaves petioled cuneate obovate retuse at the base, remotely serrulated; racemes simple, solitary; drupe oval; nut compressed, tubercled on the flattened sides, with a thickened margin. Ram Ghaut. Syn. E tuberculatus, Roxb. Flor. Ind. ii, p 594.

XXX. OLACACEÆ.

1. OLAX, Linn.

1. O Wightiana, Wall.—A scandent shrub, with ovate or oblong smooth leaves, upperside shining, under pale; racemes axillary, usually compound; flowers white, appear in February; fruit smooth, oblong, more than half covered by the closely adherent calyx.

2. BURSINOPETALUM, Wight.

1. B Arboreum, Wight Ic. 956.—A large tree; leaves ovate oblong acuminated; flowers terminal, small; calyx conical, adhering to the ovary; petals 5, ovate-pointed, leathery; fruit drupaceous, of the size of a small plum, ovoid. Parwar Ghaut; not common; flowers in April and May. Thwaites refers this to Araliaceæ.

3. MAPPIA, Jacq.

1. M Oblonga, Miers in Taylor's Ann. of Nat. Hist. x, p 40.—A middle-sized tree; leaves elliptic oblong acuminated, venous; flowers terminal, cymose panicled, of a yellowish white, very fœtid; drupe succulent, olive-shaped, purple when ripe. The Ghauts opposite Goa; common. Closely allied to the Stemonurus fœtidus of Wight's Ic. 955, if really distinct.

4. PLATEA, Blume.

1. Axillaris, Thwaites Enum. p 44.—Diœcious glabrous; leaves shortly petioled, acuminate, membranaceous; cymes axillary, solitary or twin, as long as the petiole, male few-flowered, female 2 to 5-flowered; calyx minutely 4 to 5-toothed; petals 4 to 5, united at the base into a tubular corolla; fruit ovoid. Chorla and Parwar Ghauts. Syn. Gomphandra polymorpha, Wight. Illust. i, 103; Stemonurus axillaris, Miers in Ann. of Nat. Hist. vol. x, p 41.

XXXI. AURANTIACEÆ.

1. ATALANTIA, Corr.

1. Monophylla, DC. *Prod.* 1, 535.—A large climbing shrub armed with small thorns; leaves ovate or oblong; racemes short, sessile, pedicles long, slender; flowers white, appear in November, fruit size of a nutmeg, very much like a lime. On the Ghauts; common. Native name "Ran" or "Makur limboo" Syn. Limonia monophylla, Linn. Roxb. Cor. i, *t.* 82; Fl Ind. ii, 378; Trichilia spinosa, Willd. ii, 554; DC. *Prod.* 1, 623; Rheede Mal. iv, *t.* 12.

2. LIMONIA, Linn.

1. Oligandra, Dalz. in Hook. Jour. Bot. ii, 25, 8.—Shrubby, climbing, thorny, thorns numerous, short recurved; leaves petioled, trifoliolate; leaflets elliptic, obtusely acuminated, slightly crenated; flowers axillary, racemes panicled, about as long as the leaf; petals 5, linear oblong; stamens 5, filaments free; fruit size of a pea, 5-celled; flowers in November and December. Ram Ghaut.

2. Acidissima, Linn.—A shrub, spines solitary; leaves pinnate, leaflets 2 to 3 pair; leaflets oblong retuse crenated; petioles broadly winged; flowers corymbose, corymb umbelliform peduncled, 2 to 3 together from the axils of the fallen leaves; fruit 1 to 4-celled, globose; flowers in April and May. Padshapore, Falls of Gokak, Mr. Law.

3. GLYCOSMIS, Corr.

1. Pentaphylla, DC.—An erect growing shrub; leaves pinnate, leaflets 3 to 5, oblong; panicles contracted; flowers small, white; fruit size of a pea, whitish, when ripe, pulpy. G chylocarpa of W. and A. *Prod.* p 93. Appears to be the same species; at least, it is certain there is but one species in this Presidency. Native name "Kirmira." Very common in the jungly parts of the Concan. Syn. Limonia 5-phylla, Retz. Roxb. Fl Ind. ii, 381, Cor. Pl *t*, 84.

4. SCLEROSTYLIS, Bl.

1. Atalantioides, W. and A.—A shrub armed with solitary strong spines; leaves simple, elliptic emarginate, shining, crenulated; racemes small, few-flowered, axillary and terminal; fruit small, oval, succulent, 2-celled. On the hill-fort of Raighur. Syn. Limonia bilocularis, Roxb. Fl Ind. ii, 377.

5. BERGERA, Kœnig.

1. Kœnigii, Linn.—A small tree; leaves pinnate; leaflets small, alternate ovate acuminated serrated pubescent; panicles corymbiform, terminal, many-flowered; flowers in February. On the Ghauts; common. DC. *Prod.* 1, 537; Roxb. Cor. *t.* 112; Murraya Kœnigii, Spr. *syst.*

6. PIPTOSTYLIS, Dalz.

1. Indica, Dalz. in Hook. Jour. Bot. iii, p. 33, Pl ii.—Shrubby, 6 to 7 feet high, unarmed; leaves unequally pinnate; leaflets alternate, subcoriaceous glabrous, ovate, obtusely acuminate, shining; panicles terminal corymbiform, as long as the leaf; flower small, white; berry small, 1 to 2-celled by abortion; cells one-seeded. Parwar Ghaut; flowers in March.

7. MURRAYA, Kœnig.

1. Paniculata, Herb. Sm.—An evergreen shrub or small tree, leaflets 5, elliptic ovate, tapering, acute at the base; peduncles

terminal, few-flowered ; flowers rather large, white, fragrant ; berry when ripe red, oblong-pointed, usually one-seeded. Common on the higher Ghauts, at Rohe in the Concan. Syn. Murraya exotica, Roxb. Fl Ind. ; Chalcas paniculata, Linn. ; Lour. Fl Cochin, 331.

8. CLAUSENA, Burm.

1. Willdenowii, W. and A. *Prod.* 1, 96.—Shrubby, young branches, leaves, and racemes, glabrous ; leaflets 5 to 11, alternate, ovate or ovate-acuminated oblique at the base, crenulated ; panicles racemiform axillary ; stigma 4-lobed ; fruit oblong. Chorla Ghaut, east of Goa. Syn. Amyris dentata, Willd. sp. ii, 337 ; Icica dentata, DC. *Prod.* ii, 78 ; Wight Ic. *t.* 14.

2. Simplicifolia, Dalz. in Hook. Jour. Bot. iii, 180.—A tree ; leaves simple oval oblong, attenuated towards the base, dotted with black, glabrous ; flowers from the upper axils in trichotomous cymes, longer than the leaves ; buds linear oblong ; sepals rounded ; petals linear obtuse, silky at the base inside ; stigma 4-lobed ; ovary 4-celled, cells 2-seeded ; fruit at length glabrous, of the size of a pea. Tulkut Ghaut ; flowers in August and September.

9. PARAMIGNYA, Wight.

1. Monophylla, Wight Illust. p 108, *t.* 42.—A scandent shrub, armed with stout thorns ; leaves ovate oblong, 3 inches long, 2 broad ; fruit size of an apple, when ripe pulpy, 4-celled ; seeds one above another. Parr Ghaut, jungles at Virdee, throughout the South Concan as far north as the Sawitree river. Native name " Kurwa Waguttee."

10. LUVUNGA, Hamilt.

1. Elentherandra, Dalz. in Hook. Jour. Bot. ii, 258.—Shrubby climbing, thorny, spines axillary reflexed, scarcely curved ; leaves trifoliolate long-petioled, leaflets broad-elliptic or obovate coriaceous glabrous, entire ; flowers axillary, panicle spicate, spikes shorter than the petiole ; stamens free. The Ghauts ; common ; flowers in January ; fruit in May ; fruit resinous and odoriforous, size of an olive ; found also in Ceylon.

11. FERONIA, Corr.

1. F Elephantum, Corr.—A large tree ; leaves small pinnated ; leaflets 5 to 7, obovate, common petiole slightly winged ; racemes lax, few-flowered ; fruit spherical, large as a billiard-ball, scurfy, hard ; commonly called Wood Apple. Deccan and Guzerat ; common. Rumph. Amb. ii, *t.* 43 ; Roxb. Fl Ind. ii, p 411 ; Wight Ic. Fl i, *t.* 15. Leaves have the odour of anise seed.

12. AEGLE, Corr.

1. A Marmelos.—A tall thorny tree; leaves pinnate; leaflets 3, rarely 5; peduncles axillary, few-flowered; flowers rather large, on long pedicles; fruit large, spherical, smooth, full of pulp, which is very valuable in dysentery. They are regularly sold in the Calcutta bazars. Native name "Bil." Syn. Feronia pellucida, Roth. nov. sp. p 384; Cratæva marmelos, Linn; Rheed. Mal. iii, *t.* 37. Wild in many parts of the Deccan.

XXXII. CLUSIACEÆ.

1. GARCINIA.

1. Purpurea.—A tall slender tree, with drooping branches and dark-green leaves, red when young; fruit spherical, smooth, full of purple juice. It is eaten, and has an agreeable acid flavour. From it the Portuguese at Goa make a syrup, and the seeds furnish the concrete oil called "Kokum," so useful in healing chaps. In the Southern Concan; common.

2. XANTHOCHYMUS, Roxb.

1. Ovalifolius, Roxb.—A middling-sized tree; leaves oval, shining; flowers lateral fascicled, berry oval, size of a walnut, found in March and April. It has a smooth green rind, and is full of yellow juice. On the Ghauts; pretty common. Syn. Stalagmitis ovalifolius, Don.; S cambogioides, Moore's Cat. of Ceylon Pl; Cambogia gutta, Burm. Fl Ind.

2. Pictorius, Roxb.—A middling-sized tree with a dense coma of thick dark-green polished leaves, each upwards of a foot in length; fruit size of an apple, pointed, bright yellow, which yields a large quantity of pretty good gamboge. On the Southern Ghauts; one tree, probably planted, grows in the island of Caranjah. Syn. Stalagmitis pictorius, G. Don.

3. MESUA, Linn.

1. Ferrea, Linn.—An elegant tree, with coriaceous oblong lanceolate leaves, shining above and glaucous beneath; flowers large, white, like a Cistus. Southern Concan, Warree, where it is called "Nagchumpa." Syn. M speciosa, DC. *Prod.* 1; Calophyllum nagassarum, Burm. Ind. p 21.

4. CALOPHYLLUM, Linn.

1. Inophyllum, Linn. DC. *Prod.* 1, 562.—A small crooked tree, with beautiful dark-green shining elliptic leaves; racemes lax,

axillary and terminal; flowers white, fragrant; fruit spherical, smooth, green. Oil called "Woondy" is extracted from the seeds, and the crooked stems furnish excellent knees for boats. Common in the Malwan talooka and sandy shores of Southern Concan. Syn. Balsamarina inophyllum, Lour. Hook. Pot. misc. ii, 355, *t.* 17.

2. Speurium Choisg. in DC. *Prod.* 1.—A tree with cuneate obovate leaves, very much smaller than those of the last, inserted on the authority of Nimmo as inhabiting the Southern Concan, though not seen there by other botanists. It is plentiful, however, at Honore, in Canara. Syn. C calaboides, Don in Mill. Dict.; C apetalum, Willd; C calaba, Linn.

3. Angustifolium, Roxb. Fl Ind. ii. 608.—Leaves short, petioled lanceolate, lucid, finely veined; flowers in axillary fascicles; pedicles with a cyathiform apex. Neelkoond and Woolwee Ghauts, south-west from Dharwar. Poon tree; yields the Poon spars for ships' masts.

5. CALYSACCION, Wight.

1. Longifolium, Wight. Illust. i, 130.—A tree; leaves oblong oval obtuse, coriaceous, delicately reticulated; flowers in clusters on the thick branches, small, white, streaked with red. The flowers are an article of commerce, and are exported to Calcutta and lately to Europe; they are used for dyeing silk. The globular flower-buds were sent to London under the erroneous name of Nagkesur. Maratha name "Suringee." Common in the Rutnagherry Collectorate and elsewhere. Syn. Calophyllum longifolium, W. and A. *Prod.*

XXXIII. HIPPOCRATEACEÆ.

1. HIPPOCRATEA, Linn.

1. H Indica, Willd. DC. *Prod.* 1, 558,—Glabrous; leaves elliptic-acute at the base, obtuse or acute at the apex, serrulated, shining; panicles dichotomous corymbiform; flowers minute, yellow; carpels 1 inch long, oblong striated, each 2-seeded; valves boat-shaped. Along the Ghauts; pretty common. Native name "Kazurati." Roxb. Fl Ind. i, 165; H disperma, Vahl. enum. ii, p 28.

2. H Grahamii, Wight Illust. i, 134.—Shrubby, twining, glabrous; leaves coriaceous entire, broad ovate, or suborbicular acuminate; panicles very numerous, large, many-flowered, on the summits of the branches; petals linear spathulate obtuse; carpels obovate obtuse emarginate. H obtusifolia, Grah. Mss. Common on the Ghauts.

2. SALACIA, Linn.

1. PRINOIDES, DC. *Prod.* 1, 571.—Shrub; leaves oblong acuminate, serrulate, coriaceous, smooth, shining; pedicels fascicled on an axillary tubercle; flowers very small, appear in December; fruit globose, fleshy red, like a cherry, one-seeded, eatable. Native name "Neesul Bondee." In the Warree country; not very common. Tonsella prinoides, Willd.; Johnia coromandeliana, Roxb. Fl Ind. i, 169.

2. S ROXBURGHII.—A shrub; leaves oblong lanceolate, bluntly acuminated, coriaceous, nearly quite entire; pedicels many, on an axillary tubercle; flowers greenish, minute; fruit large, globose, rough and dry, size of a crab-apple, 2 to 3-seeded. Ram Ghaut; flowers in February. Johnia salacioides, Roxb. Fl Ind. i, 168.

3. S OBLONGA, Wall.—A glabrous shrub; leaves elliptic-oblong, thin, coriaceous, entire (in Bombay specimens); peduncle axillary short, 3-flowered; pedicels equal to the peduncle, petals long and connivent; fruit size of a small orange, 8-seeded; seed large, angular. Chorla Ghaut; flowers greenish-yellow, large for the genus.

4. S BRUNONIANA, W. and A. *Prod.* 1, 105.—Glabrous, branches terete, leaves oblong, or elliptic, obtusely acuminated, minutely serrated, coriaceous; pedicels few, on an axillary tubercle, one-flowered, as long as the petiole; calyx shortly and obtusely 5-toothed, petals ovate, sessile, coriaceous. Ram Ghaut.

XXXIV. MALPIGHIACEÆ.

1. HEPTAGE, Gaert.

1. MADABLOTA, Gaert. fr. ii, 169, *t.* 116.—A climbing shrub; leaves ovate, acuminated; flowers in terminal racemes, white and yellow; carpels unequally 3-winged. On the Ghauts, and in the Concans; pretty common; flowers and fruit in January and February. The bark is a very good subaromatic bitter, Dr. Lush. Syn. Molina racemosa, Cav. dissert. ix, *t.* 263; Gaert. racemosa, Roxb. Fl Ind. ii, p 368; Banisteria bengalensis, Linn; B unicapsularis, Lam.; Rheed. Mal. vi, *t.* 59. Maratha name "Huludwail," or yellow climber. Juss. Archives du Mus d'hist. Nat. iii, 500, *t.* 16. Syn. Madablota Sounnerat voy. Ind. ii, *t.* 135; Banisteria tetraptera, Roxb. Cor. *t.* 18, Lonn. loc. cit.; Calophyllum akara, Burm. Ind. 121; Luccowia fimbriata, Dennite.

2 ASPIDOPTERYS, Juss.

1. ROXBURGHANA, A. Juss.—A climbing shrub with broadly ovate acuminate shining leaves, smooth on both sides; panicles

axillary and terminal; carpels each surrounded with an oblong linear entire wing. Syn. Hiræa indica, Roxb. Fl. Ind. ii, p 448; Trioptesis indica, Willd. sp. Kandalla Ghaut and in the Concans. Juss. in Archives de Museum d'hist Natur. iii, 508, *t.* 17.

2. CORDATA, Juss. loc. cit. 513.—Leaves roundish cordate acuminate, upperside slightly hairy, underside tomentose; petioles and panicles also tomentose; flowers in October. Near Penn. Syn. Hiræa cordata, Heyne; Wall. Pl as. rar. i, p 13, *t.* 13. The true Hiræas are American.

XXXV. ANCISTROCLADEÆ, Planchon.

1. ANCISTROCLADUS, Wall.

1. HEYNEANUS, Wall. Cat. No. 7262.—A handsome subscandent shrub, with deep-green oblong leaves, and small white flowers in terminal racemes, which appear in March; calyx and corolla about equal; stamens 10, alternately shorter; stigmas 3; fruit small, with three very long wings. Kandalla, Parr Ghaut, Meera Dongur, Ram Ghaut, &c. Syn. Wormia, Vahl.; Valli modagam, Rheed. Mal. vii, *t.* 47. This shrub has curious hooks on the branches, which, no doubt, assist in its support.

XXXVI. SAPINDACEÆ.

1. CARDIOSPERMUM, Linn.

1. HELICACABUM, Linn.—An annual climber, with delicate supra-decompound leaves, small white flowers, and inflated membranaceous, bladdery capsule; seeds black, with a white spot. Common in hedges. The root is diaphoretic, diuretic, and aperient. Wight. Ic. Pl *t.* 508.

2. SCHMIEDELIA, Linn., Rheed.—An extensive climber; leaves trifoliate; leaflets ovate or oblong acute serrated; racemes axillary, solitary, simple or bifid; flowers small, white; fruit small baccate. Meera hills; near Penn. Rheed. Mal. v, *t.* 25.

3. VILLOSA.—A tomentose climbing shrub, with ternate leaves; leaflets oblong, serrulate, softly villous beneath, 6 to 8 inches long; racemes axillary and terminal, very hairy; flowers numerous, small, hairy. Common in Southern Concan.

2. SAPINDUS, Linn.

1. LAURIFOLIUS.—A pretty large tree, with large abruptly pinnate leaves; leaflets 3 pair, ovate lanceolate, entire, glabrous;

flowers in large terminal panicles; fruit of tree globular; berries combined, rather hairy; used as soap. Common about villages; a doubtful native. Syn. trifoliata, Linn.

2. EMARGINATUS, Vahl.—Leaves abruptly pinnate; leaflets 2 to 3 pair, oblong retuse or emarginate, upperside glabrous, under very downy; racemes panicled, terminal; fruit usually 3-lobed, lobes very hairy on the inside. This and the preceding are called "Rhete"; the fruit of both is used medicinally, also for washing silk. Syn. S detergens? Roxb. Is said to have virtues in epilepsy.

3. CUPANIA, Plum.

1. CANESCENS, Pers.—Leaflets 2 pair, obovate or oblong, glabrous; racemes simple or panicled from the old leafless shoots; capsule ovoid triangular, brown, velvetty; flowers white, appear in February. Ram Ghaut and Kandalla; Graham, Beemasunker; Koosur Ghaut and Beemasunker, Gibson. Syn. Molinæa canescens, Roxb. Fl Ind. ii, p 243; Sapindus tetraphyllus, Vahl. Symb. iii, p 54. Maratha name "Kurpa."

4. NEPHELIUM, Linn.; EUPHORIA, Lam.

1. LONGANUM, Camb.—Leaflets 2 to 4 pair, entire, upperside shining, under pale, glaucous, strongly nerved; panicles lax, terminal; fruit size of a cherry, eatable when young, bluntly muricated; flowers in February and March, white. The wood of this tree is hard, close-grained, and white, Roxb. Near Parr; Ram Ghaut. Syn. Dimocarpus longan, Lour; Euphoria longana, Lam.; Scytalia longan, Roxb. Fl Ind. ii, p 270; Nephelium Bengalense, Don in Mill. Dict. Maratha name "Wumb." Bot. Reg. *t.* 1729.

5. SLEICHERA, Willd.

1. TRIJUGA, Willd.—A tree, leaflets 3 pair, oblong or broadly lanceolate, entire, nearly glabrous; racemes axillary, or below the leaves; drupe globose-pointed, covered with stout prickles; flowers white, in February and March, minute. The natives eat the fruit, and also make oil from it. Native name "Koosimb." Common on the Ghauts. Syn. Melicocea trijuga, Juss.; Stadmannia trijuga, Spr.; Cassambium pubescens, Ham. in Wern. Trans. "Koon," Gaert. *t.* 180. The bark is astringent; the wood hard, and used for various purposes, as sugar mills, &c.; the bark is rubbed up with oil to cure the itch, Roxb.

6. DODONÆA, Linn.

2. BURMANNIANA, DC.—A scandent shrub; leaves simple oblong lanceolate cuneate, clammy; flowers small, greenish, in terminal panicles; capsules emarginate at both ends, winged. Kandalla; near Belgaum; common. "Dawa-ka-Jhar" of the natives, according to Grah. Cat.; Syn. D augustifolia, Roxb. Fl Ind. ii, p 256; Ptelea viscosa, Burm. Ind. Zeyl. *t.* 23. "Lutchmee," Maratha.

XXXVII. MELIACEÆ.

1. NAREGAMIA, W. and A.

1. ALATA, W. and A. *Prod.* 1, 117.—A very small shrub, 1 foot; leaves trifoliolate; leaflets cuneate obovate, entire petiole margined; flowers large, white, on longish axillary peduncles; capsule 3-cornered 3-valved. East of Panwell; rare, Nimmo. Plentiful on the sides of nullahs at Vingorla. Syn. Turrea alata, Wight Mss.; Nela naregam, Rheed. Mal. x, *t.* 22.; Wight Ic. *t.* 90. "Kapoor Bendy," Maratha.

2. TURRÆA, Linn.

1. VIRENS, Linn. DC. *Prod.* 1, 620.—A shrub, 3 to 4 feet high; leaves elliptic lanceolate acuminate, quite smooth; flowers few, white, long, slender; calyx and fruit with silky hairs. Pretty common on the Ghauts. Smith Ic. i, *t.* 10.

3. MELIA, Linn.

1. COMPOSITA, Willd. sp. iii, 559.—A larger tree than the last; leaves bi-tripinnate; leaflets 3 to 7 pair to each pinnate, ovate acuminated, crenulated, glabrous, young shoots, petioles, and panicles mealy; flowers white; drupe, round, size of a plum; flowers in March. Parr Ghaut, Tullawaree, &c. Syn. M robusta, Roxb. Fl Ind. ii, 397.

4. AZADIRACHTA, Adr. Juss.

1. INDICA, Juss.—A middle-sized tree; leaves simply pinnated; leaflets unequal-sided, glabrous, serrated; panicles axillary; flowers white, appear in May; drupe with a one-seeded nut. The leaves and bark are very bitter; the former are used to preserve books from the attacks of the boring worm, also in fomentations; of great efficacy in rheumatism. The bark is a febrifuge. The oil of the pericarp is said to possess antispasmodic virtues. Native name "Neem." Syn. Melia azadiracta, Linn. DC. *Prod.* 1, 622; Roxb. Fl Ind. ii, 394; Rheed. Mal iv, *t.* 52.

5. MALLEA, Adr. Juss.

1. ROTHII, Juss. Mem. Mus. xix, *t.* 13, *f.* 6.—Shrubby; leaves unequally pinnated; leaflets 4 to 6 pair, unequal-sided, entire, or serrated above the middle; peduncles axillary, with the flowers in a corymb or panicle; flowers small, white; berry small, red, ripens in March. Katruj Ghaut, near Poona; between Ram Ghaut and Belgaum. Syn. Melia baccifera, Roth. nov. sp. 215; Ekebergia indica, Roxb. Fl Ind. ii, 392.

6. NEMEDRA, Adr. Juss.

1. N NIMMONII, Dalz.—A tree; leaves pinnate; leaflets 2 to 3 pair; flowers in axillary racemes, small, white; fruit pear-shaped, size of a plum, indehiscent, abounding in a white resinous juice. Kandalla, hills near Nagotna, jungle near Rohe, an interesting discovery of the late Mr. Nimmo. Its only congener is in New Holland. Native name "Boorumb." Syn. Epicharis exarillata, Nimmo.

7. AMOORA, Roxb.

1. A CUCULLATA, Roxb. Cor. Pl *t.* 258.—A tree; leaves pinnate; leaflets 2 to 4 pair; obliquely ovate lanceolate obtuse, smooth; male panicles axillary, drooping, about as long as the leaves; fruit bearing peduncles 3 to 6-flowered, young fruit like small pears, with a smooth coriaceous epicarp, when ripe, nearly spherical. Parwar Ghaut. Syn. Andersonia cucullata, Roxb. Fl Ind. ii, 212.

8. EPICHARIS, Blum.

1. E EXARILLATA, Arnott.—A tree; leaves pinnate; leaflets 4 to 6 pair, taper-pointed, entire, smooth on both sides, 6 inches long, 2 to 3 broad, panicles axillary short, rigid; flowers small, pale-yellow; capsule globose, size of an apple, smooth; when ripe yellow; seeds like chesnuts, polished, dark-purple. Near Kandalla and Vingorla; flowers in August and September. Guarea binectarifera, Roxb. Fl Ind. ii, 240.

9. WALSURA, Roxb.

1. W PISCIDIA, Roxb. Fl Ind. ii, 387.—A tree; leaves ternate; leaflets oblong entire, smooth, 2 to 3 inches long, and one broad; flowers in terminal panicles, numerous, yellowish white; berry size of an olive, oblong, dark-brown, velvetty. Ram Ghaut; plentiful. The bark is used to poison fish.

10. HEYNEA, Roxb.

1. H Trijuga, Roxb. Fl Ind. ii, 390.—A small tree, with pinnate leaves; leaflets 3 to 4 pair, ovate oblong acuminate entire; flowers in axillary long-peduncled cymes, small, white, appear in March and April; fruit cherry-like, red, fleshy, opening from the apex, like that of Xanthoxylon rhetsa. Common all along the Ghauts. Juss. Mem. Mus. xix, 235, *t.* 18, *fig* 17. Native name "Limbara."

XXXVIII. CEDRELACEÆ.

1. SOYMIDA, Adr. Juss.

1. Febrifuga, Juss.—A large tree; leaves pinnate; leaflets 3 to 6 pair, oval oblong obtuse; panicles large, terminal, or in the axils of the upper leaves; fruit-capsule oblong obovate, size of an apple, 5-celled, 5-valved, dehiscing from the apex. Guzerat, Adjunta jungles, Sindwah Ghaut, Khandeish jungles, Jowar jungles. Native name "Rouen" or "Ruhin." Syn. Swietenia febrifuga, Roxb. Cor. i, *t.* 17; Fl Ind. ii, 398. A useful tonic in intermittent fever, not more than 4 to 5 drachms to be administered in 24 hours, Ainslie.

2. CHICKRASSIA, Adr. Juss.

1. Nimmonii, I. Grah. Wight's Illust. No. 10.—A large tree; leaves pinnate; leaflets tomentose, capsule 4 to 5-valved, size of an apple. Jungles at Rohe; the flowers appear in January and February. This tree differs from C tubularis, Juss., in being tomentose or velvetty, and 4 to 5, not 3, valved. The timber resembles an inferior kind of cedar, and, as such, is exported from Malabar. This is probably the C velutina, Wall. list No. 1270.

3. CEDRELA, Linn.

1. Toona, Roxb. Cor. *t.* 238; Fl Ind. i, 635.—A large tree; leaves abruptly pinnate; leaflets 6 to 12 pair, ovate lanceolate acuminated, entire or slightly toothed; panicles drooping; flowers numerous, small, white; capsule oblong, rather larger than a field bean, 5-celled, 5-valved. Jungles at Rohe, ravines at Kandalla, &c. The timber is like inferior mahogany, and is much used in Bengal furniture, bedsteads, chairs, &c. The powdered bark, though not bitter, when mixed with a small portion of the powdered seed of Guilandina bonduc, W. and A. ("Sagurgota" of the Marathas), is a good substitute for Peruvian bark in the cure of remitting and intermitting fevers, Roxb.; Wight Ic. *t.* 161.

4. CHLOROXYLON, DC.

4. Swietenia, DC.—A tree; leaves abruptly pinnate; leaflets 10 to 20 pair, semi-cordate, oblong, pale-coloured, small, unequal sides, pellucid dotted; panicle large, terminal, capsules 3-celled, 3-valved; wood close-grained, yellow, excellent for the turner; some specimens are of great beauty, equal to the wood of the sugar maple of N. America. Native names "Billoo" and "Hulda." Yields wood-oil. Grows in the vicinity of Belgaum, also at the Falls of Gokak; Alleh Bela hills, Dr. Gibson. Syn. Swietenia chloroxylon, Roxb. Cor. *t*, 64; Fl Ind. ii, 400; Juss. Mem. Mus. xix, *t*. 23, *f*. 2; Wight Illust. Bot. i, *t*. 57.

XXXIX. AMPELIDEÆ.

1. CISSUS, Linn.

1. C. Quadrangularis, Linn.—Smooth, climbing, root tuberous; stem herbaceous dichotomous, obtusely quadrangular articulated; stipules biauricled, adnate; leaves thick, fleshy, cordate rounded, entire or trilobate; umbels contracted, few-flowered; fruit ovoid, smooth, red, 1-seeded, Willd. sp. Fl i. p 657; Saclanthus quadrangularis, Forsk. Descr. 33, Ic. *t*. 2. Guzerat, in hedges. Used by the Arabs to sleep upon in complaints of the spine. Native name "Hursanker."

2. Repanda, Vahl. Symb. iii, 18.—Young parts tomentose, stems terete; stipules oblong; leaves cordate roundish, shortly acuminated, entire, repand-toothed; tendrils none; umbels compound; flowers in June. Common. Syn. Vitis repanda, W. and A. *Prod.*; C indica, Rottl. DC. *Prod.* 1, 628.

3. Latifolia, Vahl. Symb. iii, 18.—Young parts densely pubescent, young shoots 4-angled; stipules oval, adnate; leaves broad cordate acuminate with bristly serratures, underside covered with dense rusty-coloured tomentum; fruit size of a pea, black and smooth when ripe. The Concan; common. Syn. Vitis adnata, Wall.; V repens, Wall.

4. Repens, Lam. DC. *Prod.* 1, 628.—Glabrous, pale-green, young shoots glaucous; stipules cordate rounded; leaves cordate ovate acuminate, with sharp spiniform teeth with compound umbels of flowers; fruit globose. The Concan. Syn. Vitis repens, W. and A.; Rheed. Mal. vii, *t*. 48.

5. Trilobata, Lam.—Glabrous; stipules oval; leaves 3 foliolate, upper ones often only deeply 3-cleft; leaflets bristle-toothed, oblong lanceolate, lateral ones unequal-sided; fruit globose, 1-seeded, DC. *Prod.* 1, 629. The Concan. Syn. Vitis Rheedei, W. and A. *Prod.*; Rheede Mal. vii, *t*. 45.

6. Carnosa, Roxb. Fl Ind. i, 409.—Stem compressed striated; stipules oblong; leaves 3-foliolate on longish petioles; leaflets stalked, roundish or ovate or obovate, crenate, serrated; cymes peduncles compound; berries black. Syn. C cinerea, Lam; Rheed. Mal. vii, 9; Rumph. Amb. v, *t.* 166. *f.* 2; C cœnata, Vahl; C obtusifolia, Lam; Hook. Comp. Bot. Mag. i, 161, *t.* 9.

7. Muricata, Dalz. Mss.—Unisexual, all glabrous, except the inflorescence; stem woody, branches with muricated bark; leaves petioled trifoliolate; leaflets stalked, subcoriaceous, serrated, oblong acuminated; umbels axillary, twice compound; fruit globose, size of a large cherry, white when ripe. Monkeys are very fond of it. Southern Ghauts; plentiful in Canara. Vitis muricata, Wall.; W. and A. *Prod.* p 128.

8. C Edulis, Dalz. in Hook. Jour. Bot. ix, p 248.—Root fibrous; stem quadrangular broadly 4-winged; stipules lunate entire; leaves shortly-petioled cordate ovate entire, serrulated; umbels short-peduncled; fruit globose, acrid, 1-seeded, size of a small pea. Common. Long confounded with the C quadrangularis of Linn; Syn. Vitis quadrangularis, Wall.; C quadrangularis, Roxb. Fl Ind. i, 407. Used in curries by the Bengalees.

9. C. Vitiginea, Roxb. nov. Linn.—Nearly glabrous, scarcely climbing; leaves very large, shining, broadly cordate, shortly acuminated; stipules cordate, cymes on long peduncles; flowers reddish; berry black when ripe, 1 to 2-seeded. A very common bush in the Deccan, Roxb. Fl Ind.

10. Pedata, Lam., Roxb. Fl i, 413.—Young parts softly pubescent; stipules cordate acute; leaves pedate, leaflets 7 to 11, oblong lanceolate acuminated, membranaceous, serrulate; peduncles axillary or opposite the leaves; fruit flattened on the top, 4-lobed, white, 4-seeded. The Concans and Ghauts. Syn. Vitis pedata, Wall.; W. and A. *Prod.* p 128; C heptaphylla, Retz. obs.; Rheede Mal. vii, *t.* 10. The Deccan, Gornehr.

11. Auriculata, Roxb. Fl Ind. i, 411.—Root tuberous, young shoots succulent, and petioles and inflorescence softly pubescent; leaves 5-foliolate; leaflets oblong, obovate or rhomboid, shortly acuminated, serrulated; berries smooth, shining, red, size of a cherry. At Vingorla. Syn. Vitis auriculata, Wall.

12. Discolor, Dalz. in Hook. Jour. Bot. ii, 39.—Glabrous; stem and branches acutely angular, red; stipules broadly ovate obtuse; leaves petioled, ovate or oblong lanceolate acuminated, truncate or slightly cordate at the base, serrated, deep-green above, purple, and shining beneath; umbels opposite the leaves twice the length of the petiole; petals red, cohering; berries black, shining, size of a large pea. Shady jungles of the Concan; flowers in August; fruit in October.

13. C SETOSA, Roxb. Fl Ind. 1, 410.—Herbaceous, climbing, bristly all over, even to the fruit; leaves sessile, ternate; leaflets fleshy, grossly bristle-serrate about 4 inches long, oval and waved; pedicels all recurved in fruit; berries red, ovoid; every part of the plant is acrid. About Jooneer; not seen elsewhere.

14. C ARANEOSUS, Dalz.—Climbing; all floccose except the upper surface of the leaves; leaves dark-green, pale beneath, cordate acute, simple or trifoliate; leaflets oblong acute, unequal-sided at the base; peduncles opposite the leaves, many-flowered, cirriherous, rather long; fruit spherical, smooth, 1 to 4-seeded, size of a pea; rare. On the highest Ghauts west of Jooneer.

2. VITIS, Linn.

1. V INDICA, Linn.—Branches, petioles, and peduncles villous; leaves cordate, scarcely angled or lobed, toothed, underside tomentose, upper floccose, at length somewhat glabrous; racemes peduncled, cylindric; peduncles cirriferous; flowers bisexual; fruit globose; flowers in May.

3. LEEA, Linn.

1. L STAPHYLEA, Roxb.—Shrubby, branches round, smooth; leaves from compound to super-decompound; leaflets from oblong to linear lanceolate, with a long tapering point coarsely serrated; cymes terminal, large; flowers greenish-white; berry size of a small cherry, flattened, 5 to 6-grooved, 5 to 6-celled; cells 1-seeded. Common in the Concan and Ghaut jungles. Wight Ic. *t.* 78; Illust. *t.* 58.

2. L MACROPHYLLA, Roxb. Fl Ind. i, 653.—Stem herbaceous, erect, flexuose-jointed; leaves very large simple, broad cordate, toothed, smooth on both sides; cymes terminal, large; flowers numerous, small, white; berry depressed, size of a small cherry, smooth, black and succulent when ripe. Hills in the Concan; pretty common; root tuberous, and employed in the cure of guinea-worm.

XL. GERANIACEÆ.

1. MONSONIA, Linn., Fil.

1. M SENEGALENSIS, Guill. and Perr. Tent. Fl Senegamb. i, 131.—A very small plant 3 to 4 inches high; leaves ovate cordate, acute or lanceolate, remotely toothed, pubescent and villous, long-petioled; stipules villous; flowers axillary, long-peduncled; peduncles solitary, 1-flowered, with two bracteoles; corolla and calyx about equal; flowers pink; fruit often longer than the whole plant. Dry pastures in the Deccan; not common. Syn. Erodium

chumbulense, Munro in Wight Ic. *t.* 1074; Monsonia lawiana, Stocks MS.; Geranium lawianum, Graham's Catalogue.

XLI. OXALIDEÆ.

1. OXALIS, Linn.

1. O Corniculata, Linn.—A weed, the pest of gardens, stems decumbent, rooting; leaves palmately trifoliolate; leaflets obcordate, pubescent; peduncles 2 to 5-flowered; capsule linear oblong, many-seeded, densely pubescent. Syn. O pusilla, Roxb. Fl Ind. ii, 457; O repens, Thunb. Wight Ic. *t.* 18.

2. BIOPHYTUM, DC.

1. B Sensitivum, DC. *Prod.* 1, 690.—A small plant with a short stem; leaves umbellate at its apex, abruptly pinnated; leaflets 10 to 14 pair, obliquely obovate or oblong; peduncles from among the leaves, several together, pubescent; flowers numerous, umbellate, yellow. Common in the Concan during the rains. Rheed. Mal. ix, *t.* 19; Bot Reg. xviii, *t.* 68.

XLII. BALSAMINEÆ.

1. IMPATIENS, Linn.

1. I Acaulis, Arnott in Hook. Comp. Bot. Mag. i, 325.—Smooth leaves, orbicular or oblong, rounded or cordate at the base, bracts ovate acute; pedicels elongated; sepals small, ovate obtuse, spur very slender, elongated. Syn. I scapiflora, Hook. Bot. Mag. *t.* 3587. The Ghauts.

2. I Rivalis, Wight Contr. Ind. Bot. i, 13, *t.* 8.—Herbaceous; root tuberous; all the leaves radical ovate oblong, rather oblique at the base, remotely bristle-serrated, hairy above, pale beneath; scape racemed, many-flowered; flowers pedicelled, large, upper sepal obtuse gibbous, hiding the column of fructification, lateral minute, lower ovate, attenuated into a slender spur, double the length of the petals; seeds hispid. The Ghauts; flowers in July and August. Supposed to be only a variety of the preceding.

3. I Stocksii, Hook. Fl. and Thoms.—Small, quite smooth; leaves broadly ovate, membranaceous; bracts ovate acute; sepals broadly ovate obtuse, lip saccate at the base, spur none, wings 3-lobed; leaves only 1 inch long. The Southern Ghauts. Jour. Proc. Linn. Soc. iv, p 119.

4. I Chinensis, Linn. sp. Pl.—Glabrous; stem erect, angled; leaves subsessile linear acute, opposite, remotely serrated, glaucous

beneath; pedicels solitary or fascicled; sepals linear, spur slender elongated, incurved, vexillum orbicular acuminate, wings semiobovate, auricled at the base. Syn. I fasciculata, Lam.; Wight Ic. 748; Bot. Mag. 4631; I heterophylla, Wall. in Roxb. Fl* Ind. ii, 458. The Concans.

5. I OPPOSITIFOLIA, Linn.—Leaves opposite, from narrow linear lanceolate to broad obovate lanceolate, acute, membranaceous, slightly serrated, serratures bristly; pedicels axillary, solitary or in pairs, not half the length of the leaves, very slender; lower sepal cucullate, with a very short conical, nearly straight spur. Spr. *syst.* i, 808; Syn. Balsamina oppositifolia, DC. *Prod.* i, 686; I rosmarinifolia, Retz. Very common in the Concans.

6. I TOMENTOSA, Heyne.—Leaves short-petioled, oblong lanceolate, acute serrated, slightly hispid above; pedicels solitary or twin, along with the flowers, pubescent; sepals linear lanceolate acuminate; spur very short, obtuse, incurved; capsule oblong glabrous, few-seeded; seeds black, shining. Syn. I reticulata, Wall.; I ramosissima, Dalz. in Hook. Jour. Bot. iii, 230. Flowers in September. Phoonda Ghaut.

7. I LAWII, Hook. Fil. and Thoms. loc. cit. p 122.—Stems erect branched, and with the leaves beneath quite smooth; leaves shortly oblong, obtuse at the base, sessile, the upper ones smaller, cordate, stem-clasping, remotely serrated, a little rough above; pedicels short; flowers large; sepals linear falcate; vexillum orbicular; lip small, without a spur. Southern Concan. A very beautiful species.

8. I INCONSPICUA, Benth. in Wall. Cat. 4741.—Small-branched, diffuse, smooth; leaves narrow oblong, linear or lanceolate, serrate; pedicels puberulous; flowers minute; sepals linear subulate; lip boat-shaped, acuminate, without a spur. Syn. I pusilla, Heyne. A very inconspicuous and variable plant.

9. I KLEINII, W. and A. *Prod.* 140.—Erect, with spreading branches; leaves opposite, from obovate and obtuse to lanceolate and acute, with a large gland on each side near the petiole, upperside hairy on the veins, under glaucous; pedicels solitary or twin, in fruit reflexed; lateral sepals linear, posterior concave, hairy, lower one with slender spur twice the length of the flower. Syn. Balsamania minor, DC. *Prod.* 1, 686. Very common in the rains.

10. I DALZELLII, Hook. and Thom. loc. cit.—Quite smooth, branched; leaves all shortly-petioled, ovate or oblong lanceolate, cordate at the base, acuminate, spinulously serrulate, slightly hairy above, pale beneath; flowers middling-sized, yellow; sepals linear lanceolate acuminate; lip saccate, terminated by a short spur; vexillum broadly cowled, winged on the back; stem 8 to 14 inches high. The South Concan.

11. I LATIFOLIA, Linn. sp. Pl.—Smooth; leaves subopposite or subverticelled, long-petioled, lanceolate or ovate lanceolate, acuminate, crenate serrate and bristly on the margin; flowers large; sepals small ovate cuspidate; lip acuminate concave; spur elongated, slender; vexillum reversely cuneate, horned. Syn. I cuspidata, Wight and Arn. in Hook. Comp. Bot. Mag. ii, 321; I bipartita, Wight and Arn. loc. cit. i, 322; I floribunda, Wight in Madr. Jour. v, p 7. Concan common.

12. I BALSAMINA, Linn. Willd. sp. Pl i, 1175,—A weed, herbaceous, erect, simple; leaves alternate petioled, glabrous, acuminated at both ends, acutely and often deeply serrated; petioles glanduliferous; pedicels 1 to 2 or more aggregate shorter than the leaves; lateral sepals minute lanceolate, anterior one pubescent, infundibuliform with a slender spur; capsule ovate, tomentose, and hairy. Very common; the double varieties are often of great beauty.

13. SCABRIUSCULA, Heyne in Roxb. Fl Ind. ed. Wall. ii, 464.—Low, erect, branched, pubescent and tomentose; leaves few, shortly-petioled, lanceolate acuminate serrate; pedicels short; sepals very small; lip boat-shaped, tomentose; spur none. Allied to I balsamina, but much smaller, leaves broader, and lip without a spur. The South Concan.

14. I PULCHERRIMA, Dalz. in Hook. Jour. Bot. ii, p 37.—Stem erect, glabrous; leaves alternate long-petioled ovate acuminated, crenate serrated; serratures bristly, somewhat roughish above, glaucous and quite smooth beneath; petioles glandular towards the apex; pedicels axillary, 2 to 3 together, one-flowered, half the length of the leaf; flowers large, rose-coloured, 2½ inches in diameter; the petals divided to near the base; the lobes cuneate obovate; fruit bearing pedicels erect, drooping at the apex; spur 2 inches long, filiform. Shady jungles in the Warree country; flowers in August. Hook Bot. Mag. 4615.

XLIII. PITTOSPORACEÆ.

1. PITTOSPORUM, Banks.

1. FLORIBUNDUM, W. and A. *Prod.* p 154.—A small tree; leaves thinly coriaceous, elliptic lanceolate, glabrous, margins waved; racemes terminal, compact, many-flowered; flowers white, small; capsule 2-valved, compressed, 3 to 4-seeded, size of a pea. All along the range of the Ghauts. The clubs of the Australians are made of the wood of P bicolor. Syn. Celastrus verticillata, Roxb. Fl Ind. i, 624; Senacia nepalensis, DC. *Prod.* 1, 367. Maratha name "Yekuddy." P zeylanicum, Wight Illust. i, 173.

XLIV. ZYGOPHYLLEÆ.

1. TRIBULUS, Tournef.

1. T TERRESTRIS, Linn.—A humifuse procumbent plant; leaves abruptly pinnate, opposite, stipuled; leaflets 5 to 6 pair; peduncles one-flowered, solitary, axillary; flowers yellow; fruit angular, prickly. The Deccan, Guzerat, Kattywar. DC. *Prod.* 1, 704. Belongs, with other species of the genus, to the desert flora. "Gokhroo," Marathi and Hindoostanee.

2. FAGONIA.

1. F MYSORENSIS, Roth. nov. sp. 215.—A suffrutescent much-branched plant; leaves opposite, 2-stipuled, stipules often thorny, one-foliolate; leaflets linear cuspidate; stipules spinous, very sharp, longer than the leaf; fruit capsular, 5-coccous, pubescent. Common in the Deccan. Wight Illust. i, *t.* 64. Has a fanciful reputation as a suppurative in cases of abscess from thorns; a drug in the bazar, under the name of "Dumaso," used for cooling the mouth.

3. PEGANUM, Linn.

1. HARMALA.—Herbaceous plant, with multifid leaves, lobes linear; flowers white, terminal; capsule spherical, 3-celled. Indapoor, in the Poona Collectorate, also Beejapore; apparently wild. Very common in Sind, extending to the west coast of Africa; capsules sold in the bazar under the name of "Hurmaro."

XLV. XANTHOXYLACEÆ.

1. XANTHOXYLON, Linn.

1. RHETSA, DC. *Prod.* 1, 728.—A tree with prickles over every part of it; bark corky; leaves equally pinnated; leaflets 8 to 16 pair, lanceolate, unequal-sided, entire, glabrous; panicles terminal; capsule size of a pea, globose, 2-valved, opening at the apex. The seed has a strong flavour of pepper; flowers minute, yellow, appear in November; fruit in February. Parr village, Twemlow; Kandalla, Arbuckle; at Banda, in the Warree country. Native name "Seesul." Syn Fagara rhetsa, Roxb. Fl Ind. i, 417; Rheed. Mal. v, *t.* 34.

2. TRIPHYLLUM, Juss.—A small tree without prickles; leaves trifoliolate; leaflets oblong, entire; flowers small, white, in axillary panicles, appear in April and May; capsule obovate, smooth, size of a field-bean. Found all along the Ghauts. Syn. Fagara triphylla, Linn. sp. Pl. ed. Willd. i, 666; Roxb. Fl Ind. i, 416. The capsules of X hastile are the Tejbul of the bazars, used for intoxicating fish.

2. TODDALIA, Juss.

1. Aculeata, Pers. DC. *Prod.* 2, 83.—A shrub or small tree with prickly stem and branches; leaves digitately trifoliolate; leaflets sessile, from oblong to broad lanceolate crenulate glabrous, pellucid dotted; racemes simple or compound axillary; flowers small, white; fruit size of a small cherry, 5-furrowed, 3 to 5-celled; has a pungent taste like black pepper. Near tank at Kandalla ?; Koomba Ghaut; abundant, Dr. Gibson; in Canara; plentiful. Syn. T asiatica, Lam.; T nitida, Lam; T rubricaulis, Willd.; Scopolia aculeata, Smith Roxb. Fl Ind. i, 616; Paullinia asiatica, Linn.; Rheede Mal. v, *t.* 41. The bark of the root is employed as a cure in jungle intermittent fevers, Roxb. The new genus Dipitalum, Dalz., found in Canara, is, with good reason, supposed to be the Toddalia bilocularis of W. and A. *Prod.* 149.

3. AILANTHUS, Desf.

1. Excelsa, Roxb. Fl Ind. ii, 450; Cor. *t.* 23.—A tall tree; leaves abruptly pinnated, young ones tomentose, older glabrous; leaflets coarsely toothed at the base; flowers fascicled in large-branched terminal panicles, appear in January and February; carpels samaroid, oblong compressed, membranaceous reticulated, swollen in the middle. Common about Broach and Baroda, Lush; Deccan, Dr. Gibson; wood light, used for sword-handles; of little use, Roxb.; Wight. Illust. Bot. i, *t.* 67.

2. Malabarica, DC.—Leaves with the leaflets entire; fruit broadly linear, rounded at both ends; flowers small, white, in terminal racemes, appear in February and March. DC. *Prod.* 2, p 89; Rheed. Mal. vi, *t.* 15. Ravines at Nagotna; Corondia, near Kandalla ? Yields a resin from the bark. Common in Canara. Canarese name "Muddhedoop." Punt Suchew's country, at Oodhur Raneeshwur.

XLVI. OCHNACEÆ.

I. OCHNA, Linn.

1. O Nana, Hamilton, in Wall. list 3761.—A very small shrub with narrow oblong lanceolate leaves, minutely serrulated, shining; flowers loosely pedicellate on axillary peduncles, rather large and showy, bright-yellow. South Concan. During several years in which Mr. Law and ourselves traversed the Concan in all directions, we have not met with any other member of this family, except this low shrub, two feet high at the most. Syn. O moonii, Thwaite's Enum. ?

XLVII. STAPHYLEACEÆ.

1. TURPINIA, Vent.

1. T Nepalensis, Wall.—A tree; leaves opposite unequally pinnated; leaflets 3 to 5-oblong lanceolate acuminated, coriaceous; flowers white, in opposite panicles; berry of the size of a large pea, scarcely fleshy, 3-celled; cells 1 to 3-seeded. Wight Ic. *t.* 972. Parwar Ghaut.

XLVIII. CELASTRACEÆ.

1. PLEUROSTYLIA, W. and A.

1. P Wightii, W. and A. *Prod.* 1, 157.—A shrub; leaves elliptic-oblong, entire whitish, opposite, shortly-petioled; peduncles axillary and terminal, very short, few-flowered, fruit small, indehiscent, 1 to 2-celled. The Ghauts, Wight Ic. *t.* 155.

2. EUONYMUS, Linn.

1. E Goughii, Wight Ic. *t.* 215.—Shrubby, glabrous, ramuli compressed; leaves somewhat triple-nerved, shortly-petioled, quite entire, oblong, ovate, acute at both ends, peduncles axillary, short, 1 to 3-flowered; petals 5, orbicular, fringed. Mangellee Ghaut.

3. CELASTRUS, Linn.

1. Paniculata, Willd. sp. i, p 1125.—A climbing unarmed shrub; leaves alternate, broadly oval, or ovate or obovate, with a sudden short acumination, slightly serrated, glabrous; racemes terminal, compound, elongated, erect or pendulous; flowers white; capsule globose, 3-celled, 3 to 6-seeded. Common on the Ghauts and in the Concans. The ghaut variety has an erect abbreviated panicle; oil is extracted from the seeds for burning and for medicine used in rheumatism. Maratha name "Kangoonee." Roxb. Fl Ind. i, 621; Syn. C nutans Roxb. loc. cit.; C rothiana, Schult.; DC. *Prod.* 2, p 8; Ceanothus paniculata Heyne in Roth. nov. sp. p 154; Scutia paniculata, Don in Mill. Dict. ii, 34; Wight Illust. i, *t.* 72; Ic. Pl. *t.* 158.

2. Rothiana, W. and A. *Prod.* p 159.—A shrub unarmed; leaves coriaceous, glabrous, broadly obovate, crenate, serrated, cuneate at the base, and tapering suddenly into the petiole; cymes much shorter than the leaves, dichotomous, fascicled from the tubercles of the older branches; capsules turbinate, 3-lobed, bright red when ripe, each lobe the size of a pea. Jungly hills in the Concan and Ghauts, common. Syn. C serrulata, Roth. nov. sp. p 156.

3. MONTANA, Roxb. Fl Ind. i, 620.—A shrub, thorny; leaves elliptic or obovate, tapering into the petiole, minutely and sharply crenate, serrated, coriaceous, glabrous; whitish-glaucous when dried; cymes axillary, lax, peduncled, twice as long as the petiole; capsules somewhat globose, 3-angled, about the size of a pea. Hills in the Deccan, at Koondiana in Guzerat, also in Sind. Roth. nov. sp. 154; Syn. C crenata, Roth. loc. cit. 156; Catha montana, Don in Mill. Dict. p 10. Young branches often pointed with a thorn. Much used as dunnage for roofs of houses. Native name "Mal Kangonee."

4. ELÆODENDRON, Jacq.

1. ROXBURGHII, W. and A. *Prod.* p 157.—A small tree; leaves opposite, elliptical or ovate crenate; serrated, young ones glaucous; cymes lax, dichotomous, divaricated about half the length of the leaves, usually with a solitary flower in the forks; drupe round, hard, size of a cherry; flowers small, yellow. Sattara and Kamatkee Ghauts; Beemasunker, Dr. Gibson; Syn. Nerija dichotoma, Roxb. Fl Ind. i, 646; Rhamnus nerija, Spr. *syst.* supp. p 86. Maratha name "Tamrooj."

5. LOPHOPETALUM, Wight.

1. L WIGHTIANUM, Arnott. Ann. Nat. Hist. iii, 151.—A middle-sized tree; leaves elliptic-oblong, a little acuminated, obtuse at the base, quite entire; corymbs terminal panicled; flowers with 5 divisions; ovary 3-celled; fruit sharply triangular, hard, 4 inches long; seeds oblong, compressed, surrounded by a long linear wing. Wight Ic. *t.* 162.

XLIX. RHAMNACEÆ.

1. VENTILAGO, Gaert.

1. MADRASPATANA, Gaert. fr. i, 223.—A large climbing shrub; leaves alternate, coriaceous, short-petioled, orbicular to ovate acuminated, acute or obtuse or cordate at the base, crenate, serrated or entire; flowers fascicled on long leafless branches, forming a panicle; small greenish fruit, size of a pea, with a long linear membranaceous wing. Khandalla, the Ghauts generally, and at Baitsee; flowers and fruit in January. Native names "Lokundie," "Kanwail." Cordage is made of the bark, As. Res. vi, 352; Roxb. Fl Ind. i, 629; Syn. V denticulata, Willd. DC. *Prod.* 2, 38.

2. BOMBAIENSIS, Dalz. in Hook. Jour. Bot. iii, 36.—Branchlets, petioles, and flowers covered with fulvous tomentum; leaves lanceolate acute at the base, unequal, acuminated at the apex,

crenated, crenatures with callous points, glabrous on both sides, shining; flowers fascicled in the axils of the leaves, shortly-pedicelled. Chorla Ghaut; flowers in February. This species is distinguished from the preceding by the very different inflorescence, while the costal veins in the leaf of the preceding are double in number, and form a much larger angle with the midrib.

2. ZIZYPHUS, Lournef.

1. Rugosa, Lam. Encycl. Meth. iii, 319.—A large straggling thorny shrub; leaves broadly oval serrated; cymes long-peduncled, forming a large terminal panicle; drupe obovate, small, white, eatable, and very palatable. Common. Native name "Toorun." Syn. Z latifolia, Roxb. Fl Ind. i, 607; Z paniculata, Roth. nov. sp. l p 161; Z obliqua, Heyne, in Roth. nov. sp. p 160. The edible fruit is a great support to the people of the Ghauts from March to the middle of May.

2. Xylopyra, Willd. sp. i, p. 1104.—A tree; prickles solitary or in pairs or wanting; leaves broadly elliptical or orbicular obtuse, serrulated, underside pale, softly pubescent, finely reticulated; cymes short; nut size of a large cherry, round, hard, 3-celled. The Ghauts; common. Native name "Gootee." The nuts used for blackening leather, Dr. Gibson. Syn. Z elliptica, Roxb. Fl Ind. i, 610; Z caracutta, Roxb. loc. cit. 612; Z rotundifolia, Roth. nov. sp. 160; Z orbicularis, Schult. in DC. *Prod.* 2, p 21; Rhamnus xylopyras, Retz. obs. ii, p 11. Wood excellent for torches.

3. Jujuba, Lam. Encyc. Meth. iii, 318.—A common tree, prickly, prickles often wanting; leaves elliptic or oblong obtuse, serrulated, upperside glabrous, underside covered with a dense, short, tawny tomentum; cymes sessile or shortly-peduncled; drupe spherical; nut rugose, hard and thick; flowers fœtid. Produces a kind of Kino from the bark, useful in medicine. DC. *Prod.* 2, p 21; Roxb. Fl Ind. i, p 508; Z. Syn. trinervia, Roth. nov. sp. p 158; Z sororia, Schult. in DC. *Prod.* 2, p 21; Rhamnus jujuba, Linn.

4. Nummularia, W. and A. *Prod.* p 162.—Shrubby, branched from the base, slender flexuose, spreading; thorns in pairs, the upper one straight, slender; leaves ovate or elliptic, or orbicular serrulated, underside with a dense grey tomentum; cymes sessile, very short. Common in Guzerat; very troublesome to sportsmen. Syn. Z microphylla, Roxb. Fl Ind. i, p 613; Z rotundifolia, Lam.; DC. *Prod.* 2, p 21; Rhamnus nummularia, Burm. Ind. p 61.

5. Oenoplia, Mill.—A climbing thorny shrub; leaves obliquely ovate, acuminated, slightly serrulate, underside shortly tomentose; cymes short; drupe globose. Common in the Concan, also Deccan. DC. *Prod.* 2, p 21; Roxb. Fl Ind. i, p 611; Z napeca, Roth. nov. sp. p 159; Roxb. loc. cit. 613.

3. SCUTIA, Comm.

1. Indica, Brogn. Ann. Soc. Nat. x, p 363.—A straggling thorny shrub ; leaves smooth, small, obovate obtuse or retuse, coriaceous, generally quite entire ; flowers axillary, shortly umbellate ; fruit usually tricoccous, girt by the persistent tube of the calyx. Common along the higher Ghauts. Native name "Cheemat." Syn. Rhamnus circumscissus, Linn. ; Roxb. Fl Ind. i, p 603 ; R myrtinus, Burm. Ind. p 60 ; Ceanothus circumscissa, Gaert. *t.* 106 ; C zeylanica, Heyne, in Roth. nov. sp. p 153 ; Celastrus zeylanica, Roth. in Schult. DC. *Prod.* 2, p 9 ; Catha zeylanica, Don in Mill. Dict. ii, 10.

4. COLUBRINA, Rich.

1. Asiatica, Brogn. in Ann. Soc. Nat. x, p 369.—A large, smooth, dark-green shrub ; leaves ovate acuminated crenate, serrated glabrous, shining ; cymes about the length of the petioles ; flowers few, appear in the cold weather ; fruit capsular dehiscent, tricoccous, size of a pea, very smooth. Elephanta and the Ghauts ; plentiful near the sea at Rutnagherry. Syn. Ceanothus asiaticus, Linn. ; Roxb. Fl Ind. i, p 615 ; C capsularis, Forsk. DC. *Prod* 2, p 32 ; Pomaderis capsularis, Don in Mill. Dict. ii, 39.

5. GOUANIA, Jacq.

1. G Leptostachya, DC. *Prod.* 2, p 40.—A climbing shrub, branches glabrous ; leaves ovate acuminated, slightly cordate at the base, crenate serrated glabrous ; racemes of flowers long, interrupted, axillary, or in terminal panicles ; fruit small, glabrous, triangular, scarcely winged. At Banda, in the Warree country. Syn. G tiliaefolia, Roxb. Fl Ind. i, 632.

6. RHAMNUS, Linn.

1. Wightii, W. and A. *Prod.* 1, 164.—Unarmed, glabrous ; leaves opposite or nearly so, elliptical, with a short sudden acumination, sharply and closely serrated ; pedicels axillary, fascicled, scarcely longer than the flower, much shorter than the petiole ; petals cuneate, obovate, not flat, as stated by W. and A., but folded ; ovary 3 to 4-celled ; styles 3 to 4, connected to the middle ; fruit size of a pea. Highest hills in the Northern Ghauts. Native name "Rugt Rorar." The bark is esteemed very medicinal as a tonic and déobstruent.

L. TEREBINTHACEÆ.

1. ODINA, Roxb.

1. O Wodier, Roxb. Fl Ind. ii, 293.—A large tree; leaves unequally pinnated; leaflets 3 to 4 pair, subsessile oblong-ovate acuminated, glabrous, entire, paler beneath; racemes terminal fascicled, pendulous; flowers very small, purple; fruit kidney-shaped, size of a french-bean, when ripe, red. Very common. Native name "Shimtee." Royle Illust. *t.* 31, *fig* 2. A quantity of gum exudes from the trunk, used by the natives as a medicinal plaster in Ceylon.

2. HOLIGARNA, Roxb.

1. H Longifolia, Roxb. Fl Ind. ii, p 80.—A tree; leaves petioled alternate, cuneate oblong, acute or acuminated entire, glabrous when old; petioles with a subulate soft deciduous process on each side about the middle; panicles terminal and axillary; fruit inferior, oval; pericarp thick, containing between its laminæ cells full of thick acrid juice, used in Malabar as a varnish. Roxb. Cor. *t.* 282. Canarese name "Hoolgeree."

3. GLYCYCARPUS, Dalz.

1. G Racemosus, Dalz. in Hook. Jour. Bot. ii, p 39.—A small polygamous tree; leaves alternate petioled, simple oblong entire; petiole naked; flowers racemose, small, white; petals 4, oblong linear; stamens 4; drupe size of a cherry, transversely oblong; seed one, large, covered with a sweet eatable pulp; colytedons deeply plano-convex. The Ghauts. Syn. Holigarna racemosa, Roxb. Fl Ind.; Pegia colebrookiana, Wight Ic. *t.* 236; the female plant.; Syn. H racemosa, Roxb. Fl Ind. ii, p 82. Native name "Amberee."

4. MANGIFERA, Linn.

1. M Indica, Linn. Spr. *syst.* i, p 17.—A tree with a splendid coma, thick and umbrageous in the wild state; leaves lanceolate acuminated, glabrous, shining, coriaceous; panicle terminal, much-branched; flowers small, white; drupe obliquely oblong, or slightly reniform; nut compressed, woody, 2-valved; valves grooved and covered with fibrous filaments. From this tree, so well-known, there issues a soft, reddish-brown gum resin like bdellium, dissolving entirely in alchohol, and in a great measure in water. DC. *Prod.* 2, 63; Roxb. Fl Ind. i, 641; Rheed. Mal. iv, *t.* 1 and 2; Tussac flore desantilles ii 57, *t.* 15; Rumph. Amb. *t.* 25, 61 ? M. domestica, Gaert. A singular variety, with double and triple fruit, is to

be found in gardens at Hydrabad, in Sind, and leads to the suspicion that the solitary carpel in this tree is solitary by abortion. The normal number would seem to be five.

5. SEMECARPUS, Linn.

1. S Anacardium, Linn.—A tree; leaves oblong obovate, rounded at the apex, whitish and tomentose beneath (in Bombay specimens); panicles terminal, bracteolated; fruit heart-shaped; pericarp full of a corrosive resinous juice, used for marking linen. Native name "Biboo." Warree country; Deccan and Concan; common.

2. S Grahamii, R. Wight Ic. *t.* 235.—Leaves cuneate lanceolate, acute, coriaceous, glabrous above, pubescent beneath; petiole short, furnished with four subulate bodies, as in Holigarna; panicles racemose contracted, congested towards the summit of the branches; calyx truncated, cup-shaped; ovary and young fruit covered with rusty-coloured hairs. The hilly parts of the Concan; common. Meera hills and near Thul, and elsewhere in forests.

6. BUCHANANIA, Roxb.

1. Latifolia, Roxb. Fl Ind. ii, 385.—A tree; leaves broadly oval or obovate obtuse; branches of the panicles hirsute; flowers small, greenish-white; drupe compressed, ovoid globose; nut very hard. The kernel is used in native confectionery, and abounds in a bland oil. Barria jungles, east of Baroda, Dr. Gibson; near Belgaum, Law; Salsette, Nimmo; at Baitsee, in the Warree country. Native names "Pyal" and "Charolee."

7. CANARIUM, Linn.

1. C Strictum, Roxb. Fl Ind. u iii.—A tall straight tree, young parts and inflorescence covered with ferruginous tomentum; leaves pinnated, 2 feet long; leaflets 4 pairs and 1 odd one, ovate oblong, or linear oblong, with a sudden acumination, minutely crenulate on the margin, at length glabrous and shining above, hairy beneath, on the nerves, 5 inches to a foot long. Meera hills and Punt Suchew's country. Native names "Googul" and "Dhoop." Produces a medicinal gum, aromatic, of a yellow colour.

LI. CHAILLETIACEÆ.

1. MOACURRA, Roxb.

1. M Gelonioides, Roxb. Fl Ind. ii, 69.—A small tree; leaves alternate short-petioled, broad lanceolar entire, taper-pointed,

thin and smooth, 3 to 4 inches long; flowers numerous, small, collected in small axillary, solitary, short-peduncled fascicles; capsule transversely oval, 2-lobed, size of a nutmeg, covered with a grey down dehiscing, showing inside a beautiful red arillus. Ram Ghaut; plentiful.

LII. HOMALINEÆ.

1. HOMALIUM, Jacq.

1. H ZEYLANICUM, Benth. in Jour. Proc. Linn. Soc., vol. iv, p 35.—A tree; leaves petioled, oval-elliptic or ovate-acuminate, somewhat toothed, shining, glabrous; racemes elongated, slightly tomentose; flowers small, white; leaves 3 to 4 inches long. Syn. Blackwellia zeylanica, Gardner in Calc. Jour. Nat. Hist. vii, 452; B tetrandra, Wight Ic. *t.* 1851. Ram Ghaut.

LIII. CONNARACEÆ.

1. CONNARUS, Linn.

1. MONOCARPUS, Linn. sp. Pl 678.—An erect shrub; leaves 3 to 5 foliolate; leaflets oval oblong acuminated, shining on both sides, coriaceous; panicles terminal elongated; flowers small, yellowish-white; fruit a capsule, pod-like, stalked, slightly kidney-shaped, red when ripe, extremely ornamental when covered with its bright-red fruit. On the Southern Ghauts; common. Lam. Encycl. Meth. ii, 95; Spr. *syst.* iii, 78; Syn. Omphalobium pinnatum, DC. *Prod.* 2, 86; O indicum, Gaert. *t.* 46; Rheede Mal. vi, *t.* 24. Native name " Soonder."

2. ROUREA, Aubl.

1. SANTALOIDES, W. and A. *Prod.* 144.—A climbing shrub; leaflets 2 to 4 pair, ovate, narrow blunt acuminated, coriaceous, shining; panicles axillary and terminal, few-flowered; fruit ovoid-pointed, rather fleshy, not pod-shaped as W. and A. remark, though they had never seen the fruit. Syn. Connarus sàntaloides, Vahl. Symb. iii, 87. The leaves are like those of Santalum. Warree country, Ram Ghaut, &c. Syn. Connarus santaloides, Vahl. Symb. iii, 8.

LIV. LEGUMINOSÆ.

Sub-Order.—I. PAPILIONACEÆ; II. LOTEÆ.

1. HEYLANDIA, DC.

1. Latebrosa, DC. *Prod.* 2, 123.—Herbaceous plant, hairy dichotomous; leaves on short petioles, obliquely cordate ovate; flowers axillary, solitary, subsessile, small, yellow; legume compressed, 1 to 2-seeded; more or less hairy. Syn. H hebecarpa, DC. loc. cit.; H leiocarpa, DC. loc. cit.; Hallia hirta, Willd. sp. iii, 169; Hedysarum latebrosum, Linn. Maut.; Crotalaria uniflora, Roxb. Fl Ind. iii, 271.

2. CROTALARIA, Linn.

1. Anthylloides, Lam. Encyc. Meth. ii, 195.—Annual, erect, all clothed, except the upperside of the leaves, with close-pressed brownish hairs; stipules minute setaceous; leaves oblong to oblong linear; flowers axillary and solitary, and in terminal racemes; calyx very hairy, longer than the corolla; legume glabrous, sessile, broader upwards, shorter than the calyx; flowers pale-yellow, open in the evening. Southern Concan, DC. *Prod.* 2, 129; C stricta, Roxb. Fl Ind. iii, 265; C Roxburghiana, DC. loc. cit.

2. Fulva, Roxb. Fl Ind. iii, 266.—Shrubby, erect, branched, densely clothed, particularly on the young parts, with soft white or fulvous hairs; leaves oblong lanceolate mucronate, silky on both sides when young; racemes terminal and from the upper axils; calyx densely silky; legume sessile oval, villous, enclosed in the enlarged calyx, 2-seeded. Ram Ghaut.

3. Burhia, Ham. in Wall. Cat.—Shrubby, spreading, much-branched; branchlets with silky pubescence; leaves oblong, with adpressed hairs; calyces very hairy; legume ovoid, few-seeded, very hairy. At Cambay. A member of the desert flora, Walp. Repert. v, p 436.

4. Juncea, Linn. sp. Fl 1004.—Erect branched, more or less clothed with shining, silky pubescence; stipules and bracts setaceous; leaves from narrow linear to ovate lanceolate, obtuse mucronate or acute; racemes elongated, terminating each branch; calyx densely covered with rusty tomentum; legumes sessile oblong, broader upwards, twice the length of the calyx, tomentose, many-seeded. This is the cultivated "Tag," yielding one of the best kinds of Indian hemp; DC. *Prod.* 2, 125; Roxb. Fl Ind. iii, 259. Syn. C Bengalensis, Lam. Encycl. Meth. ii, 196; C tenuifolia, Roxb. Fl Ind. iii, 263; C fenestrata, Bot. Mag. *t.* 1933.

5. Leschenautlii, DC. *Prod.* 2, 125.—Erect branched,

glabrous except on the underside of the leaves; stems terete; stipules minute triangular acuminated reflexed; leaves cuneate, narrow obovate, obtuse, upperside glabrous, minutely dotted, under villous; racemes terminal elongated; flowers numerous, distant, much larger than the quite glabrous calyx; legume oblong, broader upwards, glabrous, four times the length of the calyx, many-seeded. On the highest Ghauts; common. Native name "Dingala."

6. PEDUNCULARIS, Grah. in Wall. list 5369.—Erect, tall, sparingly branched, glabrous all over; stipules wanting; leaves oblong to narrow linear acuminated; racemes terminal elongated, lax; flowers distant, very large, on long pedicels; legume cylindric-oblong, attenuated at the base, glabrous, many-seeded. South Concan and at Vingorla; very common. W. and A. *Prod.* 186; Syn. C lutescens, Dalz. in Hook. Jour. Bot.

7. SERICEA, Retz. obs. iii, 26.—Erect-branched, glabrous, except on the underside of the leaves; stems obtusely angled; stipules large semisagittate, reflexed; leaves lanceolate cuneate at the base, mucronate pellucid dotted, upperside glabrous, underside glaucous, with adpressed silky pubescence; racemes terminal, elongated, many-flowered; legume oblong glabrous, shortly stalked, many-seeded. In pasture grounds, Bombay; Roxb. Fl Ind. iii, 273, Syn. C spectabilis, Roth. nov. sp. 341; DC. *Prod.* 2, 125; C juncea; Willd. ? sp. Pl iii, 974 (non Linn).

8. RETUSA, Linn. Spr. *syst.* iii, 237.—Erect-branched, nearly glabrous, except the underside of the leaves; stipules and bracteas subulate; leaves cuneate oblong, retuse or rounded, minutely pellucid dotted; racemes elongated, many-flowered; calyx glabrous; legume oblong, broader upwards, sessile glabrous, many-seeded. Common in sandy soil, in company with the following. Maratha name "Ghagree"; flowers in February and March. Roxb. Fl Ind. iii, 272; Syn. Lupinus cochinensis, Lour.; DC. *Prod.* 2, 410.

9. VERRUCOSA, Linn. Spr. *syst.* iii, 237.—Herbaceous, erect, much-branched; branches angled; stipules lunate; leaves ovate, suddenly and shortly acuminated at the base, nearly glabrous; racemes terminal and leaf-opposed; flowers largish, blue; legume cylindric-oblong, sessile, softly pubescent, many-seeded. Roxb. Fl Ind. iii, 273; Syn. C angulosa, Lam. Encyc. Meth. ii, 197; Cœrulea, Jacquin Ic. rar. *t.* 144. Very common.

10. BIFARIA, Linn. Suppl. 322.—Herbaceous, procumbent, clothed with somewhat rigid pubescence; branches slender, elongated; leaves from orbicular to oblong, or narrow linear pubescent, or at length nearly glabrous; racemes terminal and leaf-opposed, 1 to 2-flowered; calyx harshly pubescent; legumes obovoid, hispidly pubescent or hairy, mottled with purple. Ram

Ghaut, Law; Belgaum, Ritchie. DC. *Prod.* 2, 127; Syn. C dichotoma, Roth. nov. sp. 340.

11. FILIPES, Benth. in Hook. Lond. Jour. Bot. ii, 472.—Prostrate, ciliated with long hairs; stem filiform, very slender; stipules none; leaves obliquely cordate ovate or sublanceolate; peduncles very slender, 1 to 2-flowered; calyx divisions lanceolate, ovary many-ovuled; legume ovoid glabrous, twice as long as the calyx; leaves scarcely half an inch long; flowers the size of those of Heylandia, ovules about 20; legume 3 lines long. Common about Bombay, Salsette, &c.

12. EPUNCTATA, Dalz. in Hook. Jour. Bot. iii, 210.—Suffruticose diffuse, branched from the base; branches round, filiform, naked at the base, with the racemes and leaves beneath, strigosely pubescent; stipules minute spreading, sometimes wanting; leaves without dots, linear oblong, at length glabrous above; racemes terminal, 4 to 10-flowered; bracts linear equalling the short pedicels; calyx half the length of the corol; upper lip deeply bifid, lower trifid segments subulate; legume cernuous, smooth, transversely reticulated, oblong, a half longer than the calyx, 20-seeded. South Concan; common. Closely allied to C viminea of R. Graham.

13. LINIFOLIA, Linn. f. suppl. 322.—Cespitose, suffruticose diffuse, branched from the base, more or less strigose; stipules wanting; leaves from cuneate to linear oblong obtuse, slightly mucronate, strigose beneath; racemes terminal, elongated, many-flowered; calyx densely covered with short hairs; legume oblique, roundish-ovoid, sessile glabrous, scarcely so long as the calyx, 8 to 12-seeded. Kandalla, Graham; Surat, in company with C orixensis. DC. *Prod.* 2, 128; Syn. C cæspitosa, Roxb. Fl Ind. iii, 269; C diffusa, DC. *Prod.* 2, 126; C tecta, Heyne in Roth. nov. sp. 335; C montana, Heyne in Roth. p 334.

14. NANA, Burm. Fl Ind. 156, *t.* 48, *f.* 2.—Cespitose hairy, branched from the base; stipules wanting; leaves oblong, broader upwards, obtuse; flowers 2 to 3, on short leaf-opposed peduncles, or 5 to 6 in nearly sessile terminal umbels; calyx very hairy, as long as the corolla; legume ovoid sessile, glabrous, black, a half longer than the calyx. Malwan, on the sea shore. DC. *Prod.* 2, 127; Syn. C biflora, Willd. sp. iii, 978.

15. UMBELLATA, Wight Cat. No. 700.—Branched from the base very hairy; branches ascending, elongated, twiggy; stipules wanting; leaves oblong, slightly acute; flowers numerous, forming a dense terminal umbel; calyx very hairy, as long as the corolla; legume globose, sessile, black, glabrous, scarcely longer than the calyx, 6 to 8-seeded. At Vingorla; plentiful; Ram Ghaut, Law.

16. TRIQUETRA, Dalz. in Hook. Jour. Bot. ii, p 34.—Annual, branched from the base; branches prostrate, with spreading hairs,

acutely 3-sided; stipules ovate acute reflexed; leaves oblong elliptic, slightly cordate at the base, glabrous above, with spreading hairs beneath; racemes opposite the leaves, 3-flowered, 6 to 7 times longer than the leaf; legume oblong, with adpressed hairs, stalked, 3 or 4 times longer than the calyx, many-seeded. District of Malwan; flowers in September.

17. ROSTRATA, W. and A. *Prod.* 1, 191.—Shrubby, very rigid, much-branched; stipules long subulate; leaves trifoliolate, on a very short petiole; leaflets very small, broadly obcordate, upperside nearly glabrous, under pubescent; racemes few-flowered, terminating the branchlets; legume pubescent, ovate, obliquely-beaked, seeds 2. On the sandy soil at Domus, also in Kattywar. DC. *Prod.* 2, 133.

18. LABURNIFOLIA, Linn. sp. Pl 1005.—Shrubby erect, glabrous; stipules wanting; leaves trifoliolate; leaflets broadly oval, usually acute at both ends; racemes elongated, terminal, and leaf-opposed, many-flowered; flowers large, yellow, long-pedicellate; legume stalked, glabrous, cylindric-oblong, 3 times as long as broad. DC. *Prod.* 2, 130; Roxb. Fl Ind. iii, 275. Southern Concan, Nimmo; Syn. C pendula, Bert. DC. loc. cit.; C pedunculosa, Desv. DC. loc. cit.; C lavulium pedunculosum, Desv. in Ann. Soc. Nat. ix, 407.

19. ORIXENSIS, Roxb. Fl Ind. iii, 276.—Herbaceous procumbent; leaves trifoliolate; leaflets obovate, upperside glabrous; racemes elongated, leaf-opposed, slender, many-flowered, bracteas cordate acuminate; flowers small, on long filiform pedicels; legume stalked, glabrous, short-cylindrical, a half longer than broad, few-seeded. DC. *Prod.* 2, 131. At Surat, amongst grass.

20. QUINQUEFOLIA, Linn. sp. Pl 1006.—Annual, erect-branched; stems hollow; leaves 5-foliolate; leaflets longer than the petioles, from lanceolate to narrow-linear; racemes terminal, much elongated, many-flowered; flowers large, distant; legumes clavate oblong, glabrous, attenuated at the base into a stalk. DC. *Prod.* 2, 131; Roxb. Fl Ind. iii, 279; Syn. C heterophylla, Linn. suppl. 323. On the margins of rice fields, Salsette, &c.

3. INDIGOFERA, Linn.

1. ECHINATA, Willd. sp. iii, 1222.—Herbaceous prostrate; branches angular; leaves simple obovate, minutely dotted; racemes on very short peduncles, 6 to 8-flowered; legumes crescent-shaped, with hooked bristles on the convex margins; seed solitary, flat, reniform. Very common. DC. *Prod.* 2, 222. Roxb. Fl Ind. iii, 370; Syn. H nummulariæfolium, Linn. sp. p 1051; H rotundifolium, Vahl. Symb. ii, 81; H erinaceum, Poir. Encycl. Meth. vi, 393; Onobrychis rotundifolia, Desv. DC. *Prod.* 2, 348.

2. LINIFOLIA, Retz. Obs. iv, p 29.—Diffuse procumbent, white, with adpressed silvery hairs; leaves subsessile lanceolate or narrow linear; racemes very short, sessile; legumes globose, one-seeded, very small. A common weed. DC. *Prod.* 2, 222; Roxb. Fl Ind. iii, 370; Syn. Hedysarum linifolium, Linn. suppl. 331; Sphacridiophorum, Desv. Jour. iii, p 125.

3. CORDIFOLIA, Heyne. Roth. nov. sp. 357.—Diffuse, covered with long white hairs; leaves broadly ovate cordate subsessile; racemes capituliform, sessile, 3 to 6-flowered; legumes oval, hoary, 2-seeded. Very common. DC. *Prod.* 2, 222.

4. GLANDULOSA, Roxb. Fl Ind. iii, p 372.—Diffuse, young parts softly pubescent; leaves petioled trifoliolate; leaflets oblong obovate, underside glandular dotted; racemes sessile, oval, dense, many-flowered, short; legumes oval, twice as long as broad, hairy, 4-angled; angles slightly winged and toothed; seeds 2. Common. DC. *Prod.* 2, 223.

5. TRIQUETRA, Dalz. in Hook. Jour. Bot. ii, p 36.—Stems several, from a woody root, acutely 3-edged, prostrate, ascending at the apex, glabrous; leaves subsessile elliptic mucronate, strigose and pellucid dotted beneath; stipules subulate; racemes axillary elongated, 3 to 4 times longer than the leaf, many-flowered; flowers purple; fruit bearing peduncles reflexed; legume linear mucronate, 4-sided and 4-winged, about 5-seeded. Rocky hills in the district of Malwan.

6. ENNEAPHYLLA, Linn. Maut. 272.—Procumbent, young parts and leaves pubescent, with adpressed whitish hairs; branches prostrate, 2-edged; leaves pinnate; leaflets 3 to 5 pair, obovate oblong; racemes sessile, short, oval, dense, many-flowered; legumes oval, pubescent; seeds two. At Surat. DC. *Prod.* 2, 229; Roxb. Fl Ind. iii, 376. Syn. Hedysarum prostratum, Linn. Maut. i, 102; Burm. Ind. *t.* 55, *f* 1.

7. ASPALATHOIDES, Vahl. in Herb. Juss.—Shrubby erect, young parts whitish; branches numerous spreading; leaves sessile, digitately 3 to 5-foliolate; leaflets narrow cuneate, small; peduncles solitary, one-flowered; flowers very small; legumes cylindrical, pointed straight, 4 to 6-seeded. Near Belgaum. DC. *Prod.* 2, 231; Syn. I aspalathifolia, Roxb. Fl Ind. iii, 371; Aspalathus indicus, Linn. sp. Pl 1001; Lespedeza juncea, Wall. Rheed. Mal. ix, *t.* 37. Common in the Deccan.

8. UNIFLORA, Ham. in Herb. Banks.—Stems prostrate, long, slender; leaves pinnately trifoliolate; leaflets narrow cuneate, oblong acute; peduncles solitary filiform, one-flowered, twice the length of the leaves; legumes linear oblong terete-pointed, 3-seeded. Southern Maratha Country, Law; Roxb. Fl Ind. iii, 374.

9. TENUIFOLIA, Rottl.—Herbaceous, branched diffuse; leaves

short-petioled, pinnated; leaflets about 4-pair, cuneate oblong, sprinkled on both sides with whitish hairs; peduncles longer than the leaves, with a few subsessile flowers towards the apex; legume compressed pointed, slightly torulose, sutures thickened. At Unkleswur, near Broach. W. and A. *Prod.* p 200.

10. TRIFOLIATA, Linn. Amœn. iv, 327.—Suffruticose branched; branches slender diffuse, ascending; leaves long-petioled, palmately trifoliolate; leaflets cuneate obovate, pubescent on both sides, glandular beneath; racemes sessile very short, dense, many-flowered; flowers minute; legumes straight deflexed, sub-compressed, torulose, with a prominent nerve on each side of the sutures. At Domus. DC. *Prod.* 2, 223; Syn. I prostrata, Willd. sp. iii, 1226; DC. loc. cit. 233; Roxb. Fl Ind. iii, 373; I leschenaultii, DC. loc. cit. 223; I multicaulis DC. loc. cit.

11. PAUCIFOLIA, Delile. Fl d'Egypt, p 107, *t.* 37, *f.* 22.—Shrubby, erect-branched, hoary and glaucous; leaves pinnated; leaflets 1 to 5, alternate, oblong lanceolate; racemes solitary, sessile, longer than the leaves, many-flowered; legumes linear, slightly compressed, torulose, pendulous and curved upwards, 5 to 8-seeded. Surat and throughout Guzerat. DC. *Prod.* 2, 224; Syn. I argentea, Roxb. Fl Ind. iii, 374; Bremontiera animoxylon; B burmanni. DC. *Prod.* 2, 353.

12. WIGHTII, Graham in Wall. list 5458.—Suffruticose, erect-branched, hoary, with adpressed silky hairs; leaves pinnated; leaflets 5 to 10 pair, small, oblong oval, slightly retuse mucronate; racemes short, many-flowered; flowers small; legumes few, erect, cylindrical, stout, straight, sharp-pointed, 10 to 12-seeded; seeds cylindric. At Belgaum.

13. TINCTORIA, Linn. sp. Pl 1301.—Suffruticose erect; leaves pinnated; leaflets 5 to 6 pair, oblong obovate, cuneate at the base; racemes shorter than the leaves, sessile, many-flowered; legumes approximated towards the base of the rachis, nearly cylindrical, slightly torulose, deflexed and curved upwards; seeds 10, cylindrical, truncated. DC. *Prod.* 2, 224; Roxb. Fl Ind. iii. 379; Syn. I indica, Lam. Encycl. Meth. iii, 245. Found apparently wild in many parts of the Concan. This is the Indigo plant; the "Neel" of the natives.

14. CŒRULEA, Roxb. Fl Ind. iii, 377.—Shrubby erect, closely covered with whitish pubescence; leaflets 4 to 5 pair, obovate emarginate, terminal largest; racemes solitary, sessile, short; flowers small; legumes terete, short, five times as long as broad, deflexed, and curved upwards, slightly torulose, 3 to 4-seeded. The wild original of the preceding? In hedges at Dhej, Broach Collectorate. Roxburgh says he has extracted a finer indigo from the preceding. Syn. I tinctoria; B brachycarpa. DC. *Prod.* 2, 224.

15. **Pulchella**, Roxb. Fl Ind. iii, 382.—A shrub; branches angled; leaves pinnated; leaflets 8 to 10 pair, obovate or broad-elliptic, emarginate mucronate; racemes the length of the leaves, sessile, many-flowered; flowers large, bluish-purple, showy; legumes slightly deflexed, cylindrical, thick, straight, sharp-pointed, 10 to 12-seeded. An Alpine species; all along the highest Ghauts. Syn. I purpurascens, Roxb. loc. cit. 383; I cassioides, Rottl. DC. *Prod.* 2, 225. Native name "Chimnatee." Ind. Gibsonii, Graham's Catalogue.

16. **Trita**, Linn. Suppl. 335.—Herbaceous or suffruticose, erect, rigid, more or less hairy; leaves pinnately trifoliolate, ; leaflets oval or oblong, mucronate; racemes sessile, the length of the leaves; legumes deflexed or horizontal, 4-angled, straight rigid, sharp-pointed; seeds 6 to 10, 4-sided. Very common. DC. *Prod.* 2, 232; Roxb. Fl Ind. iii, 371; Syn. I cinerea, Willd. sp. 1225; Roxb. Fl Ind. iii, 372; I canescens, Lam. Enc. Meth. iii, 251.

17. **Kleinii**, W. and A. *Prod.* 204.—Herbaceous procumbent; leaves pinnated; leaflets alternate, about 9, obovate oblong, glaucous and strigose beneath; racemes peduncled, equal to the leaves, many-flowered; flowers small; legumes crowded, imbricately reflexed, straight linear, 4-angled, with a subulate rigid straight point; seeds 8 to 10, 4-sided. At Belgaum.

18. **Hirsuta**, Linn. sp. Pl 1862.—Erect-branched, hairy all over except the leaves; leaves pinnated; leaflets opposite, 2 to 5 pair, oblong obovate, large; racemes dense peduncled, longer than the leaves; legumes reflexed, straight, 4-angled, mucronate, hairy, 4 to 6-seeded. A large coarse species; a common weed in the South Concan. DC. *Prod.* 2, 228; Roxb. Fl Ind. iii, 376; Rheede Mal. ix, *t.* 30.

4. PSORALEA, Linn.

1. **Corylifolia**, Linn. sp. 1075.—Annual, erect, 3 to 4 feet high; leaves simple, rarely ternate, roundish ovate repand-toothed; racemes dense, spicate, on long axillary solitary peduncles; legume very short, indehiscent, 1-seeded. A common plant in waste places. Roxb. Fl Ind. iii 387; Syn. Tufolium unifolum, Forsk. Native name "Bawurcheen."

5. TEPHROSIA, Pers.

1. **Suberosa**, DC. *Prod.* 2, 249.—A small tree; ends of the branches and young shoots tomentose; leaves pinnated; leaflets 6 to 10 pair, elliptic-oblong, obtuse mucronulate, underside clothed with silky pubescence; racemes terminal, rose-coloured; legume long, straight, silky, contracted between the seeds, linear-com-

pressed; seeds 6 to 8, reniform. Rocky hills eastward of Belgaum. Wasera Ghaut, Dr. Gibson; seeds used to poison fish. Native name "Sooptee." Syn. T sericea, DC. loc. cit.; Cylisu sericens, Willd. sp. 1121; Robinia suberosa, Roxb. Fl Ind. iii, 327; R sennoides, Roxb. loc. cit. 328.

2. SENTICOSA, Pers. Syn. ii, 330.—Shrubby, diffuse; leaves pinnated; leaflets 1 to 3 pair, obcordate, underside whitish, with a fine pubescence; flowers in pairs, axillary, towards the extremities of the branches nearly sessile; legumes compressed, slightly curved at the point, 3 inches long. On hills in the Concan; common. DC. *Prod.* 2, 254; Syn. Galega senticosa, Linn. Amœn. iii, 19.

3. PURPUREA, Pers. Syn. ii, 329.—A weed, shrubby erect, much-branched; leaves pinnated; leaflets cuneate oblong; racemes leaf-opposed, peduncled, longer than the leaves; legumes slightly compressed, spreading, linear-falcate, obtuse, with a short point. DC. *Prod.* 2, 251. Common. Syn. T lancæfolia, Link. Enum. ii, 252; Galega purpurea, Linn. sp. 1063; Roxb. Fl Ind. iii, 386; Galega lancæfolia, Roxb. loc. cit. 386; G colonila and sericea, Ham. in Linn. Trans. xiii, 545.

4. TENUIS, Wall. list 5970.—Annual, diffuse; stems filiform strigose, ascending; leaves simple linear or narrow elliptic mucronate, 3-nerved; peduncles axillary, solitary or twin, shorter than the leaf, 1-flowered; corolla with long claws to the petals; legumes compressed, linear straight, margins thickened, valves cohering between the seeds, 7 to 8-seeded. The Concans; flowers in August. Syn. Macronyx strigosus, Dalz. in Hook. Jour. Bot. ii, p 35.

II. LOTEÆ.

1. WISTERIA, Nutt.

1. RACEMOSA, Dalz. Mss.—A large climbing shrub; leaves alternate, unequally pinnate; leaflets 6 to 8 pair, oval acute, entire, smooth, 2 inches long, 1 broad; racemes axillary, erect, many-flowered; flowers large, rose-coloured; legumes straight, pendulous, very protuberant at the seeds, and flatly compressed between them; seeds 5 to 6, oblong, white. Near Belgaum. Syn. Robinia racemosa, Roxb. Fl Ind. iii, 329; Tephrosia racemosa, W. and A. *Prod.* 210.

2. W PALLIDA, Dalz. Mss.—A large climbing shrub; leaflets about 5 pair and an odd one, ovate or ovate-oblong acute, with waved margins; stipules subulate; racemes axillary, solitary, long, slender, from the axils of the uppermost young undeveloped leaves; flowers small, pale-yellow, crowded; legumes straight, linear narrow, about 5 inches long and half inch broad, very protuberant at the seeds, compressed flat all around and between them; seeds

4 to 5, distant. In the Dangs; very rare. Wassoorna forest, Dr. Gibson. This is, perhaps, the Robinia ferruginea of Roxb. Fl Ind. iii, 329.

2. SESBANIA, Pers.

1. Aculeata, Pers. Syn. ii, 316.—Herbaceous, annual, erect, sparingly branched, glabrous; leaves abruptly pinnated; leaflets 20 to 40 pair, linear obtuse mucronate; racemes axillary peduncled lax, few-flowered; flowers pretty large, on slender pedicels; legumes nearly terete, long, sharp-pointed. Very common. Syn. Aeschynomene opinulosa, Roxb. Fl Ind. iii; 333; Ae. cannabina Roxb. loc. cit. 335; Ae. bispinosa, Jacq. Ic. rar. 3, *t.* 564; Coronilla aculeata, Willd. sp. iii, p 1147.

2. Procumbens, W. and A. *Prod.* 215.—Annual, diffuse, armed with inoffensive prickles; leaflets minute, 20 pair; peduncles axillary, short, 2 to 3-flowered; legumes linear erect cuspidate. Very common. Syn. Aeschynomene procumbens, Roxb. Fl Ind. iii, 337.

III. HEDYSAREÆ.

1. GEISSASPIS, W. and A.

1. Cristata, W. and A. *Prod.* 218.—Procumbent herbaceous plant; leaves equally pinnated; leaflets 2 pair, cuneate obovate, retuse, dotted; racemes axillary and terminal, on longish peduncles; bracteas large, orbicular, margins ciliated bristly; flowers solitary in each bractea, small, orange-coloured; legume 1 to 2-jointed, tumid in the middle, thin at the margins. Very common in pasture lands.

2. ZORNIA, Gmelin.

1. Angustifolia, Smith in Ree's Cycl.—Annual diffuse; leaflets 2, oblong or lanceolate mucronate, bracteas sagittate ovate acute ciliated, pellucid dotted; legumes 2 to 5-jointed, pubescent, prickly. Very common. DC. *Prod.* 2, 316; Syn. Hedysarum diphyllum and Linn.; Roxb. Fl Ind. iii, 353.

2. Zeylonensis, Pers. Syn. ii, 318.—Leaflets 2, oblong or ovate mucronate; bracteas sagittate ovate acute, opaque dotted; legumes 2 to 3 times the length of the bracteas, prickly, glochidiate. Very common. DC. *Prod.* 2, 317; Syn. Z zeylanica, Spr. *syst.* iii, 311; Hedysarum conjugatum, Willd sp. iii, 1178.

3. AESCHYNOMENE, Linn.

1. Indica, Linn. sp. 1061.—Annual procumbent; branches slender, humifuse; leaflets 15 to 20 pair, linear obtuse; peduncles

axillary, slender, few-flowered; flowers pale-yellow; legumes long-stalked, 6 to 10-jointed, warty when ripe. Common about Surat. Syn. Hedysarum nalitali, Roxb. Fl Ind. iii, 365; Rheede Mal. ix, *t.* 18; Ae. pumila, Linn. sp. 1061; DC. *Prod.* 2, 321; Ae. diffusa, Willd. sp. p 1164.

NOTE.—Aeschynomene aspera, Linn., is the Sola of Bengal, from which sun-hats are manufactured.

4. SMITHIA, Aiton.

1. S HIRSUTA, Dalz. in Hook. Jour. Bot. iii, p 135.—Annual erect 1½ foot high, stem and branches hirsute, with spreading yellow hairs; leaflets 3 to 4 pair, obovate cuneate, unequal-sided, ciliate on the margin; flowers between capitate and racemose; peduncles longer than the leaf, 10-flowered; calyx sparingly covered with long hairs, upper segment cuneate truncate emarginate, lower cuneate obovate entire; flowers yellow. Foonda Ghaut; flowers in September.

2. SENSITIVA, Ait. Hort. Kew. iii, 496.—Leaves 3 to 6 pair, oval obtuse, glabrous, with ciliated margins and midrib; flowers forming a sessile or peduncled short raceme; calyx segments striated oblong lanceolate, upper entire, lower sometimes 3-toothed at the apex; legume 4 to 6-jointed, warted. It is var. with the racemes sessile 2-flowered; that is common. The S geminiflora of Roth. nov. sp. p 352; DC. *Prod.* 2, 323; Roxb. Fl Ind. iii, 342. Eaten as a pot-herb. Smithia conferta, Sm. DC. *Prod.* 2, 323.

3. RACEMOSA, Heyne in Wall. list No. 5670.—Leaflets cuneate oblong retuse, bristly on the margin; flowers forming a peduncled short raceme; pedicels and calyx glandular and hairy, upper lip of calyx broad truncated, slightly emarginate, lower shortly 3-cleft; legume 4-jointed, slightly warted. Near Belgaum.

4. CAPITATA, Dalz. in Hook. Jour. Bot. iii, p 208. (non Desv.)—Stem glabrous branched; leaflets 9 to 15 pair, linear oblong obtuse ciliated, common petiole hispid; stipules adnate ovate lanceolate, terminated by a bristle; flowers in a spherical head, numerous, terminal; peduncles glabrous, shorter than the leaf; bracts obovate lanceolate as long as the calyx; calyx glabrous, reticulately veined, the lips rounded undivided-toothed, the teeth long and bristly; legumes smooth, joints 6 to 7. Parwar Ghaut; flowers in October.

5. SETULOSA, Dalz. loc. cit.—3 to 4 feet high; stem dichotomously branched, hispid, with small bristles; leaflets 5 to 7 pair, linear oblong obtuse, glabrous, ciliated on the margin; common petiole hispid; stipules adnate, with a long bristly acumination; flowers in a terminal leafless panicle; calyx striated, the lips quite

entire, minutely ciliated, very unequal, upper larger, round, lower oblong acute; legume prominently reticulated, with 10 to 12 joints. Found along with the preceding.

6. BIGEMINA, Dalz. loc. cit.—One foot high, branched from the base; branches filiform hirsute, with bulbous spreading hairs; leaflets 2 pair, obovate cuneate, ciliated on the margin, terminated by a bristle; racemes axillary, peduncled, few-flowered; calyx scariose, with longitudinal dichotomous veins, upper lip cuneate emarginate mucronate, lower 3-lobed, lateral lobes obtuse, middle one longer, acuminated; legume coarsely tubercled, joints 7. Parwar Ghaut.

7. PURPUREA, Bot. Mag. *t.* 4283.—Stem glabrous, erect-branched; leaflets oblong, with long points, ciliated; stipules adnate ovate, terminated by a bristle; racemes terminal and lateral; peduncles bristly, as long as the leaf; bracts ovate; lips of the calyx entire striated ciliated; flowers purple, with a white spot on the vexillum and wings. Bombay Presidency; discovered by Mr. Law.

8. BLANDA, Wall. Cat. 5669, Wight and Arn. *Prod.*—Racemes glandular and hairy; upper lip of calyx broad emarginate truncated, lower 3-lobed; leaflets cuneate oblong, middle nerve without bristles; racemes elongated; legume reticulately nerved, not tubercled or warty. At Belgaum.

5. ALYSICARPUS, Necker.

1. NUMMULARIFOLIUS, DC. *Prod.* 2, 353.—Procumbent, diffuse branched; leaves oval-obtuse, cordate at the base; racemes short; flowers approximated; legume several times longer than the calyx, almost cylindrical. Very common. Syn. Hedysarum nummularifolium, Willd. sp. iii, 1173; H cylindricum, Poir. Encyc. Meth. v, 400.

2. VAGINALIS, DC. loc. cit. 353.—Suffruticose diffuse; leaves from oval-obtuse and cordate, to cordate-lanceolate and linear; racemes terminal elongated; calyx 5-cleft, strongly nerved; legume 3 to 6-jointed, several times longer than the calyx, slightly contracted between the joints; joints a little inflated reticulated, pubescent; flowers bright-red. Common in pastures. Syn. Hedysarum vaginale, Linn. sp. 1051; Roxb. Fl Ind. iii, 345; H varium, Roth. nov. sp. p 354; H bupleurifolius, Roxb. Fl Ind. iii, 346. Found at Surat only; roots covered with minute round tubes like warts.

3. BUPLEURIFOLIUS, DC. *Prod.* 2, 352.—Diffuse, glabrous; leaves linear-lanceolate; racemes terminal, few-flowered; flowers in distant pairs, small, pale, inconspicuous; calyx deeply 4-cleft; legumes glabrous, 3 to 5-jointed, scarcely contracted between

the joints, as long, or twice as long, as the calyx. Common. Syn. Hedysarum bupleurifolium, Linn. sp. 1081; H graminium, Retz. obs. 5, p 26; Roxb. Fl Ind. iii, 346.

4. LONGIFOLIUS, W. and A. *Prod.* 1, 233.—Herbaceous, erect-branched; stems round, glabrous; leaves shortly-petioled, linear lanceolate, rather obtuse, scarcely cordate at the base, glabrous above, puberulous beneath; stipules large, longer than the petiole; racemes spiked, very long; pedicels short approximated; calyx 4-divided to near the base, segments erect, oblong, striated, hairy ciliated, upper shortly bifid; legume scarcely constricted between the seeds, reticulated, pubescent, 5 to 6-seeded, twice as long as the calyx. Wight Ic. *t.* 251; Hedysarum longifol, Rottl. in Spr. *syst.* iii, 317. Roots like Liquorice.

5. STYRACIFOLIUS, DC. *Prod.* 2, 353.—Branches diffuse, hairy; leaves from cordate oval to linear lanceolate, a little hirsute beneath; racemes terminal or leaf-opposed, short, dense, hairy; legume glabrous, 2 to 4-jointed, much contracted between the joints, scarcely longer than the calyx. At Surat. A cylindracens, Desv. in Ann. Soc. Nat. ix, 417; Hedysarum scariosum, Spr. loc. cit.

6. BELGAUMENSIS, Law in Wight's Ic. *t.* 92.—Leaves trifoliolate; leaflets linear oblong, terminal one much the largest; calyx deeply 4-cleft, upper segment bifid; joints of the legume compressed irregularly, reticulated, pubescent. Ram Ghaut, Belgaum; flowers in September.

7. PUBESCENS, Law in Wight's Ic. *t.* 250.—Herbaceous, erect, stems round, hairy; leaves simple short-petioled linear lanceolate acute, 3-nerved, glabrous above, pubescent beneath; racemes terminal spicate; flowers subsessile; calyx 4-parted to the base, clothed with long silky hairs; legumes terete, much-contracted between the seeds. Belgaum; common.

8. PARVIFLORUS, Dalz. in Hook. Jour. Bot. iii, 211.—Herbaceous, erect; stem branched, glabrous at the base, covered with spreading hairs in the upper part; leaves simple and trifoliolate, oblong-elliptic mucronate, somewhat cordate at the base, strigose beneath; stipules shorter than the petioles; calyx almost 5-divided, segments subulate; legume half necklace-shaped, reticulated, twice as long as the calyx, 5 to 6-seeded. Phoonda Ghaut; flowers and fruit in November.

6. URARIA, Desv.

1. PICTA, Desv. Jour. Bot. iii, 122.—Erect, young parts clothed with hooked hairs; leaves simple and pinnated, simple ones oblong ovate, compound ones with 2 to 4 pair leaflets, which are linear lanceolate obtuse; racemes terminal long, spike-like, rigid; legume

3 to 6-jointed, curled inwards. Near Penn. Beautifully figured in Jacquin Ic. rar. *t.* 567.

7. DESMODIUM, Desv.

1. Umbellatum, DC. *Prod.* 2, 325.—A shrub; leaves trifoliolate; leaflets oval obtuse, whitish, pubescent beneath; flowers 10 to 12, white, somewhat umbellate, legumes 3 to 4-jointed, thick margined. South-east of Surat; near Belgaum, Law.

2. Congestum, Wall. list 5723; W. and A. *Prod.* 224.—Shrubby; leaves trifoliolate; leaflets oblong lanceolate; stipules lanceolate acuminated; peduncles axillary, solitary, very short; flowers numerous, umbellate, white; legumes compressed, slightly pubescent, 4 to 6-jointed. Island of Caranjah, and other places; pretty common. Syn. Hedysarum umbellatum, Roxb. Fl. Ind. iii, 360.

3. Triquetrum, DC. *Prod.* 2, 326.—Erect-branched; branches triangular; leaves simple cordate, ovate or linear oblong acuminated; petioles winged; racemes axillary and terminal, many-flowered; legumes hairy, 5 to 8-jointed, straight on one side, crenated on the other; flowers small, violet-coloured. Very common. Hedysarum triquetrum, Linn. sp. p 1052; H alatum, Roxb. Fl Ind. iii, 348.

4. Latifolium, DC. *Prod.* 2, 327.—Shrubby; branches terete, spreading; leaves simple, broadly cordate or ovate, repand-crenated, pubescent above, tomentose beneath; racemes axillary and terminal; flowers numerous, violet; legumes densely clothed with hooked hairs, 4 to 5-jointed, crenated on one side, notched to the middle on the other. Meera hills near Penn, and other hilly places in the Concan. Syn. Hedysarum latifolium, Roxb. Fl Ind. iii, 350; Roth nov. sp. 355.

5. Gangeticum, DC. *Prod.* 2, 327.—Stems irregularly angled, with rigid white hairs; leaves simple ovate cordate at the base; racemes axillary and terminal, very long, lax; legume 6 to 8-jointed, hispidly puberulous, straightish on one side, deeply notched on the other; joints semiorbicular; flowers violet-coloured. Near Penn, Malabar hill, &c. Syn. D maculatum, DC. loc. cit.; Hedysarum gangeticum, Linn. sp. Pl p 1052; Roxb. Fl Ind. iii, 348; H collinum, Roxb. Fl Ind. iii, 348; D maculatum, Linn. sp. 1051.

6. Polycarpum, DC. *Prod.* 2, 334.—Suffruticose, procumbent, often rooting at the joints; leaves trifoliolate; leaflets oval or obovate retuse, lateral leaflets smaller; petiole slightly margined; racemes axillary and terminal, many-flowered, strobiliform before expansion; legumes ercet, hispid, 5 to 6-jointed, straight on one margin, notched into the middle on the other. Hills north-east of Penn; Ram Ghaut, Law. Syn. D heterocarpum, DC. loc. cit.;

D capitatum, DC. loc. cit.; D angulatum, DC. loc. cit.; Hedysarum purpureum, Roxb. Fl Ind. iii, 228.

7. RENIFORME, DC. *Prod.* 2, 327.—Procumbent, diffuse; branches filiform; leaves simple-petioled, roundish reniform, glabrous on both sides; flowers axillary and solitary, or in terminal racemes; legumes 5 to 6-jointed, even on one side, notched on the other. Common in subalpine jungles. Syn. Hedysarum reniforme, Linn. sp. Pl 1051.

8. TRIFLORUM, DC. *Prod.* 2.—Procumbent; leaves trifoliolate; leaflets orbicular obovate or obcordate; peduncles axillary, solitary or fascicled, 1 to 3-flowered; legume hispidly pubescent, 3 to 6-jointed, even on one side, notched to the middle on the other. Very common. Syn. Hedysarum triflorum, Linn. sp. Pl 1057; D heterophyllum, DC. *Prod.* 2, 334; H reptans, Roxb. Fl Ind. iii, 354; Sagotia triflora, Derch. and Walp, Linn. xxiii, 738.

8. ALHAGI, Tourn.

1. MAURORUM, Lour. DC. *Prod.* 3, 352.—A small shrub; leaves obovate oblong, glabrous; peduncles axillary; spinescent; flowers few, reddish, in racemes on the peduncles; legume stalked, terete, few-seeded, contracted here and there irregularly. In Guzerat, very common; Southern Maratha Country, Law; Deccan, rare. The camel thorn; much in use as a material for tatties in the hot weather.

9. TAVERNIERA.

1. CUNEIFOLIA.—A shrub 2 to 3 feet high, branched from the base, twiggy, glaucous; leaves simple and trifoliolate, oval or obovate, smooth, dotted on the upper surface; flowers on short racemes; axillary 3 to 5 together, pink; legume notched on both sides, 2-seeded, covered with soft bristles. Near Gogo, in Kattywar; plentiful; Deccan, waste places. Syn. Hedysarum gibsonii, Graham, in Cat. Bomb Pl. The root is sweet, hence the Maratha name "Jetimud," which is also the name of Liquorice.

10. PUERARIA, DC.

1. TUBEROSA, DC. *Prod.* 2, 240.—Root an immense tuber; stem twining; leaves trifoliolate; leaflets large, roundish, beneath silky villous; stipules cordate; racemes simple and branched, as long as the leaves; flowers of a beautiful blue; legumes very hairy, linear-pointed, 2 to 6-seeded, much contracted between the seeds. On Caranjah hill, and other places; pretty common. The bruised root is used as a cataplasm to reduce swelling of the joints, Roxb.; Syn. Hedysarum tuberosum, Roxb. Fl Ind. iii, 363.

11. CLITORIA, Linn.

1. TERNATEA, Linn. DC. *Prod.* 2, 233.—Herbaceous plant; stem twining, leaves unequally pinnated; leaflets 2 to 3 pair, oval or ovate; peduncles short, axillary, solitary, one-flowered; legume linear compressed, straight, many-seeded; flowers large, blue. Very common in hedges. Roxb. Fl Ind. iii, 321; Rheede Mal. viii, *t.* 38; Paxton Mag. Bot. vii, 147, cum icone.

2. BIFLORA, Dalz. in Hook. Jour. Bot. iii, p 34.—Herbaceous, erect; stem striated with lines of hair; leaflets ovate or lanceolate acute, strigose beneath; stipules general and partial setaceous; peduncles very short, 2-flowered; bracts small lanceolate acuminate, bracteoles large ovate acuminate; calyx tubular, hairy, the teeth with bristly points; ovary silky; flowers blue, half the size of those of C ternatea. Concan; common. Fort Sewnere.

12. GLYCINE, Linn.

1. LABIALIS, Linn. suppl. p 325.—Twining, stems slightly hairy; leaflets ovate oblong, slightly coriaceous, upperside glabrous and shining, under pale-green, sparingly hairy; stamens monadelphous; calyx with short adpressed whitish hairs; legumes with adpressed pubescence sharp-pointed, point bent up and rigid, upper lip of calyx bifid. Syn. G debilis Ait, DC. *Prod.*; G parviflora, Lam. in DC. loc. cit.; Teramnus labialis, Spr. *syst.* iii, 235; T parviflorus, Spr. loc. cit.

2. WARREENSIS, Dalz. in Hook. Jour. Bot. iii, 211.—Stamens diadelphous; leaflets ovate oblong, rather membranaceous, glabrous above, strigose beneath, lateral leaflets unequal-sided; racemes compound, 2 to 3 times longer than the leaf, many-flowered; flowers approximated; legume transversely veined, covered with adpressed white hairs; 6-seeded; seeds distant; calyx strongly nerved, upper lip entire. In Warree; flowers in the cold season.

3. PENTAPHYLLA, Dalz. in Hook. Jour. Bot. iv, p 334.—Stem round, twining, strigose; leaflets 2 pair, with an odd one, lanceolate mucronate, strigose on both sides; flowers axillary, interruptedly spicate; spikes straight, rigid, solitary or twin, shorter than the leaf; legume much compressed, linear acute, terminated by a straight short mucro, many-celled, 1½ inch long, 4 lines broad, thickened on the sutures. In the Warree country; flowers in the cold season.

13. SHUTERIA, W. and A.

1. VESTITA, W. and A. *Prod.* 207.—Herbaceous, twining; leaves pinnately trifoliolate, lateral leaflets ovate, terminal rhom-

boidal; racemes axillary, shorter than the leaves, many-flowered; flowers 2 or more from each bractea; calyx very hairy; legume linear compressed, continuous; 5 to 6-seeded, with cellular partitions between the seeds. Between Parwar Ghaut and Tullawaree. Syn. Glycine vestita, Graham in Wall list; Wight Ic. *t.* 162.

14. GALACTIA, P. Browne.

1. Simplicifolia, Dalz. in Hook. Jour. Bot. iii, p 209.—Stem creeping, filiform, hispid, with brown hairs pointing backwards; leaves simple-petioled ovate; stipules adnate nerved acute, partial stipules at the apex of the petiole setaceous; flowers axillary and terminal, racemose fascicled, purple; racemes shorter than the leaf; legume covered with brown hairs, linear, slightly compressed, many-celled; seeds orbicular, compressed. Near Tullawaree; flowers in October. At Hurrychunder.

15. JOHNIA, W. and A.

1. J Congesta, Dalz. Mss.—Stems filiform, twining, clothed with fine white soft reflexed hairs; leaves trifoliolate; leaflets small, broad ovate, very acute, 1¼ inch long; stipules oblong acute, strongly 4-nerved, fixedly a broad base, 2 lines long; peduncles axillary, solitary, not longer than the stipules, 2 to 3-flowered; legumes reflexed, compressed flat, linear, slightly falcate-pointed with the remains of the style, puberulous, 5 to 6-seeded; valves united between the seeds. Sewnere hill-fort.

16. CANAVALIA, Adans.

1. Virosa, W. and A. *Prod.* 253.—Biennial, twining, trifoliolate; leaflets oval or ovate; flowers rather large, of a beautiful rose-colour, racemose, subsecund; legumes large (6 inches), 3-keeled on the upper suture, 6 to 8-seeded. W. and A. say that they have never found diadelphous stamens in this genus; they are certainly so in this plant, as asserted by Roxburgh and DeCandolle. Called "Gowara" by the natives, who recognise two kinds, one bitter, the other sweet. The latter is probably the cultivated species C gladiata. Syn. Dolichos virosus, Roxb. Fl Ind. iii, 301. Common in hedges.

2. Stocksii, Dalz. Mss.—Scandent, very long; stem round, smooth, common; petioles 3 to 8 inches long, channelled on the upper surface, and swelled at the base; stipules linear-obtuse from a broad base, nearly half inch long; lateral leaflets broad oval, nearly orbicular, 3-nerved, with a short sudden acumination, rather unequal-sided, 5 inches long, 4 inches broad, smooth on both sides, rather

membranaceous; terminal leaflet cuneate towards the base; flowers of a beautiful bluish-purple, 1¼ inch long, several on the apex of a very long naked, sharply-angular peduncle (12 to 15 inches); upper lip of calyx minutely bidentate, lower lip trifid, teeth triangular, middle one longest. Budgee hill in Braminwara range, Deccan; very rare.

17. MUCUNA, Adans.

1. Monosperma, DC. *Prod.* 2, 406.—Perennial; leaflets ovate pubescent when young; racemes corymbiform, drooping; legume semioval, obliquely plaited, one-seeded, and covered with stiff ferruginous burning hairs; seed kidney-shaped, with a large hilum. Common in the hilly jungles; Ram Ghaut; flowers in December. Syn. Carpogogon monospermum, Roxb. Fl Ind. iii, 283.

2. Prurita, Hook. in Bot. Misc. ii, 308.—Annual; branches hairy; leaflets ovate, sprinkled with silvery hairs beneath; racemes peduncled, drooping; legume shaped like the letter S, armed with tawny stinging hairs. Cowitch, used to kill intestinal worms, which they do by mechanical action. Very common in hedges. Syn. Dolichos pruriens, Roxb. in E. I. C. Mus. *t.* 284; Carpogogon pruriens, Roxb. Fl Ind. iii, 283; Stizolobium pruriens, Spr. *syst.* iii, 252; Rheed. Mal. viii, *t.* 35; Rumph. Amb. v, *t.* 142; Hook. Bot. Misc. ii, Suppl. *t.* 3.

18. ERYTHRINA, Linn.

1. Indica, Lam. Encyc. Meth. ii, 391. (*a*)—Arboreous; trunk armed with black prickles; leaves pinnately trifoliolate; leaflets glabrous, entire, the terminal one broadly cordate; racemes terminal, horizontal; flowers bright-scarlet, appear in March; legume long, torulose, 6 to 8-seeded, blackish; seeds largish, dark-red. DC. *Prod.* 2, p 412; W. and A. *Prod.* 260; Roxb. Fl Ind. iii, 249; E corallodendron B, Linn. sp. 992. Employed as a support for the black-pepper plant, also for vines. A very common tree. Wight Ic. *t.* 58. Native name "Pangara;" wood used for sword-sheaths.

2. Stricta, Roxb. Fl Ind. iii, p 251.—Arboreous, armed with numerous white prickles; leaflets glabrous entire, terminal one reniform, cordate-pointed; racemes terminal, horizontal; flowers large, bright-scarlet; legume lanceolar-pointed, smooth, light-brown; seeds 2 to 3, oval and smooth. A new genus (Micropteryx) has been proposed for this, and the following by Walpers in the Linn. xxii, 740. Elephanta; the Ghauts, Graham; Southern Concan; pretty common.

3. Suberosa, Roxb. Fl Ind. iii, 253.—Arboreous, bark corky; leaflets white, with down beneath, terminal one rhomboid and

acuminated ; racemes axillary or sometimes terminal ; flowers as in E indica, but smaller ; legume 2 to 3-seeded ; seeds remote. Mawul districts, east of the Ghauts ; Guzerat, Dr. Gibson ; Khandeish Auld. The wood of these three species is soft and worthless.

19. BUTEA, Roxb.

1. Frondosa, Roxb. Fl Ind. iii, 244.—Arboreous ; leaves pinnately trifoliolate ; leaflets large, roundish-ovate, coriaceous, entire, slightly hoary beneath ; racemes terminal and axillary, rigid, covered with greenish velvetty tomentum ; flowers very large, orange-red, silky, appear in February ; legume linear, thin, downy, with one seed within its apex. Pretty common throughout the Presidency. Native name "Pullus Kakria." In Guzerat. This tree yields a beautiful ruby-coloured astringent resin called gum Butea, used for precipitating indigo ; the flowers are used as a dye. Wight, in Hook. Bot. Misc. iii, 102 ; Suppl. *t*. 32.

2. Parviflora, Roxb. Fl Ind. iii, 248.—A large woody climbing shrub ; panicles axillary and terminal ; flowers small, white, appear in November ; lateral leaflets obliquely oblong, terminal round obovate ; legume broad linear flat, covered with brown-velvetty down ; seed large, thin, reniform. Meera hills, near Penn, and other hilly places south of Panwell. Native name "Phulsun."

3. Superba, Roxb. Fl Ind. iii, 247.—Shrubby, twining ; racemes simple lax ; pedicels twice the length of calyx ; calyx segments shortish-acuminate ; corol 4 to 5 times longer than calyx ; vexillum ovate acute. Native name "Pullus Wail." This takes the place of Parviflora in the Northern Concan.

20. PHASEOLUS, Linn.

1. Trinervius, Heyne, in Wall. list No. 5603 ; W. and A. *Prod.* 245.—Twining, branches and petioles covered with long-spreading or deflexed hairs ; leaflets ovate acuminated, sometimes lobed at the base ; peduncles much longer than the leaves ; flowers yellow, forming a kind of cylindrical head ; legumes horizontal cylindrical, hairy. Very common.

2. Trilobus, Ait. Roth. nov. sp. 344.—Procumbent, diffuse ; petioles elongated ; leaflets roundish entire, or 3-lobed ; peduncles much elongated, ascending ; flowers few, small, somewhat capitate, yellow ; legumes cylindrical, smooth or slightly hairy, 6-seeded. Very common on the roadsides and borders of cultivated fields. Roxb. Fl Ind. iii, 298 ; Syn. Glycine triloba, Linn. Maut. 516 ; Dolichos trilobus, Linn. Maut. i, 101 ; D stipulaceus, Lam. Encyc. Meth. ii, p 300 ; P trilobus, Willd. sp. iii, 1035. Native name "Arkmutt."

3. SEPIARIUS, Dalz. in Hook. Jour. Bot. ii, p 33.—Glabrous, twining; leaflets somewhat membranaceous, broadly ovate acuminate mucronate, 3-nerved at the base, lateral leaflets unequal-sided; stipules adnate, ovate lanceolate; peduncles about twice the length of the leaf; flowers between racemose and capitate; divisions of the calyx subulate, 3-nerved, upper lip deeply bidentate; flowers large, rose-coloured; legume round straight, many-seeded, covered with brown shining hairs; root tuberous. Very common in the Northern Concan; flowers in September.

4. SETULOSUS, Dalz. in Hook. Jour. Bot. ii, p 33.—Twining, all covered with reddish-brown scattered bristles pointing backward; leaflets glabrous herbaceous, rhomb-ovate, scarcely acute, ciliated on the margin; lateral leaflets unequal; stipules adnate, ovate obtuse ciliated, many-nerved; calyx glabrous campanulate, upper lip truncated, lower shortly 3-toothed, the teeth obtuse; flowers yellow; legume straight round, slender, rough, with minute bristles 2 inches long; seeds cylindric, 10 to 12. Malwan; flowers in September.

5. PAUCIFLORUS, Dalz. in Hook. Jour. Bot. iii, p 209.—Twining; root fibrous; stem striated filiform, slightly hispid, with white hairs pointing backwards; leaves membranaceous, rhomb-ovate acuminate, as long as the petiole; stipules lanceolate-acute, adnate below the middle; peduncles shorter than the petiole, flowers 2 to 3, terminating the peduncles; flowers small, yellow; legume round, straight, 2 inches long, quite smooth; 9 to 10 seeded, seeds cylindrical truncate at both ends. Southern Concan; common.

6. C GRANDIS, Dalz.—Erect, 4 to 5 feet high; stem herbaceous, piped as thick as one's finger, 5-angled, sparingly clothed with brown reversed bristly hairs; leaves pinnately trifoliolate, very large; stipules very large, foliaceous, adnate, the free part below bilobed; leaflets sparingly sprinkled on both sides with minute adpressed bristles, lateral leaflets unsymmetrically bilobed, terminal, deeply 3-lobed; lobes ovate, with a short and sudden blunt acumination; peduncles axillary, solitary, longer than the leaf, covered with reflexed bristles, many-flowered at the apex; flowers small for the size of the plant; pale-yellow, with large oval bracts below the calyx; legumes cylindric torulose, obtuse at the apex, 3 inches long, as thick as a goose-quill, covered with black adpressed bristles. A very remarkable species on the highest Ghauts east of Bombay.

21. CAJAMUS, DC.

1. KULNENSIS, Dalz. in Hook. Jour. Bot. ii, 264.—Stem twining filiform, pubescent, with spreading fulvous hairs; leaves ternately

trifoliolate; leaflets rhomboid-ovate, shortly acuminated; roughish above, pubescent and covered with wax-coloured glands beneath; stipules ovate-acuminated ciliated, stipels setaceous; racemes axillary, about 6-flowered, as long as the leaf, flowers yellow; legumes linear oblong, narrow at both ends, clothed with long, soft viscid hairs, 5-seeded, obliquely constricted between the seeds. Near Kulna, in the Warree country.

2. GŒNSIS, Dalz. loc. cit.—All over villous, with soft yellow hairs; stem twining; leaves pinnately trifoliolate; leaflets ovate rounded, shortly acuminated, with waxy-looking glands beneath; stipules triangular acuminated; stipels setaceous; racemes axillary and terminal, peduncled, many-flowered, 2 or 3 times longer than the leaf. At the base of Chorla Ghaut.

3. C GLANDULOSUS.—Stems round, twining, the whole plant covered with a close, short tomentum, yellowish or whitish; leaves long-petioled, pinnately trifoliolate; leaflets rhomboid-ovate, the lateral ones acute, all as broad as long, covered on the underside with brown resinous glands; flowers large, yellow racemed, in pairs; raceme peduncled, axillary or terminal, solitary, longer than the leaf; pedicels half an inch long, retrofracted in fruit; legume linear, nearly straight hispid, with yellow bristly hairs, pointed, 7 to 8-seeded, obliquely constricted between the seeds; calyx with the upper lip entire. At Malwan and Wagotun, Southern Concan.

NOTE.—The species of this genus may be known by a sinus near the bottom of the alaæ.

22. CANTHAROSPERMUM, W. and A.

1. PAUCIFLORUM, W. and A. *Prod.* 255.—Biennial, twining; leaflets obovate rugose; peduncles shorter than the petiole, few-flowered; flowers small, yellow; legume linear, softly hairy, transversely constricted between the seeds, 3 to 8-seeded. Very common in the Concan. Syn. Cajanus scarabæoides, Pet. Thouan, Graham in Wall. L. Dolichos scarabæoides, Linn. sp. 1020; D medicaginens, Roxb. Fl Ind. iii, 315 (as to description and character); Rhyncosia scarabæoides, DC. *Prod.* 2, 387; R biflora, DC. loc. cit.; Ltizolobium scarabæoides, Spr. *syst.* iii, 253; Roxburgh says the "callosities of the banner are very sharp"; W. and A. that there are no callosities. Roxburgh also says "the calyx has the upper part entire"; W. and A. that it is "split at the apex." Bentham considers this genus the same with Atylosia of W. and A.

23. LEUCODICTYON, Dalz.

1. MALVENSIS, Walp. Dalz. in Hook. Jour. Bot. ii, p 264.—A twining plant; stems several, filiform, from a woody root; leaves

pinnately trifoliolate; leaflets linear-oblong obtuse-mucronulate, reticulated with white veins; flowers axillary, on a short peduncle, solitary or twin, purple; legume linear-compressed, mucronate, 4 to 5-seeded, obliquely constricted between the seeds. Climbing on the stems of grasses, in rocky ground in the Malwan district.

24. ATYLOSIA, W. and A.

1. Lawii, Wight Ic. *t.* 93.—Shrubby, erect, tomentose; leaflets obovate, as long as the petiole; flowers axillary, solitary; peduncles shorter than the petiole; legumes short, 2-seeded, involved in the persistent corolla, pubescent. The Ghauts; common.

25. PSEUDARTHRIA, W. and A.

1. Viscida, W. and A. *Prod.* 209.—Diffuse prostrate; leaves trifoliolate; lateral leaflets obliquely ovate, terminal rhomboid-ovate; racemes filiform, elongated; flowers purple, in threes, on longish pedicels; legume continuous membranaceous, veined and covered with hooked hairs, flat linear, round at the apex, 3 to 4-seeded. Common. Syn. Hedysarum viscidum, Linn. *syst.* Pl iii, 506; Roxb. Fl Ind. iii, 356; Desmodium viscidum, DC. *Prod.* 2, 336; Glycine viscida, Willd. Pers. Syn. ii, 308; Wight Ic. *t.* 286.

26. RHYNCOSIA, Lowr.

1. Medicaginea, DC. *Prod.* 2, 386.—Twining; leaves trifoliolate; leaflets roundish cuneate at the base, underside slightly pubescent, dotted with numerous brownish glands; racemes few-flowered; flowers very shortly pedicelled; calyx segments subulate; legume pubescent or nearly glabrous, scimitar-shaped, 2-seeded. Very common in the hedges in Guzerat, Deccan. Syn. R rhombifolia, DC. loc. cit.; Dolichos medicagineus, Lam. Encyc. Meth. ii, 297; D scarabæoides, Roxb. Fl Ind. iii. as to character and description; Glycine rhombifolia, Willd. sp. iii, 1065; R crovidia, DC. loc. cit.

27. CYLISTA, Ait.

1. Scariosa, Ait. Hort. Kew. iii, 512.—A perennial shrubby climber; leaves trifoliolate; leaflets oblong or ovate acuminated, downy; racemes axillary short-peduncled; segments of calyx very large, thin, scariose, reticulated; flowers yellow, hid by the calyx; legumes obliquely oval, downy, enclosed within the calyx, 1-seeded. Very common in hedges and open jungles. Roxb. Fl Ind iii, 320.

28. CYANOSPERMUM, W. and A.

1. TOMENTOSUM, W. and A. *Prod.* 259.—Suffrutescent, twining, tomentose; leaves trifoliolate; leaflets broadly ovate, acute; racemes axillary, simple, short; flowers yellow; legume of one or two spherical lobes, about as long as the calyx; seeds of a beautiful dark-blue, polished, round. Chorla and Parwar Ghauts; rather rare. Syn. Cylista tomentosa, Roxb. Fl Ind. iii, 319; Cor. *t.* 221; Wight Illust. *t.* 81. Belgaum jungles; Ghauts south of Beemasunker.

29. FLEMINGIA, Roxb.

1. CONGESTA, Roxb. Fl Ind. iii, 340.—Shrubby, erect, young parts villous; leaves trifoliolate; leaflets ovate-lanceolate, pubescent beneath, dotted with numerous black glands; racemes dense, oblong, shorter than the petiole, almost sessile, aggregated; flowers numerous, striated with orange and purple; legume the length of the calyx, subreniform, 2-seeded. Warree jungles. Native name "Dowdowla." Syn. Crotalaria macrophylla, Willd. sp. Pl iii, 982; Rhyncosia crotalarioides, DC. *Prod.* 3, 387.

2. STROBILIFERA, Br. in Ait. Hort. Kew. iv, 350; DC. *Prod.* 2, 351.—Shrubby, erect, leaves simple-ovate, dotted with minute glands beneath; racemes terminal or axillary; bracteas large, reniform folded, imbricated in two opposite rows; flowers pure white, enclosed within the bracteas; legume of one joint, pubescent, 1 to 2-seeded. Very common. Syn. Hedysarum strobiliferum, Linn. sp. 1053; Roxb. Fl Ind. iii, 350; Zornia strobilifera, Pers. Syn. ii, 319.

3. TUBEROSA, Dalz. in Hook. Jour. Bot. ii, p. 34.—Root tuberous, branched from the base; branches prostrate, very long, filiform; leaves trifoliolate; leaflets narrow lanceolate acute, lateral leaflets unequal-sided; stipules linear subulate, cuneate at the base, caducous; racemes axillary dichotomously panicled, few-flowered, longer than the leaf; flowers twin on the apex of the peduncle; legume glabrous, as long as the calyx, 2-seeded; flowers lilac. Malwan district; flowers in September.

4. PROCUMBENS, R. Wight Ic. *t.* 987.—Herbaceous, diffuse, procumbent hairy; leaves palmately trifoliolate; middle leaflet obovate, lateral ones ovate, slightly unequal at the base, hairy above, nearly glabrous beneath; peduncles longer than the leaves; flowers capitate; legume shorter than the calyx, usually 1-seeded. Phoonda Ghaut. The flowers are of a dark, dull purple colour.

30. PYCNOSPORA, Br.

1. NERVOSA, W. and A. *Prod.* 197.—Suffrutescent, diffuse, branched; leaves trifoliolate; leaflets cuneate obovate, paler and

strongly nerved on the underside; racemes terminal, many-flowered; flowers small, purplish; legumes oblong inflated, one-celled; seeds numerous. Near Vingorla. The pods are very like those of Crotalaria.

31. ABRUS, Linn.

1. PRECATORIUS, Linn. *syst.* p 533.—Twining; leaves abruptly pinnated; leaflets 8 to 20 pair, linear oval-obtuse; racemes axillary peduncled, nearly as long as the leaves, many-flowered; flowers rose-coloured; legumes oblong compressed, 4 to 6-seeded; seeds called Goonch (Vahl.) by the natives, bright red, polished, with a black spot, used for weighing. Supposed to be narcotic, but this is denied by the author of the flora of Jamaica (Dr. Macfadyen), who says they are only indigestible. The roots possess exactly the properties of the Liquorice roots of the shops. Very common in hedges. Roxb. Fl Ind. iii, 258; Syn. Glycine abrus, Linn. sp. 1025.

32. PTEROCARPUS, Linn.

1. MARSUPIUM, Roxb. Fl Ind. iii, 234.—A tree; leaves unequally pinnated; leaflets 5 to 7 alternate, elliptical emarginate, 3 to 5-inches long; panicles terminal, large, flowers numerous, yellowish white; legume obtuse at the base, surrounded by a waved, downy membranaceous wing, rugose and woody in the centre; seed solitary. A dark-red gum resin called "Kino" is produced from wounds in the bark. Native name "Bibla." Common in some parts of the Concan; Parnera hill-fort and Dang jungles. "Honee" is the name in the Southern Maratha Country.

33. BRACHYPTERUM, W. and A.

1. SCANDENS, W. and A. *Prod.* 264.—A woody climber; leaves unequally pinnated; leaflets 3 to 5 pair, opposite, oblong lanceolate; panicles axillary, longer than the leaves; flowers numerous, white; legume linear lanceolate, 2 to 3-seeded, with a narrow margin along the seminiferous suture. Common throughout the Concan. Syn. Dalbergia scandens, Roxb. Fl Ind. iii, 232; Cor. *t.* 192; Rheed. Mal. vi, *t.* 22.

2. B CANARENSE, Dalz.—Like the last; leaflets 7 to 10 pair; panicles terminal, shorter than the leaf, composed of simple racemes of beautiful pink flowers, which are fascicled in threes on a common peduncle; ovary hirsute, with 2 to 3 ovules; legume very flat, oval, or elliptic-pointed at both ends, and winged on both sides, 1 to 1½-inch long. At Garsuppa; in flower in April. A much handsomer species than the preceding. Syn. Pongamia canarensis, Dalz. in Hook. Jour. Bot. ii, p 37.

3. B ROBUSTUM.—A tree; leaflets 13 to 21, oblong or elliptic-mucronulate; young ones silky; racemes simple elongated; flowers fascicled; ovules 6 to 8; legume elongate-lanceolate, with a narrow wing, acute at both ends. Syn. Dalbergia robusta, Roxb.; Wight Ic. *t.* 244. We are not acquainted with this, but as it was found in Dr. Stock's herbarium, it must grow in some parts of the Presidency. The inflorescence and flowers resemble those of B scandens.

34. PONGAMIA, Lam.

1. GLABRA, Vent. Malm. *t.* 28.—Arboreous; leaves unequally pinnated; leaflets opposite, 2 to 3 pair, ovate, sometimes obovate acuminated, glabrous; racemes axillary, many-flowered, half the length of the leaves; flowers rose-coloured; legume oblong, thick, and somewhat woody, 1 to 2-seeded. Very common in the Concan. A middling sized tree, with light-green foliage like the beech. Oil is extracted from the seeds; DC. *Prod.* 2, 416; Syn. Galedupa indica, Lam. Encycl. Meth. ii, 594; Roxb. Fl Ind. iii, 239; Robinia mitis, Linn. sp. 1044; Dalbergia arborea, Willd. sp. iii, 901. Native name "Karunj." The oil of the seeds is an excellent remedy in itch or mange.

35. DERRIS, Lour.

1. D ULIGINOSA, DC. *Prod.* 2, 416.—A twining shrub, growing always near the sea; leaflets 1 to 2 pair, ovate or oblong, bluntly acuminated; racemes axillary compound elongated; flowers rose-coloured, appear in March; legume oval or orbicular, thinly coriaceous, one-seeded, seminiferous suture margined. Very common. Syn. Galedupa uliginosa, Roxb. Fl Ind. iii, 243; Robinia uliginosa, Willd. iii, 1133. This species seems, with great probability, to be a species of Brachypterum; in habit and in the reticulated winged pod, it comes much nearer to that genus than to the Pongamia glabra.

2. D HEYNEANA, Benth. in Pl. Jungh. i, p 252.—Glabrous or slightly clothed with rufous tomentum, a woody climber; leaflets 5 to 7, ovate or oval-oblong, obtusely acuminate; coriaceous; flowers small, pale-pink, in large graceful drooping panicles; legume thickish, coriaceous, strongly reticulately veined, linear oblong, 2 to 3-seeded, winged all round. We should prefer seeing this species placed in the Brachypterum group, to which it seems naturally to belong.

36. DALBERGIA, Linn.

1. LATIFOLIA, Roxb. Fl Ind. iii, 221.—A large tree; leaflets 3 to 7, orbicular emarginate; panicles axillary, branched and

divaricating; flowers small, white, legume lanceolate, thin, brittle, not dehiscing spontaneously, 1 inch broad, 2½ long, 1-seeded. Southern Concan; Southern Maratha Country. This furnishes the well-known blackwood so much used for furniture. It sinks in water.

2. Volubilis, Roxb. Fl Ind. iii, 231.—A climbing shrub; leaflets about 5 pair, alternate or nearly opposite, small, oval-obtuse, glabrous; panicles terminal and axillary, large-branched, spreading; flowers very small, numerous, blue; legume linear oblong-obtuse, membranaceous waved, smooth, 2 to 3 inches long, 1 broad, 1 to 2-seeded. Native name "Alei." Kandalla hills; throughout the Concan; flowers in February and March.

3. Paniculata, Roxb. Fl Ind. iii, 227.—A tree; leaflets 5 to 6 pair, alternate, obovate-oblong or oval emarginate, glabrous, 1½ inch long; panicles terminal, leafy, large; flowers numerous, small, white, tinged with blue; calyx blackish-purple; legume lanceolate, 1 to 2-seeded. Common in the Mawul districts above the Ghauts, Dr. Gibson. Native name "Passee." The wood of this tree is white and firm.

4. Oojeinensis, Roxb. Fl Ind. iii, 220.—A large tree; leaves ternate; leaflets subrotund, 4 inches long, 3 broad, with waved margins; racemes axillary and terminal, rarely compound; flowers numerous, rather small, of a pale rose-colour, somewhat fragrant; legume linear oblong-obtuse, veined and villous on the outside; seeds 1 to 3. North Concan; Dang forests, Dr. Gibson. The wood of this tree is highly valued for its toughness, and is used for carriage poles, &c. It is light-coloured, heavy, and close-grained. Native name "Tunuz." This now forms the genus Oujeinia in Hedysareæ, and ought to be removed from this place.. The bark affords a fine Kino, and is used medicinally in bowel-complaints.

5. Sympathetica, Nimmo in Grah. Cat. p 55.—A large scandent shrub, running over high trees; the trunk is armed with strong, blunt thorns, from 6 to 10 inches long, beautifully and fantastically curved; leaves pinnate; leaflets numerous, small, 11 to 15, obovate-oblong, very obtuse, emarginate; cymes of flowers axillary, dense, shorter than the leaf; legume 1-seeded, 1½ to 2 inches long, or 3 when 2-seeded. Common in the Concan jungles.

6. Monosperma, Dalz. in Hook. Jour. Bot. ii, 36.—A twining shrub; leaflets 5, alternate, obovate or cuneate-oval, mucronulate, quite glabrous above, glaucous beneath; petioles and peduncles pubescent; racemes axillary, solitary or twin, simple, few-flowered, much shorter than the leaf; calyx leaves rounded; corolla white, twice the length of the calyx; stamens monadelphous; legume crescent-shaped, one-seeded. Hills in the Malwan district; flowers in June.

7. D Lanceolaria, Linn., DC. *Prod.* 2, 417.—A tree; leaflets 11 to 15, oval or broadly oblong, very obtuse or retuse, smooth,

1 to 1½ inch long; panicles almost leafless, lax, with rufous pubescence, very large; flowers large for the genus; legume stalked, 1 to 3-seeded, 1½ to 4 inches long, 8 to 9 lines broad. Syn. D frondosa, Roxb. Fl Ind. iii, p 226; D arborea, Heyne in Roth. nov. sp. p 330. Native name "Dandous." Concans, rare; Lulling Ghaut in Kandeish.

37. SOPHORA, Linn.

1. Heptaphylla, Linn., Wight Ic. *t.* 1155.—Shrubby; leaflets 5 to 9 pair, elliptic-oblong acute, with recurved margins, glabrous above, strigose with adpressed rusty pubescence beneath; stipules rigid subulate; racemes leaf-opposed, lax, about the length of the leaves; legume slender, covered with strigose pubescence, attenuated at the apex, much contracted between the seeds; seeds 2 to 4, oval, smooth. Hills east of Belgaum.

38. GUILANDINA, Linn.

1. Bonduc, Linn. sp. p 545.—A climbing armed shrub, stem and petioles with hooked prickles; leaves abruptly bipinnated; leaflets oval or ovate, 3 to 8 pair; flowers spicately racemose, yellow, appear in the rains; legume ovate ventricose compressed, covered with straight prickles. Native name "Sagurgota." Common in hedges. DC. *Prod.* 2, 480; Syn. Cæsalpinia bonducella, Flem. in As. Res. xi, p 159; Roxb. Fl Ind. ii, p 357. The powdered seeds, mixed with pepper, are an excellent febrifuge, Dr. Gibson. They are very bitter; pounded small and mixed with castor-oil, they are a valuable external application in incipient hydrocele; the leaves fried with a little castor-oil, are a valuable discutient in cases of Hernia humoralis.

Note.—Seeds large, grey, used to procure abortion. Sagurgota means sea-nut; and there is reason to suspect that this is not a native of the East Indies, but of the West.

39. CÆSALPINIA, Linn.

1. Paniculata, Roxb. Fl Ind. ii, 364.—A scandent armed shrub; branches and petioles covered with numerous sharp-recurved prickles; leaves bipinnated; pinnæ, 3 to 4 pair; leaflets 3 to 4 pair, ovate lanceolate, glabrous, shining above, rusty-coloured beneath; flowers terminal panicled, yellow, fragrant; legume obliquely oval cuspidate, compressed, tumid in the middle, glabrous, one-seeded. Pretty common in the Concan. Syn. C scandens, Roth. nov. sp. p 209; Guilandina paniculata, Lam. Encyc. Meth. i, 435. Garden at Hewra.

2. Mimosoides, Lam. Encyc. Meth i, 457.—Climbing, stem and branches armed with numerous straight prickles, young parts coloured, armed with prickles and glandular bristles; pinnæ of the leaves 12 to 30 pair; leaflets 8 to 16 pair, linear oblong, glabrous; racemes simple, leaf-opposed and terminal; legumes short, obliquely truncated, cuspidate turgid, hairy, 2-seeded. Jungles in the Warree country; plentiful; flowers in January. DC. *Prod.* 2, 482; Syn. C simora, Ham. in Roxb. Fl Ind. ii, 359.

3. Sepiaria, Roxb. Fl Ind. ii, 360.—Climbing; branches and petioles armed with short, strong recurved prickles; pinnæ of the leaves 6 to 10 pair; leaflets 8 to 12 pair, linear, oblong obtuse; racemes axillary, solitary; calyx coloured; flowers yellow, appear in December, also in March and April; legumes linear oblong, smooth, with a long cuspidate point, 4 to 8-seeded. At Banda; more plentiful in the Deccan. Native name "Chillur." DC. *Prod.* 2, 484.

Note.—The famous Arambooli lines between Tippoo's and the Travancore country were made of this.

40. WAGATEA, Dalz.

1. Spicata, Dalz. in Hook. Jour. Bot. iii, p 89.—Shrubby, climbing; branches and petioles armed with many recurved thorns; leaves bipinnate; pinnæ 5 to 6 pair; leaflets 5 to 6 pair, oblong obtuse, coriaceous, shining above; flowers in terminal tapering spikes, 1 to 2 feet long, scarlet and orange-coloured; legumes linear, coriaceous, much swollen at the seeds, and constricted between them. Common in the jungles of the Concans. Syn. Cæsalpinia digyna, Graham's Catalogue, p 60. South of Panwell, also on the Ghauts.

41. MEZONEURUM, Desf.

1. Cucullatum, W. and A. *Prod.* 283.—Scandent armed, pinnæ of the leaves 3 to 7 pair; leaflets 4 to 5 pair, ovate-pointed, coriaceous, shining on the upperside; panicles terminal and axillary, composed of a few rigid racemes; flowers greenish-yellow, appear in January and February; legume unarmed, foliaceous, ovate-oblong compressed, with a wing along the seminiferous suture. The higher Ghauts; common. Native name "Ragee." Syn. Cæsalpinia cucullatta, Roxb. Fl Ind. ii, 358.

42. CASSIA, Linn.

1. Fistula, Linn. sp. p 540.—A small tree; leaves pinnated; leaflets about 5 pair, broadly ovate, obtuse or retuse, glabrous;

racemes terminal, long lax drooping; flowers yellow, showy; legumes cylindric-pendulous, smooth. Common. Native name "Bawa." Roxb. Fl Ind. ii, p 333; C rhombifolia? Roxb. loc. cit. 334. Called also "Gurmala"; the pulp is a safe purgative.

2. SOPHORA, Linn. sp p 542.—Annual, erect-branched, glabrous; leaflets 6 to 12 pair, lanceolate acute, with a clavate gland near the base of the petiole; racemes terminal or axillary, and few-flowered; legumes long linear turgid, glabrous, many-seeded; sutures keeled. A common weed. DC. *Prod.* 2, 492; C purpurea, DC. loc. cit. 497; C torosa, DC. loc. cit. 491; C coromandeliana, DC. loc. cit. 492; Syn. Senna sophera, Roxb. Fl. Ind. ii, 347; S purpurea, Roxb. loc. cit. 342; S esculenta, Roxb. 346.

3. SENNA, Swartz.—Perennial, herbaceous, diffuse; leaflets 4 to 6 pair, obovate-obtuse mucronate glabrous; racemes axillary few-flowered, much shorter than the leaves; legumes lunate broad, thin obtuse; valves crested at the seeds. Guzerat, Burn; Sind, plentiful. Syn. C obovata, Collad.; C obtusa, Roxb. Hort. Bengal, 31; S obtusa, Roxb. Fl Ind. ii, 344; C burmanni, Wight in Madras Jour. 1837. Deccan; common in Beemthuree District east, also Southern Maratha Country.

4. MONTANA, Heyne in Roth. nov. sp. p 214.—A shrub or small tree; leaflets 10 to 12 pair, oval oblong obtuse, pointed with a deciduous bristle, glabrous on both sides when old, but all the young parts are covered with a fulvous pubescence; peduncles glabrous, many-flowered, axillary, or forming a large terminal panicle; flowers long-pedicelled, rather small; legumes linear straight, thin, glabrous and shining, when ripe hard and woody. At Virdee and on the Chorla Ghaut. DC. *Prod.* 2, 499; C setigera, DC. loc. cit.; Senna glauca, Roxb. Fl Ind. ii, 351.

5. AURICULATA, Linn. sp. 542.—A small shrub; leaflets 8 to 12 pair, oval-obtuse or retuse, mucronate; stipules large, obliquely cordate, acute; racemes axillary, nearly as long as the leaves, many-flowered; flowers showy, yellow; legumes thin, compressed, straight. Very common in Guzerat and in the Deccan. DC. *Prod.* 2, 496; Syn. Senna auriculata, Roxb. Fl Ind. ii, 349. The bark is much used for tanning leather. Native names "Turwar," "Aroul."

6. OCCIDENTALIS, Linn. sp. 539.—An annual, erect-branched, glabrous; leaflets 3 to 5 pair, ovate-lanceolate, very acute; flowers longish pedicelled, upper ones forming a terminal raceme; legumes long, nearly cylindric, slightly compressed. A common weed. This, as well as the following, has a heavy, sickening smell. DC. *Prod.* 2, 497; Syn. Senna occidentalis, Roxb. Fl Ind. ii, 343.

7. TORA, Linn. sp. 538.—Annual, with spreading branches; leaflets 2 to 3 pair, cuneate obovate obtuse; flowers long-pedicelled; upper ones forming a short terminal raceme; legumes very long,

sharp-pointed, 4-sided, many-seeded, each suture 2-grooved. A common weed. Native name "Sakla." Syn. C obtusifolia, Burm. Ind p 95; C fœtida, Sal. *Prod.* 326; C gallinaria Collad monogr. p 96; Senna toroides, Roxb. Fl Ind. ii, 341.

8. PUMILA, Lam. Encyc. Meth. i, 651.—Suffruticose procumbent branches a little hairy; leaflets 12 to 30 pair, with a stalked peltate gland close to the lowest pair, linear oblong, unequal-sided, mucronate; flowers supra-axillary, 1 to 3 together; legumes flat linear, 6 to 7-seeded, constricted between the seeds. A low prostrate specimen. Common in pastures in the rains. DC. *Prod.* 2, 504; Syn. Senna prostrata, Roxb. Fl Ind. ii, 352.

43. IONESIA, Roxb.

1. ASOCA, Roxb. Fl Ind. ii, 218.—A small handsome tree; leaves abruptly pinnated; leaflets 4 to 6 pair, lanceolate; cymes terminal and axillary, large, globular, crowded with flowers of a beautiful orange-colour; legume scimitar-shaped, compressed, a little turgid, 4 to 8-seeded. This tree in full blossom is a most beautiful object; very common about the Ghauts in the Southern Concan. DC. *Prod.* 2, 487; Syn. I pinnata, Willd. sp. ii, 287; Saraca arborescens, Burm. Ind. p 85, *t.* 25, *fig.* 2. Native name "Jassoondie," "Asok."

44. TAMARINDUS, Linn.

1. INDICUS, Linn. sp. p 48.—A large and handsome tree; leaves abruptly pinnated; leaflets numerous; flowers racemose, yellow, legume stalked, linear, curved more or less, slightly compressed, 3 to 12-seeded, with a pulpy sarcocarp, having purgative properties. Common in Salsette, Guzerat, &c. Native name "Umlee." The red-fruited variety is much valued. Tussæ flore des Antilles, iii 112, *t.* 35.

45. BAUHINIA, Linn.

1. MALABARICA, Roxb. Fl Ind. ii, 321.—Arboreous; leaves transversely broad, oval-cordate at the base, glabrous; leaflets rounded, united above the middle; racemes axillary, corymbiform, almost sessile; legume long-stalked, linear, marked longitudinally with waved lines 1½ foot long, 1 inch broad. Discovered in fruit at Banda in February; rare.

2. RACEMOSA, Lam. Encycl. Meth. i, p 390.—A small crooked tree; leaves cordate at the base; leaflets roundish or broadly obovate, united to the middle; racemes solitary, terminal or leaf-opposed, much longer than the leaves; flowers white, small; legumes linear, woody, thick, many-seeded. Very common in the

Concan. Native name "Aupta." Worshipped by the Hindoos on the Dussera festival; the leaves are used for making native cigars. Also called "Wuna rajah," or king of the jungle; said to be mentioned in the Vedas. Syn. B parviflora, Vahl. Symb. iii, p 55; DC. *Prod.* 2, 514; Roxb. Fl Ind. ii, 323. This forms the new genus Piliostigma hochst.

3. VAHLII, W. and A. *Prod.* p 297.—Climbing to an immense extent, often arboreous; young shoots, petioles, and peduncles covered with a thick rusty-coloured tomentum; leaves roundish, deeply cordate at the base, underside tomentose; leaflets oval obtuse, united to above the middle; racemes terminal, corymbiform; legumes pendulous, 1 to 1½ foot long, covered with brown tomentum, 8 to 12-seeded. The Thul Ghaut; ravines at Kandalla. Native name "Chamboolee." Syn. B racemosa, Vahl. Symb. iii, p 56, *t.* 62; DC. *Prod.* 2, 515; Roxb. Fl Ind. ii, 325. The large seeds are eaten raw; when ripe, they taste like cashew-nuts; the leaves are employed to line baskets, and for thatching houses.

46. CYNOMETRA, Linn.

1. RAMIFLORA, Linn. sp. p 509.—A shrub; leaves pinnated; leaflets 1 to 3 pair, oblong acuminated or emarginate; peduncles solitary, few-flowered, springing from the branches among the leaves; legume nearly half orbicular, thick, tumid fleshy, tubercled and rugged on the outside. Southern Concan; very rare. DC. *Prod.* 2, p 509; Rumph. Amb. i, *t.* 63; Wight and Arnott's *Prod.* 293.

47. HARDWICKIA, Roxb.

1. BINATA, Roxb. Fl Ind. ii, 423.—A tree; leaves abruptly pinnated; leaflets 1 pair, opposite, obliquely ovate obtuse; racemes axillary panicled; corolla none; legume lanceolate, 2-valved, opening at the apex; seed solitary in the apex of the legume, thin and membranous on one edge. In the Lulling Pass between Malligaum and Dhoolia, Dr. Gibson and Lieutenant Auld; other parts of Kandeish, and in Nimar.

48. ENTADA, Linn.

1. PUSÆTHA, DC. *Prod.* 2, 425.—An immense climbing shrub; leaves bipinnated; pinnæ 1 to 2 pair; leaflets 2 to 5 pair, glabrous, oblong-obovate or ovate, emarginate, spikes solitary or in pairs, long, slender, axillary; flowers yellow, appear in March; legumes of extraordinary size, 2 to 3 feet long, 4 to 5 inches broad, constricted between the seeds; seeds very large. Native name "Gardul."

Common along the Ghauts. Syn. E monostachya, DC. loc. cit.; E Rheedei, Spr. *syst.* ii, 325; Pusætha No. 6441, Linn. Fl Zeyl.; Mimosa No. 219, Linn. Fl Zeyl.; M scandens, Linn. sp. p 1501; Roxb. Fl Ind. ii, 554; M Entada, Linn. sp. p 1502; Acacia scandens; Willd. loc. cit. 1057. An infusion of the spongy fibres of the trunk used with advantage for various affections of the skin in the Philippines, where it is called "Gogo," Adams; the seeds are eaten roasted in Soonda.

49. PROSOPIS, Linn.

1. Spicigera, Linn. Maut. p 68.—A tree, armed with prickles; leaves pinnated or bipinnated; leaflets 7 to 10 pair, oblong linear obtuse, glabrous; spikes axillary, several together, slender elongated; legumes cylindric, filled with mealy pulp. Very common in Guzerat, where it is called "Sumree." Generally found covered with numerous perforated knots or galls, the work of a species of cynips. DC. *Prod.* 2, 446; Syn. Adenanthera aculeata, Roxb. Fl Ind. iii, 371. Grows also in the south of Persia. The flowers are almost the same as those of Entada, Burm. Fl Ind. *t.* 25, *f.* 3.

Note.—Also called Sounder. This is the tree to which (in the Deccan) the processions during Dussera proceed. In Sind very plentiful.

50. DICHROSTACHYS, DC.

1. Cinerea, W. and A. *Prod.* 271.—A thorny shrub; leaves pinnated; pinnæ 5 to 10 pair; leaflets numerous, linear ciliated; spikes usually solitary, rarely 2 to 3 together, drooping, somewhat cylindric, one-half of the spike yellow, the other rose-coloured; legume thick and coriaceous, curved and twisted, jointed; joints one-seeded. Common in the Deccan. Syn. Mimosa cinerea, Linn. sp. 1505; Roxb. Fl Ind. ii, 561; Desmanthus cinereus, Willd. sp. iv, 1048; DC. *Prod.* 2, 445; Acacia cinerea, Spr. *syst.* iii, 143.

51. NEPTUNIA, Desm.

1. Oleracea, Lour. Benth in Hook. Jour. Bot. iv, 354.—Annual, floating and throwing out roots; leaves bipinnated; pinnæ 2 to 3 pair; leaflets 8 to 12 pair; stipules obliquely cordate; peduncles axillary, solitary, longer than the leaves; flowers in oblong solitary spikes; legume stalked, oblique at the base, oblong falcate, 6 to 8-seeded. Tanks throughout the Concan. DC. *Prod.* 2, 444; Syn. Mimosa natans, Roxb. Fl Ind. ii, 553; M prostrata, Lam.; Desmanthus natans, Willd. sp. iv, 1044; D lacustris, Willd.; D stolonifer, DC. loc. cit. 444.

2. Triquetra, Benth. loc. cit.—Bitriennial, prostrate; stem

compressed; leaves bipinnated; pinnæ 2 to 3 pair; leaflets 10 to 12 pair; stipules subulate; peduncles axillary, solitary, flower-heads globular, yellow; legumes linear oblong, equal-sided, 4 to 6-seeded; flowers in August. Common in pastures about Surat. DC. *Prod.* 2, 444; Syn. Mimosa triquetra, Vahl. Symb. iii, 102; Roxb. Fl Ind. ii, 552; M natans, Linn. Suppl. p 439; Desmanthus triquetris, Willd. sp. iv, 1045.

52. MIMOSA, Adans.

1. HAMATA, Willd. sp. iv, 1033.—An armed much-branched shrub; branches, petioles, and peduncles pubescent, and covered with scattered prickles; leaves bipinnated; pinnæ 4 pair; leaflets 7 to 8 pair, minute, linear oval approximated, pubescent; peduncles longer than the leaves, bearing one head of rose-coloured flowers; legumes linear falcately curved, pubescent. Common about Surat and in the Deccan. Native name "Arkur." DC. *Prod.* 2, 427; Syn. M armata, Rottlr. Spr. *syst.* ii, 206.

2. RUBRICAULIS, Lam. Encycl. Meth. i, p 20.—A large straggling prickly shrub; leaves bipinnated; pinnæ 5 pair; leaflets 10 to 12 pair, oblong linear, pubescent; peduncles one-headed, several together in the upper axils; legume sessile, compressed flat, glabrous, obscurely jointed. Malabar Hill, &c.; common. DC. *Prod.* 2, 429; M octandra, Roxb. Fl Ind. ii, 564; M Rottleri, Spr. *syst.* ii, 206; M spinosiliqua, Rottler.

53. XYLIA, Benth.

1. DOLABRIFORMIS, Benth. in Hook. Jour. Bot. iv, 417.—A tall unarmed tree, glabrous or tomentose on the younger parts; stipules small; leaves bipinnate; pinnæ one pair, with an elevated gland between; leaflets 2 to 6 pair, outer ones often 6 inches long; peduncles fascicled, axillary or sub-racemose, 2 to 3 inches long; heads of flowers globose, tomentose; of a pale greenish colour; legume 4 to 5 inches long, $1\frac{1}{2}$ to 2 inches broad. Mimosa acacia, Willd. sp. iv, 1055; Inga, DC. *Prod.* 2, 439; I xylocarpa, Roxb. Cor. Pl i, 68, *t.* 100; Mimosa acle, Blanco Fl. Filipin. 738. Native names "Jamba" and "Yerool"; timber excellent. Southern Concan and Waree; common.

54. ACACIA.

1. A EBURNEA, Willd. sp. Pl iv, 1081.—Branchlets and leaves with ferruginous hairs; spines straight, some of them long and ivory white; pinnæ 2 to 4 pair, small; leaflets 6 to 8 pair, very small, linear obtuse, a little hairy; peduncles axillary, bracted in the middle; legume stalked, narrow linear falcate, quite smooth, 2 to 3

inches long, 2 lines broad, rather glaucous. Common in the Deccan in dry barren places. Native name "Murmut."

2. A Sundra, DC. *Prod.* 2, 458.—A very large tree with white bark, all smooth; branchlets dark-coloured; thorns twin, recurved, small or wanting; pinnæ 10 to 15 pair; leaflets 20 to 30 pair, linear; spikes of white flowers axillary, shorter than the leaf; flowers sessile, glabrous; legume broad linear flat. Mimosa sundra, Roxb. Cor. Pl iii, 225; A chundra, Willd. sp. iv, 1078. Common in the Deccan.

3. Catechu, Willd. sp. iv, 1079.—A small tree; branchlets and petioles white, with a short pubescence; thorns infrastipulary, twin, slight recurved or none; pinnæ 10 to 30 pair; leaflets 30 to 50 pair, linear puberulous and ciliated; spikes axillary, rather lax, shorter than the leaf; flowers white; legume broad linear flat. Salsette and the Concans common; also Deccan, but stunted; flowers in July. Syn. Mimosa catechu, Linn. Fl Ind. ii, 563; M suma, Roxb. loc. cit.; A polyacantha, Willd. sp. iv, 1079; A wallichiana, DC. *Prod.* 2, 458.

4. Arabica, Willd. sp. iv, 1085.—A tree, glabrous or tomentose, pubescent; thorns very small or long subulate, or strong, finally white, straight or slightly recurved; pinnæ 4 to 8 pair; leaflets 10 to 20 pair, oblong linear obtuse, green, glabrous; peduncles axillary, with a bract in the middle; heads of flowers globose; legume flat linear, necklace-shaped. Common in the Deccan and in Guzerat. It is the variety δ which is found in India, having the legume covered with hoary tomentum. Syn. A nilotica, Delile Fl Ægypt. Ill. 31; A vera, Willd. sp. iv, 1085; Mimosa arabica, Roxb. Cor. ii, *t.* 149. The timber of this tree is excellent for cart and gun-wheels, and agricultural implements. There is a singular variety with the branches erect, like a cypress in growth, and very handsome, called "Ram Kanta." Another variety, called "Eree Babool," has the timber softer, and the pods broader, with a thicker margin, and the bark much cracked.

5. Tomentosa, Willd. sp. iv, 1087.—A tree; branches and petioles velvetty with tomentum; thorns sometimes minute, sometimes very long, stout, and dark-coloured; pinnæ 10 to 12 pair; leaflets 20 to 30 pair, linear obtuse, pubescent; peduncles axillary, with a bract in the middle; heads of flowers white, tomentose; legume broadly linear, flat, falcately sub-contorted, coriaceous; pinnæ 1 to 1½ inch long; leaflets 3 lines long; legume 3 to 4 lines broad. Rare; in the Deccan and Kandeish jungles. Syn. Mimosa tomentosa, Roxb. Fl Ind. ii, 558.

6. Leucophlæa, Willd. sp. iv, 1063.—A tree; thorns straight; pinnæ of the leaves 5 to 12 pair; leaflets 12 to 30 pair, obliquely oblong, linear obtuse rigid; heads of flowers shortly peduncled,

disposed in a large leafless tomentose panicle; legume narrow linear, slightly twisted, thick, flattened. Common in the Southern Maratha Country and the Sholapore districts. A spirit is distilled from the bark, and the trees are farmed on account of Government, Mr. Law. Syn. A alba, Willd. DC. *Prod.* 2, 469; Mimosa leucophlæa, Roxb. Fl Ind. ii, 558. Native name "Hewur."

7. LATRONUM, Willd. sp. iv, 1077.—Thorns straight, here and there very large; pinnæ 2 to 5 pair; leaflets 6 to 15 pair, small linear, or oblong obtuse; spikes cylindric lax, slightly interrupted; legume broadly falcate, oblong flat, coriaceous, glabrous. In the Eastern Deccan; common. Syn. Mimosa latronum, Roxb. Fl Ind. ii, 559.

8. CONCINNA, DC. *Prod.* 2, 464.—A large scandent shrub; prickles numerous, recurved; pinnæ 4 to 6 pair; leaflets 12 to 18 pair, half oblong obtuse, glabrous; leaflets pale-green, distant, half inch long 1⅓ inch broad; racemes but little branched; peduncles one inch long, heads of flowers small; legume 3 to 5 inches long, one inch broad, succulent, contracted between the seeds. Used as soap for washing. Native name "Chickakai." The leaves are acid, and are used in cookery instead of Tamarind, Nimmo. Jungles in the Concan; common; also Ghaut jungle. Syn. Mimosa concinna, Willd. sp. iv, 1039; Roxb. Fl Ind. ii, 564; M rugata, Lam. Encycl. Meth i, p 20; M abstergens, Spr. *syst.* ii, p 207.

9. A PROCERA.—A great tree unarmed, with white bark and pinnate leaves; leaflets 10 to 12 pairs, obliquely oblong unequal, with a large gland at base of petiole; legume reddish, leafy, 8 inches long. Native name "Kinye." Timber very useful, especially the dark heart wood. Common near the Ghauts in the Deccan, and still more so in the Concan.

10. PINNATA, Willd, sp. iv, 1090.—A scandent shrub; prickles scattered, numerous, straight, or at length recurved; pinnæ 8 to 20 pair; leaflets beyond 30 pair, narrow linear glabrous; heads of flowers globose panicled; legume glabrous or reddish, with minute tomentum. Common in the Concan. Syn. M torta, Roxb. Fl Ind. ii, 566; M ferruginea, Rottler. in Spr. *syst.* ii, 207; A arrophila, Don. *Prod.* Fl, Nepal; A megaladena, Desv. Jour. Bot. 1814, *t.* 69; A prensans, Lowe Bot. Mag. *t.* 3408. The bark much used by fishermen for their nets, and is an article of commerce.

11. CÆSIA, W. and A. *Prod.* 1, 278.—A scandent shrub, armed with numerous scattered recurved prickles; pinnæ 8 to 15 pair; leaflets 15 to 40 pair, oblong linear falcate, rather acute; heads of flowers globose, paniculate; legume subfalcate, glabrous. The Concans. Syn. A intsioides, DC. *Prod.* 2, 278 (?); A arar, Ham. in Wall. Cat. 5258; Mimosa cæsia, Roxb. Fl Ind. ii, 565 (?) The Concans.

Supposed to be a variety of the following, with more numerous leaflets.

12. Intsia, Willd. sp. iv, 1091.—A climbing shrub, with numerous small recurved scattered prickles; pinnæ 4 to 8 pair; leaflets 8 to 20 pair, obliquely oblong obtuse, glabrous; heads of flowers white, globose panicled; legume subfalcate, glabrous, purple, 4 inches long and one inch broad, obtuse at apex. Syn. Mimosa intsia, Linn. sp. p 1508; Roxb. Fl Ind. ii, 565. At Cambay; flowers in October; Unkleswur.

55. ALBIZZIA, Darazni.

1. Lebbek, Benth. in Hook. Jour. Bot. iii, 87.—A large tree; leaves bipinnate; pinnæ 2 to 4 pair; leaflets 5 to 3 pair, obliquely oval-oblong, very obtuse, unequal-sided, subsessile; peduncles elongated, fascicled, sub-racemose in the supreme axils; heads of flowers large, many-flowered; legume very long, glabrous, Common; flowers in May, white, very fragrant. Syn. Acacia lebbek, Willd. DC. *Prod.* 2, 466; A speciosa, Willd. DC. *Prod.* 2, 467; Mimosa sirissa, Roxb. Fl Ind. ii, 544; Albizzia latifolia, Boivin. Encycl. The timber of this tree is strong and durable.

2. Odoratissima, Benth. loc. cit. p 88.—A tree; pinnæ 3 to 8 pair; leaflets 8 to 25 pair, broadly oblong, very unequal-sided, glaucous beneath; panicle of flowers many-headed, heads few-flowered; flowers pubescent, ovary subsessile, glabrous. This has much smaller flowers than the preceding. The Concans. Syn. Acacia odoratissima, Willd. DC. *Prod.* 2, 466; Albizzia micrantha, Boivin. loc. cit.; Mimosa odoratissima, Roxb. Fl Ind. ii, 546. This large and handsome tree has particularly hard and strong timber.

3. Amara, Boivin loc. cit.—A tree; branchlets and petioles tomentose; pinnæ 7 to 11 pair, approximated; leaflets many-pair, small, oblong linear falcate; peduncles in the upmost axils fasciculate subracemose; heads 12 to 20-flowered, ovary stipitate, glabrous. Common on the banks of the Krishna; about Nalutwar, Law; on Matheran Hill; and Deccan, common. Syn. Acacia amara, Willd. DC. *Prod.* 2, 469; A wightii, Grah. W. and A. *Prod.* 1, 274; Mimosa amara, Roxb. Fl Ind. ii, 548. Native name "Lullei."

4. Stipulata, Boivin. loc. cit.—A tree; stipules large, membranaceous, acuminated deciduous; pinnæ 7 to 20 pair; leaflets many-paired, oblong-linear falcate acute; peduncles racemose, paniculate, heads 10 to 20-flowered; ovary subsessile, glabrous; legume flat, thin linear lanceolate, glabrous. Common on the Ghauts; flowers in April and May, pinkish. Syn. Acacia stipulata, DC. *Prod.* 2, p 469; Mimosa stipulacea, Roxb. Fl Ind. ii, 549.

56. PITHECOLOBIUM, Martius.

1. P BIGEMINUM, Mart. Herb. Fl Bras. p 115.—A tree; pinnæ 1 to 2 pair; leaflets 2 to 4 pair, ovate or oblong-acuminate, 2 to 3 inches long, a gland in the middle of the petiole; flowers capitate, few, puberulous, sessile; legume spirally twisted, the exterior margin entire. Southern Concan. Syn. Mimosa bigemina, Vahl. Symb. ii, p 103; Inga bigemina, Willd. sp. Pl.

LV. DRUPACEÆ.

1. PYGEUM, Linn.

1. P ZEYLANICUM, Gaert. Fruct. i, 218, *t.* 46, and P acuminatum, Colebrooke, in Linn. Trans. xii, 360, *t.* 18.—A tree; leaves alternate oblong acuminate, quite entire, glabrous; racemes long slender axillary; flowers yellowish-white; fruit small, smooth, obtusely and slightly bilobed. Hill-fort of Munohur and Parwar Ghaut; at Mahableshwur, pretty common.

2. ROSACEÆ; RUBUS, Linn.

1. R LASIOCARPUS, Smith, W. and A. *Prod.* 1, 299; Wight Ic. *t.* 232.—Stems round, long, rooting at the extremities, glabrous, glaucous, armed with curved prickles; branches and petioles tomentose and prickly; leaves pinnated; leaflets 3 to 7, ovate, obovate or lanceolate, terminal one roundish and often 3-lobed, smooth above, white and tomentose beneath, irregularly toothed and serrated; panicles racemose, chiefly terminal; carpels tomentose. Syn. R albescens, Roxb. Fl Ind. ii, p 519; R mysorensis, Heyne. Highest Ghauts to the southward.

2. R WALLICHIANUS, W. and A. *Prod.* 1, 298.—Petioles, peduncles, and pedicels armed with recurved prickles, and densely hispid with brown hairs; leaves pinnately trifoliolate; leaflets nearly orbicular, toothed, serrated, green on both sides; panicles large compound, somewhat corymbose, axillary and terminal. R hirtus, Roxb. Fl Ind. ii, 518, along with the preceding.

3. RUGOSUS, Smith in Ree's Cycl.—Shrubby, armed with small scattered prickles; branches, calyx, and underside of the leaves villous, with tawny tomentum; leaves simple cordate, 3 to 5-lobed, reticulated and pitted underneath, scabrous above; racemes axillary and terminal, few-flowered. Mahableshwur, and along the higher

Ghauts; pretty common. DC. *Prod.* 2, 567; Syn. R alceæfolius, Poir Encycl. Meth. vi, 247; DC. loc. cit.; R reflexus, Kew. Bot. Reg. *t.* 461; R moluccanus, Roxb. Fl Ind. ii, 518; R hamiltonianus, Seringe in DC. loc. cit.

LVI. SAXIFRAGACEÆ.

1. VAHLIA, Thunb.

1. Viscosa, Roxb. Fl Ind. ii, p 89.—Herbaceous, pubescent, slightly glutinous; leaves oblong-lanceolate or linear; flowers in pairs, almost sessile, yellow; capsules nearly globose; seeds minute. Island of Caranjah, and Guzerat; common. Syn. V sessiliflora, DC. *Prod.* 4, p 54; Oldenlandia digyna, Retz. Obs. iv, p 23.

LVII. COMBRETACEÆ.

1. COMBRETUM, Löffl.

1. C Wightianum, Wall., W. and A. *Prod.* 1, 317.—A scandent shrub; leaves elliptic-obovate, with a short sudden acumination, coriaceous, shining above; spikes of flowers axillary, on longish peduncles, elongated, lax; tube of the calyx 2 to 3 times longer than the ovary; fruit 4-winged. Wight Ic. *t.* 227; Syn. C laxum, Roxb. Fl Ind. ii, 231; Rheed. Mal. vii, *t.* 23. Hilly parts of the Concan, not uncommon; at Vingorla. Native name "Peeloka."

2. C Ovalifolium, Roxb. Fl Ind. 2, 226.—A climber like the last; leaves ovate or elliptic-obtuse, or slightly acute. minutely dotted above; spikes of yellowish-white; flowers axillary and terminal, appear in April and May; tube of calyx not longer than the ovary; wings of the fruit smooth, semicircular. Jungles in the Concan and Ghauts, common. Wight in Hook. Bot. Misc. Suppl. *t.* 22. Native name "Zelloosey," also "Peelookha." Is much used as hoops for the Motes employed in drawing water from tanks and wells.

2. LUMNITZERA, Willd.

1. L Racemosa, Willd.—A shrub; leaves cuneate obovate retuse, attenuated at the base, crenated or entire, thick and veinless; spikes of small white flowers, short, axillary; stamens 10, alternately shorter. Salt-water creeks, Southern Concan. Syn. Petaloma alternifolia, Roxb. Fl Ind. ii, 372; Rheed. Mal. vi, *t.* 37. In fruit in October.

3. CONOCARPUS, Gaert.

1. C Latifolia, Roxb. Fl Ind. ii, p 442.—A large erect tree with white bark; leaves elliptic or obovate-obtuse or emarginate, smooth; heads of flowers aggregated, on branched peduncles; fruit coriaceous, scale-like, closely imbricated. Meera hills, and other elevated jungly places in the Concan. The timber is good for cart-axles, and the tree produces a very white, hard, and valuable gum. Wight Ic. 994. Native name "Daura" or "Dabria."

4. GETONIA, Roxb.

1. G Floribunda, Roxb. Cor. Pl i, *t.* 87; Fl Ind. ii, p 428.—A climbing shrub, with opposite short-petioled leaves, resinous dotted beneath, the young ones tomentose; panicles of greenish-white flowers, erect; fruit small, drupaceous, dry, ovate-oblong, between round and pentagonal. Extremely common in the Concan and Ghauts, not found in Ceylon. Native name "Wooksey" or "Bagoolee."

5. TERMINALIA, Linn.

1. T Belerica, Roxb. Cor. Pl *t.* 198; Fl Ind. ii, p 431.—A large handsome tree; leaves collected about the extremities of the branchlets, large, long-petioled obovate-obtuse or shortly acuminated, quite entire, generally smooth; spikes of small yellowish-green; flowers axillary solitary, almost as long as the leaves; drupe small, roundish, covered with a grey silky down. Native name "Bherda."

2. T Chebula, Retz. Obs. v, p 31.—A large tree with shortly-petioled leaves, which are ovate or oblong, obtuse or cordate at the base, when young clothed with silky hairs; petiole with a pair of glands at the apex; spikes terminal, often panicled; drupe oval, about 1½ inch long. This is the Heerda tree, of which the fruit is an article of commerce, for the large quantity of tannin which it contains. The fruit of T citrina is sometimes imported into Bombay from the North-Western Provinces, and is highly valued for some imaginary properties.

3. T Glabra, W. and A. *Prod.* Var. tomentosa, Roxb.—An erect-growing tree of middling size; leaves linear oblong obtuse, somewhat cordate at the base, crenulate, with turbinate glands on the midrib; drupes ovoid, coriaceous, winged. The Ainee tree, much valued and in great demand for a variety of purposes. Common in the jungles at the foot of the Ghauts, and near the Ghauts in the upper country.

4. T Arjuna, Roxb. Fl Ind. ii, 438.—A tree with smooth bark

and horizontal branches; leaves linear-oblong with cordate base, smooth, with two sessile glands underneath; flowers in April and May. Common in the jungles south-east of Surat. The bark is in great repute as a tonic and vulnerary. Native name "Arjoon Sadura." This tree is of great size in the Belgaum and Soonda forests. In the Deccan, but rare. Koorun at Mooee Zillah, Poona.

5. T Berryi, W. and A. *Prod.* 1, 314.—A tree, with smooth bark and drooping branches; leaves from lanceolate to linear oblong, smooth, with two sessile glands on the apex of the petiole; spikes terminal, somewhat panicled. Banks of the Kaleenuddee and Gutpurba Rivers. Syn. Pentaptera angustifolia, Roxb. Fl Ind. ii, 437.

6. T Paniculata, W. and A. *Prod.* 1, p 315.—A tree, with diverging branches; leaves linear-oblong with a cordate base, coriaceous, wrinkled above, with sessile umbilicate glands beneath, near the base; spikes of flowers forming compound panicles; drupe with three unequal wings. Common along the foot of the Ghauts in the Southern Concan. Native name "Keerijul." Pentaptera paniculata, Roxb. Fl Ind. ii, p 442.

LVIII. MELASTOMACEÆ.

1. OSBECKIA, Linn.

1. Leschenaultiana, DC. *Prod.* 3, p 142.—Annual, herbaceous; stems 4-angled, slightly branched, the angles clothed with hairs; leaves ovate-strigose, quite entire, ciliated, 3-nerved; flowers very small, terminal, nearly sessile-aggregated; calyx urceolate, covered with spreading bristles, segments 4, deciduous; anthers 8. truncated. Syn. O truncata, Don in W. and A. *Prod.* 1, 322; Wight Ic. *t.* 996. Common in pastures in the Concan, Caranjah, &c. This is the only one we have met with.

2. MELASTOMA, Linn.

1. M Malabaricum, Linn. sp. p 559.—A shrub, about 3 feet high; branches 4-angled, ultimate ones compressed; leaves elliptic-oblong, somewhat acute, obtuse at the base, entire, upperside strigose, under hirsute on the nerves and veins, and harshly pubescent between them; corymbs terminal, 1 to 5-flowered, almost sessile; flowers rose-coloured, handsome, large. The fruit when ripe bursts irregularly and exposes a dark-coloured pulp, which is eaten, and stains the mouth of a black colour. The Concan; comes as far north as Bankote.

3. SONERILA, Roxb.

1. S. Scapigera, Hook. in Jour. Bot. vii, p 672; Ic. *t.* 23.—A plant, 3 to 4 inches high, stemless, quite smooth; leaves radical cordate, serrate, long-petioled; flowering scapes as long as the leaf; pedicels umbellato-racemose, longer than the flower; calyx segments 3, triangular-acute; petals obovate-acute; stamens as long as the style. The Ghauts near Bombay; flowers in the rains.

4. MEMECYLON, Linn.

1. M Edule, Roxb. Cor. Pl i, *t.* 82.—Arborescent; branches terete; leaves shortly-petioled, ovate or oblong, or elliptic-lanceolate, 1-nerved; peduncles axillary, and below the leaves on the older branches; flowers conglomerated, of a beautiful purple; fruit globose, crowned with the 4-toothed limb of the calyx; 1 to 2-seeded. Common along the higher Ghauts. Native name "Anjun." Wood, known by the name of "Kurpa," very strong. Syn. M tinctorium, Kœnig.; M heyneanum, Benth.; Wight Ic. *t.* 278.

2. M Terminale, Dalz. in Hook. Jour. Bot. iii, 121.—A shrub, 2 to 3 feet high; branches dichotomous, slender, terete; leaves sessile, lanceolate-acuminate; peduncles axillary and terminal, solitary, half inch long; flowers umbelled; pedicels half the length of the peduncle; fruit globose, dry unilocular, of the size of a large pea. On the Southern Ghauts. Perhaps the smallest of the Indian species.

LIX. MYRTACEÆ.

1. SYZYGIUM, Gaertn.

1. S Jambolanum, DC. *Prod.* 3, 259.—A large handsome tree, with whitish bark; leaves oval or oblong, feather-nerved, coriaceous; cymes panicled-lax, usually lateral on the former year's branches, occasionally axillary or terminal; calyx shortly turbinate, truncated; berry olive-shaped, often oblique. Syn. S caryophyllifolium, DC. loc. cit. A very common tree. "Jambool," Maratha. The timber is excellent for building; the astringent bark yields an extract like the gum "Kino" of Malabar, and the fruit is a favourite food of the flying-foxes, and is much eaten by the poorer classes.

2. S Caryophyllæum, Gaert.—A small tree; leaves obovate-obtuse, or suddenly acuminated, somewhat coriaceous, inconspicuously dotted; cymes of small white flowers, corymbose, trichotomous, terminal; fruit globose, 1-seeded. Southern Concan; always on the banks of streams, also on the Ghauts. Wight Ic. *t.* 540. The berries are eaten in Ceylon.

3. S Zeylanicum, DC. *Prod.* 3, p 260.—Arborescent; leaves ovate or oblong, much-acuminated, coriaceous, shining on the upperside; flowers shortly pedicellate, forming axillary or terminal compound cymes; calyx pruinose elongated clavate; berry white, globose, 1-seeded. Syn. Myrtus zeylanica, Linn. A most beautiful tree, very like a gigantic myrtle, confined to the higher Ghauts to the south of the Presidency.

4. S Rubicundum, W. and A. *Prod.* 1, 330.—Leaves narrow-oblong, attenuated at both ends, coriaceous, pellucid dotted; cymes corymbose, terminal, longer than the leaves; flowers minute; calyx 4-lobed, shortly turbinate. On the higher Ghauts on banks of Jambool streams.

5. S Salicifolium, Wall.—A shrub, with narrow-lanceolate leaves; flowers small, white, in lax panicles from the naked branches. The beds of rivers on the higher Ghauts. Wight Ic. 539. The wood is much used for rafters. Maratha name "Pan Jambool."

Note.—S gibsonii, Grah. Cat. No. 579, in the Olea dioica.

2. EUGENIA, Willd.

1. E Willdenovii, DC. *Prod.* 3, 265.—A tree; leaves short-petioled, oblong, narrowed at the base, acuminated with a blunt point, coriaceous, shining, veined, not dotted; peduncles filiform, solitary or in pairs, axillary or on the leafless branchlets, with two subulate bracteoles under the calyx. Syn. E zeylanica, Willd. sp. ii, p 963. Phoonda Ghaut. Wight Ic. 545.

3. JAMBOSA, Rumph.

1. J Pauciflora, Wight Ic. 526.—A middling-sized tree; leaves short-petioled, lanceolate, attenuated towards the base, ending in a long, slender acumen; pedicels solitary from the extreme axils, 1-flowered; calyx tube cylindrical, long and slender; flowers reddish; fruit ovoid. On the higher Ghauts opposite Bombay.

2. J Lanceolaria, Wight Ic. 613.—A small tree; leaves short-petioled, narrow-lanceolate; flowers terminal, about 15, corymbose, fascicled; flowers large, rosy, and somewhat fragrant; berries irregularly round-lobate, size of a small apple. Syn. Eugenia lanceolaria, Roxb. Fl Ind. iii, p 494. Ram and Neelkoond Ghauts.

LX. BARRINGTONIACEÆ.

1. BARRINGTONIA, Forst.

1. B Racemosa, Roxb. Fl Ind. ii, p 634.—A stout timber tree; leaves broad lanceolate serrulate, smooth on both sides, 3 to 12

inches long; racemes of showy pink; flowers lateral and terminal, long, pendent; fruit drupaceous, size of a pullet's egg, smooth. Severndroog Talooka; rather rare. It is a southern species, and plentiful in Canara.

2. B Acutangula, Gaert. Fr. ii, p 97, *t.* 101.—A middle-sized tree, something like an oak; leaves cuneate obovate, serrulate; racemes of pretty scarlet; flowers long, pendulous, much smaller than in the preceding; fruit oblong, 4-sided, sharp-angled. Native name "Tiwur." Common on the banks of creeks in the Southern Concan; between Indapoor and Dasgaum; flowers in April.

2. CAREYA, Roxb.

1. C Arborea, Roxb. Cor. iii, *t.* 218; Fl Ind. ii, p 638.—A middle-sized tree, with large obovate or oblong serrulate leaves; flowers few, in terminal short spikes, very large, white; fruit of the size and appearance of an apple. Extremely common in the Southern Concan; also near Indapoor. Native name "Koomba." The bark is used by matchlock men; the timber is useful, and stands water well; calyx of the flowers are sold in the bazars under the name of "Waekoomba."

LXI. RHIZOPHORACEÆ.

1. RHIZOPHORA.

1. R Mucronata, Lam.—A small tree; leaves oval long cuspidate, segments of the calyx triangular-ovate; peduncles 3 to 6 flowered, germinating embryo, subulate clavate acute. Syn. R candelaria, W. and A. *Prod.* 1, 10; Wight Ic. *t.* 238. Salt marshes along the coast; common.

2. BRUGUIERA, Lam.

1. Rheedei, Blume Mus. Bot. Lugd. Bot. i, p 138.—Leaves elliptic-oblong, acute at both ends, calyx tube unribbed, limb 11 to 13 divided; petals hirsute at the base, sparingly hairy along the margin, divisions rather obtuse, with 3 bristles at the apex, with a longish one in the sinuses, germinating radicle cylindric, rather obtuse, smoothish. Syn. B rumphii, Bl.; and B wightii, Bl.; Wight Ic. *t.* 139. Common on the sea-coast.

3. KANILIA, Blume.

1. K Parviflora, Blume loc. cit. p 320.—A small shrub; leaves oblong or lanceolate, rather obtuse, narrowed at the base; peduncles 3, or many-flowered in cymes; calyx tube ribbed,

divisions of the limb short lanceolate acute, erect in the fruit, ovary 3-celled; germinating radicle cylindric, rather obtuse. Syn. Bruguiera parviflora, W. and A. *Prod.* 1, 311; Rhizophora parviflora, Roxb. Fl Ind. ii, p 461. Salt marshes; not common.

4. CARALLIA, Roxb.

1. C Integerrima, DC. *Prod.* 3, p 33.—A small tree, with corky bark and obovate dark-green polished leaves, quite entire; peduncles short axillary trifid; flowers small; stigma 5-lobed; fruit size of a pea. Syn. C integrifolia, Graham Cat.; C zeylanica, Arnott; C chinensis, Arnott. Wood strong and fit for furniture. The Ghauts; pretty common. Native name "Punschi."

LXII. LYTHRACEÆ.

1. ROTALA, Linn.

1. R Verticillaris, Linn. Maut. p 175.—Herbaceous, aquatic; leaves in verticles 4 to 8, linear-acute; flowers axillary, solitary minute, sessile; capsule covered by the calyx, 1-celled; seeds very numerous. In ditches, tanks, &c.; common.

2. AMELETIA, DC.

1. A Floribunda, Wight Hook. Ic. Pl *v* ix, p 826.—Annual, erect, quite smooth, branched upwards; leaves alternate linear, the upper ones especially, cordate, stem-clasping; peduncles very slender, on terminal branches; racemes spiked, bracteated; bracteoles almost as long as the calyx; flowers pink; monoicous; stamens long exserted. Syn. Nimmonia floribunda, Wight in Madr. Jour. vi, p 34, *t.* 20. On bare rocky ground on the highest Ghauts; also below the Ghauts at Sivapore.

2. A Tenuis, Wight Ic. *t.* 257 b.—Stems somewhat procumbent at the base, afterwards erect, most slender; leaves opposite, orbicular; spikes terminal; flowers solitary, longish-pedicelled, from the axil of a linear bract; bracteoles large, stamens included; capsule ovate, 2-valved. Banks of the Penn River; not common.

3. A Rotundifolia, Wight. Ic. *t.* 258.—Stems diffuse procumbent; branches erect; leaves large, orbicular, opposite, sessile; spikes congested near the extremities of the branches; flowers solitary in the axils of broad ovate-cordate or orbicular bracteas; bracteoles very minute; stamens longer than the calyx; capsule 4-valved.

4. A Indica, DC. *Prod.* 3, p 76.—Procumbent; leaves obovate

opposite, spikes axillary; flowers sessile, solitary, in the axils of obovate bracts; bracteoles subulate, membranaceous, shorter than the tube of the calyx; stamens as long as the calyx. Common in watery places. Wight Ic. *t.* 257 A; Ammania repens, Rottler, in DC. *Prod.* 3, 80, No. 3.

3. AMMANIA, Hæst.

1. A MULTIFLORA, Roxb. Fl Ind. i, 426.—Stem erect, 4-sided, angles sharp, sides convex; branches cross-armed; leaves opposite, sessile linear, with an enlarged cordate base, stem-clasping; peduncles axillary, almost always solitary, about as long as the smaller leaves, generally 3-flowered, or sometimes 9-flowered, petals large, roundish, red. Water holes in the Deccan; tetrandrous.

2. A OCTANDRA, Linn.—Herbaceous; stem 4-angled; leaves linear lanceolate sessile, acutely auricled at the base; peduncles axillary, very short, 1 to 3-flowered; calyx 4-angled, angles winged; capsule 4-celled; flowers minute, bright red. In wet ground; common.

3. A SALICIFOLIA, Monte.—Leaves lanceolate, attenuated at the base; flowers almost sessile, 2 to 3 in the axils of the opposite leaves; calyx half globose; capsule 1-celled, opening transversely. At Malwan; found also in Egypt and Italy. Syn. A verticellata, Lam. Illust. *t.* 77, *fig* 3. Sometimes the petals are wanting.

4. A BACCIFERA, Linn.—Leaves lanceolate, attenuated towards the base; flowers very minute, aggregated in the axils of the leaves, almost sessile; calyx in fruit cup-shaped; petals none. Common. The leaves are exceedingly acrid, and are used for raising blisters. Syn. A vesicatoria, Roxb. Fl Ind. i, 426.

4. GRISLEA, Löfl.

1. TOMENTOSA, Roxb. Fl Ind. ii, 233.—A shrub; leaves opposite, entire, lanceolate sessile, underside hoary and dotted with black glands; peduncles axillary, several-flowered; flowers red, rather handsome; capsule oblong. Very common throughout the Concan and above the Ghauts, and in Gujarat to the south; flowers in the cold weather. Flowers used as a dye in Kandeish, Dr. Gibson. Native name "Dhauree." Syn. Lythrum fruticosum, Linn. sp. p 641.

5. LAWSONIA, Linn.

1. ALBA, Lam. DC. *Prod.* 3, p 90.—A much-branched shrub; leaves small, opposite, entire, oval-lanceolate, glabrous; flowers in a large panicle, very numerous, white; capsule globose membrana-

ceous, size of a pea; seeds numerous, angled. Generally cultivated as a hedge in gardens, but indigenous in Guzerat. Used by women for staining their hands and feet of an orange-colour. Native name "Mendie." It is the Henné of Egypt. Syn. L spinosa, Linn.; Roxb. L inermis, Linn.; Fl Ind. ii, 258.

6. LAGERSTRŒMIA, Linn.

1. Parviflora, Roxb. Fl Ind. ii, 505.—A very large tree, with very white bark; leaves from oblong or oval-obtuse to ovate-acute, pale beneath; peduncles axillary, 3 to 6-flowered; flowers small; white; capsule, small oblong, 3 to 4-celled. Very common in the Warree country; also on the Ghauts. Produces a very useful reddish timber, called Benteak. Native name "Naneh," also "Bondareh."

2. Reginæ, Roxb. Fl Ind. ii, p 505.—A tree; leaves oblong, glabrous; panicles large, terminal; flowers large, purple, very showy; calyx tomentose, longitudinally furrowed and plaited. Jungles near Nagotna, at Vingorla, and very common throughout the Southern Concan. Maratha name "Taman." Syn. L flosegina, Retz. Obs. i, p 20; Adambea glabra, Lam. Encycl. Meth. i, 39. Wood very valuable; tough and almost indestructible.

3. Lanceolata, Wall. List 2120.—A tree; leaves oblong-lanceolate, smooth, rather glaucous; flowers small, white; capsule very like an acorn, exceedingly hard. Common in the Warree Country and Southern Ghauts.

7. SONNERATIA, Linn.

1. Acida, Linn. DC. *Prod.* 3, 231.—A small tree; leaves opposite, entire, thick, veinless, oval-oblong; flowers, large, solitary; fruit baccate, nearly globose, many-celled. In salt marshes, Sion Causeway, Rutnagherry, Vingorla, &c.; flowers in March. Syn. Rhizophora caseolaris, Linn.

LXIII. ONAGRACEÆ.

1. JUSSIÆA, Linn.

1. J Repens, Linn. Maut. p 381.—Herbaceous, glabrous, creeping or floating, rooting at the joints; leaves oblong obovate-obtuse or retuse-petioled; flowers on longish pedicels; tube of the calyx cylindrical, attenuated at the base; lobes 5, lanceolate-acute; petals 5, obovate-retuse, yellow. Common on margins of tanks.

2. J Villosa, Lam.—Tall, suffruticose; leaves from broadly lanceolate to linear acuminate, tapering into a short petiole; flowers axillary, almost sessile, yellow; calyx lobes broadly lanceolate or ovate, 4 to 5, much shorter than the rounded obovate petals.

Lam. Encycl. Meth. iii, p 331; Syn. J exaltata, Roxb. Fl Ind. ii, 401; J fruticosa, DC. At Vingorla, and on the Ghauts.

2. LUDWIGIA, Roxb.

1. L Parviflora, Roxb.—Erect, annual, glabrous, branched; leaves lanceolate; flowers axillary, subsessile, yellow; capsule obsoletely 4 to 5-angled, 2 to 3 times longer than broad, 4 to 5-celled. Concan; very common. Syn. L perennis, Linn. sp. p 173; Rheed. Mal. ii, *t.* 49.

LXIV. HALORAGEÆ.

1. MYRIOPHYLLUM, Vaill.

1. M Tetrandrum, Roxb.—An aquatic floating herbaceous plant; leaves verticellate, lower ones divided into capillary segments; flowers small, verticelled in the axils of the floral leaves, monœcious; stamens 4; carpels nearly smooth, and even blunt on the back. Roxb. Fl Ind. i, 451. In tanks, common.

2. TRAPA, Linn.

1. T Bispinosa, Roxb. Cor. iii, 234; Fl. Ind. i, 428.—Herbaceous, floating plant; lower leaves opposite, upper alternate, tomentose beneath; flowers axillary; peduncles shorter than the petioles; fruit 2-horned, horns opposite, straight-conical, very sharp. We have eaten the fruit boiled, and find it very like potatoes. Native name "Shingaree." Water Chesnut of Anglo-Indians. An important article of food in some parts; chiefly found in tanks in Guzerat.

LXV. CUCURBITACEÆ.

1. ZANONIA, Linn.

1. Z Indica, Linn.—Herbaceous, smooth, climbing, diœcious; leaves rather large, elliptic, 3-nerved; flowers racemose, on long axillary peduncles, pale-yellow, small; fruit obconico-cylindric, like candle extinguishers. Very rare; found only near Vingorla; the fruit is ripe in May.

2. ZEHNERIA, Endl.

1. Z Garcini, Stocks in Hook. Jour. Bot. iv, p 149.—Stems smooth, climbing; tendrils simple; leaves deeply 3 to 5-lobed, bristle-toothed, more or less scabrous; bracteas axillary, large, reniform ciliated; flowers minute; berries red, small, hammer-shaped,

or inverse reniform, 2-seeded; seeds oblong, thickest at the margin. Not common; at Domus and on the Kattywar coast, plentiful. Syn. Bryonia garcini, Willd.

2. Z Cerasiformis, Stocks loc. cit.—Stems, leaves, and bracts as in the preceding; fruit globose, scarlet, clustered, like cherries; seeds 2, rather large, convex on one side and concave on the other. This is one of the most beautiful of climbers, when covered with its cherry-like fruit. Found in hedges at Gundar, in Guzerat, and in Sind plentiful.

3. AECHMANDRA, Arnott.

1. A Epigæa, Arn. in Hook. Jour. Bot. iii, 274 (1841).—Stem glabrous, often very flexuose at the joints, tendrils simple; leaves somewhat fleshy on longish petioles, cordate, sometimes only obtusely-angled, usually 3-lobed, lobes rounded, the lateral ones broader and slightly 2-lobed, all remotely and slightly toothed; male flowers minute, yellow, shortly racemose, on the apex of a long, naked, smooth peduncle; female flowers solitary, sessile, in the same axils as the male; berry stalked, ovoid, smooth-beaked, green at the base, scarlet above. Guzerat and the Deccan, pretty common; also in Sind. Seeds brown, with white corded margins.

2. A Cenocarpa, Dalz. Mss.—A climber like the last, but with the lobes of the leaves lanceolate-acute, the middle one much longer than the others; male flowers about 15; peduncle 1½ inch long; fruit sessile, exactly narrow-conical, smooth, orange-red, except the cup-shaped base, which remains green; seeds black, ovate, scarcely compressed, sides bulging. Hedges in Guzerat; near Malpor and Gundar.

3. A Rostrata, Arn. loc. cit.—Stems slender, hairy or pubescent; tendrils simple; leaves on longish petioles, roundish-cordate, sinuate-toothed, pubescent; male flowers from 2 to 7 together on an axillary peduncle; small, yellow; female solitary, very shortly peduncled; berry roundish-depressed, slightly grooved, with a long sudden beak, hairy, scarlet; seeds bulging on each side, with a very thin margin. Syn. Bryonia rostrata, Rottler. Hedges in Guzerat. In these three species, the stamens are certainly opposite the segments of the corolla. In the first, the horns of the anthers are scarcely visible; in the second, they are more developed; in the last, they are very long; æstivation of corolla decidedly valvate; the fruit is 4-celled in all, one cell above the other, and the beak of the fruit falls off like a Calyptra. A fourth species, all velvetty, grows in Sind. A velutina, Dalz. Mss.

4. MUKIA, Arnott.

1. M Scabrella, Arnott. loc. cit.—All hispid and scabrous;

tendrils simple; leaves cordate, lobed or angled; flowers short-peduncled; male, fascicled; female 1 to 4, in different axils from the male; berry globular, scarlet, size of a pea, smooth or sprinkled with a few bristly hairs; seeds surrounded by a narrow zone, rugose, from numerous shallow hollows. Syn. Bryonia scabrella, Linn. Common in every hedge. Native name "Chirati."

5. BRYONIA, Linn.

1. B Laciniosa, Linn.—Climbing; stems smooth; leaves palmately 5-lobed, more or less deeply divided, segments oblong-lanceolate, acuminated serrated; petioles muricated; male flowers fascicled, female solitary in the same axil; berry size of a cherry, round, smooth, pale-red, with white streaks. Linn. sp. p 624. Common in hedges.

2. B Umbellata, Herb. Madr.—Diœcious; root tuberous; leaves shortly petioled, cordate or sagittate or hastate at the base, the lobes longer than the petiole, 3 to 5-lobed, or palmately 5-partite, sinuate and sharply toothed; male flowers umbelled or shortly racemose, at the apex of a long slender peduncle; female on a different plant, solitary, short-peduncled; berry oval or oblong, size of a pigeon's egg, smooth, red when ripe. Common in hedges. Native name "Gometta." Syn. Momordica umbellata, Roxb. Fl Ind. iii, p 710.

3. B Mysorensis, Herb. Madr.—Stems glabrous, smooth; tendrils simple; leaves cordate, repand-toothed, 5-angled or lobed; male flowers in a simple or proliferous umbel, at the apex of a long, slender peduncle; female shortly peduncled, solitary, rarely umbellate, at the apex of a long peduncle; berry longish-oval, glabrous, copiously marked before maturity with small, shallow pits; seeds smooth, flat on the sides. Not common; found only in the Warree Country.

6. CITRULLUS, Necker.

1. C Colocynthis, Arnott. loc. cit.—Creeping; stems scabrous; leaves glabrous and nearly quite smooth above, copiously muricated beneath, with small, white, hair-bearing tubercles, many-cleft and lobed, the lobes obtuse; tendrils short and simple; female flowers solitary; calyx tube globose and hispid; fruit globose, glabrous, variegated longitudinally with green and yellow, often only yellow, especially when ripe. Eastern Deccan and Guzerat. Native name "Indrayeen." Syn. Cucumis colocynthis, Linn. Extends over Africa and Arabia, even to the shores of Spain. Mentioned in the Old Testament under the names of "Paka" and "Pakuot." From the fruit of this plant compound extract of Colocynth is

prepared in large quantities at Hewra, for the supply of the medical stores.

2. C Vulgaris, Schrader in Linn. *t.* xii, p 412.—Leaves larger and softer than in the preceding; fruit also larger, uniform in colour or sometimes marbled, glaucous, with a whitish powder, pulp sweet and eatable, sometimes very bitter. This is the "Dilpussund" of Guzerat gardeners, and is a very good vegetable. We know not whether it is a native of the country or not, but we place it here, as there has been much confusion of ideas regarding it. The common Water Melon is a variety of this species, altered by long cultivation. Syn. Cucumis citrullus, Linn.; C fistulosus, Stocks in Hook. Jour. Bot. iii, p 74, *t.* 3.

7. MOMORDICA, Linn.

1. M Dioica, Roxb. Fl Ind. iii, p 709.—Diœcious; root tuberous, perennial; leaves longish-petioled, cordate at the base, from entire to 3 to 4-lobed; peduncles slender, male with a bracteole close to the flower, cucullate, female with a smallish one near the base; flowers largish, yellow; fruit ovate muricated, bursting irregularly, showing the red arillas of the seed, which are black, shining, and almost spherical. Very common. Native name "Kurtoli."

2. M Charantia, Linn. sp. 1433.—Stems hairy; leaves palmately 5-lobed, sinuate-toothed; peduncles slender, with a reniform bracteole; male ones with the bracteole about the middle, female with it near the base; fruit oblong-ovate, or almost spherical, tubercled. Native name "Kurela." Syn. M muricata, Willd; M Roxburghiana, Don; Cucumis africanus, Lind. in Bot. Reg. *t.* 980. Common as food after having been steeped in salt-water.

8. LUFFA, Tournef.

1. L Amara, Roxb. Fl Ind. iii, p 715.—Leaves 5 to 7-lobed, when young whitish, and soft to the touch, at length rough; male racemes long-peduncled; fruit 3 to 4 inches long, ovoid, longitudinally ribbed, lid deciduous; flowers pale-yellow, closely allied to L acutangula. Native name "Ran Toorai." Common in hedges.

2. L Echinata, Roxb. loc. dit.—Diœcious; leaves somewhat hairy, about 5-lobed, repand-toothed; tendrils bifid; flowers white, 1 inch in diameter; male racemes longer than the leaves; fruit roundish-oval, clothed with long, straight, soft bristles. Not common; found only at Gundar, in Guzerat.

9. TRICHOSANTHES, Linn.

1. T Cucumerina, Linn.—Annual, climbing; leaves broadly cordate, 3 to 7-angled or lobed, toothed or serrated; tendrils

3-cleft; male flowers white, fringed, shortly racemose, at the apex of a long peduncle; female solitary, short-peduncled; fruit 2 to 4 inches long, ovate-pointed. Very common in hedges in Guzerat, also in Southern Concan; flowers from August to October. Syn. T laciniosa, Willd. sp. iv, 601. "Junglee Parole" of the Marathas. Has a reputation in fevers.

2. T Palmata, Roxb. Fl Ind. iii, p 704.—Perennial climbing; leaves deeply lobed, tendrils 3-cleft; male flowers racemose; pedicels short, each furnished with an ovate-toothed bracteole; fruit globose, size of an orange and of the same colour, and not unlike that of the Nux-Vomica. This plant is much esteemed in diseases of cattle, and is called "Mukal" or "Koundal." In jungles near the Ghauts, common; elsewhere rare.

10. CUCUMIS, Linn.

1. C Trigonus, Roxb. Fl Ind. iii, 722.—Root perennial, all over rough and scabrous; stems creeping, slender, very little branched; leaves polymorphous, 3 to 5 to 7-lobed, or sometimes many-lobed; female flowers few, larger than the male ones; ovary densely covered with long hairs; fruit small, oval, longitudinally striped with light and dark-green, yellow and smooth when ripe; pulp bitter. Syn. C pseudo colocynths, Royle Illust. *t.* 47, *fig* 2; C eriocarpus, Boiss. Diagnos. ser. ii, p 59. Common all over the Deccan; extending from the Nelgherries to Cashmere, and also Beloochistan, whence it was brought by Sir Bartle Frere.

2. C Pubescens, Willd. sp. iv, 614.—Annual, all hirsute or hispid, or scabrous; leaves cordate at the base, sometimes reniform, sometimes 3 to 7-lobed, with the sinuses rounded, ovary pubescent and hirsute; fruit (in the Peninsular variety) covered with small bristles, 1 to 1½ inch long, oval or oblong. Common in the Deccan; fruit eaten. In Sind it is cultivated and sold in the bazars under the name of "Chiber." Syn. C maderaspatanus and turbinatus, Roxb. Fl Ind. iii, 723. Nandin considers this as the parent of the Cucumis Melo, or Sweet Melon. The variety found in Sind was published by Dr. Stocks in Hooker's Journal as C cicatrisatus, vol. iv, p 148. The Cucumis prophetarum is common in Sind.

11. COCCINIA, W. and A.

1. C Indica, W. and A. *Prod.* 1, p 347.—Diœcious, climbing, smooth; leaves entire or 5-angled or lobed, or deeply palmately 5-cleft; peduncles solitary, axillary, 1-flowered; corolla large, white; fruit oblong, red when ripe. Syn. Bryonia grandis, Linn.; Rheed. Mal. viii, *t.* 14; Rumph. Amb. v, *t.* 166. Hedges, common.

LXVI. PASSIFLORACEÆ.

1. MODECCA, Linn.

1. M Palmata, Lam.—Root large, woody, fusiform, appearing above the ground; leaves from cordate acuminate (on young plants) to palmately 3 to 5-lobed, smooth, with two flat glands at the base, and one below each sinus between the lobes; fruit globular, size of a Crab-apple, of a bright orange-yellow. Rare, found only at Malwan and in southern jungles above the Ghauts; in flower in April. The description, under Graham's No. 625, refers to the Trichosanthes. Syn. Modecca tuberosa, Roxb. Fl. Ind. iii, p 134.

LXVII. BEGONIACEÆ.

1. BEGONIA, Linn.

1. Crenata, Dryander.—First described from specimens taken from Salsette to England by Dr. Hove in 1789, *vide* Linn. Trans. vol. i, p 162; a delicate herbaceous plant, with semicordate leaves, and pink or white flowers. Common on rocks and trees in the rainy season.

2. Integrifolia, Dalz. in Hook. Jour. Bot. vol. iii, p 230.—Root tuberous; stem herbaceous; leaves obliquely ovate-obtuse, cordate at the base, margins entire, hispid, with white hairs on both sides, blood-red below, peduncles dichotomous; flowers small, white; capsules glabrous, 3-winged, one of the wings larger than the others; stem 6 to 8 inches high; leaves 7 inches long, 4 broad. On rocks on the Ghauts; flowers in the rains. Found also in Ceylon, according to DeCandolle, but not named in Thwaites' Enumeration.

3. Trichocarpa, Dalz. loc. cit.—Root tuberous; stem herbaceous, half a foot high, leaf one radical, large, unequally cordate acuminate, sinuate-dentate, wrinkled, minutely lacerated on the margin, green on both sides, hispid on both sides; flowers terminal umbelled; pedicels hispid, an inch long; capsule hispid, with three equal obtuse wings; leaves 7 inches long and broad; flowers white, 2 inches in diameter. Grows with the preceding.

4. B Concanensis, Alph. DC. in Annales des. Soc. Nat. Tom. xi, p 126.—Tuberous; stem short, herbaceous, smooth; leaves ovate acute-cordate, palmately 7 to 9-nerved, undulate-dentate, and with smaller teeth, hairy; stipules ovate-lanceolate, bracts lanceolate, slightly ciliated; capsule turbinate, with the larger wing ovate-triangular. This we do not know; the specimens were from the Hookerian herbarium.

LXVIII. CRASSULACEÆ.

1. KALANCHOE, Adans.

1. Ritchieana, Dalz. in Hook. Jour. Bot. iv, p 346.—1½ foot high, herbaceous, glaucous; stem simple erect, succulent, 4-sided; leaves oblong, narrower towards the base, perfoliate, decussate, thick and fleshy, with the margin obscurely toothed, lower ones approximated, glabrous, upper ones viscid and glandular, smaller, inflorescence terminal; racemes panicled, viscid and glandular; calyx 4-divided to near the middle; corolla nearly twice as long as the calyx, divisions of the limb oblong, mucronate. On the hill of Caktay, between Belgaum and Sholapore, Dr. Ritchie.

2. Laciniata, DC. Pl Gr. *t.* 100.—Leaves decompound and pinnatifid, the segments oblong-acute, coarsely toothed, upper ones nearly entire; sepals lanceolate acuminate, spreading; cyme panicled; flowers yellow. Syn. Cotyledon laciniata, Linn. Wild on the hills near Dharwar.

3. Pinnata, Pas. Syn. p 446.—Fleshy, erect, suffruticose, with thick ovate-crenated opposite leaves, and terminal panicles of pendulous tubular yellowish-red flowers. Very common in the Warree Country and near Belgaum. Syn. Bryophyllum calycinum; Colytedon rhizophylla, Roxb. Fl Ind. ii, 456; Bot. Mag *t.* 1409.

2. TILLAEA, Linn.

1. T Pentandra, Royle; Edgeworth in Linn. Trans. xx, 50.—Stems creeping; branches erect, leafy; leaves opposite subperfoliate, rather fleshy, subulate acute, mucronate; flower bearing branchlets, axillary solitary, sessile, or shortly peduncled; sepals 5, subulate; petals 5, lanceolate-acute; carpels minute, 2-seeded; seeds ovoid, shining. Concan. This we have not seen, but it was found in Dr. Stock's Herbarium as growing in the Concan.

LXIX. UMBELLIFERÆ.

1. HYDROCOTYLE, Tournef.

1. H Asiatica, Linn.—A slender herbaceous plant; leaves orbicular reniform, crenated, attached by the margin, 7-nerved, glabrous; petioles and peduncles fascicled; umbels capitate, shortly peduncled, 3 to 4-flowered; fruit orbicular, reticulated, with 4 ribs on each of the flat sides. In moist places in the rains; not common. Wight Ic. *t.* 565.

2. HELOSCIADIUM, Koch.

1. H Heyneanum, DC. *Prod.* 4, p 106.—Annual, glabrous, 2 feet high; stem erect, slightly branched; leaves long-petioled, ternate, segments shortly petioled, lanceolate acuminate or tripartite, toothed; umbels long-peduncled, without involucre or involucels; rays 5 to 20, elongated, partial umbels 5 to 8-flowered; fruit orbicular, glabrous. The Concans; flowers in August and September. Syn. Anethum trifoliatum, Roxb. Fl Ind ii, p 96, not Apium trifoliatum, as stated by W. and A.

3. PIMPINELLA, Linn.

1. Involucrata, W. and A. *Prod.* 1, p 369.—Stem erect, 2 to 3 feet, dichotomous, glaucous; leaves ternate, cut and pinnated, or sometimes entire in the upper leaves, lobes in the lower leaves linear-oblong and short; umbels with 6 to 8 rays; leaflets of the involucre and involucel about 6, subulate entire, styles reflexed; fruit slightly ribbed, minutely muricated all over. Very common in the Concans. Syn. Apium involucratum, Roxb. Fl Ind. ii, p 97; Ptychotis roxburghiana, DC. *Prod.* 4, p 109.

2. P Lateriflora, Dalz.—1 to 1½ foot high, puberulous, erect; leaves ternate, leaflets twice ternately divided, lobes of the lower leaves lanceolate, of the upper linear, all acute and mucronate; peduncles long, slender, leaf-opposed; umbels 3 to 10, involucre of 3 to 7 subulate leaflets; involucel leaves similar, about 7, as long as the pedicels; flowers pink; fruit densely covered with small granular tubercles. Ravines in the Deccan; common.

3. Adscendens, Dalz. in Hook. Jour. Bot. ii, p 261.—Stems diffuse ascending; leaves radical-pinnated, half a foot long; leaflets 6 pair, rounded-ovate, truncate or cuneate at the base, coarsely and unequally crenate serrate, stem leaves few; leaflets 1 to 2 pair, uppermost ones much divided; flowers white; fruit ovate, minutely bristly. Banks of rivers in the Concan. The whole plant smells like Parsley.

4. Monoica, Dalz. loc. cit. iii, p 212.—Stem 6 to 8 feet high, round, glabrous, smooth, simple below, branched above; branches alternate and bifarious, lower leaves long-petioled, pinnately trifoliolate, partial petioles long, leaflets cordate lanceolate with minute cartilaginous teeth, upper leaves multifid, divisions filiform or reduced to mere sheaths; involucre one-leaved or none; involucel few-leaved, terminal; umbels fruit-bearing, lateral ones male; fruit covered with pellucid granules; flowers white, appear in November on the highest Ghauts.

4. POLYZYGUS, Dalz.

1. Tuberosus, Dalz. Mss. in Hook. Jour. Bot. ii, p 260.— Glabrous, one foot high; roots tuberous; stem erect with few branches, angled and furrowed above; leaves twice ternate; leaflets three times ternate, pinnately divided, segments cuneate and ovate, unequally serrated; umbels terminal and axillary, naked; involucre none; involucel 3-leaved; flowers white; fruit compressed on the back, smooth, shining, many-ribbed; commissure with 8 vittæ. Malwan; flowers in June and July.

5. PASTINACA.

1. Glauca, Dalz. loc. cit. vol. iv, p 293.—Glabrous glaucous; stem rigid, scarcely branched; leaves radical, somewhat coriaceous, long-petioled, pinnately divided; leaflets 3 to 5, sometimes entire, more frequently deeply 2 to 3-lobed; lobes obovate mucronate entire; involucre and involucel leaves few, lanceolate; flowers yellow; fruit broadly oval; vittæ linear, solitary between the ribs; commissure with 2 vittæ. In pastures near Belgaum. Native name "Kolund." The root is eaten, and has the taste and odour of a Carrot.

2. P Grandis.—3 feet high; root large, woody, perennial, all quite smooth; leaves mostly radical, long-petioled, bipinnate; leaflets trilobate; lobes large rounded, margins crenate serrate, shining on both sides; cauline leaves 1 to 2, biternate; stem as thick as the little finger at the base, round, smooth, striated; involucre and involucel leaves oblong or obovate-obtuse, partial rays numerous, many-flowered; flowers yellow; fruit large, broadly obovate; commissure with 4 linear vittæ. The Ghauts near Bombay. Native name "Baphullee."

6. HERACLEUM.

1. Concanense, Dalz. in Hook. Jour. Bot. ii, p 260.—2 feet in height, all hispid with spreading hairs; stem striated, dichotomously branched; leaves twice ternate; leaflets 3-lobed, or ternately cut, segments ovate, cuneate at the base, unequally serrated, upper leaves reduced to a sheathing petiole; involucre 1 to 3-leaved; involucel 5-leaved, the leaflets ovate acuminate, 3-nerved; flowers white; fruit ovate, glabrous; dorsal vittæ 10; commissure with 6 vittæ. Hills in the Concan; flowers in July.

2. H Pinda.—1 to 1½ foot high; root perennial, as thick as the finger, the whole plant clothed with long, weak, white, flat hairs; stem erect-branched; leaves mostly radical, long-petioled, bipinnately divided; segments cuneate at the base, coarsely toothed, the teeth mucronate; umbels terminal, with 6 to 8 rays; radii unequal;

involucre of 1 to 3 broad ovate acute foliaceous leaflets, partial of 3 leaflets of the same shape on the exterior side; flowers white, exterior petals large obcordate, deeply bilobed; seeds smooth 6 vittæ on the back, 2 on the commissure. On Hursur and Hurry-chunder hill-forts; flowers in July and August. Eaten by the natives, who call it "Pinda."

3. H GRANDIFLORUM.—Root as in the preceding; stem short, smooth, covered by the sheathing bases of the leaves; leaves long-petioled trifoliolate; leaflets deeply 3-lobed, segments pinnatifid acuminate, sparingly strigose above, smooth and pale beneath, margins ciliated; umbels terminal, with about 12 rays; involucre of one many-nerved, rounded or oblong-acuminate leaflet; involucels 3, rhomboid-ovate, acuminate, as long as the rays; flowers white, outer petals very large, deeply divided; fruit not seen, has much the character of Tordyliopsis. Along with the preceding.

4. H TOMENTOSUM.—2 feet high; stems, petioles, and rays shortly tomentose; leaves on very long petioles, tripinnate; leaflets small, cuneate at the base, closely and sharply toothed, teeth ending in a bristle-point, slightly puberulous on both sides; involucre of one long capillary leaflet; involucel of 3 filiform leaflets; fruit not seen, and the genus doubtful. The leaves are very like those of Dasyloma Bengalense. Found along with the preceding.

5. H SPRENGELIANUM, W. and A. *Prod.* 1, p 372.—Stem branched, furrowed, harshly puberulous towards the top; leaves with scattered hairs, often densely villous beneath; segments acute or rounded; petals equal; fruit nearly orbicular; vittæ on the back linear-acute, a little shorter than the fruit; vittæ on the commissure 4 to 6, the exterior ones much shorter. Wight Ic. *t.* 1008. On the road between Belgaum and the Ram Ghaut.

7. BUPLEURUM, Tournef.

1. B FALCATUM, Linn. Var. ramosissimum, W. and A. *Prod.* p 370.—Perennial, diffuse and much-branched; leaves oblong-linear with a long mucro, narrowed towards the base, amplexicaul 5 to 9-nerved; general umbels with 5 to 8 rays, partial with 8 to 12 flowers; leaflets of involucre and involucel about 5, oblong-linear mucronate; fruit strongly ribbed; interstices with 1 to 2 vittæ. In the Dharwar Collectorate.

LXX. ARALIACEÆ.

1. HEDERA, Linn.

1. H WALLICHIANA.—A strong woody climber with digitate leaves; leaflets 8 to 10, long-petioled, oblong-pointed, quite entire,

coriaceous; thyrses numerous at the ends of the branches; flowers pedicelled and umbelled, numerous; berry 6-celled. W. and A. *Prod.* 1, 377. At Moolus, foot of the Ram Ghaut, and other similar places; pretty common.

LXXI. ALANGIACEÆ.

1. ALANGIUM, Linn.

1. A LAMARCKII, Thwaites' Enum. Pl Zeyl. i, 133.—A small tree, with the branches more or less spinescent; leaves narrow-oblong or ovate-lanceolate; flowers few, axillary fascicled, whitish; petals 6 to 10, linear reflexed; berry small, oval. Elephanta; Virdee jungles; Concans, not uncommon; also common in Deccan wastes. Syn. A decapetalum, Hexapetalum, and Tomentosum, Lam.

LXXII. LORANTHACEÆ.

1. LORANTHUS, Linn.

1. L WALLICHIANUS, Schult.—Glabrous; branches terete; leaves somewhat alternate, ovate, obtuse, acute at the base; racemes 1 to 3 axillary, a half shorter than the leaves, fascicled at the knots of the branches, simple; flowers small-pedicelled, bractes lateral cucullate; petals 4, linear-cuneate; berry almost globular, at length reflexed. Schult. *syst.* vii, p 100; L terrestris, Heyne; L tetrandrus, Heyne. Parwar Ghaut.

2. L CAPITELLATUS, W. and A. *Prod.* p 382.—Glabrous; branches terete, young shoots 2-edged; leaves oblong-lanceolate, short-petioled; petiole sharply keeled; flowers sessile capitate, few together; heads axillary, sessile, limb of the calyx entire; flower-buds 6-angled above; segments of corolla cuneate linear, spreading. Chorla Ghaut, parasitic on Gnidia eriocephala.

3. ELASTICUS, Desv. in Encyc. Meth. iii, 599.—Glabrous, dichotomous; branches terete; leaves sessile, oblong or ovate-lanceolate, thick and coriaceous, obscurely 5-nerved; flowers subsessile, fascicled around the knots of the branches; corolla 5-cleft, one of the fissures deeper than the others; segments long narrow-linear, revolute; fruit ovoid. Vingorla; flowers in July.

4. INVOLUCRATUS, Roxb. Fl Ind. i, 552.—Leaves short-petioled, ovate and ovate-cordate, 3 to 4 inches long; umbellets axillary, crowded, subsessile; involucres 4-leaved, 4-flowered, leaflets ovate-lanceolate, smooth; corol tube villous, border 5-parted; segments linear revolute; ovary sericeous. Beemasunker, Dr. Gibson.

5. OBTUSATUS, Wall.—Branches speckled; leaves opposite or

alternate, ovate-obtuse, glabrous; racemes 1 to 2, axillary, as long or longer than the leaves, simple; flowers pedicelled; flower-bud sharply 4-angled; petals 4, linear; berry nearly globose. Rotunda Ghaut, Mahableshwur; flowers in May.

6. LONICEROIDES, Linn sp. p 473.—Glabrous; branches terete, young ones slightly 2-edged; leaves ovate or oblong-lanceolate acuminated; peduncles axillary, solitary, opposite to the petiole, bearing at the apex a few sessile flowers; bracts 3 at the base of each ovary, roundish acute concave; corolla tubular, curved, equally 6-cleft; segments cuneate, linear, spreading. Island of Caranjah; the Concans. Syn. L coriaceus, Desv.; L umbellatus, Heyne in Roth. nov. sp. p 192.

7. BUDDLEOIDES, Desv. in Encyc. Meth. iii, p 600.—Branches terete, glabrous; young shoots sometimes tomentose; leaves from elliptic to cordate-ovate, thinnish, firm, at first furfuraceous on the underside; peduncles axillary crowded, very short, few-flowered; flower-bud clavate; fruit turbinate. On Asanna and Kurmul trees at Kandalla; flowers in February and March. Syn. L scurrula, Roxb. Fl Ind. i, 550; L Heynei, DC. *Prod.* iv, p 300.

8. LONGIFLORUS, Desv. loc. cit. p 498.—Glabrous; leaves usually opposite, sometimes alternate, from linear to oblong-lanceolate or ovate-obtuse; racemes axillary, solitary or in pairs, simple, many-flowered, much shorter than the leaves; bractes concave oblique; close to the ovary; corolla long infundibuliform curved; segments 5, linear recurved, one of the fissures deeper than the others; flowers greenish-white. The commonest species in the Concan; extends into Guzerat. Syn. L. bicolor, Roxb. Cor. *t.* 139; Fl Ind. i, 548; L kœnigianus, Agardh in Schult. *syst.* vii, p 108.

9. L LAGENIFERUS, Wight Ic. 306—Glabrous; branches terete; leaves opposite petioled, elliptic, oblong-obtuse, rounded at the base; peduncles fascicled, having at the apex a large campanulate 4 to 5-lobed involucrum, inside of which are 4 to 5 flowers. This curious species, which is pretty common on the higher hills, extends to Malabar.

10. L CUNEATUS, Heyne; Wight Ic. *t.* 305.—Covered with a grey pubescence when young; branches terete; leaves alternate or fascicled in pairs, narrow-oblong or obovate-obtuse, cuneate at the base; umbels peduncled; flowers 2 to 5, shortly-pedicelled, clothed with short tomentum; corol tubular, 5-cleft; segments linear. Parwar Ghaut and Tullawarree. Syn. L goodeniiflorus and Candolleanus, W. and A. *Prod.* Found also at Gondabyle.

3. VISCUM, Tournef.

1 V ANGULATUM, Heyne.—Leafless; stems and older branches terete or obscurely many-angled, dichotomous, younger ones

opposite or verticillate, 4-angled, jointed equal between the joints; flowers sessile, opposite or verticillate at the joints; berries nearly globose. Chorla Ghaut, growing on Olea paniculata; flowers in April.

LXXIII. RUBIACEÆ.

1. SPERMACOCE, Linn.

1. Hispida, Linn. Maut. p 558.—Herbaceous, diffuse, hairy or scabrous; leaves from obovate-oblong to roundish; bristles of the stipules longer than the hirsute sheath; flowers few, axillary sessile, white; tube of the corolla wide; capsule 2-seeded. A common weed.

2. KNOXIA.

1. Corymbosa, Willd. sp. 1, p 582.—Stem somewhat shrubby, erect, more or less hirsute; leaves lanceolate, hispid on the upper-side, under pubescent; cymes corymbose, often very compound; flowers white, numerous; fruit 2-celled; cells one-seeded. On Wag Donger, near Vingorla; flowers in August. Syn. K teres, DC. *Prod.* 4, 569; K exserta, DC. loc. cit; Spermacoce teres, Roxb. Fl Ind. i, 367; S exserta, Roxb. loc. cit; S sumatrensis, Retz. Obs. iv, p 23.

3. GEOPHILA, Don.

1. G Reniformis, Don.—Herbaceous creeping plant; petioles and peduncles hirsute or pubescent; leaves roundish-cordate; peduncles 2 to 3-flowered, shorter than the leaf; corolla tubular, hairy in the throat, with 5 ovate recurved lobes. At Vingorla. Syn. Psychotria herbacea, Linn. sp. p 245.

4. PSYCHOTRIA.

1. Ambigua, W. and A. *Prod.* 1, p 433.—Shrubby, erect, glabrous; leaves oblong-lanceolate, tapering at the base; corymbs terminal. peduncled, trichotomous, lax, somewhat fleshy; flower-bud clavate and curved; corolla tubular, white, 6 to 8 times longer than the calyx; fruit globose, with ten small ribs. Parwar Ghaut.

5. GRUMILEA.

1. Vaginnans, Dalz. Mss.—Shrubby, erect, glabrous; leaves large obovate; stipules ovate or lanceolate-acute, caducous, 1½ to 2 inches long, combined into a sheathing tube; corymb terminal peduncled, panicle-shaped, trichotomous, puberulous; flowers small,

white; fruit like black pepper. Chorla Ghaut. Syn. Psychotria vaginnans, W. and A. *Prod*. p 434. Mahableshwur; rare.

6. SAPROSMA, Blume.

1. Indicum, Dalz. in Hook. Jour. Bot. iii, p 37.—A shrub; branches round dichotomous, glabrous; leaves sessile obovate-elliptic, attenuated towards the base, entire, margins recurved; stipules solitary between the petioles, sheathing the stem; flowers few, terminal, fascicled, very shortly pedicelled; berries ovoid, smooth, blue, very fœtid, crowned with the calyx teeth, one or two-seeded. Chorla Ghaut. Syn. Dysidodendron glomeratum, Gardn. in Calc. Jour. Nat. Hist. " vii, p 3. Thwaites thinks this plant is a Serissa.

7. PAVETTA, Linn.

1. Indica, Linn. sp. p 160.—A shrub about 3 feet high; leaves oval oblong acuminated, upper surface glabrous and shining; stipules broad, corymbs terminal and from the upper axils; flowers white; corolla half inch long. Caranjah Hill; the Ghauts; common. Syn. P alba, Vahl. Symb. iii, p 11; Ixora paniculata, Lam. Encycl. Meth. iii, 344; I pavetta, Roxb. Fl Ind. i, 386. "Paput," Maratha.

2. Siphonantha, Dalz. in Hook. Jour. Bot. ii, p 133.—A shrub; leaves membranaceous elliptic-oblong, suddenly acuminated, attenuated into a short petiole; stipules cuneate mucronate, hairy within; corymbs axillary and terminal; tube of the corolla very long (1½ inch); style long and slender, twice the length of the corolla; flowers white. Parpoolee Ghaut; flowers in May.

3. Brunonis, Wall.; Wight Ic 1065.—Soft and villous all over; leaves obovate; stipules and bracteas broad, membranous; peduncles trichotomous, with the branches dense and corymbose; lobes of the calyx triangular-obtuse. Syn. Pavetta villosa, Roth. nov. sp. p 88. In hedges at Vingorla.

8. IXORA.

1. Coccinea, Linn. sp. p 159.—Shrubby, 2 to 3 feet high, glabrous; leaves opposite oblong-obtuse; stem-clasping, coriaceous; corymbs terminal, crowded; flowers numerous, of a beautiful crimson; berry size of a large pea, smooth, fleshy when ripe, purple. This is the indigenous red-flowered species in the Presidency. The Concans; common. We have seen this in Ceylon, whence Linnæus obtained his specimens. It is highly probable that I. bandhuca of Roxb. Fl Ind. i, 376, is identical. Syn. I grandiflora, DC. *Prod*. 4, 486; Hook. Bot. Misc. Suppl. *t*. 35; I obovata, Heyne in Roth. nov. sp. p 90.

2. Nigricans, Br.—Shrubby, glabrous; leaves oblong-lanceolate, shining on both sides, turns black in drying; corymbs trichotomous, large, open; flowers white, lax, one inch long; berries globose. Very common in thick-shaded jungles of the Ghauts. "Katkoora" of the Marathas.

3. Parviflora, Vahl. Symb. iii, p 2, *t.* 52.—A small erect-growing tree; leaves short-petioled, from linear-oblong to cuneate-obovate, coriaceous, and hard shining corymbs and panicles, terminal trichotomous; flowers very small, numerous, white or pink. Common on the Ghauts. This makes excellent firewood. Syn. I arborea, Smith in Ree's Cycl.; I pavetta, Andr. Bot. Rep. *t.* 78; I decipiens, DC. *Prod.* 4, 488. Native name "Koorat;" makes good torches.

4. I Pedunculata, Dalz. in Hook. Jour. Bot. iii, p 121.—A shrub; leaves shortly-petioled, elliptic, coriaceous, glabrous; stipules triangular, shortly cuspidate; panicle terminal trichotomous, small, lax, terminating a long naked peduncle; flowers numerous, small, pink. Near Parwar Ghaut, Kala Kooda, and Beemasunker; flowers in February.

9. CANTHIUM, Lam.

1. C Umbellatum, Wight Ic. 1034.—A most beautiful tree, with dark-green, oval, coriaceous leaves; young branches 4-sided; flowers axillary, white, umbelled on the apex of a short, stout peduncle; fruit obovate, didymous, warted, size of a large pea. Pretty common in stony places above the Ghauts, and very ornamental. The wood is close-grained, of a light-chocolate colour, but black in the centre. Native name "Ursool."

2. C Leschenaultii, W. and A. *Prod.* p 426.—Shrubby, climbing; old branches armed with short supra-axillary thorns; young shoots long, slender, often unarmed; petioles shortish-twisted; leaves opposite, or 3 to 4-verticillate, oblong, much acuminate, acute at the base; cymes axillary, short-peduncled, 3 to 5-flowered; segments of the corolla linear-lanceolate acuminate, reflexed; drupe obcordate, black when ripe. At Moolus, foot of Ram Ghaut. Wight Ic. 826.

3. C Parviflorum, Lam.—Shrubby, usually with opposite horizontal thorns a little above the axils, sometimes unarmed; leaves ovate glabrous, often fascicled on the young shoots; racemes short, axillary, few-flowered; drupe obovate, slightly emarginate, compressed, furrowed on each side, ripe in July. Ghauts between Belgaum and Nepanee, Deccan; rare. Native name "Keernee."

4. C Rheedei, DC. *Prod.* iv, p 474.—Shrubby, armed with supra-axillary thorns; branches hirsute; leaves ovate or oval-lanceolate, acuminate, upperside shining, under with a tuft of hairs in the axils of the nerves; flowers axillary, shortly-pedicelled,

few, fascicled, or in a short raceme; drupe obovate, emarginate. This we have not seen. Said by Graham to grow in the Concan, and at Sewree Fort, Bombay.

10. MORINDA, Vaill.

1. M Bracteata, Roxb. Fl Ind. i, 544.—A small tree, quite glabrous; leaves large, oval-oblong, pointed at both ends, shining; stipules broader than long, rounded; heads of flowers short-peduncled, leaf-opposed, solitary bracteate; bracteas few, foliaceous; corolla long, infundibuliform, white; berries concreted into a roundish smooth fruit. At Malwan and Vingorla. We have not seen this species further north.

2. M Citrifolia, Linn.—Somewhat arboreous, glabrous, branchlets 4-angled; leaves oval, attenuated at both ends, shining; stipules membranaceous, obtuse; heads of flowers short-peduncled. without bracts; flowers white. Very common in many places. Native name "Aal" or "Bartoondie." The roots are used in dyeing. M tinctoria, Roxb. Fl Ind. i, 543.

3. M Tomentosa, Heyne in Roth nov. sp. p 147.—A small tree; young branches 4-angled, tomentose; leaves roundish-ovate acuminate, shortly tomentose on both sides; stipules bifid; peduncles axillary, solitary, longer than the petiole, tomentose; heads without bracts, few flowers; flowers white; flowers in April. Common in Concan, south of Poorundur Fort in the Deccan. Syn. M mudia, Ham. in Linn. Trans. xiii, 536.

11. VANGUERIA, Comm.

1. Edulis, Vahl. Symb. iii, p 36.—A small tree; leaves ovate or oblong, membranaceous, glabrous; cymes below the leaves from the old cicatrices; flowers greenish-white; fruit round, smooth, size of an apple, containing 5 one-seeded nuts; the flowers appear in the cold weather. Common in the Concan and on the Ghauts. Syn. V spinosa, Roxb. Fl Ind. i, 536 (?); V cymosa, Gaert. Fr. p 74, *t.* 193; V madagascariensis, Gmel. syst.; V commersonii, Desf.; Vanauga chinensis, Rottr. Native name "Aloo." Fruit is eaten, but is by no means palatable.

12. SANTIA, W. and A.

1. Venulosa, W. and A. *Prod.* p 422.—Shrubby; branches and young shoots glabrous; leaves short-petioled, elliptic-oblong, shortly-pointed, glabrous above, hirsute on the nerves beneath; veins numerous, transverse, prominent on the upperside; peduncles

axillary, short, hirsute, bearing 3 to 4 flowers at their apex ; drupe somewhat globose, crowned with the erect subulate teeth of the calyx. On the Ghauts, but very rare.

13. HAMILTONIA, Roxb.

1. Mysorensis, W. and A. *Prod.* p 423.—A small erect-growing shrub, with slender rigid branches ; leaves oblong or oval-lanceolate, with a short rigid pubescence ; panicles corymbose, trichotomous pubescent ; flowers fascicled, small, white. In rocky places. Island of Caranjah ; on the Ghauts ; pretty common. Native name " Geedesa."

14. DENTELLA, Forst.

1. Repens, Forst.—An herbaceous, annual, creeping plant ; stems filiform, branched, glabrous ; leaves oblong, attenuated at the base ; flowers small, white, tender, axillary solitary, alternate, very shortly pedicelled ; capsule hirsutely villous, 2-celled ; seeds numerous. Common in moist situations. Syn. Oldenlandia repens, Linn. Maut. p 40 ; Hedyotis repens, Lam.

15. HEDYOTIS, Linn.

1. Leschenaultiana, W. and A. *Prod.* p 411.—Herbaceous, rooting at the base ; stems long, straggling, hairy, particularly towards the extremities ; leaves broadly ovate acuminated, obtuse or cordate at the base ; bristles of the stipules 2 to 6 on each side, longer than the sheathing portion ; corymbs hirsute, terminal peduncled ; calyx increasing and becoming foliaceous after flowering ; corolla blue, with a long, slender tube. At Belgaum. Syn. Putoria indica, DC. (?) *Prod.* 4, 577.

2. Aspera, Heyne, in Roth nov. sp. p 94.—Annual, erect, simple all over rough, with minute white warts ; leaves linear acuminated ; stipules with 1 to 3 long, subulate points ; cymes terminal, long-peduncled ; flowers usually in pairs, pale-blue, with long slender tubes. Surat and Deccan ; flowers in August. Syn. Oldenlandia aspera, DC. *Prod* 4, 428.

3. Trinervia, Rœm. and Schult. iii, p 197.—Herbaceous ; branched, procumbent ; stems slender, glabrous or slightly hairy ; leaves petioled, roundish-ovate or oval, small, 3-nerved ; stipules bipartite ; flowers shortly pedicelled, 1 to 4 in the axils of the leaves ; corolla rotate, 4-partite, white ; capsule hirsutely villous. At Malwan ; flowers in July. Syn. H rotundifolia, Spr. Pug. ii, p 33 ; H serpyllifolia, Poir. Encycl. Meth. Suppl. iii, p 14 ; Oldenlandia trinervia, Retz. Obs. iv, p 23.

4. Burmanniana, Br.—Annual, procumbent; branches elongated; leaves linear or linear-lanceolate; peduncles solitary, axillary alternate, shorter than the leaves, 1 to 3-flowered; corolla white, shortly tubular; capsule roundish-ovate, glabrous. A common weed. Syn. H biflora, Lam. Illust. No. 1427; H diffusa, Willd. sp. i, 566; Oldenlandia biflora, Lam. Encycl. Meth. iv, 533; Gerontogea biflora, Cham. and Schult. in Linn. iv, 155.

5. Heynei, Br.—Annual or biennial erect, dichotomous, glabrous; branches acutely 4-angled; leaves linear or linear-lanceolate; pedicels 1-flowered, axillary, solitary or in pairs in the opposite or alternate axils, shorter than the leaves; capsule roundish-ovate, crustaceous, opening across the apex. Equally common with the preceding. Syn. H herbacea, Willd. sp. i, 566; Oldenlandia herbacea, Roxb. Fl Ind. i, 424.

6. Latifolia, Dalz. in Hook. Jour. Bot. ii, p 133.—Stem erect, glabrous, quadrangular, almost 4-winged, trichotomous; leaves ovate-acute, rounded at the base, short-petioled, slightly hispid on the prominent nerves beneath, 1½ inch long, 1 inch broad, lower stipules truncate, glabrous, upper ones with 3 to 6 ciliated bristles; flowers few, minute, pale rose-coloured, on longish trichotomously branched peduncles; calyx 4-toothed, tube of the corolla 3 to 4 times longer than the calyx teeth; capsule with the calycine teeth about the middle, splitting to the base, 4 to 12-seeded, seeds cup-shaped. Malwan; flowers in July; closely allied to H Rheedei.

7. Fœtida, Dalz. loc. cit.—Four inches high, erect, glabrous, scarcely branched, stems acutely 4-sided; leaves linear, with recurved margins, scabrous above, 1 inch long; flowers purple, capitate, clustered in threes or fives on the apex of longish peduncles, very fœtid; calyx 4-divided, the teeth with callous points; capsule much-compressed, crowned by the distant calyx teeth, dehiscing only within the calyx, 4 to 12-seeded, Malwan; common in stony ground in the rains.

8. Carnosa, Dalz. loc. cit—Herbaceous, much-branched, ascending, glabrous; leaves lanceolate elliptic-obtuse, thick and fleshy, attenuated into a short petiole, the margins recurved, 1 inch long, 5 to 6 lines broad; flowers and capsules exactly as in the preceding, and supposed therefore to be a variety of it, the differences in the leaves, &c., being caused by the influence of the salt spray. On the sea shore at Malwan.

9. Lancifolia, Dalz. loc. cit.—Herbaceous, erect-branched; leaves lanceolate acuminate, pubescent above and on the nerves beneath; stipules pubescent, furnished with 4 to 5 ciliated bristles; peduncles with spreading hairs; flowers numerous, in heads of 5, corolla with a long slender tube 6 to 7 times longer than the calyx teeth; capsule hispid, compressed, crowned with the spreading

teeth, dehiscing only within the calyx, 4 to 6-seeded. Phoonda Ghaut; flowers in September.

10. H SENEGALENSIS, Cham. and Schult. in Linn. 1829, p 156.—One foot high; leaves linear, floral ones subulate; stipules with 2 bristles; flowers shortly-pedicelled near the apex of the branches, distant, few; lobes of corolla lanceolate; flowers of a dingy white. Barren places in the Deccan; flowers rather smaller than those of African specimens; we have found this in the province of Lus, near Sonmeanee. Syn. Kohautia senegalensis, DC. *Prod.* 4, p 430.

16. OPHIORHIZA, Linn.

1. HARRISONII, Wall.—Herbaceous; stems, petiole, peduncles, and nerves on the leaves, beneath pubescent; leaves ovate or roundish-ovate, acutish, green above, pale beneath; peduncles terminal, corymbose, and dichotomously branched at the apex. Wight Ic. 1162. Ram Ghaut.

17. WENDLANDIA, Bartl.

1. NOTONIANA, W. and A. *Prod.* p 403.—A shrub, young shoots hirsute; leaves petioled, oblong, upperside glabrous, under glaucous, and subpubescent; stipules triangular ovate, branches of the panicle hirsute; flowers numerous, crowded, white, forming interrupted spikes, delightfully fragrant. Ram Ghaut and Warree country, common; flowers in January and February. Banks of the Yeena, Mahableshwur. Syn. W. thyrsoidea, Roth. nov. sp. p 149; Canthium thyrsoideum, Rœm. and Schult. v, 207; Cupia thyrsoidea, DC. *Prod.* iv, 394. Quoina river banks; Northern Ghauts, rare.

18. HYMENODICTYON, Wall.

1. OBOVATUM, Wall.—A large tree; leaves obovate acuminate, glabrous; stipules ovate-acute, floral leaves lanceolate, coloured, bullate; panicles racemed, slender, scarcely branched; flowers small, inconspicuous, greenish; flowers in July. Island of Caranjah, Ram Ghaut, &c. Syn. Cinchona obovata, Spr. *syst.* Suppl. p 73. Native name "Kurwei." Ghaut jungles, common.

2. EXCELSUM, Wall. in Roxb. Fl Ind. ii, p 149.—Arboreous; leaves from oblong to roundish-ovate, pubescent; stipules cordate, floral leaves oblong, bullate, coloured; panicles terminal and axillary; flowers fascicled, small, greenish-white, fragrant. The bark is bitter and astringent, hence the native name "Kurwah." Along the Ghauts. The wood is firm, close-grained, and very useful. The bark of these has none of the properties of their congeners. Roxb. Syn. Cinchona excelsa, Roxb. Fl Ind. i, 529.

19. NAUCLEA.

1. Parviflora, Roxb. Fl Ind. i, 513.—A tree, glabrous; branches brachiate; stipules oval, leaves petioled, ovate or oval, or obovate-obtuse, or with a short, blunt point; general peduncles opposite, terminal, bearing a pair of small deciduous leaves, partial ones scarcely so long as the globose head of flowers; limb of the calyx very short, almost truncated. Native name "Kuddum." The Concans; the Mawul districts. The wood is used for gun-stocks and building. It soon rots when exposed to wet. Syn. N parviflora, Pers. Syn. i, 202; N orientalis, Linn. (?); Cephalanthus pilulifer, Lam. Encycl. Meth. i, 678.

2. Cordifolia, Roxb. Fl Ind. i, p 514.—A tree; stipules oval; leaves petioled, cordate-roundish, pubescent above, tomentose beneath; general peduncles axillary, 1 to 3 together, bearing at the apex a pair of scariose roundish deciduous bracts; partial one longer than the globose head of flowers; calyx segments clavate, corolla pubescent. This tree yields the Hedoowood, a very inferior wood, used for making packing boxes for opium, &c. Roxburgh says it is beautiful, and that it answers very well for furniture. It is good for planking where not exposed.

3. N Elliptica.—A large tree; leaves elliptic-acute at both ends, rather thick and coriaceous, shining, glabrous; peduncles axillary and terminal, solitary, 2½ inches long; heads of flowers globose, 1 inch in diameter, stigmas long exserted, thick, smooth, with a round head; corol tubular, wider upwards, yellowish white, 4½ lines long, divisions short, oval-obtuse, with a mucro on the back below the apex; calyx divisions subulate, hairy; leaf with the petiole 7 inches long and 3 broad. Native name "Phooga." Near Sura, and the village of Hoolun, not far from Chorla Ghaut.

20. ARGOSTEMMA, Wall.

1. Glaberrimum, Dalz. in Hook. Jour. Bot. iii, p 345.—Four to 5 inches high, erect; leaves 4, verticelled, lanceolate acuminated, unequal, and with unequal sides; inflorescence umbelled trichotomous, shorter than the leaves, umbels few-flowered; flowers pentamerous, filaments much swellon at the apex, adhering together. On trees in the Warree country.

2. A Cuneatum, Dalz. loc. cit.—Stem pubescent; leaves 2 to 4 verticelled, subsessile, ovate, unequal, sparingly puberous on both sides; peduncle simple, glabrous, umbel short, many-flowered; bracts foliaceous, cuneate; flowers tetramerous; calyx and pedicels pubescent; anthers without beaks. On rocks at the Chorla Ghaut; flowers in August.

21. STYLOCORYNE, Cav.

1. WEBERA, A. Rich.—Shrubby, glabrous; leaves lanceolate-oblong, shining; corymbs trichotomous terminal; calyx limb 5-cleft, tube of corolla short, bearded at the mouth, segments of the limb recurved, stigma 10-ribbed, berry 2-celled, globose; flowers white. The young shoots are frequently covered with a resinous exudation. Southern Concan. Syn. Webera corymbosa, Willd. sp. i, 1224. Rondeletia asiatica, Linn. sp. 244; Canthium corymbosum, Pers. Syn i, 200; Cupia corymbosa, DC. *Prod.* 4, 394; Tarenna zeylanica, Gaert. Fr. i, 139; Polyozus madraspatana, DC. loc. cit. 495.

22. GRIFFITHIA, W. and A.

1. FRAGRANS, W. and A. *Prod.* p 400.—A rigid glabrous shrub, with opposite thorns; leaves petioled, from obovate to oblong, cuneate at the base, coriaceous; stipules roundish, ovate cuspidate; flowers in an umbel-like corymb, white; fruit size of a large pea, South Concan. Syn. Gardenia fragrans, Kœnig. Roxb. Cor. *t.* 197; Posoqueria fragrans, Roxb. Fl. Ind. i, 717; Randia malabarica, Lam. Encyc. Meth. iii, 25; Stylocoryne pandaki; DC. *Prod.* 4, 377; S malabarica, DC. loc. cit.

23. RANDIA, Houst.

1. DUMETORUM, Lam. Illust. *t.* 156, *fig.* 4.—A small thorny tree; leaves oval-obtuse, cuneate at the base, glabrous; flowers solitary, terminal on the young shoots, white or yellowish; fruit size of a small apple, slightly grooved longitudinally. Very common on the Ghauts. Syn. Gardenia dumetorum, Retz. Obs. ii, p 14; G spinosa, Linn. Suppl. p 164; Posoqueria dumetorum, Roxb. Fl Ind. i, p 713; Ceriscus malabaricus, Gaert. i, *t.* 28. Native name "Ghela."

2. LONGISPINA, DC. *Prod.* 4, 386.—A tree armed with long straight thorns; leaves from obovate to oblong cuneate at the base, glabrous; flowers 1 to 3, at the extremities of young axillary shoots; fruit ovoid, size of a small wood-apple. Kandeish jungles. The Ataveesy, rare, Dr. Gibson. Syn. Posoqueria longispina, Roxb. Fl Ind. i, 716.

3. ULIGINOSA, DC. *Prod.* 4, 386.—A thorny tree; branches 4-angled; leaves short petioled, oblong, cuneate at the base, glabrous, shining; fruit size of a lemon, smooth, yellow, South Concan. Syn. Gardenia uliginosa, Retz. Obs. ii, p 14; Posoqueria uliginosa, Roxb. Fl Ind. i, 712.

24. DISCOSPERMUM, Dalz.

1. Sphærocarpum, Dalz. in Hook. Jour. Bot. ii, p 257.—A middle-sized tree; branchlets with the bark pale; leaves opposite, elliptic, coriaceous, glabrous, petioled, with hollow hairy glands in the axils of the primary veins; stipules between the petioles solitary, triangular cuspidate, persistent; flowers in the opposite axils, small sessile, clustered; calyx deeply 4-lobed; fruit nearly an inch in diameter, globose, fœtid, indehiscent, 2-celled, seeds in each 5 to 6, compressed lenticular, with membranaceous partitions between them. The Ghauts, latitude 16°. Syn. D dalzellii, Thwaites in Enum. Pl, Ceylon, p 158.

2. Apiocarpum, Dalz. loc. cit.—Like the preceding; the fruit pear-shaped, with a circular ring somewhat below the apex. In the same locality.

25. GARDENIA, Ellis.

1. Lucida, Roxb. Fl Ind. i, 707.—A large shrub, unarmed, with resinous buds; leaves oblong or oval, or obovate, smooth, hard, and shining; flowers somewhat terminal, large, white, fragrant, with a long tube; berry drupaceous, oblong; nut very hard, thick, and bony. Common in the Concan jungles. This, as well as G Gummifera, furnishes the Decamalee resin, sold in every bazar; it is greenish-yellow, of a repulsive odour, and is effectual in cleaning sores and in cutaneous diseases. Syn. G resinifera, Roth. nov. sp. p 150.

2. Latifolia, Ait. Hort, Kew. i, 294.—Arboreous, unarmed; leaves opposite, or in threes, very shortly petioled, oval or obovate, glabrous; flowers terminal, solitary, very shortly pedicelled; fruit nearly globose, large. Duddi on the Gutpurba, Law; Kandeish jungles, Auld; Nagotna; the Tull Ghaut. Syn. G enneandra, Kœnig; G latifolia, Roxb. Fl Ind. i, p 706.

3. Gummifera, Linn. Suppl. p 164.—Arborescent, unarmed, with resinous buds; leaves sessile, from narrow elliptic-oblong to ovate oblong-obtuse, or bluntly pointed; flowers terminal, almost sessile, 1 to 3 together; corolla with long slender tube; fruit drupaceous, even oblong. Duddi on the Gutpurba; very common, Law; also on barren plains south of Dharwar. Syn. G arborea, Roxb. Fl Ind. i, 708. North Canara. Decamalee is of the greatest use in medical practice for keeping flies off putrid sores.

4. Montana, Roxb. Fl Ind. i, 709.—A tree with short rigid spines; leaves oblong-obtuse, nearly sessile, upperside glabrous and shining; flowers 3 to 6 together, fascicled from the young leafless shoots; berry drupaceous, roundish; nut hard and bony, with 4 to 6 pointed receptacles; fruit size of a pullet's egg. In the Ataveesy, rare, Law.

26. MUSSÆNDA.

1. FRONDOSA, Linn. sp. 231.—A somewhat scandent shrup; leaves oval-acuminated; flowers corymbose, terminal, of a deep golden yellow, one of the calyx segments produced into a large white oval leaf; fruit glabrous, obovoid. Hills in the Concan; very common, also on the Ghauts. Syn. M flavescens, Ham. in Linn. Trans. xiv, p 203; M belilla, Ham. loc. cit.; M glabra, Vahl. Symb. iii, 38; M corymbosa, Roxb. Fl Ind. i, p 556 (?).

LXXIV. GALIACEÆ.

1. RUBIA, Tournef.

1. CORDIFOLIA, Linn. Maut. p 197—A perennial herbaceous climbing plant, stem rough; leaves in fours, long-petioled, oblong or ovate-acute, more or less cordate, 3 to 7-nerved, prickly on the margins and middle nerve; panicles axillary, peduncled trichotomous, corolla rotate, 4 to 3-parted; fruit somewhat globose, didymous, red or black. Common on the higher Ghauts. Syn. R munjista, Roxb. Fl Ind. i, 374; R munjith, Desv. Jour. Bot. ii, 207. This furnishes the Munjeet of commerce, or Indian Madder, an article of export, but chiefly from Kelat through Sind.

LXXV. COMPOSITÆ.

SUB-ORDER.—I. VERNONIACEÆ, Adenoon.

1. INDICUM, Dalz. in Hook. Jour. Bot. ii, p 344.—A branched, erect plant, 1½ foot high; stem angular, scabrous, and hispid; leaves broad, elliptical-acute at both ends, coarsely serrated, glandular and rough; panicles of flowers corymbose; flowers blue. Phoonda Ghaut; flowers in September. No. 795 of Graham's Catalogue, under Ethulia. Near Belgaum, Law.

2. VERNONIA.

1. CINEREA, Less. in Linn. p 291.—Stem herbaceous, erect-branched, rather hoary, with closely-set short hairs; leaves petioled, lowermost rounded, the others obovate-oblong, somewhat toothed, rather hoary beneath; corymb lax, dichotomous; heads of flowers peduncled; involucre scales lanceolate linear-acuminated; flowers purple. A common weed. Syn. Conyza cinerea, Linn. 1208; Serratula cinerea, Roxb. Fl Ind. iii, p 406; Conyza mollis, Willd. sp. iii, p 1924.

2. CONYZOIDES, DC. in Wight. Bot. Ind. ii, p 6.—Stem erect, herbaceous, striated, minutely pubescent beneath; leaves ovate or

oblong-lanceolate, acuminated, attenuated into a short petiole, serrated, pubescent beneath ; corymb compound, branched, many-headed ; involucre scales linear-lanceolate acuminated, shorter than the disc. The Ghauts.

3. DECANEURUM, DC.

1. MOLLE, DC. *Prod.* 5, p 67.—Stem herbaceous, erect, rather smooth, or roughish with minute bristles, tomentose at the apex ; leaves ovate lanceolate acuminated, coarsely and irregularly serrated, tomentose and hoary beneath ; peduncles axillary, one-headed ; bracts foliaceous, close under the head of flowers ; like the leaves. South Concan. Syn. D epileium, DC. in Wight Contr. p 7 ; D scabridum, DC. loc. cit.

2. MICROCEPHALUM, Dalz. in Hook. Jour. Bot. iii, p 231.—Stem branched, scabrous, and pubescent ; leaves petioled, elliptic-acuminate, gradually attenuated into the petiole, pubescent above, hoary and tomentose beneath ; heads of flowers shall, solitary at the apex of the branches ; scales of the involucre squariose, hoary and tomentose beneath, exterior ones lanceolate-acuminate, bristle-pointed, ciliated ; seeds smooth, shining, without ribs. The Parwar Ghaut ; flowers in November ; when freshly gathered, smells like Chamomile.

4. ELEPHANTOPUS, Cass.

1. SCABER, Linn. sp. 1313.—Stem dichotomously branched, strigose ; radical leaves rough crenated, wedge-shaped, gradually attenuated towards the base ; stem leaves broadly cordate, ovate-acuminate, hoary ; flowers purple. Common under the shade of trees in the Concan and Ghauts.

SUB-ORDER.—II. EUPATORIACEÆ.

1. ADENOSTEMMA.

1. LATIFOLIUM, Don. *Prod.* 181.—Stem erect-branched, pubescent towards the apex ; leaves petioled, broadly ovate-rhomboid, or subcordate, coarsely serrated ; panicle corymbose hirsute, many-headed ; scales of involucre rough on the back, seeds muricated and tubercled. Jungles in the Concan ; common ; flowers white. Syn. Lavenia latifolia, Spr. *syst.* iii, p 445 ; A strictum, Bot. Mag. *t.* 2410 (?).

2. RIVALE, Dalz. in Hook. Jour. Bot. iii, 231.—Stem erect, round, glabrous ; leaves linear lanceolate, long-attenuated at the base, serrate-toothed, glabrous ; panicle corymbose, lax, few-headed ;

scales of the involucre linear or linear-spathulate, obtuse, herbaceous. Margins of rivulets near Rohee Bunder. Syn. Ageratum aquaticum, Roxb. Fl Ind. iii, 416.

2. EUPATORIUM, Tournef.

1. Divergens, Roxb. Fl Ind. iii, p 414.—Shrubby, 6 to 8 feet high, branches diverging; leaves short-petioled, elliptic-recurved, serrate-dentate, rugose, when young downy, when old scabrous, 1 to 6 inches long; corymbs terminal compound; flowers purple, very numerous, heads with 5 to 8 flowers. Common on the Ghauts; flowers in February. This has been strangely confounded by DeCandolle with Decancurum divergens, but it is a true Eupatorium. Native name "Boondar." Mahableshwur, common.

Sub-Order.—III. ASTEROIDEÆ.

1. CALLISTEPHUS, Cass.

1. Concolor, Dalz. in Hook. Jour. Bot. ii, 344.—A small glaucous plant, root woody, perennial, branches ascending, radical; leaves oblong-obovate, toothed towards the apex; stem leaves linear-oblong, toothed or entire, glandular-dotted, glabrous; outer scales of involucre linear-obtuse, inner erect foliaceous, glandular-dotted; peduncles terminal, solitary, 1-headed; flowers yellow. In rocky ground near Malwan; flowers in September and October.

2. C Wightianus, DC. *Prod.* 5, p 275.—A rigidly erect annual; leaves sessile, oblong linear-entire or serrated, shortly mucronate; branches leafy, compressed at the apex, minutely puberulous; exterior scales of the involucre foliaceous, linear-oblong; flowers large, yellow. Wight Ic. 1089. Common in the Deccan.

2. LEUCOBLEPHARIS, Arnott.

1. L Subsessilis, Arn. in Mag. Zool. and Bot. ii, p 422.—Herbaceous, glabrous simple; root thick, woody; leaves alternate subsessile, elliptic-obtuse, or attenuated at both ends, entire 3-nerved; cluster of flowers globose, terminal subsessile; bracts foliaceous, longer than the flowers; seeds black, shining, plano-convex. The Ghauts. Blepharispermum subsessile. Wight Ic. 1093.

3. SPHÆRANTHUS, Vaill.

1. S Mollis, Roxb. Fl Ind. iii, 446.—Annual, winged; leaves sessile, decurrent, long obovate, bristle serrate, downy and glutinous;

heads of flowers solitary, leaf-opposed, or terminal peduncled, globular, rose-coloured or purple; peduncles winged. Very common.

4. DICHROCEPHALA, DC.

1. LATIFOLIA, DC. *Prod.* 5, p 372.—Stem erect, with scattered hairs; leaves obovate, attenuated into the petiole, coarsely toothed, often subpinnatifid at the base; flower bearing branches almost naked; pedicels rigid-spreading, longer than the globose head of flowers. Ram Ghaut, during the rains. Syn. Cotula bicolor, Roth. Cat. Bot. ii, p 116; Sphæranthus africanus, Burm. Ind. 185, *t.* 60, *f.* 2; Grangea latifolia, Lam. Illust. *t.* 699, *f.* i; Hippia bicolor, Smith in Ree's Cycl. 18, N. 2; Cotula latifolia, Pers. Enchir. ii, p 464; D erecta, L'Her. Mss.

5. GRANGEA, Adans.

1. MADRASPATANA, Poir. Dict. Suppl. iii, p 825.—Stems procumbent or diffuse, villous; leaves sinuato-pinnatifid, the lobes obtuse; peduncles terminal or opposite the leaves; heads of flowers yellow, solitary, subglobose. Rice fields, in the cold weather. Syn. Artemisia madraspatana, Linn. sp. 1190; Cotula madraspatana, Willd. sp. iii, 2170; Grangea adansonii, Cass. Dict. xix, p 304.

6. CYATHOCLINE, Cass.

1. STRICTA, DC. *Prod.* 5, p 374.—An erect-branched, delicate plant; leaves tender, pinnately divided, the lobes somewhat linear, coarsely and regularly serrated; flowers corymbose, terminal, purple. Banks of streams in the Concan jungles. Syn. Tanacetum viscosum, E. and F; Artemisia stricta, Heyne. Herb.

2. LAWII, Wight Ic. *t.* 1150.—Leaves nearly all radical, minute, sub-bipinnatifid, pubescent; stems slender, erect, dichotomously branched, often with a capitulum in the fork; flowers yellow; the whole plant 3 to 4 inches in height. The Ghauts.

7. CONYZA, Lessing.

1. ABSINTHIFOLIA, DC. in Wight Contr. p 16.—Erect, much-branched, pubescent; leaves obovate oblong-mucronate, attenuated towards the base, lower ones coarsely toothed, upper entire; panicle corymbose, much-branched, many-headed; involucre scales linear-acuminate, shorter than the flowers. The Ghauts. Syn. Baccharis trifurcata, Trevir in Nov. Act. Acad. Nat. Cur. xiii, p 210; C pinnatifida, Roxb. Fl Ind. iii, p 430.

2. ADENOCARPA, Dalz.—Stem rather woody below, much-branched from the base, pubescent and scabrous all over; leaves linear or spathulate, stem-clasping, auricled at the base, and entire or distantly toothed, mucronulate; corymb terminal dichotomous, 8-flowered; flowers small, yellow; hermaph florets 10 to 12; achenia glabrous, covered with yellow resinous-looking glands. Hab. Hursur fort, near Jooneer, Hurrychunder, &c.; involucre scales lanceolate-acute, scabrous with membranous margins, rough and hairy.

8. BLUMEA, DC.

1. AMPLECTENS, DC. in Wight. Contr. p 13.—Stem herbaceous, as round, hairy, branched; young leaves villous, older ones almost glabrous, cauline leaves ovate, somewhat stem-clasping, acutely toothed, lower ones cut at the base; peduncles few, subterminal, a little longer than the leaf, with spreading hairs; heads of flowers solitary. Common on the roadsides. Syn. Conyza amplexicaulis, Lam. Dict. ii, p 85.

2. BIFOLIATA, DC. loc. cit. under Conyza.—Stem herbaceous, ascending, round-branched, slightly hairy; leaves acutely toothed, lower ones ovate, attenuated at the base, upper ones sessile, oblong; pedicels elongated, slender, terminated by a solitary head of flowers. Common about Surat.

3. MURALIS, DC. *Prod.* 5, p 440.—Glabrous below, glandular and hairy at the apex; stem herbaceous, erect, simple round; leaves lyrate, pinnately lobed, narrowed into the petiole, lobes coarsely toothed, panicle elongated, lax; flowers yellow, shorter than the involucre. Common on old walls, a tall species, the leaves very tender. Bassein Fort.

4. GLOMERATA, DC. in Wight Contr. p 15.—All over hirsutely villous, of an ashy hue; stem erect, round-branched, branches disposed in a leafy panicle, having sessile clustered heads of flowers in interrupted spikes. The Concans.

5. HOLOSERICEA, DC. *Prod.* 5, p 442.—All clothed with long silky hairs; stem round, erect, scarcely branched; leaves oblong, attenuated at the base, acute, deeply and acutely serrated, covered with silky, close-pressed hairs; panicle elongated, interrupted, lower branches longer than the leaves, racemose at apex. The Concans.

6. LONGIFOLIA, DC. *Prod.* 5, p 446.—Stem tall, herbaceous, erect, simple below; leaves 9 inches to a foot long, oblong serrated, acute at both ends; panicle elongated, many-headed; involucre scales linear, glabrous. At Tullawaree, on the Ghauts; 6 to 8 feet high.

7. ALATA, DC. *Prod.* 5, p 446.—Stem herbaceous, erect-branched along with the leaves, covered sparingly with a rufous pubescence; leaves linear or elliptic-oblong, toothed, running down

the stem into wings; peduncles axillary; panicles racemed, few-headed; heads of flowers drooping. On the Ghauts. Syn. Conyza alata, Roxb. Fl Ind. iii, 430; Erigeron alatum, Don. *Prod.* 171.

8. Leptocladea, (?) DC. *Prod.* 5, p 443.—Glabrous below, ashy villous above; stem herbaceous, erect, round-branched; branches twiggy, panicled, bearing sessile heads, solitary or clustered in an interrupted spike; leaves rather glabrous, obovate-oblong, gradually attenuated to the base, almost petioled, coarsely and sharply serrated at the apex; involucre scales linear-acuminate, the length of the flowers; male flowers 12 to 15.

9. PLUCHEA, Cassini.

1. Wallichiana, Less. in Linn. 1831, p 150.—A tall shrub, branches and young leaves puberulous; leaves obovate subsessile, distantly and acutely serrated, mucronate; corymbs terminating the branches, very numerous; flowers pink. Guzerat, near Dhej. Only one bush of this has been seen in the whole country, and we suspect it is not really indigenous, though the specimen was not near any house or garden.

10. EPALTES, Cass.

1. Divaricata, Cass. Bull. Philom, 1818, p 139.—Stem herbaceous erect, much-branched; leaves linear-oblong, attenuated at the base, decurrent along the stem, remotely toothed; peduncles shorter than the leaf, almost without bracts; involucre scales very acute, longer than the disc; flowers pink. Syn. Ethulia divaricata, Linn. Maut. 110; Burm. Ind. 176, *t.* 58, *fig.* 1; Pluk Alm. *t.* 21, *fig.* 4.

11. VICOA.

1. Indica, DC. Wight Contr. p 10.—Leaves auricled at the base, lanceolate-acuminate, serrated or nearly entire, more or less puberulous on both sides, rays twice as long as the disc. Syn. Inula indica, Willd. sp. iii, p 2092; Linn sp. 1237; Doronicum calcuratum, Roxb. Fl Ind. iii, p 434; Burm. zeyl. 124, *t.* 55, *f.* 2; Pluk. Alm. *t.* 149, N. 4, *f.* 3; Aster indicus, Willd. sp. iii, p 2041, nov. Linn.

1. V Cernua, Dalz.—A shorter plant than the preceding, with oblong lanceolate leaves; heads of flowers drooping, distinguished by having always one or two bristles as pappus to the ray flowers. Elevated parts of the Concans; flowers in October.

12. CÆSULIA, Roxb.

1. Axillaris, Roxb. Cor. i, p 64, *t.* 93; Fl. Ind. iii, p 447.—Glabrous, ascending; leaves alternate linear-lanccolate, acuminated

at both ends, distantly serrated, dilated at the base, somewhat stem-clasping; floral branchlets axillary, very short; floral leaves 2 to 3, coloured, orbicular, surrounding the head of flowers; flowers pale-violet and white. Andr. Bot. Rep. *t.* 431; Meyera orientalis, Don *Prod.* Fl Nep. 180; Melananthera orientalis, Spr. in Litt; leaves 3 inches long.

13. ECLIPTA, Linn.

1. Erecta, Linn. Maut. 286 (?); Willd. sp. iii, p 2217.—Stem erect, strigose, with adpressed hairs; leaves oblong lanceolate, acuminated at both ends; pedicels solitary or twin, 5 times longer than head of flowers. Very common. Syn. Verbesina alba, Linn. sp. 1272; Cotula alba, Linn. *syst.* Nat. ii, p 564; Micrelium asteroides, Forsk. Descr. 152; Ecl. adpressa, Mœnch. Meth.; Dill. Elth. *fig.* 137; Rumph. Amb. vi, p 18, *f.* 1; Pluk Alm. *t.* 109, *fig.* 1.

2. Prostrata, Linn. Maut. 286.—Stem prostrate or ascending, strigose, with adpressed hairs; branches somewhat hirsute; leaves oval or oblong-lanceolate, attenuated at the base, slightly serrated and undulated, rough; peduncles 2 to 3 times longer than the head of flowers. Syn. Verbesina prostrata, Linn. sp. ii, p 1272; Cotula prostrata, Linn. *syst.* ii, 564; Micrelium tolak, Forsk. descr. 153; Dill. Elth. *f.* 138; Pluk Alm. *t.* 118, *f.* 5.

14. BLAINVILLEA, Cass.

1. Latifolia, DC. in Wight Contr. p 17.—Leaves rhomboid-acuminate, coarsely toothed, sparingly pubescent; branches and petioles hairy, opposite, uppermost ones dichotomous; peduncles generally shorter than the petiole; awns of the achenium bearded at the base. Syn. Eclipta latifolia, Linn. Fil. suppl. 378; Verbesina lavenia, Roxb. Fl. Ind. iii, 442.

15. SIEGESBECKIA.

1. Orientalis, Linn. sp. 1269.—Leaves ovate, cuneate at the base, acuminated at the apex, coarsely toothed, uppermost ones oblong-lanceolate; exterior scales of the involucre twice the length of the inner. Near Belgaum. Linn. Hort. Cliff. *t.* 23; Ic. Pluk. Alm., p 58, *t.* 380, *f.* 2. We found this in Australia also.

16. XANTHIUM, Tourn.

1. Indicum, Roxb. Cat. Calc. 67.—Fruit-bearing; involucre oval, pubescent between the prickles and at the base of the beaks, beaks hooked at the apex. X orientale, Linn. sp. 1400; X chinense,

Nill. Dict. No. 5 (?); X strumarium, Delile Illustr. Fl Egypt. No. 891 (?) Has a reputation in diseases of the ears: the juice is used.

17. WEDELIA, Jacq.

1. Calendulacea, Less. Syn. p 222.—Non. Rich.—Leaves oblong-lanceolate, attenuated at the base, strigose and hairy on both sides, slightly serrated at the apex; peduncles 1-headed, solitary, axillary, 3 times longer than the leaf; outer involucre scales oblong subacute, longer than the disc. Syn. Verbesina calendulacea, Linn. sp. 1272; Willd. sp. iii, p 2226; Lam. Illust. *t.* 686, *f.* 1; W bengalensis, Rich in Pers. Erch. ii, p 10; Jægena calendulacea, Spr. *syst.* iii, p 500; Burm. Zeyl. 52, *t.* 22, *fig* 1.

18. WOLLASTONIA, DC.

1. Biflora, DC. *Prod.* 5, p 546.—Leaves petioled, ovate, long acuminated at the apex, acutely serrated, a little rough and hairy above, smoother below; peduncles 1 to 3-headed, one terminal, 1 to 2 from the uppermost axils; involurce scales lanceolate, achenium bare, or with one awn. Syn. Verbesina biflora, Linn. sp. 1272; Willd sp. iii, p 2226; Wedelia biflora, DC. in Wight Contr. p 18; Acmella biflora, Spr. *syst.* iii, 591; Rheed. Mal. x, *t.* 40.

19. GUIZOTIA, Cass.

1. Oleifera, DC. Mem. Soc. Hist. Nat. Genev. v, 7 cum. tav. 2.—Stem pubescent at the apex; leaves semiamplexicaul, subcordate or ovate-lanceolate, remotely serrated, a little rough; exterior scales of the involucre broadly ovate foliaceous. Syn. Polymnia abyssinica, Linn. Fil suppl. p 383; Verbesina sativa, Roxb. Cat. Calc. p 62; Bot. Mag. *t.* 1017; Parthenuim luteum, Spr. nov. *Prod.* p 31; Heliopsis platyglossa, Cass. Dict. 24, p 332.

20. BIDENS, Linn.

1. B Wallichii, DC. *Prod.* 5, p 598.—Lower leaves pinnately divided, upper ternately divided, segments ovate-acuminate, inciso-serrate or dentate, lateral ones obliquely attenuated at the base; heads of flowers long-peduncled, loosely corymbose; achenia linear angular striated, glabrous, with 3 awns at the apex. Syn. B chinensis, DC. in Wight Contr. p 19; Agrimonia moluccana, Rumph. Amb. vi, *t.* 15 *f.* 2. Deccan gardens, grounds, and plains, common.

22. SCLEROCARPUS, Jacquin.

1. S Africanus, Jacq. Ic. rar. *t.* 176.—Annual, erect; stem rough; leaves broadly ovate, acutely serrated, petioled alternate 3-nerved; heads of flowers yellow, solitary subsessile, at the apex of the branchlets. Found originally on the River Senegal, and afterwards in Northern India, by Royle; but supposed by De-Candolle to be introduced into the latter country. This does not appear to be the case, as it is found truly wild on the highest hills around Jooneer; flowers in July and August.

23. SPILANTHES, Jacq.

1. S Acmella, Linn. *syst.* veg. 610.—Stem slightly rooting at the base, erect or ascending; leaves petioled, ovate-lanceolate, 3-nerved, entire or toothed, rather glabrous; peduncles three times longer than the leaf; heads of flowers ovate; ligulæ 5 to 6, very small; achenia ciliated, with 1 to 2 awns. Syn. Verbesina acmella, Linn. Maut. 475; Acmella linnæi, Cass. Dict. 24, p 330. Supposed to include Pseudo, Acmella, and Calva. Chorla Ghaut.

24. GLOSSOCARDIA, Cass.

1. Bosvallea, DC. in Wight Contr. p 19.—A small annual, with many stems, diffuse; leaves alternate, much-divided, linear at the base; heads of flowers solitary, yellow, on short, naked peduncles. Common. Syn. Verbesina bosvallea, Linn. Suppl. p 379; Willd. sp. iii, p 2223; Roxb. Fl Ind. iii, p 443; G linearifolia, Cass. Dict. xix. p 62. Much used in female complaints.

25. GLOSSOGYNE, Cass.

1. G Pinnatifida, DC. in Wight Contr. p 19.—Glabrous, erect; stems dichotomous; leaves alternate, crowded, short, pinnately divided; lobes linear, acute-entire, uppermost small, linear, undivided; heads of flowers erect; yellow, awns on the seeds widely-spreading. Southern Maratha Country.

26. ARTEMISIA, Linn.

1. Indica, Willd. sp. iii, p 1846.—Erect, suffruticose; leaves ashy and tomentose beneath, lower pinnatifid, upper trifid, uppermost undivided, or with lanceolate lobes; lobes of the lower leaves toothed or cut; heads of flowers racemose-panicled, ovate; panicle leafy, spreading, partial racemes pendulous before flowering, young involucre a little tomentose, at length glabrous; exterior scales foliaceous, acute, interior membranaceous obtuse; corol

naked. Roxb. Fl Ind. iii, p 419. Native name "Downa." The flowers are sold in the bazars.

27. GNAPHALIUM, D. Don.

1. INDICUM, Linn. sp. 1200.—Stems several, herbaceous, diffuse, tomentose; leaves obovate-oblong or oblong-linear, mucronate, more or less tomentose, lowest attenuated at the base, upper sessile; heads of flowers aggregated into an interrupted simple or branched spike; involucre scales linear-obtuse, scariose, straw-coloured or reddish. Syn. G multicaule, Willd. sp. iii, 1888; G Polycaulon, Pers. Enchir. No. 105; G strictum, Roxb. Fl Ind. iii, 424; Pluk. Alm. *t.* 187, *f.* 5.

28. GYNURA, Cass.

1. G SIMPLEX.—Tall, erect, unbranched, glabrous; stem at the base as thick as the finger, angled; leaves large, oblong-obovate, sessile, coarsely sinuate-toothed, 5 inches long, 2 to 3 broad; stem distantly clothed with leaves to the apex; corymb terminal of 5 to 7, heads of deep orange-coloured flowers; heads 9 lines long; bracteoles linear-acute, one-third the length of the heads. This comes near to G angulosa of DC. *Prod.* from Nepal. On the highest hills around Jooneer.

29. DORONICUM, Linn.

1. RETICULATUM, Wight Ic. *t.* 1151, B.—Herbaceous, erect, ramous; stem and branches glabrous; leaves somewhat rhomboidal, coarsely and unequally dentate; teeth mucronate, rough and arancosely pubescent above, tomentose between the veins beneath; capitula laxly corymbose, longish-pedicelled; ligulæ 10 to 12, sterile; throat hairy within; pappus none; disc flowers numerous; achenium ribbed, conical, hairy. Island of Caranjah.

2. D HEWRENSE, Dalz.—Stem erect, striated, pilose; leaves oblong or lanceolate, attenuated at the base, and auricled, coarsely toothed, pubescent above, ciliated on the margin, and hispid on the prominent nerves beneath; peduncles axillary or terminal, long, slender, with 1 to 3 heads of flowers, which are small and yellow; ligulate flowers 3 only in each head; the ligulæ very small, oval; disc florets about 12. Common in rocky places around Jooneer; flowers in July and August.

30. MADACARPUS, R. Wight.

1. BELGAUMENSIS, Wight Ic. *t.* 1152.—Annual, erect, hirsute; leaves ovate, crenate-dentate, auricled at the base, pubescent above,

tomentose beneath; capitula corymbose; scales of the involucre linear mucronate; ligulæ about 8 (4-nerved); style and stigma none; achenia 10-nerved; nerves, hispid; pappus none. At Belgaum.

31. ECHINOPS, Linn.

1. E ECHINATUS, Roxb.—Erect, much-branched; leaves pinnatifid, pubescent and viscid above, hoary and tomentose beneath; divisions ovate-lanceolate, waved plain; heads of flowers terminal, solitary, globose spinous; florets pale-lilac; tube slender; divisions linear-acute, revolute; pappus short, brush-like; ovary very hairy. Guzerat and the Deccan; common. Roxb. Fl Ind. iii, p 447.

32. AMBERBOA, Isn.

1. INDICA, DC. *Prod.* 6, p 558.—Stem erect-branched, furrowed and angular, naked at the top; leaves glabrous or rough, lanceolate, coarsely toothed, uppermost few, linear, entire. Guzerat. Syn. Serratula indica, Klein in Willd. sp. iii, p 1642; Athanasia indica, Roxb. Fl Ind. iii.

33. TRICHOLEPIS.

1. PROCUMBENS, Wight Ic. *t.* 1139.—Stem flexuose, short, ramous; branches diffuse, procumbent, angularly striated, subglabrous; leaves shortly pubescent or subglabrous, those of the stem lyrate, of the branches sinuately pinnatifid, the lobes spinously mucronate; involucrum ovate; scales ovate at the base, araneose, terminating in a prickle-like appendage; flowers purple. Flowers in the cold weather; common in light soils in Guzerat. Syn. Carduus ramosus, Roxb. Fl Ind. iii, p 407.

2. T RADICANS, DC. *Prod.* 4, p 564.—Stem branched; branches spreading; leaves obovate or oblong-linear, sharply serrated; the teeth bristle-pointed, smooth, dotted; heads of flowers small, terminal, purple. Common in ravines in the Deccan. Syn. Carduus radicans, Roxb. Fl Ind. iii, 408.

3. T GLABERRIMA, DC. loc. cit.—Tall, erect, smooth, with the stem angled; leaves linear lanceolate acuminate, stem-clasping, distantly spotted with black specks; florets 7 lines long; heads of flowers as in the preceding, only a little larger. The Concan and Deccan; common.

4. T MONTANA.—A coarser species; leaves obovate-oblong, very coarsely toothed, or sometimes pinnatifid, differs from the last also in having long, slender stigmas. The Ghauts.

34. DICOMA, Less.

1. LANUGINOSA, DC. *Prod.* 7, p 36.—Erect, much-branched, wooly; scales of the ovate involucre prickly, nearly glabrous externally; leaves oblong, soft, quite entire; heads of flowers apparently axillary, but really terminating; very short axillary branches; achenium 10-ribbed, villous. Near Gogo, in Kattywar; also in the Deccan. Wight Ic. 1140.

35. MICRORHYNCHUS, Less.

1. SARMENTOSUS, DC. *Prod.* 7, p 181.—Stem filiform, procumbent, bearing roots and leaves here and there; leaves crowded, sinuate-pinnatifid, lobes obtuse or subacute; peduncles 1-headed, rather shorter than the leaf, having at the top scaly bracts, which are scarious on the margin. Very common in sandy ground. Syn. Prenanthes sarmentosa, Willd. sp. iii, p 1540; Lactuca sarmentosa, Wight Contr. p 27; Launæa pinnatifida, Cass. Ann. d'Soc. Nat. 23, p 85.

36. BRACHYRAMPHUS, DC.

1. HEYNEANUS, Wight Ic. *t.* 1146.—Stem erect, glabrous, terete, naked above; leaves rigid, subradical, runcinate, coarsely setoso-ciliate, the rest glabrous, stem-clasping; capitula cylindrical, short-pedicelled, remotely fascicled along the branches; achenia compressed, striated, slightly muricate, shortly beaked. Common on old walls, &c. Syn. Lactuca heyneana, DC. *Prod.* 7, p. 140.

2. SONCHIFOLIUS, DC. *Prod.* 7, p 177.—Glabrous, stem erect, leafy at the base, naked at the top, sparingly branched; leaves membranaceous, stem-clasping, obovate, somewhat runcinate and waved, bristle-ciliated on the margin; capitula remotely spicato-racemose; pedicels very short, a little scaly; achenia oblong, subcompressed, transversely muricated, attenuated into a short beak; pappus white, soft. Common. Lactuca remotiflora, DC. in Wight. Contr. p 26.

37. NOTONIA, DC.

1. N GRANDIFLORA, DC. in Deless, Ic. Selec. iv, *t.* 61.—A shrub, fleshy, smooth; stem thick, round, marked with the scars of fallen leaves; leaves oblong or obovate-entire; flowers terminal, corymbose, few, pale-yellow. Graham, in Cat. No. 773, has mistaken for this the Kleinia nerufolia of the Canary Islands. High rocky precipices in the Deccan. This genus was named by DeCandolle after Mr. Benjamin Noton, of Bombay, who collected many curious plants on the Nelgherries, where he found the present species.

2. N Balsamica.—Suffruticose, glaucous, and perfectly smooth, four feet high; leaves rather fleshy petioled, lanceolate, long attenuated at the base; flowers terminale, corymbose, at the apex of the tall, nearly naked, stem; branches of the corymb few, simple, 2 to 3-flowered; pedicels short club-shaped, angular or slightly winged, each with 2 lanceolate bracts at its apex; involucre of 5 to 7 unequal linear-acute leaflets, united into a tube, 8 lines long; florets about 15, a half longer than the involucre; pappus as long as the florets; achenia cylindric, mutic, striated, smooth; has a strong balsamic odour; leaves 3 to 4 inches long, 1 inch broad in the middle. Habitat below the Kamatkee and several other of the more inland Ghauts of the Deccan; rare.

LXXVI. LOBELIACEÆ.

1. LOBELIA, Linn.

1. L Trigona, Roxb. Fl Ind. ii, p 111.—A small, herbaceous, glabrous plant, with diffuse branches, and 3-angled stems; leaves subsessile, ovate, subcordate, repand-dentate mucronulate; pedicels slender, longer than the leaf; flowers small, of a deep blue. Syn. L stipularis, Roth. in Rœm. and Schult. *syst.* v, p 67. Common in pastures in the Concan.

2. L Nicotianæfolia, Heyne in Roxb. Fl Ind. i, 506.—A tall, erect plant, with hollow stems; leaves long, subsessile, lanceolate-acute, with large white flowers in terminal racemes. "Dawul" and "Deonul" is said by Graham to be the Maratha name, but in the Southern Ghauts the people call it "Bokenul," or tubular poison plant; "Boke" being a tree of the order Euphorbiaceæ, said to be poisonous. Common on the Ghauts; seeds extremely acrid.

LXXVII. CAMPANULACEÆ.

1. CEPHALOSTIGMA.

1. C Hirsutum, Edgew. in Linn. Trans. xx, p 81.—Stem erect, flexuose, pilose, angled, ramous; leaves alternate, sessile lanceolate, acuminated at the base, glabrous, margin denticulate; peduncles terminal, pubescent, naked; tube of the calyx hairy; capsule globose, 3-celled. Syn. Wahlenbergia perotifolia, Wight Ic. 842. The Concans; flowers in September; found also in Abyssinia.

2. C Flexuosum, Hook. Fil. and Thoms. in Proc. Linn. Soc. ii, p 9.—Stem hispid and pilose, very slender, flexuous, panicle-branched above; branches filiform; leaves sessile, broad ovate oblong-obtuse, slightly sinuate-dentate; flowers on very slender pedicels. A plant, 5 to 8 inches high, with the stem angled, and leaves three-quarters of an inch long, having a more slender stem and broader leaves than the preceding. The Concans.

2. WAHLENBERGIA.

1. W Agrestis, Alph. DC. *Prod.* 7, p 434.—Stem erect-branched from the base, hairy below; leaves approximated at the base, linear-narrow, almost entire, margins waved; peduncles often dichotomous, with very short bracts, calyx lobes erect linear, very narrow; corol tubular, bluish-white. capsule obovoid. Syn. W dehisceus, A. DC.; W. indica, A. DC. At Mahableshwur, and on other high Ghauts.

LXXVIII. GOODENOVIEÆ.

1. SCÆVOLA, Linn.

1. S Taccada, Roxb. Fl Ind. ii, p 146.—A shrub, with obovate, smooth, shining, entire leaves; peduncles axillary, short, dichotomous; flowers whitish, with a cleft tube; berries spherical, small, white when ripe. Syn. Lobelia taccada, Gaert; Buglossum littoreum, Rumph Amb. iv, *t.* 54 (?). On the sea-shore near Rutnagherry, also at Raree Fort. A species with purple fruit (S uvifera) grows at Kurrachee.

LXXIX. GESNERACEÆ.

1. DIDYMOCARPUS, Wall.

1. Cristatus, Dalz. in Hook. Jour. Bot. iii, 225.—Stem herbaceous, 8 to 9 inches high, simple erect, round, fleshy; leaves large, opposite-petioled, broadly cordate, ovate-obtuse, slightly hairy on both sides, inflorescence in the opposite axils and connate with the petioles, crested hairy, shorter than the leaf, consisting of numerous pedicels, rising upwards, and united below into a short thick peduncle; corolla white, half inch long; capsule long, slender, curved, pubescent, seeds 5-angled, oblong. On rocks near Parwar Ghaut; flowers in September and October. Allied to D crinita, Jack.

2. KLUGIA, Schlt.

1. Scabra, Dalz. Mss.—Stem terete, herbaceous, scabrous; leaves obliquely ovate-acute, entire, penni-nerved, upperside of the leaf and nerves beneath scabrous; flowers disposed in a long terminal raceme, alternate, drooping, of a deep-blue colour; pedicels shorter than the filiform bract, lower lip of corolla subentire, with a triangular acute apex; leaves 4 inches long. Warree country; flowers in the rains. Syn. Rhyncoglossum scabrum, Dalz. in Hook. Jour. Bot. ii, 140.

3. EPITHEMA, Blume.

1. Zeylanica, Gardner in Wight Ic. Pl *t.* 1354.—Pilosely hispid all over; inferior leaves opposite, or solitary by abortion, petioled, broad ovate-cordate, doubly serrate-dentate, the upper ones opposite, sessile; peduncles terminal, 1 to 3 elongated, spicate at the apex; spikes dense, secund, circinate, bracteate at the base; bracts cordate, cucullate, obtuse, dentate. On the Ghauts in the southern portion of the Presidency; flowers during the rains.

4. ÆSCHYNANTHUS, Jack.

1. Perottettii, Alph. in DC. *Prod.* 9, p 261.—Leaves lanceolate, rather obtuse at the base, obtusely acuminated at the apex, glabrous; lateral nerves few, oblique; umbels 3 to 5-flowered; pedicels twice the length of the calyx; flowers red, two inches long; capsule three inches long. Parwar Ghaut; flowers in October. Syn. Ae. zeylanica, Gardner (?) in Wight Ic. *t.* 1347 (?).

LXXX. LENTIBULARIACEÆ.

1. UTRICULARIA.

1. Reticulata, Smith Exot. Bot. *t.* 119.—Annual, twining; leaves linear oblong-obtuse; stem branched, many-flowered; scales ovate, acute, sessile; bracts tern, ovate-lanceolate; calycine segments ovate acuminate equal; flowers rather large, blue, the throat reticulated with darker veins; spur conical, about equal to the lower lip. Common in rice fields in the rains.

2. Nivea, Vahl. Enum. i, p 203.—3 to 4 inches high, leafless; scales adnate, with the base free; flowers few, white, the upper lip linear-erect, 2-toothed, lower ovate, half the length of the conical spur; capsules nodding, globose. At Vingorla; in the rains.

3. Stellaris, Linn. Fil Suppl. p 86.—Aquatic; leaves verticelled, bipinnatifid, segments capillary, bearing bladders near the base; scape ascending, many-flowered; flowers yellow, calycine segments ovate-obtuse, upper lip of corolla entire, lower longer than the sac-formed spur. In tanks throughout the Concans.

4. Albocœrulea, Dalz. in Hook. Jour. Bot. iii, p 279.—Scape round, erect, 4 to 6 inches high, root with bladders; leaves soon falling off, spathulate obscurely 3-nerved, 2 to 3 lines long, also bearing bladders; scales few, acute, fixed by their base; flowers few, blue and white, upper lip round, entire or emarginate, lower very much larger, twice as long as the acute-descending spur. Vingorla. S U smithiana, Wight Ic. (?)

5. Decipiens, Dalz. loc. cit.—Scape round, 3 to 9 inches high, straight or twining, root with bladders; leaves deciduous, obovate

spathulate, 2 to 4 lines long; scales few, acute, fixed by the base; flowers few, purple, upper lip obovate, cuneate emarginate, lower much larger, entire or emarginate about the length of the acute-depending spur. Vingorla, in the rains. Syn. U affinis, Wight Ic. *t.* 1580, *fig* 1.

6. ORBICULATA, Wall. list. No. 1500, DC. *Prod.* 8, p 18.—One to 2 inches high; leaves radical, rounded, obovate, entire, attenuated into a very slender petiole, scape very slender, erect, 3 to 4-flowered; pedicels twice the length of the flower; flowers purple, the lower lip with a yellow spot in the centre; seeds oblong, covered with glochidate bristles. On the face of moist rocks in the Concans. Syn. U pussilla, Grah. Cat. Bomb. Pl p 165; U glochidiata, Wight Ic. *t.* 1581. The seeds are curious and beautiful objects.

7. U ARCUATA, Wight Ic. *t.* 1570 and 1571.—Flowers few, calyx lobes subequal, upper a little larger, broadly ovate or cordate-ovate, upper lip of corolla suborbicular, obovate or obcordate, entire, or more or less deeply emarginate, lower lip large, entire, rarely emarginate, spur long, slender, linear subulate, pendent, or falcately curved. Concans and Belgaum. Bombay, gathered by Jacquemont.

LXXXI. PRIMULACEÆ.

1. ANAGALLIS, Tournef.

1. A ARVENSIS, Linn. sp. 211.—Stems procumbent, branched; branches elongated, quadrangular, shortly winged; leaves opposite or tern, ovate sessile, acutish; peduncles longer than the leaf; calyx-leaves linear lanceolate; flowers blue or rose-coloured. Deccan. Found from Europe to New Holland.

LXXXII. MYRSINACEÆ.

1. MAESA, Forsk.

1. INDICA, DC. *Prod.* 8, p 80.—A shrub; leaves alternate, oblong acute, grossly serrate, smooth, 3 to 6 inches long; racemes axillary and terminal, simple, branched and panicled; flowers numerous, very small, diverging, pure white; fruit size of a small pea; used to poison fish; seeds numerous, angular. Very common along the Ghauts. Syn. Baeobotrys indica, Roxb. Fl Ind. i, 557. Native name "Atkee."

2. EMBELIA, Juss.

1. BASAAL, Alph., DC. *Prod.* 8, p 87.—A shrub, 4 to 5 feet high; leaves ovate, acute, entire; racemes lateral, one-third shorter than the leaf; flowers very small, greenish-yellow; petals acumi-

nated; berries size of a pepper corn, globose, red when ripe. Vingorla, plentiful.

2. E GLANDULIFERA, R. Wight Ic. 1207.—Shrubby, glabrous; leaves ovate-lanceolate, obtusely acuminate, entire, furnished with numerous hollow glands on either side of the midrib; flowers small, panicled or racemose axillary; petals elliptic, puberulous; fruit small, globose. The Ghauts.

3. E RIBES, Burm. Ind. 62, *t.* 23.—Branches glabrous; leaves ovate, obtusely acuminate, entire, coriaceous, shortly petioled; panicle many-flowered, much-branched; petals elliptic-ciliated; fruit like pepper corns, sold in all the bazars under the name of "Waiwurung." The Ghauts.

3. ARDISIA, Swartz.

1. HUMILIS, Vahl. Symb. p 40.—A handsome evergreen shrub; leaves obovate lanceolate obtuse, entire, coriaceous, narrowed into the petiole, quite smooth; racemes axillary and terminal umbellate, drooping, shorter than the leaf; calycine lobes rounded, subciliate; flowers of a beautiful rose-colour, shining; segments of corolla lanceolate-acute. Common on the Ghauts to the south. Syn. Tonus humilis, Burm. Zeyl. *t.* 103; Anguillaria zeylanica, Gaert. Fr i, *t.* 77; A solanacea, Roxb. Fl. Ind. i, 580; Bot. Mag. *t.* 1677; A umbellata, Roxb. Fl Ind. i, 582. Native name "Dikna."

4. ÆGICERAS.

1. MAJUS, Gærtn. Fr. i, p 216.—A milky shrub; leaves obovate, rounded-obtuse, often retuse; flowers pure white, fragrant, in terminal umbels; fruit elongated, falcate, 3 to 4 times longer than the pedicel. Common in salt marshes, in company with the different species of Mangrove. Syn. Mangium fruticosum corniculatum, Rumph. Amb. iii, *t.* 77; Rhizophora corniculata, Linn. sp. p 635; Aeg. fragrans, Kœnig. Ann. of Bot. i, *t.* 3; Aeg. obovatum, Blum. This tree is well described in Arrian's account of Alexander's expedition. No. 816 of Graham's Catalogue is most probably Blackwellia.

LXXXIII. JASMINACEÆ.

1. JASMINUM, Linn.

1. SAMBAC, Ait. Hort. Kew. i, p 8.—Shrubby, somewhat climbing; branches and petioles hairy; leaves simple, shortly-petioled, ovate or subcordate, often acute, rather smooth; racemes terminal, few-flowered; calycine lobes about 8, subulate. Native

name "Bhut Mogra." Syn. Nyctanthes sambac, Linn. sp. p 8; Mogorium sambac, Lam. Illust., p 23; J fragrans, Salisb. *Prod.* 12. Cultivated for its fragrant flowers, but supposed to be indigenous.

2. PUBESCENS, Willd. sp. i, 36.—Branchlets hirsute; leaves opposte, shortly-petioled, cordate mucronate, tomentose beneath; flowerss ubsessile, in terminal umbels; calycine lobes 6 to 9, filiform hirsute; corol lobes oval mucronate. South Concan. Syn. Nyctanthes pubescens, Retz. Obs. v, p 9; Nyct. hirsuta, Linn. sp. p 8; J hirsutum, Willd i, p 36; Bot. Mag. *t.* 1931; Bot. Reg. *t.* 15; Nyctanthes multiflora, Burm. Ind. v, *t.* 3; Mogorium pubescens, Lam. Dict. iv, p 213; Rheed. Mal. *t.* 54 and 55.

3. LATIFOLIUM, Roxb. Fl Ind. i, p 93.—Shrubby, climbing, leaves cordate and oblong-acute, glabrous; corymbs terminal, diffuse; calycine lobes 5 to 7, subulate; corol lobes 8 to 12, linear cuspidate; berries kidney-shaped and oblong. Very common in Ghaut Districts; flowers large, white, fragrant. Syn. J trichotomum B latifolium, Roth. nov. sp. p 7. Native name "Koosur."

4. J ROTTLERIANUM, R. Wight Ic. 1249.—Everywhere except the flowers hairy; branches terete; leaves elliptic-obtuse at the base, acute at the apex; petioles jointed in the middle; peduncles 3, terminal, bearing fascicle of white flowers on the apex; bracts linear lanceolate, acuminate; lobes of corolla 5 to 7, oblong mucronate. Sivapore jungles, Warree.

5. J BRACTEATUM, Roxb.—Scandent; branches terete, elongated, velvetty; leaves ovate oblong, acute, villous, with short petioles; fascicle terminal, subsessile, 3 to 11-flowered; bracts broadly ovate-cordate; calyx lobes subulate; lobes of corolla oblong, obtuse, apiculate. Found on Mount Aboo by Dr. Stocks. Wight Ic. 1248.

2. SCHREBERA, Roxb.

1. SWIETENIOIDES, Roxb. Cor. *t.* 101.—A tall tree, glabrous; leaves imparipinnate; leaflets 3 to 4 pair, obliquely ovate-acuminate; panicles terminal, trichotomous, minutely bracteated; flowers whitish; capsule pyriform, hard bilocular, bivalved. Common below the Thul Ghaut, not found in the South. Native name "Moka." Wood white, close-grained, and excellent for turners.

LXXXIV. SAPOTACEÆ.

1. CHRYSOPHYLLUM, Linn.

1. ROXBURGHII, Don. Gen. *syst.* Gard. iv, p 33.—A very large tree; leaves 3 to 4 inches long, alternate lanceolate, acuminate, glabrous; pedicels axillary, fascicled, recurved, as long as the petiole; fruit of the size and appearance of an apple, very pulpy

and glutinous, 5-seeded. On Chorla Ghaut and in the Soonda Jungles; fruit ripe in March. Indigenous also in Silhet. DC. *Prod.* 8, 162. Syn. C acuminatum, Roxb. Fl Ind. i, 599. Native name "Tursiphul" (?).

2. SAPOTA, Plum.

1. Tomentosa, DC. *Prod.* 8, 175.—A tree, frequently armed with blunt thorns; leaves oval, undulated, bluntly acuminated, young ones covered with tawny tomentum; flowers numerous fascicled, axillary, of a dull white, appear in February and March; berry ovate, size of an olive. Common along the higher Ghauts. Sambre are fond of the fruit, Dr. Gibson. Syn. Sideroxylon tomentosum, Roxb. Fl Ind. i, 602. Native name "Kanta Koomla" or "Koombul."

3. ISONANDRA, Wight.

1. Candolliana, R. Wight Ic. 1220.—Arboreous; leaves obovate oblong; bluntly acuminate, tapering at the base, glabrous beneath; flowers rather small, axillary, sessile; corolla deeply 4-cleft; lobes emarginate, much longer than the stamens. On the Ghauts, not uncommon. The famous Gutta-percha tree belongs to this genus.

4. BASSIA, Kœnig.

1. B Longifolia, Linn. Maut. p 563.—A large tree; leaves lanceolate, acute at both ends; petioles slightly villous; pedicels half the length of the leaf, suberect; corolla 8 to 9-divided; stamens 16 to 20, in a double series. Confined entirely to the southern limits in the latitude of Dharwar; in Canara, common.

2. B Elliptica, Dalz. in Hook. Jour. Bot. iii, p 36 (1851).—A tree; leaves elliptic or elliptic-obovate, shortly and obtusely acuminate, coriaceous, smooth on both sides; pedicels axillary, twin or tern, 3 to 4 times longer than the petiole, in fruit erect; filaments in one series, those opposite the corol lobes are in pairs, those alternate with them single; fruit oblong, smooth, along with the preceding. This tree has been found to yield a kind of Gutta-percha; the date of publication has been mentioned, because in a pamphlet on this tree, published by Dr. Cleghorn in 1858, that gentleman states that he could find no account of it, and that he believed the tree was unknown to naturalists.

3. Latifolia, Roxb. Fl Ind. ii, 526.—A large tree, branched like an oak; leaves elliptic-oblong or oval, membranaceous, subacute, 4 to 8 inches long; pedicels about the apex of branchlets, subumbellate, reflexed, covered with tawny tomentum; berry oblong, of the size of a small apple, 1 to 4-seeded. The Concans; much

more plentiful in Gujarat and Rajwara. The Mowah tree, from the flowers of which the Mowra spirit is distilled. The seeds yield a large quantity of thick oil. The wood is hard and very strong, and proper for naves of wheels, Roxb. The oil is used in making soap in the Kaira Zillah.

5. MIMUSOPS, Linn.

1. Elengi, Linn. sp. p 497.—A rather small but handsome tree, with dark-green shining leaves, elliptic-oblong, obtusely acuminated, glabrous; pedicels axillary fascicled; flowers white, the calyxes covered with rusty-coloured tomentum; berry ovoid, 1 to 2-seeded. Wild in the ravines of the Ghauts; in fruit in September. Native names "Buckhool," "Wowlee," &c. Roxb. Fl Ind. ii, 237.

2. Hexandra, Roxb. Pl Cor. i, p 16, *t.* 15.—A small rigid tree; leaves obovate-elliptic, emarginate, smooth and shining on both sides, 3 to 5 inches long; flowers axillary, 1 to 6, on pedicels shorter than the petiole; berry of the size and shape of an olive, 1 to 2-seeded, yellow edible. Roxb. Fl Ind. ii, 238. The Concans and Gujarat. Native name "Kernee." The wood is tough, and used for making sugar-mills, &c.

LXXXV. SYMPLOCACEÆ.

1. HOPEA, Linn.

1. Spicata, DC. *Prod.* 8, 254.—A middle-sized tree; leaves oblong lanceolate acute, serrated, glabrous; racemes axillary, nearly simple, scarcely longer than the petiole; flowers yellowish-white; drupe size of a pea, urceolate; seeds fluted. On the Ghauts, pretty common. Syn. Symplocos spicata, Roxb. Fl Ind. ii, 540; Eugenia laurina, Willd. sp. ii, 967; Bobua laurina, DC. *Prod.* iii, 24; Myrtus laurina, Retz. Obs. iv, p 27.

2. Racemosa, DC. *Prod.* 8, 255.—A small tree; leaves oblong lanceolate-acuminate, glabrous, subdenticulated, shining above; racemes simple axillary, equalling the petiole, hairy; drupe narrow-oblong, smooth, half an inch long, purple when ripe. On the Ghauts, common. Syn. Symplocos racemosa, Roxb. loc. cit. p 539; S theæfolia, Don. *Prod.* Fl Nep. p 145.

LXXXVI. EBENACEÆ.

1. DIOSPYROS, Dalech.

1. D Chloroxylon, Roxb. Cor. Pl p 38, *t.* 49.—A tree, with deeply cracked bark, sometimes with the branches thorny; branch-

lets tomentose; leaves small (2 inches long) elliptic-obovate, or oblong-obtuse, pubescent above, tomentose beneath; male flowers axillary fascicled (3 to 6); calyx 4-divided, divisions ovate, pubescent on the outside; corolla scarcely twice the length of the calyx, 4-lobed; female flowers solitary sessile, with 8 anthers; stigmas 4, bifid; ovary glabrous, 8-celled, anthers in the male flowers 16, in unequal pairs, a 4-lobed rudimul in the centre; anthers dehiscing, on each side of the apex; flowers small, white, appear in the beginning of June. Common about Surat, on the north side, also in Nassick Districts; fruit size of a large pea. Syn. D capitulata, Wight Ic. 1224 and 1588 (?). Native name "Ninei"; fruit eatable.

2. PANICULATA, Dalz. in Hook. Jour. Bot. iv, p 109.—Arboreous, branches glabrous; leaves lanceolate-oblong, obtusely acuminated, short-petioled, coriaceous, glabrous; male flowers numerous, panicled in the axils of the fallen leaves; panicles shorter than the leaf, with the buds and pedicels sooty velvetty; calyx 5-divided, segments foliaceous, reticulately veined, broadly oval-obtuse; corolla sooty and velvetty outside, twice as long as the calyx, the 5 divisions oblong-obtuse, as long as the tube; female flowers lateral solitary, with their pedicels as long as the petiole; female calyx increasing with the fruit; fruit ovoid, densely tomentose, included in the enlarged calyx. Chorla Ghaut and Raighur; flowers in the cool season.

3. PRURIENS, Dalz. loc. cit.—Branchlets softly hairy; leaves narrow-oblong, acuminate, subsessile, hirsute on both sides; male flowers twin, on an axillary peduncle, 3 times longer than the petiole; female flowers, axillary and lateral solitary, subsessile; fruit ovoid-conical, densely clothed with fulvous stinging hairs, the size of a large cherry. Grows in the same place as the preceding.

4. NIGRICANS, Dalz. loc. cit.—Arboreous; leaves oblong or lanceolate-acuminated, membranaceous, glabrous, 4 inches long; male flowers in threes, sessile, on the apex of a very short peduncle; calyx villous turbinate, the limb 4-divided, divisions ovate-acute, ciliated, spreading; corolla glabrous, with a short tube, divisions narrow-linear, 3 to 4 lines longer than the tube; stamens 26, in twos, threes, or fours; female flowers not seen. Chorla Ghaut.

5. GOINDU, Dalz. loc. cit.—Arboreous; leaves ovate oblong, rounded or truncate at the base, obtuse at the apex, glabrous, shortly-petioled; male flowers in threes, on an axillary peduncle as long as the petiole; female flowers axillary, solitary; calyx 4-divided, the divisions short, rounded, glabrous; corolla urceolate, segments of the limb 4, rounded; staminá 16; fruit globose, size of a cherry, yellow when ripe; flowers in April to June; allied to D cordifolia, Roxb. Common on the Ghauts. No. 830 of Graham's

Catalogue; D cordifolia, Wight Illustr. *t.* 148 (non. Roxb.); Wight Ic. 1225. Native name "Goindu."

6. Candolliana, Wight Ic. 1221.—Arboreous glabrous; leaves elliptic-oblong, obtusely acuminate, flowers axillary aggregated sessile; calyx 4 to 5-cleft; of the female, revolute on the margin; corolla tubular, 4 to 5-cleft; stamens of the male 10, filaments united by pairs, of the female 4 to 5, sterile; fruit ovoid, hard, about the size of a nutmeg. Distinguished from all the others by its veinless leaves. The Ghauts, common.

7. D Exsculpta, Ham. in Linn. Trans. xv, p 111.—A small tree; branchlets, peduncles, and flowers clothed with ferruginous tomentum; leaves large, broad-elliptic, tomentose beneath; peduncles of male flowers as long as the petiole, 3-flowered; fruit size of a pigeon's egg, smooth, eatable. Native name "Timboornee." No. 826 of Graham's Catalogue; Wight Ic. 182 and 183.

8. D Montana, Roxb. Cor. Pl. *t.* 48.—A small tree, with or without thorns on the stem; leaves ovate-acute, obtuse at the base, smooth, membranaceous, male racemes 5 to 6-flowered, double the length of the petiole; female flowers solitary; drupe globose, slightly depressed, rather hard, olive-coloured. This species is not unlike D Goindu, but has much larger leaves and fruit, and more numerous flowers. The Ghauts to the north; hills around Hewra.

2. HOLOCHILUS, Dalz.

1. H Micranthus, Dalz. in Hook. Jour. Bot. iv, p 290.—A middle-sized tree; leaves elliptic or oblong, attenuated at the base, obtusely acuminated, shortly petioled, coriaceous, smooth; flowers minute, white, axillary solitary, sessile, diœcious; calyx tube entire truncated; corol tubular, 3-divided to the middle; stamens in the female flower 6, sterile; fruit cylindric-oblong, hard, dry, 1 inch long, 6-celled; seeds solitary, pendent. On the Southern Ghauts; flowers in February and March; male flowers not yet seen.

3. MABA, Forst.

1. M Nigrescens, Dalz.—A small tree with rigidly erect branches, young branchlets covered with rusty or tawny pubescence; leaves small, shining, subsessile, ovate or oval-acute, margins slightly recurved and undulated; leaves beneath, especially on the margin and midrib, clothed with tawny adpressed hairs. Pretty common in the Ghaut jungles. Native name "Ruktroora." The leaves turn black in drying, and appear quite veinless. Allied to M Guineensis.

LXXXVII. AZIMACEÆ, Gard. and Wight.

1. AZIMA, Lam.

1. A Tetracantha, Lam. Illustr. Gen. *t.* 807.—Diœcious, shrubby; branches opposite, tetragonal, spreading, thorny; leaves opposite-petioled, acute, entire, smooth; flowers axillary, clustered, very shortly peduncled; berries white. At Gokak; Dharwar fort; also the Hubshee's Country near the sea, &c. Syn. Monetia barlerioides, Herit. Wight Illustr. *t.* 153.

LXXXVIII. AQUIFOLIACEÆ.

1. ILEX, Linn.

1. I Wightiana, Wall., Wight Ic. 1216.—A tree, glabrous; leaves ovate-elliptic or elliptic-acuminate, entire, coriaceous; umbels of flowers numerous, axillary, or from the scars of the fallen leaves; pedicels about the length of the peduncles, often longer; corolla white, 5 to 6-cleft; berry 5 to 6-seeded, size of a small pea, red when ripe. The Ghauts; flowers in March and April.

LXXXIX. APOCYNACEÆ.

1. CARISSA, Linn.

1. Carandas, Linn. Maut. p 52.—A very common thorny shrub; leaves oval, shortly petioled, coriaceous, glabrous, shining above; peduncles terminal, 3 to 5-flowered, shorter than the leaf; flowers white, like a Jasmine; berry oval, reddish or purple, ripe in May, eatable. Syn. Lycium malabaricum, Pluk. Alm. *t.* 305. *fig.* 4; Carandas, Rumph. Amb. vii, p 57; Echites spinosa, Burm. Ind; Capparis carandas, Gmel. *syst.* i, p 806. Native name "Corinda."

2. Lanceolata, Dalz. Mss.—A thorny shrub; leaves 3 to 4 inches long, lanceolate, coriaceous, glabrous; fruit size of a plum, purple when ripe, glutinous, far superior in flavour to the preceding. Ram Ghaut; fruit ripe in May.

3. Hirsuta, Roth. nov. sp. p 128.—Branches thorny, tomentose; leaves roundish or ovate, hairy on both sides, 1 to 1½ inch long; peduncles terminal and axillary, 3 to 7-flowered, shorter than the leaf; berry globose, of the size of a pea, smooth, dark-purple. Hills eastward of Belgaum. Syn. C villosa, Roxb. Fl Ind. ii, 525; Wight. Ic. *t.* 437.

2. OPHIOXYLON, Linn.

1. Serpentinum, Linn. Willd. *syst.* iv., p 979.—A very small shrub; leaves opposite or verticelled in threes, oblong-acute,

undulate, 3 to 6 inches long; cymes subterminal from the uppermost axils; flowers numerous, small, white or rosy; peduncles and pedicels at length bright-red; berries ovoid, 1-seeded, small, shining. The Concans, common. Syn. O trifoliatum and Album, Gaert. Fr. ii, p 129; Rumph. Herb. Amb. vii, 30 (?). Used to poison tigers.

2. NEILGHERRYENSE, R. Wight Ic. 1292.—Shrubby, erect, glabrous; leaves confined to the terminal ramuli, older branches naked; leaves oblong-elliptic, broader towards the apex, acute at both ends; corymbs axillary, cymose trichotomous; flowers white; berries connate at the base, ovoid, dark, brownish-purple when ripe.

3. TABERNÆMONTANA, Plum.

1. CRISPA, Roxb. Fl Ind. 2, p 24.—A shrub, with dichotomous branches; leaves oblong-acute undulated, glabrous, 4 to 8 inches long; peduncles arising from the forks, few-flowered; pedicels elongated; flowers large, white, the margins of the petals crisped and curled, follicles curved, oblong-acute, 2 inches long, yellow when ripe. On the Ghauts, pretty common. Wight Ic. *t.* 470; Syn. T alternifolia, Linn. sp. p 308.

2. CORONARIA, Br. in Hort. Kew. ii, p 72.—A shrub very like the preceding; leaves opposite unequal, elliptic-oblong, acute at the base, obtusely acuminated; peduncles from the forks twin, erect, dichotomous, 4 to 6-flowered; flowers white, fragrant at night. On the Meera hills, near Penn. The double variety is common in gardens. Roxb. Fl Ind. ii, p 23; Wight Ic. *t.* 477; Syn. Nandi ervatam; Rheed Mal. ii, *t.* 54 and 55; Flos Manilhanus, Rumph. Amb. iv, p 87; Nerium divaricatum, Linn sp. p 306; Jasminum zeylanicum, Burm. Zeyl. *t.* 39; Nerium coronarium, Jacq; Bot. Mag. *t.* 1865.

4. VINCA, Linn.

1. PUSILLA, Murr. Act. Goett. 1772, p 66, *t.* 2, *fig.* 1.—A small annual herbaceous plant, stem erect, quadrangular, glabrous; leaves narrow lanceolate, rough on the margin; flowers very small, white, solitary in the axils of the leaves; follicles slender, 1½ inch long. Wag Donger, near Vingorla. The Deccan, common; Syn. V parviflora, Retz. Obs. ii, No. 33; Roxb. Fl Ind. ii, p 1; Catharanthus pusillus, Don. *syst.* Gard. iv, p 95.

5. VALLARIS, Burm.

1. HEYNEI, Spr. *syst.* i, p 635.—A twining shrubby plant; leaves elliptic, acuminated, glabrous; racemes subcorymbose, pubescent; flowers rather large, white, rotate; the lobes of the corolla

obtuse; follicles oblong, large, six inches long, 2 inches thick. In the Concans; common even in the Deccan. Syn. Peltanthera solanacea, Roth. nov. sp. p 132; Echites dichotoma, Roxb. Fl Ind. ii, p 19.

6. WRIGHTIA, R. Br.

1. TOMENTOSA, Rœm. and Schult. *syst.* iv, p 414.—A small tree; leaves elliptic-lanceolate or elliptic, attenuated at the base, pubescent, with dark-coloured tomentum; corymbs dense, rigid, terminal; flowers yellowish; follicles 8 to 9 inches long, scabrous. Very common on the Northern Ghauts. Yields a yellow juice, which may be serviceable as a dye. Syn. Nerium tomentosum, Roxb. Fl Ind. ii, p 6; W tomentosa, Wight Ic. 443; W pubescens, Roth. nov. sp. 120 and 397. Native name "Kala Inderjow."

2. TINCTORIA, Br. Mem. Wern. Soc. i, 73.—A small tree; leaves elliptic-lanceolate and ovate, obtusely acuminated, glabrous, membranaceous, panicles terminal, lax, many-flowered; flowers white, fragrant, appear in April; follicles very long and slender, pendulous, as thick as a quill. Jungles south of Nagotna, and many other places. The wood of this tree is remarkably white and close-grained, coming nearer to ivory than any other I know of, Roxb. Indigo is made from the leaves and tender branches. Native name "Kala Koora."

3. WALLICHII.—A shrub; leaves elliptic-obovate, acute at the base, obtusely acuminated, covered all over with dark-brown tomentum; calycine lobes broadly ovate-rounded; scales inside ovate-rounded, half the length of the lobes; flowers and follicles very like those of Tomentosa. In the Warree Country, very common; a native also of Burmah.

7. HOLARRHENA, R. Br.

1. ANTIDYSENTERICA, Wall. list No. 1672.—A shrub; branches, leaves, and peduncles glabrous; leaves elliptic, very obtuse at the base, acute or abruptly acuminated at the apex; cymes many-flowered, terminal; flowers puberulous, white, appear in April and May; follicles 1 foot long. Very common in the Concans. Syn. Chonemorpha antidysenterica, Don. Gen. *syst.* Gard. iv, p 79; Wight Ic. *t.* 439. This plant furnishes the officinal Conessi bark, used in fever and diarrhœa, and which contains an uncrystallisable alkaloid. Native name "Dowla Koora."

8. ALSTONIA, R. Br.

1. SCHOLARIS, Br. Mem. Wern. Soc. i, 75.—A large spreading tree; leaves in verticels of 5 to 7, obovate-oblong, acute at the

base, obtuse at the apex, glabrous and shining above, paler beneath; cyme globose, compound, many-flowered; flowers greenish-white, subsessile, fascicled, pubescent, woolly in the throat, follicles a foot long. Pretty common in the jungly parts of the Concan; very large trees in Rairee Fort. Native name "Satween." Wight Ic. *t.* 422; Syn. Pala, Rheed. Mal. i, *t.* 45; Lignum scholare, Rumph. Amb. ii, p 246; Echites scholaris, Linn. The bark possesses very powerful tonic properties, and may prove useful in agues; a common rustic medicine in bowel disorders, Nimmo; the wood is as bitter as Gentian. (*Vide* Pharmac. Journal 1852 accounts by Dr. Gibson of its virtues.)

9. HELIGME, Blume.

1. H Rheedei, R. Wight. Ic. 1303.—Twining, glabrous; leaves ovate-acute, short-petioled, corymbs trichotomous, many-flowered; calyx lobes ovate-obtuse, ciliated; corolla rotate, hairy within, filaments beautifully twisted into a spiral column; follicles 2-celled, seeds comose at the apex. Near Banda, in the Warree Country.

10. ELLERTONIA, Wight.

1. E Rheedei, Wight Ic. *t.* 1295.—A scandent shrub with opposite or verticellate leaves, which are elliptic-acuminate, coriaceous, glabrous; corymbs axillary, or several, from the ends of the branches, longish-peduncled, cymose, many-flowered; corolla hypocrateriform, revolute; follicles terete, divaricated. In the Warree Country.

11. CHONEMORPHA, G. Don.

1. Macrophylla, G. Don. Gen. *syst.* Gard. iv, p 76.—A large climbing shrub; branches strong, covered with ovate warts; leaves broadly oval cuspidate, subcordate at the base, pubescent beneath, membranaceous, 10 to 12 inches long, 6 to 10 inches broad; cymes erect, stalked, shorter than the leaf, subpubescent; flowers large, white, fragrant, coriaceous; follicles a foot long, rather slender and pretty smooth. At Banda, in the Warree Country. Wight Ic. *t.* 432; Syn. Echites macrophylla, Roxb. Fl Ind. ii, p 13.

12. AGANOSMA, Don.

1. A Doniana, R. Wight Ic. 1306.—Everywhere glabrous, except the inflorescence; leaves elliptic, cuspidately acuminate; corymbs terminal, compact, pilose; lobes of the calyx linear-lanceolate, longer than the tube of the corolla; follicles terete, tomentose, divaricated. Phoonda Ghaut.

2. A Concanensis, Hook. Ic. Pl ix, *t.* 841.—Climbing, glabrous; leaves broad-elliptic, ovate, very shortly acuminated, cordate at the base, membranaceous, remotely penninerved; peduncles axillary, shorter than the leaf; cymes compound dense; sepals triquetrous, acuminate; corol tube short, divisions of the limb oblong-obtuse, spreading; stamens exserted, glands 5, large, obtuse. South Concan; rare.

13. BEAUMONTIA, Wall.

1. B Jerdoniana, Wight Ic. 1314 & 1315.—A climbing shrub; leaves obovate, abruptly acuminate, 8 to 10 inches long; cymes terminal, many-flowered; corolla large, infundibuliform, 4 inches long; follicles cylindric, 9 to 10 inches long, and about 1 thick; calyx lobes narrow-lanceolate. Warree and the Southern Maratha Country; in Canara, plentiful.

14. ICHNOCARPUS, R. Br.

1. I Frutescens, Br. in Mem. Wern. Soc. i, p 61.—A climbing shrub; leaves small, elliptic-acute at both ends, hairy beneath; cymes terminal, many-flowered, covered with reddish tomentum; flowers very small, white; follicles 6 inches long; leaves 1 to 3 inches long. Common in the Warree Country, climbing over trees. Southern Maratha Country, Law; Dharwar Collectorate; Wight Ic. *t.* 430; Syn. Apocynum floribus fasciculatis, Burm; Thes. Zeyl. *t.* 12; Apocynum frutescens, Linn. sp. 312; Echites frutescens, Roxb. Fl Ind. ii, p 12.

15. ANODENDRON, DC.

1. Paniculatum, DC. *Prod.* 8, 443.—An immense climbing shrub, glabrous; leaves opposite, entire, obtusely cuspidate, coriaceous; cymes axillary and terminal, trichotomous, panicled; flowers very numerous, small, pale-yellow; follicles attenuated upwards, from an ovoid base, somewhat woody, smooth, 4 inches long. Very common on the Ghauts. Syn. Echites paniculata, Roxb. Fl Ind. p 17; Wight Ic. *t.* 396; Gymnema nepalense of Graham's Catalogue, p 120. Native name "Lamtanee"; flowers in January and March.

XC. ASCLEPIADEÆ.

1. HEMIDESMUS, R. Br.

1. H Indicus, R. Br. Mem. Wern. Soc. i, 56.—A twining, glabrous plant; leaves from ovate to narrow-linear, cuspidate;

cymes subsessile or shortly-peduncled; flowers small, deep purple inside; follicles slender, straight. A very common plant. The root is used as a substitute for Sarsaparilla, and from its aroma seems to have active properties. Wight Ic. 594; Syn. Periploca indica, Willd. sp. i, p 1251; Asclepias pseudosarsa, Roxb. Fl Ind. ii, 39; Deless Ic. v, 24, *t.* 55.

2. CRYPTOLEPIS, R. Br.

1. Puchanani, Rœm. and Schult. *syst.* iv, 409.—A milky shrub, with dark-coloured cracked bark, coming off in thin laminæ, climbing, smooth; leaves opposite, short-petioled, broad-elliptic, with a short subulate point, bright-green above, whitish and glaucous beneath, transversely veined; corymbs axillary, short-peduncled; flowers subsessile, pale-yellow; corol segments ligulate. Royle Trans. Linn Soc. xix, 53, *t.* 5; C reticulata, Royle Illustr. Him. Pl. p 1, 270; Nerium reticulatum, Roxb. Fl Ind. ii, p 9. Common in Bombay, Elephanta, the Concans, &c., and Ghauts. Wight Ic. *t.* 49.

3. TOXOCARPUS, W. and A.

1. Crassifolius, Wight Contr. p 61.—Branches sparingly pubescent; leaves oval-acuminate, glabrous on both sides, paler beneath, and with a narrow recurved margin; branches of the cyme elongated, panicled; flowers small, sessile, fascicled; divisions of the corolla reflexed at the apex, densely bearded with white hairs (collapsed tubes) within. The Ghauts. Wight Ic. *t.* 598.

4. HOLOSTEMMA, R. Br.

1. H Rheedei, Spr. *syst.* i, 851.—A twining, glabrous shrub; leaves broadly ovate-cordate, with a wide sinus, acuminated, glabrous; umbels shortly-peduncled; flowers pretty large, thick, and fleshy, red and white, fragrant; follicles ventricose, smooth. Wight Ic. 597. Very common in hedges, Bombay and the Concans. Syn. Asclepias annularis, Roxb. Fl Ind. ii, p 37; Sarcostemma annulare, Roth. nov. sp. p 178. Found also above the Ghauts.

5. CYNANCHUM.

1. Pauciflorum, R. Br.—Twining, glabrous; leaves ovate acuminate, reniformly cordate, with diverging auricles; umbels few-flowered; peduncles shorter than the petioles; flowers glabrous, on short pedicels; crown equaling corolla, with a 10-cleft plicate border, naked inside; anthers lanceolate-acuminate, bifid at the point; alternate ones very short, and emarginate or truncate. At Moosee, near Poona.

6. CALOTROPIS, R. Br.

1. C GIGANTEA, R. Br. Mem. Wern. Soc. p 28.—A tall, hoary shrub; leaves large, stem-clasping, oblong-ovate, downy beneath, 4 to 6 inches long; umbels simple or compound, interpetiolar, half the length of the leaves; flowers large, of a pale-purple; follicles ovoid ventricose, green, herbaceous. Common in the Concan, not in Gujarat. Lind. Bot. Reg. xvii. *t.* 58. The active principle Mudarine is extracted from this plant, and has the property of coagulating by heat, and becoming fluid again on exposure to cold. Syn. Asclepias gigantea, Willd. sp. i, 1264. An excellent alterative, and powerful as a remedy in cutaneous diseases.

2. C PROCERA, R. Br. in Hort. Kew. ii, p 78.—A shrub like the preceding, but generally smaller; leaves ovate or oval, with a cordate base, and with a short and sudden acumination, 4 inches long; umbels peduncled, nearly as long as the leaves; flowers as in the preceding; follicles obovoid, downy, as large as an egg. The Deccan and Guzerat, also in Sind, Persia, Arabia, and Africa. Syn. C wallichii, Wight Contr. p 53; C hamiltonii, Wight loc. cit; C heterophylla, Wall. in Wight Contr. p 54; Wight Ic. 1278. From this plant has been extracted hemp of the finest quality, very strong and silky. Handkerchiefs of fine quality have been made from it.

7. SARCOSTEMMA, R. Br.

1. S BREVISTIGMA, W. and A. Contr. p 59.—Leafless, twining; umbels terminal, or at the apex of short lateral branchlets; pedicels and calyx smooth; divisions of corolla ovate, rather obtuse, smooth; exterior staminal corona with 10 folds; interior ones gibbous on the back, and longer than the gynostegium; flowers white. Common in the Deccan in stony places; flowers in June. Syn. Asclepias acida, Roxb. Fl Ind. ii, p 31; Jacq. Voy. *t.* 113.

2. INTERMEDIUM, DeCaisne in DC. *Prod.* 8, p 538.—Twining, leafless; branches round, glabrous; peduncles terminal or axillary; umbels many-flowered, sub-globose; divisions of corolla oblong-lanceolate, waved, glabrous; follicles linear or oblong obtuse; flowers white, appear in the rains. Throughout the Deccan; Isle of Perim, Dr. Lush. Syn. Sarcostemma viminale, Wight Contr. p 59. Used in the culture of Sugar-cane to keep off White Ants. Wight Ic. 1281.

8. PENTATROPIS, R. Br.

1. MICROPHYLLA, W. and A. Contr. p 52.—A twining glabrous plant; leaves oval-mucronulate, rounded at the base, glabrous, fleshy, shortly-petioled; umbels subsessile, few-flowered; pedicels

filiform; flowers greenish; divisions of the corol lanceolate, reflexed. Bombay, Salsette, Gujarat, and Deccan, plentiful. Syn. Asclepias microphylla, Roxb. Fl Ind. ii, p 35; Heyne in Roth. nov. sp. p 177; Wight Ic. 352. A type of the desert Flora.

9. OXYSTELMA, R. Br.

1. Esculentum, R. Br. Mem. Wern. Soc. i, p 40.—Twining, perennial; leaves linear or linear-lanceolate, mucronate, glabrous; peduncles 1 to 5-flowered; margins of corolla ciliated; flowers large, pale rose-coloured, streaked with purple; follicles oblong, obtusely acuminated, very handsome. The Concans and Deccan, rare. Syn. Periploca esculenta, Linn. Fil. suppl. p 168; Willd. sp. Pl 1250; Roxb. Cor. *t.* 11; Asclepias rosea, Roxb. Fl Ind. ii, p 40.

10. DŒMIA, R. Br.

1. Extensa, R. Br. loc. cit.—Twining, perennial; branches hoary and hairy; leaves subrotund, cordate, acuminate, pubescent, membranaceous; peduncles and pedicels long, slender; flowers drooping, dull-white; follicles covered with soft bristles, and with a curved beak. Northern Concan, and Gujarat; flowers in January. Syn. Cynanchum extensum, Ait. Hort. Kew. i, 303; C cordifolium, Retz. Obs. ii, p 15; Asclepias echinata, Roxb. Fl Ind. ii, p 44; A convolvulaceæ, Willd. sp. Pl i, 1269; A dœmia, Forsk. Fl Ægypt, p 51; Wight Ic. 596.

11. TYLOPHORA, R. Br.

1. Carnosa, Wall., Wight and Arn. Contr. p 49.—Twining, glabrous; stems and branches slender; leaves fleshy-ovate or elliptic-ovate mucronate, shining, paler beneath; petioles pubescent above; peduncles longer than the petioles, several flowered; pedicels filiform; flowers small, purple, inside leaflets of the staminal crown suborbicular; leaves 1 to 2 inches long, 6 to 9 lines broad. Wight Ic. *t.* 351.

2. Tenuissima, Wight and Arn. Contr. p 49.—Twining, glabrous; branches slender; leaves oblong-lanceolate, subcordate at the base, cuspidate, veinless, revolute on the margin; peduncles flexuous, having several filiform pedicels at the bends; flowers small; leaflets of the staminal crown ovate-oblong. Wight Ic. 588; Syn. Asclepias tenuissima, Roxb. Fl Ind. ii, p 44; Rœm. and Schult. *syst.* vi, p 85.

3. Asthmatica, Wight and Arn. Contr. p 51.—Twining, glabrous, or pubescent; branches slender; leaves ovate or somewhat rounded-acuminate, often cordate at the base, glabrous above;

petioles nearly round without glands; peduncles shorter than the leaf, bearing towards the apex, 2 to 3 sessile, few-flowered umbels; flowers rather large, long-pedicelled, divisions of the corolla acute. Wight Ic. 1277; Syn. Asclepias asthmatica, Roxb. Fl Ind. ii, p 33; Willd. sp. p 1270; Cynanchum vomitorium, Lam. Encycl. ii, p 235; C ipecacuana, Willd. Jaterb. der. Pharm; C indicum, Burm; C viridiflorum, Bot. Mag. *t.* 1929; Pluk. *t.* 336, *f.* 7.

4. Fasciculata, Ham., Wight and Arn. Contr. p 50.—Erect, or scarcely twining, glabrous; leaves approximated, ovate, rather obtuse, rather fleshy, decreasing in size upwards; peduncles erect, flexuous, bearing at the flexures 2 to 3 few-flowered fascicles. Southern Concan. Wight Ic. *t.* 848.

12. COSMOSTIGMA, Wight.

1. Racemosum, Wight Contr. p 41.—Shrubby, climbing; branchlets piped; leaves broadly-ovate or rounded-acuminate, obtuse or cordate at the base, glabrous; peduncles interpetiolar; corymbose racemose at the apex; flowers small, yellow, marked with ferruginous dots; follicles large, linear oblong-obtuse, smooth. Common in hedges; flowers in the rains. Syn. Asclepias racemosa, Roxb. Fl Ind. ii, p 32; Deless. Ic. Select. v, 35, *t.* 84; Wight Ic. 591.

13. GYMNEMA, R. Br.

1. Sylvestre, R. Br. Wern. Soc. i, 33.—Shrubby, climbing, all except the upperside of the leaves softly pubescent; leaves ovate or ovate-lanceolate, attenuated at both ends, or obscurely cordate at the base; peduncles as long as the petioles; umbels twin, many-flowered; flowers crowded, small, yellow; follicles slender, attenuated, glabrous. The Ghauts and Southern Maratha Country, Law; Wight. Ic. *t.* 349; Syn. G parviflorum, Wall. Tent. Fl Nep. p 50; Periploca sylvestris, Willd. sp. i, 1252; Asclepias geminata, Roxb. Fl Ind. ii, p 45; Wight Ic. 349.

14. BIDARIA, Endl.

1. Elegans, DeCaisne DC. *Prod.* 8, p 623.—Twining; branches slender, smooth; leaves cordate-ovate or oval-acuminate, waved on the margin, quite smooth; petioles puberulous; umbels at first shortly peduncled, after elongated spirally, of the same length as the pedicels; flowers small, greenish-yellow; follicles acuminate, 3 inches long, 3 to 4 lines thick. On the higher Ghauts. Syn. Gymnema elegans, Wight Contr. p 46.

15. LEPTADENIA, R. Br.

1. Reticulata, Wight Contr. p 47.—Shrubby, bark corky, twining, younger branches ash-coloured, pubescent; leaves ovate or lanceolate-acute, glabrous or pubescent; umbels lateral, many-flowered, as long as the petiole; segments of the corolla revolute on the margin, bearded within; flowers greenish-yellow; follicles cylindrical oblong-obtuse. Very common, particularly near the sea. Syn. Cynanchum reticulatum, Retz. Obs. ii, p 15; Asclepias suberosa, Roxb. Fl Ind. ii, 38; Secamone canescens, Smith in Ree's Cycl; Wight Ic. 350.

2. Jacquemontiana, DeCaisne Etud. Asclep.—An erect, much-branched, broom-like shrub; branches twiggy, slender; leaves narrow-linear (on the younger branches only); umbels few-flowered, very shortly-peduncled; flowers very small, yellow; follicles 4 inches long, slender, smooth. On the sea-shore south of Gogo, plentiful. DeCaisne describes this as leafless, but this is a mistake. Very common in Sind, where it is called "Kip." Ropes are made from it.

16. HETEROSTEMMA, W. and A.

1. Wallichii, Wight. Contr. p 42.—Twining; branches with two opposite lines of hairs; leaves ovate-acuminate glabrous, 4 to 8 inches long; peduncles very short, few-flowered; flowers fuscous within; follicles 4 inches long, smooth, purple, blunt-pointed; seeds few. Near Malwan; flowers in September.

2. Urceolatum, Dalz. in Hook. Jour. Bot. iv, p 295.—Stem twining, purple, puberulous; leaves petioled, herbaceous, glabrous, broadly ovate, acute-cordate at the base, and furnished with a gland; umbels very shortly-peduncled, few-flowered; corolla deeply urceolate, reddish-purple, 8 to 10 lines long. On hills near Belgaum, also at Rewadunda; flowers in July.

17. HOYA, R. Br.

1. Pallida, Lind. Bot. Reg. 951.—Parasitic, climbing; leaves ovate lanceolate-acuminate, fleshy, veined; umbel of flowers compact, hemispherical. Very like H carnosa, but much paler, and the divisions of the corolla more acute. Very common on trees.

2. Pendula, Wight. Contr. p 36.—Twining; leaves oval oblong-acute or broadly ovate-acuminate; peduncles longer than the petiole, pendulous, many-flowered; corolla pubescent within; flowers in the rains. Hills near Nagotna; Southern Concan, Nimmo. Syn Asclepias pendula, Roxb. Fl Ind. ii, p 36; Rheed. Mal. ix, *t.* 13; Wight Ic. 474.

3. RETUSA, Dalz. in Hook. Jour. Bot. iv, p 294.—Parasitic, pendulous, glabrous; branches long, filiform, terete; leaves short-petioled, linear, 3-sided, fleshy, glabrous, retuse at the apex; flowers on a very short axillary peduncle, solitary or twin fascicled, long-pedicelled; flowers white, shining. Dandelly jungles; flowers in the rains; has the habits of H pauciflora, R. Wight Ic. *t.* 1269.

4. VIRIDIFLORA, R. Br. Wern. Soc. i, p 27.—Twining; leaves ovate or cordate-acuminate, smooth on both sides; peduncles often as long as the petiole, and with pedicels glabrous; flowers, grow in drooping umbels, which appear in May; follicles divaricate, thick-obtuse, covered with rusty-coloured farina, or smooth. Very common in hedges. Maratha name "Doree," owing to its being used as rope. Wight in Hook. Bot. Misc. ii, p 98; Suppl. *t.* 1; Rheed. Mal. ix, p 25, *t.* 15; Asclepias volubilis, Linn. Suppl. 170; Willd. sp. i, p 1279; "Hirun Doree," Maratha name.

18. CEROPEGIA, Linn.

1. JACQUEMONTIANA, DeCaisne in DC. *Prod.* 8, 641.—Herbaceous, twining, hairy; leaves ovate or ovate-lanceolate, subcordate or rounded at the base, pubescent on both sides; peduncles hispid, shorter than the leaf, several-flowered; sepals linear-lanceolate; corolla club-shaped, base ventricose, greenish, of a lurid purple below, spotted above; divisions oblong, broader upwards, smooth; follicles straight, smooth; root tuberous, about 2 inches long. Near Vingorla; near Karlee, Jacq.

2. JUNCEA, Roxb. Cor. i, p 12, *t.* 10.—Twining, glabrous, rather fleshy; leaves small, sessile, lanceolate-acute; peduncles few-flowered, sepals subulate; corolla club-shaped; ventricose at the base; divisions ligulate-ciliated, connate; follicles attenuated, smooth. Kasersaye jungles, Lush.

3. VINCÆFOLIA, Bot. Mag. *t.* 3740.—Twining, pubescent; leaves subcordate or broadly ovate-acuminate, shortly-petioled; peduncles with spreading hairs, few-flowered; tube of corolla ventricose at the base, white spotted; divisions oblong erect, connivent, ciliated, dark-purple. Near Bombay, Nimmo. Comes near to the first species.

4. BULBOSA, Roxb. Cor. i, p 11, *t.* 7.—Twining, glabrous, fleshy; lowest leaves nearly orbicular, uppermost ones ovate, apiculate, almost veinless, smooth; peduncles shorter than the leaf, several-flowered; corol tube subclavate, divisions ciliated, violet-coloured within; root bulbous. Wight Ic. 845; Roxb. Fl Ind. ii, 28. Malabar Hill, Island of Caranjah, &c. Hook. Bot. Misc. Suppl.; Wight Ic. *t.* 845.

5. ACUMINATA, Roxb. Cor. i, p 12, *t.* 8.—Twining, glabrous,

fleshy ; leaves linear-lanceolate, attenuated at the apex ; peduncles few-flowered ; corolla shaped as in the genus ; root bulbous ; leaves 2 to 4 inches long, 4 to 6 lines broad. About Dharwar, Law. Roxb. Fl Ind. ii, 29.

6. Lushii, Grah. in Bot. Mag. *t.* 3300.—Twining, glabrous ; leaves linear-acuminate, fleshy, channelled, glaucous ; base of the corol-tube globose, inflated, greenish; divisions linear-ciliated, cohering at the apex, violet-coloured within. Kasersaye jungles, Lush.

7. Tuberosa, Roxb. Cor. i, p 12, *t.* 9.—Twining, fleshy, glabrous ; lowest leaves almost orbicular, upper ovate, or ovate-oblong cuspidate ; peduncles sometimes twin, few or many-flowered, as long or longer than the leaves ; divisions of the corolla ligulate, hairy, cohering at the apex ; follicles slender, round. The Concans, Nimmo. Syn. C mucronata, Roth. nov. sp. p 179 ; C biflora, Linn. ; C candelabrum, Roxb. Fl Ind. ii, 27 ; C longiflora, Poir. Encycl. Suppl. ; Wight Ic. 353.

8. Angustifolia, Dalz. in Hook. Jour. Bot. ii, p 259.—Herbaceous, erect, pubescent, 5 to 6 inches high ; root tuberous ; stem round ; leaves narrow-linear, lanceolate-acute, hairy on the margins of the upperside, glabrous and pale beneath ; flowers outside of the axils, solitary, ascending ; corolla slightly ventricose at the base ; tube cylindrical, segments of the limb narrow-linear ; spathulate as long as the tube ; flowers purple, with a green base. Rocky pasturage near the sea ; district of Malwan ; flowers in July.

9. Ophiocephala, Dalz. loc. cit.—All hispid, twining ; leaves broad-lanceolate, rounded or cordate at the base, acuminated at the apex, hispid on both sides ; peduncles outside of the axils, longer than petiole, hispid, 3 to 4-flowered ; sepals linear-subulate, spreading ; corol tube ascending, ventricose at the base, dark-purple, glabrous ; divisions of the limb one-third shorter, oblong-obtuse, attenuated towards the apex, purple, yellow, and green ; follicles linear, smooth, 4 to 5 inches long, spotted with purple. On Caranjah hill.

10. Oculata, Hook. Bot. Mag. *t.* 4093.—Stem herbaceous, twining, glabrous ; leaves cordate ovate-acuminate, rather hairy, ciliated, with glands at the base ; peduncles with spreading hairs, 4 to 6-flowered; tube of the corolla much inflated at the base, globose, broader than the limb ; segments of the limb oblong, erect, connivent, ciliated, yellow below, with black spots, deep-green above ; lobes of the outer staminal crown attenuated, emarginate, of the inner narrow-linear, straight, entire. Bombay, whence the plant figured was received.

11. C Attenuata, Hook. Ic. Pl ix, 867.—Erect ; leaves linear, long and slenderly attenuated ; younger ones slightly pilose ; peduncle axillary, solitary, 1-flowered ; calyx lobes subulate, ciliated

spreading; corol-tube long, inflated at the base; lobes of the limb as long as the tube, slender, filiform. S. Concan, near Vingorla.

19. CARALLUMA, R. Br.

1. FIMBRIATA, Wall. Pl. As. rar. *t.* 8.—Erect, fleshy, leafless; stems quadrangular, toothed along the angles; flowers at the top of the branches solitary, or twin, or in threes, drooping, shortly-pedicelled; divisions of the corolla fringed. Sparingly scattered over the Deccan. Native name "Makur Sing." Anglice, Monkey's-horn. Eaten as a vegetable; flowers in June.

XCI. LOGANIACEÆ.

1. MITREOLA, Linn.

1. OLDENLANDIOIDES, Wall. list No. 4350.—A small, erect, herbaceous plant; stem somewhat quadrangular, glabrous; leaves ovate or oblong-acute or obtuse, attenuated at the base; cymes dichotomous; flowers subsessile on the branches, secund, small, white; capsule shaped like a mitre. Island of Caranjah. DC. *Prod.* 9, p 9.

2. MITRASACME, Lab.

1. PUSILLA, Dalz. in Hook. Jour. Bot. ii, p 136.—Stem 3 to 4 inches high, erect, glabrous, obtusely quadrangular; leaves linear-subulate acute, glabrous, veinless; pedicels axillary, solitary or twin, 2 to 3 times longer than the leaf; calyx 4-divided to the middle; lobes lanceolate-acute; corolla white, segments oblong, rather obtuse, shorter than the tube, throat hairy; capsule globose, a little shorter than the calyx. Malwan; flowers in August and September. This was afterwards named M indica by Wight Ic. 1601; its proper name should be M crystallina, Griffith in Notulæ iv, p 87.

3. STRYCHNOS, Linn.

1. S COLUBRINA, Linn (?) A, DC. *Prod.* 9, p 14 (?)—Smooth, scandent; cirrhi for the most part bifurcate; leaves ovate or elliptic, obtuse or scarcely acuminate; cymes lax, axillary, and terminal; flowers generally of 5 parts; tube of the corolla shorter than the lobes. Syn. S bicirrhosa, Leschen. A, DC. *Prod.* 9, p 16; Rheed. Hort. Mal. viii, *t.* 24. Chorla Ghaut; Meria Donger, near Penn; fruit size of an olive. We suspect that the S axillaris of Colebrooke is also a native of the Southern Ghauts, but our specimens are insufficient to determine.

2. NUXVOMICA, Linn. sp. 271.—A pretty large tree, no hooks or tendrils; leaves petioled-ovate, quite smooth; corymbs terminal,

greenish-white; berry globose, of the same size and colour as an orange; seeds several, light-grey, silky, furnishes the powerful poisonous principle Strychnine, so valuable in paralysis of the lower extremities; used also as a tonic in bowel-complaints. Native name "Kajra." Extremely common throughout the Warree Country and Concan southward. The wood is exceedingly bitter, particularly that of the root, and is used in the cure of intermittent fevers.

3. Potatorum, Linn. Fil. Suppl. 148.—A tree; leaves very shortly-petioled, elliptic-acute, glabrous, membranaceous; corymbs axillary, opposite, shorter than the leaf; berry 1-seeded; flowers white, odorous; berries black, half inch in diameter. Arawud jungles, Dr. Gibson; Southern Maratha Country, Law. The seeds are used for clearing muddy-water, hence called Clearing-nuts.

XCII. GENTIANEÆ.

1. OPHELIA, Don.

1. O Minor, Griseb. in DC. *Prod.* 9, p 126.—A small, erect, herbaceous plant; stem subterete, filiform, sparingly branched; branches erect, 1 to 3-flowered; leaves short, cordate-ovate, or ovate-glabrous, obscurely 3-nerved, cauline ones sessile, terminal cyme lax, 3 to 5-flowered; flowers of a beautiful blue, with a pale spot at the base of each of the four segments. In springy, wet ground on the highest Ghauts opposite Bombay; flowers in July.

2. Multiflora, Dalz. in Hook. Jour. Bot. ii, p 135.—Stem quadrangular, 4-winged, ascending, densely-leafy; leaves round-ovate, stem-clasping, 5-nerved, mucronulate, glabrous, decussate; cymes many-flowered; calyx divisions lanceolate-acuminate; corolla white, 4-divided; segments ovate-elliptic, their rounded pits surrounded by long fringes; filaments united at the very base. Mahableshwur. Syn. Swertia decussata, Nimmo in Grah. Cat. Bomb. Pl. p 249. Forms an excellent substitute for Gentian. Sold in the bazar at Marh as a bitter.

3. Pauciflora, Dalz. loc. cit. iii, p 211.—Stem erect, 4-winged, glabrous, branched towards the top; leaves sessile, lanceolate-acuminate, 3 nerved; cymes few-flowered; calyx segments subulate, as long as the corolla; corolla white, 4-divided, the segments obovate-elliptic, their pits large, round, covered with a fringed scale, and surrounded by a short fringe. The Ghauts; flowers in September.

2. EXACUM, Linn.

1. Bicolor, Roxb. Fl Ind. i, 397.—Herbaceous, erect, two feet high; stem quadrangular; leaves sessile, ovate lanceolate acute, 5-nerved; cyme terminal, contracted; flowers large, white,

tipped with blue. Salsette and the Concans ; pretty common in pasture lands. Syn. E tetragonum, Roxb. Fl Ind. i, 398 ; Grisebach, in DC. *Prod.* 9, 44, has made some mistake about this plant. He says the flowers are not a quarter of an inch in size, although Roxburgh describes them as large and beautiful. Sebæa carinata, Grah. Cat. p 124.

2. Pumilum, Griseb. in DC. *Prod.* 9, 46.—A small plant ; stem quadrangular ; leaves sessile, oblong-lanceolate, rather obtuse, 3-nerved ; segments of the calyx subulate, winged ; flowers small, bluish-purple. Very common among grass during the rains. Grisebach's specimens were from Bombay ; he has made a slight mistake in describing the calyx as wingless.

3. Petiolare, Griseb. in DC. *Prod.* 9, 46.—Stem almost simple, quadrangular ; leaves long-petioled, broadly ovate-obtuse, 5-nerved ; calyx segments acute, the wings semiovate ; flowers pedicelled, larger and paler than in the preceding. Island of Caranjah, during the rains. DC.'s specimens were collected by Baron Hugel.

3. ERYTHRÆA, Ren.

1. Roxburghii, Don. *syst.* Gard. iv, p 203.—A small herbaceous plant ; stem erect, 4 to 5 inches high ; lowermost leaves rosulate obovate, oblong-obtuse ; stem ones linear-acuminate ; cymes dichotomous, spreading ; flowers of a beautiful pink, starlike. Common in cultivated fields after the rains. Syn. Chironia centaureoides, Roxb. Fl Ind. i, 584; Chironia brachiata, Willd.

4. HIPPION, Sprengel.

1. Orientale.—Stem ascending, simple 4-sided, leafy from the base ; leaves opposite, subsessile, linear-lanceolate or oblong, 3-nerved ; calyx with bracts ; the lobes obtuse, longer than the capsule ; flowers small, white, sessile in the opposite axils. Gujarat, common ; Concan, rare. Syn. Stevoglia orientalis, Grisebach in DC. *Prod.* 9, p 65 ; Cicendia hyssopifolia, W. and A. in Hook. Comp. Bot. Mag.

5. CANSCORA, Lam.

1. Decurrens, Dalz. in Hook. Jour. Bot. ii, p 136.—Stem erect, broadly 4-winged ; branches opposite and alternate ; leaves decurrent, lower ones oblong, attenuated towards the base, upper ovate or lanceolate-acute ; calyx without wings, 3 lines long ; corolla small, pale rose-coloured or white. In rice fields, Southern Concan ; flowers in October and November.

2. Pauciflora, Dalz. loc. cit.—Stem erect, 4-winged, scarcely branched ; leaves very small, lower ovate-obtuse, upper oblong-

acute, all sessile, 3-nerved, rough on the margin alone; panicle lax, few-flowered; flowers long-pedicelled, solitary; pedicels 4-winged, thickened upwards. Malwan, in grassy places; flowers in September.

3. Alata, Wall Cat.—Stem 4-winged above, below simple and tetragonal; leaves ovate-oblong, rather acute; floral ones orbicular or slightly kidney-shaped; central flowers sessile, sometimes none; calyx with a semiovate wing. Near Vingorla.

4. Diffusa, R. Br. *Prod.* p 451.—Stem obsoletely winged; very much branched; leaves ovate-acute; central flowers pedicelled, sometimes wanting; calyx wingless; corolla pink or rosy. We have failed to find any difference between C lawii (Wight Ic. 1327, *fig.* 1,) and this species. Common in rocky parts of the Concan. Syn. Pladera virgata, Roxb. Fl Ind. i, 417; Exacum diffusum, Willd.

6. LIMNANTHEMUM, Gmel.

1. Cristatum, Griseb. Gent. p 342.—An aquatic plant; leaves cordate-orbicular, roughish above, glandular beneath; calyx segments ovate-lanceolate; segments of the corolla waved-ciliated, with a longitudinal crest within; flowers white, cymose, inserted on the petiole; capsule 1 to 2-seeded; seeds muricated. Tanks in the Concan. Syn. Menyanthes cristata, Roxb. Cor. ii, p 3, *t.* 105; Villarsia cristata, Spr. *syst.* i, p 582; Hook. Jour. i, p 123; Menyanthes indica, Bory.

2. Indicum, Griseb. Gent. p 343.—Leaves cordate-orbicular, membranaceous, roughish; calyx segments ovate; segments of the corolla fringed on the margin, destitute of crest within; flowers white; arising from the petiole; capsule many-seeded; seeds muricated. Tanks in the Concans and Deccan; flowers white, rather smaller than in the preceding. Syn. Menyanthes indica, Linn. sp. Pl i, p 207; Villarsia indica, Vent. Choix. p 9.

3. Aurantiacum, Dalz. in Hook. Jour. Bot. ii, 136.—Umbels axillary; leaves small, orbicular, deeply cordate, shining above, glandular dotted and purple beneath; corolla orange-coloured, half inch long; segments of the limb wedge-shaped, broadly and deeply emarginate, fringed on the margin, bearded at the base; seeds lenticular, muricated; capsule ovate-obtuse, 12-seeded. Near Malwan; flowers in September.

4. Parvifolium, Griseb. in DC. *Prod.* 9, p 141.—A minute plant; leaves cordate-orbicular, small (½ inch) membranaceous; petioles bearing the flowers, immediately below the leaf; capsule many-seeded; seeds minute, rough. Very common in tanks, but difficult to find, on account of its small size; at Malwan, Surat, &c. Syn. Villarsia parvifolia, Wall. Cat. 4351.

XCIII. OLEACEÆ.

1. OLEA.

1. ROXBURGHIANA, Rœm. and Schult. *syst.* Maut. i, p 77.—A small but handsome tree; leaves oblong, attenuated at the base, quite entire, glabrous, waved; panicles axillary, and springing from beneath the leaves, lax, many-flowered; flowers white, appear in the hot weather; fruit small, purple. Common on the Ghauts. Syn. O paniculata, Roxb. Fl Ind. i, p 105; O roxburghii, Spr. *syst.* i, p 34.

2. DIOICA, Roxb. Fl Ind. i, p 106.—A pretty large tree; leaves oblong, acute at both ends, remotely and acutely serrated, 4 to 8 inches long, quite smooth; panicles springing from below the leaves, short and few-flowered; drupe in size and colour like the common Sloe. Khandalla, Mahableshwur, Wag Donger, near Vingorla; flowers in July. The timber is excellent, and put to various uses. Native name "Parrjamb," also "Karamba."

2. LIGUSTRUM, Tourn.

1. L NEILGHERRENSE, Wight Ic. 1243.—Arboreous, glabrous; leaves ovate, elliptic-acute, or cuspidately-acuminate, coriaceous; thyrses of white fragrant flowers, on the ends of the branches lax; fruit black, linear-oblong, small. Syn. Phillyrea microphylla, Graham's Cat. p 108. All along the Ghauts, from Hurrychunder to the Parwar Ghaut below Goa.

3. LINOCIERA, Swartz.

1. MALABARICA, Wall. list No. 2828.—A small tree; leaves elliptic-obtuse, attenuated towards the base, smooth on both sides; racemes axillary, much shorter than the leaf, few-flowered; pedicels bearing 1 to 3 sessile flowers at the top; pedicels and calyx pubescent; petals linear-channelled. Khandalla, Ram Ghaut, &c. The flowers, which appear in November and December, have the fragrance of ripe apples, Law.

XCIV. BIGNONIACEÆ.

1. BIGNONIA, DC.

1. B XYLOCARPA, Roxb. Fl Ind. iii, p 108.—Arboreous, glabrous; leaves bitripinnate; petiole sharply-angular, leaflets petioled; ovate or oblong-acuminated, membranaceous, reticulately veined; panicle corymbose; branches dichotomous; calyx unequally

5-toothed; corolla campanulate, shortly-tubular; lobes rounded; capsule round-linear, incurved, woody, tubercled; flowers white, fragrant. Native name "Kursing." Thul Ghaut; Jowar jungle, near Nagotna; Parr Ghaut, &c.; the Dangs in Kandeish. Syn. Tecoma xylocarpa, Don's *syst.* iv, p 225. An oily substance, distilled from the wood, is powerful in cutaneous diseases.

2. SPATHODEA, Beauv.

1. S Falcata, Wall. List No. 6517.—A small tree; leaves unequally pinnate, 2 to 3 pair, oval, rounded, entire, slightly hairy; racemes terminal, few-flowered; calyx cylindrical, oblique; flowers white, about 1 inch long, fragrant; capsule linear, 1 foot long, variously twisted. Near Nagotna village; below Kandalla Ghaut; Duddi; Southern Maratha Country, Law. Syn. Bignonia spathacea, Linn. Fil. Suppl. 283; S Rheedei, Spr. *syst.* ii, 835; S longiflora, Pers. Ench. ii, 172.

2. S Crispa, Wall. List. No. 6515.—Arboreous; leaves unequally pinnate; leaflets 1 to 3 pair; branchlets and racemes pubescent and velvetty; leaflets oval-oblong, acuminated at both ends, quite entire; raceme terminal, few-flowered; corol tube slender elongated; lobes much curled and crisped; flowers pure white, fragrant; capsule pod-like, elongated, obtusely-acuminated, pendulous. Duddi on the Gutpurba, Law. Syn. Bignonia crispa, Buchanan in Roxb. Fl Ind. iii, 103; B atrovirens, Roth. nov. sp. p 284; S atrovirens, Spr. *syst.* ii, 835.

3. HETEROPHRAGMA, DC.

1. H Roxburghii, DC. *Prod.* 9.—A large timber tree; branches round; leaves opposite or tern, glabrous, simply pinnated, 4 to 5 pair; leaflets ovate, acute, serrated; panicle terminal, tomentose, and velvetty; flowers whitish, with a pink margin; pod thick, linear, about a foot long and 2 inches broad, 4-celled; flowers in March and April. Very common on the Ghauts. Native name "Warus." Bignonia 4-locularis, Roxb. Cor. ii, *t.* 145; Spathodea roxburghii, Spr. *spst.* ii, 825. The wood is serviceable for planks.

2. Chelonioides, DC. *Prod.* 9, p 210.—A tree, glabrous; branches round; leaves unequally pinnated, 4 pair; leaflets elliptic-cuspidate, acuminate; panicle terminal, lax, ultimate branchlets, 3-flowered; calyx coriaceous, 2 to 3-lobed, or 5-toothed; corolla between campanulate and bilabiate, the lobes ciliated; capsule very long, roundish, glabrous. The Ghauts, common; flowers yellowish, fragrant, appear in May and June. Syn. Bignonia

chelonoides, Linn. Fil. Suppl. 232; Willd sp. iii, p 304; Roxb. Fl Ind. iii, p 106; "Padri," Rheed. Mal. vi, *t.* 26. Native name "Padel."

2. Suaveolens, DC. in *Prod.* 9, p 211.—A tree; leaves pinnate; leaflets 2 to 4 pair, oval-acuminate, almost entire; panicle terminal, lax, somewhat brachiate; calyx 5-toothed; flowers dark-purple, fragrant, appear in March and common in the April; capsule pod-shaped, cylindric. Common in the Dandelly jungles, Dr. Gibson. One tree grows in the Island of Caranjah. Syn. Bignonia suaveolens, Roxb. Fl Ind. iii, p 104; Tecoma suaveolens, Don. Gen. *syst.* iv, 224. Native name "Purul."

4. TECOMA, Juss.

1. Undulata, Don. Gen. *syst.* iv, p 223.—A tree, glabrous; leaves petioled, simple, linear-lanceolate obtuse, waved, entire; racemes terminating the lateral branchlets, few-flowered; calyx campanulate, shortly and broadly 5-lobed; corolla large, orange-yellow, campanulate; capsule long, slender, linear-compressed, smooth. Western Kandeish; Bunass River, Gujarat. One tree grows at Dhoolia and another at Domus, both planted. Syn. Bignonia undulata, Roxb. Fl Ind. iii, 101; Smith Exot. Bot i, *t.* 19.

5. CALOSANTHES, Blume.

1. Indica, Blume. Bijdr. 760.—A tree; leaves opposite, pinnate, leaflets on the branches of the petiole 2 to 3 pair, petioletted, subcordate, ovate-acuminated; panicle terminal, erect; flowers fleshy, of a dark, lurid appearance, fœtid, appear in the rains; pod 2 feet long, 3 inches broad, straight and flat. Salsette jungles, and throughout the Concan and Ghauts. Syn. Bignonia indica, Var. and Linn. sp. 871; Lam. Dict. i, 428; B indica, Willd. sp. iii, 306; Roxb. Fl Ind. iii, 110; B pentandra, Lour. Coch. ii, 460; Spathodea indica, Pers. Ench. ii, 173; Rheed. Mal. i, p 77, *t.* 43; Ham. Tr. Linn. Soc. viii, p 514.

XCV. SESAMEÆ.

1. SESAMUM, Linn.

1. S Indicum, DC. Pl Rar. Gard. Gen. p 18, *t.* 5.—An annual plant; leaves opposite, or upper ones alternate, ovate-oblong or lanceolate, the lower ones often 3-lobed, or 3-divided; flowers solitary in the axils, rose-coloured, handsome, but of offensive odour; capsule velvetty and pubescent, mucronate. From the seeds of this plant, which is only to be seen cultivated, is obtained the oil called "Jinjelly." This plant is nowhere found wild.

2. PEDALIUM, Royen.

1. P Murex, Linn. sp. 892.—A low annual succulent herb; leaves petioled, oval, inciso-dentate, obtuse, a little cuneate at the base; pedicels axillary, 1-flowered, shorter than the petiole, without bracts; flowers yellow; fruit corky, with 4 conical spines, from the base. The fruit is sold in the bazars under the name of Gokroo; it is mucilaginous, and the leaves infused in water render it mucilaginous. On the sandy shores of Kattywar, and Deccan.

XCVI. CONVOLVULACEÆ.

1. EVOLVULUS, Linn.

1. Hirsutus, Lam. Encycl. iii, 538.—A very small herbaceous plant, cespitose procumbent, covered with adpressed hairs; leaves ovate-oblong, subsessile, less than half an inch long; peduncles 1-flowered, as long as the leaf or longer; flowers of a beautiful deep blue, very small. Common everywhere in grassy places.

2. CRESSA, Linn.

1. Cretica, Linn. sp. 325.—A very small, shrubby, diffuse plant; leaves ovate-sessile, very small, acute, numerous, ashy or hoary pubescent; flowers small, white or pink, subsessile, in the superior axils, forming a many-flowered head. Very common in cultivated fields in the cold weather. Sibth. Fl Grae. *t.* 256; Syn. C humifusa, Lam. Encycl.; Quamoclit minima, Tournef.; C indica, Retz. Obs. iv, p 24; C australis, Br. *Prod.* Fl nov. Holl., &c. &c.

3. BREWERIA, R. Br.

1. Roxburghii, Chois. DC. *Prod.* 9, p 438.—Stem twining, branched; branchlets rusty-coloured; leaves ovate-cordate, subacuminate, long-petioled, ferruginous; peduncles 3, many-flowered, scarcely so long as the petiole; flowers white, pretty large. Near Vingorla; flowers in October and November. Syn. Convolvulus semidigynus, Roxb. Fl Ind. ii, p 47, ed. Wall; Wight. Ic.

4. PORANA, Burm.

1. Racemosa, Roxb. Fl Ind. i, p 566.—Herbaceous, climbing to a great height; leaves cordate, acuminate, glabrous or pubescent, long-petioled; panicles racemose, leafy, few-flowered; calyx increasing with the fruit, becoming scariose; corol white, tubular, small. Mahableshwur and the higher Ghauts; common. Native

name "Bhowree." Syn. P dichotoma, Ham. ex. Don. Fl. Nep. 99; P cordifolia, Ledeb. Dinetus racemosus; Sev. Br. Fl Gard. 127.

5. PALMIA, Endl.

1. Bicolor, Endl. Gen.—Stem twining, hairy; leaves ovate-cordate, entire, or with waved angles; peduncles most frequently 1-flowered, longer than the leaves; bracts on the peduncle ovate-lanceolate, leafy, acute, pubescent; corolla less than an inch, yellow and purple; capsules hairy, one-celled. The Concans, near Penn. Syn. Convolvulus bicolor, Vahl. Symb. iii, p 25; Bot Mag. 2205; Ipomæa bicolor, Sw. H. Suburb. 2, p 289; C sublobatus, Linn. Supp. 135; C involucratus, Bot. Reg. 318; Hewittia bicolor, Stendel.; C bracteatus, Vahl.; Thutereia bicolor, Chois. DC. *Prod.* 9, 435.

6. ANISEIA, Chois.

1. Calycina, Chois. DC. *Prod.* 4, p 429.—Stem twining, hairy; leaves oblong, cordate-acuminate, glabrous-petioled; peduncles shorter than the petioles, 1 to 3-flowered; exterior sepals sagittate; corolla tubular, white; capsule pointed; seeds silky. Surat and Broach. Syn. Convolvulus calycinus, Roxb. Fl Ind; C hardwickii, Spr. *syst.* iv, p 60; Ipomæa cardiosepala, Hochst. in Un. Itiner. No. 207 and 384.

2. Uniflora, Chois loc. cit. p 431.—Stems prostrate; leaves oblong-linear, very shortly petioled, mucronate, glabrous, 1 to 2 inches long; corolla white, hairy on the outside; capsule silky within. Southern Concan. Syn. Convolvulus uniflorus, Desv. Encycl. 3, p 544; Burm. Ind. 47, *t.* i, *f.* 2; C emarginatus, Vahl. Symb.; C rheedei, Wall. Fl Ind. ii, p 70; Wight Illust. *t.* 8; Ipomæa uniflora, Rœm. and Schult.

7. CONVOLVULUS, Linn.

1. Arvensis, Linn. sp 218.—Stem slender, prostrate or twining, striated, angled; leaves narrow-sagittate, subauricled; peduncles 1 to 2-flowered, with 2 small bracts; sepals ovate-obtuse; corolla rosy; capsule smooth. Very common in the black soil of Gujarat, also in the Deccan; flowers in the cold weather. Syn. C chinensis, Kew. Bot. Reg. *t.* 322; C malcolmi, Roxb. Fl Ind. 474.

2. Parviflorus, Vahl. Symb. iii, p 29.—Stems weak, twining, pubescent; leaves cordate, ovate-acute, glabrous-petioled; peduncles longer than the petioles; flowers white, umbelled, numerous, small, appear in October. Island of Caranjah; Surat, &c. Syn. Ipomæa paniculata, Burm. Ind. p 50, *t.* 21, *f.* 3; Ip. parviflora, Pers. Ip. timorensis, Blum. Bijdr; C multivalvis, Br. *Prod.*

3. Microphyllus, Luber. in DC. *Prod.* 9.—Stems prostrate, elongated, hirsute; leaves lanceolate, attenuated at the base into a very short petiole, half an inch to 1 inch long; flowers axillary, sometimes solitary, sometimes in twos or threes on the rudiment of a branch, rotate, white or pale-pink; capsule globose, smooth; seeds smooth. Very common in Gujarat, also in Sind, Egypt, and Arabia.

4. C Rottlerianus, Chois. DC. *Prod.* 9, p 403.—Erect, herbaceous, scarcely branched, slender; leaves linear-acute, subsessile, 1 to 2 inches long; peduncles 2-flowered, very slender, longer than the leaves; calyx leaves broad-ovate, with a long acumen, hairy; flowers small, starlike, pink; corolla twice as long as the calyx; capsule round, smooth, size of a small pea. In Kattywar and Deccan, sparingly; flowers in October.

8. CALONYCTION, Chois.

1. Speciosum, Chois DC. *Prod.* 9, p 345.—Stem sometimes prickly, climbing to a great height; leaves large, quite smooth, cordate-petioled, pointed; peduncles very long, 1 to 5-flowered; flowers very large, pure white, opening at sunset. A very variable plant; in hedges. Syn. Ipomæa bonanox, Linn. sp. 228; Bot. Mag. *t.* 752; Ip. grandiflora, Roxb. Fl Ind.; Ip. longiflora, Willd.; Ip. latiflora, Bot Reg., note 917; Ip. roxburghii, Steudel; C roxburghii, Don.; Convolvulus muricatus, Linn.; C muricatum, Don. Native name "Goolchandnee."

9. IPOMÆA, Linn.

1. Reptans, Poir. Encycl. Suppl. iii, p 460.—Stems creeping and rooting, fistulous, smooth; leaves sagittate, lanceolate; petioles glabrous; peduncles 1 to 5-flowered, nearly as long as the petioles; sepals ovate, glabrous; corolla tubulose, campanulate, of a pretty rose-colour. In tanks; very common in Gujarat, where it is used as a pot-herb by poorer natives.

2. Pescapræ, Sw. Hort. Sub. p 289.—Stems creeping to a great length; leaves subrotund, bilobed, parallel-veined, rather fleshy; peduncles, 1 to many-flowered, a little longer than the petiole; sepals ovate-lanceolate; corolla rosy or purple. Common on sandy beaches, where it serves to bind the sand. Syn. C pescapræ, Linn. sp. 226; Convolvulus brasilianus, Linn.; C marinus, Rumph. Amb. v, 433; C bilobatus, Roxb. Fl Ind.; C bauhinæfolius, Sal.; C carnosus, Spr. *syst.*, &c. &c.

3. Reniformis, Chois. DC. *Prod.* 9, p 351.—Stem creeping and rooting; leaves kidney-shaped, waved, and dentate on the margin, obtuse; petioles hairy; peduncles very short, 1 to 2-flowered;

corolla small, yellow. Common in places where water has lodged; flowers in the cold weather. Syn. Convolvulus reniformis, Roxb. Fl Ind. ii, p 67; C gangeticus, Linn.; Evolvulus emarginatus, Burm. Ind. *t.* 30, *f.* 1; E gangeticus, Linn. sp. 391. Found both in the Concan and Deccan, and often overlooked.

4. TRIDENTATA, Roth. Cat. ii, p 19.—Herbaceous, annual; stem filiform, angular; leaves sessile, oblong-linear, truncate at the apex, often 3-toothed, auricled and toothed at the base, scarcely an inch long, smooth; peduncles 1-flowered, longer than the leaf; sepals ovate, awned; corolla pale-yellow. Near Bassein and Ghore Bunder. Syn. Convolvulus tridentatus, Linn. sp. p 157; C viscidus, Roxb. Cat. 14; Evolvulus tridentatus, Linn. sp. 392.

5. FILICAULIS, Blum. Bijdr. p 721.—Stem elongated, rarely twining, filiform, angular; leaves linear or linear-lanceolate, shortly-petioled, hastate and denticulate at the base, quite smooth; peduncles longer than the leaf, 1 to 2-flowered; pedicels clavate; sepals ovate-acuminate; corolla small, pale-yellow. Common in the Concans and Deccan also. Syn. Convolvulus filicaulis, Vahl. Symb. iii, p 24; C hastatus, Desv.; C simplex, Pers., &c. &c.

6. CAMPANULATA, Linn. sp. 228.—A large, climbing plant; stem striated, glabrous; leaves large, cordate-acute, glabrous, veined with red beneath, long-petioled; peduncles many-flowered, as long as the petioles; sepals ovate-rounded, glabrous; corolla large, pale-rosy, deeper coloured at the base; seeds silky. Hilly parts of the Concan; Warree, common. A very handsome species. Syn. Convolvulus campanulatus, Spr. *syst.* i, 607.

7. TURPETHUM, Br. *Prod.* 485.—Stems angular; leaves cordate, sometimes entire, sometimes sinuate-angled or crenated, pubescent and velvetty on both sides; peduncles thick, 1 to 4-flowered; bracts ovate-lanceolate, velvetty, deciduous; exterior sepals large; flowers white; seeds smooth; root thick, purgative. Gujarat, very common; Deccan. Bot. Mag. 2093; Syn. Convolvulus turpethum, Linn.

8. VITIFOLIA, Sw. Hort. Suburb. p 289.—Stem round, hairy or pubescent; leaves cordate, palmately pentafid; lobes unequal, irregularly crenate and dentate; peduncles many-flowered; flowers large, handsome, yellow; appear in the cold weather. In a jungle near Roha, plentiful; hilly parts of the Concan generally.

9. PESTIGRIDIS, Linn. sp. 230.—Stems round, hairy; leaves palmately 5 to 7-lobed; lobes ovate-acute, silky and hairy; peduncles many-flowered, as long as the leaf; heads of flowers surrounded by 6 to 8 ovate-linear hairy bracts; corolla white, hairy. Very common in hedges. Syn. Convolvulus pestrigidis, Spr.; C begoniæfolius, Sal.

10. PILOSA, Sw. Hort. Sub. p 289.—Stems hairy, herbaceous; leaves broadly-cordate, entire or slightly 3-lobed, the middle lobe acuminate, 2 to 6 inches long, long-petioled; peduncles longer than the petioles; flowers many, cymose; sepals linear, hairy; corolla tubular, white; capsules glabrous; seeds villous. A common weed. Syn. Convolvulus pilosus, Roxb. Fl Ind. ii, 55.

11. PILEATA, Roxb. Fl Ind. ii, p 94.—Stem slender, villous; leaves cordate-acuminate, petioled, glabrous; pedúncles shorter than the petiole; flowers 3 to 6, sessile, in a boat-shaped perfoliate involucre; bracts obovate, hirsute; corolla tubular campanulate; capsule glabrous. Jungles in the Southern Concan; rare. Syn. Convolvulus pileatus, Spr. *syst.* iv. p 61.

12. SESSILIFLORA, Roth nov. sp. 117.—Stem herbaceous, covered with hairs pointing downwards; leaves cordate ovate-lanceolate or sagittate; flowers axillary, 1 to 12, subsessile or very shortly-pedicelled; sepals acuminate subulate, hairy; corolla scarcely longer than the calyx; capsule hairy; seeds glabrous. Fort of Severndroog. Syn. Ipomæa sphærocephala, Sw. Hort. Sub.; Convolvulus sessiliflorus, Spr. *syst.*; C hispidus, Vahl. Symb. iii, p 29; C sphærocephalus, Roxb. Fl Ind.; Wight Ic. *t.* 169.

13. OBSCURA, Bot. Reg. 239.—Stem herbaceous, elongated; leaves cordate-acuminate, glabrous or puberulous, acute, reticulated beneath, long-petioled; peduncles longer than the petioles, 1 to 3-flowered; pedicels thick, articulated; sepals oblong-ovate, glabrous or puberulous; flowers yellow; base of tube purple; capsule glabrous. Common about Bombay; the Deccan. Syn. Convolvulus obscurus, Linn. sp. 220; C gemellus, Vahl. Symb. iii, p 27; Ipomæa solanifolia, Burm. Ind. p 49.

14. SEPIARIA, Kœn. in Roxb. and Wall. Fl Ind. ii, p 90.—Twining; leaves cordate-oblong; peduncles many-flowered; heads of flowers dense; sepals oblong, ovate-acute or obtuse; corolla pinkish, tubular, funnel-shaped. Common in every hedge. Syn. Convolvulus maximus, Vahl. Symb.; C striatus, Vahl. Symb.; Ipomæa striata, Roth nov. sp. iii.

15. CHRYSEIDES, Bot. Reg. 270.—Stems twisted, glabrous; leaves oblong-cordate, subhastate, entire or oftener angled, sometimes 3-lobed, acuminate, glabrous, 1 to 2 inches long; petioles long, muricated and warty at the base; peduncles rigid, longer than the petioles, 2 to 7-flowered, dichotomous, a solitary flower in the forks; sepals ovate retuse-mucronate; corolla very small, yellow, bell-shaped, five lines in diameter; capsule depressed, wrinkled, glabrous, 4-angled. Muneree, in the Warree Country; rare. The flowers open at 9 A.M.

16. COPTICA, Roth nov. sp. p 110.—Herbaceous, procumbent; leaves palmate or pedate, lower lobes shorter, bifid, all serrated,

glabrous; petioles compressed; peduncles longer than the petiole, 1 to 2-flowered; sepals wrinkled, muricated, ovate-oblong, glabrous, mucronulate, two lines long; corolla white; tubular, shortly 5-lobed; capsule glabrous. The open glades about Khandalla, creeping amongst the grass. Grah. Cat. p 132; Convolvulus copticus, Linn. Maut. 559; Roxb. Fl Ind. i, p 477.

17. Rhyncorhiza, Dalz. in Hook. Jour. Bot. iii, 179.—Root an ovoid compressed beaked tuber; stem filiform, climbing, glabrous; leaves long-petioled, palmately divided into 7 lobes; lobes unequally pinnatifid, acuminate; peduncles axillary, solitary, filiform, 1 to 2-flowered, longer than the leaf; flowers middle-sized, yellow. Near Tulkut Ghaut; flowers in August and September.

10. BATATAS.

1. Paniculata, Chois. DC. *Prod.* 9, p 339.—Root tuberous; stems thick, twining, glabrous; leaves large, palmately 5 to 7-lobed; lobes ovate-lanceolate; peduncles much longer than the petioles, many-flowered, dichotomous; sepals ovate, rounded-concave, very obtuse; corolla purple, handsome, narrowed at the base; seeds with long hairs. A very common but handsome plant; flowers in the rains. Syn. Convolvulus paniculatus, Linn. sp. 223; C insignis, Spr. *syst.* i, 592; C roseus, Kunth.; Ipomæa paniculata, Br. *Prod.* 486; Bot. Reg. *t.* 62; Ip gossypiifolia, Willd.; Ip insignis, Bot. Mag. 1790.

2. Pentaphylla, Chois. DC. *Prod.* 9, 339.—Stems twining, hirsute; leaves digitate; leaflets 5, elliptic-lanceolate, entire; peduncles as long as the petioles, hirsute, 1 to 3-flowered; sepals very hairy, lanceolate-acute; corolla a little longer than the calyx, white; capsule and seeds smooth. A common weed. Syn. Convolvulus pentaphyllus, Linn. sp. 223; C hirsutus, Roxb. Fl Ind. i, 479; C munitus, Wight Illust. *t.* 7; C nemorosus, Rœm. and Schult. iv, 303.

11. PHARBITIS.

1. Laciniata, Dalz. in Hook. Jour. Bot. iii, 178.—Root fibrous; Stem filiform, creeping or twining, angular-twisted; leaves shortly-petioled, divided into 7 lobes; lobes very narrow-linear, between serrated and pinnatifid, the teeth unequal mucronate; peduncles axillary, solitary, angular-clavate, 1 to 3-flowered, shorter than the leaf; corolla white, with a long, slender tube, purple within; calyx leaflets oblong-mucronate, thick, fleshy, 3-ribbed, wrinkled; capsule 3-celled; cells 2-seeded; seeds silky. In the district of Malwan; flowers in August; unfolds its flowers only at sunset.

12. RIVEA.

1. Hypocrateriformis, Chois. DC. *Prod.* 9, 326.—Stems twining, pubescent; leaves rounded-obtuse, cordate, covered on the underside with white hairs; peduncles 1-flowered, sometimes axillary, solitary; sometimes disposed like a spike at the apex of the branchlets; sepals ovate-obtuse, unequal, hairy outside; corolla with a very narrow tube. Bombay and the Concans. Syn. Convolvulus hypocrateriformis, Desv. Encycl. iii, 561; C caudicans, Rœm. and Schult. iv, 302; Lettsomia uniflora, Roxb. Fl Ind. i, 495.

2. Bonanox, Chois. loc. cit.—Twining; leaves rounded-cordate, emarginate, sometimes hairy; peduncles shorter than the petiole, commonly 3-flowered; sepals ovate, cordate-obtuse; corolla large, pure white, expanding at sunset, perfuming the air with the scent of cloves. Roxb. and Grah. Cat. p 127. To me the fragrance is that of Honeysuckle. Syn. R fragrans, Nimmo; Lettsomia bonanox, Roxb. Fl Ind. i, 494; Argyreia bonanox, Sw.

3. R Ornata, Chois. Conv. p 27, *t.* 3.—Stem erect, whitish; leaves large, orbicular, cordate or kidney-shaped, smooth above, whitish and tomentose beneath; peduncles elongated, between spiked and panicled, or umbellate; sepals ovate-lanceolate, villous; tube of white corolla slender, with a flat, spreading limb. The high Ghauts west of Jooneer.

13. ARGYREIA, Lour.

1. Speciosa, Sw. Hort. Sub. p 289.—A very large climber; stem tomentose; leaves very large, cordate-acute, smooth or nearly so above, covered with white, silky hairs beneath; peduncles as long as the petioles; flowers somewhat umbellate or capitate; sepals ovate, very obtuse, tomentose; corolla 2 inches long, somewhat cylindric, pale rose-coloured; fruit berried, 4-celled; cells 1-seeded. This does not agree with the genus as given by Chois. as the fruit is 4-celled, as in Rivea. Bombay and the Deccan, called "Elephant Creeper." Syn. Convolvulus nervosus, Burm. Ind. 48, *t.* 20; C speciosus, Linn. Suppl. 137; Ipomæa speciosa, Pers. *syn.*; Lettsomia nervosa, Roxb. Fl Ind. i, 488. "Sumoodr. Shok," Mark.

2. Setosa, Chois. DC. *Prod.* 9, 332.—Covered with close-pressed hairs; leaves cordate-ovate, or rounded-acuminate, smooth above, strigose beneath; peduncles longer than the petioles, rigid; flowers numerous, corymbose; bracts reniform, orbiculate-obtuse; sepals of the same shape; corolla 1½ inch long, tubular, rather hairy, whitish. Near Viziadroog; Surat, Law. Syn. Ipomæa strigosa, Roth. nov. sp. p. 113; Lettsomia setosa, Roxb. Fl Ind. i, 490; Convolvulus strigosus, Spr. *syst.* i, 600; fruit 2-celled.

3. CUNEATA, Bot. Reg. 661.—An erect-growing shrub, glabrous; leaves obovate-cuneate, emarginate, glabrous above, hairy beneath, scarcely petioled; peduncles shorter than the leaf, 3 to 6-flowered; bracts minute, linear; sepals ovate-obtuse; corolla tubular, an inch long, deep purple. Common in the Mawul districts and Deccan; fruit 4-celled, according to Wight. Syn. Convolvulus cuneatus, Willd. sp. i, 873; Lettsomia cuneata, Roxb. Fl Ind. i, p 491; Ipomæa atrosanguinea, Hook. Bot. Mag. *t.* 2170.

4. ELLIPTICA, Chois. DC. *Prod.* 9, 330.—Climbing; leaves ovate or obovate-elliptic; villous, peduncles very long, bearing at the apex a corymbose panicle of flowers; sepals very obtuse, hairy outside, corolla an inch long, rose-coloured; fruit a berry, size of a large pea, orange-coloured, 2-celled. On the Ghauts, common. Native name "Bondwail." Syn. Convolvulus laurifolius, Roxb. Fl Ind. i, 470.

1. MALABARICA, Chois. DC. *Prod.* 9 331.—Stem pubescent; leaves cordate, rounded-acute, glabrous, or slightly hairy; peduncles as long as, or longer than, the petiole, many-flowered at the apex; sepals lanceolate-acute, hoary, the margins revolute; corolla white or cream-coloured, the bottom deep-purple. The Ghauts, common. Syn. Convolvulus malabaricus, Linn. sp. 221; Ipomæa malabarica, Rœm. and Schult; Rheed. Mal. xi, *t.* 51.

2. AGGREGATA, Chois. DC. *Prod.* 4, 333.—Hoary, tomentose; leaves ovate-cordate, smooth above, hoary beneath, very obtuse; peduncles longer than the petioles; flowers numerous, capitate; bracts ovate-orbiculate, hoary, obtuse; sepals ovate-obtuse; corolla small, 8 lines long, Southern Maratha Country, Law. Syn. Lettsomia aggregata, Roxb. Fl Ind. i, 488; Ipomæa imbricata, Roth nov. sp. p. 112; Convolvulus imbricatus, Spr.

3. A SERICEA, Dalz.—Twining, tomentose; leaves ample, broad, cordate-acuminate, hispid on the upper surface, white and silky, with adpressed pubescence beneath; petiole 2 inches long; peduncles axillary, simple, bearing a head of 6 to 8 flowers, enveloped in large, foliaceous, linear-oblong bracts; calyx and outer surface of corolla with long, white hairs; flowers large, pink; ovary 4-celled; berry small, orange-coloured. Southern Concan, common; also on the high hills west of Joonere; flowers in September. This comes near to A argentea, which has the flowers in a kind of loose umbel, while in this they are in a dense head. No. 985 of Graham's Catalogue.

14. ERYCIBE, Roxb.

1. PANICULATA, Roxb. Fl Ind. i, 585.—A large, climbing shrub, covered with tawny tomentum; leaves elliptic-acute at the base, abruptly acuminated at the apex, smooth; panicles terminal

and axillary, longer than the leaf; flowers in clusters along the rachis, yellow; berry oblong, black, size of a small cherry. Jungly parts of the Concan; flowers in April. Syn. Erimatalia rheedei, Rœm. and Schul. *syst.* v, 331; Cotonia glauca, Vahl. Roxb. Cor. *t.* 159.

2. Wightiana, Grah. Cat. p 137.—A climbing shrub, with rigid stems; leaves petioled, coriaceous, shining, oblong-acuminate, attenuated at the base; racemes about the length of the leaves; corolla almost rotate, white; divisions cuneate, bilobed, their lower part clothed outside with rusty tomentum, very fragrant; calyx segments rounded, clothed with rusty hairs; stigma large, convolute; leaves 4 inches long, $1\frac{1}{2}$ to 2 broad; flowers in November. Phoonda Ghaut.

XCVII. HYDROPHYLLACEÆ.

1. HYDROLEA, Linn.

1. Zeylanica, Willd. i, 1327.—Herbaceous, annual, creeping; stems round, smooth; leaves alternate, lanceolate, entire, smooth; flowers numerous, about the extremities of the branchlets, or solitary, opposite to the leaves or between them, of beautiful deep-blue; capsules superior, 2-celled. Common on the margin of tanks and other wet places; flowers in the cold season. Syn. Nama zeylanica, Linn. sp. Pl 327; Rheed. Mal. x, *t.* 28. May be safely used as a bitter tonic.

XCVIII. EHRETIACEÆ.

1. EHRETIA, Linn.

1. Lævis, Roxb. Fl. Ind. i, 597.—A tree; leaves shortly-petioled, ovate or oval-entire, glabrous; corymbs lateral or sub-axillary, dichotomous, many-spiked; pedicels and calyx rather hairy; corolla subrotate; flowers small, white; fruit berried, dividing into 4. Near Malwan, south-east of Surat, Law; Beemasunker; flowers in October. Syn. E punctata, Roth. nov. sp. p 126; Bewneria lævis, Don.

2. RHABDIA, Mart.

1. Viminea, Dalz.—A much-branched shrub; branches twiggy; leaves obovate-cuneate, small, smooth; flowers axillary, few, corymbiform, corolla campanulate; flowers small, pink; berries size of a small pea, orange-red when ripe. In the beds of the Concan rivers, pretty common. Syn. Ehretia cuneata, Wight Ic. *t.* 1385.

3. COLDENIA, Linn.

1. PROCUMBENS, Linn. sp. 182.—Herbaceous; stems procumbent, hirsute; leaves shortly-petioled, obovate, plicate, coarsely-toothed, with adpressed hairs above, hirsute beneath; flowers axillary, solitary, sessile, white; nuts rugose, rough. Common in rice-fields, in the cold weather.

4. HELIOTROPIUM, Tourn.

1. ROTTLERI, Lehm. Asp. p 66.—Shrubby; stems short, dividing into many horizontal prostrate branches; branchlets and leaves strigose; leaves subsessile, ovate lanceolate-acutish; spikes lateral, 1 to 2 inches long; flowers subsessile, secund, the underside of the rachis bearing the bract; bracts ovate, strigose; calyx lobes ovate-acute, a little shorter than the corol tube; corolla hairy externally, throat closed with hairs; fruit strigose, globose. At Domus.

2. SUPINUM, Linn. sp. 187; B Malabaricum, Benth. in Royle. Illustr. 306.—Herbaceous; stems ascending; leaves oval, obtuse, plicate, hoary, and tomentose on both sides; spikes mostly solitary; calyx 5-toothed, shut, very hirsute; corol scarcely longer than the calyx, white. Common in rice-fields, in the cold weather. Lyn. H malabaricum, Retz. Obs. iv, p 24; Piptoclaina malabarica, Don. Gon. *syst.* iv, 364.

3. COROMANDELIANUM, Lehm. Asp. 46, and obovatum.—Herbaceous, pubescent, erect; leaves obovate obtuse mucronate, clothed with soft, white hairs; spikes terminal, generally paired; flowers numerous, small, white, placed in a waved row on the upperside of the spikes. Beemasunker.

4. MARIFOLIUM, Retz. Obs. 2, p 8.—Suffruticose; stems procumbent, diffuse, much-branched; leaves and calyx strigose; leaves linear-lanceolate, acute, revolute on the margin, racemes subspicate, solitary, alternate, the uppermost ones twin; flowers minute, white, with yellow eye; nuts densely-hispid. At Vingorla.

5. LAXIFLORUM, Roth. nov. sp. p 102.—Erect-branched, strigose with minute adpressed hairs; leaves linear-lanceolate, entire; racemes simple, subspicate, solitary or twin, elongated; flowers rather lax; lobes of the calyx strigose, as long as the tube of the corolla, nuts globose, strigose, not glabrous as described by Roth. Worlee hill, Island of Bombay; Deccan.

5. TOURNEFORTIA, Linn.

1. T SUBULATA, Hochst.—Stem suffruticose, erect, sparingly-branched, clothed with stiff, bristly hairs; leaves linear-lanceolate.

pilose on both sides; racemes axillary, very long and slender; flowers secund; corolla tubular, segments spreading, acuminated; anthers 3-toothed at the apex; flowers yellowish. Near Gogo; flowers in November.

6. TIARIDIUM, Lehm.

1. INDICUM, Lehm. Asp. 14.—Stem erect, herbaceous, branched, hairy; leaves opposite and alternate-petioled, cordate-ovate, or oval, rugose; spikes terminal, solitary, simple; fruit bifid, glabrous, mitre-shaped, segments devaricate. A common weed, generally found on rubbish; flowers lilac. Syn. Heliotropium indicum, Linn.; H anisophyllum, Beauv.; T anisophyllum, Don. Gen. *syst*. iv, p 364.

XCIX. BORAGINACEÆ.

1. SERICOSTOMA, Stocks.

1. PAUCIFLORUM, Stock's Mss.—Shrubby, very much branched, suberect; leaves linear-lanceolate, 1 inch long, 2 lines broad; flowers spiked, terminal, or on short branches opposite the leaves; flowers fasciculate; calyx segments ovate-acute, strigose; corol white, small, the throat thickly clothed with white hairs; seeds hard, tubercled, shining. One of the commonest plants on the Coast of Kattywar. Wight Ic. *t*. 1377. This does not seem to differ from Lithospermum.

2. CYNOGLOSSUM, Linn.

1. MICRANTHUM, Desf. Cat. H. Par. 1804, p 220.—Stem branched, hispid, with spreading hairs; younger branches and racemes with hoary adpressed pubescence; leaves lanceolate-acute, denticulate, rough, with hairs above, softly hairy beneath; racemes without bracts; calyx lobes ovate-obtuse, nearly as long as the corolla; flowers blue, with a white eye, appear towards the end of the rains. Concan, Khandalla, &c. Syn. C canescens, Willd. Enum i, p 180; C racemosum, Roxb. Fl Ind. ii, p 6. Nuts scarcely one line in length, ovate-rounded, sub-compressed, bristly all over.

2. GLOCHIDIATUM, Wall List. 922.—Stem erect-branched, hispid; hairs of the stem and leaves spreading, tuberculate at their base, branches rather angular; leaves lanceolate-acuminate, attenuated at the base; racemes terminal, solitary or twin, without bracts; calyx lobes ovate oblong-obtuse, silky and strigose; fruit with a hairy ring surmounted by long teeth, which have 5 to 6 recurved hooks at their apex. Parr Ghaut; flowers in November.

3. Cœlestinum, Lindl. Bot. Reg. 1839, *t.* 36.—Pubescent; stem erect-branched; radical leaves cordate-petioled ovate, subacute; stem ones ovate-acute, cuneate at the base; racemes without bracts, often twice bifid; calyx lobes ovate, rather obtuse; corol tube the length of the calyx, limb spreading; flowers pale-blue; nuts ovate-compressed, covered with hooked bristles round the margin. Near Vingorla. Syn. Echinospermum coelestinum, Wight Ic. *t.* 1394. At Mahableshwur, common.

3. TRICHODESMA, R. Br. *Prod.* 496.

1. Amplexicaule, Roth. nov. sp. p 104.—Erect, all over hispid with scattered spreading hairs; lower leaves opposite sessile linear-oblong, upper ones alternate, cordate, stem-clasping, broadly ovate acuminate; pedicels lateral and opposite the leaves, 1-flowered; calyx lobes shortly and obtusely auriculate; limb of the corolla; with scattered hairs inside; lobes rounded, mucronulate. Around Bombay (Polydore Roux.) Very like T indicum. Native name "Chota Kulpa." A common weed.

2. Zeylanicum, R. Br. loc. cit.—Stem erect, sparingly covered with scattered bristles; leaves opposite, subsessile, oblong-lanceolate, attenuated at the base, bristly; pedicels hispid, lateral, long, 1-flowered disposed in a raceme; calyx lobes ovate-lanceolate, villous; flowers pale-blue. A common weed. Syn Borago zeylanica, Linn. Mant. 202; Trichodesma kotschyanum Fenzt; Leiocarya kotschyana, Hochst. in Flora 1844, p 30.

C. CORDIACEÆ.

1. CORDIA, Plum.

1. C Latifolia, Roxb. Fl Ind. ii, p 330.—A tree; the branchlets angled, and the petioles smooth; leaves petioled, ovate-rounded, sometimes slightly cordate, slightly repand, entire, smooth above, paler beneath, and with the nerves a little hairy; panicles terminal and lateral, rather shorter than the leaf; calyx irregularly toothed, hirsute within; corol lobes 5, linear-oblong; flowers white; drupe 1 inch in diameter, yellow when ripe, full of a glutinous pulp. Common in Gujarat, where it is called "Burgoond;" still commoner in Sind, where it is called "Gedooree." The timber is tough, and much used for agricultural implements in Sind.

2. C Myxa, Linn. sp 272.—Branches round and smooth; leaves petioled ovate, repand-dentate on young trees, smooth above, roughish beneath; panicles terminal, rarely lateral; flowers white, appearing in March and April; berry smaller than the preceding, ovoid mucronate, and is an article of native materia medica, being

found in all bazars. Native name "Bhokur" in Bombay; "Lessooree" in Sind. The timber is good; also used in making Bird Lime.

3. C Wallichii, G Don. Gen. *syst.* iv, p 379.—Arboreous; leaves broad, ovate-rounded, more or less cordate, 3-nerved acute, smooth above, densely tomentose and white beneath; corymbs lateral and terminal, dichotomous; calyx campanulate, velvetty, irregularly toothed. Native name "Duhiwun." Between Malsej Ghaut and Ahmednuggur; thinly throughout the Braminwara range of hills.

4. C Rothii, Roem. and Schult. *syst.* p 798.—A small tree; leaves subopposite, lanceolate, obtuse, mucronate, entire rough; panicles terminal and lateral, rather shorter than the leaf, many-flowered; flowers small, white; fruit size of a pea, orange-yellow. Native name "Goondnee." Gum issues from the wounded bark; the wood is very tough, and useful; common everywhere. The "Lyar" of Sind (C subopposita) is very like this tree. Syn. C angustifolia, Roxb. Fl Ind. ii, p 338.

CI. SOLANACEÆ.

1. DATURA, Linn.

1. D Alba, Neesab. Es. in Trans. Linn. soc. xvii, 73—Annual (?); leaves ovate-acuminate, repand-dentate, unequal at the base, smooth; stems herbaceous; capsules nodding, covered with prickles. A common and well-known plant, of which there are several varieties. Rheed. Hort. Mal. ii, *t.* 28; Datura metel, Roxb. Fl Ind. ii, 238; Rumph. Amb. v, *t.* 87.

2. D Hummatu, Bernhardi Journ. Pharm. *v* xxvi, Var. B fastuosa.—Leaves smooth; calyx with 5 angles; corolla often double and treble; flower violet-coloured outside, white within; fruit tubercled. Almost as common as the preceding. These plants are intoxicating and narcotic; the root is used in violent headaches and epilepsy; poultices are made of the leaves, for repelling cutaneous tumours; the bruised seeds are applied to boils.

2. SOLANUM, Tournef.

1. Indicum, Linn. sp. Pl 268.—A prickly shrub; prickles on the stem compressed, recurved; leaves solitary or twin, ovate, sinuate lobed or pinnatifid, unequal at the base, tomentose, prickly, of 2 colours; racemes subcymose, placed between the leaves; calyx prickly; berries globose, size of a cherry, yellow when ripe. Common. Syn. S violaceum, Jacq. frag. *t.* 133; S canesceus, Blume Bijdr. 701; S pinnatifidum Roth. nov. sp. 129; S heynei, Rœm. and Schult. *syst.* 669; S agreste, Roth. loc. cit. 130.

2. Jacquini, Willd. sp. Pl. i, 1041.—Herbaceous, procumbent, perennial, completely armed with prickles; leaves ovate-oblong, subcordate, sinuate-pinnatifid, the divisions acute; racemes few-flowered; berries yellow when ripe, the size of a plum. Very common. Syn. S diffusum, Roxb. Fl Ind. ii, 250; S xantho carpum, Schrad and Wendl. sert. Hann. 1, 8, *t.* 2; S virginianum, Jacq. Ic. rar. *t.* 332.

3. Neesianum, Wall Cat. Suppl. No. 248.—Stem suffruticose; branches quadrangular, roughish towards the apex; lower leaves solitary, upper twin, densely and minutely scabrous above, oblong lanceolate-acuminated at both ends, one smaller than the other; flowers lateral, fascicled; calyx quite entire; berry size of a pea, smooth and red, 2-celled. Phoonda Ghaut.

4. Verbascifolium, Linn. sp. Pl. 184.—A small tree; leaves solitary, ovate-acute, quite entire, hairy above, white and tomentose beneath; corymbs terminal, dichotomous; flowers small, white; berry size of a small cherry. Near Dharwar, Lush. Syn. S pubescens, Roxb. Fl Ind. i, 564; S erianthum, Don. *Prod.* Fl nep. 96; S bicolor, Willd. Reliq.

5. Trilobatum, Linn. sp. Pl. 270.—Stems climbing, prickly; leaves 3-lobed, obtuse glabrous; petioles and peduncles prickly; racemes terminal and lateral, somewhat umbellate; corolla deeply 5-divided, purple; fruit scarlet, size of a large pea. Hedges in Gujarat, common. Burm. Ind. 57, *t.* 22, *fig.* 2. Syn. S acetosæfolium, Lam. Illustr. Gen. No. 2381. Deccan.

6. Giganteum, Jacq. Coll. Bot. iv, 125; Ic. rar. Pl *t.* 328.—A prickly shrub; prickles tomentose at the base; leaves large, oblong-lanceolate entire, covered on the underside with a mealy tomentum; cymes lateral, dichotomous, many-flowered; berries round, red, size of a pea; flowers purplish-violet. On the higher Ghauts, common. Syn. S niveum, Vahl. Symb. ii, 41; S farinosum Wall. in Roxb. Fl Ind. ii, 255. This is a native of the Cape of Good Hope also.

7. S Torvum, Var B inerme.—3 to 4 feet high; leaves slightly repand, ovate or cordate-acute, tomentose; peduncles lateral, corymbose, many-flowered; berry size of an apple. In the Southern Maratha Country; but we suspect had escaped from cultivated fields. Syn. S multiflorum, Roth nov. sp. 130.

3. PHYSALIS, Linn.

1. P Somnifera, Link Enum. Pl Hort. Bowl. i, 180.—Shrubby; branches flexuose, round, downy; leaves double, short-petioled, ovate, slightly repand, smooth, pubescent or tomentose; flowers axillary, subsessile, crowded, small, greenish; berry red, smooth,

size of a pea. P flexuosa, Roxb. Fl Ind. i, 561; Linn. sp. 1, 261. A widely-spread plant, growing also at the Cape of Good Hope, the Canary Isles, Greece, Mauritius, Sind, and Persia. The root and leaves are powerfully narcotic and diuretic, the seeds are employed to coagulate milk, like the Puneeria in Sind—a plant of the same family.

CII. SCROPHULARIACEÆ.

1. CELSIA.

1. C Coromandeliana, Vahl. Symb. iii, 79.—Herbaceous, pubescent and viscid; lower leaves lyrate, floral ones cordate, stem-clasping; peduncles longer than the calyx; calycine segments, ovate, slightly toothed, or oblong-lanceolate, entire; flowers largish, yellow; filaments bearded with purple hairs. Ryeghur Fort; waste places in the Deccan.

2. LINARIA, Vent.

1. L Ramosissima, Wall. Cat. 3911, and Pl As. rar. *t.* 153.—Glabrous; branches elongated, very slender; leaves alternate-petioled, smooth, triangular hastate, lower ones sometimes acutely 5 to 7 lobed; pedicels longer than the petiole; flowers yellow, with a short-curved spur; capsule glabrous. Bassein Hills; near Belgaum, Ahmedabad, Deccan, and Sind, plentiful.

3. LINDENBERGIA, Link. and Otto.

1. L Urticaefolia, L. and O. Ic Select. Pl Hort. Bowl. 95.—An annual, downy plant, erect or ascending; leaves ovate-serrate; flowers solitary, axillary, yellow; corol 3 times the length of the calyx. On the wall of Bombay Fort and other similar places, common. Syn. Stemodia ruderalis, Vahl. Symb. ii, 69; Brachycoris parviflora, Schrad. Ind. Sem. Hort. Gœtting. 1830.

4. STEMODIA, Linn.

S. Viscosa, Roxb. Cor. Pl *t.* 163.—Herbaceous, erect, pubescent and viscid; leaves sessile, ovate-oblong, acute-dilated, cordate and stem-clasping at the base; flowers axillary, solitary-pedicelled, dark-blue. Common on rice fields in the cold weather.

5. MAZUS, Lour.

1. M Rugosus, Lour. Fl Cochin 385.—A delicate annual; leaves cuneate-oblong, coarsely toothed, glabrous; calycine seg-

ments ovate-lanceolate-acute; corolla about twice as long as the calyx, pale-blue, the throat white and yellow. On garden-walks in the rains; Tanna. Syn. Hornemannia bicolor, Willd. Enum. 634; Lindernia japonica, Thunb. Fl Jap. p 253 (?).

6. LIMNOPHILA.

1. CONFERTA, Benth. in DC. *Prod.* 10, p 387.—Glabrous, procumbent; leaves sessile, oblong, rather obtuse, serrate-crenated, narrow at the base; floral ones similar; flowers axillary, subsessile, solitary or aggregated on little branches; calyx-segments lanceolate-subulate; flowers blue, scarcely longer than the calyx. At Malwan; flowers in September. Syn. Stemodia sessilis, Benth. Scroph. Ind. p 23.

2. L MENTHASTRUM.—Erect, smoothish; leaves petioled, ovate-oblong, narrowed at both ends; floral leaves of the same shape, longer than the calyx; flowers axillary, sessile, clustered in globose heads; calyx deeply 5-divided, lanceolate-subulate; leaves 2 to 3 inches long, with glandular dots on the underside; corol 5 lines long. Tulkut Ghaut; flowers in September. Syn. Herpestes rugosa, Roth. nov. sp. p 290.

3. GRATIOLOIDES, R. Br. *Prod.* 442.—Annual, erect, stoloniferous; stems round, jointed, smooth; lower leaves verticelled, above pinnatifid or lobed, uppermost linear-lanceolate, all are serrated towards the apex, less than an inch long; peduncles solitary, axillary, longer than the leaves. On the margins of tanks, common. Syn. Gratiola trifida, Willd. sp. Pl i, 104; Hottonia indica, Linn. sp. Pl 208; Hydropityon pedunculatum, Lor. in DC. *Prod.* 1, 422; Columnea balsamica, Roxb. Fl Ind. iii, 97; Limnophila myriophylloides, Roth. nov. sp. 294. Submersed leaves capillary.

4. ROXBURGHII, G. Don.—Root creeping; stems annual, erect; leaves opposite, subsessile, oblong, serrated; flowers solitary axillary, subsessile; stems emitting capillary leaves at the knots near the root; leaves 2½ inches long, 1 inch broad; corolla campanulate, purple. Syn. Capraria gratissima, Roxb. Fl Ind. ii, 92.

5. RACEMOSA, Benth. in Wall. Cat. 3907.—Emersed leaves, lanceolate, opposite or subverticellate, 3-nerved, entire, or the lowest divided; racemes dense, many-flowered; calyx membranous, smooth, pedicelled; flowers purple. On the borders of tanks, &c. Syn. Cyrilla aquatica, Roxb. Fl Ind. iii, 115; L hyssopifolia, Roth. nov. sp. 297 (?).

6. GRATISSIMA, Blume Bijdr. 749.—Stem round-striated; all the leaves in threes, sessile, linear-lanceolate, serrated; peduncles

racemose, glandular and hairy, as well as the calyx. Margins of ponds, &c.

7. HERPESTES.

1. Monnieria, Kunth. nov. Gen. sp. ii, p 336.—Glabrous, stem-creeping; leaves obovate, oblong-obtuse, entire, rather fleshy; peduncles longer than the leaf; flowers pale-blue. On the margins of tanks; grows all over the world. Syn. Gratiola monniera, Linn. sp. p 24; Lemosella calycina, Forsk.; Septas repens, Lour.; Bramia indica, Lam., and no less than twelve others.

2. Hamiltoniana, Benth. DC. *Prod.* 10, p 400.—Small, erect; leaves lanceolate entire, narrow at the base; flowers subsessile, axillary, opposite, solitary; upper segment of calyx very broad, cordate. At Malwan, plentiful.

8. DOPATRIUM, Ham.

1. Junceum, Ham. Mss.—Stem elongated, scarcely branched; floral leaves minute, obtuse; lower ones obovate, entire; capsule globose; corolla about three times longer than the calyx. In swampy places, common. Syn. Gratiola juncea, Roxb. Pl Cor. ii, p 18, *t.* 129; Morgania juncea, Spr. *syst.* ii, p 803.

9. BONNAYA, Link and Otto.

1. Brachiata, Link and Otto, Abbild. ii, p 25, *t.* 9.—Erect, much-branched; leaves sessile, oblong or obovate, sharply serrated; flowers racemose, pink; capsules spreading, twice the length of the calyx. Pretty common in pastures during the rainy season. Syn. Gratiola serrata, Roxb. Fl Ind. i, 140; B pussilla, Benth. Scroph. Ind. p 33. Stems 2 to 8 inches high.

2. Veronicæfolia, Spr. *syst.* i, p 41.—Stem decumbent or creeping at the base; flower-bearing branches ascending; leaves subsessile, narrow at the base, oblong, rather thick, sharply serrated, lower ones nearly entire; flowers racemose; capsules 2 to 3, longer than the calyx. Common. Syn. Gratiola veronicæfolia, Retz. Obs. 4, p 8; Roxb. Cor. *t.* 154; B marginata, Spr. *syst.* i, p 41; G racemosa, Roth. nov. sp. p 9.

3. Verbenæfolia, Spr. *syst.* i, p 42—Leaves subsessile, oblong-lanceolate or nearly linear, entire or serrated; flowers racemose; capsules 2 to 3 times longer than the calyx; leaves narrower and not so much serrated as in the preceding. Southern Concan. Syn. Gratiola verbenæfolia, Colsm. Vahl. Enum i, p 96; G racemosa, Roxb. Fl Ind. i, 139; G roxburghiana, Rœm. and Schult. *syst.* i, p 123.

4. GRANDIFLORA, Spr. *syst.* i, p 41.—Stem diffuse, rather creeping; ovate-oblong or lanceolate, sessile, serrated; flowers axillary, uppermost ones racemose; capsules linear, scarcely twice as long as the calyx. Southern Concan. Syn. Gratiola grandiflora, Roxb. Cor. *t.* 179; G pulegiifolia, Vahl. Enum. i, 98; B pulegiifolia, Spr. *syst.* i, p 41.

5. OPPOSITIFOLIA, Spr. *syst.* i, 41.—Erect; leaves oblong or lanceolate, slightly serrated; lower peduncles opposite the leaves, reflexed in fruit, uppermost ones racemose; capsules linear, 4 lines long. The Concans. Syn. Gratiola oppositifolia, Roxb. Cor. *t.* 155; G minima, Roth. nov. sp. p 8 (?).

6. REPTANS, Spr. *syst.* i, p 41.—Stem creeping and rooting; leaves rounded or obovate-oblong, sharply serrated, narrowing into the petiole; capsules spreading, 2 to 3 times longer than the calyx. Southern Concan. Syn. Gratiola reptans, Roxb. Fl Ind. i, p 140; G melloides, Koen. in Vahl. Enum. i, p 99; Bonnaya melloides, Spr. *syst.* i, p 41; G ciliata, Vahl. Enum. i, p 97; B ciliata, Spr. *syst.* i, p 41.

10. ILYSANTHES, Rafin.

1. I HYSSOPIOIDES, Benth. in DC. *Prod.* 10, p 149.—Stem diffuse, elongated, lax; leaves oblong or lanceolate, remote, narrow at the base, upper ones small-linear; peduncles elongated, filiform; corolla 3 to 4 times longer than the calyx. Common in the rains. Syn. Gratiola hyssopioides, Linn. Maut. p 174; Morgania hyssopioides, Spr. *syst.* ii, p 803; Bonnaya hyssopioides, Benth. Scroph. Ind. p 34; Wight Ic. 857.

11. VANDELLIA.

1. V HIRSUTA, Ham. in Benth. Scroph. Ind. p 36.—Hirsute, erect, much-branched; leaves ovate-crenate, lower ones narrowing into the petiole, upper sessile, or slightly stem-clasping; racemes elongated (2 inches); calyx-segments lanceolate-subulate; capsules subglobose. Vingorla. Syn. Gratiola viscosa, Hornem. Hort. Hafu. p 19; Hornemannia viscosa, Willd. Enum. p 654; Titmannia viscosa, Reich. Ic. Exot. i, p 26, *t.* 38.

2. LAXA, Benth. Scroph. Ind. p 36.—Diffuse, clothed sparingly with long hairs; leaves subsessile, broadly-ovate, rounded or cordate at the base; pedicels axillary, and in lax racemes, many times longer than the calyx; flowers pretty large, white. At Vingorla.

3. PEDUNCULATA, Benth. Scroph. Ind. p 37.—Glabrous; leaves very shortly-petioled, ovate or ovate-lanceolate, crenated or

entire, upper ones slightly cordate; pedicels axillary, many times longer than the calyx; capsules oblong-linear. Vingorla. Syn. Torenia diffusa, Roxb. Fl Ind. ii, p 95; V roxburghii, Don. *syst.* Gard. and Bot. iv, 549; Gratiola cordifolia, Vahl. Enum. i, 97; Bonnaya cordifolia, Spr. *syst.* i, 42.

4. V Crustacea, Benth. Scroph. Ind. p 35.—A very common plant, diffuse; leaves shortly-petioled, ovate, coarsely crenated; peduncles axillary or subracemose, 6 to 12 lines long; corolla scarcely twice as long as the calyx, small, of a light-purple colour. Syn. Capraria crustacea, Linn. Maut. p 87; Torenia crustacea, Cham. and Schlect. in Linn. ii, 570; Gratiola lucida, Vahl.; Morgania lucida, Spr. *syst.* ii, p 802; Torenia varians, Roxb. Fl Ind. iii, p 96 (?); with many others.

12. GLOSSOSTIGMA, Arnott.

1. G Spathulatum, Arnott. in Nov. Act. Nat. Cur. p 18.—Cespitose, creeping; stems stoloniferous and rooting at the nodes; leaves fascicled, linear spathulate, entire, very small; pedicels solitary in the axils of the leaves; calyx and corolla minute. Margins of tanks and other moist places. Syn. Microcarpæa spathulata, Hook. Bot. Misc. ii, p 101; Suppl. *t.* 4.

13. BUDDLEIA, Linn.

1. B Asiatica, Lour. Fl Cochin, p 72.—Arboreous, covered with a fine tomentum; leaves lanceolate-acuminate, entire or serrulate, smooth above; spikes long and slender; flowers in threes, sessile; tube of the corol nearly twice the length of the campanulate calyx. Hills near Penn. Syn B discolor, Roth. nov. sp. p 83; Wight Ic. 894; B salicina, Lam.

14. TORENIA, Linn.

1. Asiatica, Linn. sp. p 862.—Glabrous or slightly hairy; leaves petioled, ovate or ovate-lanceolate, serrate-crenate; calyx elongated, acute at the base, winged with 3 to 5 prominent ribs; corolla twice as long as calyx, showy, pink. Wight Ic. 862. The Concans, pretty common. Syn. T vagans and hians, Roxb. Fl Ind. iii, p 96; leaves 1 to 2 inches long; corolla 1½ inch. Bot. Mag. *t.* 4249.

2. Cordifolia, Roxb. Cor. Pl ii, p 52, *t.* 161.—Stem trailing, glabrous or slightly hairy; leaves petioled, ovate serrate-crenate; calyx with 3 rather broad wings, rounded at the base; corolla nearly twice as long as the calyx. Bot. Mag. 3715. At Vingorla.

3. Bicolor, Dalz. in Hook. Jour. Bot. iii, p 38.—Stem creeping and rooting; leaves petioled triangular, scarcely cordate at the base, crenate-serrated; calyx linear incurved, equally 5-ribbed; corolla an inch long, curved, under-lip white, the rest of a deep-violet. Flowers beautiful, axillary, in twos or threes. Near Vingorla. Well worthy of a place in gardens.

15. ARTANEMA, Don.

1. Sesamoides, Benth. Scroph. Ind. p 39.—Two feet high; stem acutely 4-sided; leaves petioled, oblong or ovate-lanceolate, entire or serrated; pedicels shorter than the calyx; corolla sub-campanulate, half an inch long; flowers in terminal racemes. The Concans, rare. Syn. Columnea longifolia, Linn. Maut. p 90; Achimenes sesamoides, Vahl. Symb. ii, p 71; Diceros longifolius, Pers. Syn. ii, 164.

16. STRIGA.

1. Orobanchioides, Benth. in Comp. Bot. Mag. i, p 361, *t.* 19.—Glabrous or puberulous, branched; leaves minute, scale-like; stems rigid, erect, 6 to 12 inches high, of a reddish hue; flowers numerous, rose-coloured; parasitic on the roots of different species of Lepidagathis and Euphorbium. Common in rocky ground in the Northern Concan, and hilly parts of Deccan. Syn. Buchnera gesnerioides, Willd. sp. iii, p 338; B orobanchioides, Br. in Salt. Voy.; B hydrabadensis, Roth. nov. sp. p 292; Orobanche indica, Spr. *syst.* ii, 817.

2. Euphrasioides, Benth. loc. cit. i, 364.—Glabrous, rough; leaves linear-entire or few-toothed, elongated; spikes slender, interrupted; calyx with 15 striæ, which all reach to the apex of the segments; flowers white. Syn. Buchnera euphrasioides, Vahl. Symb. iii, p 81; B angustifolia, Don *Prod.* Fl Nep. p 91; S glabrata, Benth. loc. cit. p 364. Very common.

3. Hirsuta, Benth. in DC. *Prod.* 10, p 502.—Very rough; leaves linear-elongated, or lower ones lanceolate; calyx with 10 striæ, of which 5 run into the sinuses between the segments; flowers red, white, or yellow. Very common; turns black in drying. Syn. S lutea, Lour. Fl Cochin, p 22; Buchnera asiatica, Linn.; Campuleia coccinea, Hook. Exot. Fl iii, *t.* 203; B coccinea, Benth. Scroph. Ind. p 40.

4. Densiflora, Benth. in Comp. Bot. Mag. p 363.—Glabrous, very rough; leaves lanceolate-linear, floral ones scale-like; spikes rather thick when young, densely-flowered, afterwards elongated, interrupted; flowers white, not distinguishable from S euphrasioides, but may be always known by the calyx having only 5 striæ up the

centre of the segments. About Surat. Syn. Buchnera asiatica, Vahl. Symb. iii, p 81 (?); B densiflora, Benth. Scroph. Ind. p 41; leaves spreading and recurved.

5. SULPHUREA, Dalz. Mss.—All scabrous; stem slender, quadrangular; leaves very narrow-linear, acute, 8 to 12 lines long, scarcely half a line broad; flowers very shortly-pedicelled; pedicel with 2 subulate bracts; calyx prominently 15-nerved, 5 to 5½ lines long, divided to the middle, divisions linear, strap-shaped; corolla yellow; tube as long as calyx, and pubescent towards the apex; upper lip broad, almost truncate, lower 3-lobed; lobes obovate, all ciliated, about 1 to 1¼ line in length. A very distinct species, coming nearest to Euphrasioides, but having a calyx about double the length, with the divisions long and exactly linear. Found on wet rocks on Sewnere Hill-fort, along with Ophelia minor.

17. BUCHNERA, Linn.

1. B HISPIDA, Ham. in Don. *Prod.* Fl Nep. p 91.—1 to 2 feet high, scarcely branched, leafy at the base; leaves oblong or lanceolate-toothed, upper ones linear; spike terminal, slender, interrupted, many-flowered; flowers light-purple, curved like those of Striga. Island of Caranjah, in the rains.

18. RAMPHICARPA, Benth.

1. R LONGIFLORA, Benth. in Comp. Bot. Mag. i, 368—A low, much-branched plant; leaves pinnately divided into linear segments; flowers white, with a very long, slender tube, and regular limb; capsule furnished with an incurved oblique beak. Common in Ghaut pastures during the rains. Syn. Buchnera longiflora, Arnott in Nov. Act. Nat. Cur. 18, p 356.

19. CENTRANTHERA, Br.

1. C HISPIDA, R. Br. *Prod.* p 438.—Erect, hispid, about 1 foot high; leaves opposite, sessile, linear, almost entire, very rough; flowers axillary, solitary subsessile, somewhat trumpet-shaped, of a deep-purplish red. Hilly parts of the Concan, but not common.

20. SOPUBIA, Hamilton.

1. S DELPHINIFOLIA, G. Don. Gard. Dict. iv, p 560.—An annual, erect, elegant plant; leaves opposite, irregularly pinnatifid, with filiform segments; flowers axillary, solitary, short-peduncled, large, rose-coloured; capsule oblong, the length of the calyx. Common in cultivated fields during the rains. Gerardia delphini-

folia, Linn. sp. p 848; Euphrasia coromandeliana, Roth. in Spr. *syst*. ii, p 775. There is a variety with small flowers.

CIII. ACANTHACEÆ.

SUB-ORDER I.—THUNBERGIEÆ.

1. THUNBERGIA.

1. FRAGRANS, Roxb. Fl Ind. iii, p 33.—Climbing; leaves oblong-acute, cordate, angular and subhastate at the base, slightly scabrous; peduncles axillary, solitary, one-flowered, round, downy, 1 to 2 inches long; flowers large, pure white; capsule flat and beaked. Common in the Concans. Roxburgh has made some mistake about the fragrance, as this species is not fragrant.

2. HEXACENTRIS, N. ab E.

1. H MYSORENSIS, Wight Ic.—Climbing; leaves elliptic-oblong, acuminate-crenate, 3-nerved, reticulated; flowers large, handsome, in a pendulous raceme, either of a golden-yellow throughout, or with the limb of an orange or blood-red colour. Within the latitude of the Dharwar Zillah, though not within the presidency limits. Hook Bot. Mag. 4786.

3. ELYTRARIA, Vahl.

1. E CRENATA, Vahl. Enum. i, p 106.—Stemless; leaves obovate-oblong, crenated, villous on the nerves beneath; scape long, slender, simple; flowers spiked, white; bracts ovate, ciliated. Under the shade of trees at Koondiana, in the Broach Collectorate. Though said to be common in other parts of India, this is the only spot in which we have seen it. Syn. Justicia acaulis, Linn.

4. NELSONIA, R. Br.

1. TOMENTOSA, Willd. sp. Pl i, 419.—Herbaceous, prostrate, villous; lower leaves petioled, elliptic-obtuse, upper subsessile, smaller; spikes ovate; bracts rounded-elliptic, obtuse-mucronulate; corolla purple, a little longer than the calyx. In the Warree jungles, common. Syn. Justicia tomentosa, Roxb. Fl Ind. i, 132; N origanoides, Roem. and Schultz *syst*. i, p 173; J origanoides, Vahl. Enum. p 122; J vestita, Roem. and Schultz *syst*. Mant. i, 145; J bengalensis, Spr. *syst*. i, p 82; J lamiifolia, Roxb. Fl Ind. i, p 136.

5. EBERMEIERA, N. ab E.

1. Glauca, N. ab E.—Stem erect, a foot high, pubescent and rough, spikes leafy, axillary and terminal; leaves oblong, attenuated into the petiole, glabrous entire; calyx pubescent and glandular; corolla very small, tubular; capsule oblong-obtuse, glabrous. Southern Concan.

6. ERYTHRACANTHUS, N. ab E.

1. Elongatus, N. ab E.—Herbaceous; leaves oblong-oval or oblong-pubescent, rough, obtuse at both ends; racemes axillary and terminal, simple or compound, elongated lax-flowered; common peduncle very short; bracts lanceolate; leaves red on the underside; capsule oblong. Warree jungles. Syn. Adenosma elongatum, Bl. Bijdr. p 757.

Sub-Order II.—HYGROPHILEÆ.

7. PHYSICHILUS, N. ab E.

1. Serpyllum, N. ab E. in DC. *Prod.* 11, p 81.—Diffuse-branched, creeping; leaves strigose and hirsute, those on the stem nearly orbicular, floral ones oblong or oblong-lanceolate; flowers purple, axillary, subsessile, collected into a terminal spike. Island of Bombay; the Concan, common.

8. NOMAPHILA, Blume.

1. Pinnatifida, Dalz. in Hook Jour. Bot. iii, p 38.—All glandular and pubescent; leaves petioled, deeply pinnatifid, linear-lanceolate, the segments linear, oblong-obtuse, serrulated; flowers in the opposite axils of the leaves, sessile, or clustered in terminal heads; flowers purple. The river-banks of the Southern Concan; flowers in January and March.

9. HYGROPHILA, R. Br.

1. Salicifolia, N. ab E. DC. *Prod.* 11, p 92.—Herbaceous; stem erect, 1 to 2 feet high; lower leaves obovate or oblong, rather obtuse, upper lanceolate, attenuated at both ends; flowers axillary, clustered, about 7 together, pale-blue; calycine segments subulate, hirsute; capsule narrow-compressed, quadrangular, half an inch long. Wet places in the Southern Concan. Syn. Ruellia salicifolia, Vahl. Symb. iii, p 84; Roxb. Fl Ind. i, p 50; R longifolia, Roth. nov. sp. p 306.

10. CRYPTOPHRAGMIUM, N. ab E.

1. Latifolium, Dalz. in Hook. Jour. Bot. ii, 137.—Suffruticose glabrous; leaves very long-petioled, rounded-ovate, acuminate, truncate at the base, crenulate, 1 foot long, 4½ inches broad; spikes axillary, short, trichotomous; flowers yellowish-white; capsule 4 times longer than the calyx. Chorla Ghaut. Syn. Phloganthus latifolius, Wight Ic. *t.* 1537.

2. Glabrum, Dalz. loc. cit. ii, 338.—Herbaceous; leaves elliptic-acuminate, denticulate, glabrous, running down with a wing into the petioles; spike terminal, compound; the branches opposite, nearly a foot long. In shady places in the Southern Concan.

11. ENDOPOGON, N. ab E.

1. Integrifolius, Dalz. in Hook. Jour. Bot. ii, 342.—A shrub; leaves narrow-elliptic or lanceolate-acuminate, running down with a wing into the petiole; bracts and bracteoles linear, ciliated with long hairs, and as long as the calyx; flowers blue, rather large; rachis short, quadrangular, viscous and glandular. Hills near Panwell.

12. PETALIDIUM, N. ab E.

1. Barlerioides, N. ab E., DC. *Prod.* 11, p 114.—Shrubby; leaves oblong, crenate-dentate, somewhat glaucous; peduncles axillary, solitary, 1-flowered; flowers an inch long, white or pale-blue; bracteoles large, opposite, covering the calyx. The Ghauts; hills near Panwell. Syn. Ruellia barlerioides, Roth. nov. sp. p 310; R bracteata, Roxb. Fl Ind. iii, p 47; Bot. Mag. *t.* 4053; Eranthemum barlerioides, Roxb. Fl Ind. i, 114.

2. P Patulus, N. ab E. DC. *Prod.* 11, p 126.—Stem erect; leaves ovate, oval or oblong-obtuse, hoary and puberulous; flowers fascicled in threes or fives, or solitary, smaller than in the preceding, white; bracteoles oval or oblong, longer than the calyx. The flowers open in the evening, and fall off in the morning; while in the preceding, the flowers open in the morning.

13. DIPTERACANTHUS, N. ab E.

1. Dejectus, N. ab E., DC. *Prod.* 11, p 125.—Stem herbaceous, suffrutiscent at the base, creeping, procumbent or ascending; leaves long-petioled, ovate-elliptic, acute at both ends, entire, strigose or rough on the veins; flowers pretty large, blue, axillary, sessile, solitary; capsule half an inch long, oblong, narrow at the base, 12 to 16-seeded. Common in Bombay and the Concans; flowers in October. Syn. Ruellia repens, Blume Bijdr. p 794; R rigens, Roxb. Fl Ind. iii, p 44.

14. RUELLIA, Linn.

1. Dura, N. ab E., DC. *Prod.* 11, p 146.—Stem quadrangular, procumbent, hispid and bristly; leaves oblong-obtuse, subcrenate, attenuated into the petiole, hispid; spikes axillary subsessile and terminal, somewhat capitate, subtended by subovate hirsute bracts; flowers middle-sized, blue; capsule 8-seeded, shorter than the calyx. About Surat, common.

2. Elegans, Bot. Mag. *t.* 3389.—Herbaceous, erect, pubescent; stem with opposite branches; leaves ovate-acuminate, coarsely serrated; flowers of a bright blue, axillary, short-peduncled, subcapitate or terminal subsolitary; capsule as long as the calyx, 6 to 8-seeded. In the Concans, common. Syn. Hemigraphis elegans, N. ab E. The anthers are not unilocular, as stated by N. ab. E. DC. *Prod.* 11, p 722.

3. Latebrosa, Roxb. Fl Ind. iii, p 46.—Creeping; leaves opposite, short-petioled, broad-oval, coarsely toothed, hairy, about an inch long, and nearly as broad; flowers axillary, solitary sessile, light-blue, collected also in small terminal bracted heads; bracts ovate-lanceolate, as long as the calyx. Below trees on the Island of Caranjah; the Deccan. Syn. Hemigraphis latebrosa, N. ab E. in DC. *Prod.* 11, p 723; Ruellia ebracteata, Dalz. in Hook. Jour. Bot. ii, 342.

15. ASYSTASIA, Blum.

1. Coromandeliana, N. ab E., DC. *Prod.* 11, p 165.—Stem erect; branches numerous, almost smooth; leaves cordate-ovate or suborbiculate-cuspidate, glabrous; racemes axillary, elongated, secund, straight; flowers large, pale-blue; capsule an inch long. Very common, often cultivated in gardens, where there are white-flowered varieties. Syn. Justicia gangetica, Linn. Amœn. iv, p 290; Ruellia secunda, Roxb. Fl Ind. iii, p 42; Vahl. Symb. iii, p 84.

2. Violacea, Dalz. in Hook.—Stem ascending, jointed, smooth, striated, obtusely quadrangular; leaves ovate or oblong-acute, entire, lower ones attenuated into the petiole, upper rounded at the base, short-petioled or subsessile; racemes terminal, secund, solitary or twin; flowers an inch long, of a deep-blue, somewhat 2-lipped, the lower lip of a dark violet; the throat spotted with purple. The Concans. A very handsome species.

3. Lawiana, Dalz. in Hook. Jour. Bot. iv, 344.—Stem herbaceous, erect, quadrangular, knotted, trichotomous; leaves elliptic-oblong acute, suddenly narrowing into a petiole of 1 inch, roughish above, hispid on the nerves beneath; spikes terminal, solitary, short; flowers approximated, sessile, opposite, decussate; bracts and

bracteoles lanceolate, foliaceous, 3-nerved, villous; flowers small, white, shorter than the bracts. Near Dharwar; flowers in the rains. Syn. Strobilanthes mysorensis, N. ab E. in DC. *Prod.* 11.

16. STROBILANTHES.

1. Heyneanus, N. ab E. in DC. *Prod.* 11, p 184.—Stems about a foot high, herbaceous, strigose, and hirsute; leaves elliptic-cuspidate, running down into a long petiole, crenate-serrate, hirsute; spikes axillary, compound, shorter than the leaf, subglobose, glabrous; bracts orbicular, ventricose; calyx short, the segments oblong-obtuse, glabrous; corolla half an inch long. Chorla Ghaut.

2. Sessiloides, Wight Ic. Pl Ind. Or. *t.* 1512.—A low, suffruticose plant; branches numerous, spreading, hairy all over; stem erect, quadrangular; leaves sessile, rounded-cordate, serrate, blistered, reticulate, coriaceous; spikes axillary and terminal, short; flowers blue, numerous, handsome; bracts broadly-cordate, cuspidate, entire. Phoonda Ghaut, in abundance.

3. Grahamianus, Wight loc. cit. *t.* 1520.—A tall branched-shrub; stem quadrangular; older branches glabrous, tuberculated; leaves broadly ovate-cuspidate, acuminate, crenate-dentate, running down into a long petiole, hirsute, with stellate hairs above, pubescent beneath, reticulately veined; peduncles axillary, or on the naked branches, trifid, shorter than the petiole; spikes ovate-oblong, glabrous; bracts orbicular, ventricose, corolla large, blue; capsule short-compressed, 4-seeded; seeds pubescent. Comes nearest to S callosus.

4. Warreensis, Dalz. in Hook. Jour. Bot. ii, 341.—Stem suffruticose, dichotomously branched, knotty and smooth; leaves oblong-acuminate, running gradually into the petiole, glabrous on both sides, repand-toothed; spikes in the opposite axils peduncled, simple, solitary, drooping; peduncles jointed in the middle; flowers small, spotted with purple. The Warree Country.

5. Tetrapterus, Dalz. loc. cit. 342.—Shrubby, subscandent, glabrous; leaves oval, shortly acuminated, running down the petiole and along the stem, crenate, coriaceous, shining above; spikes axillary opposite, and terminal solitary, peduncled; bracts herbaceous, rhomb-cuneate, long-cuspidate, ciliated; corolla somewhat 2-lipped, white; leaves 9 to 10 inches long. The Warree Country.

6. Asperrimus, N. ab E., DC. *Prod.* 11, p 183.—Stem rigid, rough, and tuberculated, hirsute at joints; leaves elliptic-acute, running down like a wing into a petiole, shorter than the leaf, crenated, hispid, and bristly; peduncles axillary, trichotomous; spikes ovate; bracts broadly oval, ventricose, glabrous, lower ones more remote and smaller; rachis hirsute. Well marked by the small foramina left on the falling off of the rigid hairs on the leaf. The Ghauts.

7. CALLOSUS, N. ab. E. in Wall. Pl. As. Rar. iii, p 85.—Shrubby, 6 feet high; stem verrucose; leaves elliptic-cuspidate, running down into a long petiole, with minute callous teeth on the margin, scabrous and ciliated; spikes axillary, compound, shorter than the leaf; bracts orbicular, ventricose, lower more remote, sterile; branches as thick as a goose-quill, 4-sided, glabrous, often rough with warts and grey points; leaves 7 to 10 inches long; flowers. deep-blue; seeds quite smooth. The Ghauts; flowers in August.

8. NEESIANA, R. Wight Ic. *t.* 1523.—Suffruticose; ramuli subterete, glabrous; leaves unequal, elliptic-ovate; acuminate-acute, and subunequal at the base, coarsely crenate-serrated; stillato-hirsute, densely lineolate above, sparingly pubescent beneath; peduncles axillary, often trifid, numerous and subpanicled towards the end of the branches, bibracteolate about the middle; spikes short, ovate-capitulate; bracts foliaceous, acuminate, retuse at the point, clothed with viscid pubescence; calyx and shorter bracteoles densely pilose; corolla sparingly pubescent without, bristly hirsute within. Salsette, and hills throughout the Concans; common.

17. BARLERIA, Linn.

1. TERMINALIS, N. ab E. in DC. *Prod.* ii, p 225.—Stem strigose; leaves oval-oblong, running down with a wing into a long petiole; flowers spicate; spikes destitute of bracts, crowded at the apex of the branches; bracteoles lanceolate, nearly as long as the calyx; calyx pubescent, ciliated; the larger segments subequal; oval-acute, entire; flower deep-blue, 2 inches long. The Ghauts; flowers in November and December. This is No. 1184 of Graham's Catalogue.

2. COURTALLICA, N. ab E. loc. cit. p 226.—Stem fruticose; leaves oblong, glabrous, shining, attenuated at both ends; spikes axillary and terminal, short, hairy, and glandular; bracts and bracteoles linear subulate; flowers 1¼ inch long, blue and yellow. On Chorla Ghaut.

3. DICHOTOMA, Roxb. Fl Ind. iii, p 39.—Suffruticose, adpressed, strigose; stem with opposite branches; leaves elliptic-oblong, attenuated at both ends, petioled; spikes axillary and terminal; flowers white, secund; bracts linear-lanceolate, pectinate, ciliated; larger calycine segments ovate-subulate, serrate. Near the village of Penn. Though certainly a native of India, it has never been found truly wild. It is a favourite plant of the Brahmins, and is often found planted near temples.

4. CRISTATA, Linn. sp. Pl, p 887.—Herbaceous, all over strigose, with adpressed hairs; leaves elliptic, attenuated at both ends, petioled; peduncles axillary, very short, few-flowered; bracts linear

subulate, ciliated; larger calycine segments unequal, elliptic-oblong, ciliate and serrated; flowers blue, an inch long. Bombay and the Concans.

5. MONTANA, N. ab E. loc. cit. p 232.—Herbaceous, erect, 2 feet high, all quite smooth, diandrous; leaves oblong-elliptic, attenuated into the petiole, a little scabrous on the margin; flowers axillary, solitary, sessile, opposite; bracteoles linear; larger calycine segments equal, elliptic, herbaceous; flowers of a beautiful rose-colour, 2 inches long, appear in September. Island of Caranjah; Cross Island, &c. This is No. 1182 of Graham's Catalogue. Syn. B purpurea, Lodd. Bot. Cab. *t.* 344.

6. GIBSONI, Dalz. in Hook. Jour. Bot. ii, 339.—Suffruticose, 3 to 4 feet high, diandrous, all quite smooth; leaves elliptic-acute at both ends, glaucous beneath, ciliolated on the margins; flowers spicate; spikes short, terminal, solitary; bracts small, foliaceous, narrow-ovate, obtusely-acuminate; bracteoles linear-acute; larger calycine segments oval, subequal, quite entire; flowers of a beautiful pink colour. The Ghauts, and on the Brahminwara Range.

7. GRANDIFLORA, Dalz. loc. cit.—Stem fruticose; leaves elliptic-acuminate, attenuated into the petiole, upper ones subsessile, quite smooth on both sides; flowers short-pedicelled, solitary in the opposite axils, very large, pure white; bracts inserted on the middle of the pedicel, short-subulate; larger calycine segments equal, herbaceous, ovate-acute, glabrous, 10 to 12-nerved; smaller ones narrow-subulate, half the length; flower upwards of 4 inches long. The Mangellee Ghaut. This is by far the showiest of the genus.

8. ELATA, Dalz. loc. cit. iii, 227.—Shrubby, 6 feet high; stem round-strigose, swollen at the joints; leaves herbaceous unequal, long-petioled, elliptic-acuminated, suddenly attenuated into the petiole, pubescent on both sides; spikes terminal, and in the upper axils, solitary, short-spreading, stout, 2 to 3-flowered; flowers very shortly pedicelled, secund; pedicels subtended by lanceolate, foliaceous bracts as long as the calyx; flowers 3½ to 4 inches long, the tube reddish-purple, the limb blue. Phoonda Ghaut; flowers in November.

9. PRIONITIS, Linn. sp. Pl, p 887.—Shrubby; leaves elliptic-oblong, attenuated at both ends, glabrous; flowers axillary, verticelled, sessile, and terminal spicate; flowers yellow; fertile bracteoles subulate and spinous; larger calycine segments ovate-entire, glabrous, pointed with spines. Very common in hedges. Coletta veedla, Rheed. Hort. Mal. ix, *t.* 41.

18. ASTERACANTHA, N. ab E.

1. LONGIFOLIA, N. ab E., DC. *Prod.* 11, 247.—Herbaceous, erect; stem quadrangular; leaves lanceolate, attenuated at both

ends, serrulate, ciliated; flowers sessile in the axils, verticelled, blue, surrounded by rigid spines. In swampy places, very common. Syn. Barleria longifolia, Linn. Amœn. Acad. iv, p 320; Willd. sp. iii, p 375. It is a kind of religious service among the Hindoos to collect a lac of these flowers to present them to their idols. The ceremony is called "Lackotee." The seeds have considerable diuretic powers, and are called "Talimkhana."

19. NEURACANTHUS, N. ab E.

1. Sphærostachyus, Dalz. in Hook. Jour. Bot. ii, 140.—Stems many, from a perennial root, erect, simple, obtusely quadrangular, pubescent and scabrous; leaves opposite, oblong-truncate or sub-cordate at the base, obtuse at the apex, pubescent and scabrous on both sides; spikes in the opposite axils sessile, globose, densely silky and tomentose; bracts orbicular, suddenly acuminate, reticulately veined; corolla blue, subentire; the limb ventricose and rotate. Malabar Hill; Island of Caranjah, &c. Syn. Lepidagathis sphærostachya, N. ab E. in DC. *Prod.* 11, p 254 (?); N lawii, Wight Ic. *t.* 1532.

2. Trinervius, Wight Ic. Pl. *t.* 1532.—Branches round, glabrous, and shining; leaves shortly-petioled, subobovate-mucronate, glabrous; spikes axillary, secund, dense, terminal one as long as the leaves; bracts ovate-acute, coriaceous, densely hairy, 3 to 5-nerved; calycine lobes lanceolate, pubescent; corolla obsoletely 5-lobed; flowers small, blue. Hills near Alibaug, &c.

20. LEPIDAGATHIS, Willd.

1. Grandiflora, Dalz. in Hook. Jour. Bot. ii, 138.—Stem erect, suffruticose, quadrangular, glabrous, 3 to 4 feet high; leaves ovate-acuminate, entire, glabrous, attenuated into the petiole; spikes axillary and terminal, simple or trifid, long, slender, densely woolly; bracts, bracteoles, and upper lip of calyx of the same shape, obtuse, 3-nerved, reticulately veined, woolly; corolla deeply bilabiate, large, blue, with 2 lines of yellow hairs in the throat. The Ghauts.

2. Prostrata, Dalz. loc. cit.—Stem shrubby, creeping and rooting, glabrous, obtusely quadrangular; younger branches softly tomentose; leaves small, sessile, opposite or tern, elliptic, spinous-pointed, younger ones tomentose; bracts, bracteoles, and calyx segments lanceolate, spinous-pointed; spikes rarely axillary, more frequently terminal and simple at the apex of short ascending branches. Malwan.

3. Lutea, Dalz. loc. cit.—Stems several, erect, filiform, dichotomously branched from the base, velvetty and tomentose; leaves

linear-folded, 3-nerved, minutely hispid above, glabrous beneath; spikes clustered about the root, velvetty and tomentose; bracts ovate-orbicular, with a long spinous point; anterior and posterior segments of calyx rhomb-cuneate, spinous-pointed, lateral ones linear; flowers small, yellow. Malwan, on rocks; leaves 2 inches long, 2 lines broad.

4. Mitis, Dalz. loc. cit. iii, 226.—Stem branched, diffuse; branches trichotomous, glabrous, almost 4-sided; leaves sessile, linear-oblong, acute, glabrous on both sides, minutely ciliated on the margin; spikes clustered about the root into a ball 2 to 3 inches in diameter; bracts acuminated from a broad base; bracteoles and calyx-segments linear-acute, all without points, somewhat cartilaginous, smooth at the base, silky and villous at the lip; flowers white, spotted with pink and yellow. On rocks at Fonda Ghaut; flowers in November.

5. Clavata, Dalz. loc. cit. ii, 340.—Stems several, from a woody root 1 foot, high, simple, ascending, obtusely quadrangular, glabrous, naked at the base; spikes terminal, solitary, simple, oblong quadrangular; leaves small, sessile, ovate-acuminate, spinous-pointed, glabrous, entire, coriaceous, rigid; bracts densely imbricated in 4 rows, of the same shape as the leaves, along with the bracteoles and calyx, silky and tomentose. Chorla Ghaut.

6. Rigida, Dalz. loc. cit. p 341.—Stem erect, suffruticose, covered with soft, spreading hairs; leaves linear-lanceolate, folded, gradually attenuated into the base, glandular and pubescent on both sides; spikes terminal on the short branchlets, cylindric, 1 to 1½ inch long, compound at the base, glandular and pubescent; bracts linear-subulate, calyx 4-divided; dorsal segment oblong-acute, 3-nerved, anterior divided to the middle, lateral subulate, all spinous-pointed; leaves 3 to 4 inches long. Ram Ghaut.

7. Gœnsis, Dalz. loc. cit. p 340.—Stem herbaceous, dichotomous, diffuse; leaves broadly ovate-acute, 1½ to 2 inches long, softly pubescent, repand-dentate; spikes terminal on bitrifid peduncles, lax, few-flowered, 1 to 1½ inch long; bracts broadly ovate, rather obtuse; bracteoles linear, and with the calycine segments densely glandular, pubescent. The Warree Country; closely allied to L fasciculata, N. ab E. A native of Ceylon.

8. Cristata, Willd. sp. Pl iii. 1, p 400.—Stem suffruticose, diffuse; leaves lanceolate or oblong; spikes all clustered about the root, in a subglobose head of various sizes; bracts and bracteoles oblong-attenuated, mucronate; calyx 4-divided; segments acuminate, bristle-pointed, lower one bifid; corolla 4 lines long, pubescent, whitish. Wight Ic. 455; Roxb. Cor. Pl. *t.* 267.

21. ÆTHEILEMA, R. Br.

1. Reniforme, N. ab E. in DC. *Prod.* 11, p 261.—Stem herbaceous; leaves ovate, unequal at the base, repand, pubescent, one of the pair smaller; spike bearing branches axillary, shorter than the leaves; bracts kidney-shaped, membranous, ciliated, as well as the upper ovate division of the calyx; flowers whitish, scarcely longer than the calyx. At Banda, in the Warree Country, and the Ghauts generally. Syn. Ruellia imbricata, Vahl. Symb. ii, p 73; R dosiflora, Retz. Obs. vi, p 31; R glutinosa, Roxb.; Aeth. parviflorum, Spr. *syst.* ii, 826; Phaylopsis parviflora, Willd. sp. iii, 342.

22. BLEPHARIS, Juss.

1. Molluginifolia, Juss. Pers. Syn. ii, p 180.—Hispid and bristly; stem creeping; leaves in fours, oblong-sublinear, densely serrulate, scabrous on the margin, the two opposite one half smaller; flowers axillary, alternate, sessile; bracteoles boat-shaped, pointed with a bristle, and strongly ciliated. Bassein; the Concans generally. Syn. B repens, Roth. nov. sp. 321; Acanthus repens, Vahl. Symb. ii, 76.

2. Bœrhaavifolia, Juss., DC. *Prod.* 11, p 266.—Stem creeping; leaves in fours, ovate-rhomboid or oblong, repand-dentate, the two opposite smaller; flowers axillary, sessile or peduncled; bracteoles flat, wedge-shaped, ciliated with bristles at the apex; flowers pale-blue, with a yellow spot on the under lip. A common weed. Syn. B madraspatensis, Var. B. Roth. nov. sp. p 320; B procumbens, Roth. loc. cit.

3. Asperrima, N. ab E., DC. *Prod.* 11, p 267.—Stem herbaceous, suberect; leaves oblong or ovate, entire or remotely denticulate, opposite; bracteoles in fours, white, with green veins, cuneiform, trifid, and lanceolate; flowers blue, solitary, or in pairs in the opposite axils, subsessile. Very common on the Ghauts.

23. DILIVARIA, Juss.

1. Ilicifolia, Juss. Gen. p 103.—A shrub, 2 to 4 feet high, spinous or unarmed, glabrous; leaves elliptic-sinuate, dentate-spinous, waved, ending acutely in a short petiole; spike many-flowered; flowers blue, with bracts and bracteoles, very like the English Holly in its foliage. In salt marshes, common, Syn. Acanthus dolvaria, Blanco in Fl Philipp. p 487; A ilicifolius, Blume Bijdr. p 806; A malabaricus, Petiver.

24. CROSSANDRA, Salisb.

1. Axillaris, N. ab E. in DC. *Prod.* 11, p 281.—Shrubby, erect; leaves in fours, oblong, glabrous, rather smooth; spikes axillary, alternate, shorter than the leaf; bracts pubescent, scabrous, naked on the margins; spike tetragonal; flowers orange-coloured. About Dharwar, Wight Ic. *t.* 460.

25. ROSTELLULARIA, Reichen.

1. R Peploides, N. ab E. in Wall. Pl. As. rar. iii, p 101.—Branches diffuse, spreading; leaves ovate-obtuse, glabrous; spikes dense at the apex, interrupted and leafy at the base; bracts, bracteoles, and calyx-segments oblong-spathulate, with white margins; whole plant smooth and glaucous. About watercourses in the Deccan.

2. Diffusa, N. ab E. DC. *Prod.* 11, 371.—Stem procumbent, diffuse; leaves lanceolate-elliptic or rounded, glabrous or sparingly hairy; spikes compressed, slender; calycine-segments lanceolate, membranous on the margin, minutely ciliated; bracts of the same shape, and shorter than the calyx; flowers small, pale-purple. In pastures, common. Syn. Justicia diffusa, Wild. sp. Pl i, p 87; J procumbens, Vahl. Enum. i, p 140.

3. Procumbens, N. ab E. loc. cit.—Stem procumbent or ascending; leaves from ovate to lanceolate, ciliated, hairy; spikes subtetragonal; calyx-segments and bracts lanceolate, linear, equal, hairy ciliated. Very like the last, of which it is probably merely a variety.

4. Crinita, N. ab E. DC. *Prod.* 11, p 373.—Stem procumbent, ascending, trichotomous, pubescent; leaves elliptic or ovate, hairy; spikes terminal, sessile, short; apices of the calyx-segments and the setaceous equal; bracts very rough, with spreading hairs; flowers pale-purple, very small; capsule oval, glabrous, white. Vingorla; flowers in August. Dr. Thomas Anderson, who has paid considerable attention to this genus in Ceylon, considers Rotundifolia, Procumbens, Crinita, and Royeniana, as varieties of one species.

26. ADHATODA, N. ab E.

1. Ramosissima, N. ab E. in DC. *Prod.* 11, p 385.—Shrubby, creeping; leaves broadly ovate, obtusely acuminated, glabrous; spikes axillary and terminal, secund, rather lax; bracts and bracteoles ovate-lanceolate, acuminate, glabrous, white, reticulated with green veins; flowers of a dull-white colour. Common on the higher Ghauts. Syn. Justicia ramosissima, Roxb. Fl Ind. i, p 130.

2. Trinervia, N. ab E. loc. cit.—Suffruticose; stem procumbent; leaves lanceolate or oval, obtuse sessile, glabrous; spikes terminal secund, slender; bracts and bracteoles oblong-lanceolate, acuminate, reticulately veined, much smaller than the last species. On Wag Donger, near Vingorla. Syn. Justicia trinervia, Vahl. Enum. i, p 156; Dicliptera trinervia, Juss. Ann. Mus. ix, p 169.

3. Vasica, N. ab E. loc. cit. p 387.—A shrub, 4 to 5 feet high; leaves elliptic-oblong, attenuated at both ends, glabrous; spikes axillary, opposite, ovate, long-peduncled; bracts herbaceous, glabrous, ovate; flowers rather large, white, with brown spots. On the Ghauts, pretty common. Used in making hedges in Gujarat and Ghaut villages. Roxburgh says the wood is good for making charcoal for gunpowder. Syn. Justicia adhatoda, Linn. Fl Zeyl. p 16.

4. Wynaadensis, N. ab E. in DC. *Prod.* 11, p 406.—Shrubby; stems long, slender, terete, smooth; leaves oblong, attenuated at both ends, lower ones crenate-dentate; spikes axillary, spreading and drooping, glandular and pubescent; flowers solitary, opposite, pubescent, quarter of an inch long; bracts ovate deciduous; bracteoles linear-subulate, shorter than the calyx. Jungly parts of the Concan, common. Syn. Gendarussa wynaadensis, N. ab E. in Wall. Pl As. rar. iii, p 104.

27. HEMICHORISTE, N. ab E.

1. H Montana, N. ab E. in Pl As. rar. iii, p 102.—Shrubby, smooth; leaves large, oblong-entire, attenuated into the petiole; thyrsus of whitish flowers, terminal, six inches to a foot in length; corolla upwards of an inch long. The Ghauts, pretty common. This may be easily mistaken for an Adhatoda, which it much resembles.

28. JUSTICIA, N. ab E., Linn.

1. Ecbolium, Linn. Fl Zeyl. p 17.—Shrubby; leaves elliptic-oblong, attenuated at both ends, pubescent or glabrous; spikes terminal, tetragonal; bracts oval, quite entire, ciliated, mucronate, as long as the capsule; flowers greenish or azure-coloured; capsule half an inch long. Hills throughout the Concans; Island of Bombay. Bot. Mag. *t.* 1847.

29. RHINACANTHUS, N. ab E.

1. Communis, N. ab E. in DC. *Prod.* 11, p 442.—Shrubby, 4 to 5 feet high; leaves oblong or ovate-oblong; panicles axillary and terminal, bitrichotomous, spreading; flowers small, white; corolla with a long, slender, compressed tube. Mahableshwur;

generally to be found in gardens. The roots, rubbed up with lime-juice and pepper, are used to cure Ringworms; the roots boiled in milk are reckoned by native doctors aphrodisiacal. Syn. Justicia nasuta, Linn. sp. Pl. p 63; J scandens, Vahl. Symb. ii, p 7.; J sylvatica, Lour. Cochin i, p 26; Dianthera paniculata, Lour. Cochin i, p 32.

30. ERANTHEMUM, Linn.

1. Roseum, Rœm. and Schult. *syst.* i, p 175.—Leaves elliptic, glabrous, scabrous on the veins beneath; spikes axillary-peduncled, imbricated; bracts oval, somewhat wedge-shaped, acute, ciliated, with long hairs, reticulately veined. Around Bombay, Perottet. 2; leaves 5 inches long, 2 broad; corolla 1¼ inch long.

2. Nervosum, R. Br. *Prod.* p 333.—Stem quadrangular; leaves ovate or elliptic, acuminated at both ends, subcrenate or entire, glabrous; spikes axillary, opposite, imbricated; bracts elliptic, long and acutely cuspidate, reticulated with veins; diameter of the limb of the corolla as long as the tube; flowers blue. The Concans. Syn. E pulchellum, Roxb. Fl Ind. i, p 111; Justicia nervosa, Vahl. Enum. i, 164; Bot. Mag. *t.* 1358; J pulchella, Roxb. Pl Cor. p 41, *t.* 177.

3. Montanum, Roxb. Fl. Ind. i, 110.—Stem quadrangular; leaves oblong, attenuated at both ends, repand-crenate, glabrous; peduncles terminal, trichotomous, and the spikes pubescent and viscid; bracts lanceolate, attenuated, ciliated. The Ghauts near Dharwar. Syn. E capense fol. lanceolato-ovatis petiolatis, Linn. Fl Zeyl. No. 15; Willd. sp. Pl. i, p 51; Wight Ic. *t.* 466; Bot. Mag. *t.* 4031; E montanum, Roxb.; E fastigiatum, Spr. *syst.* i, 89; Justicia fastigiata, Lam. Illust. p 41.

4. Crenulatum, Wall. in Bot. Reg. *t.* 879.—Shrubby, erect; leaves oblong, acuminated at both ends, repand-crenate, glabrous; raceme terminal, simple or compound, or several axillary aggregated simple; flowers somewhat fascicled, subverticelled or secund, white; bracts and bracteoles subulate, short, and with the calyx glandular and scabrous. In the Warree jungles. Syn. Justicia latifolia, Vahl. Symb. ii, p 4; Willd. sp. Pl i, 88; E diantherum, Blume Bijdr. p 792.

31. RUNGIA.

1. Parviflora, N. ab E. in DC. *Prod.* 11, p 469.—Stem diffuse or creeping; leaves oval or lanceolate, rather obtuse; fertile bracts suborbicular, mucronate or unpointed, nerved and veined, glabrous, ciliated, with membranous margin, sterile ones oval or oblong, margined on one or both sides, acute ciliated; bracteoles membranous margined, emarginate mucronate; corolla small, upper lip

acute; flowers of a fine blue. Common. Syn. Justicia parviflora, Retz. Obs. v, p 9; J pectinata, Roxb. Cor. *t.* 153; Fl Ind. non Linn.

2. POLYGONOIDES, N. ab E. loc. cit. p 471.—Stem creeping at the base; common bracts suborbicular, mucronulate, 3-nerved; bracteoles boat-shaped, ciliated, and with a broad, membranous margin; leaves unequal, obtuse, lower oval, upper lanceolate. A plant like Polygonum aurculare; spikes axillary, clustered; gathered in Bombay by Polydore Roux.; spikes subglobose, of the size of a pea.

3. REPENS, N. ab E. loc. cit. p 472.—Leaves oblong, lanceolate-acute; stem creeping; bracts ovate-cuspidate, without nerves, with a broad, white margin, subciliated; bracteoles lanceolate; flowers small, pink. Very common all over the Presidency. Syn. Justicia repens, Linn. Fl. Zeyl. p 20; Roxb. Pl. Ind. i, 133; Dicliptera repens, Rœm. and Schult. *syst.* i, 171; D retusa, Juss. Ann. Mus. ix, 269.

4. R ELEGANS, Dalz.—Stem somewhat angular, covered with soft, white hairs; leaves sessile-ovate or ovate lanceolate-acuminate, puberulous on the upper surface, pale beneath, with prominent nerves; flowers in a sessile terminal spike, 1 inch long; bracts all broad, ovate-cuspidate, ciliate, with a broad, white, scarious margin; flowers large for the genus, of a beautiful blue, half an inch long; capsule ovoid, glabrous, 4-seeded. High hills around Joonere; flowers in August.

32. DICLIPTERA, Juss.

1. BIVALVIS, Juss. in Ann. Mus. ix, p 268.—Leaves ovate oblong-acute at the base, hispid and scabrous; peduncles axillary, longer than the petiole, trifid, heads 2 to 3-flowered; bracts ovate, somewhat rounded, dilated, bristle-pointed, 5-nerved, hispid, margins naked; corolla half an inch long, pubescent, pink-coloured; branches hexangular. Syn. Justicia bivalvis, Linn. sp. Pl. i, p 23; Vahl. Symb. ii, p 13.

2. BURMANNI, N. ab E. DC. *Prod.* 11, p 483.—Stem obsoletely quadrangular; branches pubescent and scabrous; leaves oval or lanceolate-acute at both ends, mucronate; umbels axillary, simply or doubly in fours or fives, very shortly-peduncled; proper involucre 2-leaved; leaflets unequal, spathulate, lanceolate, pointed with a bristle, ciliated; capsule orbicular. Syn. Justicia chinensis, Burm. Fl. Ind. p 8, *t.* 4, *f.* 1; Vahl. Symb. i, p 4.

3. ROXBURGHIANA, N. ab E. DC. *Prod.* 11, p 483.—Leaves ovate, acute at both ends; umbels axillary, in fours or fives, 3 to 5-divided; leaflets of proper involucre unequal, obovate mucronulate,

ciliated, 3-nerved, veined; capsule oval, somewhat rounded, compressed, hirsute, very like the preceding. Syn. Dicliptera chinensis, Rœm. and Schultz *syst.* i, 146; Justicia chinensis, Roxb. Fl Ind. i, 125.

4. MICRANTHES, N. ab E. loc. cit. p 484.—Leaves ovate-acuminated; umbels axillary, subsessile, 3 to 5-divided; flowers in heads of three; leaflets of proper involucre unequal, sessile, oblong, partial ones in fours, lanceolate-pointed, ciliated; capsule sessile, oblong, tetragonal; seeds glochidiate. Gujarat; on Sagurghur, near Alibaug. Syn. Justicia chinensis, Vahl. Symb. ii, p 13; D spinulosa, Hœhott. in Kotsch. it. Nub.; J cuspidata, Vahl. Symb. ii, p 9.

33. PERISTOPHE, N. ab E.

1. BICALYCULATA, N. ab E. DC. *Prod.* 9, p 496.—Stem hexagonal, rough and hairy; leaves ovate-acuminate, glabrous or puberulous; peduncles axillary, bitrifid, their branches dichotomous; flowers solitary; common involucre of one leaf linear, double the length of the flower-head; calyx small, membranaceous; corolla rosy, pubescent, nearly half an inch long. A common weed. Syn. Justicia bicalyculata, Vahl. Symb. ii, p 13; Roxb. Fl. Ind. i, 127; J malabarica, Ait. Hort. Kew. i, 27; Dianthera malabarica, Linn. Suppl. No. 85.

34. HYPŒSTES.

1. LANATA, Dalz. in Hook. Jour. Bot. ii, 343.—Suffruticose; stem glabrous, ascending, geniculate; leaves lanceolate-acuminate, entire, slightly hispid above, glabrous beneath; branches of the inflorescence trichotomous, covered with a white wool; heads few-flowered, 1 to 3, sessile in the opposite axils of the floral leaves; flowers light-purple. In Northern Concan; near Rohe.

35. HAPLANTHUS.

1. VERTICILLARIS, N. ab E. in DC. *Prod.* 11, p 513.—Stem herbaceous, simple, erect, naked and smooth at the base; leaves ovate-oblong, attenuated at both ends; branches assuming the form of short, rigid spines, which are bifid at the apex; flowers of a pale-lilac, half an inch long; Syn. Justicia verticillata, Roxb. Fl Ind. i, 135.

2. TENTACULATUS, N. ab E. loc. cit.—Leaves oval-obtuse, smaller than in the preceding; axillary branches verticelled, bifid, longer than the leaves. A much stouter species than the preceding. Jungles in the Concan; rarer than the preceding. Syn Ruellia tentaculata, Linn. sp. Pl 826; R aciculata, Roth. nov. sp. 301.

36. ANDROGRAPHIS.

1. Paniculata, N. ab E. loc. cit. p 515.—Stem erect, 4-sided, smooth; leaves lanceolate, attenuated into the petiole, entire, smooth, 2 to 3 inches long; racemes terminal, horizontal, long, secund; flowers remote, rose-coloured, long-pedicelled; capsules subcylindric, many-seeded. Syn. Justicia paniculata, Burm. Fl Ind. p 9; Roxb. Fl Ind. i, 119; Cara caniram, Rheed. Mal. iv, p 109, *t.* 56. This is the Kreat of the Indian bazars, so famous as a substitute for Gentian. Kreat or Chiryata, however, is the original name of some species of Ophelia which grow on the Himalayas, and which are used in the same manner as bitter tonics. The virtues are extracted by cold water.

2. A Echioides, N. ab E. in Wall. Pl. As. rar. iii, p 117.—Herbaceous, hirsute; leaves oblong-subsessile, entire or slightly crenate; racemes, or rather spikes, axillary, rigid-spreading; flowers whitish, with dark-purple spots, secund; capsules 4-seeded. In the sides of ravines in the Deccan, not very common; flowers in August and September. Syn. Justicia echioides, Linn. Fl Zeyl. p 21. This appears to be much commoner in other parts of India.

CIV. VERBENACEÆ.

1. PRIVA, Adans.

1. Leptostachya, Juss. Ann. Mus. vii, p 70.—Perennial; stem and branches puberulous; leaves subcordate, ovate-acuminate, coarsely crenate-serrate, hispid on both sides, pale beneath; fruit bearing calyx subglobose, hoary, with hooked pubescence; capsules obcordate; flowers small, white, in terminal racemes. On old walls at Dapoorie, Lush. Syn. Tortula aspera, Roxb. in Willd. sp. Pl iii, p 359; Streptium asperum, Roxb. Cor. ii, p 25, *t.* 146.

2. LIPPIA, Linn.

1. Nodiflora, Rich. in Michx. Fl Bor. Am. ii, p 25.—Creeping, all strigose, with adpressed hairs; stems filiform; leaves cuneate-spathulate, sharply serrated in the upper half; peduncles axillary, solitary; heads of flowers ovoid, and afterwards cylindric. Common in grassy and sandy places. Syn. Verbena nodiflora, Linn. sp. Pl p 28; V capitata, Forsk. Descr. p 10; Blairia nodiflora, Gaert. Fr. *t.* 56; Zapania nodiflora, Lam. Illust. *t.* 17, *f.* 3.

3. LANTANA, Linn.

1. Alba, Mill. Ex. Link. Enum. Pl Hort. Berol. ii, p 126.—Shrubby, erect, straight; branches twiggy, 4-sided, strigose and

hairy; leaves opposite, short-petioled, elliptic or rounded-ovate or subcordate, acuminated at ends, coarsely serrate-crenate, much wrinkled, scabrous above, hoary and villous beneath; peduncles axillary, spreading, thickened upwards; heads of flowers hemispherical, light-purple; throat yellow, scentless; fruit dark-violet, of the size of a pea. About Dharwar, and other parts of Deccan, thinly scattered. Syn. L indica, Roxb. Fl Ind. iii, p 89; L dubia, Royle Illust. Him. Pl, *t.* 73, *f.* 3; L collina, DeCaisne in Jacq. voy. *t.* 141.

4. SYMPHOREMA, Roxb.

1. Involucratum, Roxb. Fl Ind. ii, p 262.—Stem woody, climbing; branches, inflorescence, and underside of the leaf covered with soft tomentum; leaves opposite, short-petioled, oval or rounded-elliptic, obtuse at the base, 3-nerved, with a short, obtuse, acumen, the margin almost entire, or irregularly repand-toothed or serrate; inflorescence terminal panicled, consisting of long-peduncled bifid cymes; involucre 6 to 8-seeded, 7 to 9-flowered; flowers white. The Concans, between Nagotna and Alibaug.

5. TECTONA, Linn. Fil.

1. Grandis, Linn. Fil. Suppl. p 151.—The Teak tree; branches quadrangular; leaves opposite, large, ovate or subelliptic-acuminated, short-petioled, shining above; cymes axillary, dichotomous, or collected in a terminal panicle; flowers numerous, small, white; drupes enclosed in the inflated calyx; nut 4-celled, one-seed in each; seeds thick, oily. Endlicher states that the flowers are diuretics; that the foliage supplies a red dye, which is true. The timber has no rival for durability; it abounds in oil and silex. The Tunuj (Dalbergia oojeinensis) is, perhaps, superior to Teak.

6. PREMNA, Linn.

1. Cordifolia, Roxb. Fl Ind. iii, p 78.—A thick, bushy shrub, erect, 3 to 6 feet high; branches twiggy, villous; leaves short-petioled, cordate or cordate-ovate acuminated, quite entire, shining above; panicle of flowers small, terminal, in a close corymb; flowers greenish-white; drupe like a pea; nuts rough; flowers appear in April and May. Kandalla. The leaves smell like Colts-foot, Graham.

2. Scandens, Roxb. Fl Ind. iii, p 82.—A large, climbing shrub; branches and cymes pubescent; leaves ovate-oblong or subcordate, cuspidate-acuminate, quite entire, glabrous, shining above; panicle terminal; corymbose rather large; flowers very small, greenish-white; drupe like a pea, black, smooth. Kandalla.

3. LATIFOLIA, Roxb. loc. cit. p 76.—A shrub, erect-branched; leaves petioled, rounded-cordate or oval, quite entire, or obsoletely repand in the upper part; panicles corymbose, terminal and axillary; flowers small, greenish; the flowers appear in July. Very common in hedges in the Concan.

7. CALLICARPA, Linn.

1. CANA, Linn. Mant. ii, p 196.—A tall shrub; branches, peduncles, and petioles covered with white down; leaves lanceolate-elliptic or ovate-oblong, short-petioled, obtuse or rounded at the base, entire or crenate-wrinkled, hoary and tomentose beneath; cymes axillary, many-flowered, dichotomously branched; the peduncle shorter than the petiole; flowers pale-red, appear in February and March. Common on the Ghauts; leaves ½ to 1 foot long, 2 to 4 inches broad. The bark is subaromatic and slightly bitter, Graham. Syn. C heynei, Roth. nov. sp. p 82; C wallichiana, Walp. in Wight Ic. *t.* 1480.

8. CLERODENDRON, Linn.

1. PHLOMOIDES, Linn. Suppl. p 292.—A large shrub; leaves opposite, membranaceous, ovate or oval-rhomboid acuminate, rather obtuse, irregularly and bluntly serrated in the middle of the margins; panicles terminal, leafy below; cymes trichotomous lax; flowers white, fragrant. Very common in hedges throughout Gujarat; the Deçcan.

2. SERRATUM, Spr. *syst.* Veg. ii, 758.—Suffruticose; branchlets quadrangular, furrowed, glabrous; leaves opposite or in threes, papery, obovate-oblong or lanceolate, remotely serrate-toothed; panicles terminal, raceme-like, hoary and farinaceous; flowers pale-blue. Meera hills, near Penn; Kandalla and Mahul districts. Native name "Barungee." Syn. Volkameria serrata, Linn. Mant. 1, p 90; V farinosa, Roxb. Fl. Ind. iii, 64; C ternifolium, Don *Prod.* Fl Nep. 103; C javanicum, Walp. Rep. iv, p 113.

3. INFORTUNATUM, Linn. Fl Zeyl. p 232.—An under-shrub, 2 to 3 feet high; branchlets quadrangular; leaves long-petioled, rounded or ovate-cordate, the upper ones ovate-entire or dentate-strigose, and hairy on both sides; panicle terminal, large-spreading, naked; flowers white; the calyces increasing and turning red after the flower withers; drupe black, within the increased calyx. Common at Vingorla, Belgaum, &c. Syn. Volkameria infortunata, Roxb. Fl Ind. iii, 59; C viscosum, Vent. Jard. de Malm. *t.* 25; Petasites agrestis, Rumph. Amb. iv, p 180.

4. INERME, R. Br. in Ait. Hort. Kew. iv, p 65.—A weak, climbing branched shrub; leaves small, smooth, shining, oval or

elliptic; cymes axillary, as long as the leaf, 3-flowered, collected into a terminal corymbose panicle; flowers white; the tubes long and slender. Common along the Coast, near the sea. Syn. Volkameria inermis, Linn. Fl Zeyl. p 231; C buxifolium, Spr. *syst.* ii, 750.

9. GMELINA.

1. Arborea, Roxb. Fl Ind. iii, 84.—An unarmed tree; branchlets and young leaves covered with a mealy tomentum; leaves long-petioled, cordate-acuminate, quite entire, when old smooth above, tomentose and ashy beneath; panicles terminal and axillary, tomentose, racemed; cymes few-flowered; flowers yellow, about an inch long, with a wide mouth. Drupe yellow when ripe. Common in the Concans; yields a valuable wood, light and strong; some specimens somewhat resemble Satinwood. Syn. Premna arborea, Roth. nov. sp. p 287. Grows remarkably well in Sind, where it was introduced by Dr. Gibson. Its cultivation ought to be encouraged, as, perhaps, no wood combines so much lightness and strength.

10. VITEX.

1. Bicolor, Willd. Enum. Hort. Ber. p 606.—A shrub; branchlets, panicle, and underside of the leaves white, with a fine tomentum; leaves petioled, 3 to 5-foliolate; leaflets lanceolate, long-acuminated, entire or coarsely cut and crenated; panicle terminal, pyramidal; flowers light-blue; berry black, size of pea. A very common shrub. Native name "Neergoonda." This is No. 1150 of Graham's Catalogue.

2. Alata, Heyne in Roth. nov. sp. 316.—A small tree; branchlets with obtuse angles, densely tomentose; leaves trifoliolate; the petiole with a broad wing; leaflets ovate or elliptic-oblong, narrow at both ends, acuminate, quite entire, subcoriaceous, shining above, pubescent or hoary and glandular-dotted beneath; panicle terminal-compound, spreading pyramidal; flowers pale-yellow, tinged with blue; petioles three inches long, with a broad-veined wing. Southern Maratha country, Law.; Wursai jungles.

3. Altissmia, Linn. Fil. Suppl. 294.—A large tree, with the branchlets quadrangular, compressed, and channelled; petioles and back of the leaf white, with a short, woolly pubescence; leaves long-petioled, trifoliolate; leaflets elliptic or elliptic-oblong, acuminated at both ends, entire; panicle hoary, with a dense tomentum, terminal, compound, spreading, pyramidal; cymes interruptedly verticelled; corolla small, lower lip woolly; flowers white, tinged with blue. Ravine near Nagotna; in Canara, plentiful.

4. Leucoxylon, Linn. Fil Suppl. 293.—A small tree; leaves

long-petioled, 3 to 5-foliolate; leaflets elliptic or ovate-oblong, shortly and obtusely acuminated, attenuated into the petiole, entire subcoriaceous, shining and glabrous above; cymes axillary, long-peduncled; corymbose, many-flowered; lower lip of corolla densely woolly; drupe large, obovate, black when ripe. Warree Country; flowers in February. Southern Concan, Kandalla, Southern Maratha Country. Native name "Sherus." Syn. Wall. Rothia leucoxylon; Roth. nov. sp. 317, Deccan, rare.

CV. OROBANCHACEÆ.

1. PHELIPÆA, Tournef.

1. P INDICA, G. Don *syst.* iv. p 632.—Scape simple or branched, with scales here and there; calyx 4-toothed; teeth lanceolate-subulate from a broad base; corol tubular, infundibuliform, curved, purple, widened in the throat; flowers spiked, terminal, parasitic. On Tobacco plants in Deccan and Guzerat; found also in the Caucasus, whence it may have come with Tobacco plants originally. Syn. Orobanche indica, Roxb. Fl Ind. iii, p 27.

2. ÆGINETIA, Linn.

1. Æ INDICA, Roxb. Cor. Pl. 1, p 63, *t.* 91.—Scape simple elongated, naked, bearing at its apex a large, curved, purple flower, something like a tobacco-pipe; calyx spathe-like, lax, split in front, acute. Parasitic on the roots of bushes. Kandalla, Salsette, &c. Wight Ic. 895.

3. CHRISTISONIA, Wight.

1. C STOCKSII, Hook. Ic. Pl. *v* ix, *t.* 836.—Scape thick, fleshy, imbricately scaly; scales broadly ovate, concave-obtuse; flowers racemose; pedicels elongated, erect, without bracts; calyx tubular, cylindric; limb 5-divided; lobes triangular, rather obtuse; corolla pubescent, of a bluish-white colour; the lobes spreading and rounded. Parasitic on the roots of Strobilanthes; flowers in the rains. Salsette. Syn. C calcarata, Wight Ic. 1426.

2. C. LAWII, Wight Ic. 1427.—Scape thick, fleshy, irregularly shaped; base of the subsessile flowers ebracteolate, embraced by a few loose scales; calyx tubular, 5-toothed, regular; corol tubular, twice the length of the calyx, lobes suborbicular; flowers large, pale-purple, with yellow spots. Salsette and between the Ram Ghaut and Belgaum; flowers in August.

CVI. LABIATÆ.

1. OCIMUM, Linn.

1. O Canum, Linn. Bot. Mag. *t.* 2452.—Stem herbaceous, erect, pubescent; leaves petioled, ovate, narrowed at both ends, denticulate or entire, rather hoary beneath; petioles ciliated; verticels of the fruit bearing raceme, numerous, approximated; calyx small, a little ciliated; corolla half longer than the calyx to double the length. Very common; grows all over the world. Africa is supposed to be its native country. Nearly allied to O basilicum, but the flowers are only half the size. Syn. O americanum, Linn. Amœn. 4, p 276; O album, Roxburgh and others; O stanimeum, Bot. Mag. 2452.

2. O Basilicum, Linn. sp. p 833.—Stem erect or ascending; leaves petioled, ovate or oblong, narrowed at the base, slightly toothed, glabrous; verticels of the fruit-bearing raceme separated by a space longer than the calyx, or more rarely loosely approximated in a branched raceme; calyx ciliated; corolla twice its length. This species has been long in cultivation throughout Asia and Africa. The Indian varieties are divided into Pilosum and B. glabratum. In the former, the stem is ascending, much-branched; leaves small, oblong-entire; petioles and verticels very hairy. In the latter, the stem is erect; petioles and calyx scarcely ciliated; leaves scarcely dentate; racemes elongated.

3. O Gratissimum, Linn. sp. p 832.—Stem rather glabrous; leaves petioled, ovate-acute, crenated or coarsely toothed, narrowed at the base; glabrous or pubescent along the veins; floral leaves like bracts, lanceolate-acuminate, hastate at the base; racemes simple or slightly branched, pubescent; calyces pedicelled; lateral teeth minute, upper united into a bimucronate lip; corolla scarcely longer than the calyx; stamens exserted. A shrub, several feet high; racemes slender, many-flowered. Syn. O zeylanicum, Burm. Thes. Zeyl. p 174; O frutescens, Mill. Dict; O petiolare, Linn. Cam. Dict; O gratissimum, Jacq. Ic. rar. iii, p 495.

4. O Adscendens, Willd sp. iii, p 166.—Stem prostrate; branches pubescent; leaves petioled, ovate-oblong, obtuse, slightly toothed, narrowed at the base, pubescent; floral leaves like bracts, deciduous; racemes simple; calyx in fruit drooping, the tube striated; wings of the upper tooth reaching to the middle of the calyx; lateral teeth truncated, lower very shortly setaceous, acuminated; corolla twice the length of the calyx; stamens much exserted. Common all over India. O indicum, Roth. nov. sp. p 273; Plectranthus indicus, Spr. *syst.* ii, 690; O cristatum, Roxb. Hort. Bengh. p 65. Stems rising from a thick base 6 to 9 inches long.

5. O Sanctum, Linn. Mant. p 85.—Stems hairy; leaves petioled; oval-obtuse, dentate, pubescent; floral leaves like bracts, sessile, shorter than the pedicels; racemes slender, simple, or slightly branched; calyx shorter than the pedicel, drooping, glabrous; throat within naked, upper tooth obovate-concave, shortly decurrent; corolla scarcely longer than the calyx. Common almost everywhere. Sacred to Hindoos. Syn. Basilicum agreste, Rumph Amb. v, 265; O zeylanicum, Penenne, Burm. Thes. Zeyl. p 174; O frutescens, Burm. Ind. p 129; O inodorum, Burm. Ind. p 130; O monachorum, Linn. Mant. 58; Plectranthus monachorum, Spr. *syst.* ii, 690; O tenuiflorum, Lam; Lumnitzera tenuiflora, Spr. *syst.* ii, 687; O villosum, Roxb. Hort. Beng. 44 (?) The whole plant has often a purple hue. The flowers are pale-purple, and not inodorous, stated by Bentham. This plant goes through the ceremony of marriage about the end of October.

2. AJUGA.

1. A Disticha Anisomeles Ovata, Roxb. Fl. 3, p 2; Marrubium Indic. Burm. Thes. Zeyl. *t.* 71; Rheede Mal. 10, *t.* 88; Wight in Hook. Bot. Misc. 2 *t.* 7.—A tall annual, with 4-seeded stems, and branches opposite; leaves cordate-serrate; flowers spiked alternate, with narrow-lanceolate or subulate hairy bracts; upper lip of the corolla narrow, greenish, overhanging; under lip larger, recurved longer, bialate, with purple segments. The plant has a strong savour of black currants. Near to and on the Ghauts, common.

3. ACROCEPHALUS, Benth.

1. Capitatus, Benth. in Wall. Pl. As. Rar. ii, p 18.—Stem procumbent; leaves ovate or lanceolate, sub-glabrous; heads of flowers terminal; lower lip of calyx 4-toothed; stem slender, very much branched at the base. On the Meera hills, near Penn and at Mahar, sparingly; Southern Maratha Country, Law. Syn. Prunella indica, Burm. Ind. 130; Ocimum capitellatum, Linn. Mant. 276; O capitatum, Roth. nov. sp. 276; Hook. Ic. Pl *t.* 456.

4. MOSCHOSMA, Reichb., Consp. 171.

1. Polystachyum, Benth. in Wall. Pl As. Rar. ii, p 13.—1 to 2 feet high; stem acutely quadrangular, angles smooth or scarcely rough; leaves long-petioled, ovate, rather acute-crenate, rounded or cuneate at the base; racemes numerous, slender, 2 to 4 inches long; flowers minute, purplish; verticels 6 to 10-flowered, lax, approximated. The Concans. Syn. Ocimum tenuiflorum, Burm. Ind. p 129; O polystachyum, Linn. Mant. p 567; Plectranthus parviflorus, Br. *Prod.* p 506; P micranthus, Spr. *syst.* ii, 691.

5. ORTHOSIPHON, Benth.

1. O Pallidus, Royle Benth. Lab. p 708.—Smooth; stem ascending; leaves petioled, ovate-obtuse, coarsely cut and toothed, entire and cuneate at the base; tube of the small white corolla as long as the calyx; spike short, terminal. Very common in the Deccan; flowering from June to October. Is very like an Ocimum, and may be easily mistaken for one of that genus.

2. Glabratus, Benth. in Wall. Pl. As. rar. ii, p 14.—Stems ascending, branched, glabrous; leaves long-petioled, ovate-acute, toothed, rounded or subcordate at the base, glabrous; corolla sub-incurved; tube twice the length of the calyx; flowers light-purple. Common in the rains. Syn. Ocimum thymiflorum, Roth. nov. sp. p 269 (?); Plectranthus thymiflorus, Spr. *syst.* ii, 690; Pallidus deccan; flowers in June.

6. PLECTRANTHUS.

1. Wightii, Benth. Lab. p 41.—Stem herbaceous, erect-branched; leaves petioled, broadly ovate or rounded-acuminate, cordate at the base; lower floral leaves like them; upper and the bracts membranaceous, rounded spathulate, shorter than the peduncle and pedicels; calyx oblong, incurved, striated; mouth oblique bilabiate; corolla inflated, declinate. Ram Ghaut, Law; leaves 1½ to 2 inches.

2. Rotundifolius, Spr. *syst.* ii, p 690.—Stem procumbent at the base, rooting; branches erect, thick, fleshy; leaves petioled, ovate-rounded or cuneate, running into the petiole, smooth, thiok; floral leaves bract-like; racemes simple; verticels rather lax, many-flowered, approximated; corolla three times longer than the calyx, declinate. The Concans. Syn. Germanea rotundifolia, Poir. Dict. ii, 763; Coleus rugosus, Benth. in Wall. Pl. As rar. ii, p 15.

3. Cordifolius, Don. *Prod.* Fl Nep. p 116.—Pubescent or tomentose, hoary; stem herbaceous, erect; leaves petioled, broadly ovate-crenate, cordate at the base; floral leaves bract-like, ovate-cuneate; racemes lax, panicled; verticels secund, few-flowered; corolla scarcely twice as long as calyx; tube bent in the middle, the throat dilated; flowers small, pale-blue. About Kandalla; Sawunt Warree.

7. COLEUS.

1. Barbatus, Benth. in Wall. Pl. As. rar. ii, p 15.—Stem fruticose at the base, ascending, tomentose and hispid; leaves petioled, ovate-crenate, softly tomentose, younger ones strigose hispid; floral leaves membranaceous, broadly ovate-acuminate, in

flowering deciduous; verticels distant, 6-flowered; calyx in fruit deflexed, hispid. Caranjah Hill; Deccan hills. Cultivated for the roots, which are pickled, Law. Syn. Plectranthus forskolei, Willd. sp. iii, p 169; P barbatus, Andr. Bot. Rep. *t* 594; P comosus, Bot. Mag. *t* 2318; Ocimum asperum, Roth. nov. sp. p 268; P asper, Spr. *syst*. ii, p 690; P monadelphus, Roxb. Hort. Beng.

2. C Zatarhendi, Benth Lab. p 50.—Leaves fleshy, rigid, broadly ovate, acute-crenated, villous, truncate at the base. On the sandy coast north of Bassein. Syn. Ocymum zatarhendi, Forsk. Fl. Ægypt Arab. 109; Plectranthus crassifolius, Vahl. Symb. i, p 44.

8. ANISOCHILUS, Wall.

1. A Carnosus, Wall. Pl As. rar. ii, p 18.—Stem erect, tetragonal; leaves petioled, ovate-rounded, obtuse-crenated, cordate at the base, or rounded; thick, fleshy, hoary and tomentose, or villous on both sides; spikes long-peduncled, at length cylindric; floral leaves ovate-obtuse; upper lip of calyx acute, glabrous, membranaceous, ciliated on the margin. Rheed Mal. x, *t*. 90; Syn. Lavandula carnosa, Linn. Amœn. x, p 56, *t*. 3; Plectranthus dubius, Spr. *syst*. ii, p 691.

2. A Decussatus, Dalz.—Stem round, coloured, smooth below, hoary above; leaves on longish petioles, broad, ovate-acute, truncate or cordate at the base, crenated, shortly tomentose beneath, sprinkled on both sides with ruby-coloured glands; spikes shortly-cylindric, pointed on long-naked peduncles, brachiately disposed; floral leaves cordate-acute; calyx densely woolly, upper lip deflexed, rounded with a sudden point, lower truncate; corolla bluish-purple, velvetty and villous; anthers 4, perfect, blue; stigmas 2, filiform, acute. On the highest Ghauts opposite Bombay, in rocky places; flowers in August. A beautiful plant, the dark-red spike contrasting well with the flowers.

3. A Adenanthus, Dalz.—Spikes dense, pyramidal; floral leaves lanceolate-acuminate, pubescent, 3-nerved, 3 lines long; calyx minute, oblique truncate, scarcely toothed, tomentose on the outside; corolla grandular-dotted, 5 lines long, tomentose outside, lower lip long, entire, boat-shaped, upper 3 to 4-lobed, rounded, obtuse, short. Near Dharwar; Bababooden hills. Unfortunately the lower part of our specimens has been lost.

9. LAVANDULA, Tournef.

1. L Perottetii, Benth. Lab. p 151.—Softly villous; stems leafy; leaves deeply pinnatifid; lobes oblong or linear-toothed, green on both sides, villous; floral leaves broadly ovate-acute, as long as

the calyx; spikes dense, villous; flowers solitary, alternate. Hills at Sattara, flowering in November. Syn. L lawii, Wight Ic. 1439.

2. L BURMANNI, Benth. loc. cit.—Slightly pubescent; leaves bipinnatifid, segments linear-entire; floral leaves membranaceous, dilated at the base, acuminated and setaceous at the apex, longer than the calyx; spikes short, dense; flowers solitary, approximated, either white or of a beautiful deep-blue. Common in the Deccan, where it is called "Gorea." Syn. Bysteropogon bipinnatus, Roth. nov. sp. 225. There is a white-flowered variety.

10. POGOSTEMON, Desf.

1. P PANICULATUS, Benth. in Wall. Pl As. rar. 1, p 30.—Stem erect, pubescent; leaves unequal-ovate, cut and serrated, narrow at the base; verticels globose, secund, remote; racemes terminal; bracts broadly ovate, membranaceous, as long as the calyx; calyx pubescent; teeth lanceolate. Syn. Elsholzia paniculata, Willd. sp. iii, p 59. Southern Concan.

2. P PLECTRANTOIDES, Desp. Ann. Muss. ii, p 154, *t.* 6.—Covered with hoary pubescence; stem erect; leaves ovate-cuneate or rounded at the base, doubly serrated; flowers subsecund, clustered, spicate, ovate, cylindric-peduncled, panicled; bracts broad, ovate, glandular-dotted, longer than the calyx; calyx hirsute, glandular; teeth broad, lanceolate-acute. Near Chicklee, Surat Collectorate.

3. P HEYNEANUS, Benth. in Wall. Pl As. rar. 1, p 31.—Stem ascending, pubescent; leaves subglabrous, ovate, narrow at the base, irregularly crenated; verticels many-flowered, subsecund, interruptedly spicate; spikes panicled; bracts ovate or lanceolate, equal to the calyx or a little shorter. Between the Ram Ghaut and Belgaum. Syn. Origanum indicum, Roth. nov. sp. p 265. This is not the Pach plant, as supposed by Graham. Pach is a distinct specis (P patchouli). We do not know its native country, but the leaves are imported from Singapore. As it thrives admirably in our gardens, the growing of it in quantity would be a good speculation.

4. PURPURICAULIS, Dalz. in Hook. Jour. Bot. ii, 336.—Stem erect, suffruticose, purple, shining; leaves broadly ovate-acuminate, coarsely double-toothed, attenuated into the petiole, subglabrous; verticels dinudate, approximated; panicles axillary and terminal lax, pyramidal; bracts ovate and lanceolate, equal to the calyx; leaves 7 inches long 3½ broad. Has the odour of black currants. Very common in the hilly parts of the Concan and on the Ghauts; grows to the height of 5 to 6 feet. Syn. D frutescens, Graham's Catalogue No. 1109.

5. PURPURASCENS, Dalz. loc. cit. 337.—Stem herbaceous, quadrangular, 4-furrowed, softly tomentose with spreading hairs; leaves.

broadly ovate-acute, cuneate at the base, doubly-serrated, wrinkled, softly villous on both sides; lowest verticels sessile in the axils of the upper leaves, upper terminal, simply spicate, approximated; bracts under the calyx ovate-acute, leafy, reticulately veined, equal to the calyx; calyx pentagonal, villous; segments triangular subulate, 3-nerved. Common in shady woods in the Concan; leaves 4 to 5 inches long, 2 to 2½ broad.

11. DYSOPHYLLA, Blume.

1. Rupestris, Dalz. in Hook. Jour. Bot.—Perennial, erect; stems round, woody, 3 to 4 feet high; leaves 4-fold, spreading, short-petioled, linear-lanceolate, serrated, rugose, downy, 2 to 3 inches long; spikes terminal solitary, cylindric, covered with innumerable small rose-coloured flowers; corol tube twice the length of the calyx; segments reflexed. Near Vingorla. Syn. Mentha quadrifolia, Roxb. Fl Ind. iii, p 5. Grows on dry ground, and is quite distinct from D quadrifolia of Bentham, for which Roxburgh's plant is given as a synonym.

2. Tomentosa, Dalz. in Hook. Jour. Bot. ii, 337.—Softly tomentose all over, with spreading hairs; stem creeping; branches several, simple, erect; leaves verticelled, 6 to 9 together, linear-acute, quite entire, much longer than the internodes, covered beneath with scattered glands, margins revolute; floral leaves of the same shape; calyx tuberculate glandular, densely tomentose; segments triangular ovate-obtuse, shorter than the hairs; stems 10 to 12 inches long; leaves 4 lines long. In rice fields near Malwan.

3. Erecta, Dalz. loc. cit.—Stem erect-branched, rather hispid; leaves verticelled, 9 to 12 together, narrow linear-obtuse at the apex, papillose and rough on both sides, glandular-dotted beneath, equalling the internodes; floral leaves filiform, with a thick oblique head, as long as the calyx; calyx villous; segments erect obtuse, 7 to 8 inches high; leaves 7 to 8 lines long. Near Malwan.

4. Gracilis, Dalz. loc. cit.—Stem erect, straight, 9 inches high, sparingly branched above, rough, with soft spreading hairs; leaves verticelled in sevens, narrow linear-acute, longer than the internodes, 4 lines long, distantly and minutely toothed towards the apex; floral leaves linear-acute, densely ciliated, longer than calyx and corolla; upper tooth of the corolla the smaller and quite entire. On the Ghauts.

5. Myosmoides, Benth. in Wall. Pl. As. rar. 1, p 30.—Tomentose and silky; stem erect; leaves opposite, shortly-petioled, oblong or lanceolate; floral ones minute; spikes dense; calyx tomentose; the teeth very short, straight; corolla minute, red. Beds of watercourses at Mahableshwur. Syn. Mentha myosmoides, Roth. nov. sp. p 257.

6. STELLATA, Benth. in Wall. Pl. As. rar. i, p 30.—Stem creeping; branches erect; leaves verticelled, 6 to 8 together, narrow-linear, almost equal to the internodes, quite entire; floral ones subulate; calyx villous; the segments erect, rather acute, nearly allied to D tomentosa, but distinct. About Belgaum, Law; at Banda, in rice fields. Syn. Mentha quaternifolia, Roth. nov. sp. p 256 (?).

12. COLEBROOKIA, Smith.

1. TERNIFOLIA, Roxb. Pl Cor. iii, p 40, *t*. 245.—A small shrub; leaves oblong-elliptic, narrow at both ends, serrulate, softly pubescent above, tomentose beneath, with the branches and spikes verticelled in threes; flowers very minute, white; the spikes very dense. On the Ghauts, very common. Scarcely differs from C oppositifolia of Sm. Exot. Bot. ii, p 111. A native of Nepaul.

13. MICROMERIA, Benth.

1. MALCOLMIANA, Dalz. Mss.—Herbaceous; branches elongated, simple, slender, villous; leaves small, shortly-petioled, ovate-obtuse, crenated, pubescent on both sides; verticels of flowers distant, dichotomously cymose, peduncled, few-flowered, contracted into a kind of umbel; flowers minute. On the banks of the Yeena, Mahableshwur. In its aromatic and carminative qualities, it rivals the Peppermint. Syn. Marrubium malcolmianum, Dalz. in Hook. Jour. Bot iv, p 109.

14. NEPETA, Linn.

1. N BOMBAIENSIS, Dalz.—Branched, 1 foot high; stem quadrangular, pubescent; leaves long-petioled, softly villous on both sides, cordate, ovate-obtuse, crenated; flowers axillary, peduncled; peduncle as long as the petiole, with about 5 pedicelled flowers, subtended by a pair of lanceolate-acute bracts; calyx pilose, deeply ribbed, upper lip much longer than the lower, of 3 acute ciliate teeth; lower of 2 subulate teeth, increasing with the fruit; corol small, pale-blue, with purple spots. Allied to N graciliflora, Benth. Old walls and rocks on Sewnere Fort; flowering in July and August.

15. SALVIA, Linn.

1. PLEBEIA, Br. *Prod*. 501.—Stem herbaceous, erect-branched, pubescent; leaves petioled, oblong, wrinkled; verticels lax, about 6-flowered, racemose; racemes paniculate; calyx campanulate; upper lip quite entire; teeth of the lower lip obtuse; corolla scarcely longer than the calyx. At Kandalla and Island of Caranjah.

Syn. S brachiata, Roxb. Hort. Beng. p 4 ; Fl. Ind. i, 146 ; Ocimum fastigiatum, Roth. nov. sp. p 277 ; Lumnitzera fastigiata, Spr. *syst.* ii, 687. Seeds used for killing vermin.

16. SCUTELLARIA, Linn.

1. Discolor, Coleb. in Wall. Pl. As. rar. i, p 66.—Stem rooting at the base, leafy, ascending, rather naked above ; leaves petioled, ovate-obtuse, crenated, rounded or cuneate at the base, strongly nerved and purple beneath ; floral leaves minute ; racemes elongated, somewhat branched at the base; flowers scattered, secund. Parwar Ghaut, Mahableshwur, &c. ; in Canara, plentiful. Syn. S indica, Don *Prod.* Fl Nep. p 109.

17. ANISOMELES, R. Br.

1. Heyneana, Benth. in Wall. Pl. As. rar. i, p 59.—Glabrous or very slightly pubescent ; leaves ovate or oblong-lanceolate, narrow at the base ; cymes long-peduncled, secund, few-flowered ; calycine teeth lanceolate-acute. Bombay, Salsette, &c., common. Branches elongated, slender, acutely quadrangular ; leaves pale-green on both sides, serrate-crenate ; cymes unilateral, at the apex of the peduncles.

2. Ovata, Br. in Ait. Hort. Kew. ii, 364.—Hirsute, more rarely subglabrous ; leaves ovate-acuminate or rounded, truncate, subcordate or rounded at the base, broadly crenate ; verticels many-flowered, dense ; calycine teeth lanceolate-acute ; corolla purple, the lip darker in colour. A suffruticose plant 2 to 4 feet high. Very common everywhere. Syn. A disticha, Heyne in Roth. nov. sp. p 254 ; Nepeta amboinica, Linn. Suppl. 273 ; Ballota disticha, Linn. Mant. p 83 ; Ajuga disticha, Roxb. Fl Ind. iii, p 2 ; Marrubium indicum, Burm. Ind. 127 ; Ballota mauritiana, Pers. Syn. p 2.

3. Malabarica, Br. in Bot. Mag. *t.* 2071.—Tomentose and villous ; leaves oblong-lanceolate, narrow at the base, serrato-crenate in the upper part, soft, tomentose or woolly; verticels many-flowered, dense, or cymes large, at length elongated ; floral leaves and bracts subulate, very soft ; corolla rosy or purple, the throat hairy within. On the Ghauts, pretty common. Syn. Nepeta malabarica, Linn. Maut. 566 ; Ajuga fruticosa, Roxb. Fl Ind. iii, p 1.

18. LEUCAS, Benth.

1. Longifolia, Benth. Lab. p 744.—Stem herbaceous, erect, villous ; leaves linear-subentire, rather glabrous ; verticels 6 to 10-flowered ; bracts minute ; calyx turbinate, tubular, the mouth equal ; teeth very short, setaceous, straight. Half a foot to a foot high ;

leaves 2 to 3 inches long, with one or two teeth, sessile, narrow at the base. About Poona.

2. BIFLORA, Br. *Prod.* 504.—Herbaceous, diffuse; leaves ovate, coarsely toothed, pubescent on both sides, half an inch long; verticels 2-flowered; bracts minute; calyx tubular, mouth equal, teeth subulate. The Concans. Syn. Phlomis biflora, Vahl. Symb. iii, p 77; non. Roxb.; Wight Ic. 866.

3. COLLINA, Dalz. in Hook. Jour. Bot. ii, 338.—Suffruticose, erect; branches quadrangular, tomentose, with adpressed hairs; leaves petioled, ovate, lanceolate-acute, cuneate at the base, coarsely crenate-serrate, softly pubescent and green above, hoary and tomentose beneath; verticels 10-flowered; bracts linear or narrow-spathulate, hirsute, ciliated, half the length of the calyx; calyx tomentose, turbinate, tubular, mouth equal, teeth erect subulate, alternately shorter; leaves 3 to 4 inches long. Southern Concan.

4. STELLIGERA, Wall. Pl. As. rar. i, p 61.—Herbaceous, erect, a little hoary; stem hirsute; leaves oblong, lanceolate-obtuse, serrated, scabrous and hispid above; calyx tomentose, mouth truncate, villous within; teeth (10) and bracts subulate, soft, spreading, their apices revolute; leaves 2 to 3 inches long, green above, pale beneath; verticels an inch in diameter; flowers white. The Ghauts.

5. CILIATA, Benth. in Wall. Pl. As. rar. i, p 61.—Herbaceous; stem erect, adpressed, pubescent, or rough with reflexed hairs; leaves ovate-lanceolate or oblong serrate-crenate, green on both sides, hairy and pubescent; bracts linear, ciliate, hairy; calyx tubular, hirsute, mouth truncate, equal, teeth elongated, subulate, hairy, spreading like a star. Near Banda, between Roha and Thul.

6. ASPERA, Spr. *syst.* ii, p 743.—Herbaceous, hairy and pubescent; leaves oblong or linear, subcrenate, green; verticels dense, equal; bracts oblong-linear or subulate, hairy; calyx smooth at the base, striated at the apex, subincurved, mouth oblique, teeth short. A rough, hispid plant, half a foot high. On the sea-shore at Alibaug, &c. Syn. Phlomis aspera, Willd Enum. Hort. Berol. ii, 621; P plukenetii, Roth nov. sp. p 261; P esculenta, Roxb. Fl Ind. iii, p 10.

7. CEPHALOTES, Spr. *syst.* ii, p 743.—Herbaceous, hairy and pubescent; leaves ovate or oblong, subserrate, green, verticels subsolitary, large, globose, densely many-flowered, bracts ovate, lanceolate-acute, imbricated; calyx striated and subvillous at the apex; mouth oblique, teeth subulate, short; uppermost leaves coming out of the top of the verticel. Coast of Kattywar; at Ahmedabad, Law. Syn. Phlomis cephalotes, Roth nov. sp. p 262; Leucas capitata, Desf. Mem. Mus. Par. ii, p 8, *t.* 4.

8. LINIFOLIA, Spr. *syst.* ii, p 743.—Herbaceous, erect, slightly pubescent or tomentose; leaves oblong linear-entire, or remotely

serrated; verticels dense, subequal, many-flowered; bracts linear, hoary; calyx elongated above; mouth very oblique, lower teeth very short, upper largest. A very common plant in cultivated fields. Syn. Phlomis linifolia, Roth. nov. sp. p 260; P zeylanica, Roxb. Fl Ind. iii, p 9; Leonurus indicus, Burm. Ind. p 127; Herba admerationis, Rumph. Amb. vi, p 39; L lavandulæfolia, Sm. in Rees Cycl. v. 20.

9. L Urticæfolia, Br. *Prod.* p 504.—Herbaceous, finely tomentose and hoary; verticels many-flowered, globose; calyces hairy membranaceous; mouth oblique, lengthened below, split above; teeth 8 to 10, very short, setaceous; verticels nearly 1 inch in diameter, distant; leaves petioled, broadly ovate, coarsely serrate-crenate, rounded or cuneate at the base; flowers white. At Cambay. Found also in Abyssinia and Arabia, also in the Punjaub.

19. LEONOTIS, Br.

1. Nepetæfolia, Br. *Prod.* 504.—Herbaceous, 6 feet high; leaves membranaceous, ovate-crenate; verticels large globular; teeth of calyx spinous, uppermost largest, ovate; corolla orange-coloured, about twice the length of the calyx. Common on heaps of rubbish. Scarcely indigenous; supposed to be originally from Africa. Syn. Phlomis nepetæfolia, Linn. sp. 820; P spinosa, Vand. in Rœm. Script. Hisp. p 81 (?); Leonurus globosus, Mœnch. Meth. p 400; L nepetæfolius, Mill. Dict. N. 2; Stachys mediterranea, Vell. Pl Plum. ii, *t.* 2.

CVII. CHENOPODEACEÆ.

1. OBIONE, Gaert.

1. Stocksii, Wight Ic. *t.* 1789.—Stem shrubby, very ramous ascending or diffuse, branches round, glabrous, unarmed; leaves alternate, short-petioled, elliptic-obtuse, tending to obovate, smooth, glabrous, whitish, and glaucous; sheath of the bracts conical, limbs orbicular, free, entire; disk smooth. Gujarat; common near the sea.

2. ARTHROCNEMUM, Moq.

1. Indicum, Moq. Chenopod. Enum. p 113.—Stem suffruticose, procumbent, articulated; branches herbaceous, alternate, divaricate, articulations short, clavate, thick, spongy, truncate and sub-bifid at the apex; spikes lateral, alternate or opposite, large, cylindric-obtuse. Common on salt ground. Syn. Salicornia indica, Willd. nov. Aet. Hist. Nat. v, p 111, *t.* 4, *f.* 1; Wight Ic. *t.* 737. Native name "Muchoor."

3. SUÆDA, Forsk.

1. Nudiflora, Moq. in Ann. Soc. Nat. 23, p 316.—Stem shrubby, ascending, branched; branches erect, spreading, puberulous; leaves rather short, oblong or obovate, attenuated at the base, very obtuse, rigid, glabrous; flowers axillary, sessile, 5 to 10 densely clustered hermaphrodite; upper clusters at length naked and spiked; seed beaked, shining. Native name "Morus." Syn. Salsola nudiflora, Willd. sp. ii, p 2323.

2. Indica, Moq. loc. cit.—Stem shrubby, very diffuse, branched; branches ascending, glabrous; leaves half round, attenuated below, obtuse, rigid, a little mealy; upper ones minute, oblong; flowers axillary, sessile, 3 to 5 clustered; seed obtuse-beaked, shining. Wight Ic. *t.* 1796; Syn. Salsola indica, Willd. sp. i, p 1317.

CVIII. NYCTAGINACEÆ.

1. BŒRHAAVIA, Linn.

1. Diffusa, Linn. sp. 4.—Herbaceous plant, with numerous slender prostrate branches, spreading close on the ground; leaves opposite, unequal, petioled cordate, with waved and often coloured margins; peduncles solitary, intra-axillary; leaves green on both sides; flowers minute, red, sessile on the apex of the pedicels. A very common weed. Syn. B procumbens, Roxb. Fl Ind. i, 146.

2. Repanda, Willd sp. i, p 22.—Stem elongated, climbing, glabrous; leaves cordate, lanceolate-acuminate, sinuate and repand on the margin; flower-bearing peduncles forming a loose panicle; terminal umbels 3 to 6-flowered; fruit clavate, rough with glandular knobs; flowers pink, larger than in the preceding. In hedges, Surat, climbing to the height of 6 feet. Syn. Valeriana chinensis, Linn. sp. 47; Burm. Ind. xv, *t.* 6, *f.* 3; Astrephia chinensis, Dufr. Valer. p 51; B umbellata, Wight.

3. Stellata, Wight Ic. *t.* 875.—Decumbent; leaves succulent, ovate-cordate, obtuse-mucronate; racemes long-peduncled; flowers verticelled, subsessile, interruptedly subspicate; ovary club-shaped elongated, furrowed, with 5 elongated viscid glands at the apex; flowers white, Wight (stem-climbing, Dalz; flowers pink.) In Kattywar.

4. Repens, Linn.—Herbaceous, creeping, diffuse; leaves ovate-obtuse, sinnate-repand, pubescent, white beneath; peduncles axillary, short, bearing small umbels; flowers small, deep-pink, 2 to 3-androus; fruit ovate-elliptic, ribbed viscous. Common in the Deccan plains, also in Sind, Arabia, and neighbouring desert countries.

5. Fruticosa, Dalz.—Shrubby, erect, all viscid and tomentose; leaves small, ovate, with a truncate base, sometimes triangular,

much-wrinkled on the underside; flowers umbellate, small pink, on an axillary peduncle, as long as the leaf; pedicels slender, nearly as long as the peduncle; flower 4½ lines long, filaments 3-long, exserted, fruit linear-oblong, sulcated, pubescent, tuberculated along the ribs from top to bottom. On Sewnere Fort and the Ghauts east of Bombay; flowers in September.

CIX. POLYGONACEÆ.

1. POLYGONUM, Linn.

1. Glabrum, Willd. ii, 447.—Annual, suberect, smooth, reddish; leaves narrow-lanceolate, short-petioled, tapering to each end, smooth on both sides, entire, 5 to 7 inches long; stipules ragged; racemes of flowers long, slender, and smooth; flowers numerous, rose-coloured, heptandrous; style 3-cleft, seed ovate, compressed. A native of ditches, rivulets, &c.; pretty common. Roxb. Fl Ind. ii, 287; Rheede Mal. x, *t.* 80; and xii, *t.* 77. Native name "Ruktroora," a name also applied to a species of Ebenaceæ and a Rhamnus used medicinally by the Ghaut people. Wight Ic. 1799.

2. Rivulare, Kœnig Mss.—Annual; branches erect; leaves narrow-lanceolate, pretty smooth, 5 to 6 inches long; stipules short, ciliated; flowers octandrous, seed triangular. Roxb. Fl Ind. ii, 290; Grows in the same sort of situations as the preceding.

3. Chinense, Willd. ii, 453.—Scandent, flexuose; leaves oblong, truncate at the base; bracts auricled; peduncles sub-panicled, terminal; flowers in globular pedicelled heads, white. An alpine plant, confined to the Ghauts; flowers octandrous. Wight Ic. *t.* 1806.

4. Elegans, Roxb. Fl Ind. ii, 291.—A very small species, prostrate; stems numerous-spreading; leaves alternate, bifarious, very shortly-petioled, lanceolate, smooth; stipules membranaceous with torn and ciliated margins; flowers axillary, very small, rose-coloured. On waste ground where water has lodged; banks of the Nerbudda. Syn. P linifolium, Roth nov. sp. 207; P indicum, Roth; Wight Ic. *t.* 1808.

CX. AMARANTACEÆ.

1. DEERINIGA, R. Br.

1. Baccata, Moq. in DC. *Prod.* 13, p 236.—Stem suffruticose, angled, decumbent; leaves 2 to 3 inches long, ovate or cordate-ovate acute; spikes elongated, loosely branched; flowers very shortly-pedicelled, solitary; sepals at length reflexed; spikes 3 to 4 inches long, slender. Syn. Celosia baccata, Retz. Obs. v, p 23;

Deeringia celosioides, R. Br. *Prod.* 1, 413; Bot. Mag. *t.* 2717; Wight Ic. *t.* 728; D indica, Blume Bijdr. 542; D celosioides and indica, Spr. *syst.* i, 816.

2. CELOSIA, Linn.

1. Cristata, Moq. in DC. *Prod.* 13, p 242.—Stem herbaceous, erect, branched, quite glabrous; leaves petioled, ovate, ovate-lanceolate or subcordate-ovate, sometimes lanceolate-acute, glabrous; spikes subsessile, ovate-pyramidal, sometimes dilated, compressed, truncated, or subentire or branched at the apex; flowers very short-pedicelled, digynous; sepals longer than the bracts, obsoletely keeled, somewhat 3-nerved; utricles ovato-globose. Syn. C castrensis, Cristata, and Coccinea, Linn. sp. p 297; Bot. Reg. 1834; Amarantus indicus cristatus, Rumph Amb. v, p 236, *t.* 84; C comosa, Retz. Obs. vi, p 26; C cernua, Roxb. Fl Ind. ed. Wall. ii, 509; Andr. Bot. Rep. *t.* 635; wight Ic. *t.* 730.

2. Argentea, Moq. loc. cit.—Stem herbaceous, erect, glabrous, branched; leaves somewhat petioled, linear-lanceolate, narrow or sublinear, rarely ovate, acute, glabrous; spikes long-peduncled, ovato-cylindric, or cylindric cuspidate; flowers sessile, digynous; sepals much longer than the bracts, mucronulate, 3-nerved; utricles between ovate and pear-shaped. Syn. C argentea, Linn sp. p 296; C marilandica, Retz. Obs. iii, p 27 B; C linearis, Sw. Hort. Brit. p 569 (at Bombay, Roux.); C argentea, Poir. Dict. v, p 36; Y margantacea; C margantacea, Linn. sp. p 297.

3. AMARANTHUS, Kunth.

1. Paniculatus, Moq. loc. cit..—Stem erect, obsoletely furrowed, striated, pubescent, greenish; leaves petioled, oval or ovate-lanceolate, attenuated at both ends, roughish, pale-green, sometimes purple on the margin; panicle much-branched; spikes erect or spreading, cylindric, rather acute; flowers rather dense, greenish-red or blood-red; calyx rather shorter than the bracts; utricles longer than the calyx, 2 to 3-toothed at the apex. A paniculatus, Linn. sp. p 1406; A cruentus, Linn. loc. cit.; Y Mill. Ic. *t.* 22; A sanguineus, Linn. loc. cit.; Willd. Amar. p 32, N. 24, *t.* 2, *f.* 4; and p 29, N. 21; and p 31, N. 23, *t.* 2, *f.* 3; and p 27, N. 19, *t.* 3, *f.* 5.

2. Tristis, Linn. sp. p 1404, N. 6.—Stem erect, striated, angular, glabrous, green; leaves long-petioled, somewhat rhombovate or ovate-obtuse, glabrous, glaucous, green, a little ash-coloured; panicles sparingly branched; spikes suberect, narrow-cylindric, rather obtuse, terminal one longer and flexuous, lateral middling-sized and rather distant; flowers rather dense, pale or yellowish-

green; calyx scarcely longer than the bracts; utricles the same length as the calyx, bi or trifid at the apex. Syn. Blitum indicum, 2; Rumph. Amb. v, p 231, *t.* 82, *f.* 2; Amaranthus tristis, Willd. Amarant. p 21, N. 14, *t.* 5, *f.* 10; Wight Ic. *t.* 514; A dubius, Mart. Hort. Erlang. 1814, p 197; A tristis, Wight Ic. *t.* 713.

3. SPINOSUS, Linn. sp. p 1407, N. 22.—Stem erect, not angled, obsoletely striated, quite glabrous, reddish; leaves long-petioled, rhomb-ovate or deltoid, sometimes lanceolate-oblong, obtuse, sub-emarginate, glabrous, dark-green, with 2 thorns in the axils; panicles sparingly branched; spikes erect, cylindric-acute, terminal one long and somewhat rigid; flowers dense, green; calyx as long as the bracts; utricles as long as the calyx, bi to trifid at the apex. Syn. Blitum spinosum, Rumph. Amb. v, *t.* 83, *f.* i.

4. EUXOLUS, Rafin.

1. OLERACEUS, Moq. loc. cit.—Stem erect or ascending, striated, glabrous, whitish; leaves petioled, ovate, very obtuse, emarginate, rather wrinkled, pale-green; spikelets axillary, shorter than the petiole, a little branched; spike terminal, erect, abbreviated, thickish, rather obtuse, dense rigid; flowers closely clustered, pale-green; calyx twice the length of the bracts; utricles ovate, rather acute, smooth. Amaranthus oleraceus, Linn. sp. p 1403, N. 1. Aubl. Guy. ii, p 855; Willd. Amarant. p 17, *t.* 5, *f.* 9; Wight Ic. *t.* 715 (?); Pyxidium oleraceum, Mœnch. Meth. p 359; Pentrius oleraceus, Rafin. Fl. Tell p 42; Albersia oleracea, Kunth Fl Berol. ii, p 144.

5. PSILOTRICHUM, Blume.

1. SERICEUM, Dalz. Mss.—Stem erect, tomentose; leaves petioled, broad-ovate, acuminate, silky; peduncles axillary, longer than the leaf, 2 to 3 inches long, round, bifid or trifid, rigid, tomentose; spikes 1 to 1½ inch long, flexuose. Kattywar. Syn. Achyranthes sericea, Kœn. in Roxb. Fl Ind. ii, p 502; Wight Ic. *t.* 726.

6. AERVA, Forsk.

1. JAVANICA, Juss. Ann. d'Mus. ii, p 131.—Stem herbaceous, erect or ascending, branched, round, obsoletely striated, tomentose hoary; leaves alternate, very shortly-petioled, obovate-lanceolate, lanceolate or oblong-lanceolate, obtuse, shortly mucronate, tomentose, hoary; spikes solitary, sessile ascending, long, cylindric-obtuse, woolly; flowers white; calyx a little longer than the bracts; sepals 1-nerved. At Cambay. Syn. Iresine javanica, Burm. Fl Ind. p 212, *t.* 60, *f.* 2; Celosia lanata, Linn. sp. p 298, N. 7; Illecebrum

javanicum, Ait. Hort. Kew. ed. i, 1780-81, p 289; Aerva tomentosa, Forsk. Fl Ægypt. Arab. p 122 and 170, N. 66; Lam. Dict. i, p 46; Achyranthes alopecuroides, Lam. Dict. i, p 548, N. 16; Aerva Ægyptiaca, Gmel. *syst.* Nat. p 1026; Achyranthes javanica, Pers. Syn. i, p 259; A incana, Roxb. Fl Ind. ed. Wall. ii, p 495; A javanica, Wight Ic. *t.* 876.

2. SCANDENS, Wall. List No. 6911.—Stem suffruticose, climbing, branched, round, striated, pubescent, green; leaves alternate, very shortly-petioled, elliptic or oblong, acuminated at both ends, very acute mucronulate, pubescent, green; spikes solitary or twin, sessile or shortly-peduncled, spreading, ovate-oblong or ovate-pyramidal, rather acute, woolly; flowers whitish; calyx twice as long as the mucronate bracts (Bombay, P Roux. 1835) Wight Ic. *t.* 724; Achyranthes scandens, Roxb. Fl Ind. ed. Wall. ii, p 503.

3. LANATA, Juss. Ann. Mus. ii, p 131.—Stems herbaceous, ascending, much-branched, round, striated, a little tomentose, ash-coloured; leaves shortly-petioled, obovate-obtuse, shortly mucronate, pubescent on both sides, ashy or hoary and glaucous; spikes solitary or in twos or threes, sessile, horizontal, ovate-obtuse, woolly; flowers white, hoary; calyx twice as long as the bracts; sepals one-nerved. Mill. Ic. *t.* ii, *f.* 1; Wight Ic *t.* 723; Achyranthes lanata, Linn. sp. p 296; Lam. Dict. i, p 548; Illecebrum lanatum, Linn. Mant. p 344; Willd. sp. i, p 1204; Achyranthes villosa, Forsk. Fl Ægypt Arab. p 48, N. 64; Amaranthus lanatus, Dum. Cours. ed. i, 1802, p 640, N. 21.

7. AERVA.

1. BRACHIATA, Mart. Beitrag. Amarant. p 83, N. 3.—Stems herbaceous, ascending, much-branched, striated, glabrous, green; leaves opposite or alternate, shortly-pétioled, oblong-oval or obovate oblong-obtuse, mucronulate, glabrous, bright-green; spikes 3 to 4 together, subsessile, spreading, oblong-linear, obtuse, villous; flowers snow-white; calyx twice the length of the bracts (proper near Bombay, P. Roux.); Syn. Achyranthes brachiata, Linn. Mant. p 50; Roth. nov. sp. Pl. p 159; Illecebrum brachiatum, Linn. Mant. p 23; Willd. sp. 1, p 1203; Pseudanthus brachiatus, Wight Ic. *t.* 1776.

2. MONSONIA, Mart. loc. cit.—Stem suffruticose, ascending, branched, striated, tomentose, hoary; leaves verticelled or opposite, sessile, linear-subulate, acute-mucronate, hairy, green; spikes solitary, shortly-peduncled, erect, oblong-ovate or ovate-cylindric, obtuse, woolly; flowers pinkish, shining. Syn. Celosia monsonia, Retz. Obs. ii, p 13, N. 26; Illecebrum monsonia, Linn. Fil. Suppl., p 161. Achyranthes pungens, Lam. Dict. i, 546.; Achyr. monsoniæ, Pers. Syn. i, 258; Wight Ic. *t.* 725.

8. AMBLOGYNA, Raf.

1. A Polygonoides.—Stem from a span to a foot long; decumbent or ascending, angular and striated, smooth, red or green; branches diffuse-flexuose; leaves rhomb-ovate or obovate-cuneate at the base, obtuse, emarginate, smooth, green, glaucous beneath, about an inch long; clusters of flowers much shorter than the petiole, roundish, 6 to 8-flowered. Very common in all cultivated lands. Syn. Amaranthus polygonoides, Linn. sp.; Wight Ic. *t.* 512.

9. MENGEA, Schaner.

1. M. Tenuifolia, Moq. in DC. *Prod.* 13, p 271.—Branched from the root; branches distant-spreading; leaves small, obovate-obtuse, much attenuated towards the base, the nerves prominent beneath; clusters of flowers shorter than the petiole, subternate, few-flowered; bracts lanceolate-obtuse. Common everywhere. Native name "Ghol." This and the preceding, along with the Amaranthus, form the staple pot-herbs of the Natives; and, when young, are as good as Spinach.

10. ACHYRANTHES.

1. Aspera, Linn. sp. p 295.—Stem erect, striated, pubescent, of a dusky-ash colour; branches spreading obsoletely, 4-sided; leaves shortly-petioled, obovate-rounded, sometimes somewhat rhomb-rounded, suddenly attenuated at the base, very obtuse and very shortly acuminated, pubescent, pale-green; spikes long, slender, twiggy, lax, flowered; flowers shining, greenish; lateral bracts with an awn as long as the limb. It is B indica Var. which is found in Bombay, with the leaves slightly undulated, rather soft and pubescent. Syn. Amaranthus spicatus, Dicbam.; Pluk. Phyt. *t.* 10, *f.* 4; Mill. Ic. *t.* 11, *f.* 2; A obtusifolia, Lam. Dict. i, 545.

11. DIGERA, Forsk.

1. Arvensis, Forsk. Fl. Ægypt. Arab. p 65.—Stems annual, striated, glabrous; leaves ovate or somewhat acute or obtuse, thin, somewhat wrinkled, green, sometimes reddish on the margin; spikes slender, somewhat panicled, 5 to 6 inches long, erect, rather rigid; bracts ovate-mucronate, whitish; flowers rose-coloured, very small. Common in the rains. Syn. Achyranthes polygonoides, Retz. Obs. ii, p 12; A digera, Poir. Dict. Suppl. 1. 2, p 11; Chamissoa commutata, Spr. *syst.* 1, p 815; Desmochæta muricata, Wight Ic. *t.* 732; Achyranthes alternifolia, Linn. Mant. 50 and 344; A muricata, B; Willd. sp. i, 1193; D muricata, Mart. Beitr.

Amar. p 77; Cladostachys alternifolia, Sweet. Hort. Brit. p 570; Chamissoa arabica and Muricata, Spr. *syst.* i, p 815.

12. CYATHULA.

1. Prostrata, Blume Bijdr. p 549.—Stem herbaceous, prostrate or ascending, angular, glabrous; branches somewhat quadrangular, hairy; leaves very shortly-petioled, obovate, rhomb or ovate lanceolate-acuminate, pubescent, green above, glaucous beneath; spikes twiggy; slender, lax-flowered; flowers pale-violet; hooks 15 to 20, as long as the calyx, yellowish. Syn. Achyranthes prostrata, Linn. sp. 296; Cyathula geniculata, Lour. Fl. Cochin, p 102; Desmochæta prostrata, DC. Cat. Mon. Hort. 1813, p 102; Wight Ic. *t.* 733; Pupalia prostrata, Mart. Beitr. Amarant. p 113; Centaurium ciliare minus, Pluk. Alm. p 93, et Phyt. *t.* 82, *f.* 2; Achyranthes debilis, Dict. Suppl. I. 2, p 10; Desmochæta micrantha, DC. loc. cit., N. 4.

13. PUPALIA, Juss.

1. Atropurpurea, Moq. in DC. *Prod.* 13, p 331.—Stem suffruticose, glabrous, branches ascending, obtusely and obscurely 4-seeded, hispid and pubescent, leaves opposite, long-petioled ovate-acuminate, obsoletely mucronulate, hispid and rough, dark-green; calyx twice as long as the bracts; hooks numerous, long, dark-purple. Common in Gujarat. Syn. Achyranthes lappacea, Linn. sp. ed. ii, p 95; Celosia lappacea, Med. Bot. Beob. p 160; Achyranthes atropurpurea, Lam. Dict. i, p 546; Desmochæta atropurpurea, DC. Cat. Hort. Monsp. p 102; Wight Ic. *t.* 731.

2. Lappacea, Moq. loc. cit.—Stem herbaceous, erect, villous and pubescent; branches spreading, somewhat quadrangular, rather tomentose; leaves opposite, shortly-petioled, oval, attenuated at both ends, acuminate-mucronate, shortly villous, hoary and glaucous; calyx a little longer than the bracts; sepals woolly, 3-nerved; hooks, few, long, yellow. Common in some parts of Gujarat and Kattywar. Syn. Achyranthes lappacea, Linn. sp. ed. i, p 204; A echinata, Retz. Obs. ii, p 12; A patula, Linn. Fil. Suppl. p 160; A lappacea, Echinata, and Patula, Willd. sp. i, 1193; A styracifolia, Lam. Dict. i, p 546; Cadelari lappacea, Medic. Monad. p 92; Desmochæta flavescens, DC. loc. cit. p 102; D patula, Rœm. and Schult. *syst.* v, p 550.

3. Orbiculata, R. Wight. *t.* 1783.—A spreading procumbent plant; stem prostrate; leaves orbicular, retuse, acute at the base, short-petioled, densely villous when young, becoming smoother by age; fascicles densely tomentose, many-flowered, globular, remote,

with long, brown bristles. The Ghauts. Syn. Achyranthes orbiculata, Heyne. Wall. Cyathula orbiculata, Moq. in *Prod.* 13, p 325.

14. ALTERNANTHERA, Mart.

1. A Sessilis, R. Br. *Prod.* p 417.—Stem herbaceous, creeping, branched, articulated, a little compressed, striated, pubescent on 2 sides; leaves shortly-petioled, ovate-lanceolate or obovate, entire or denticulate on the margin, glabrous, bright-green; heads of flowers much shorter than the leaf, 2 to 4 together, spherical; flowers shining, whitish; calyx 2 to 3 times longer than the lateral bracts. A common weed. Wight Ic. 617; Syn. Achyranthes triandra, Roxb. Fl. Ind. ed. Wall. ii, 505; Gomphrena sessilis, Linn. sp. ed. ii, p 300.

CXI. PLUMBAGINEÆ.

1. PLUMBAGO, Tournef.

1. P Zeylanica, Linn. sp. i, p 215.—Stems shrubby, subscandent, striated, much-branched, leaves ovate or oblong, rather acute, shortly and abruptly attenuated into a short stem-clasping petiole; flowers white, disposed in elongated spikes; rachis glandular; corol with a slender tube, divisions of the limb cuneate, retuse. Common on rocky places in the Concans. Grows from Cabool to New Holland.

2. VOGELIA, Lam.

1. V Arabica, Boiss. in DC. *Prod.* 12, p 696.—An erect under shrub, of a singular whitish, glaucous hue; branches twiggy, striated, dichotomous; leaves ovate or obovate, sessile or perfoliate, coriaceous, smooth; flowers small, on long, slender spikes; corolla tubular, the limb small, divisions emarginate, mucronulate; sepals lanceolate, undulated. Hunmunt Ghaut and Mount Aboo. Syn. V indica, Gibson in Wight Ic. 1075. It has been found from seed brought from the Cape by Sir W. Harris, that our Indian plant does not differ from the Arabian and African one.

CXII. SALICACEÆ.

1. SALIX, Linn.

1. S Tetrasperma, Roxb. Cor. Pl. i, p 66, *t.* 97.—Catkins lateral peduncled, male long, lax, and few-flowered; female cylindric, rather dense, elongated; peduncle furnished with 3 to 6 leaves, scales oblong-spathulate, grey and puberulous; nectary six times

shorter than the pedicel ; capsule long-pedicelled, ovoid, glabrous ; leaves lanceolate, elongated, long-acuminated, generally glaucous beneath, quite entire or serrulated. Wight Ic. 1954, and S. ichnostachya 1953. Native name "Walloonj" or "Bucha." On the banks of rivulets on the Ghauts, and some way inland ; flowers in the cold weather.

CXIII. HERNANDIACEÆ.

1. SARCOSTIGMA, Wight and Arnott.

1. S Kleinii, W. and A.—A climbing, branched shrub, leaves alternate, short-petioled, oblong-oval acuminate, coriaceous, glabrous, prominently reticulated ; racemes paired, axillary, very long, interrupted, pendulous, the flowers forming numerous sessile fascicles ; fruit about the size of a large nutmeg, oval, in long, pendent racemes, of a bright orange colour ; seed exalbuminous. At Chorla Ghaut, and along the Ghauts to the south of this point. The ripe fruit is to be found in April. Wight Ic. 1854.

CXIV. THYMELACEÆ.

1. LASIOSIPHON, Fresen.

1. L Speciosus, DeCaisne in Jacq. Voy. p 147, *t.* 150.—A shrub, with scattered, very shortly-petioled, willow-looking leaves, lanceolate, oblong rather acute ; heads of flowers terminal, surrounded by an involucre of oblong, rather hoary, leaflets ; calyx hairy, the lobes ovate-obtuse, with 5 linear bifid scales half their length. Common on the higher Ghauts, as opposite Kandalla, Carlee, &c. &c. ; Syn. Gnidia eriocephala, Graham's Cat. p 176.

CXV. LAURACEÆ.

1. MACHILUS, Nees.

1. Macrantha, Nees.—As mall tree with spreading branches ; leaves large, elliptic-acute, glaucous beneath, glabrous, penninerved ; panicles large, pubescent ; fruit globose, somewhat depressed, black, size of a large currant. Parwar Ghaut, plentiful. Wight Ic. *t.* 1824.

2. Glaucescens, Wight Ic. *t.* 1825.—Leaves oblong-lanceolate, acute at both ends or acuminate, glaucous ; panicles thyrsoid, forming terminal tomentose corymbs ; fruit globose, slightly depressed, about the size of a small gooseberry. The Ghauts. Syn. Phœbe glaucescens, Nees ; Wight Ic. 1825.

2. ALSEODAPHNE, Nees.

1. Semicarpifolia, Nees.—Arboreous; leaves obovate, cuneiform, glaucous, glabrous, penninerved beneath; panicles terminal, cymosely umbelled on the ends of the branches. The Ghauts. Wight Ic. *t.* 1826.

3. BEILSCHMIEDIA, Nees.

1. Roxburghiana, Nees.—Arboreous with a straight trunk, and wide-spreading branches; leaves opposite and alternate, broad lanceolar shining, veined; racemes solitary, under the leaves, or axillary, filaments without glands; nectaries 9; anthers bilocular; berries oblong, glaucous. Wight Ic. *t.* 1828; Laurus bilocularis, Roxb. Fl. Ind. ii, p 311. Common on the Ghauts.

4. CRYPTOCARYA, R. Br.

1. Floribunda, Nees.—A tree; leaves oval-oblong, abruptly shortly-acuminate, coarsely venoso-reticulate and glaucous beneath, glabrous and shining above, pubescent on the veins beneath; panicles axillary, the terminal one dichotomous, naked, yellowish, tomentose. Plentiful at Tullawaree. Wight Ic. *t.* 1829.

5. TETRANTHERA, Jacquin.

1. Apetala, Roxb. Fl. Ind. iii, p 819.—A middle-sized tree; leaves petioled, oval-obtuse, smooth, shining above, 3 to 5 inches long, 2 to 3 inches broad; petioles one inch long, round and smooth; peduncles solitary axillary, as long as the petioles, 3 to 4 cleft; pedicels shorter than the peduncles, each supporting a small umbellet of minute flowers; male involucre 4-leaved, containing 8 to 12 pedicelled corollets; leaflets orbicular, concave, caducous, perianth none; calyx campanulate; female flowers on a separate tree; involucre and calyx as in the male; berry globular, smooth, black when ripe and almost dry, of the size of a pea, resting on the clubbed pedicel. At Vingorla; flowers in June. Syn. tomentosa, Roxb. Ex. Wight Ic. *t.* 1834; flowers apetalous; umbels axillary, solitary, peduncled; leaves elliptic-oblong, somewhat acute at both ends, beneath, with the petioles and young branchlets, whitish tomentose. Common on the Ghauts.

6. CYLICODAPHNE, Nees.

1. Wightiana, Nees.—A tree with broad-lanceolate leaves, crowded about the ends of the branches, under surface clothed with

rusty-brown pubescence; umbels racemed, axillary; racemes solitary, shorter than the leaves, clothed with rusty pubescence; fruit glabrous, the berry half immersed in the cup-shaped truncated tube of the perianth. Wight. Ic. *t.* 1833.

7. LITSAEA, Juss.

1. ZEYLANICA, Nees.—Leaves oblong or lanceolate, attenuated at both ends, acuminate, triple-nerved, glaucous beneath; ribs of the leaves, petioles, and young branches finely yellowish silky; flower-buds globose, contracted at the base. Parwar Ghaut. Wight. Ic. *t.* 132 and 1844.

SUB-ORDER.—CASSYTHACEÆ.

1. CASSYTHA, Linn.

1. FILIFORMIS, Linn. Willd. sp. ii, 487.—A parasitic, herbaceous plant, leafless, consisting of long twining cord-like stems from a papilliform root; flowers small, in simple or compound spikes; flowers like those of the preceding order; fruit size of a pea, one-seeded, a little fleshy. Hook. Exot. Fl. *t.* 167; Jacq. Amer. Stirp. *t.* 79. Very common in hedges.

CXVI. SANTALACEÆ.

1. OSYRIS, Linn.

1. WIGHTIANA, Wall. List 4036.—Shrubby, very ramous, glabrous; young shoots 3-sided, with prominent, sharp angles; leaves from oblong-elliptic lanceolate to elliptic-obovate mucronate; male flowers umbellato-capitulate; peduncles axillary, shorter than the leaves, 6 to 8-flowered; female peduncles axillary, 1 to 3-flowered, lengthening as the fruit advances; ovary conical; limb of the perianth 3-lobed; style short; stigma 3-lobed; fruit size of a small Sloe, red when ripe. Wight Ic. *t.* 1853. Common on the Ghauts.

2. SPHÆROCARYA, Wall.

1. S LEPROSA, Dalz. in Hook. Jour. Bot. iii, p 34.—A tree; leaves oblong, coriaceous, glabrous, rounded at the base, acute at the apex; flowers subsessile, clustered on a scaly, axillary tubercle; calyx with 5 very short semiorbicular divisions; petals linear-acute; filaments adnate to the petals; fruit spherical, nearly an inch in diameter, covered with scurfy scales. In the Warree Country; flowers in the cold season.

3. SANTALUM, Linn.

1. S ALBUM, Linn. sp. p 497.—A small tree, with ovate-elliptic leaves, acute at the base, 1½ to 2½ inches long; panicle of flowers terminal and lateral, shorter than the leaf, its divisions 3-flowered; flowers small, purplish; berry size of a large pea, dark-purple, shining. A native of the Southern Maratha Country, but planted in gardens as far north as Gujarat, where it thrives well. This yields the Sandal-wood of commerce; all the other species of this genus belong to Australasia. Found also in some Kooruns south-west of Poona.

CXVII. ELÆAGNACEÆ.

1. ELÆAGNUS, Linn.

1. E. KOLOGA, Schlecht. in DC. *Prod.* 14, p 611.—A large climbing shrub; branchlets densely covered with ferruginous, shining scales; leaves elliptic, acute or obtuse, green and smooth above along with the flowers, silvery and shining beneath; flowers axillary, pedicelled, deflexed, on short leafy branches; fruit elliptic, sive of an Olive, eatable. Common on the Ghauts. Syn. E conferta, Graham's List; E latifolia, Wight Ic. 1856. Native names "Nurgi" and "Ambgool."

CXVIII. ARISTOLOCHIACEÆ.

1. ARISTOLOCHIA, Tournef.

1. A. ACUMINATA, Willd. iv, 157.—Perennial, twining, smooth; leaves petioled, cordate entire, somewhat acuminate; racemes axillary, simple or compound, drooping, shorter than the leaves; petioles 1 inch long, slightly channelled; corol with a funnel-shaped tube, and long, linear, acute laminæ; capsule pear-shaped, about 2 inches long, dehiscing, with 5 valves. Very rare; we have seen this on the banks of the Chapora River at Muneree, in the Warree Country; also on Parr Ghaut leading to Mahableshwur.

2. A INDICA, Willd. iv, 157.—Shrubby, twining; leaves petioled, linear-wedgeformed or obovate, 3-nerved, pointed, waved smooth, 2 to 4 inches long; racemes axillary, shorter than the leaves; flowers erect, dark-coloured; capsules oblong, pendulous. Hills throughout the Concan, not very common. "Sampsun"

3. A BRACTEATA, Retz. Obs. 80.—Stem and branches weak, trailing on the ground; leaves reniform, glaucous; flowers axillary, solitary-peduncled; peduncles furnished at the base with a kidney-shaped, curled, sessile bract; flowers of a dark-purple colour, hairy

inside. In the black soil of Gujarat and the Deccan. This and the preceding are nauseously bitter. These plants have a reputation as antidotes to snake-bites, but their qualities in this respect are more than doubtful. A. indica has, however, decidedly active qualities as a remedy in bowel affections, and Bracteata, a merited reputation as an antiperiodic in intermittent fevers. "Keeramar," Maratha.

2. BRAGANTIA, Lour.

1. B WALLICHII, R. Br.—Diœcious; leaves oblong-lanceolate, 3-nerved at the base; tube of the perianth smooth, lobes of the limb acutish; anthers 9, triadelphous; pistil very short; stigmas 9, radiating, united at the base, three of them bifid; fruit like a siliqua, slender, about 4 inches long, terete. Southern Concan, rare. At Kullumbeest, in the Warree Country; Canara, common. Wight Ic. 520.

CXIX. PIPERACEÆ.

1. PIPER, Linn.

1. SYLVESTRE (Lam.), Miquel *syst.* p 314.—Stem shrubby, scandent, rooting; leaves membranaceous, pellucido-punctate, glabrous, green above, glaucous beneath, ovate-acuminate, oblique at the base, or in the lower ones somewhat cordate and equal, 7-nerved, the three middle ones extending to the apex; male catkins peduncled, filiform, pendulous; bracts linear-oblong; female about the length of the leaves; bracts linear-oblong; female about the length of the leaves; bracts oblong, roughish beneath; stigmas 4-reflexed, deciduous. Miquel in Hook. Jour. Bot. v, p 552; Wight Ic. *t.* 1937.

2. PEPEROMIA, Ruiz. and Pavon.

1. PORTULACOIDES (Dietr. Miq.), Miquel *syst.* p 130.—Succulent, glabrous, sparingly branched, creeping, deeply rooting, leafless below; leaves opposite, upper ones ternate, short-petioled, succulent, glanduloso-punctate, obovate, oblong, or subspathulate, obsoletely 3, rarely 5-nerved; catkins axillary and terminal, solitary, longish-peduncled, shorter than the peduncles, cylindrical obtuse. Common on the Southern Ghauts on moist rocks, or on branches of trees. Miquel in Hook. Jour. Bot. v, p 550; Wight Ic. *t.* 1922.

CXX. EUPHORBIACEÆ.

1. EUPHORBIA, Linn.

1. E NIVULIA, Ham. in Linn. Trans. xiv, 286.—A large shrub; branches round, naked below, leafy at the apex; stipulary

spines naked, paired, spirally set; leaves tongue-shaped, mucronate, very fleshy, 4 to 6 inches long (the branchlets come off in whorls of four); peduncles solitary or twin, in the axil of the fallen leaf, half an inch long, 3-flowered at the apex, of which the central one comes out first in February, while the lateral ones are but undeveloped buds. The centre flower consists of five thick, fleshy scales, alternate, with five thinner scales fringed on the margin and imbricate in æstivation; stamens 40, in 5 bundles, each bundle of 7 to 8 stamens, surrounded by branched and tattered fringes; ovary of the central flower abortive. Wight Ic. 1862; Syn. E neriifolia, Hort. Beng. 36; Tithymalus zeylanicus, Pluk. Alm. 369; Rheed. Mal. ii, *t.* 43. Gujarat and Sind, common.

2. E Neriifolia, Willd. sp. ii, 885.—Shrubby, often arboreous; branches sharply 5-angled; stipulary thorns twin; leaves subsessile, oblong, about 3 inches long, and much less fleshy than those of the preceding. Bombay, Concan, and Deccan. The common Milk-bush. Native name "Thor." Syn. Ligularia, Herb. Amb. iv. 88, *t.* 40; E ligularia, Hort. Beng.

3. E Antiquorum, Willd. sp. ii, 881.—A large, leafless shrub; branches spreading, triangular, armed with double spines at the protuberances of the angles; peduncles solitary or in pairs, 3-flowered; flowers in the cold season. Rheed. Mal. ii, *t.* 42. A rather scarce species. In Severndroog Fort; Goregaum, in the Concan; Falls of Gokak.

4. Acaulis, Roxb.—Stemless, unarmed; root very large, fusiform, perennial; leaves radical, fleshy, cuneiform, with curled margins; peduncles from the crown of the root 5 to 7-flowered. The leaves are often spotted, as if with blood. The root is used medicinally. Mahableshwur, Braminwara range, Sawunt Warree.

5. E Rothiana, Spr.—An erect, smooth, herbaceous plant; leaves oblong-lanceolate, tapering towards the base, glabrous; whorls 3 to 5-branched; branches 2, or in the old plants, 3 times dichotomous, with broad, cordate, subperfoliate bracts at each fork; flowers solitary in the fork. Wight Ic. 1864. On the Ghauts; in fields at Dasgaum; in the black soil of Gujarat. A glaucous, dichotomous plant, one foot high; flowers in the cold weather. E lacta, Roth; E glauca, Roxb. Fl Ind. ii, 473.

6. E Strobilifera, Dalz. in Hook. Jour. Bot. iii, p 229.—2 to 3 feet high, smooth; stem erect, round, naked at the base, dichotomously branched towards the top; flowers racemose, terminal on the branches; bracts cordate, ovate-oblique, mucronate, imbricated scariose, reticulated, 1 to 2 inches long; capsule pubescent; petaloid scales oblique, somewhat wedge-shaped. On rocks in the Warree Country; flowers in February; leaves none. Syn. E rupestris, Law (?) in Graham's Catalogue, p 251.

7. E THYMIFOLIA, Willd. ii, 898.—A common weed; stems red, hairy, prostrate; leaves opposite, obliquely ovate-serrate; calyx and corol of four semilateral parts each. Commonly found on gravel walks.

8. E HIRTA, Willd. ii, 897.—Annual, hairy, obliquely-erect, with the apices recurved; leaves opposite, obliquely-oblong, serrulate; flowers small, numerous, in globular, axillary, shortly-peduncled clusters. A common weed.

9. E PARVIFLORA, Willd. ii, 898.—Very like the last, but easily distinguished by its smoothness, and its having fewer flowers; leaves obliquely-oblong, serrulate, smooth; flowers few, peduncled between the leaves. Not so common as the preceding.

10. E UNIFLORA, Roxb. Fl Ind. ii, 473.—Annual, dichotomous, diffuse, filiform, smooth; leaves somewhat linear, with the base obliquely-cordate, and serrulated towards the apex; flowers solitary; capsules smooth. Rather rare. Our specimens are from Dasgaum, in the Concan.

2. EXCŒCARIA, Linn.

1. E AGALLOCHA, Willd. iv, 864.—A small tree; leaves about the extremities of the branchlets alternate, petioled, ovate or ovate-cordate, serrulate, smooth; flowers in aments, axillary; male ones often crowded; female solitary; capsule 3-lobed, with 3 recurved styles; the flowers are triandrous, and very fragrant. In salt marshes, not very common. The white, milky juice is said to be highly acrid and dangerous.

3. FALCONERA, Royle.

1. F MALABARICA, R. Wight Ic. 1866.—A small tree, with thick, spreading branches; leaves large, ovate-oblong or lanceolate-serrate, quite smooth, biglandular at the base; flowers in long, naked, rigid spikes, appearing when the tree is destitute of leaves; fruit purple, size of a pea. Found sparingly on the hills from Nassick to Vingorla. The milky juice is of a highly poisonous nature. No. 1314 of Graham's Catalogue.

4. MICROSTACHYS, Juss.

1. M MERCURIALIS, Juss. Euphorb.—Annual, erect-branched; leaves ovate-cordate, serrate, smooth, from 1 to 2½ inches long; racemes axillary, solitary, as long as the leaves, filiform, cernuous, few-flowered; male perigonium 3-leaved, oval-pointed; female 6-leaved; stigma 3-cleft, spreading; capsule 3-celled. Southern Concan. Syn. Tragia mercurialis, Willd. iv, 324.

2. M CHAMÆLEA, Juss.—Erect, slender, and smooth, with narrow-linear leaves. Common about Vingorla.

5. TRAGIA, Linn.

1. T INVOLUCRATA, Willd. iv, 324.—A perennial, twining plant, the tender parts hairy; leaves petioled, oblong, 3-nerved, pointed, serrate, hairy; stipules cordate; racemes leaf-opposed, peduncled, erect, 1 to 2 female flowers on each, with the calyx pinnatifid. A formidable plant; a sting from the hairs is very painful. In shady places on the Ghauts, common.

2. T CANNABINA, Willd. iv, 326.—Shrubby, climbing, 4 to 5 feet high; leaves petioled, 3-divided, serrate, hairy, 2 to 4 inches long; stipules half lanceolate; racemes erect, many-flowered; male flowers numerous on the upper part of the raceme, very small, yellow, each with three bracts; female flowers beneath the male, two on each raceme, with the calyx-leaflets pinnatifid. This plant also stings like the Nettle. In hedges in Gujarat and the Deccan.

6. ACALYPHA, Linn.

1. A CILIATA, Willd. iv, 522.—A common weed, annual; leaves ovate-acuminate serrate; spikes axillary, shorter than the petioles; involucres pectinated tomentose, one-flowered.

2. A INDICA, Willd. iv, 523.—An annual weed; leaves petioled, round-ovate, 3-nerved, serrate, smooth, minutely dotted, 2 inches long; involucre cup-shaped, striated, smooth, toothed. Wight Ic. 877; Rheed. Mal. x, *t.* 81, 83.

7. MACARANGA, Thouars.

1. M ROXBURGHII, Wight, under Ic. 1883.—A small tree, with entire peltate ovate-cordate leaves, 3-nerved, hairy beneath; petioles as long as the leaves; panicles thin, axillary, erect; flowers minute; filaments three, as long as the calyx; capsule round, size of a pea, fleshy, covered with clammy, waxy grains. Very common in the Concan and Ghaut jungles. Syn. Osyris peltata, Roxb. Fl. Ind. iii, p 755. Native name "Chanda." Wight Ic. 817.

8. GIVOTIA, Griffith.

1. ROTTLERIFORMIS, Griff., Wight. Ic. 1889.—A small, ramous tree; leaves alternate-cordate, or somewhat lobed, clothed with white stellate pubescence beneath, subglabrous above; petioles often furnished with 1 to 2 prominent glands; panicles terminal; flowers congested or subcapitate on the ends of the ramuli; pedicels

jointed, usually furnished with a filiform bract; stamens about 15, hairy at the base; fruit oblong, about the size of a pigeon's egg; nut very hard; seed oily; wood very porous; used for making imitations of fruit at Gokak. Sparingly found in the northern parts of the Deccan, also in the Southern Maratha Country.

9. JATROPHA, Kunth.

1. J Glandulifera, Roxb. Fl. Ind. iii, 688.—A short, stout shrub, dichotomously branched above; leaves alternate-petioled, sometimes entire, but generally palmately lobed; lobes 3 to 5, oblong or lanceolate, acutely serrate, each serrature ending in a capitate bristle; panicles terminal, short, few-flowered; bracts bristly; male flowers small, of a pale, greenish-yellow colour; capsule 3-lobed, smooth, oblong, size of a small filbert. Employed by the natives in the same manner as the following. At Punderpore, in the Deccan, plentiful.

2. J Nana, Dalz.—A shrub, 1 to 1½ foot high, all smooth; root woody, as thick as the finger; stem round, smooth, very little branched; branches erect; leaves large for the size of the plant, sessile or shortly-petioled, broadly-ovate, entire or trilobate; lobes obtuse, central much the largest, 4 to 6 inches long and broad, pale beneath, 3-nerved; flowers panicled, terminal, few, 3 to 5 on each division; stipules minute; flowers solitary, pedicelled, subtended by a subulate bract half its length; calyx leaves six, small, subulate; fruit obovoid, flattened at the top, slightly six-sulcated, of the same size as the preceding. Rare, in waste, stony places near Poona. Native name "Kirkundee." Employed in Ophthalmia as a counter-irritant.

10. HEMICYCLIA, Wight & Arnott.

1. Sepiaria, W. and A., Edin. New. Phil. Jour. xiv, 297; Wight Ic. *t.* 1872.—A middle-sized tree; leaves glabrous, oblong or obovate-retuse, slightly toothed or waved on the margin; flowers numerous, minute, whitish, 2 lines broad; male flowers with 8 to 11 stamens surrounding a flat disk, no rudiment of ovary; female flowers with concave crenated stigma; drupe nearly round, red. Thwaites in Hook. Jour. Bot. vii, p 271. Wood very hard and close-grained.

2. H Venusta, Thwaites in Hook. Jour. Bot. vii.—A small-branched tree; extreme branches slender, gracefully drooping on all sides; leaves oblong elliptic-lanceolate, acuminate, waved on the margin, entire, glabrous; flowers axillary; males fascicled, short-pedicelled; male calyx 4-parted, tomentose, concave, 2 exterior

concealing the others in æstivation; female flowers in pairs; stigma large, sessile. Hills in the Dharwar Zillah. Syn. Astylis venusta, Wight. Ic. 1992.

11. ROTTLERA, Roxb.

1. R DICOCCA, Roxb. Fl Ind. iii, 829.—A half-scandent shrub, about 5 feet high; leaves large, round-cordate, 3-nerved; racemes terminal and axillary; capsule dicoccous, tomentose. In the Southern Concan, very common.

2. R MAPPOIDES, Dalz. in Hook. Jour. Bot.—Arboreous, diœcious; leaves long-petioled, cordate-peltate, acuminate when old, smooth above, beneath densely clothed with a whitish or ferruginous, starry tomentum; male flowers spiked; spikes axillary, compound; flowers clustered 5 to 6 together, naked; female spikes terminal, 4 to 5 inches long, densely covered with ferruginous tomentum. Differs in some important particulars from Roxburgh's R peltata, to which it is nearly allied. Syn. R peltata, Wight Ic. 1873. Canara, common.

3. R AUREOPUNCTATA, Dalz. in Hook. Jour. Bot. iii, p 122.—A diœcious shrub; leaves opposite, oblong-obovate, acuminate, attenuated towards the base, shortly-petioled, smooth and shining above, sprinkled beneath with stellate hairs, and golden-coloured scales; stipules linear caducous; flowers racemose; racemes simple, axillary and terminal, shorter than the leaf; male flowers fascicled, about 5 together; calyx 4-divided, divisions broadly ovate, reflexed; female raceme 4 to 5-flowered; calyx spathaceous, split on one side; capsule 9 lines in diameter, clothed with soft hairy bristles. Noticed in Graham's list under 1334. Shady jungles in the Ghauts and hilly parts of the Concan; Meera Hills.

4. R URANDA, Dalz. loc. cit. p 229.—A shrub; branchlets glabrous; leaves narrow-oblong, obtusely acuminate, coriaceous, shining, attenuated into the petiole, serrulated, the serratures callous-pointed; male flowers racemose, smooth; racemes axillary, solitary, shorter than the leaf; female flowers axillary, solitary, with a very long peduncle, naked and smooth, 3 inches long; capsules bilocular, smooth. Well distinguished by the unusually long peduncles of the solitary female flowers. Phoonda and other Ghauts; in flower and fruit in November.

5. R TINCTORIA, Willd. iv, 823.—Arboreous; leaves alternate ovate-oblong, 3-nerved, with 2 glands at the base; panicles axillary and terminal; capsules covered with a red, mealy powder, used to dye red. Common in the Concan and Ghaut jungles. Native name "Shendree."

12. TREWIA, Linn.

1. T Nudiflora, Willd. iv, 834.—A rather large tree, with opposite cordate-acuminate leaves, something like those of the Bendy tree; male flowers in pendulous racemes, the female solitary; fruit a berry, 3 to 4-celled. Very plentiful at Banda, in the Warree Country; also at Bassein; between Nagotna and the Pass leading to Indapore. The native name is "Petaree," as stated by Graham. "Petaree" is also the Rottlera dicocca; Wight Ic. 1870-71; Rheed. Mal. i, *t.* 42.

13. ADELIA, Linn.

1. A Neriifolia, Roxb. Fl Ind. iii, 849.—A diœcious shrub, 2 to 3 feet high; leaves alternate, linear-lanceolate, willow-like; spikes of flowers red, axillary, solitary, slender. Common in the beds of rivers along with Trichaurus ericoides. Wight Ic. 1868.

2. A Retusa, J. Graham Cat. p 185.—A low shrub; leaves alternate, sessile, obovate-cuneate, retuse, slightly crenate; flowers axillary, 2 to 3 together; stamens very numerous. The flowers appear in March and April. Pretty common in the beds of the Deccan rivers. Wight Ic. 1869; male only.

14. CROTON, Linn.

1. C Umbellatum, Willd.—A shrub, 5 to 6 feet high; leaves ovate oblong-acuminate, entire, glabrous on both sides; flowers terminal, small, white, umbelled. Chorla Ghaut; flowers in the cold weather. Wight Ic. 1874.

2. C Hypoleucos, Dalz. in Hook. Jour. Bot. iii, 123.—Small tree, monœcious; branches, petioles, and rachis covered with ferruginous tomentum; leaves elliptic, acute at both ends, entire, long-petioled, covered sparingly above and densely beneath with white, stellate, silvery scales, and having 2 to 4 stipitate glands at the base; racemes axillary and terminal, as long as the leaves; male flowers numerous, above; female few, below. In shady jungles on the Concan Hills. Native name "Panduray." We do not think that this differs from the C bicolor of Roxb. (Fl. Ind. iii, p 680), who says it is a native of Sumatra.

3. C Oblongifolium, Roxb. Fl. Ind. iii, p 685.—Arboreous; leaves large, oblong, serrate, obtuse-pointed, smooth on both sides, 2-glanded at the base; racemes terminal, generally solitary, erect, shorter than the leaves; flowers male and female mixed, small, of a pale-greenish colour; capsule globular, fleshy, six-furrowed, tricoccous. Southern Concan, rare; in the fort of Banda. Native name "Gunsoor." Used medicinally by the natives to reduce Swellings.

4. C Gibsonianus, Nimmo in Grah. Cat. p 251.—A tree, 15 feet high, with smooth, whitish bark; leaves oval-acuminate entire, of a yellowish-green, sometimes reddish; inflorescence in lateral spikes; male flowers below the female; calyx 5-divided, that of the female flower larger and increasing with the fruit; capsule greenish-yellow when ripe, of the size of a cherry; seeds spotted, not unlike those of the Castor Oil plant. Hurrychunder and hills of Alun, and Koorun near Nassick. Used as a remedy for Rheumatism.

5. C Lawianus, Nimmo loc. cit.—A small tree, with oblong-lanceolate, coriaceous, smooth leaves, larger than the preceding, 4 to 5 inches long; capsule spherical, trilobate, nearly an inch in diameter, smooth, surrounded by the enlarged foliaceous wax-like calyx leaves. Beemasunker, Meera Hills, &c.

15. AGROSTISTACHYS, Dalz.

1. A Indica, Dalz. in Hook. Jour. Bot. ii, p 41.—A rare shrub, rising to the height of 5 to 6 feet; leaves alternate, petioled, oblong, long-acuminated at both ends, serrate-dentate, smooth, 12 to 15 inches long; male flowers in grass-like spikelets, above the axils, small; female flowers on a separate bush, solitary, pedicelled; capsule 3-celled; seeds solitary, of the size of a pea. Near Tulkut Ghaut.

16. BALIOSPERMUM, Blume.

1. B Polyandrum, Wight Ic. 1885.—Suffruticose; leaves large, oval, often lobed, toothed or coarsely and remotely serrated; spikes axillary, about the length of the petioles, 1 to 2; female flowers at their base; anther cells transverse; ovary 3-celled; style deeply 3-cleft; capsule hispid. Northern hills of Caranjah; Ghauts to the north of Braminwara range; Kotool. Syn. Croton polyandrum, Roxb. Fl Ind. iii, 682. This is the "Jumalgota" of the native druggists; one seed is a dose for an adult.

17. CROZOPHORA, Necker.

1. C Plicata.—An annual, erect plant, having a hoary appearance; leaves 2½ inches long, petioled, broad-cordate, waved, sublobate; racemes terminal, few-flowered; petals elliptic, covered with stellate scales on the outside, and 3 lines of white hairs on the inside; capsule rough. Common in fields in the Raighur Talooka, Deccan and Gujarat in the cold weather. Syn. C tinctorium, Burm.; bark very tough.

2. C Prostrata, Dalz.—Procumbent, humifuse; leaves 1 inch long, dark-coloured, much wrinkled and bullate; inflorescence as in the preceding. We believe this to be a very distinct species, never having seen intermediate forms. Syn. Croton plicatum, Willd. (?) Found commonly in dried-up water-holes.

18. BRIEDELIA, Willd.

1. B Scandens, Willd. iv, 979.—Shrubby, scandent, with long, weak branches, their extremities flower-bearing and pendulous; leaves alternate, short-petioled, oval-entire, downy beneath, with numerous prominent parallel veins; flowers small, axillary, crowded, yellowish-green; berries black, succulent when ripe. Common in the hilly parts of the Concan. Syn. Cluytia scandens, Roxb. Cor. Pl *t.* 173.

2. B Montana, Willd. iv, 978.—A tree with short, thick trunk, and spreading branches; leaves obovate or cuneate, smooth, entire, 2 to 3 inches long; veins as in the preceding; flowers small, green, axillary, crowded, sessile; berry globular, succulent, size of a pea. The flowers appear in April; the tree is with or without thorns, according to situation and soil. Syn. B spinosa, Willd. loc. cit.; Cluytia spinosa, Roxb. Cor. *t.* 172. Native name "Asauna." The wood is excellent, and stands exposure to water. On the Ghauts, common.

19. ANOMOSPERMUM, Dalz.

1. A Excelsum, Dalz. in Hook. Jour. Bot. (1851), p 228.—Arboreous, monœcious; leaves alternate, stipuled, coriaceous, smooth shining, elliptic, acute at both ends, 6 to 7 inches long; flowers axillary, fascicled on longish pedicels; male and female mixed; calyx 5-leaved, much larger than the petals; fruit-bearing pedicels drooping; capsules smooth, about an inch in diameter. Syn. Actephila neilgherrensis, Wight Ic. 1910 (1852). Closely allied to the Cluytia collina and Patula of Roxburgh. As Miers has a genus of the same name in Menispermaceæ, it is doubtful whether this will stand. Hab. Phoonda Ghaut; seed without albumen.

20. PHYLLANTHUS, Swartz.

1. P Madraspatensis, Linn., Var. Gracilis, Roxb. Fl Ind. iii, 655.—Perennial, erect, twiggy, 2 to 3 feet high; leaves bifarious, oblong or cuneate-lanceolate; flowers axillary, 3 to 5 males, and 1 female; capsule smooth; styles 3, bifid at apex; seeds brown, beautifully marked like basket-work. Wight Ic. 1895, *fig.* 3; dehiscence of anthers longitudinal.

2. P NIRURI, Linn.—Annual, erect-branched; branches herbaceous, ascending; floriferous branchlets filiform; leaves elliptic, mucronate entire, glabrous; male and female flowers in separate axils, male on the lower ones; dehiscence of anthers transverse, glands in the female bifid and trifid; capsule globose, smooth, 2 seeds in each cell; seeds triangular. A common weed. Wight Ic. 1894.

3. P SIMPLEX, Willd.—Perennial, diffuse; branches flattened; leaves bifarious, lanceolate, sessile, smooth, entire, three-quarters of an inch long; stipules obliquely cordate; flowers axillary, male and female mixed; capsule minutely tubercled; seeds black, muricated; dehiscence of anthers transverse; styles divided to the base. This is an example of Wight's genus Macræa, separated by him on account of the filaments being separate.

4. P POLYPHYLLUS, Willd.—A shrub; floriferous branchlets many-leaved; leaves linear, obtuse-mucronate, minute; flowers axillary; female ones above; stamens monadelphous; anthers vertical, cohering. Fringes the banks of rivers towards the Ghauts. Wight Ic. 1895, *fig.* 2; Syn. P lawii, Graham's Cat. p 181.

21. MELANTHESA, Blume.

1. M TURBINATA, Wight. Ic. 1897.—Shrubby or arboreous; floriferous branchlets bifarious; leaves oval-obtuse, entire, sometimes unequal-sided; flowers axillary, male and female in the same axil; male flower turbinate, six-lobed; female calyx deeply 6-lobed, enlarging with the fruit, red; fruit when ripe dry and capsular; seeds 3, angular, arilled at the base. Malabar and Worlee Hills, Bombay; Concan jungles, common. Syn. Phyllanthus turbinatus, Roxb. Fl Ind. iii, 666.

22. ANISONEMA, Juss.

1. A MULTIFLORA, Wight Ic. 1899.—Shrubby, climbing, primary branches twiggy; young shoots pubescent; floriferous branchlets angular; leaves oval-obtuse, bifarious; flowers axillary aggregated, several males, and usually one female; male flowers purplish; berries size of a pea, dark-purple or black, very common, almost always near water or damp places. This species extends to Sind, where it is found in the forests of great size, climbing to the tops of the highest trees. Syn. Phyllanthus multiflorus, Willd.

23. CERATOGYNUM, Wight.

1. C. RHAMNOIDES, Wight Ic. 1900.—1 to 1½ foot high, a little shrubby; young shoots angular; leaves alternate, short-

petioled, spreading, broad-oval; exterior ones largest, below whitish, entire, half to three-quarters of an inch long; male flowers racemed from the lower axils; female flowers in the upper axils, solitary, short-peduncled, drooping; flowers curious; capsule size of a pea. Rare, at Vingorla; flowers in July. Syn. Phyllanthus rhamnoides, Willd. iv, 580.

24. EMBLICA, Gaert.

1. E Officinalis, Gaert.—Arboreous, branched; floriferous branchlets many-leaved; leaves linear-oblong, obtuse at both ends; flowers axillary, clustered, small, yellowish; appear at the beginning of the hot season; drupe fleshy, globular, smooth, striated; nut obovate, obtusely triangular, 3-celled; seeds 2 in each cell. The fruit is ripe in October. Native name "Awla." The wood is hard and durable, particularly under water; the bark is strongly astringent, and is employed in the cure of Diarrhœa; the fruit is made into pickles. Syn. Phyllanthus emblica, Willd. iv, 587. Concans and Deccan.

25. GLOCHIDION, Forst.

1. G Lanceolarium, Dalz.—Arboreous, smooth; leaves short-petioled, lanceolate, obtusely acuminate, shining; flowers axillary fascicled; the male flowers on longish slender peduncles; female few and sessile; stipules obliquely ovate-acute; capsule small, depressed, turnip-shaped, grooved, 6-celled, 12-valved; seeds 2 in each cell. Very common on the Ghauts. No. 1328 of Graham's Catalogue. Syn. Bradleia lanceolaria, Roxb. Native name "Bhoma." The wood is hard and durable.

2. G Nitidum, Dalz.—Subarboreous; leaves large, sessile, ovate-oblong, acute, shining smooth; fascicles of flowers very shortly-peduncled, supra-axillary; male and female mixed; capsules subglobular, small; apex a little depressed, 5 to 6-celled, 10 to 12-striated, 10 to 12-valved; flowers in January. Near water in the Southern Concan; at Vingorla. Syn. Bradleia nitida, Roxb. Fl Ind. iii, p 699.

26. STYLODISCUS, Bennet.

1. S Trifoliatus, Benn. in Horsf. Pl. Jav.—A large tree of quick growth; trunk erect; branches spreading, forming an extensive, close, shady head; leaves petioled, ternate; leaflets oblong-acuminate, serrated, smooth, 4 to 6 inches long; panicles axillary or supra-axillary, as long as the leaves, composed of numerous small greenish flowers; calyx 5-leaved; corol none; stigma peltate, with 10 rays; capsule size of a small cherry, round, smooth, 3-celled. Wood very hard; Chorla Ghaut, plentiful. Native name "Boke." Syn. Microclus rœperianus, W. and A.

Edin. Phil. Jour. xiv, 298; Bischofila, Blume Bijdr. 1163; Andrachne trifoliata, Roxb. Fl Ind. iii, 728.

27. FLÜGGEA, Willd.

1. F LEUCOPYRUS, Willd.—Shrubby, diœcious; leaves small, obovate-cuneate, subretuse; flowers small, axillary, crowded; male flowers pentandrous; calyx 5-leaved; leaflets oval-concave; berries round, pure white, smooth, size of a small pea, succulent; 3-celled. Wight Ic. 1875. Common in the Concans. Syn. Phyllanthus retusus, Roxb. Fl. Ind. iii, p 657.

2. F VIROSA, Dalz.—A poor-looking thorny shrub, with oval or elliptic leaves, larger than the preceding, narrowed towards the base, 2 to 2½ inches long; berry size of a pea, covered with a white fleshy pulp, 3-celled. Malabar and Worlee Hills, Bombay. We have not seen this in any other locality. The bark is used to intoxicate fish. Syn. Phyllanthus virosus, Willd. iv, 578. Juice of leaves fatal to worms in sores.

28. PROSORUS, Dalz.

1. P INDICA, Dalz. in Hook. Jour. Bot. iv, p 345.—An alpine tree with oval or oblong leaves, and very numerous, small, fascicled male flowers, which appear with the young leaves in March; fruit small, capsular, of a bluish tinge, in threes. Figured in Hooker's Journal 1855; found also by Thwaites in Ceylon, where the wood is used for building purposes, being white and tough. On the Ghauts to the southward.

29. PUTRANJIVA, Wallich.

1. ROXBURGHII, Wall.—A tree with narrow-oblong, acutely-serrulate leaves, with the base oblique, smooth, shining, waved; male flowers short-peduncled, numerous, minute, yellow, collected into globular heads in the axils, sometimes on short axillary racemes; female racemes small, simple, from last year's branchlets; styles 3, short, with large crescent-shaped stigmas; drupe obovate or oval, of the size of a large gooseberry, smooth, white; nut oval-pointed, very hard, rugose, 1-celled. Nagotna, Kandalla, Kennery, and Alibaug Jungles; Belgaum. Wight. Ic. 1876; Syn. Nageia putranjiva, Roxb. Fl. Ind. iii, 766.

CXXI. SCEPACEÆ.

1. SCEPA, Lind.

1. S LINDLEYANA, Wight Ic. 361.—A small, diœcious tree;

leaves alternate, short-petioled, oblong-acuminate, coriaceous, smooth; male flowers amentaceous, diandrous, with a 4-leaved perigonium; female flowers in very short, axillary racemes; perigonium 4 to 6-leaved, in a double series; fruit size of a pea, generally 2-celled, of which one is abortive. Very common in the Southern Concan. This is very probably No. 1346 of Graham's Catalogue.

CXXII. STILAGINACEÆ.

1. ANTIDESMA, Burm.

1. A Lanceolatum, Tulasne, Ann. Des. Soc. Nat. xv, 195.—Shrubby, smooth; leaves long-lanceolate; stipules ensiform; spikes terminal, filiform; male flowers 3 to 4-androus (4 seems to be the normal number); stigmas also very irregular, there being 3 to 4 or 5 divisions; flowers in March. Tulkut Ghaut and Virdee. Wight Ic. 766.

2. A Diandrum, Tulasne loc. cit.—A small tree; leaves short-petioled, oval or oblong, acuminate entire, smooth; 2 to 4 inches long, and 1 to 2 broad; stipules narrow-lanceolate; spikes terminal, filiform, many-flowered; flowers very small; male calyx obtusely 4-toothed; styles 2, spreading, one of them always 2-cleft; drupe minute, succulent, 1-celled. At Vingorla; flowers in the rains. Syn. Stilago diandra, Willd. iv, 714.

3. A Pubescens, Willd. iv, 763.—A small tree; leaves alternate, short-petioled, oval, entire, downy, 2 to 4 inches long, 2 to 3 broad; stipules subulate; spikes numerous, terminal, and from the exterior axils, those of the male tree much longer and more slender; flowers very small, greenish-yellow; calyx 5-leaved; leaflets ovate, hairy; filaments 5, spreading, longer than the calyx; drupe minute; nut one-seeded, eatable. On the hills near Vingorla; flowers in June. Wight Ic. 821.

4. A Paniculatum, Willd. iv, 764.—A small tree; leaves short-petioled, round-oval, often emarginate, entire, villous, 1 to 3 inches long, and nearly as broad; spikes terminal and axillary, panicled, downy; flowers numerous, minute, sessile, greenish-yellow; male calyx 5-leaved, female calyx 5-toothed; stigma of 5 stellate divisions; berry small, round, smooth, dark-purple when ripe, of a pleasant, subacid taste. This differs from the last in having much broader and rounder leaves, and branched, not simple spikes. At Vingorla; flowers in June. Wight Ic. 820.

CXXIII. ULMACEÆ.

1. CELTIS.

1. C Roxburghii, Planch. Ann. Soc. Nat., ser. iii, *t.* x, p 302.—

A small tree; leaves obliquely ovate-cordate acuminate, glabrous, 3-nerved; flowers pentandrous; male ones from the base of the young shoots, or solitary under the bisexual ones; bisexual flowers on slender, villous, axillary racemes; germ 1-celled, containing one ovule, pendulous from the apex of the cell. On the Ghauts, common. Celtis trinervia, Roxb. Fl Ind. ii, p 65.

2. SPONIA, Commerson.

1. S Wightii, Planch. loc. cit. p 264.—A small tree of quick growth; leaves ovate-oblong cuspidate, cordate and unequal at the base; younger ones with a white pubescence beneath; cymes very shortly-peduncled, as long as or a little longer than the petiole; male flowers dense; female more lax; stigmas 2, equal, covered with long threads; berry small. Common in the hilly parts of the Concan. Native name "Gol." Syn. Celtis orientalis, Roxb. Fl. Ind. ii, p 65; Wight Ic. *t.* 1971.

3. HOLOPTELÆA, Planch.

1. H Integrifolia, Planch. loc. cit. p 259.—A large tree; leaves alternate short-petioled, ovate, sometimes cordate-entire, smooth, shining; stipules lanceolate; flowers polygamous; male and bisexual mixed in cymes along the naked branches; capsule orbicular, leafy, compressed, emarginate, 1 to 2-celled, indehiscent. The wood of this tree is of good quality and much used. Syn. Ulmus integrifolia, Roxb. in Willd sp. Pl. i, 1326; Wight Ic *t.* 1968. Concans, common. Maratha name "Wawulee."

CXXIV. URTICACEÆ.

1. FLEURYA, Gaudichand.

1. F Interrupta, Wight Ic. 1975.—Herbaceous, erect, bristly all over; young branches and under-surface of the leaves pubescent; leaves long-petioled, cordato-ovate, acute or acuminate, coarsely serrated, triple-nerved; peduncles axillary, solitary, as long or longer than the leaves, bearing small lateral panicles at unequal distances; male calyx 4-parted; stamens 4, achenium ovate compressed, winged round the margin, tubercled on the disks. Syn. Urtica interrupta, Linn. A common weed in gardens.

2. GIRARDINA, Gaudichand.

1. G Heterophylla.—Leaves broad-cordate, 7-lobed; lobes oblong, acute, coarsely serrated, clothed on both sides with fine whitish down, armed above with thin, scattered prickles, thickly

clothed beneath with the same; male and female flowers in distinct, glomerate peduncled spikes. Common on the slopes of the Ghauts. A formidable plant; the least touch of any part produces most acute pain. The bark of this, as of many other of the order, makes good flax. Syn. Urtica heterophylla, Willd. iv, 362; Gerardina leschenaultiana, DeCaisne, Wight Ic. 1976.

3. SPLITGERBERA, Miquel.

1. S Scabrella.—Shrubby, spreading; leaves large, opposite, cordate, spreading, serrate harsh, 3-nerved; spikes axillary, erect, cylindric; male flowers crowded, short and in the lower axils; female above and generally solitary. Syn. Urtica scabrella, Roxb. Fl. Ind. iii, p 581; Wight Ic. 691. Common in the hilly jungles of the Concan; Meera Hills.

4. ELATOSTEMMA, Forster.

1. E Oppositifolium, Dalz. in Hook. Jour. Bot. iii, p 179.—Herbaceous, about 1 foot high; stem simple, smooth, naked at the base; leaves rather long-petioled, opposite, lanceolate-acuminate, coarsely dentate-serrate, 3-nerved, sparingly hairy above, quite smooth beneath; upper ones the largest; heads of flowers solitary peduncled, in the alternate axils; peduncles shorter than the petiole; common receptacle flat, discoid, simple; male and female flowers mixed. The Ghauts; flowers in September.

2. E Cuneatum, Wight Ic. 2091.—Erect, simple; leaves obovate cuneate, unequal-sided, crenately serrated towards the apex, pilose on both sides, above mixed with scattered, bristly hairs; receptacles sessile, unisexual; fertile flowers few, sessile, mixed with numerous, pedicelled, 3 to 4-lobed sterile ones; nuts oval-ribbed. On old walls, Mahim woods; Bombay; also at Belgaum.

5. CONOCEPHALUS, Blume.

1. C Niveus, Wight Ic. No. 1959.—Arboreous, erect-branched; leaves ovate-lanceolate, acute or acuminate, 5-nerved, acutely serrated, somewhat bullate above, prominently reticulate and white beneath, strigosely hispid on both sides; inflorescence axillary cymose; fruit capitate, drupaceous; drupes small, yellow, globose. Bœhmeria ramiflora, Spr. (?). Native name "Capsee." Common in the Concan and Ghaut jungles.

2. C Concolor, Dalz.—Shrubby; leaves very large (1 foot), irregularly scattered, 3-nerved, perfectly smooth, oblong-ovate, acute, green on both sides; female flower axillary. At the Phoonda Ghaut.

6. POUZOLZIA, Gaudichand.

1. P INDICA, Wight Ic. 1980-81.—Ascending, lax; leaves triple-nerved, alternate, short-petioled, uniform, reduced in size towards the ends of the branches, ovate-lanceolate, subacuminate, pilose; flowers few, axillary, glomerate, tetrandrous; fruit ovate, 8-ribbed, apiculate. Common in gardens as a weed. Syn. Panetaria indica, Linn.

2. P PENTANDRA, Wight Ic. No. 20, under No. 2096.—Stem ramous, 4-sided towards the apex; leaves sessile, narrow-lanceolate, cordate, pilose on both sides, scabrous above; flowers pentandrous, fruit-winged, cordate. Island of Caranjah. Syn. Urtica pentandra, Roxb. Fl Ind. iii, 583.

3. P. INTEGRIFOLIA, Dalz. in Hook. Jour. Bot. iii, p 134.—Suffruticose, 3 to 4 feet high; root thick; stem compressed, with a line of hairs on each side; leaves opposite, sessile, with a cordate base, lanceolate-acuminated, 3-nerved, entire, pubescent, 3 to 4 inches long; flowers male and female together, clustered in the axils of the leaves; male perianth 4-parted; filaments flattened; female fruit-bearing perianth 2 to 3-winged, with 8 to 10 ribs between the wings. Phoonda Ghaut; flowers in September. Wight Ic. 1979, *fig*. 1.

4. P STOCKSII, Wight Ic. No. 18.—Straggling, ramous, seeking support, and then ascending; stem and branches 4-angled, furrowed between, glabrous; petioles short, connected by a broad, scarious stipule; leaves glabrous, except the hispid margin, from oval-obtuse at both ends, to cordate-ovate, obtuse; floral ones sessile, narrow ovate-lanceolate obtuse; flowers few, axillary, pentandrous; fruit ovate, ribbed, or broadly 2 to 3-winged. Belgaum, Deccan.

CXXV. MORACEÆ.

1. EPICARPURUS.

1. ORIENTALIS, Blume.—Arboreous; leaves alternate, short-petioled, obovate cuspidate acuminate, serrated towards the apex, very rough above; male flowers capitate; heads axillary aggregated, short-peduncled; females axillary, 1 to 2 together, longish-pedicelled; fruit drupaceous, 1-seeded, tertacrustaceous; cotyledons very unequal, exalbuminous. Syn. Trophis aspera, Willd. A small, scraggy-looking tree, with very rough leaves, used in polishing wood.

2. UROSTIGMA, Gasparrini.

1. U BENGALENSE, Gaspar.—Branches dropping roots, which form stems; bark smooth and of a light ash-colour; leaves

alternate, about the extremities of the branchlets, petioled ovate-cordate, 3-nerved, entire, 5 to 6 inches long, 3 to 4 broad, smooth and shining when old; fruit paired, axillary, sessile, of the size and colour of a cherry, downy. The well-known Banyan tree. Syn. Ficus bengalensis, Linn.; F indica, Roxb. Native name "Wur."

2. U Religiosum, Gaspar.—A large and handsome tree; leaves long-petioled, ovate-cordate narrow-acuminate, entire or repandly undulate towards the apex, quite smooth; fruit paired, axillary, sessile, vertically compressed, when ripe of the size and colour of a small, black cherry. The Peepul tree.

3. U Lambertianum, Miquel in Hook. Jour. Bot. vi, p 565.—Leaves long-petioled, ovate-oblong, margins obsoletely repand-undulate, abruptly and obtusely acuminate, truncate at the base, between membranaceous and coriaceous, shining, 3-nerved; fruit axillary, twin, sessile globose, glabrous, with 3 bracts at the base, puberulous on the back. Bombay, Lambert in Herb. Hooker.

4. U. Infectorium, Miquel loc. cit.—Leaves rather long-petioled, membranaceous, oblong or sublanceolate-oblong, moderately and acutely acuminated, obtuse, or rounded, or subcordate at the base, quite entire, or very slightly repand; fruit small, sessile, twin, globose, smooth, when ripe white. Syn. Ficus infectoria, Roxb. Fl Ind. iii, p 551; Wight Ic. 665 (excluding F infectoria, Willd). The Concans.

5. U Pseudotjiela, Miquel loc. cit.—A very large tree; leaves long-petioled, ovate-oblong, pointed, entire, firm, smooth on both sides, shining, particularly above, with numerous simple and parallel veins, 4 to 6 inches long, 2 to 3 broad; fruit paired, axillary, sessile, a little turbinate, smooth, size of a cherry, when ripe purple. This it appears is not the Tjiela of Rheede as supposed by Roxburgh. Syn. Ficus tjiela, Roxb. Fl Ind. iii, p 549; Wight Ic. 668. On the Ghauts. Native name "Peepree."

6. U Retusum, Miquel loc. cit. 581.—Leaves moderately petioled, broadly obovate or somewhat rounded, dilated at the apex, very shortly and obtusely apiculate or retuse, slightly emarginate, between membranaceous and coriaceous, veins half-spreading, about 10 on each side, rather distinct, the rest capillary, finely reticulated; petioles deeply-furrowed on the upperside; fruit axillary twin, sessile; bracts puberous. Miquel's specimens were from Bombay; comes very near to the following; perhaps too near to be distinct. It differs in the branchlets, stipules, and young fruit being quite glabrous, the branches much dilated at the apex, for the most part retuse, or abruptly ending in a short peak. This species is the true "Nandrook" of the Natives.

7. U Nitidum, Miquel loc. cit.—Branchlets somewhat 3-cornered; leaves with moderate or rather long petioles, elliptic or obovate or subrhombeo-elliptic, obtusely and shortly subapiculate acute or subcuneate at the base, slightly 3-nerved, veins on each side several, subimmersed, or distinct beneath, confluent near the margin, but with no submarginal nerve, coriaceo-membranaceous; stipules ovate-lanceolate, smooth or puberulous; fruit axillary, twin sessile, globose, smooth, size of a pea with 3 obtuse bracts; petioles with a narrow groove in front. Syn. Ficus nitida, Thunb.; Wight Ic. 642; Ficus benjaminea, Roxb. Fl Ind. iii, p 550; Rheed. Mal. iii, *t* 55.

8. U Benjamineum, Miquel loc. cit.—Branchlets slender, flexuose, weak, hanging; petioles round, rather short; leaves ovate or elliptic-ovate acuminate, coriaceous, like parchment, surrounded by a smooth margin; veins capillary horizontal, united into an arched nerve; fruit axillary, sessile, like peas; bracts 3, ovate-obtuse, deciduous; leaves 2 to 3½ inches long, 1 to 1½ broad; fruit smooth, shining, greenish-yellow, with a dash of purple. Syn. Ficus striata, Roth., whose specimens were received from the Southern Maratha Country.

9. U Dasycarpum, Miquel loc. cit.—Branchlets and fruit densely tomentose; leaves shortly-petioled, broadly ovate or elliptic, shortly and obtusely acuminate, rounded or slightly cordate at the base, repand-undulate, thickly coriaceous, smooth above, beneath with the petioles tomentose and pubescent; costal veins 8 to 10, spreading, confluent at the margin, much reticulated and very prominent beneath; fruit axillary, sessile, generally twin, ellipsoid obtuse at both ends, bracts 3, obtuse, membranaceous, pubescent. Bombay, Lam. in Herb. Hook.

10. Cordifolium.—A tree, having much the appearance of the Peepul; leaves on very long petioles (6 to 8 inches), broad-cordate, with a short and sudden acumination, rather membranaceous with waved margins, finely reticulated beneath (lateral veins spreading and prominent), perfectly smooth; fruit paired, sessile, round, smooth, black, of the size and appearance of a black cherry. On the Ghauts. Native name "Paeer."

11. U Volubile, Dalz.—A climbing shrub, and often a tree with a stem as thick as a man's arm; leaves alternate, very shortly petioled, somewhat ovate, suddenly acuminated, very unequal-sided, cuneate towards the base; lateral nerves 3 to 4 on each side, prominent-spreading, uniting in arches, pale-green, hard, and roughish to the touch, though smooth, 3 to 4 inches long, sometimes a little toothed on the margin; fruit small, like the Nandrook. Native name "Datir." Rocky places on the Ghauts.

3. FICUS, Linn.

1. F Acutiloba, Miquel.—Branchlets puberulous, when old smooth, shining, dark-coloured; leaves moderately petioled, ovate-oblong, 3 to 5-lobed, base obtuse, 3-nerved; lobes elliptic or lanceolate-acute, denticulate, middle one longer, subsinuate or coarsely toothed on both sides, especially beneath, scabrous and harsh; fruit axillary, solitary peduncled, small, between pear-shaped and globose, with 3 bracts at the base. Allied to F repens, and Heterophylla; 1370 of Graham's list; Malabar Hill, Bombay; the Ghauts, &c.

2. F Asperrima, Roxb. Fl. Ind. iii, p 554.—Branches at length smooth; leaves alternate or opposite, oblong-acuminate, obtuse at the base, remotely toothed upwards, rigid, very rough and harsh, 3-nerved, and with 3 to 4 costal veins on each side; fruit axillary, peduncled, globose, hoary, pubescent and scabrous. Bombay, common. Wight Ic. 633.

3. F Heterophylla, Linn.—All rough and harsh; leaves alternate, shortly-petioled, rigid, membranaceous, above roughish, and of a deep-green, below pale, oblong-acute, acute at the base, serrated, entire or 3-lobed or subpinnatifid, of all shapes; fruit axillary, solitary, rarely twin, between turbinate and globose. Common in moist places. Wight Ic. 659.

4. COVELLIA, Gasp.

1. C Oppositifolia, Gasp.—A small tree, native of the banks of rivulets; trunk erect; young shoots scabrous and covered with much short, white hair, fistulous, and interrupted at the insertion of the leaves; leaves opposite, short, round or oblong, slightly serrate, glandular in the axils of the veins beneath, shining above, downy beneath; fruit axillary and peduncled, racemed on the naked, woody branches, round, about the size of a large nutmeg, covered with short, white hair, with several equi-distant ridges. Syn. Ficus oppositifolia, Willd sp. iv, p 1151; Sycomorphe roxburghii, Miquel 1375 of Graham's Catalogue.

2. C Glomerata, Miquel loc. cit.—A large tree, generally found about villages and on the banks of rivers; trunk crooked, thick, and high; bark of a rusty-greenish colour and rough; leaves alternate, petioled, oblong or broad-lanceolate, tapering equally to each end, entire, very slightly 3-nerved, smooth on both sides; racemes compound or panicled, issuing immediately from the trunk or the large branches; fruit pedicelled, nearly as large as common figs, clothed with soft down, and most frequently full of worms. Native name "Oombur."

3. C Dæmonum, Miquel.—Shrubby; leaves generally opposite, cuneate-oblong, pointed, serrate, scabrous above, downy beneath, with a green gland in the axils of the veins; fruit for the most part in pairs in radical, withering racemes, often under-ground, of the size of a large nutmeg, obovate, very hairy, obscurely ridged. Ficus dæmona, Kœn. Wight Ic. 641. Common; generally near the sea.

CXXVI. ARTOCARPACEÆ.

1. ANTIARIS, Leschenault.

1. A Saccidora, Dalz. in Hook. Jour. Bot. iii, 232.—A stately forest tree; leaves stipulate, alternate, oblong-elliptic, dentate-serrulate, scabrous, on short petioles; flowers on a convex, fleshy, pedicelled receptacle, tetrandous; fruit purple, the size of a filbert, containing one seed. Hills in the Concan; Kandalla Ghaut; Warree Country. Syn. Lepurandra saccidora, Nimmo in Grah. Cat. Bomb. Pl. p 193; Wight Ic. 1958. Native name "Jassoond."

2. ARTOCARPUS, Linn.

1. Hirsuta, Lam. Encyc. iii, 201.—Leaves elliptic-obtuse, or rounded at both ends, glabrous above, hairy, especially in the nerves beneath; male catkins long-cylindrical, about the thickness of a quill, at first ascending or erect, afterwards pendulous; females oval, about the size of an egg; fruit globose echinate. Punt Suchew's Country. Native name "Ranphunnus" and Patphunnus.

2. A Lakoocha, Roxb. Fl. Ind. iii, 524.—A middling-sized tree, with a short, thick trunk; leaves alternate short-petioled, oval entire, generally pointed, smooth above, downy beneath, 4 to 12 inches long, 2 to 6 broad; aments axillary; male subsessile, about the size of a nutmeg, female short-peduncled, globular; fruit with a pretty smooth surface, of an irregular roundish form, yellow when ripe, eatable; ripe in July. Caranjah Hill and Bassein, not common.

3. A Integrifolia, Willd. iv, 184—Leaves petioled, oval, of a firm, coriaceous texture, of a deep, shining green above; male ament of the size of a man's thumb, female oblong; fruit very large, oblong-muricated; seeds of the size of a nutmeg. The well-known Jack tree. Native name "Phunnus." The wood is excellent, becoming by age very like Mahogany; in colour bright-yellow when newly cut. Formerly much used for furniture, but has gone completely out of fashion, having been superseded by Blackwood.

CXXVII. PODOSTEMACÆ.

1. MNIOPSIS, Mart.

1. M HOOKERIANA, Tulasne Ann. Des. Sc. Nat. (3 ser.) xi, 104.—A minute plant, moss-like, with the stems densely leafy and cespitose, and a frond beneath like a lichen, creeping on stones in running water; flowers terminal, solitary, or sometimes a little branched, having one forked filament, each division bearing a perfect anther; capsule spherical, smooth, 2-celled, surmounted by 2 stigmas. Common in the running streams of the Concan, flowering as soon as its head is above water; the whole plant is only 1 to 1½ inch high. Wight Ic. 1918, *fig*. 4.

2. TERNIOLA, Tulasne.

1. T PULCHELLA, Tulasne Monogr. Podostem. p 189.—Rhizome thin-linear, branched, short; flower bearing here and there leaves linear, marked with a whitish line in the middle, distichous, interior ones the flower-bearing bud, verticelled and united at the base; pedicel of middling length. Concan rivers. Syn. Lawia pulchella, Tulasne; Mnianthus pulchellus, Walpers.

2. T LONGIPES, Tul. loc. cit.—Rhizome thin, broadly linear, sparingly branched; leaves long-linear acute, marked with a whitish line, near to the flower inserted in a circle, and at the same time united downwards; flowers long-pedicelled. Concan rivers. Syn. Mnianthus longipes, Wal. Ann. iii, 443.

3. FOLIOSA.—Rhizoma spreading lichen-like, lobed and free on the margin; buds for the most part on the free margin; leaves numerous fascicled, round at base of the pedicel, long, linear-pointed, no sheath; pedicel 2 to 3 times the length of the leaves. Rivers in Salsette, Law. This is a very distinct species, and most easily recognised by its tufts of well-formed leaves, and no sheath. Syn. Dalzellia foliosa, Wight Ic. 1919, *fig*. 2.

4. LAWII.—Rhizoma spreading, margins free, gemmiferous leaves surrounding the sheath, few, short, broader than those within, somewhat lanceolate, those of the sheath very numerous, short, needle-shaped, recurved; pedicels shortish; capsule ovoid, scarcely angled. Salsette, Law. Very distinct from the preceding in the character of its leaves and sheaths. Syn. Dalzellia lawii, Wight Ic. 1919, *fig*. 3.

5. PEDUNCULOSA.—Rhizoma spreading, margins free, lobed, gemmiferous; leaves all aggregated and united to form the sheath, short bristle-like; peduncle 6 to 8 times the length of the sheath, very slender; capsule ovoid, round or scarcely angled. Salsette, Law. Syn. D pedunculosa, Wight Ic. 1919, *fig*. 4.

CXXVIII. GNETACEÆ.

1. GNETUM.

1. G Scandens, Roxb. Fl. Ind. iii, 518.—A stout scandent shrub; young shoots round, smooth, jointed and swollen at the insertion of the leaves; leaves opposite, short-petioled, oblong, firm, glossy, entire, rather obtuse; peduncles axillary and terminal, with one or two opposite pairs of peduncled, cylindrical aments, and a terminal one; scales of the aments short cyathiform; drupe oblong, of the size of an olive, when ripe smooth, of a reddish orange-colour, one-celled; pulp intermixed with many tender spiculæ; nut of the shape of the drupe. Very common in the thick jungles. Native name "Koombul" or "Oomblee"; flowers in March and April.

CXXIX. SMILACEÆ.

1. SMILAX, Linn.

1. S Ovalifolia, Roxb. Fl. Ind. iii, p 794.—Stems climbing, cylindric, woody, larger parts armed with sharp, strong, incurved prickles; tendrils paired, simple; leaves alternate, short-petioled, oval, 5 to 7-nerved smooth, entire; petioles short-winged, channelled; umbels axillary, compound; umbellets globular; berries red, smooth, succulent, 2 to 3-seeded. Native name "Gootee." Common in the jungles.

2. S Macrophylla, Roxb. loc. cit. 793.—Scandent; stem and branches cylindric and prickly; leaves short-petioled, round entire, 5-nerved, glossy; tendrils petiolary, undivided; female peduncles axillary solitary, branched, each with a large globular umbellet of greenish-yellow, pedicelled flowers; umbellets much larger than in the preceding; berries size of a pea, red, smooth, 1 to 2-seeded, in dense, round balls. Rarer than the preceding; on the Southern Ghauts, Chorla.

CXXX. ASPARAGINEÆ.

1. ASPARAGOPSIS, Kunth.

1. A Sarmentosa, Kunth. Enum. v, p 97.—Stems woody, climbing, very much branched; branches grooved and ribbed; branchlets rather rough; thorns subulate straight, turned downwards; leaves linear-mucronulate; racemes many-flowered, flowers white; berries red; root woody, with oblong, fleshy tubers, which are often candied for the table. Wild in Gujarat and on Deckan Hills; fruit ripe in February. Often found in gardens.

CXXXI. DIOSCORINEÆ.

1. DIOSCOREA, Linn.

1. D Triphylla, Linn. sp. 1462.—Twining; branches furrowed, a little hairy, and armed with small prickles; leaves scattered, ternately 3-divided, membranaceous, with pellucid lines; segments cuspidate, terminal one elliptic-oblong, lateral obliquely ovate; male racemes axillary, in threes, generally all simple; rachis and pedicels clothed with whitish hairs; capsules obovate-oblong, pubescent. Rheed. Mal. vii, *t* 33. The root is said by Graham to be intoxicating and intensely bitter. Common in the Concan.

2. D Oppositifolia, Linn. sp. 1463.—Root, as in all the species, tuberous, perennial; stems twining, slender, round, smooth, annual; leaves opposite-petioled, oval, acute, waved, 3 to 7-nerved; male flowers very numerous, in axillary panicles; female flowers few, in axillary spikes; flowers in the rainy season. The roots are eaten by the Natives. On the Ghauts, common.

3. D Pentaphylla, Willd. Herb. No. 18411.—Branches prickly, furrowed, rather hairy; leaves digitate, 5-divided, membranaceous, puberulous; segments oblong-acuminate cuspidate; stipulary prickles twin; female spikes axillary twin, simple, scarcely longer than the petiole; male-flowers numerous, greenish-white, and exquisitely fragrant. They are sold in the bazar, and eaten as greens. Common in the Concan, and on the Ghauts. Rumph. Amb. v, p 359, *t*. 127.

2. HELMIA, Kunth; DIOSCOREA, Auct.

1. H Bulbifera.—Smooth and bull-bearing; branches terete; leaves scattered, cordate, subrotund ovate-acuminate cuspidate, 9-nerved, membranaceous; male spikes axillary, simple, about 5 together, or compound panicled; segments of the flower 6, lanceolate-acute; female spikes about 3 together, longer than the leaf; capsules oblong, smooth, of the texture of parchment. Native name "Caroo-Karunda. Bombay and Concans, common.

2. H Dæmona, Kunth. Enum. v, 439.—Root tuberous; stems annual, twining, armed; leaves ternate; leaflets obovate-cuneate, 3 to 5-nerved, very large, acute entire, both sides villous when young; petioles armed with small prickles; male spikes axillary compound, drooping, sometimes leaf-bearing; 6 to 18 inches long; female flowers on a different plant; spikes axillary solitary, pendulous. At Vingorla; Hills in Concan, rare. Syn. Dioscorea dæmona, Roxb. Fl Ind. iii, 805; Wight Ic. 811.

CXXXII. JUNCAGINACEÆ.

1. POTAMOGETON, Linn.

1. P INDICUS, Roxb. Fl. Ind. i, 452.—Stem branched, creeping, round, smooth, knotty; leaves alternate, floral ones opposite, petioled, narrow-lanceolate or elliptic-oval, shining, smooth, entire, obsoletely many-nerved; stipules solitary axillary; sheathing as long as the petioles, divided to the middle; peduncles solitary axillary, or opposite the leaves, round, thick, smooth, about as long as the cylindric spike; sepals with long claws, roundish, concave persistent; stamina 4. Pretty common in tanks and lakes; in waterholes of the high Hill-forts of Western Deccan.

2. P PERFOLIATUS, Linn. sp. 182.—Stem round, slightly branched; all the leaves submersed and of one shape, sessile, semi-amplexicaul with a cordate base, ovate or ovate-lanceolate, obtuse, membranous, pellucid; stipules united into a sheath, embracing the stem; fruit rather obliquely obovate, compressed, obtusely angled. In the stream around Dapoorie Garden, and most probably in other streams of the Deccan; a native also of Europe, North America, and New Holland.

3. P PECTINATUS, Linn. sp. 183.—Stem round; all the leaves submersed, extremely narrow, half-round and channelled, divided into tubular compartments, having sheathes at the base; spikes long-peduncled, interrupted; peduncles thread-like. In the large tank at Gogo, most plentiful; a native of Europe, Asia, and America, but not seen in India by any previous observer.

4. P CRISPUS, Linn. sp. 183.—Stem branched, rather compressed; leaves all submersed, uniform sessile, oblong-linear, obtuse or shortly acuminate, sharply denticulate, waved and crisp on the margin, membranous, pellucid; fruit obliquely and broadly ovate, terminated by a slightly recurved, compressed, subulate beak. Syn. P tuberosum, Roxb. Fl. Ind. i, 472. Tanks in the Concans.

2. APONOGETON, Linn.

1. MONOSTACHYUM, Linn. Suppl. 214.—Root tuberous; leaves radical, long-petioled, linear-oblong, cordate at the base, pointed, entire, smooth, 3 to 5-nerved, 3 to 6 inches long and about one broad; scapes as long as the leaves; spikes densely flowered; calyx of 2 wedge-shaped concave leaflets; flowers hexandrous; capsules smooth, pointed, 1-celled, 4 to 8-seeded. Tanks in the Dharwar and Belgaum Collectorates.

CXXXIII. ALISMACEÆ.

1. SAGITTARIA, Linn.

1. S TRIANDRA, Dalz. in Hook. Jour. Bot. ii, 144.—Root fibrous; leaves long-petioled, linear-spathulate, 3-nerved, much longer than the scape, obtusely keeled on the back; scape erect, simple, round, obtusely trigonal at the apex; flowers triandrous, verticelled, shortly-pedicelled, inconspicuous; female flowers on the lower part of the spike. In water-holes, Malwan Talooka; flowers in August.

2. S OBTUSIFOLIA, Linn. sp. 1410.—Root fibrous; leaves radical, erect, long-petioled, ovate-sagittate; basal lobes divaricate, tapering to long, narrow, fine points, smooth, many-nerved; scapes tall, erect, 5 to 6-angled, striated, branched and verticelled at the apex; flowers numerous, small, white; drupes small, numerous, collected in globular heads, turbinate, dry and wrinkled. Pretty common in water-holes in Gujarat; at Gundar, where it is called "Nulkoot." Goats are very fond of the leaves. This plant is certainly much nearer to Alisma than to Sagittaria.

CXXXIV. BUTOMACEÆ.

1. BUTOMOPSIS, Kunth.

1. B LANCEOLATA, Kunth. Enum. iii, p 164.—Aquatic; leaves radical, long-petioled, lanceolate; scape as long as the leaves, 6 to 12-flowered; flowers pedicelled, erect, umbelled; exterior sepals elliptic-obtuse, herbaceous; interior petaloid; stamina 8 to 9; carpels 6 to 7; papery rostrate; seeds numerous, very minute. Syn. Butomus lanceolatus, Roxb. Fl Ind. ii, 315. Rare; at Chicklee, in the Surat Districts.

CXXXV. PONTEDERACEÆ.

1. PONTEDERIA, Linn.

1. P VAGINALIS, Linn. Willd. ii, 23.—Root perennial, creeping; leaves radical, narrow-cordate, pointed-entire, smooth, glossy, 5 to 7-nerved; petioles long, fistulous, smooth, those bearing a raceme swelled about the middle; raceme short-peduncled, with about a dozen handsome blue hyacinth-like flowers. Margins of tanks and water-holes, common.

2. P HASTATA, Willd. ii, 24.—Leaves triangular or hastate-pointed, many-nerved, very smooth and glossy; posterior angles generally obtuse; flower-bearing petioles swelled near the apex, and there split to allow of the passage of the raceme; flowers

numerous-pedicelled, of a beautiful, bright-blue, violet colour. In the same situations as the preceding.

CXXXVI. LILIACEÆ.

1. METHONIA, Herm.

1. M Superba, Lam. Encycl. iv, 133.—A climbing plant, with bulbous, biennial root; stem herbaceous; leaves cirrhiferous; inferior oblong; superior ovate-lanceolate; perigonium of six lanceolate, undulate leaflets, yellow, with a scarlet base; capsule 3-celled, 3-valved. Syn. Gloriosa superba, Linn.; Roxb. Fl. Ind. ii, 143; Rheed. Mal. vii, *t.* 57. Pretty common in hedges; flowers large. Native names "Buchnag," "Kalawee," "Karianag." Root is said to be poisonous.

2. URGINIA, Steinh.

1. U Indica, Kunth. Enum. iv.—Bulb tunicated; leaves numerous, radical ensiform, nearly flat, 6 to 18 inches long; scape erect, round, smooth, naked, 2 to 3 feet long; raceme long, erect; flowers remote, long-pedicelled, drooping, inconspicuous, of a dingy, brownish colour, appear long before the leaves. Sandy shores of the Concan, common; at Hurnee, abundant. Generally called "Jungly Piaz." Syn. Scilla indica, Roxb. Fl. Ind. ii, 147.

3. UROPETALUM, Gawler.

1. U Montanum, Dalz. in Hook. Jour. Bot. ii, p 142.—Root a small, tunicated bulb; scape round, about a foot high; raceme drooping, about 8-flowered; leaves linear, folded, as long as the scape; corolla white between, tubular and campanulate, 8 lines long; exterior divisions oblong-obtuse, a little longer than the tube; interior united to the middle, all glandular at the apex; bracts scarious, acuminated, longer than the pedicels; capsule stalked, 3-lobed; cells 3 to 4-seeded. In the Western Deccan, in pastures, also at Belgaum; flowers in August.

2. U Concanense, Dalz. loc. cit.—Scape round, 8 to 10 inches high; raceme drooping, 3 to 4-flowered; leaves half round, fleshy, filiform, few, deeply grooved above, a half shorter than the scape; corol white, tubular, an inch and a-half long; exterior divisions half the length of the tube, spreading; interior united to the middle, all linear-oblong, obtuse, papillous and glandular at the apex; capsule 3-lobed; cells 6-seeded; seeds flat, black, shining, and smooth. In rocky places in the Malwan Talooka; flowers in August.

4. LEDEBOURIA, Roth.

1. L Maculata, Dalz. loc. cit.—Leaves obovate, glabrous, wedge-shaped, attenuated into the petiole, purple spotted, and never bearing bulbs ; flowers like those of the following, appear in June. Common in the Concans and Deccan.

2. L Hyacinthina, Roth. nov. sp. 195.—Root bulbous, as in the preceding ; leaves of a light-green colour, linear-oblong, undulated, smooth, pretty long, bearing bulbs at the apex ; scapes bearing a many-flowered raceme, of small, bluish, hyacinth-like flowers. Kunth has confounded both species under this name. Bot. Mag. 3226 ; Syn. Anthericum hyacinthoides, Willd. ; Erythronium indicum, Rottl. fide Spring. This, as far as we know, is confined to the Southern Concan.

5. PHALANGIUM, Juss.

1. Tuberosum, Kunth. Enum. iv, p 598.—Roots very many, fleshy, terminated by a small, oblong tuber ; leaves radical, ensiform, waved on the margin ; scape round, naked ; flowers panicled or simply racemed, fascicled, small, white. There is some doubt as to Roxburgh's Anthericum tuberosum being this species, as he describes the flowers as large as snow drops ; possibly Roxburgh's plant may be a species of the following genus, which has flat (not angular) seeds. Very common in both Concans and Deccan.

6. CHLOROPHYTUM, Gawler; HARTWEGIA, Nees.

1. C Anthericoideum, Dalz. in Hook. Jour. Bot. ii, 141.—2 feet high ; roots many, tuberous ; leaves radical ensiform, slightly folded, margins waved, shorter than the naked scape, with 2 to 3 very short, simple branches ; flowers racemose, solitary or twin ; pedicels half-an-inch long, articulated near the base ; filaments covered with minute, papillose vesicles ; capsule triquetrous ; seeds in each cell 5 to 6, compressed reniform ; testa black. The papillose vesicles on the filaments place this in the genus Hartwegia ; but this does not differ in any other respect from Chlorophytum. It may be easily mistaken for the preceding, being very like it. In the district of Malwan ; flowers in July.

2. C Parviflorum, Dalz. loc. cit.--8 to 10 inches high, smooth ; tubers oblong, hanging from the fibres of the root ; leaves erect, grass-like, linear folded, striated, longer than the scape ; scape simple, few-flowered ; flowers solitary or sometimes twin, with acuminate bracts ; filaments smooth, alternately a little shorter ; anthers green ; pedicels articulated in the middle, droop-

ing in fruit; capsule sharply 3-lobed, triangular; seeds in each cell 2 to 4. In rocky places near the sea, Malwan District; flowers in July.

3. C Breviscapum, Dalz. loc. cit.—Tubers oblong, pendulous, from the fibrous root; leaves flat, ensiform; margins undulated, acuminated at the apex, attenuated towards the base, striated, shining above, pale beneath; scape round, simple, or very rarely branched, half the length of the leaves; flowers rather densely racemose, twin; sepals oblong-acute, all reflexed in flowering; pedicels articulated at the apex; filaments papillose, thickened towards the apex; capsule triquetrous; cells with 1 to 3 seeds; seeds black. Malwan; flowers in July.

4. C Nimmonii, Dalz. loc. cit.—Root tuberous; leaves flat, broad-lanceolate, long-attenuated towards the base, 2 feet long, shining above, striated, shorter than the simply branched, round scape; branches of the scape from the axils of sheathing bracts, long, compressed or angular, undivided; flowers twin, distant, drooping racemose; sepals spreading, exterior acute, interior obtuse; anthers and filaments minutely papillose; capsule triquetrous; cells with only one seed. This is the largest of our species, and rises to the height of 3 feet. We have a strong suspicion that it will turn out to be identical with the C orchidastrum of Sierra Leone. Malwan; also the Ghauts opposite Bombay.

5. C Glaucum, Dalz. loc. cit.—Root a spherical, depressed, fibrous tuber; fibres from above the tuber stout vermiform; leaves recurved, lanceolate-acuminated, attenuated towards the base, glaucous, striated, slightly folded, half the length of the simple, rigidly-erect scape, which is clothed with several very sharp sheathing scales; flowers twin approximated, spreading; pedicels articulated above the middle; anthers and filaments papillose; ovary triquetrous, with 8 ovules in each cell. On the Ghauts, rather rare. The root differs from all the preceding; also the scape differs by being scaly.

CXXXVII. COMMELYNACEÆ.

1. COMMELYNA, Linn.

1. C Communis, Linn. sp. 60.—Root fibrous; stems branched, creeping; branchlets marked with a line of hairs; leaves sessile, ovate-lanceolate, acuminate, rounded at the base; margin waved; spathes opposite the leaves, rounded-cordate, acute-folded, smooth, with roughish margins; peduncles in the spathe 2, the longer one 1-flowered, the shorter 3-flowered. Common everywhere. Syn. C polygama, Willd. Enum. 67; Roth. Cat. Bot. i, p 1; C cæspitosa, Roxb. Fl. Ind. i, 174 (?).

2. C BENGALENSIS, Linn. sp. 60.—Stem branched, creeping, hairy; leaves petioled, ovate-elliptic or cordate-acute, puberulous on both sides; sheaths hairy, with the mouth ciliated; spathes shortly-peduncled, cucullate, turbinate, acute; peduncles twin in each spathe, shorter one 2-flowered; flowers bisexual, the longer hairy, one-flowered; flower barren. Common everywhere.

2. ANEILEMA, Brown.

1. A NUDIFLORUM, Br. *Prod.* 271.—Stem creeping, branched; branches erect, smooth; leaves linear-lanceolate acute, sheathing and ciliated at the base, smooth on both sides, margins a little rough; peduncles terminal, 1 to 2, elongated, with several flowers in a kind of corymb at the apex; capsules 3-celled; cells 2-seeded; leaves 2½ to 3 inches long, 2½ lines broad. Common. Syn. Commelyna nudiflora, Linn. sp. 61; Tradescantia malabarica, Linn. sp. 412.

2. A COMPRESSUM, Dalz. in Hook. Jour. Bot. iii. p 138.—Branched at the base and rooting; branches ascending, compressed, simple, smooth; leaves short, bifarious, ensiform, rather obtuse, a little folded; sheaths hispid all round; peduncles terminal, and from the axils of sheathing bracts, 1 inch long; flowers several, shortly-pedicelled, racemose; exterior sepals oblong, obtuse, smooth; interior rounded, rose-coloured; capsule oblong, 9-seeded. Malwan. Very like the preceding; but in this the leaves are shorter, more fleshy, darker in colour, and there are more seeds in the capsule. A secunda, Wight Ic. 2075.

3. A OCHRACEUM, Dalz. loc. cit.—Stems erect, simple, round, smooth, leafy; lower leaves ovate-oblong, upper cordate-ovate, acute and smaller; pedicels 6 to 7 together, axillary and terminal fascicled, articulated in the middle; flowers ochre-yellow; capsule cartilaginous, smooth; cells 7 to 8-seeded; seeds in 2 rows. In wet, rocky places of the South Concan. Syn. Dichœspermum repens, Wight Ic. 2078 (?).

4. A VERSICOLOR, Dalz. loc. cit.—Branched; branches erect round, striated, hispid, with spreading hairs; leaves distant lanceolate-acuminate, smooth, stem-clasping, 5 to 7-nerved beneath; sheaths rather long, a little hispid, furrowed and striated; pedicels axillary, fascicled, 3 to 4 together; flowers ochre-yellow, twice as large as in the preceding; capsule linear, trigonal; cells 7-seeded; seeds in a single row. Malwan. These two species are distinguished from all others by having yellow instead of blue flowers.

5. PAUCIFLORUM, Dalz. loc. cit.—2 feet high; the whole plant, except the mouth of the sheaths, smooth; leaves long-linear acuminated, narrow; sheaths of the lower leaves split, the upper suddenly transformed into short sheathing floral bracts; pedicels 1 to

3, from the axils of the bracts, twice articulated in the middle; fertile stamens 2, with orange-coloured anthers; capsule obtusely trigonal; seeds tuberculated, solitary in each cell. Allied to A vaginatum, Br.; but the much longer leaves, and 1-seeded cells, distinguish it from that species. Wight Ic. 2076.

6. A ELATUM, Dalz. loc. cit.—3 to 4 feet high; stem erect, round, smooth, leafy; leaves linear-lanceolate acute, smooth, flat, with white, undulated margins, 6 to 8 inches long, 2 inches broad; sheaths entire, 1 inch long; peduncles terminal, dichotomously branched, the branches distant and few-flowered; flowers in threes; the petaloid sepals obovate cuneate, reflexed. This remarkable species has tuberous roots. Differs from the A giganteum of R. Brown only in having bearded stamens, and from the A elatum of Kunth, in the exterior sepals being oval, obtuse, and concave, not linear, as in that species. Syn. Commelyna elata, Vahl (?). In dark, shady woods of the South Concan. Wight Ic. 2072.

7. A CANALICULATUM, Dalz. loc. cit.—6 to 7 inches high; root fibrous; stem simply branched erect, striated, alternately marked on one side with a pubescent line; lower leaves broad-linear lanceolate, upper ones cordate-oblong, all stem-clasping, smooth, channelled in the middle; peduncles terminal and axillary, solitary or twin, dichotomously branched, few-flowered; flowers rather long-pedicelled, bifarious, distant; stamens 3, perfect; anthers blue, all the filaments bearded; capsule oblong, acutely trigonal; cells 4 to 5-seeded; seeds in a single row; flowers blue. Southern Concan. Syn. A paniculatum, Wight Ic. 2075.

8. A DEMORPHUM, Dalz. loc. cit.—All except the ciliated mouth of the sheaths smooth, one foot high, a little branched at the base; branches erect, round-striated, internodes marked on one side with a pubescent line; lower leaves linear-acuminate, upper lanceolate-acute, all stem-clasping; flowers terminal, dichotomously panicled, few; pedicels and branches of the panicle with rounded, cucullate bracts; fertile stamens 3; anthers purple; fertile filaments only bearded, gland-bearing; filaments naked. The little cucullate bracts mark this species from all others. When specimens are found on a stony soil, the internodes are so much shortened as to give the plant a very different appearance, the leaves appearing all radical. Southern Concan.

9. A SEMITERES, Dalz. loc. cit.—Stem erect, simple, round, smooth, 2 to 5 inches high; leaves few, subulate fleshy, half round; sheaths entire; flowers terminal, and from the axils of the uppermost leaf dichotomously panicled, few; peduncles and pedicels red; floral sheaths truncate, one-toothed. All the filaments united at the base. Syn. Cyanotis nimmoniana, Grah. Cat. p 224; Dichœspermum juncoides, Wight. Ic. 2078.

10. A Tuberosum, Hamilton in Wall. Cat. 5207.—Root perennial, composed of several smooth, elongated tubers; stem none, except the sheathing bases of the leaves, which appear after the flowers; leaves ensiform, waved acute, smooth; racemes radical, erect, straight, smooth; scape branched above; branches each with a sheathing bract; branchlets with several pedicelled blue flowers, rather large. Southern Concan, common. Syn. Commelyna scapiflora, Roxb. Fl. Ind. i, 175. Royle has needlessly, it is thought, made this into a new genus. (Mardaunia, Royle Himal, *t.* 95). Royle states that the curious root sold in the bazars under the name of "Kala-Mooslee," is the root of this plant; but it does not bear the least resemblance to it. A scapiflora, Wight Ic. 2078.

3. CYANOTIS.

1. C Hispida, Dalz. loc. cit.—Annual, 4 to 5 inches high, all hispid, slightly branched at the base; stems erect, round, striated, red; leaves linear ensiform, fleshy, rather flat, 1 to 2 inches long, 3 to 6 lines broad; flowers terminal, sessile, capitate, few, with falcate semicordate bracts; stamens 6, fertile, long-exserted; anthers of a very deep-violet colour; filaments bearded above, with blue hairs all pointing to one side; capsule with the cells 2-seeded. On rocks. Southern Concan. Syn. Tradescantia rupestris, Law in Grah. Cat. p 223.

2. C Vivipara, Dalz. loc. cit.—Epiphytal stemless, all clothed with rufous-spreading hairs; radical leaves all linear ensiform, flat, thick, fleshy, fascicled; scapes rising from the root, filiform, rooting and viviparous; peduncles from the nodes of the scape, solitary alternate, bearing a 3 to 4-flowered umbel, with 2 bracts; bracts at the base of the peduncle small, foliaceous, oblong, acute; sheathing cells of capsule 2-seeded; valves much recurved after dehiscence; seeds cylindric. On trees at Parwar Ghaut. This is a plant of a very peculiar habit, most resembling the large C tuberosa; the tuft of radical leaves are liliaceous in appearance.

3. C Adscendens, Dalz. in Hook. Jour. Bot. iv, p 343.—Root tuberous; stems several, ascending simple, round striated, shining; leaves linear ensiform glabrous; heads terminal, many-flowered; flowers of a lovely blue. At Belgaum, in wet, grassy places.

4. C Fasciculata, Rœm. and Schultz *syst.* vii, 1152.—Woolly; stem dichotomous; leaves lanceolate, subpetioled; head of flowers terminal, few-flowered, with about 4 lanceolate-falcate sheaths; flowers rose-coloured, filaments bearded with hairs, of which the lower half are pure white, the upper half rose-coloured, 4 to 6 inches high. Common in rocky places in the Deccan. Syn. Tradescantia fasciculata, Heyne in Roth. nov. sp. p 189; C dichro-

tricha, Stocks in Wight Ic. 2086-87. The late Dr. Stocks supposed this to be a new species; but we cannot find that it differs from Heynes' plant, especially as we have found but one woolly species in the Presidency. The differently coloured hairs are not observable in dried specimens, and therefore were not seen by Roth, who described Heynes' specimens.

5. C Tuberosa, Rœm. and Schultz *syst.* vii, 1153.—Root tuberous perennial; stems several, creeping, round, 6 to 30 inches long; radical leaves 3 to 4, lily-like, ensiform, large; stem ones linear-lanceolate, sheathing, striated, villous and purple beneath; heads of flowers terminal and axillary, solitary or twin, peduncled, imbricated; bracts falcate, ciliated; flowers bluish-purple. This is a large and coarse species when compared with the others. Common in the Western Deccan, never seen in Concan. Roxb. Cor. *t.* 108.

6. Cristata, Rœm. and Schult. loc. cit. 1150.—Stem diffuse, creeping, marked with alternate, pubescent lines; leaves ovate-lanceolate, smooth, ciliated; pairs of bracts 6 to 7 lanceolate falcate, imbricated, terminal; stamens scarcely longer than the corolla. The commonest species during the rains. Syn. Commelyna cristata, Linn. sp. 62; Tradescantia cristata, Jacq. Vind. ii, *t.* 137; Bot. Mag. 1435.

7. C Axillaris, Rœm. and Schult. *syst.* vii, 1155.—Stem branched, creeping, the branches puberulous on one side; leaves linear-acute, smooth, ciliated; sheaths ciliated; flowers axillary in twos or threes, subsessile, coming out in succession. Western Deccan, not uncommon. Syn. Tradescantia axillaris, Linn. Mant. 321; Rheed. Mal. x, *t.* 13.

4. DITHYROCARPUS, Kunth.

1. D Paniculatus, Kunth. Enum. iv, p 79.—Stem-creeping with the extremities erect and smooth; sheaths with the mouth woolly; leaves lanceolate-acuminate; panicle terminal, subglobose, many-flowered, pubescent. On the Ghauts; might be easily mistaken for a grass at first sight. Syn. D rothii, Wight Ic. 2080; Tradescantia paniculata, Roxb. Cor. Pl. *t.* 109; Roth. nov. sp. 188 (?).

5. FLAGELLARIA, Linn.

1. F Indica, Linn. Willd. ii, 263.—A long, straggling, scandent, perennial plant; leaves narrow, ending in long, slender, spiral cirrhi; flowers inconspicuous; berries globose, size of a pea, smooth, red, pulpy, generally one-seeded, with 2 abortive ovules; the flowers are terminal and panicled as in the preceding plant, and are often by abortion unisexual. Among rocks near the sea, South Concan.

CXXXVIII. ORONTIACEÆ.

1. POTHOS, Linn.

1. P Scandens, Linn. sp. 1374.—Climbing and rooting on trees; stems long, very tough; leaves entire, articulated with the petiole; petioles winged, slightly stem-clasping at the base; leaves lanceolate or oblong-lanceolate acuminate, obtuse and rounded at the base; spadices axillary solitary, peduncled, recurved, subglobose. The leaves are coriaceous, smooth, 2 to 4 inches long; berries oblong, red, pulpy, 1 to 2-seeded. In the Ghaut jungles, pretty common. Rheed. Mal. vii, *t.* 40; Bot. Reg. *t.* 1337; Syn. Flagellaria repens, Lour. Coch. 263.

2. SCINDAPSUS, Schott.

1. S Pertusus, Schott. Meletem. i, 21.—Stem climbing and rooting on trees, smooth, about an inch in diameter; leaves large, long-petioled, cordate, pinnatifid on one side, and pierced on the other; spadices shortly-peduncled; spathe gibbous, acute, a little longer than the spadix; spadix cylindric-obtuse. Jungles in the Southern Concan. Syn. Pothos pertusus, Roxb. Fl. Ind.; Rheed. Mal. xii, *t.* 20, 21.

CXXXIX. AROIDEÆ.

1. CRYPTOCORYNE, Fisch.

1. C Roxburghii, Dalz.—Root fibrous, stoloniferous; leaves radical, erect, ensiform, smooth, a little curled on the margin; 8 to 12 inches long; scape about an inch long, compressed, smooth; spathe as long as the leaves, erect, twisted like a screw to a very fine point, beautifully spotted inside, with very dark-purple; capsule coriaceous, conical, 5-celled; seeds very numerous. Banks of streams and other wet places, common; flowering in October. This is the Ambrosinia unilocularis of Roxb. Fl. Ind. iii, 493; but as the fruit is not unilocular, we are obliged to alter the specific name. No. 1618 of Graham's Catalogue.

2. LAGENANDRA, Dalz.

1. L Toxicaria, Dalz. in Hook. Jour. Bot. iv, p 289.—A marsh plant, 3 feet high, with a thick creeping root or rhizome; leaves on long petioles, oblong, obtuse, entire, coriaceous, large; sheaths stipulary, opposite the leaf; scapes axillary, solitary, compressed; spathe longer than the scape, tubular at the base, attenuated into a long, slender apex; fruit compound, about 1 inch

in diameter; seeds cylindric-oblong, minute, several in each cell, erect from the base. Marshes of the Southern Concan and Belgaum Collectorate, rare. Called "Vutsunab" by the natives; it is a deadly poison.

3. ARISÆMA, Martins.

1. A MURRAYII, Bot. Mag. *t.* 4388.—Tubers the size of small potatoes; leaves peltate divided; segments 5 to 6, ovate-lanceolate acuminate; lower part of the spathe green, forming a wide tube; upper ovate convex, somewhat cucullate, acuminate; spadix subulate, bent, scarcely longer than the tube of the spathe. Mahableshwur; flowers in May, before the leaves. Snake Lily of Anglo-Indians.

2. ERUBESCENS, Schott. Meletem. i, 17; Blume in Rumph. i, 93.—Leaves peltate divided; segments 10 to 12, sessile, linear-lanceolate acuminated, entire, remotely veined; spadix club-shaped, rather obtuse, shorter than the acuminated-subfornicate spathe. Syn. Arum erubescens, Wall. Pl. As. rar. ii. 30, *t.* 156. Between Ram Ghaut and Belgaum in the rains.

3. CURVATUM, Kunth. Enum. iii, 20.—Stemless; leaflets 10 to 12, lanceolate; spathe fornicate, half the length of the curved spadix; roots tuberous; leaves with very long petioles; leaflets entire, glabrous. Syn. Arum curvatum, Roxb. Fl. Ind. iii, 506.

4. TYPHONIUM, Schott.

1. T BULBIFERUM, Dalz. in Hook. Jour. Bot. iv, 113.—5 to 6 inches high; leaves 2, cordate-hastate mucronulate, long-petioled, shining beneath; petioles 3 times longer than the leaf, striated, bulb-bearing at the apex; spathe narrow-linear, of a pale rose-colour; spadix as long as the spathe, filiform, ovule one erect, stalked, fixed to the base of the ovary. Southern Concan; flowers in June.

5. TAPINOCARPUS, Dalz.

1. T INDICUS, Dalz. in Hook. Jour. Bot. iii, 346.—Stemless; root small, tuberous, perennial; leaves long-petioled, cordate-hastate entire; basal lobes obtuse; scape long exserted; spathe convolute at the base, above narrow elongated, acuminate, flat; spadix cylindric above, slender, as long as the spathe. The scape when in fruit is contorted and bent downwards, the fruit resting on the ground. Vingorla; in the rains.

6. AMORPHOPHALLUS, Blume.

1. A Campanulatus, Bl. in DeCaisne Descr. Herb. Timor. 38.—Root perennial, tuberous, of enormous size; leaves radical, few, thrice bifid, divisions outwardly pinnatifid; segments obliquely oblong-pointed, smooth; petioles round, pretty smooth or verrucose, clouded; spathe large, leathery, campanulate, the border curled; spadix about as long as the spathe, lower and flowering part cylindric, upper part very short and broad, conical or subglobular, lobate and wrinkled. This is the cultivated Soorun; it grows wild on the banks of streams in the Southern Concan. Syn. Arum campanulatum, Roxb. Fl. Ind. iii, 509. The flowers appear long before the leaves.

2. A Sylvaticus, Kunth. Enum. iii, p 34.—Root perennial, tuberous, nearly smooth, like a potato; stem none; leaves radical, 1 to 2-petioled, thrice 2 or more lobed; lobes pinnatifid; segments lanceolate; petioles winged; scape tall, erect, round; spathe one-third the length of the spadix, which tapers to a long, subulate point. Southern Concan, common. This is probably the plant entered as Dracontium in Grah. Cat. p 229. Syn. Arum sylvaticum, Roxb. Fl. Ind. iii, 511.

7. ARIOPSIS, J. Grah.

1. A Peltata, Nimmo in Grah. Cat. p 252.—A small plant; leaf solitary, orbicular, peltate; spathe small, cucullate, a little longer than the spadix; spadix club-shaped, foraminiferous, each foramen containing 6 anthers; ovaries below adnate with the spathe. Common in the Concan; flowers in June.

8. REMUSATIA, Schott.

1. R Vivipara, Schott. Meletem. i, 18.—Stemless; root tuberous; leaves appearing after the flowers, long-petioled, peltate cordate, acuminate; peduncle with bracts short; spathe yellow. In the clefts of trees in the Ghaut jungles; it rarely flowers, but sends up several stalks, covered with minute, scaly bulbs. Syn. Arum viviparum, Roxb. Fl. Ind. iii, 496; Rheed. xii, *t*. 9.

CXL. XYRIDACEÆ.

1. XYRIS, Linn.

1. Indica, Linn. Zeyl. 14.—A rush-like plant, smooth; peduncles round, grooved, sheathed with the leaf below; leaves linear ensiform, shorter than the peduncle; spikes elliptic, many-

flowered; scales broadly obovate, rounded at the apex, shining, smooth; flowers yellow. In salt marshes in the South Concan; near Raree Fort. Rheed. Mal. ix, *t.* 7.

CXLI. ORCHIDACEÆ.

1. OBERONIA, Lindley.

1. O Recurva, Lind.—A small, stemless plant; leaves bifarious, fleshy, short acute; raceme recurved, many flowered; petals obovate, subdentate; lip subrotund, 4-lobed; lobes erose, denticulate; flowers minute, brick-red. Bot. Reg. 1839, p 14, Misc. On trees on the Ghauts.

2. O Lindleyana, Wight Ic. 1624.—Much larger than the preceding; leaves ensiform, short, fleshy, brown, slightly falcate; stem compressed; spike drooping towards the apex, densely covered with innumerable small, sessile flowers; sepals broad-ovate obtuse, entire; petals narrow-linear; lip 2-lobed at the apex; flowers straw-coloured; lip dull-orange. On trees on the Ghauts. The free, spherical, reticulate, hollow cells in the leaves of this plant are curious and beautiful objects.

2. MICROSTYLIS, Nuttal.

1. M Rheedei, Lind. Gen. and Sp. Orch.—Stem leafy; leaves oblong-lanceolate, plaited; flowers in a long, slender spike, purplish; lip truncated, dentate, largely overlapping at the base. Wight Ic. 902. In the Southern Concan; flowers in June. Syn. Malaxis rheedei, Willd.; Epidendrum resupinatum, Forst.

3. DENDROBIUM, Swartz.

1. D Lawanum, Lindl. in Proc. Linn. Soc. iii, p 10.—Young stems fleshy, ascending; leaves membranaceous, lanceolate-acute; flowering-stem leafless, concealed under lax, membranaceous, sheaths; sepals and petals ovate, rather obtuse; lip a little larger, of the same shape, concave; flowers in pairs, of a beautiful shining rose-colour. On trees on the Ghauts to the south. Syn. Dendrochilum roseum, Dalz. in Hook. Jour. Bot. iv, p 291; flowers in the cold season.

2. D Macræi, Lind. Gen. and Sp. Orch., No. 3.—A large, much-branched plant; stems many, long and pendulous, knotty, and with many oblong pseudo-bulbs; leaf 1, terminal, short-oblong, on the terminating pseudo-bulb; flowers solitary at the base of the leaf, one in front and one behind, small, white; middle lobe of the lip much dilated, and the disk with 2 longitudinal fleshy crests.

On Jambool trees at the Ram Ghaut; flowers in August. Lindley's specimens were from Ceylon.

3. D RAMOSISSIMUM, Wight Ic. 1648.—Much-branched; lower part of the stem naked, smooth, dark, shining, brownish-coloured; branchlets leafy; leaves narrow-linear, lanceolate-acute; racemes terminal, short, few-flowered; flowers small; sepals ovate-lanceolate acute, broader than the lanceolate-acute, entire petals; lip oblong obtuse, contracted near the apex, forming a suborbicular, terminal lobe; flowers whitish-yellow. Mahableshwur and other Ghauts.

4. D MICROBOLBON, A. Richard, Ann. Soc. Nat. xv, *t.* 8.—Pseudo-bulbs ovate, covered with the sheaths of fallen leaves; leaves often wanting, when present, one or two from the apex of the bulb linear-lanceolate, about the length of the scape; raceme erect, 4 to 8-flowered; bracts small, linear subulate; lateral sepals acute subfalcate, forming, with the process of the column, an acute spur; posterior divaricato-lanceolate; petals lanceolate, narrower than the posterior sepal; lip large, 3-lobed; middle lobe crenulate, suborbicular; lateral ones entire, or slightly crenate; flowers greenish-yellow, tipped with pink, with darker crimson lines. On trees in the Concan; flowers in July and August. D crispum, Dalz. in Hook. Jour. Bot. iv, p 111; D humile, Wight 1643.

5. D CHLOROPS, Lind. in Bot. Reg. 1844, Misc. 54.—Stems terete, aphyllous when bearing flowers; racemes lateral and terminal; sepals and petals ovate-lanceolate; middle lobe of the lip round, fleshy, inciso-crenate, greenish-yellow, streaked with violet. Common in both Concans; flowering in the cold season. Syn. D heymanum, Wight Ic. 909 (?).

6. D BARBATULUM, Lind. Gen. and Sp. Orch., No. 44.—Stems when flower-bearing round, leafless, enveloped in the withered sheaths of the leaves; racemes lateral and terminal, many-flowered; sepals ovate-acuminate; petals obovate-acute, larger than the upper sepal; middle lobe of lip flat, obovate, obtuse entire, bearded at the base with yellow hairs; flowers cream or nankin-coloured. Common in the Concans, flowering in the cold weather. Wight Ic. 910. Flowers much larger than in the preceding.

4. CIRRHOPETALUM, Lind.

1. C FIMBRIATUM, Hook. Bot. Mag.; Lind. Bot. Reg. 1839, p 72.—Leafless; pseudo-bulbs cespitose, irregularly angular, depressed; scapes slender, erect, furnished with remote, adpressed scales; umbels many-flowered, orbicular; lateral sepals long, linear, cohering to near the point; posterior ovate-acuminate, and with the conformable but smaller petals fimbriate on the margin; lip ovate, obtuse fleshy, shorter than the petals; lateral sepals often

cohering, cream-coloured with darker lines; petals, lip, and posterior sepal red; flowers in the cold weather. A curious and elegant Orchid. It has been called the Umbrella Orchis, from the likeness of the inflorescence. Parwar Ghaut; on trees.

5. ERIA, Lind.

1. E Braccata, Lind. in Jour. Proc. Linn. Soc. iii, p 46.—Cespitose, stemless; pseudo-bulbs orbicular, enclosed in a net-like sack; leaves about 2, elliptic-spreading; scape filiform, short, 1-flowered, furnished at the apex with a large, somewhat boat-shaped bractea; flowers large, white, resupinate, expanding sepals and petals about equal, exceeding the obscurely 3-lobed lip; lip and column yellowish. On branches of trees in the Southern Concan and Ghauts. Syn. E uniflora, Dalz. in Hook. Jour. Bot. iv, 111; E reticosa, Wight Ic. 1637. Grows also in Ceylon and the Neilgherries, where, however, the flowers are much smaller.

2. E Microchilos, Linn. loc. cit.—Pseudo-bulbs deeply bi-lobed; lobes orbicular, much-depressed, reticulated, with a white skin; leaves 3 to 4 linear, rather obtuse, rather flattened towards the top, narrowed at the base, and there sheathing the flowering scape; flowers spiked alternate, secund, minute, of a straw-colour; capsule sessile ovate, smooth; sepals acuminated from a broad base; petals similar; lip ovate, undivided, half their length. On trees, particularly the Mango, in the Warree Country; flowers in August. Syn. Dendrobium microchilos, Dalz. in Hook. Jour. Bot. iii, 345.

3. E Dalzelli, Lind. loc. cit.—Very like the last, a little more robust, but the sepals are here fringed with marginal glands; the flowers are larger and less fleshy; the lip is membranous, ovate-lanceolate. and distinctly serrulate towards the point. Southern Concan and Ghauts. Often in the hollows of trees. Syn Dendrobium dalzellii, Hook. in Jour. Bot.; D filiforme, Wight Ic. 1642; Dendrobium fimbriatum, Hook. Jour. iv, 292.

6. PHOLIDOTA, Lind.

1. P Imbricata, Lind. Gen. and Sp. Orch. p 36.—Pseudo-bulbs ovate oblong obtuse, somewhat angled; leaves solitary oblong-lanceolate, plicate, acute; spikes the length of the leaves; pendulous, slender; bracts membranaceous, concave imbricated; lateral sepals ovate, carinate; lip subglobose, cucullate; lateral lobes small, erect, middle one 2-lobed, cordate. Near Vingorla, rare. Hook. Exot. Fl. *t.* 138; Bot. Reg. 1213; Wight Ic. 907. Grows also on the Himalayas, at a height of 5,000 feet.

7. COTTONIA, Wight.

1. C Macrostachys, Wight Ic. 1755.—Epiphytal, caulescent; leaves linear distichous, obliquely emarginate; peduncles very long and wiry, bearing a few-flowered short racemes at the apex; flower-buds globose; sepals broad-obovate, obtuse; petals smaller, sub-lanceolate, cuneate at the base; lip fiddle-shaped, purple with yellow borders, velvetty, and furnished with bristly knobs and curious appendages. One of our most singular Orchids, the flower somewhat resembling a Humble-Bee. At Kulna in the Warree Country, and on Chola Ghaut, now established in Dapoorie Garden. Syn. Vanda peduncularis, Lind. Gen. and Sp. Orch, p 216; Paxton's Fl. Gard. iii, *t.* 253. Lindley's specimens were from Ceylon.

8. MICROPERA, Dalzell.

1. M Maculata, Dalz. in Hook. Jour. Bot. iii, 282.—Almost stemless; leaves flat, linear oblong, narrow towards the base, obliquely emarginate at the apex, and furnished with a mucro; racemes basal and axillary, simple, solitary, elongated, erect, many-flowered from the base, twice the length of the leaves; sepals and petals about equal, obovate; lip painted with white and rose-colour, and furnished with two horns on the sides, which lean backwards; spur shorter than the flower, saccate, obtuse, pointing forwards, hairy within, and lying under a 3-lobed laminæ; the lip in the front resembles a shoe, with the front leather turned backwards, white at the base; it is like a side-saddle. Very curious. Tulkut Ghaut; flowers in May; sepals and petals yellow, with a purple spot in the centre.

9. SACCOLABIUM.

1. S Guttatum, Lind. Gen. and Sp. Orch. 220.—Leaves linear-channelled, denticulate-truncate or præmorse at the apex; racemes pendulous, densely many-flowered; posterior sepal ovate, lateral ones unequal-sided, about twice the breadth of the lanceolate-acute petals; spur saccate, compressed, conical, hairy on the throat; laminæ of the lip broad, obcordato-cuneate, spreading; flowers pale-pink, dotted with deeper coloured spots; lip deeper pink. Salsette and the Concans. Syn. S blumei; S rheedei, Wight Ic. 1745-46, exclude the dissections.

2. S Viridiflorum, Lind. in Proc. Linn. Soc. iii, p 36.—Stemless; leaves 2, oblong, flat obtuse, emarginate; peduncle lateral, with two sheaths, few-flowered, much shorter than the leaves; sepals and petals unguiculate, obtuse; lip oval, equal to the incurved infundibular spur. Very like Oeceoclades pusilla, but with much shorter spikes, and fleshy, not membranous, flowers. On

the Ghauts; flowers greenish-white. Syn. Micropera viridiflora, Dalz. in Hook. Jour. Bot. iii, 282; the lip is beautifully painted with white and rose-colour,

3. S PAPILLOSUM, Lind. Bot. Reg. *t.* 1552.—Leaves strap-shaped, unequally 2-lobed at the apex; peduncles much shorter than the leaves; sepals and petals subspathulate; sepals equal, larger than the petals; lip 3-lobed; lateral lobes short-obtuse, middle one suborbicular, saccate at the base; flowers yellow, transversely streaked with purple; lip white, transversely streaked with rose-colour; flowers very stiff and fleshy. Exceedingly common in the Concan. Syn. Aerides undulatum, Smith; Cymbidum præmorsum, Swartz; Epidendrum præmorsum, Roxb. Cor. Pl. *t.* 43; Vanda wightiana, Wight Ic. 1670.

4. S RUBRUM, Lind.—Leaves channelled, bowed, bidentate at the apex; racemes erect, many-flowered; sepals and petals ovate-obtuse; spur cylindrical-obtuse, incurved; laminæ oval-acuminate, fleshy at the apex, bicorniculate at the base; flowers deep rose-coloured; leaves mottled with purple, pale on the under surface; flowers, like most other Orchids, in the rainy season. Salsette, pretty common.

10. SARCANTHUS, Lind.

1. S PENINSULARIS, Dalz. in Hook. Jour. Bot. iii, p 343.—Stem simple, terete, flexuose, leafy, pendulous; leaves linear-acuminate, thick, coriaceous, a little 3-edged; racemes opposite the leaves, and half their length; spur as long as the flower, horn-like, obtuse pendulous, completely bilocular; the throat closed by 2 tubercles; lip short, entire, ovate, obtuse, thick, fleshy, erect, painted with white and violet. On trees near Virdee, in the Warree Country; flowers in July and August. Syn. S pauciflorus, Wight Ic. 1747.

11. EULOPHIA, R. Br.

1. E BICOLOR, Dalz. loc. cit. p 43.—Root like a small potato; leaves 2 to 3, linear-lanceolate acute, with many folds coming after the flowers; scape a foot and a-half high, longer than the leaves, with 9 to 10 rather distant flowers, which are either purple or yellowish-green; sepals linear-oblong, acute, 7-nerved; petals oblong-obtuse, shorter than the sepals, 3-nerved in the middle; lip obtuse saccate, 3-lobed; lateral lobes short, flat, erect; middle one elongated, recurved, with crisp margins, with 10 crested veins on the disk. On the Ghauts; flowers in June. Native name "Amberkund." Wight Ic. 1690 (?).

2. E PRATENSIS, Lindl. in Jour. Proc. Linn. Soc. iii, p 25.—Leafless; stem-sheaths about 5, very acute; raceme lax, many-

flowered; sepals and petals oblong-acute; lip 3-lobed; lateral segments ovate-obtuse, about equal to the ovate-obtuse middle one; crested veins 3; spur short, conic-obtuse. Pasture lands in the Deccan, in the cold season.

3. E OCHREATA, Lind. loc. cit.—Leaves oblong-acute; scape with 3 loose sheaths; bracts linear acuminate, longer than the ovary; raceme cylindric; sepals oval-acute, concave; petals broader and flat; lip oblong, serrated, with all the veins fringed; spur small, hemispherical. A small-flowered species, with a rather dense, cylindrical raceme, 4 to 5 inches long; all the parts of the flower membranous. The Concan.

4. E HERBACEA, Lind. in Wall. Cat.—A species something like Bicolor, but the spike is shorter and thicker; the spur is also shorter, and the flowers double the size; sepals long, green, and narrow; petals broader and shorter; lip with fringed veins. The Concans; grows also on the Himalayas.

12. ÆRIDES, Lour.

1. A CRISPUM, Lind. Gen. and Sp. Orch. p 239.—Leaves strap-shaped, obliquely emarginate at the apex; panicle large, lateral branches few-flowered, terminal one long, drooping, many-flowered; sepals broad, ovate-elliptic, obtuse; petals rhombeo-spathulate; lip 3-lobed; lateral ones small, suborbicular; middle one subtriangular, crenate, truncate at the apex; spur tapering, shorter than the lip, hooked outwards; fruit short, obconical; flowers rose-coloured; lip deeper coloured. Southern Concan and Warree Country. Syn. A brookei, Bot. Reg. 1841; A crispum, Bot. Reg. 1842, *t.* 55; Saccolabium speciosum, Wight Ic. 1674-75.

2. A LINDLEYANA, Wight Ic. 1677.—Leaves fleshy, coriaceous, linear-oblong, oblique, deeply emarginate at the apex; racemes erect, few-flowered; sepals and petals obovate, suborbicular; anterior sepals somewhat larger, and, like the lip, thick and coriaceous; lip 3-lobed, attached to the point of the prolonged base of the column; lateral lobes small, ovate, ventricose above, crisp on the margins, with a large, fleshy lobe at the base, closing the spur; spur short, rigid, inflexed under the laminæ; capsules large, obovate, long-pedicelled; flowers pinkish-lilac; lip deeper coloured, sweetly fragrant. Near Vingorla, and in the Warree Country.

3. A WIGHTIANUM, Lind. Gen. and Sp. 238.—Leaves strap-shaped, oblique at the base, 2-lobed at the apex, with a tooth between; racemes straight, simple, many-flowered, longer than the leaves; sepals and petals oval; anterior ones larger; lip funnel-shaped; lateral lobes adnate to the foot of the column; the middle one subcuneate, roundish, 3-lobed at the apex; disk crested with several crisp lines; spur short, conical; middle lobe of the lip deep

lilac; capsules club-shaped, 6-angled; flowers yellow. Southern Concan. Syn. Vanda parviflora, Lind. in Bot. Reg. 1844, Misc. 57.

4. A Maculosum, Lind. Bot. Reg. 1845, *t.* 58.—Leaves coriaceous, plain, oblique at the apex, obtuse; racemes dense, nodding, subpaniculate; sepals round-oblong; petals the same, double the breadth; lip ovate, entire, with a tooth on each side at the base, and a tubercle between; flowers spotted all over with light-purple, on a pale rose-coloured ground. Pretty common in the Concan jungles.

13. CYMBIDIUM, Swartz.

1. C Aloifolium, Swartz.—Leaves long ensiform, coriaceous, oblique obtuse; racemes pendulous, many-flowered; bracts minute; petals and sepals lanceolate, somewhat obtuse; lip revolute; lateral lobes acute, middle one oblong, obtuse; petals and sepals yellowish-red; lip dark-lilac, tending to purple. One of our largest Orchids; it grows in great bunches on the branches of trees, and even on Palms. Alibaug, Chowreekhind, Salsette. Syn. Epidendrum aloifolium, Linn. sp. Pl; Ærides borassi, Smith in Rees Cyclop.; Wight Ic. 1687-88.

14. LUISIA, Gaudichand.

1. L Tenuifolia, Blume Rumph. iv, p 50.—Leaves subcylindric (terete); umbels subsessile; sepals linear-obtuse, spreading, mucronate below the point, shorter than the oblong linear obtuse subfalcate petals and lip; lip oblong convave, with 3 callosities on the disk, auricled at the base, membranaceous, 2-lobed at the apex; sepals yellowish-green; lip purple, streaked with paler lines. Southern Concan. Wight Ic. 911; Syn. Cymbidium tenuifolium, Willd. sp; Epidendrum tenuifolium, Linn.

15. GEODORUM, R. Br.

1. G. Purpureum, Roxb.—Bulbs undivided, roundish, smooth; leaves oval, many-nerved, plaited; scape longer than the leaves; spike oblong, pendulous; flowers rather distant, rose-coloured or purple, with the lip sharp-pointed. In the Warree Country. Syn. Malaxis nutans, Willd. iv, 93; Limodorum nutans, Roxb. Cor. Pl. 1, *t.* 40; Rheed. Mal. xi, *t.* 35.

2. G. Dilatatum, R. Br.—Bulb biennial, nearly round; leaves broad-lanceolate, 5-nerved, plaited, a little waved round the margins, smooth, 6 to 12 inches long, 3 to 4 broad; scape about twice the length of the leaves or shorter, with a few sheathing

bracts; flowering-spike oblong, cernuous, many-flowered; flowers rose-coloured or purple.

16. HABENARIA, Willd.

1. H ROTUNDIFOLIA, Lind. Gen. and Sp. Orch. p 306.—About 8 inches high; leaf solitary, radical, cordate, subrotund; raceme 3 to 5-flowered; petals bifid; anterior segment subulate; lip 3-partite; divisions subequal, middle one broader; flowers white; appear in July and August. Between Ram Ghaut and Belgaum; Sewnere Fort.

2. DIGITATA, Lind. loc. cit. p 307.—Leaves ovate oblong-acute, undulate; raceme long, many-flowered; flowers greenish-white; petals bipartite, divisions linear; lip 3-partite, divisions also linear. Island of Caranjah; flowers in July. Syn. H trinervia, Wight Ic. 1701.

3. FOLIOSA, A. Richard on the authority of Wight (Ic. 1700).—One foot high, leafy; leaves lanceolate-acute, 5 inches long; bracts a little shorter than the ovary; upper sepal ovate-obtuse; lateral oblong; petals bipartite; posterior divisions linear, spirally twisted; anterior setaceous; shorter lip tripartite; divisions filiform, middle one broader and longer; spur slender clavate, shorter than the ovary; flowers greenish-white, appear in August. Salsette. Syn. H laciniata, Dalz. in Hook. Jour. Bot ii, 261. Allied to H lancifolia, Rich.

4. H MODESTA, Dalz. in Hook. Jour. Bot. ii, p 262.—Stem leafy at the base, naked above; leaves (?); bracts half the length of the ovary; lip trifid; lateral divisions linear-lanceolate, free, spreading; middle one ovate-obtuse, shorter, introrse, cohering with the apices of the petals and with the upper sepal, and concealing the column; spur filiform, scarcely clavate, a little longer than the ovary; flowers greenish-white, appear in August, Salsette.

5. H CARANJENSIS, Dalz. loc. cit.—Lower leaves somewhat rounded, upper oblong-lanceolate, 3-nerved; bracts acuminated, shorter than the ovary; upper sepal rounded; petals half-ovate obtuse; lip tripartite; middle division oblong, rather obtuse, lateral ones shorter, cuneate, truncate; spur clavate, shorter than the ovary; flowers small, yellow. Island of Caranjah.

6. H CANDIDA, Dalz. loc. cit.—Stem 1 foot high, leafy; leaves sheathing at the base, linear lanceolate acute-mucronate, 3 to 5-nerved, changing above into floral bracts, which are a little longer than the ovary; upper sepal ovate, obtuse; lateral oblong-obtuse; petals entire oblong, rather acute; lip trifid, middle one broad lanceolate obtuse, lateral linear falcate, all of the same length; spur slender filiform, shorter than the ovary; flowers few, white. Allied to Heyneana. Southern Concan.

7. H Suaveolens, Dalz. loc. cit.—Stem half a foot high, leafy only at the base; leaves lanceolate-acute, erect, folded, half the length of the scape; scape angled, with one bract in the middle, few-flowered; floral bracts foliaceous, ovate-lanceolate acute, sheathing as long as the ovary; upper sepal broad-lanceolate, rather acute; lateral sepals falcate, acute, deflexed in flowering; petals and sepals alike; lip trifid; middle segment linear-acute; lateral broader and shorter, obliquely truncated and denticulate at the apex; spur pendulous filiform, scarcely clavate, as long as the ovary. Between Vingorla and Malwan, rare. Jasmine-scented Habenaria. The colour of the flowers, and the form of the lip, the same as in the following, which is also a sweet-smelling species. Syn. H decipiens, Wight Ic. 927 (?).

8. H Longicalcarata, A. Richard.—2 to 3 feet high; radical leaves numerous, oblong-elliptic, acute, upper leafless; part of the stem clothed with the sheaths of numerous depauperated leaves; flowers 1 to 2, large, long-peduncled; bracts convolute, oval-acuminated, the length of the peduncle; petals erect lanceolate; lip trifid; middle segment lanceolate, narrow; lateral ones broad, truncate, crenate; spur very long, 2 to 3 times longer than the ovary and peduncle. Grassy pastures near Belgaum, abundant. Wight Ic. 925.

9. H Heyneana, Lind.—Leaves narrow-oval acute; raceme lax, secund, few-flowered; bracts foliaceous, cucullate, somewhat ventricose acuminated, longer than the flowers; lip 3-parted; segments about equal; middle one narrow-oval; lateral ones filiform incurved; spur pendulous, filiform, shorter than the ovary; flowers pale yellowish-green. Pastures in the Warree Country, and on the Ghauts. Wight Ic. 923.

10. H Marginata, Colebrooke in Hook. Exot. Pl. *t.* 136.—Radical leaves cordate-oblong, with a white margin; raceme dense, many-flowered; lip tripartite; lateral divisions linear acuminate; middle lanceolate, obtuse, shorter; flowers of a very deep-yellow. In Caranjah; on the Ghauts around Jooneer.

11. H Diphylla, Dalz. in Hook. Jour. Bot. ii, 262.—Six inches high; leaves 2, radical, fleshy orbicular, cordate at the base, obscurely 7-nerved, pressing flat on the ground; flowers few, distant, greenish-white; cauline-bracts subulate; floral ones half the length of the ovary; upper sepal broad-ovate, 3-nerved; lateral ovate-acute, spreading; petals linear falcate acute; lip 3-divided, all the segments filiform; lateral longer than the middle one, ascending, reflexed, spirally twisted at the apex; spur pendulous, filiform, a little shorter than the ovary. Southern Concan. Syn. H jerdoniana, Wight Ic. 1715; H crassifolia, Richard (?).

12. H Rariflora, A. Richard.—Leaves oblong lanceolate-

acute, plicate, occupying the lower part of the stem ; stem slender, 1 to 2-flowered ; flowers long-peduncled, bracteated ; bracts convolute oval, acute, usually shorter than the peduncle ; petals oval, oblong, acuminate, with a longer linear appendage ; lip 3-parted ; lateral segments the longest, linear subulate, somewhat spreading ; spur longer than the ovary ; flowers white. Southern Concan.

13. H Crinifera, Lind.—3 to 5 inches high ; radical leaves oblong-lanceolate ; raceme few-flowered ; bracts acuminate, about one-third the length of the ovary ; lip 4-times longer than the sepals, unginculate at the base ; limb 4-parted ; lobes dentate, with subulate apices ; flowers white. Near Vingorla, and on trees at the Ram Ghaut.

17. CŒLOGLOSSUM.

1. C Luteum, Dalz. in Hook. Jour. Bot. ii, 263.—Leaves few, linear, acuminate, congested near the base ; scape clothed with a few ovate-acuminate scales ; spike very slender, many-flowered ; bracts acuminate, half the length of the ovary ; lip tripartite, callous at the base ; lateral segments filiform, twice the length of the middle, tongue-shaped segment ; spur filiform cylindric, as long as the ovary. Near Malwan ; flowers yellow, small, appear in August. Syn. Habenaria peristyloides, Wight Ic. 1702.

18. PLATANTHERA, Richard.

1. P Susannæ, Lind.—The giant Orchis, 3 to 4 feet high ; stem leafy, about 3-flowered ; leaves ovate oblong-acute, upper ones cucullate, acuminate ; sepals ovate-obtuse ; lateral ones oblique, upper one rhomboid ; petals linear acute ; lip 3-parted ; lateral lobes truncate pectinate ; middle one linear ; spur double its length ; flowers very large, white. Concans and Ghauts in several places, but nowhere abundant. Syn. Flos. susannæ, Rumph ; Habenaria susannæ, R. Br. ; Orchis gigantea, Smith Exot. Bot. *t.* 100 ; Hook. Bot. Mag. 3374 ; Wight Ic. 920.

2. P Brachyphylla, Lind.—Leaves 2, radical, fleshy, reniform-orbicular ; scape clothed with acuminate scales ; bracts ovate-acuminate cuculate, as long as the flowers ; sepals ovate roundish, upper ones obtuse, lateral ones acute ; petals smaller ovate ; lip deeply 3 cleft, shorter than the sepals, 3 times shorter than the clavate spur ; ovary beaked ; flowers white ; spur greenish. On the high hills around Jooneer ; flowers in June and July. Wight Ic. 1694.

19. PERISTYLUS, Blume.

1. P GOODYEROIDES, Lind.—Stem 12 to 18 inches high, erect, round, leafy, the upper ones gradually increasing in size; flowers small, white, in a densely-crowded spike, furnished with lanceolate bracts. South Concan; flowers in the rains. Syn. Habenaria goodyeroides, Spr. *syst.* iii, p 690; Bot. Mag. 3397.

2. P LAWII, R. Wight Ic. 1695.—Stem loosely vaginate at the base, 3 to 4-leaved in the middle, above naked; leaves oblong-lanceolate acute; scape longer than the leaves, slender; sepals linear-lanceolate, obtuse, narrower than the petals; lip equalling the sepals, 3-lobed at the apex; lobes all equal; spur short, bladdery. Belgaum.

3. P ELATUS, Dalz. in Hook. Jour. Bot. iii, p 344.—1½ foot high, as thick as a swan's quill; stem vaginate at the base, leafy in the middle; leaves few, spreading, elliptic, lower ones obtuse, amplexicaul, upper longer acute, with a callous mucro, all shorter than the scape, abruptly going off into acuminate scales; upper sepal rounded; lateral oblong, cucullate at the apex, with a mucro on the back; petals longer, lip almost entire, rounded, like the petals; spur spheroidal, scrotiform; bracts lanceolate-acuminate, longer than the flower; spike cylindric, many-flowered; flowers small, crowded; leaves 5 to 7 inches long, 2½ to 3 broad. Malwan; flowers in July.

20. POGONIA, Juss.

1. P CARINATA, Lind.—Root a subglobular white bulb; leaf appearing after the flowers, radical, solitary, cordate, smooth, 7-nerved; scape with 1 to 2 sheaths, bearing at the apex a raceme of many flowers; flowers large, sepals and petals unilateral, linear-lanceolate, pale-green; lip rhomboid subtrilobate, middle lobe crenate, with purple veins and spots on a pale greenish-yellow ground; capsule oval, 6-winged. Common in the Concan Jungles.

2. P FLABELLIFORMIS, Lind. Gen. and Sp. Orch. 415.—Leaf somewhat like that of the preceding, but with many folds, like that of the Borassus. We have never seen the flowers, which appear in the rains; found in the densest and shadiest thickets of the Concan, also near Dharwar.

21. SPIRANTHES, Lind.

1. S AUSTRALIS, Lind.—Radical and cauline leaves linear or linear-lanceolate, obtuse or acute, sometimes ensiform; flowers spiral, glabrous, or pubescent; bracts ovate, longer than the ovary; lip oblong, dilated at the apex, crisp, pubescent above; flowers white.

Chorla Ghaut. Grows everywhere, from Siberia to New Zealand, and most probably the same as the European species Æstivalis.

22. CHEIROSTYLIS, Blume.

1. C Flabellata, Wight Ic. 1727.—Leaves brownish, ovate, 3-nerved, acute, reticulately veined; scape pilose, few-flowered at the apex; lip orbicular, limb-spreading, deeply 2-cleft; lobes digitately 4 to 5-cleft, claw with 2 callosities at the base; flowers white; the leaves are almost transparent, and most beautifully veined. Chorla Ghaut. Syn. Goodyera flabellata, Richard in Ann. Soc. Nat. xv, *t* 12.

23. MONOCHILUS, Wallich.

1. M Longilabris, Lind. Gen. and Sp. Orch. p 486.—Stem pilose; leaves ovate, petioled, nerved; scape furnished with some sheathing scales; spike secund, few-flowered; bracts roundish, cucullate, acuminate, membranaceous, as long as the pubescent ovary; sepals ovate-acute; petals rounded at the apex, lobes of the lip oblong, coarsely crenate, with 2 involute, subulate callosities; flowers white. On Chorla Ghaut, along with the preceding. Syn. M affinis, Wight Ic. 1728.

CXLII. MARANTACEÆ.

1. PHRYNIUM, Willd.

1. Capitatum, Willd. sp. i, 17.—Root tuberous, stem none; leaves radical, long-petioled, oblong-entire, smooth on both sides, 6 to 18 inches long; petioles longer than the leaves, slender and round, flower-bearing; flowers numerous, collected into a pretty large sessile head bursting from the anterior margin of the jointed petioles, of a pale rose-colour. Common in shady jungles in the Concan.

CXLIII. BURMANNIACEÆ.

1. BURMANNIA.

1. Triflora, Roxb. Fl. Ind. ii, 117.—Flowers 1 to 3, in a terminal head; scape 4 to 6 inches high, filiform quadrangular, with 3 to 4 remote stem-clasping pointed bracts; flowers about three-fourths of an inch in length, of a beautiful purple; wings of the perianth semi-oval. At the hot-springs near Mahar. No leaves were found on this plant.

CXLIV. MUSACEÆ.

1. MUSA, Tournef.

1. Ornata, Roxb. Fl Ind. i, 666.—Root perennial, putting forth a succession of spurious stems, as in the common Plantain; from 3 to 5 feet high; leaves linear-oblong, and of a firmer texture than in the cultivated Plantain; spadix erect; spathes deciduous, 3-flowered, lanceolate; fruit linear-oblong, slightly incurved, obscurely 4 to 5-sided, the size of a man's finger; seeds many, black, tubercled; pulp none. The favourite locality of this and the following is on the sides of precipitous crags, almost inaccessible.

2. Superba, Roxb. loc. cit. p 667.—Root bulbous, with an annual spurious short stem; leaves petioled lanceolate; spadix terminal, simple, drooping; spathes broad-cordate, smooth ferruginous; flowers numerous in each spathe, berry oblong, size of a goose-egg, dry when ripe, and filled with rather large angular black seeds.—Ram Ghaut, &c. Has entirely the habit of a Crinum.

CXLV. ZINZIBERACEÆ.

1. GLOBBA, Linn.

1. Marantina, Linn., Willd. sp. i, 153.—Root tuberous; stems 12 to 18 inches high; leaves bifarious, broad-lanceolate acute, smooth above, villous and whitish underneath, margins waved; spike terminal, solitary, strobiliform, oblong; bracts ovate-cordate, with a small bulb in the axil; flowers slender, bright-yellow, fragrant, tube long and slender. On Wag Donger, in the Warree Country. Syn. G marantinoides, Wight Ic.

2. ZINZIBER, Gaert.

1. Zerumbet, Roscoe in Trans. Linn. Soc. viii, 348.—Root tuberous; stems annual, oblique, 3 to 4 feet high; leaves bifarious; broad-lanceolate, entire, smooth-waved; peduncle solitary, 1 to 2 feet high; spikes oval, compact, obtuse; bracts broad obovate; flowers large, of a pale sulphur-colour. Common about old wells, &c. in the South Concan.

2. Cassumunar, Roxb. Fl. Ind. i, 49.—Root tuberous; stems erect, round, 3 to 5 feet high; leaves bifarious, linear-lanceolate, 1 to 2 feet long, 3 inches broad; scapes radical, 6 to 12 inches long; spikes oblong strobiliform, closely imbricated with numerous, obovate acuminate villous bracts; flowers large, of a pale sulphur-colour. The Concans.

3. NIMMONII, Dalz. in Hook. Jour. Bot. iv, p 341.—Stem glabrous; leaves lanceolate-acuminated, with a very short petiole; green above, pale and covered with fine web below; spike ascending, short-peduncled, ovate, scarcely rising above the ground; bracts linear-oblong or lanceolate, inner ones bifid; outer divisions of the corolla yellowish red; lip 3-lobed, yellow; middle one ovate, rounded, capsule size of a pigeon's egg. The Concans, common; flowers in the rains. Syn. Alpinia nimmonii; Grah. Cat. Bomb. Pl. p 206; Z panduratum, Roxb. Fl. Ind. i, p 55 (?).

4. CERNUUM, Dalz. loc. cit. p 342.—Stem glabrous, somewhat curved; leaves narrow-elliptic acuminate, glabrous on both sides; spikes ovate-obtuse, very shortly peduncled, scarcely rising above the ground; bracts ovate or oblong, inner ones shortly 3-cleft, outer divisions of the corolla —— (?); middle lobe of the lip ovate, deeply bifid, variegated with white and pink; lateral lobes yellow and pink. Ram Ghaut. Flowers in July.

5. MACROSTACHYUM, Dalz. loc. cit.—Stem red, pubescent; leaves lanceolate, acuminate, dark-green above, pale and pubescent beneath; spikes one or two from the root, cylindric-elongated, long-peduncled; bracts obovate acute; flowers white; lip 3-lobed; middle one rounded, emarginate, marked with diverging purple lines; capsule obovate, pubescent, red, size of a sparrow's egg. Ram Ghaut; flowers in July. Syn. Alpinia neesana, Grah. Cat. Bomb. Pl. No. 1455; Kandalla and Mahableshwur, Graham.

3. HEDYCHIUM.

1. SCAPOSUM, Nimmo in Grah. Cat. Bomb. Pl. p 205.—Root with small oblong tubers hanging from the fibres; leaves lanceolate, glabrous, long-acuminated, long-petioled; scape erect, round, 2 feet high, a little leafy; spike terminal compact, imbricated, many-flowered; flowers in pairs, 3 times longer than the subtending lanceolate bract, pure white; outer petals oblong reflexed; inner very large, round cordate; lip bifid at the apex. Banks of rivulets in the South Concan. Syn. Monolophus scaposus, Dalz. in Hook. Jour. Bot. ii, p 143.

4. ALPINIA.

1. ALLUGHAS, Roscoe, in Linn. Trans. viii, 346.—Root tuberous; stem erect, slightly compressed, entirely covered with the sheaths of the leaves; leaves petioled, oblong, glabrous on both sides, paler beneath; panicle terminal, bending to one side; flowers numerous, large, of a beautiful rose-colour; capsule globular, smooth, when ripe black. South Concan, Nimmo. Syn. Hellenia allughas, Linn. sp. Fl. ed. Willd. i, 4.

2. Galanga, Willd. sp. i, 12.—Root tuberous, perennial; stems erect, round, smooth, 6 to 7 feet high, leafy in the upper part; leaves lanceolar, smooth on both sides; margins white and somewhat callous; panicle terminal, erect, oblong, branched; flowers greenish-white; fruit size of a small cherry, obovate, smooth, deep orange-red. The root is the Galanga major of the druggists; truly wild on Wag Donger, in the Warree Country. Syn. Galanga major, Rumph. Amb. v, *t.* 63. Native name "Koolinjun."

3. Calcarata, Roscoe in Linn. Trans. viii, 347.—Root stoloniferous fragrant; stems oblique, smooth, 2 to 4 feet high; leaves short-petioled, narrow lanceolar, fine-pointed, smooth on both sides; racemes terminal solitary erect, compound; flowers numerous, large; the lip ovate oblong, deeply coloured with purple veins on a yellow ground. Southern Concan (Nimmo), but never seen by us.

5. COSTUS, Linn.

1. Speciosus, Smith in Linn. Trans. Soc. i, 240.—Stem somewhat spiral, round, 3 to 4 feet high; leaves subsessile, spirally arranged, oblong, cuspidate, softly villous beneath; bracts obovate, obtuse, scarlet; flowers very large, white. One of the commonest, as well as handsomest, of the order. Syn. Tjana kua, Rheed. Mal. xi, p 15, *f.* 8; Tsana speciosa, Gmelin. ix; Herba spiralis hirsuta, Rumph. Amb. vi, p 143, *t.* 64, *f.* i; Banksia speciosa, Kœnig; Hellenia grandiflora, Retz.

6. CURCUMA, Linn.

1. Angustifolia, Roxb. Fl. Ind. i, p 31.—Root with small, oval tubers hanging to the fibres; leaves petioled, narrow-lanceolar, very acute, smooth on both sides; petioles 6 to 12 inches long; spike radical, crowned with a tuft of oval, purple bracts; flowers large, longer than the bracts, bright-yellow. Ram Ghaut, springing up at the beginning of the rains.

2. Decipiens, Dalz. in Hook Jour. Bot. ii, p 144.—Root with numerous almond-shaped tubers hanging from the fibres; earlier scapes lateral; later, central, 6 to 8 inches long; leaves broadly oval, glabrous, rarely velvetty beneath, long-petioled; floral bracts saccate, purple; flowers twin, purple, the lip bifid with curled margins. Malwan; flowers from June to August.

3. Zedoaria, Roxb. Fl Ind. p 23.—Tubers of the root palmate, yellow within; leaves petioled, broad-lanceolar, entire, softly downy underneath; spike 6 to 12 inches long; coma of a beautiful rose-colour; flowers yellow; lip obovate entire. The Concans; flowers in May, when the leaves begin to appear.

4. AMADA, Roxb. Fl Ind. i, p 33.—Tubers palmate, inwardly pale-yellow; leaves long-petioled; broad, lanceolate, smooth spikes; central about 6 inches high, cylindric, crowned with a tuft of pale rosy abortive bracts; flowers rather small, yellow. The Concans and Gujarat, Nimmo.

5. PSEUDOMONTANA, Grah. in Cat. Bomb. Pl. p 210.—Tubers of the root round, size of small potatoes, white inside; leaves, including the petiole, 2 to 3 feet long, tapering at both ends, 6 to 18 inches broad; scape central; coma of a beautiful dark rose-colour, waved; flowers yellow, of about equal length; flowers in September. The Concans.

6. CAULINA, Graham loc. cit.—Root with large oblong tubers, white inside; radical leaves short-petioled, 12 to 20 inches long; scape central, leafy, 3 feet high; upper leaves on the stem alternate, frequently tinged with a beautiful red; coma white; bracts green, large, loose, oval; flowers yellow, longer than the bracts. Table-land of Mahableshwur.

CXLVI. AMARYLLIDACEÆ.

1. CRINUM, Linn.

1. C ROXBURGHII, Dalz.—Root bulbous, with a fusiform crown; stem none; leaves radical, linear concave, without a keel; margins smooth, 1 to 3 feet long, three-quarters of an inch broad; scapes about the length of the leaves, a little compressed, smooth; spathe 2-leaved, with filiform bracts among the flowers; flowers large, white, subsessile; corol-tube 4 to 6 inches long; berry sub-globose. Common on the banks of the Deccan rivers; flowering in October. Syn. C asiaticum, Roxb. Fl. Ind. ii, p 127; non Willd.

2. C ASIATICUM, Linn. sp. 419.—Caulescent or stemless; leaves linear-lanceolate, very smooth; margins entire, striated beneath, 3 to 4 feet long and 5 to 7 inches broad; scapes axillary, shorter than the leaves, a little compressed; flowers numerous, 12 to 50 in an umbel, white, almost inodorous; berries roundish, the size of a pigeon's egg. The Concans. The leaves are said to be equal as an emetic to the best Ipecacuanha. Syn. C toxicarium, Roxb. Fl. Ind. ii, 134; C brevifolium, Roxb. loc. cit; Bot. Mag. *t.* 1073, 2121, 2231, 2908; Bot. Reg. *t.* 179. Native name "Nagdaun."

3. C AUGUSTUM, Roxb. Fl. Ind. ii, 136.—Bulb columnar, mostly above ground; leaves lanceolate, channelled, linearly tapering, 3 to 5 feet long, and 3 to 4 inches broad; scapes lateral, from the axils of the outermost leaves, and nearly as long; umbels composed of 30 to 40 pedicelled flowers, white or rosy, and fragrant;

tube of corol 2½ to 5 inches long. On the banks of the Gutpurba and Mulpurba rivers. Syn. C canaliculatum, Roxb. loc. cit.

2. PANCRATIUM, Linn.

1. P Parvum, Dalz. in Hook. Jour. Bot. ii, p 144.—Leaves linear-striated, rather flat, attenuated towards the base; scape compressed, striated, 3 to 4-flowered; corol-tube very long and slender; corona half the length of the limb, 12-toothed; flowers white, six inches long; capsule ovate, 3-lobed; seeds few in each cell. Concan and Ghaut hills; flowers in June. Syn. P malabathricum, Herbert Amar. 292 (?).

CXLVII. HYPOXIDACEÆ.

1. CURCULIGO, Gaert.

1. C Brevifolia, Ait. Hort. Kew.—Root perennial, somewhat fusiform; leaves sessile or short-petioled, narrow linear lanceolate, sprinkled with long, soft hairs; scape short; lower flowers only hermaphrodite; tube long, slender, pubescent; flowers yellow, star-like, just appearing above the ground. Common at the beginning of the rains.

2. C Malabarica, Wight Ic. 2043.—Leaves long-petioled, linear-lanceolate, tapering at both ends, smooth; scape racemose, the lower flowers only bisexual, all clothed with long, soft pubescence; bracts ovate, tapering from the base, subulate-pointed; leaves 2 feet long and upwards. On the Ghauts, pretty common; at Mahableshwur.

3. C Graminifolia, Nimmo in Grah. Cat. p 215.—A small species of a very different habit from the others; leaves very narrow-keeled; flowers solitary, on very long, slender peduncles. Kandalla, Belgaum, Sewnere Fort, and probably all along the Ghauts.

CXLVIII. TACCACEÆ.

1. TACCA, Forst.

1. T Pinnatifida, Forst. Pl. Exs. No. 28; *Prod.* No. 209.—Root tuberous, perennial; radical leaves petioled, 3-parted, the segments 2 to 3-parted, and finally pinnatifid, with waved margins; petioles 1 to 3 feet long; scape radical, round, smooth, naked, twice the length of the petioles; umbel simple, 10-flowered; flowers long-pedicelled, drooping, greenish, mixed with several long threads. In the Concans, common in the rains. The root yields excellent Arrowroot.

CXLIX. ZOSTERACEÆ.

1. ZOSTERA, Linn.

1. Z Marina, Linn. sp. 1374.—A salt-water plant, submersed; stems slender; leaves scattered, narrow-linear acute, 5-nerved; floral leaves shorter, swelled out above the base into a sheathing spathe; stipules united into a sheath, elongated and membranaceous; spadix the length of the spathe; fruit obliquely oblong, acuminated and beaked at the apex; seed cylindric oblong. In the Saltpans near Malwan.

CL. NAIADACEÆ.

1. NAJAS, Willd.

1. N Indica, Chamisso in Linn. iv, 501.—An aquatic, stem round dichotomous; leaves tern or opposite, elongated, very narrow-linear, remotely denticulate; sheath dentate, ciliate; ovaries axillary solitary, sessile; style bifid. Common in tanks. Syn. Caulinia indica, Willd. in Aet. Acad. Berol. 1798, 89, *t.* 1, *f.* 3; Fluvialis indica, Pers. Syn. ii, 530; N dichotoma, Roxb. Fl. Ind. iii, 749 (?).

CLI. HYDROCHARIDACEÆ.

1. HYDRILLA, Richard.

1. H Verticillata.—An aquatic, with long slender stems; leaves small, verticelled, sessile, oblong serrulate; male flowers minute, axillary sessile; calyx spathaceous murexed; perianth 3-leaved; anthers 3; female flowers on a different plant, axillary, solitary; spathe sessile, tubular; tube of the perianth filiform elongated, connate, with the ovary; the limb 6-divided; ovary 1 celled, with 3-parietal placentæ. Common in tanks. Syn. Serpicula verticillata, Roxb. Fl. Ind. iii, 578.

2. NECHAMANDRA, Planch.

1. N Roxburghii, Pl. Ann. Soc. Nat. (ser. iii.) xi, p 79.—Aquatic submersed; leaves alternate, grassy, stem-clasping, acute, many-nerved, minutely serrulated, pellucid; flowers diœcious; male spathe ovate, enclosing many flowers, thickly clustered on a conical spadix, and leaving it at the time of flowering; perianth of 6 divisions; stamens 2; female spathe tubular, bifid at the apex; tube of the perianth attenuated upwards, crowned with the 3-parted limb; stigmas 3; ovary ovate-lanceolate, 1-celled; ovules parietal.

Common in tanks. Syn. Vallisneria alternifolia, Roxb. Cor. i, 165; Wight in Hook. Bot. Misc. ii, 344, *t.* 12.

3. OTTELIA, Pers.

1. Indica, Planch.—An aquatic, with large oblong, cordate-petioled leaves, which generally grow under water; they are many-nerved and membranous; petioles 3-sided; calyx spathaceous, winged; flowers white. Common in tanks. Syn. Damasonium indicum, Willd. sp. ii, 276; Roxb. Cor. ii, *t.* 185; Bot. Mag. *t.* 1201.

CLII. PALMALES.

1. CARYOTA, Linn.

1. Urens, Linn. Zeyl. 369.—A tall, straight palm; the stem often 60 feet high, marked with annular cicatrices; leaves terminal, large, bipinnate; the leaflets cuneate, triangular, obliquely præmorse; the petioles sheathing at the base; spadices from between the leaves, long-branched, pendulous; berry roundish, size of a nutmeg, stinging, 1 to 2-seeded; seeds plano-convex, with horny albumen. Native name "Birly Mhar"; excellent fishery lines are made from the rachis of the long spadices. Sagnaster major, Rumph. Amb. i, *t.* 14; Schunda pana, Rheed. Mal. i, 15, *t.* 11.

2. BORASSUS, Linn.

1. Flabelliformis, Linn. Mus. Oiff. 13; Fl. Zeyl. 395.—The well-known Palmyra tree, one of the tallest of the tribe; leaves very large, fan-shaped; petioles serrated and spinous on the margins; male spadix composed of branched aments, densely scaly; fruit large, spherical. The outer wood of the stem is black, hard, and tough, and used for spear-handles. Syn. Carim pana, Rheed. Mal. i, *t.* 9 (the female); Am pana, Rheed. Mal. i, *t.* 10 (male.)

3. PHŒNIX, Linn.

1. Sylvestris, Roxb. Fl. Ind. iii, 787.—The common wild Date tree; leaves pinnate; leaflets folded, linear-lanceolate, straight, spinous-pointed. Roxburgh says the leaflets are fascicled, this is surely a mistake; fruit yellow when ripe, of which no use is made.

2. Acaulis, Ham. in Roxb. Fl. Ind. iii, 783.—Stemless; leaves radical pinnated; leaflets folded, ensiform, the lower spinous. Common on the Ghauts. A third species has been brought from the Ghaut jungles to Hewra Garden, where the trees are now 6 to 8 feet high. The leaves are much more slender and

delicate than in the two preceding; it does not answer the description of any in Roxburgh's Flora, but comes nearest to P paludosa.

4. COCOS, Linn.

1. C Nucifera, Linn. Fl. Zeyl. 391.—The Cocoanut tree. This invaluable tree is too well known to require description. Tenga, Rheed. Mal. i, *t.* 1 to 4.

5. CALAMUS.

1. C Rotang, Willd. ii, 202.—Stem jointed, climbing to a great extent, enveloped in the thorny sheaths of the leaves; leaves pinnate, 18 to 36 inches long; leaflets opposite or alternate, sessile, linear-lanceolate, the margins armed with minute bristles. Pretty common in the jungles towards the South. Native name "Bet." This is the common Rattan, from which baskets, &c. are made.

CLIII. PANDANACEÆ.

1. PANDANUS, Linn. Fil.

1. P Furcatus, Roxb. Fl. Ind. iii, p 744.—A large spreading bush, pretty much like the following, but with the large compound fruit of an oblong shape; drupes cuneate, crowned with an incurved, polished, sharp-forked spine. Rheed. Mal. ii, *t.* 8. Between Belgaum and the Ram Ghaut.

2. P Odoratissimus, Linn. Suppl.—A large spreading bush, with fusiform roots from the stem and branches; leaves closely imbricated in 3 spiral rows, long linear-subulate, drooping; margins and back armed with very fine sharp spines; male and female inflorescence on separate bushes; fruit almost round, 6 to 8 inches in diameter, something like a Pine-apple, and of a rich orange colour. Roxb. Fl. Ind. iii, 738. Native name "Keura." In sandy places near the sea. The Screw Pine.

CLIV. ERIOCAULACEÆ.

1. ERIOCAULON.

1. Sexangulare, Linn. Zeyl. 49; Willd. sp. 1, 485.—Stemless; leaves narrow-linear, subulate, 3-nerved, pellucid; peduncles and sheaths glabrous, the latter half the length of the leaf; peduncles with 5 furrows (6-angled, Linn.); heads glabrous, bracts (involucre)

oblong obtuse; male flowers hexandrous, female trigynous. Syn. E minimum, Lam. Encycl. iii, 275; Leucocephala spathacea, Roxb. Fl. Ind. iii, 613; leaves 10 to 15 lines long, one-third of a line broad; peduncles 2½ to 3½ inches.

2. Quinquangulare, Linn. Zeyl. 48; Willd. sp. 1, 485.—Stemless; leaves grassy, linear, sharp, 7 to 11-nerved, pellucid, minutely and obscurely strigose; sheaths shorter than the leaf, and the peduncles glabrous, the latter 5-furrowed. Syn. Leucocephala graminifolia, Roxb. Fl. Ind. ii, 612; Sphacrochloa quinquangularis, Beauv. and Desv. in Ann. Des. Scien. Nat. xiii, 47.

3. Wallichianum, Mart. in Wall. Pl. As. rar. iii, 26, *t.* 249.—Stemless; leaves grassy linear, narrow-acute, many-nerved, sub-pellucid; peduncles and sheaths glabrous; peduncles furrowed, 5-angular, twice the length of the leaves; leaves membranous, 8 to 9 inches long, 2 to 3 lines broad (half a foot long, half inch broad, Mart.); sheaths lax, membranaceous, 2½ to 3½ inches long.

4. Odoratum, Dalz. in Hook. Jour. Bot. iii, p 280.—Stemless; leaves subulate recurved, 7-nerved, 1 inch long; sheaths as long as the leaf; peduncles several, 5-angular, 6 inches high, twisted, filiform, glabrous; heads of flowers snow white, 3 lines in diameter; bracts (involucre) very short, obovate cuneate, scarious; floral ones rhomb-cuneate, clothed with opaque white hairs at the apex. In stagnant water at Malwan; flowers in September, smells like Chamomile.

5. Cuspidatum, Dalz. loc. cit.—Stemless, leaves linear ensiform, very obtuse, cuspidate, 7 to 9-nerved, glabrous 1½ inch long, 3 lines broad, one-third the length of the sheath; peduncles 9 to 10 inches long, 7-angular, glabrous; heads of flowers white, villous, bracts (involucre) ovate, shorter than the head; floral bracts obovate-cuneate, incurved and rounded at the apex. Between Vingorla and Malwan.

6. Pygmæum, Dalz. loc. cit.—Stemless; leaves flat linear acuminate, 7-nerved, twice the length of the sheath, and as long as the peduncles; sheaths striated, glabrous, acuminate and split at the apex; peduncles several, 3 to 4-angled, 1 inch high; bracts (involucre) lanceolate-acuminate, minutely striated, 3 to 4 times longer than the head, spreading. Near Malwan.

7. Rivulare, Dalz. loc. cit. p 280.—Stem simple elongated, submersed, densely leafy; leaves linear, flat, attenuated into a bristly-pointed acumen, 7-nerved, twice the length of the sheath; sheaths striated, glabrous, lacerated at the apex; peduncles terete, 10-furrowed, 7 to 18 inches long, twice the length of the leaf; leaves 4 to 9 inches long, 1 line broad. On sunken stones in the rivulets of the South Concan; flowers in the rains.

CLV. PISTIACEÆ.

1. LEMNA, Linn.

1. L Trisulca, Linn. sp. 1376.—Fronds joined crosswise, stipitate, oblong-lanceolate, denticulate near the apex, thin, submersed, flower-bearing, swimming; rootlets solitary. In standing water. Syn. Lenticula trisulca; Scop. Carn. No. 1143; Stamogeton, Reich. Consp. 44; L cruciata, Roxb. Fl. Ind. iii, 566.

2. L Globosa, Roxb. Fl. Ind. iii, 565.—Single, globular, rootless, minute, one or two together, each about the size of a grain of sand. Forms a green scum on the surface of stagnant water.

2. PISTIA.

1. P Stratiotes, Linn. Zeyl. 322.—An aquatic plant; leaves subrotund, obcordate, rosulate, waved on the margins; the nerves spreading like a fan, uniting into a truncate arc at the base; spadices axillary, solitary, seated on a short scape. Rumph. Amb. vi, *t.* 74, *fig.* 2; Rheed. Mal. xi, *t.* 32; Roxb. Cor. *t.* 268; Jacq. Amer. Stirp. *t.* 148. Common in tanks.

CLVI. CYPERACEÆ.

1. CYPERUS, Linn.

1. Squarrosus, Linn. Am. Acad. iv, 303.—Leaves linear-keeled, glabrous, longer than the culm; umbel with 3 to 5 rays; rays very unequal, with many spikes; spikes clustered, 10 to 11-flowered; involucre very long; scales sharply keeled, 3-nerved, mucronate; flowers monandrous; achenium linear triangular, one-third shorter than the scale. Syn. C madraspatanus, Willd. sp. i, 278; Pycreus squarrosus, N. ab E. in Linn. ix, 283 (?); C squarrosus, Roxb. Fl. Ind. i, 194. Cum pygmaeo conjungit, a pigmy plant, in the bottoms of dried water-holes, half an inch high.

2. Polystachyus, Rottb. Gram. 39, *t.* 11, *f.* 1.—Culm triangular, glabrous, leafy at the base; leaves shorter than the culm, flat and keeled, generally rough on the margins; umbel, with several rays, for the most part contracted; rays branched, corymbiform at the apex, many-spiked, most frequently abbreviated; involucre 3 to 6-leaved; spikes fascicled corymbiform, linear-lanceolate compressed, 20 to 22-flowered; scales ovate-elliptic, keeled, shortly mucronated; keel 3-nerved and green; stamens 2. Syn. C. fascicularis, Lam. Illustr. i, 144, *t.* 38, *f.* 2; Pycreus polystachyus and Tetraphyllus, Beauv.; C paniculatus, Rottb. Gram. 40. Grows all over the world. Roxb. Fl. Ind. i, 193.

3. Alopecuroides, Rottb. Gram. 38, *t.* 8, *f.* 2.—Culm triangular, glabrous; leaves flat, scabrous on the margins; umbel decompound, with about 9 rays; rays very unequal; umbellets 3 to 7-rayed; partial rays densely covered with spikes on every side, forming elongated cylindrical compound spikes; involucre 3 to 5-leaved (6 to 7, ex Nees) longer than the umbel; partial involucres 3 to 4-leaved, short; spikes oblong acute compressed, about 18-flowered; scales broad elliptic, mucronate, obsoletely 7-nerved. Nees C alopecuroides (?), Roxb. Fl. Ind. i, 211; Cum exaltato, Vahl. Enum. ii, 366; Subnomine alti distinguit.

4. Compressus, Linn. sp. 68.—Roxb. Fl. Ind. i, 194.—Leaves glabrous, flat, longer than the triangular culm, younger ones serrulated on the margin; umbel with 1 to 6 rays; rays 3 to 6-spiked at the top, very unequal, 1 almost undeveloped; involucre 3 to 6-leaved, very long; spikes lanceolate and linear, compressed, 24 to 36-flowered; scales keeled, acute and mucronate, many-nerved, green; achenium obovate, triquetrous, one-third the length of the scale. Syn. C pectinatus, Roxb. Fl. Ind. i, 190; C coromandelianus, Spr. *syst.* i, 217; C pectiniformis, Schult. Mant. ii, 128. The Deccan.

5. Haspan, Linn. sp. 66; Roxb. Fl. Ind. i, 210.—Culm triquetrous at the base, sometimes sheathed and leafless, sometimes leafy; leaves linear, flat, glabrous; umbel decompound, lax; involucre 2-leaved, generally shorter than the umbel; spikes in threes, or fascicled and clustered, linear compressed, 18 to 30-flowered, scales somewhat keeled, navicular, 3-nerved; achenium obovate, rounded-pointed, rough with minute tubercles. Syn. C autumnalis, Vahl. Enum. ii, 318; Scirpus autumnalis, Linn. Mant. 150; C gracilis, Muelenb. Gram. 18; C leptos, Schult. Mant. ii, 105; C camplanatus, Willd. sp. i, 270.

6. Difformis, Linn. sp. 67; Roxb. Fl. Ind. i, 195.—Culm triquetrous; leaves flat, glabrous; umbels simple or compound, with 3 to 11 rays; involucre 2 to 3-leaved, very long; spikes densely clustered into globular heads, linear compressed, 8 to 25-flowered; scales orbicular reniform, retuse, blunt, 3-nerved as the back; achenium obovate elliptic triangular, as long as the scale.

7. Iria, Linn. sp. 67; Roxb. Fl. Ind. i, 201.—Culm triquetrous, glabrous; leaves flat, flaccid, rough on the margins; umbel with 6 to 8 rays; involucre very long, 3 to 4-leaved; rays very unequal, branched and fascicled at the apex; spikes linear compressed, 8 to 20-flowered, flowers distant; scales rounded, obovate emarginate, very shortly mucronate, 5-nerved; achenium elliptic triangular mucronate, as long as the scale. Syn. C santonici, Rottb. Gram. 41, *t.* 9, *f* i; C panicoides, Lam. Illustr. i, 145. This is the only species in our list with rounded obovate distant scales. The Deccan.

8. TUBEROSUS, Rottb. Gram. 28, *t.* 7, *f.* i.—Glaucous, root tuberous, stoloniferous; culm triangular, glabrous, leafy at the base; leaves as long as the culm, rigid, flat, with the keel and margin rough; umbel simple, with about 8 rays; rays with 3 to 9 spikes, involucre 3-leaved, very long; spikes fascicled, linear compressed, 18 to 24-flowered; scales ovate-obtuse, 7-nerved; achenium somewhat rounded and elliptic, obsoletely dotted, half the length of the scale. Syn. C stoloniferous, Retz. Obs. iv, 10; C spadiceus, Lam.

9. ROTUNDUS, Linn. *syst.* Veg. 98; Roxb. Fl. Ind. i.—Root fibrous, emitting a tuber here and there; culm triangular, glabrous, leafy below, with a bulbous thickening at the base; leaves for the most part shorter than the culm, flat, with rough margins; umbel with 3 to 8 rays; rays sometimes simple, 3 to 10-spiked at the apex, sometimes trifid at the apex, with many spikes; involucre 2 to 3-leaved, longer than the umbel; spikes linear-compressed, 10 to 50-flowered; scales ovate, blunt or shortly mucronate, 7-nerved. Syn. C hexastachyos, Rottb. Gram. 28, *t.* 14, *f.* 2; N. ab E in Wight Bot. of Ind. 81 (exclude C tuberoso, Rottb., Willd., and Roxb.); C bulbosus, N. ab E. in Wight Bot. Ind. 80; C jemenicus Roxb. Fl. Ind. i, 191; C procerus, var. Bengalensis, Roxb. Fl. Ind. i, 203. The tubers are the Motha or Moostaka of native druggists, and are fragrant when burned.

10. DISTANS, Linn. Suppl. 103.—Culm triangular, glabrous, leafy at the base; leaves as long as the culm, flat, rough on the margin; umbel decompound; umbellets with many rays; partial rays 2 to 3 leaves; branches with 5 spikes; involucre 5 to 8-leaved, very long; spikes filiform, roundish, 9 to 14-flowered; scales obovate elliptic, rounded at the apex.

11. PUNCTICULATUS, Vahl. Enum. ii, 348.—Culm triangular, glabrous; leaves rigid, flat, and keeled, the margin and keel rather rough; umbel decompound, with about 8 rays, large diffuse; rays 3 to 5-divided; branches with many spikes; spikes broadly linear, 20 to 26-flowered; involucre 3-leaved (4 to 5-leaved, Roxb.), very long; scales rounded-elliptic; stamens 2; style bifid; achenium, obliquely somewhat obcordate, compressed on the sides, half shorter than the scale. C inundatus, Roxb. Fl. Ind. i, 201; C procerus, Roxb. loc. cit. 203.

12. C CAPILLARIS, Kœnig in Roxb. Fl. Ind. i, 198.—Root fibrous; culms trigonal, erect, filiform; leaves filiform, as long as or shorter than the culm; involucre 3-leaved, filiform; umbel small, composed generally of one sessile spikelet, and two pedicelled ones; spikelets linear, many-flowered, diandrous; scales membranaceous; obtuse, seed compressed, dark-coloured. The Deccan.

13. C ATER, Vahl. Enum.—Culm triangular, smooth; leaves linear-lanceolate, smooth on the margin; umbel with about six rays;

rays unequal, with 4 to 15 spikelets at the apex, the longer ones 3-divided; involucre 3 to 4-leaved, longer than the umbel; spikelets spicato-fascicled, oblong-lanceolate acute, compressed, shining and almost black; scales ovate-elliptic, obtuse. Syn. C pumilus, Rottb. Gram. *t.* 9, *f.* 4. The Deccan.

14. C Arenarius, Retz.—Stem long descending (into the sand), covered with the brown fibrous remains of withered sheaths; branches solitary, lateral, their bases covered with many-nerved mucronate sheaths; culms (above) round, short, smooth, with 3 to 4 glaucous, retro-curved, canaliculate mucronate leaves, much longer than the culm; sheaths a delicate white membrane, uniting the margins of the leaf, and truncate at the apex; spiculæ 12 to 15 in a dense head, ovate-obtuse, subtended by bracts, of which the 2 lower are long and leafy; seed obovate, smooth, trigonal. In sand on the sea-shore; scales ovate, mucronate, membrànous, with reddish brown striæ; styles 3, long and pointed.

15. C Bulbosus, Vahl.—Root with a little oval-pointed, brown bulb; culm filiform, obtusely triangular, shorter than the leaves; leaves 3 to 4, with long sheaths, very narrow, coming to a long slender fine point, channeled on the inner surface, convex on the other; spiculæ 2 to 3 lines long, about 6, reddish-brown, alternate, solitary or twin, linear lanceolate, composed of about 7 scales, the 2 lowermost spiculae subtended by leafy bracts, of which the lowermost is very long, 1 to 3 inches, and like the leaves; stamens 3, long linear; scales ovate, with a little mucro. Sandy soil near the sea.

16. C Tenuiflorus, Rottb. Gram. *t.* 14, *fig.* 1.—Root creeping; culms acutely triangular, 2 feet high, smooth, leafy below; leaves flat, nerved, roughish on the margins, shorter than the culm; involucre about 4-leaved, longer than the compound umbel; rays about 7, branched in a brachiate manner above; spikelets 2 to 8 between, spiked and fascicled, narrow-linear compressed, of a rich chesnut colour, 16 to 24-flowered; scales ovate obtuse, 7 to 9-nerved, with the keel green; style very long; seed oval, 3-cornered, smooth. Syn. C incurvatus, Roxb. Fl. Ind. i, 200. The Deccan.

17. C Umbellatus, Roxb. Fl. Ind. i, 208.—Root fibrous; culms erect, 4 to 6 feet high, smooth, bluntly angled, leafy at the base; leaves elongated, one as long as the culm; involucre 3 to 6-leaved; leaflets unequal, the largest 2 to 3 feet long; umbel decompound, with many unequal rays; spikelets numerous spiked, alternate, 3 to 4-flowered; seed elliptic, triangular, smooth. The Deccan.

18. C Flavidus, Retz. Obs. v, 13.—Root fibrous, of a dark-purple colour; culm triangular, erect, 6 to 8 inches high, naked,

smooth; leaves radical for the most part, longer than the culm, very shortly sheathing the base of the culm; involucre 2-leaved, shorter than the umbel, which is compound or decompound; umbels globose, 1 to 2 sessile, 2 to 8 unequally peduncled; peduncle very long; spikelets crowded, lanceolate monandrous, chesnut-coloured; seed obcordate, triangular, roughish, short. The Deccan. Easily recognised by its yellow hue.

2. ELEOCHARIS, Brown.

1. E CAPITATA, Br. *Prod.* 225.—Three inches high, root fibrous; culms cespitose, capillary, sulcate, sheathing at the base, leafless; spike solitary, erect, ovato-subglobose, obtuse, without bracts; scales elliptic rounded at the apex, convex, 1-nerved, of a pale-straw colour, ferruginous above; style deeply bifid; seed obovate, thickly lenticular, smooth, shining, terminated by a small tubercle. Swampy places in the Deccan; a native also of the West Indies, Mexico, Mauritius, and New Holland. Syn. Scirpus capitatus, Willd. Eleogenus capitatus, Nees in Wight Contr. 112.

3. MARISCUS, Vahl.

1. UMBELLATUS, Vahl. Enum. ii, 376.—Culm triangular, glabrous; leaves longer than the culm, membranaceous, margins and keel hispid and rough; spikes compound, 11 to 16, unequally peduncled and sessile, umbelled; involucre many-leaved, very long. Syn. Scirpus cyperoides, Linn. Mant. 181; Kyllingia umbellata, Linn. Suppl. 105.

4. COURTOISIA, N. ab E.

1. CYPEROIDES, N. ab E. in Edin. Phil. Jour. 1834, No. 34.—Culm slender, triangular, striated, glabrous, leafy at the base; leaves elongated, linear, flat, membranaceous, scabrous on the margin; umbel compound, with many rays; heads subglobose, with many spikes; involucre very long, about 4-leaved; scales ferruginous, mucronate. Syn. Kyllingia cyperoides, Roxb. Fl. Ind. i, 187; Mariscus cyperoides, Dictr. sp. ii, 348; Cyperus glomeratus, Klein.

5. KYLLINGIA, Rottl.

1. MONOCEPHALA, Linn. Suppl. 104.—Creeping; culm erect triangular, leafy at the base; leaves membranaceous, flat towards the apex, ciliated with minute bristles on the margin and keel; head solitary, globose, dense; involucre 3 to 4-leaved, very long;

spikes 1-flowered. Syn. Schœnus coloratus, Linn. sp. i, 64; Theyocephalon nemorale, Forst. Gen. 65; Scirpus cephalotes, Jacq. Vind. i, 42, *t.* 97; K triceps, Hort. Upsal. in Herb.

6. ABILDGAARDIA, Vahl.

1. MONOSTACHYA, Vahl. Enum. ii, 296.—Cespitose; culms filiform, glabrous, leafy at the base; leaves shorter than the culm, linear filiform, acute, convex on the outside; spike suberect, solitary, ovate-acute, compressed; scales keeled, mucronate. Syn. Cyperus monostachyus, Linn. Mant. 180; A rottboelliana, N. ab E. in Wight. Bot. 95; Scirpus schœnoides, Kœnig in Roxb. Fl. Ind. i, 223.

7. LIPOCARPHA, Brown.

1. ARGENTEA, Brum. Congo. 40.—Culms trigonal, leafy at the base; leaves shorter than the culm, rigid, keeled, glabrous; spikes 3 to 7, capitate, aggregate, ovate-obtuse; involucre 2 to 4-leaved, very long; scales spathulate, 5-nerved, whitish; stamen 1. Syn. Hypælyptum argenteum, Vahl. Enum. ii, 283; Scirpus senegalensis, Lam. Illust. i, 140; Hypolytrum senegalense, Rich. in Pers. Syn. i, 70; Tunga lævigata, Roxb. Fl. Ind. i, 188; Lipocarpha lævigata, N. ab E. in Wight Bot. 92.

8. ISOLEPIS.

1. SQUARROSA, Roem. and Schult. *syst.* ii, 111.—Culms filiform, 3-cornered, glabrous; leaves shorter than the culm, thin like hair, glabrous; spikes in threes, sessile, oblong-obtuse; involucre 2-leaved, very long; scales convex, obovate cuneate, about 5-nerved, Scirpus squarrosus, Linn. Mant. 181; Roxb. Fl. Ind. i, 224.

2. ARTICULATA, N. ab E. in Wight Bot. Ind. 108.—Culms roundish, sheathed, leafless; spikes many, capitate, clustered, ovate-oblong; involucre 1-leaved, continuing the culm and much longer, round, fistulous, articulated with transverse partitions; scales ovate acute. Scirpus articulatus, Linn. sp. i, 70; Roxb. Fl. Ind. i, 217; S fistulosus, Forsk. Descr. 14; Rheed. Mal. xii, 71.

9. FUIRENA, Rottl.

1. F CUSPIDATA.—Root perennial, stoloniferous; culms leafy, with the sheaths sharply triangular; mouths of the sheaths membranous; leaves about twice the length of the sheaths, spreading, rigid, linear-subulate, keeled; spikelets about 8, solitary or in twos or threes, ovoid, oblong, on pedicels of different lengths; general involucre of one rigid ciliated leaf, 1 to 1½ inch long; partial invo-

lucres shorter than the umbel; spikelets of a greenish-colour, all puberulous; glumes with blood-red streaks with transmitted light. Watery places in the Deccan. Syn. Scirpus cuspidatus, Roth. nov. sp. p 31, who has described it well, though he did not see the minute setulæ between the filaments.

10. FIMBRISTYLIS, Vahl.

1. Miliacea, Vahl. Enum. ii, 287.—Culms cespitose, compressed, quadragonal, leafy at the base, glabrous; leaves distichous, narrow-linear ensiform; sheaths compressed; umbel irregularly supra-decompound, with 3 to 4 rays; involucre and involucels 2-leaved, short, subulate; spikes subglobose, central ones sessile; scales broadly ovate, rounded and blunt at the apex. Syn. Scirpus miliaceus, Linn. sp. i, 75; Isolepis miliacea, Presl.; Trichelostylis miliacea, Nees in Wight. Bot. 103; Scirpus tetragonus, Poir.; Roxb. Fl. Ind. i, 232, with many others.

2. Quinquangularis, Kunth.—Culms cespitose, 5-angled, glabrous, leafy at the base, sometimes leafless; leaves linear, flat, acute above, scabrous on the margin; sheaths compressed, distichous; umbel irregularly supra-decompound; involucre about 5-leaved, setaceous, short; spikes ovate-acute, central ones sessile; scales keeled, broadly ovate mucronulate. Syn. Scirpus quinquangularis, Vahl. Enum. ii, 279; Roxb. Fl. Ind. i, 233; Trichelostylis quinquangularis, N. ab E. in Wight Bot. 104; Scirpus pentagonus, Roxb. Fl. Ind. i, 221; Scirpus plantagineus, Roxb. Herb.

3. F Argentea, Vahl. Enum. ii, 294.—Glaucous; culms cespitose, filiform, triangular, glabrous, leafy at the base; leaves linear filiform, canaliculate, rough on the margin; spikes several, capitate, clustered, sessile, cylindric, oblong, acute; involucre 3-leaved, very long; scales ovate acute, 3-nerved on the back. Syn. Scirpus argenteus, Rottb. Gram. 51, *t.* 17, *fig.* 6; S monander, Rottb. Gram. 50, *t.* 14, *fig.* 3; S nanus, Poir. Encycl. vi, 759.

4. F Ferruginea, Vahl. Enum. ii, 291.—Culm erect, compressed, triangular above, smooth; sheaths pubescent; leaves short, narrow-linear, roughish on the margins; umbel simple or compound; rays very unequal, with 1 to 5 spikelets; involucre 1 to 2-leaved, shorter than the umbel; spikelets ovate oblong, acute, the central ones sessile; scales ovate-elliptic, mucronate under the apex, ferruginous, a little hoary and puberulous above; stamens 3; style bifid; seed obovate, umbonate, dark-coloured, shining. Generally about 1 foot high. Banks of the Deccan streams. This is supposed with good reason to be the Indian form of the Mexican and Bourbon plant, and is synonymous with F arvensis of Vahl.

11. SCIRPUS, Linn.

1. Subulatus, Vahl. Enum. ii, 268.—Culm round, 3-cornered at the apex, sheathed; leafless, glabrous; umbel irregularly compound; involucre one-leaved, 3-cornered, subulate, as long as the umbel; spikes solitary, ovate-oblong, obtuse. Syn. S pectinatus, Roxb. Fl Ind. i, 220; Malacochæte pectinata, N. ab E. in Wight Bot. 110.

2. Grossus, Linn. Suppl. 104.—Roxb. Fl. Ind. i, 230.—Culm triquetrous, leafy at the base, glabrous; umbel supra-decompound cymiformed; involucre about 3-leaved, very long; spikes solitary, ovate-elliptic obtuse; scales convex, slightly mucronate. Syn. Hymenochæte grassa, N. ab E. in Wight Bot. Ind. 110. Common on the margins of water-holes; 2 to 3 feet high.

3. Maritimus, Linn. Fl. Lucc. 39.—Creeping; culms triquetrous; leaves flat, rough on the margin, longer than the culm; umbel simple, with few rays; rays very unequal, 1 to many-spiked, sometimes capitate contracted; involucre 3 to 4-leaved, very long; spikes ovate-oblong or cylindric; scales 2-lobed at the apex, mucronate. Scirpus corymbosus, Forsk. Descr. 14; S tridentatus, Roxb. Fl. Ind. i, 229; S affinis, Roth. nov. sp. 31.

4. Kysoor, Roxb. Fl. Ind. i, 235.—Culms 5 to 6 feet high, triangular, hispid; umbel supra-decompound; spikes ovate; seed oblong, triangular; bristles 5, villous. Allied to S grossus, Roxb.

12. RHYNCOSPORA, Vahl.

1. Articulata, Schult. Mant. ii, 49.—Spikelets subcapitate; heads fascicled corymbose; corymbs axillary, decompound, terminal, supra-decompound, many-flowered, erect; bracts setaceous; leaves broad-linear. Schœnus articulatus, Roxb. Fl. Ind. i, 189; Cephaloschœnus articulatus, N. ab E. in Edin. Phil. Jour. 1834.

13. SCLERIA, Linn.

1. Lithospherma, Willd. sp. iv, 316.—Glaucous; culms slender, triquetrous, glabrous; leaves narrow-linear, elongated, scabrous on the margin; sheaths triquetrous; ligula short, rounded; peduncles axillary and terminal, simple or branched, few-spiked; spikes in twos or threes; male and female intermixed; achenium stony, ovate elliptic. Syn. Scirpus lithospermus, Linn. sp. ed. i, 51.

14. CAREX, Linn.

1. Indica, Linn. Mant. 574.—Spikes subdecompound, subpinnated, axillary, lower peduncled; rachis angular, very rough;

spikelets alternate, subdistichous, round, acute, the female at the base; stigmas 3; fruit trigonal ovate, beaked, rough. Mahableshwur.

15. ERIOPHORUM, Linn.

1. E COMOSUM, Wall. Cat. 3446.—Root fibrous; culms cespitose, erect, 6 to 12 inches high, round, trigonal above, smooth; leaves rigid, narrow, keeled, folded, 3-cornered at the apex, rough on the margin, twice as long as the culm; involucre very long, about 5-leaved; corymb supra-decompound, umbellate; scales ovate-oblong, mucronate, one-nerved, somewhat keeled and convex. In ravines in the Western Deccan, near Joonere; a native also of Nepal.

CLVII. GRAMINEÆ.

Section.—PHALARIDEÆ.

1. COIX, Linn.

1. C LACHRYMA, Linn. sp. 1378.—A tall, coarse Grass, growing in watery places; leaves broad, flat, and glabrous; culm full of pith, half round above; spikes fascicled and peduncled at the apex of the branchlets; flowers monœcious, the male loosely spiked, rising out of an ovate, inflated, coriaceous involucre, open at the apex, and which afterwards becomes bony; female flowers enclosed within the involucre, which hardens over the subglobose seed. These hardened involucres are called Job's tears. Syn. C arundinacea, Lam. Encycl. iii, 422; Lithagrostis lachryma, Jobi. Gaert. Fr. i, 7, *t.* 1, *f.* 10.

2. C BARBATA, Roxb.—Roots annual; culms erect, cernuous at the apex, branched, jointed, smooth, sulcated, not piped, 3 to 6 feet high, and as thick as a common quill; leaves sheathing, 2 to 3 feet long, narrow, keeled; margins armed with small prickles, and clothed with numerous stiff, white hairs; mouths of the sheaths slightly bearded; spikes numerous, pedicelled, terminal, and from the exterior axils forming a large linear panicle, collected in fascicles of from 2 to 6 on a common peduncle; involucre of one hard, glossy valve, allowing free egress to the male spike, and enclosing the female flower. On the high hills around Jooneer.

Section.—PANICEÆ.

2. UROCHLOA, Beauv.

1. U CIMICINA, Kunth. Gram. i, 31; and ii, *t.* 103.—Culms erect or ascending; sheaths with scattered hairs; leaves lanceolate, from

an ovate base, smooth, ciliated; spikes in fives, digitate; spikelets solitary, or in twos or threes; glumes 3-nerved, the upper one densely ciliated on the margin; outer palea terminated by an awn. Syn. Panicum cimicinum, Retz. Obs. iii, 9; Milium cimicinum, Linn. Mant. 184.

2. U PANICOIDES, Beauv. Agrost. 52, *t.* 11, *fig.* 1.—Culms creeping near the base, the rest erect, smooth, 1½ foot high; leaves long, narrow, smooth; racemes subdigitate, 3 to 8; spikelets alternate, in 2 series, unqually pedicelled; glumes glabrous; sheaths hairy. Syn. Milium sanguinale, Roxb. Fl. Ind. i, 315; Panicum javanicum, Poir. Encycl. Suppl. iv, 274.

3. PANICUM, Linn.

(Spikes several, racemed.)

1. P FLUITANS, Retz. Obs. iii, 8; and v, 13.—Culms 2 to 3 feet high, creeping at the base; leaves long and smooth; mouths of the sheaths bearded and subciliate; spike compound; partial ones alternate, adpressed; spikelets bifarious, elliptic; lower glume very short and truncate, upper obovate, rounded, a little shorter than the paleæ; lower flower neuter, with 1 valve; seed elliptic acute, minutely wrinkled.

2. P PROSTRATUM, Lam. Encycl. iv, 745.—Culm creeping, branched, 1 to 2 feet long; nodes pubescent; sheaths either glabrous or ciliated; leaves lanceolate, from a cordate base, 1 to 2 inches long, ciliated at the base; racemes 4 to 15, crowded, alternate, much longer than the intervals; spikelets twin and solitary, oval, acute, smooth; lower glume quarter the length of the flowers; hermaphrodite floret cuspidate-mucronate, slightly wrinkled. About Surat. Syn. P procumbens, Nees. Agr. Bras. 109; Panicum setigerum, Retz. Obs. iv, 15.

3. P BRIZOIDES, Jacq. Eclog. Gram. i, *t.* 2.—Culms near the base, resting on the ground, above ascending, compressed, smooth; leaves bifarious, smooth; mouths of the sheaths bearded; spikes compound; spikelets bifarious, ovate, ventricose; both glumes ovate; lower one-third shorter than the flower; upper a little shorter than the flower; seed ovate, obtuse, smooth. Near Surat.

(Spikes subdigitate, fascicled, or panicled.)

4. P CILIARE, Retz. Obs. iv, 16.—Spikes 4 to 5 digitate undivided; flowers imbricated; outer valve of the glume very minute, without nerves; inner one half the length of the flower; leaves lanceolate, waved, rather hairy; sheaths smooth. Syn. Digitaria ciliaris, Pers; Syn. i, 85.

5. P ÆGYPTIACUM, Retz. Obs. iii, 8.—Creeping at the base; spikes 4 to 8, corymbose, smooth; flowers twin, unequally pedicelled; accessory value of the calyx minute or wanting, the others unequal, nerved, and ciliated on the margin. Syn. Digitaria ægyptiaca, Willd. Enum. 93.

6. P CONJUGATUM, Roxb. Fl. Ind. i, 288.—Culms branched, creeping, their extremities suberect; leaves short and rather broad, covered with soft hair; sheaths large, downy; spikes 2, terminal, spreading, horizontal; lower glumes minute, lanceolate; upper tapering to a fine point, 3-nerved; margins fringed.

7. P NEPALENSE, Spr. *syst.* i, 321.—Erect, 4 to 5 feet high; leaves lanceolate plicate, 1 foot long and 2 inches broad; mouths of the sheaths bearded; panicle thin; branches long, simple filiform, remote; flowers solitary, or twin, or in threes, pedicelled, with a long awn often springing from the pedicel; florets smooth. On the western side of the Ghauts. A remarkable Grass. Syn. P nervosum, Roxb. Fl. Ind. i, 311.

4. ISACHNE, Brown.

1. I ELEGANS, Dalz.—A small, elegant Grass, about 8 inches high; culms geniculate below; sheaths ciliate and with the apex bristly; leaves 2 to 3 inches long, 3 to 4 lines broad, deeply striated, and minutely serrulate on the margin; flowers panicled; panicle consisting of slender, alternate, undulating branchlets; florets solitary, pedicelled, globular; glumes green, with red margins, tuberculated and bristly 2-flowered, both flowers perfect, plano-convex. On the margins of rivulets in the Deccan. Native name "Doonda."

5. OPLISMENUS, Beauv.

1. O BURMANNI, Beauv. Agrost. 54.—Culms creeping, branched, with their extremities erect; leaves lanceolate, waved, hairy; sheaths half the length of the joints, very hairy; spikes compound, secund, erect; spikelets 4 to 8, alternate secund, adpressed; flowers generally paired, 1 sessile, the other pedicelled; glumes hairy, with long awns. Generally found under the shade of trees. Syn. Panicum burmanni, Retz. Obs. iii, 10; Orthopogon burmanni, Brown *Prod.* i, 194.

2. O COLONUS, Humb. and Kunth. nov. Gen. i, 109.—Culms below, resting on the ground and rooting, above suberect, branched, a little compressed, smooth; leaves short, smooth, tapering from the base to a sharp point; spikes compound, secund, 7 to 9, alternate, distant spikelets in 4 series; glumes scabrous, mucronate,

unequal, 3-nerved. One of the commonest Grasses about cultivated fields. Syn. Panicum colonum, Linn. sp. 84; P tetrastachyon, Forsk. Descr. 19.

3. O Crusgalli, Kunth. Gram. i, 44.—A delicate, rather rare species; culms filiform, creeping at the base, above nearly erect; leaves soft, downy; spikes compound, alternate, secund; flowers imbricated in 2 rows; glumes and outer palea of the neuter floret hispid, awned, or mucronate. Syn. Panicum crus-corvi, and P crus-galli, Linn. sp. 83, 84. Our specimens were found near Surat.

4. O Stagninus, Kunth. Gram. i, 44.—Culms 1 to 4 feet high, ascending; leaves soft and smooth; mouth only of the sheaths ciliate; spike compound, erect; partial ones alternate; spikelets ovate-oblong, tubercled, bristly and ciliate; lower glume ovate-elliptic, acute; a half shorter than the flower; upper one awned. Syn. Panicum stagninum, Willd. sp. i, 337. Generally found in wet, cultivated ground, and about ditches.

5. O Lanceolatus, Kunth. Gram i, 45.—Culms creeping and branched, with their extremities suberect; leaves lanceolate acuminate, undulated, about 4 inches long and nearly 1 broad, very unequal-sided; mouths of the sheaths bearded; panicle terminal, naked, consisting of distant-spreading spikes; florets sessile, solitary, subtended by a few long hairs; lower glume narrow, ending in a long, purple awn; upper broader, oblong and mucronate. About the foot of the Ghauts, under the shade of trees; Kineshwur. Syn. Panicum lanceolatum, Retz., and P aristatum, Retz. Obs. iv, 17.

6. ARUNDINELLA, Raddi.

1. A Tenella, Nees (?).—Six inches to 1½ foot high; culms several, from the same root; sheaths about 1 inch long, ciliate along the margins; leaves few, 1 to 3 inches long, and 3 to 9 lines broad in the middle, very tender, a little narrowed at the base, and acuminate at the apex, sprinkled on both sides with a few slender, stiff hairs; flowers in a panicle of the most delicate and slender kind; pedicels long, capillary, solitary or more frequently twin on the branches of the panicle; spikelets 2-flowered, lower flower barren, the upper fertile; glumes lanceolate acuminate, unequal, the upper larger, with a long acumen, and minutely bifid at the apex, with 3 to 5 green veins clothed with hairs rising from papilli; paleæ of the lower flower membranous, and, like the glumes of the upper flower, much smaller, of a dark-brown colour, membranous, scabrous at the apex, and with 2 tufts of bristly hairs at the base; the lower paleæ bifid at the apex, and furnished with a long, bent awn. One of the commonest Grasses at Mahableshwur, under the shade of the shrubs and trees.

2. A Stricta, Nees (?).—1 to 3 feet high ; culms rigid, wiry, smooth, round ; nodes elongated ; sheaths smooth, woolly at the apex ; leaves few, 9 to 10 inches long, with a fine point, 2½ lines broad, shortly pubescent on the upper side ; striated margins, serrulate ; flowers panicled ; branchlets subverticelled ; spikelets solitary, racemed ; the pedicels pubescent ; florets pale-purple, smooth ; glumes unequal ; lower smaller, ovate, acuminate, strongly 3-nerved ; upper acuminate, 5-nerved, twice the length ; outer or lower paleæ of upper flower slightly bifid, with a short, twisted awn, which is not longer than itself. Mahableshwur.

3. A Gigantea, Dalz.—Culms erect, round, smooth, 6 feet high, as thick as a goose-quill at the base, branched at all the lower joints ; nodes much swollen, covered by the tomentose base of the sheaths, which are ciliated along the margins, and about half the length of the joints ; leaves 1½ to 2 feet long, attenuated to a fine point, 5 to 6 lines broad in the middle, scabrous and deeply striated above, sparingly pilose ; panicle very delicate and large ; pedicels solitary or in pairs, very slender, scabrous ; flowers similar ; in all respects to the one named species. At the foot of the Ghauts, Kineshwur.

4. A Spicata, Dalz.—Culms erect, simple, 1 foot high ; leaves ensiform, and, with the sheaths, clothed with stiff, spreading hairs, 1 to 1½ inches long, 3 lines broad ; spike terminal, cylindric, 1½ inch long, densely flowered ; lower glume herbaceo-membranous, with 3 green veins, lanceolate, subulate, a little pilose, 1 line long ; upper long-attenuated and folded, 2½ lines long, and concealing within it the awn of the hermaphrodite flower. In this species, the inflorescence is like that of Setaria, and unlike its congeners, but the flowers are exactly similar to all the above species. Mahableshwur Hills, common. To this genus (Arundinella) belong the Holcus nervosus and Ciliatus of Roxb. Fl. Ind. ; also the Acratherum miliaceum of Link., and probably the Loudetia of Hochsteller. We are inclined to place the genus in the Section Andropogoneæ.

7. SETARIA, Beauv.

1. S Glauca, Beauv. Agrost. 51.—Culms erect, ramous, smooth, a little compressed, 1 to 3 feet high ; leaves sheathing, nearly bifarious, smooth ; mouths of the sheaths hairy ; spikes terminal, solitary, cylindric, 2 to 6 inches long ; involucels from below each floret consisting of a bundle of hairy bristles, which is shortly pedicelled ; glumes smooth ; hermaphrodite flower transversely undulated ; male with 2 paleæ. Syn. Panicum glaucum, Linn. sp. 83 ; Pennisetum glaucum, Br. *Prod.* i, 195. A variety

of this, with the involucels of a reddish colour, and the fertile floret transversely and deeply wrinkled and shining, is one of the commonest Grasses on the table-land of Mahableshwur, where it is called "Kolara."

2. S Verticillata, Beauv. Agrost. 51.—Culms below resting on the ground and striking root, above weak, leaning to one side, smooth; leaves sheathing, linear-lanceolate, a little downy, margins hispid; mouths of the sheaths hairy; spikes cylindric, compound subverticelled; bristles of the involucels reversely hispid; hermaphrodite florets rather smooth. Syn. Panicum verticillatum, Linn. sp. 82; Pennisetum verticillatum, Br. *Prod.* i, 195. Generally found about rubbish heaps.

8. PENNISETUM, Beauv.

1. P Aureum, Link. Hort. i, 215.—Culm 2 feet high, and with the basis of the leaves much compressed; leaves much longer than the culm, the margins at the base ciliated; spike 2 to 3 inches long, imbricated on all sides; bristles of the involucre rough, elongated, rigid, of a yellowish colour. This plant, though common all over the Deccan, is almost unknown to botanists. Native name "Mooltom."

9. CENCHRUS, Linn.

1. C Ramosissimus, Poir. Encycl. Suppl. v, 51.—Root fibrous and bulbous; culm branched above, subscandent, smooth, round; leaves flat, narrow, acuminated to a very fine point, rough on the inner surface, a little hairy; spikes terminal, solitary on the subcorymbose branches of the culm, cylindric-oblong, 2 inches in length; spikelets 2 to 4 in each involucre, ovate, acute, sessile, 2-flowered; involucre hard, coriaceous, 10 to 12-divided; divisions rigid, lanceolate-acute, unequal, smooth, but bearded at the base, on the inside as long as the spikelets. A weak Grass, growing in hedges in Gujarat; a native also of Egypt.

2. C Biflorus, Roxb. Fl. Ind. i, 233.—Culms branched from the base, spreading, 1 to 1½ foot long; leaves elongated, slender, roughish; mouths of the sheaths a little hairy; spikes terminal, solitary, cylindric, 3 to 4 inches long, involucres with only 2 spikelets, the segments subulate, hooked, hairy within, barbed and pungent. Sandy sea-shores, Domus, Gogo, &c. One of the most troublesome of Grasses. The hooked and bristly involucres fall off in the autumn at the least touch, stick to ones clothes like burs, and occasion a painful itching.

10. LAPPAGO, Schreber.

1. L Aliena, Spr., N. Ent. ii, 15.—Culms pressing on the earth, and striking roots from the joints, 6 to 12 inches long, branched; leaves short, margins ciliate and waved, glaucous; mouths of the sheaths bearded; racemes terminal, simple, 1 to 2 inches long; pedicels short, diverging, 2-flowered; flowers lanceolate, echinated on the back or outside, diverging on all sides round the rachis, the prickles pointing in 5 different directions. Syn. Lappago biflora, Roxb. Fl. Ind. i, 281. This we have found in Sind, but have looked for it in vain at Domus, the locality indicated in Graham's list.

Section.—Stipaceæ.

11. ARISTIDA, Linn.

1. A Setacea, Retz. Obs. iv, p 22.—Rhizome thick; culms erect, firm, 2 feet high, generally branched, tumid at the nodes; sheaths smooth; leaves filiform convolute, flaccid, 3 to 6 inches long; panicle rather dense, of a straw-colour, linear, contracted; branches of the panicle solitary, or several together; glumes unequal, upper bidentate at the apex, mucronate, longer than the subulate inferior one; awns of the flower 12 to 16 lines long, spreading. On dry hills. Used for making tatties; cattle do not eat it.

2. A Hystrix, Linn. Fil.—Root creeping, stoloniferous, branched; culms diffuse, ascending, 10 to 20 inches long; sheaths smooth, striated, bearded in the mouth; leaves rather glaucous, spreading in 2 ways, 1½ to 4 inches long; convolute, smooth, roughish above; panicle rigid, divisions spreading, angular, bearded at the axils; flowers as in the preceding. Found along with the former.

3. A Depressa, Retz. Obs. iv, p 22.—Culm 9 to 18 inches, ascending or procumbent; leaves rather glaucous; rays of the dense panicle rather contracted and nodding; flowers as in the genus. One of the most troublesome of all the Grasses; the ripe flowers, which fall off easily, are like barbed arrows.

Section.—Agrostideæ.

12. SPOROBOLUS, Brown.

1. S Orientalis, Kunth.—Culms branched, creeping, with 4 to 8 inches of the extremity erect, smooth, filiform, and very firm; leaves very small and smooth; panicle erect, linear; ramifications adpressed, 1 to 2 inches long; outer glume shorter than the paleæ. A small, rigid Grass, growing on stiff pasture-land. Syn. Agrostis

tenacissima, Linn. Suppl. 197; A elongata, Roth. nov. sp. 41; Agrostis orientalis, Nees.

2. S DIANDER, Beauv. Agrost. 26.—Smooth; culms erect, 1 to 3 feet high; panicle linear, its branches short, expanding; flowers twin, diandrous; paleæ nearly double the length of the glumes; seed naked, obovate, wrinkled. Syn. Agrostis diandra, Retz. Obs. v, 19; Vilfa diandra, Trinius. In moist pasture-ground, common.

3. S COROMANDELIANUS, Kunth. Gram. ii, *t.* 126.—Culms 4 to 8 inches high; panicle verticelled; branches simple, secund; inner glume as long as the paleæ, exterior one minute. Syn. Agrostis coromandeliana, Retz. Obs. iv, 19; Vilfa coromandeliana, Beauv. Agrost. 16.

13. PEROTIS, Aiton.

1. P LATIFOLIA, Ait. Kew. i, 85.—Root thin and fibrous; culm ascending, 8 to 10 inches long, branched below, slender, with the nodes and sheaths smooth; leaves acute, linear-oblong, short; margins waved and hispid; racemes terminal, erect, cylindrical, lead-coloured, about 3 inches long; spikelets linear-lanceolate, very shortly pedicelled; glumes hairy, terminating in a scabrous awn. Not very common. Our specimens are from Domus. Syn. Agrostis spicæformis, Linn. Fil.

Section.—CHLORIDEÆ.

14. CHLORIS, Swartz.

1. C BARBATA, Swartz Fl. Ind. Occ. i, 200.—Culm about 1 foot high, compressed, branched; leaves acute, a little hairy above; spikes digitate, 4 to 12; spikelets sessile, imbricated, hermaphrodite; corolla ciliate, awned; neuter of 2 awned valves. One of the commonest Grasses. Syn. Andropogon barbatum, Linn. Mant. 302; C caribæa, Spr. *syst.* i, 295.

2. C TENELLA, Roxb. Fl. Ind. i, 329.—Culms delicate, erect, smooth, about 1 foot high; leaves large in proportion to the plant, smooth and soft; spikes solitary, secund, scarcely 2 inches long; spikelets alternate, and alternately pointing two ways; flowers to each calyx 3 to 5, all perfect; glumes unequal, broad-lanceolate, smooth, acute, permanent. This is a rare Grass, according to Roxburgh, and we have not met with it in more than one place, viz. on the City walls of Surat.

15. LEPTOCHLOA, Beauv.

1. L CALYCINA, Kunth. Gram. i, 91.—Culms about 2 feet high, much covered with leaves; leaves thinly sprinkled with hairs;

panicle linear, erect, 8 to 12 inches long, composed of many sessile, expanding, alternate, secund, short spikes; spikelets occupying the underside of the spike; calyx 3-flowered; glumes equal, twice the length of the flowers, each ending in a long, sharp dagger. On the banks of the Taptee, above Surat. The L arabica is common in Sind, where it is called Drub, and is a favourite food of buffaloes.

16. DACTYLOCTENIUM, Willd.

1. D Ægyptiacum.—Root fibrous and turfy; culms ascending; proliferous, branched, sometimes rooting, 3 to 12 inches long; spikes digitate, short, 2 to 4, scarcely 1 inch long; rachis terminated by a mucro; spikelets unilateral imbricated, 3 to 5-flowered; awns of the glumes longer than the spikelet. Syn. Cynosurus ægyptiacus, Linn. Common about roadsides. D figarei takes the place of this in Sind.

17. CYNODON, Richard.

1. C Dactylon, Pers. Syn. i, 85.—Root turfy or stoloniferous; culms creeping, compressed, rooting, branched, and giving rise to new plants; leaves rather short, rigid, distichous; spikes very slender, digitate, 2 to 4, linear, smooth. Syn. Panicum dactylon, Linn. sp. 85; Digitaria stolonifera, Schrad. The "Doorba" of the Hindoos, sacred to Gunesh. The Huryalee Grass of the Deccan. Found also in all the southern parts of the world.

18. MELANOCENCHRIS, Nees.

1. M Rothiana, Nees. Ann. Nat. Hist. vii, 221.—Culms cespitose, filiform, 4 to 5 inches high, the nodes bearded; leaves short, rigid, folded, convolute at the apex, mucronate; raceme short, erect; spikelets secund, short; awns dark-coloured. A very common Grass in stony and barren places, both in Concan and Deccan. Syn. Pommereullia monoica, Roth. N. Pl. sp. 33.

Section Festucaceæ.

19. ERAGROSTIS, Beauv.

1. E Nutans, Retz. Obs. iv, 19 (Sub. Poa.)—Culm erect, simple, smooth, 3 to 5 feet high; leaves narrow-elongated, rough; panicle linear, contracted, 1 to 2 feet high; rays filiform, solitary, twin or several, approximated, adpressed; spikelets 8 to 14-flowered, pedicelled, smooth; seed oblong. In water-holes in Gujarat. Poa nutans, Roxb. Fl. Ind. i, 335.

2. E Ciliata, Nees.—Culms erect, rigid, smooth, 1 to 2 feet high; leaves pubescent at the mouth of the sheaths; panicle columnar, 2 to 4 inches high, hairy at the insertion of the branches; spikelets 6 to 12-flowered; exterior valve 3-nerved, cuspidate, with ciliated margins; seed obovate-globose, smooth, dark-coloured. Poa ciliata, Roxb. Fl. Ind. i, 336. At Domus. The panicle is much more like a spike, and resembles Dactylis lagopodioides.

3. E Cynosuroides, Retz.—Root creeping; culm stout, reed-like, clothed at the base with withered sheaths; leaves rigid, flat, or the younger root ones convolute elongated, 4 to 8 inches or a foot long; raceme compound, close, elongated, the branches scattered, dense racemose; spikelets sessile, secund, distichous, 9 to 50-flowered; florets lanceolate, ovate, shining. Syn. Poa cynosuroides, Retz. Obs. iv, 20; Briza bipinnata, Linn.

4. E Multiflora, Trinius in Act. Petropol. vi, i, 401.—Culm suberect, round, smooth, 6 to 18 inches long; leaves short; mouths of the sheaths a little hairy; panicle much longer than the rest of the plant, oblong; branches filiform, short, drooping, simple; spikelets pedicelled, very long, linear, crowded, 50 to 70-flowered, smooth; glumes obtuse. Near Gogo, on the Kattywar Coast. Syn. Poa multiflora, Roxb. Fl. Ind. i, 338.

5. E Viscosa, Trin. loc. cit.—Leaves narrow, and with the leaves glabrous; panicle thyrsiform, contracted, elongated, with the branches very short and compound; spikelets oblong, very shortly-pedicelled, 6 to 20-flowered, lower valve most frequently ciliated. Syn. Poa riparia, Willd. Malabar Hill. It is covered with a viscid, resinous substance, having a balsamic odour.

20. UNIOLA, Linn.

1. U Indica, Sprengel.—Culm decumbent at the base, branched, ascending, 1 to 2 feet high, round and smooth; leaves glaucous, rather short; mouth of the sheaths bearded; panicle ovate-oblong, half the length of the plant; branches short, simple horizontal, fascicled below, solitary above; spikelets long-pedicelled, 16 to 20-flowered, with a bluish-purple tinge, ovate. Syn. Poa unioloides, Roxb. Fl. Ind. i, 339.

21. DACTYLIS, Linn.

1. D Lagopodioides, Linn.—Culm ascending; branches simple, short; leaves short, lanceolate, from a broad base, rigid, convolute and pungent at the apex, glaucous; spike terminal, ovoid or subrotund, white, dense; spikelets about 4-flowered. Common

on salt ground, near the sea. Crypsis aculeata takes the place of this Grass in Sind. Syn. D brevifolia, Kœnig; Poa brevifolia, Kunth. Enum.

Section Bambusaceæ.

22. BAMBUSA, Schreber.

1. B Stricta, Roxb. Cor. Pl. i, *t.* 80.—Culms straight, thorny or unarmed; leaves shortly-petioled, lanceolate, rounded at the base; branches of the panicle simple and very long; clusters of spikelets very dense, oval, equidistant, about 1 inch in diameter. This small species grows very straight, and has very little hollow inside, and is the kind used for Boar-spears. Native names "Bas" and "Oodha."

2. B Arundinacea, Willd sp. ii, 245.—Culm thorny; sheaths downy, setigerous in the mouth; leaves lanceolate, rounded at the base, scabrous above and on the margins, 12 to 15 inches long, and three-fourths to 2 inches broad; spikes from all the nodes branched, compound and decompound, regularly clustered; spikelets sessile, oblong-lanceolate. The culms of this species are about 3 inches in diameter, with the nodes rather near each other. The sheaths, which fall off from the young stem, are 1 foot to 15 inches in length, white, shining, and silvery inside, with a free acuminated apex of 3 to 5 inches. Native name "Mandgay."

3. B Vulgaris, Schrad.—Culm unarmed, 20 to 50 feet high; branches green, opaque, striated and sulcated, widely piped; sheaths above hirsute with dark-coloured hairs; leaves linear lanceolate acute, 6 to 10 inches long, and 9 to 18 inches broad; spikelets oblong lanceolate, acuminate, compressed, herbaceous, 6 to 8-flowered. One of the largest species of Bamboo. Native name "Kulluk" or "Bamboo."

4. B Arundo, Klein. Nees. Linn. ix, 471.—Culm thorny; mouths of the sheaths naked; leaves (floral) ovate-lanceolate, 6 to 7 inches long, 4 to 5 lines broad, rounded at the base, shortly-petioled, smooth; spike terminal, ample, leafy, the branches spreading, simple or compound; spikelets an inch long, erect, approximated in threes, upper ones alternate, 6 to 8-flowered; culm 8 to 9 feet high. Native name "Chiwaree." On the Ghauts. Of this walking-sticks are sold at Mahableshwur.

In addition to these, there is one called Mace, found about villages; the natives say it is not to be found wild. Owing to the little attention that has been paid to them in a living state, particularly in the rainy season, when their characteristics are more easily laid hold on, these are among the most difficult of the family. The seeds of one species from the Dang are highly valued, and are made into bread ; while the young, tender shoots are eaten as a vegetable. The curious siliceous mineral called Tabasheer, which becomes transparent when soaked in water, is found in the hollows of the joints of several species.

Section ROTTBŒLLIACEÆ.

23. OROPETIUM, Trin.

1. O THOMÆUM, Trin. Fund. 98.—Culms erect, compressed, 1 inch high ; leaves bifarious, numerous, somewhat setaceous ; spikes terminal, solitary, subulate, distichous, compressed ; flowers in the excavations of the rachis all hermaphrodite. Grows on old walls. Syn. Nardus thomæa, Linn. Suppl. 105 ; Rottbœllia thomæa, Willd. sp. i. 464 ; R pilosa, Willd. loc. cit.

24. OPHIURUS, Gaert.

1. O CORYMBOSUS, Gaert. Carp. iii, 4.—A tall, coarse Grass, 3 to 5 feet high ; culms erect, round, rigid, leafy at the base ; leaves narrow, 8 to 10 inches long, ciliated at the base ; spikes axillary, somewhat fascicled, filiform, the joints alternately flower-bearing ; flowers in the excavations of the rachis ; exterior glume entire, smooth. Syn. Rottbœllia corymbosa, Linn. Suppl. 114; R punctata, Retz. Obs. iii, 12 ; Ægilops exaltata, Linn. Mant. 575. In pastures in Gujarat and the Deccan.

25. MANISURUS, Linn.

1. M GRANULARIS, Swartz Fl. Ind. i, 186.—Root fibrous ; culm branched, erect, 6 inches to one foot high, with the nodes hairy ; sheaths subinflated, papillose and hairy ; leaves lanceolate, subcordate at the base, ciliated on the margin, 1 to 3 inches long, 3 to 5 lines broad ; spikes from the sheaths solitary or several together, unequally peduncled, ½ to 1 inch long ; glume of the fertile flower very hard, rugose and tubercled. Very common on barren land. Grows also in Africa and the West Indies.

Section ANDROPOGONEÆ.

26. ANDROPOGON, Linn.

1. A CONTORTUS, Linn.—Culm erect, branched 1 to 2 feet high, between round and two-edged ; sheaths and nodes smooth ; leaves flat, setaceous, acuminated, rough to the touch ; spike solitary,

terminal, cylindric, a little drooping; rachis smooth below, where it is occupied by male and neuter flowers, above covered with short brown hair; all the awns twisted together like the strands of a rope. A very common Grass, and almost as troublesome as Aristida setacea.

2. A POLYSTACHYUS, Roxb. Fl. Ind. i, 261.—Culms 4 to 5 feet high, straight, branched; leaves ensiform, straight, acute, ciliate at the base; spikes simple, many together from the axils of the leaves, each elevated on a long-jointed sheathed peduncle, 1 to 2 inches long; lower part of the spike perfectly smooth, upper part of the rachis clothed with stiff, dark-brown hair; awns twisted together, as in the preceding. Rather a rare Grass. Our specimens were found on the western side of the Mahableshwur hills.

3. A TENELLUS, Roxb. Fl. Ind. i, 254.—A delicate tall Grass; culm 2 to 3 feet long at the base, resting on the ground, branched, scarcely so thick as a pack thread; nodes villous; leaves slender, with a few hairs near the base; spikes paired, erect, short-pedicelled, outside imbricated with 2 rows of sessile awned, hermaphrodite flowers; inside with rows of pedicelled neuter, awnless ones; rachis jointed and hairy; exterior glume oblong, striated, hairy, 3-toothed. Near Surat.

4. A MOLLICOMUS, Kunth. Gram. i, *t.* 96.—Culm and branches grooved, the apex and upper nodes villous; leaves linear, flat, roughish; sheaths keeled, smooth; spikes terminal, digitate, 2 to 4; spikelets in 4 series, clothed with silky hairs; hermaphrodite florets with long awns; sterile ones pedicelled and mutic; rachis and pedicels hairy on one side, awn rough, spirally twisted. This has hitherto been supposed to be confined to the Mauritius and Timor, but it is common in the black-soil around Surat. It grows to the height of 4 to 5 feet.

5. A SCANDENS, Roxb. Fl. Ind. i, 258.—Culms long, branched, creeping or climbing over bushes, emitting long roots from the joints, smooth and deeply grooved on one side, flower-bearing extremities erect, 1 to 2 feet long; nodes woolly; leaves sometimes a little hairy on the upper side; spikes generally from 3 to 6, terminal, short-pedicelled, subpanicled; flowers in approximate pairs, one hermaphrodite and sessile, the other male and pedicelled; glumes lanceolate, hairy. In the Deccan, common. Native name "Marwail"; sold as fodder.

6. A IWARANCUSA, Roxb.—Root perennial, with the fibres aromatic; culms erect, generally simple, 2 to 6 feet high, smooth; leaves elongated, linear; margins hispid, panicle linear, intercepted, composed of numerous fascicles of slender, pedicelled, thin spikes of 5 joints, each fascicle furnished with its own proper boat-shaped

spathe, and many chaffy bracts. The whole plant is aromatic. It is particularly mentioned by Arrian in his account of Alexander's journey through the Punjaub and Sind, and was gathered by the Phœnician followers of the army in Lus, who called it Spikenard. It is common about Kurrachee, and is used as a scent by the natives. It may be found in the Ahmedabad Zillah, but we think there must be some mistake as to its having been found in the moist Concan, as stated in Graham's Catalogue.

7. A Nardoides, Nees. Fl. Afr. Austr. 116—Culm erect, simple, tall, 6 feet high, very smooth, and like the preceding, filled with pith; ligula large, ovate; leaves from a broad amplexicaul base broadly linear, upwards of a foot in length, and nearly 2 inches broad; margins rough, sheaths smooth; spikes twin, few-flowered, between fasciculate and panicled, reflexed, forming a supra-decompound narrow, elongated panicle; rachis and pedicels silvery, strigose; spikelets smooth. A native of the South of Africa and, strange to say, also of Kandeish, where a valuable aromatic oil, called "Cusha," is manufactured from it. Syn. A calamus aromaticus, Royle; A pachnodes, Trinius.

8. A Pumilus, Roxb. Fl. Ind.—Culms branched, smooth, erect, 12 inches high; leaves rather small, particularly the floral ones, which are almost reduced to sheaths; panicle composed of numerous axillary and terminal conjugate, hirsute, secund spikes, elevated on slender-jointed peduncles, embraced by many delicate chaffy bracts at the base; flowers in pairs on the joints of the hairy rachis, one sessile bisexual, the other peduncled and male; glumes of hermaphrodite flower cuspidate. About Surat.

9. A Glaber, Roxb. Fl. Ind. i, p 267.—Root perennial; culms suberect, much-branched, smooth, 3 to 4 feet high; leaves glossy, smooth; panicle ovate verticelled, ramifications simple or 2 to 3 cleft; flowers paired, hermaphrodite one sessile and awned, male pedicelled, awnless; glumes smooth, purple-coloured; exterior valve pitted on the back. This is one of the common fodder Grasses of the Deccan. Native name "Tambut."

10. A Muricatus, Retz. Obs. iii, 95; and v, 20.—Culm erect, compressed, 5 to 6 feet high; nodes smooth; leaves linear-narrow, sub-bifarious, rigid, elongated; panicle verticelled; branches very many, simple, and spreading; joints of the rachis smooth; glumes minutely prickly on both sides, subequal, muricated. This is the Grass whose roots are aromatic, particularly when moistened with water, and from which the tatties called "Khuskus" are made. Syn. Anatherum muricatum, Beauv. Agr. *t.* 22; Andropogon squarrosus, Linn; Phalaris zizanioides, Linn.; Vetiveria odorata, Virey.

11. A ACICULATUS, Retz. Obs. v, 22.—Culms erect, rooting at the base, simple or branched, 1 to 2 feet high; nodes, sheaths, and leaves smooth, the last subradical and abbreviated, 1 to 3 inches long 2 to 3 lines broad, lanceolate; margins rough and prickly; panicle terminal, linear-oblong, 1 to 3 inches high; branches sub-verticelled, simple, hirsute towards the top with short hairs; glumes of the hermaphrodite floret subequal, the lower acuminated, upper bifid, dentate, with the awn about twice the length of the floret. The seeds of this species are exceedingly troublesome to those who walk where it grows; they stick in the stockings, and produce a disagreeable itching. Syn. Raphis trivialis, Lour. Cochin 676; Centrophorum chinense, Trin. Fund. *t.* 5; Chrysopogon aciculatus, Trin. loc. cit.

12. A VERTICILLATUS, Roxb. Fl. Ind. i, 263.—Root woody, perennial; culms erect, simple, very leafy, round, smooth; leaves 18 inches long and ¾ an inch broad; margins minutely spinous, hairy on the inside near the base; panicles erect, conical, lax, 8 to 10 inches long, composed of many verticelled, simple, filiform, waved, drooping, 3-flowered branches, as in the preceding; spikelets surrounded with much brown hair; inner glume of the hermaphrodite floret awned.

13. A PETIOLATUS, Dalz.—Culms erect, 3 feet high, simple below, dichotomously branched above, semiterete, smooth and shining; sheaths smooth, keeled, ciliated on the margin; leaves petioled, broad-lanceolate, very thin and tender, sparingly pilose on both sides, bristle-pointed, 6 to 8 inches long, 1 to 1½ inch broad; petiole 4 inches long, slender, grooved; inflorescence whitish, panicled; panicle branched below, above composed of simple alternate spikes, 1 inch in length; sessile spikelet with the glumes glabrous, the pedicelled one bearded at the base, and covered with long, white hairs, all 7 to 9-nerved; paleæ of both spikelets furnished with an awn, that of the pedicelled spikelet much larger. A remarkable Grass, the existence of a distinct petiole being extremely unusual in Grasses. There is one something resembling this in Nepal, with a petiole 1½ inch long, but the inflorescence is purple and smooth, and in other respects different. This has been called A petiolaris by Trinius.

27. APLUDA, Linn.

1. A ARISTATA, Linn.—Culm rooting at the base, ascending, branched, 2 feet high; nodes and sheaths smooth; leaves lanceolate-acute at the base, revolute on the margin, and attenuated into a short petiole, 2 to 6 inches long, 1 to 3 lines broad; panicle contracted; involucre of the rays ovate; involucel lanceolate,

bidentate; hermaphrodite flower ciliated on the back and awned. Common in hedges, climbing and supporting itself on other plants. Grows also in the Isle of France and South Africa. Syn. Andropogon glaucus, Retz. Obs. v, 20.

28. SACCHARUM, Linn.

1. S Spontaneum.—Culm, according to soil and situation, 1 foot to 12 feet high, smooth, full of pith; leaves narrow-convolute, much-acuminated to a very fine point, 2 feet long, 2 to 3 lines broad; panicle elongated, close or spreading; branches semiverticellate and spiked, joints and pedicels clothed with long, white, silky hairs; glumes acuminated, half the length of the hairs at the base, the upper one finely fringed; spikelets 1-flowered, twin; one sessile, neuter, the other pedicelled and hermaphrodite; neuter spikelets without paleæ; palea of hermaphrodite flower fringed, mutic. At Domus, scarcely 2 feet high; on the banks of the Deccan rivers 6 feet. In Sind plentiful, where it is called "Kahn." Makes excellent thatch, and the culms are made into native pens. We know of no other native species.

29. ANTHISTIRIA, Linn.

1. A Cymbaria, Roxb. Fl. Ind. p 251.—Cespitose; culms many, erect, 3 to 6 feet high, much-branched, smooth and solid; joints smooth; leaves lanceolate-elongated, smooth, 1 foot long, 3 lines broad; panicle thyrsoid, linear, leafy, erect, composed of innumerable bracted fascicles; bracts boat-shaped, ending in a long subulate point, sometimes coloured, and generally fringed with many long rigid hairs; flowers 7 in each fascicle, 4 male flowers surrounding the base of the common pedicel, sessile. Syn. Andropogon cymbarius, Linn. Mant. 303; Cymbopogon elegans, Spr.

2. A Ciliata, Linn. Diss. nov. Gram. Gen. 35.—Annual; culms erect, about 2 feet high, slender, smooth, and often coloured; leaves few, ensiform, very narrow, broadest at the base, and there more ciliated, particularly the small floral leaves; panicles sometimes drooping, though in general erect and composed of a few rather remote axillary branches; involucres longer than the flowers, smooth cuspidate; hermaphrodite florets bearded at the base; glumes hard, obtuse, a little hairy, changing by age from straw colour to dark-brown; accessory florets 6, all neuter. This and the preceding are generally found together in the same field; they form the greater part of the best specimens of Hay in the country. This latter differs scarcely, if at all, from the famous Kangaroo Grass of New Holland. It grows also in South Africa.

30. PSILOSTACHYS, Steudel.

1. P FILIFORMIS, Dalz.—One span high; culms several from one root, geniculate below; nodes slightly bearded; sheaths smooth, 1 inch long; leaves lanceolate-acuminate, 1½ inch long, 2 lines broad; spikes 2 to 3, terminal, 1 inch long, slender, about 8-flowered, dark-purple; florets sessile, alternate on the rachis, which is clothed with closely adpressed whitish, stiff hairs; glumes muricated above, subequal, acute, hardish in fruit; anthers 2, purple; paleæ much smaller than the glumes, upper one bifid, with a very long awn rising from the base behind, lower mutic, narrow, slender Mahableshwur. Syn. Andropogon filiformis, Roxb.

31. ISCHÆMUM, Linn.

1. I PILOSUM, Wight Madr. Jour. Sc. No. 7.—Culms 4 to 5 feet high, smooth; leaves glaucous, smooth, 8 to 9 inches long, 3 to 4 lines broad; spikes terminal, fascicled, 3 to 4 together, 4 to 5 inches long, white and hairy; sessile spikelet with the lower flower male, and the upper female, pedicelled floret female, all bearded with long, white hairs, upper valve of the female floret awned; glumes all minutely bifid. A regularly diœcious species. One of the greatest pests to agriculturists who love clean fields, from the difficulty of eradicating it. Common in Deccan, where it is called "Koonda"; less common in Gujarat; delights in black soil. We are strongly inclined to believe that this will be found identical with the I latifolium, Kunth, a native of the west Indies and Brazil, and also with the Spodiossogon of Siberia, as hinted by Nees.

2. I RUGOSUM, Willd. sp. iv, 940.—Culm erect, branched; leaves lanceolate, smooth; mouths of the sheaths crowned with a long 2-parted ligula; spikes terminal, and from the exterior axils paired, erect, 2 to 3 inches long; rachis jointed; flowers in pairs, one sessile, the other on a short, thick, angular clubbed pedicel; exterior glumes rugose and very hard; inner palea of hermaphrodite flower with a long-twisted awn, from the middle of its back. Gaert. Fr. iii, *t.* 181. We have a variety of this with the pedicelled spikelet having 1 male and 1 female floret, without awns, whereas this has 2 male florets with 1 awn.

3. I CONJUGATUM, Roxb. Fl. Ind. i.—Culms branched, creeping at the base, filiform, 6 to 18 inches long; sheaths smooth; leaves short, acute, with a cordate base; spikes on a clavate peduncle, conjugately united; rachis hairy and articulated; flowers in pairs, on each spike 4 to 8, one sessile, the other subsessile; glumes of both spikelets woolly, sessile, floret with an awn. Syn. Andropogon cordatifolius, Steudel.

4. I Aristatum, Linn.—Culms at the base resting on the ground and there rooting; nodes smooth; leaves cordate-lanceolate; peduncle long and naked; spikes twin, 1 inch long, joints and pedicels quite smooth, lower spikelet bitorulose on both sides, upper neuter and mutic. Syn. Andropogon imberbis, Retz. Obs. vi, 35; Meoschium aristatum, Beauv. Agr. *t.* 21, *f.* 4.

CLVIII. FILICES.

THE FERN TRIBE, Nat. Syst. 312, Cryptogamia.

ACROSTICHUM, Linn. From *akros,* highest; *stichos,* order; referring to the lines on the back of the fronds resembling the first lines of a poetry.

1. A —— (?) sp.—A small fern 4 or 5 inches high; frond simple. Rheed. *f.* 10, vol. 12, may perhaps be referred to it.

POLYPODIUM, Linn. From *polys,* many; *pous,* a foot; in allusion to the number of roots.

2. P Quercifolium, Spr. *syst.* 4, p 49; P indicum, Rumph. Amb. 6, *t.* 36; Panna Keleago marano, Rheed. Mal. 12, *t.* 11; Moris. Hist. 3, S. 14, *t.* 1, *f.* 15.—Kadic-pan, Oak-leaved Polypodium. Parasitic on the roots of trees. Nagotna, Salsette, both Concans, S. M. Country, Mr. Law. This remarkable fern has a wide range, specimens were brought from Torres' Straits by Lieutenant Kempthorne, I. N.

3. P Taxifolium, Spr. *syst.* 4, p 50; Rheed. Mal. 12, *t.* 12 and 13.—Both Concans.

4. P Adnascens, Willd. sp. 5, p 145; Niphobolus adnascens, Spr. *syst.*; Maletta mala maravara, Rheed. Mal. 12, *t.* 29.—Parasitic. Concans.

LOMARIA, W. From *loma,* an edge; in allusion to the position of the indusia, the membranous coverings.

5. L Scandens, Willd. Spr. 5, p 293; Lonchitis volubilis, Rumph. Amb. 6, *t.* 31; Burm. Zeyl. *t.* 46. Panna valli, Rheed. Mal. 12, *t.* 35.—Scandent, fronds pinnate. The Ghauts and Concans.

ASPLENIUM, Linn. From *a,* privative; *splen,* the spleen; thought to be a remedy for diseases of the spleen.

6. A Falcatum, Willd. Spr. 5, *t.* p 325; Nellapanna maravara, Rheed. Mal. 12, *t.* 18; Burm. Zeyl. *t.* 43.—Concans.

7. A Ambiguum, Willd. Spr. 5, p 343; Parapanna maravara, Rheed. Mal. 12, *t.* 15; Rumph. Amb. 6, *t.* 29; Diplazium malabaricum, Spr.—Mahableshwur.

8. A Radiatum.—A beautiful small Fern, like a miniature Palm; found growing in the chinks of old walls and rocks, Deccan (*vide* Graham, p 254).

PTERIS, Linn. A general Greek name for the *Fern Tribe*.

9. P Aquilina (?), Willd. Spr. 5, p 402; Moris. Hist. 9, S. 14, *t*. 4, *f*. 3; Blackwell *t*. 325.—The common Brake, or Bracken. Grows in great abundance at Mahableshwur.

10. P Farinosa, Willd. Spr. 5, p 397; Vahls. Sym. 3, *t*. 75.—A small fern, fronds white beneath. The banks of the Yeena, Mahableshwur; the ravines at Kandalla.

BLECHNUM, Linn. *Blechnon*, Greek name for a fern.

11. B Orientale, Willd. Spr. 10, p 407.

ASPIDIUM, Swartz. From *aspis*, a little buckler, referring to the form of the indusium.

12. A Splendens, Spr. *syst*. 4, p 100; Polypodium punctulatum, Lam. Encycl. 5, p 553; Arana panna, Rheed. Mal. 12, *t*. 31.—Grows in moist, shady ravines on the Ghauts.

13. A Parasiticum, Willd. Spr. 5, p 246; Kariwelli panna maravara, Rheed. Mal. 12, *t*. 17.—Parasitic; fronds pinnate. The Ghauts.

ADIANTUM, Linn. From *adiantos*, dry, referring to the nature of its stems.

14. A Lunulatum, Spr. *syst*. 4, p 110; Pteris lunalata, Vahl. Rheed. Mal. 12, *t*. 40.—The common Indian Maiden Hair. Appears in the rains on old walls, &c. The natives use a decoction of the plant to allay coughs, &c. This is the genus from which the Sirop-de-Capillaire is manufactured.

CHEILANTHES, Swz. From *cheilos*, lip; *anthos*, flower; alluding to the form of the indusium.

15. C Tenuifolia, Spr. *syst*. 4, p 117; Trichomanes tenuifolia; Burm. Rumph. Amb. 6, *t*. 34, *f*. 2.

ALLANTODEA, R. Br. From *allantos*, a sausage; resemblance in the form of the indusia, or membranaceous involucre.

16. A Brunoniana, Wall. Pl. Asiat. rar. 1, *t*. 52.—Moist places on Mahableshwur.

SPHÆROPTERIS, Wall. From the spherical form of the indusium inclosing the sori.

17. S Barbata, Wall. Pl. Asiat. rar. 1 to 48.—A fern with scales on the stem; jungles at Parr.

OSMUNDA, Linn. From *Osmunder*, a Celtic divinity.

18. O —— (?) sp.—A very beautiful species, growing common in the bed of the Yeena, at Mahableshwur.

LYGODIUM, Swartz. From *lygos*, a band, in allusion to the twining habit of the species.

19. L MICROPHYLLUM, Spr. *syst.* 4, p 28; Hydroglossum scandens, Willd.; Ugena microphylla, Cav. Icon. 6, *t.* 595, *f.* 2; Adiantum minus volubile, Rumph. Amb. 6, *t.* 32, *f.* 2, 3; Tsieru. Valli panna altera, Rheed. Mal. 12, *t.* 34; Bot. Cab. *t.* 742.—Stem flexuous, climbing. Kennery jungles; the Ghauts, &c.

20. L PINNATIFIDUM, Spr. *syst.* 4, p 28; Hydroglossum pinnatifidum, Willd.; Warapoli, Rheed. Mal. 12, *t.* 33.—A very beautiful scandent fern, with pinnate fronds. The Ghauts and Concans, Mahableshwur.

21. L FLEXUOSUM, Spr. *syst.* 4, p 29; Hydroglossum flexuosum, Willd.; Valli panna, Rheed. Mal. 12, *t.* 32.—A scandent fern. Kennery Jungles, Salsette, and both Concans.

GLICHENIA, Sm. In honour of the Baron *Von. Gleichen*, a German Botanist.

22. G HERMANNI, Spr. *syst.* 4, p 26; Mertensia dichotoma, Sw.; Dicranopteris, Bern. Rumph. Amb. 6, *t.* 38.

BOTRYCHIUM, Swz. From *botrys*; a bunch of grapes, alluding to the form of fructification.

23. B ZEYLANICUM, Willd. 10, p 61.—Ceylon Moon-wort, Rumph. Amb. 6, *t.* 68, *f.* 3.

OPHIOGLOSSUM, Linn. From *ophis*, a serpent; *glossa*, a tongue; alluding to the shape of the leaves.

24. O MOLUCCANUM, Willd. Spr. 5, p 58; O simplex, Rumph. Amb. 6, *t.* 68, *f.* 2; Hooker and Grev. p 45.

25. O PENDULUM, Willd. Spr. 5, p 60; Scolopendria, Rumph. Amb. 6, *t.* 37, *f.* 3.—Parasitic.

CLIX. LYCOPODIACEÆ.

THE CLUB-MOSS TRIBE, Lind., Loud. Hort. Brit. p 544.

LYCOPODIUM, Linn. From *lycos*, a wolf; *pous*, a foot; in allusion to the fancied resemblance between the roots and a wolf's foot.

1. L PHLEGMARIA, Willd. Spr. 5, p 10; Tanopavel patsja maravara; Rheed. Mal. 12, *t.* 14; Rumph. Amb. 6, *t.* 41, *f.* 1.—Indian Club-moss. Parasitic; stem dichotomous, pendulous; leaves quatern. On the Ghauts, S. Concan, Nimmo.

2. L CERNUUM, Willd. Spr. 5, p 30; Bellanpotsja, Rheed. Mal. 12, *t.* 39; Pluk. Alm. *t.* 47, *f.* 9; Burm. Zeyl. *t.* 66; Moris. Hist. 3, S. 15, *t.* 5 and 9; Rumph. Amb. 6, *t.* 40, *f.* 1.—Terrestrial. The Concans, Nimmo.

3. L CIRCINALE, Willd. Spr. 5, p 32; Pluk. *t.* 100, *f.* 3; Moris. Hist. 3, *t.* 515, *f.* 11.—The Concans.

4. L Canaliculatum, Willd. Spr. 5, p 43; Pluk. Alm. *t.* 453, *f.* 8; Dill. Musc. *t.* 65, *f.* 6.—The Concans.
5. L Plumosum, Willd. Spr. 5, p 45; Dill. Musc. *t.* 66, *f.* 8.
6. L Durvilleæi, Hooker and Grev. p 26; Rumph. Amb. 6, *t.* 39.

CLX. MARSILEACEÆ.

THE PEPPER-WORT TRIBE, Lind., Loud. Hort. Brit. p 544.

MARSILEA, Linn. Named after *Count Marsigli*, Founder of the Academy of Sciences at Bologna. Lam. Illust *t.* 538; Pluk. Alm. *t.* 401, *f.* 5.

1. M Quadrifolia.—A small annual plant, having the appearance of the Oxalis corniculata. Margins of tanks, &c.
2. ISOETES, Linn. *Isos*, equal; *etos*, the year; the plant continuing unchanged through the year.
3. I Coromandelina, Linn., Spr. *syst.* 4, p 9.—An aquatic plant, see Ainslie Mat. Ind.

SALVINIA, Linn. From *M. Salvini*, a Greek Professor at Florence.

4. S Cucullata, Linn.—An aquatic plant.

CLXI. MUSCI.

THE MOSS TRIBE, Lind., Loud. Hort. Brit. p 544.

DICRANUM, Hedw. *Dikranos*, two-headed or forked, in allusion to the teeth of the capsule.

1. D Bryoides, Sw., Spr. *syst.* 4, p 163; Hypnum bryoides, Linn. On old walls, associated with Bryum and Hypnum.

CLXII. FUNGI.

THE MUSHROOM TRIBE, Lind. Nat. Syst. p 334.

AGARICUS, Linn. From *agaria*, a region of Sarmatia.

1. A Campestris, Linn.—Common Mushroom.
2. A Ostreatus (?).—On the trunks of decayed trees; with several species of leathery Boletus.

LYCOPERDON, Linn. From *lykos*, a wolf; *perdo*, crepito; application not obvious.

3. L Pratense.—Puff-ball.

PEZIZA, Linn. From *Pezicæ*, a tribe of Fungi in Pliny.

4. P Cerina (?).—Small, cup-shaped; on old flower tubs in garden, &c.

ADDENDA ET CORRIGENDA
TO No. I.

MESEMBRYACEÆ.

1. GLINUS, Linn.

1. LOTOIDES, Linn. sp. 663.—A procumbent, diffuse, herbaceous plant, hoary, with short stellate tomentum; leaves obovate, flat, fascicled, unequal; pedicels one-flowered, axillary, twice as long as the petiole; petals 5, deeply cloven. Bombay, common. DC. *Prod.* 3, 455; Spr. *syst.* ii, 467; Syn. G dictamnoides, Lam. Illustr. *t.* 413, *f.* 2; G dictamnoides, Linn. (?).

MORINGACEÆ.

1. MORINGA, Burm.

1. M PTERYGOSPERMA, Gaert., DC. *Prod.* 2, 478.—A small tree; leaves twice and thrice pinnate; leaflets small; flowers white; seed-vessel triquetrous, long-linear, and pendulous. Syn. M zeylanica, Pers. Syn.; Guilandina moringa, Vahl.; Hyperanthera moringa, Roxb. Fl. Ind. ii, p 368. A common tree about villages; yields a large quantity of a bland gum. The seeds of this and other species yield the Ben Oil of watchmakers. The root is the Horse-radish of Anglo-Indians, and the fruit is eaten in curries. Is said to be a good rubefacient.

2. M CONCANENSIS, Nimmo in Grah. Cat. p 43.—A tree something like the last, but distinguished by very much larger and rounder leaflets, and a much more powerful odour of Horse-radish; flowers yellowish, with pink streaks; anthers 5, perfect, but only one-celled, 5-abortive, and much smaller. Flowers in November. In the jungles near Penn. We have found it also on the hills in Lus, and it very probably will be found in Arabia.

DATISCEÆ.

1. TETRAMELES, R. Br.—A large diœcious tree, with naked flexuose branches; leaves coming out after the flowers, rounded-

acute or acuminated, sometimes lobed, coarsely and unequally toothed, smooth above, beneath covered with white tomentum; spikes in the male panicle erect, female elongated, almost simple, pendular fascicled; flowers small, very numerous, yellow; male perianth 4-divided; stamina 4; female perianth 4-toothed; styles 4, opposite the teeth of the calyx, with thick obliquely truncated stigmas; ovary unilocular, with 4 parietal placentæ; ovules very numerous. A native of Java, and also of the Ghauts in this Presidency. Horsf. Pl. Jav. rar. *t.* 17.

SALVADORACEÆ.

1. SALVADORA.

1. S Persica, Linn. Willd. sp. i, 695.—A middle-sized tree, with rough, whitish bark; trunk generally very crooked; branches very numerous, and with the extremities pendulous; leaves oval or ovate, veinless, rather fleshy, smooth; panicles terminal, and from the exterior axils; flowers minute, greenish-yellow; berry very small, smooth, red, juicy, has a strong aromatic smell, and tastes much like garden Cresses; bark of the root remarkably acrid, bruised and applied to the skin it soon raises blisters, and it is used by the natives in this way. This is said to be the Mustard tree of Scripture. Found common near the sea-coast in Gujarat, and in the Hubshee's Country, and is always an indication of a salt soil.

CXV. LAURACEÆ, p 221.

8. ACTINODAPHNE.

1. A Lanceolata.—A small tree; leaves ovate lanceolate or elliptic-lanceolate, long-acuminated, coriaceous, dark-green and shining above, glaucous beneath, with prominent veins; young shoots, before expansion, concealed under a strobilus of bracts, which are larger upwards; young leaves all silky and tomentose, verticellate in 2 series, 3 and 3; flowers from out of a lateral bud, with very short, broad-cordate, fringed scales; raceme abbreviated, all tawny and silky, with reddish brown hairs; bracts to each flower large obovate, concave, sessile, caducous; flowers 8 together; perianth of 6 oval or ovate, tomentose leaflets, spreading or reflexed in flowering; stamens 9, 6 in the circumference without glands, 3 central, each with 2 bilobed, somewhat reniform, glands attached to each side of the base of the filaments. The commonest tree at Mahableshwur, next to the Jambool; most of the trees are only male.

L. TEREBINTHACEÆ, p 51.

8. GARUGA, Roxb.

1. G PINNATA, Roxb. Fl. Ind. ii, p 400.—A rather large tree, with pinnate leaves, which are deciduous in the cold weather; flowers panicled, yellowish-white, often covered with a mealy kind of substance; they appear in the hot weather; fruit size of a gooseberry, eaten by the natives both raw and pickled; it contains from 1 to 5 one-seeded nuts. Native name "Koorak." Found in many parts of the country, but nowhere in great quantity. The timber is very inferior.

LXVIII. CRASSULACEÆ, p 105.

1. KALANCHOE, Adans.

4. K OLIVACEA, Dalz.—Stem 1 foot high, terete, somewhat jointed, herbaceous; leaves ovate or broad-lanceolate, cuneate at the base, unequally crenate-serrate, fleshy, with the nerves immersed, dotted with blood-red spots, 3½ to 5 inches long, 1 to 2 inches broad; upper leaves smaller; flowering branches from above the leaves (supra-axillary) forming a cyme; pedicels, calyx, and flowers clothed with glandular viscid hairs; calyx divided to the base, segments lanceolate acuminate; corol tube swelled at the base, a half longer than the calyx, segments 4, ovate-oblong acute mucronate, of a pale-pink colour, half the length of the tube, twisted in æstivation; stamens 8, in 2 rows; glands situated behind each ovary at the base, linear bidentate; ovaries 4, flask-shaped, attenuated upwards; ovules in four rows on the inner angle. The whole plant is of an olive colour. Found only at Pandooghur, and under the cliff at Paunchgunny.

LXIX. UMBELLIFERÆ, p 108.

The fruit of Heracleum tomentosum having been since discovered, it is found not to belong to that genus.

LXXV. COMPOSITÆ, p 121.

2. VERNONIA, Linn.

3. V ANTHELMINTICA, Willd. iii, 1634.—A large, annual, erect species; stem branched, terete, clouded with elevated purple spots, 2 to 3 feet high; leaves petioled, broad-lanceolate, coarsely serrate, slightly downy, running down to the insertion of the

petioles; heads of flowers terminal, peduncled, purple; seeds cylindric. Common in the black-soil of the Deccan. The seeds are much used in native medicine, and are really effectual in bowel-complaints.

3. DECANEURUM, DC., p 122.

3. D Lilacinum, Dalz.—Stem 4 to 5 feet high, herbaceous, dichotomously branched; leaves large, 6 to 7 inches long, 3 inches broad, lower ones ovate, attenuated at both ends, upper lanceolate, all thinly clothed above with flat-jointed hairs, white and araneose beneath, repand-dentate on the margins, and with the teeth cuspidate; heads of flowers solitary terminal, of a beautiful lilac colour; involucre ovate, subtended by a few lanceolate cuspidate leaflets; outer scales small oval cuspidate, stalked; inner long linear acute, scarious-pointed, all fringed with a little white wool; pappus half the length of the corolla, caducous; achenia smooth, with 10 slight grooves. Mahableshwur Hills, also in the Concan; flowering in November.

11. VICOA CERNUA, p 126.

(Amended description.)

Leaves pendulous, oblong acuminate, narrowed at the base, slightly stem-clasping, serrate, sparingly pilose above, and on the nerves beneath wrinkled, somewhat membranous, 3 to 3½ inches long, 1 broad; uppermost leaves lanceolate-acuminate from a cordate stem-clasping base; heads of flowers solitary from the upper axils, and terminal peduncle or flower-bearing branch long, slender, pilose, with 1 to 3 small leaves, and 1 to 3 subulate bracts under the capitulum; flower-buds spherical; involucre leaves very numerous, squarrose, fine subulate, with extremely fine points; ray-florets numerous, 2 rows, linear; pappus of 4 to 5 slender bristles, almost as long as the flowers; anthers cordate; achenia cylindrical, with close-pressed bristles, which appear above like a false pappus.

26. ARTEMISIA, Linn., p 129.

2. A Parviflora, Buch.—Root perennial; stem ascending obliquely; branches several, spreading or drooping; lower leaves simple, sessile, cuneate, with the apex dentate, and some linear segments at the base, deep-green on both sides, uppermost leaves minute, entire; flowers numerous-pedicelled, very minute, ovate, drooping, green. Very common on the eastern side of the Mahableshwur Hills, and on the road towards Sattara. Dr. Buchanan's

original specimens were from Nepaul, and are described as having the young parts hoary; this is not the case with Bombay specimens; flowers in the cold weather.

33. TRICHOLEPIS GLABERRIMA, p 131.

(Description revised.)

Larger leaves below elliptic oblong, attenuated towards the base, where it forms a kind of winged petiole, acuminated at the apex, rather coarsely and sharply serrated, the serratures cuspidate on their margins, scabrous, 4 to 6 inches long, 2 inches broad, uppermost leaves linear acute, 2 to 3 inches long, 4 lines broad, with a few very distant small teeth; heads of flowers smaller than in T montana, with the scales of the involucre glabrous (not araneose); outer florets spreading; stigmas exserted, erect, and not separating one from the other, surrounded with a brush of hairs at the base; corol 7 lines long.

CXIX. PIPERACEÆ, p 225.

1. PIPER, Linn.

2. P Hookeri, Miquel in Hook. Jour. Bot. iv, 437.—Branchlets, petioles, peduncles, and nerves, on the under side of the leaves hairy; leaves between coriaceous and membranaceous, thickly pellucid dotted, smooth above, broadly ovate and equal-sided, shortly acuminate; the acumen obtuse, 5 to 7-nerved; peduncle longer than the petiole; bracts oblong, decurrent and adnate; ovary ovate; stigmas 4, short, thick, puberulous. Common on the Mahableshwur Hills, and easily distinguished by the rather long petioles being thickly clothed with whitish hairs.

CXXV. MORACEÆ, p 240.

2. UROSTIGMA, Gasparrini.

12. U Ampelos, Koenig.—A large tree; trunk short, thick, often completely concealed by numerous small, very leafy branchlets, top very large, spreading to a great distance; bark smooth, ash-coloured; leaves alternate, spreading, short-petioled, obliquely oval, obtusely pointed, a little scolloped, scabrous, and very firm, 3 to 4 inches long; petioles short-curved, channelled; fruit axillary, paired, peduncled, when ripe size of a pea, and yellow. We have met with this tree in fruit on the western side of the Ghauts, but the specimens did not come up to the above description as to its being either large or spreading. The natives called it "Datir."

If the name be correct, then it is both an erect tree and a climber, and will include our U volubile, p 242.

NOTE.—The Concan name of Ficus cordifolia is "Ashta."

CLIV. ERIOCAULACEÆ, p 279.

1. ERIOCAULON, Linn.

8. E RIVULARE.—This name having been preoccupied by Don, the species here described has been named E dalzellii by Koernicke, in the 26th vol. of the Linnæa.

9. E ROUXIANUM, Steudel, Syn. ii, 270.—Cespitose; root fibrous; stem very short; leaves linear-lanceolate, 9 to 11-nerved, rather obtuse at the apex, subpellucid, 1 to 1½ inch long, twice the length of the tumid sheaths, which are rather membranous and white at the apex; heads about 2 lines in breadth, snow-white, villous, a little shorter than the involucre. The specimens were collected by Polydore Roux, near Bombay.

10. E HETEROLEPIS, Steudel loc. cit. 271.—Cespitose; root fibrous; stem very short; leaves-lanceolate, rather obtuse, 9 to 11-nerved, scarcely one inch long; sheaths short, tumid, membranous, divided at the apex; bracts of the involucre in 2 series, scarious, the outer ones oblong-lanceolate, deciduous; interior ovate-obtuse, much shorter than the flower-heads; floral bracts cuneate ovate, ciliated at the apex. Bombay, P. Roux.

CLVII. GRAMINEÆ.

3. PANICUM, Linn., p 290.

8. P INTERRUPTUM, Willd. sp. i, 351.—Culm under the water, floating, thick, ascending, several feet high; sheaths longer than the joints, smooth; leaves smooth, narrow; raceme spike-like, slender; cylindric, erect, 4 to 8 inches long; florets small, green and smooth, on short pedicels, crowded all round the rachis, oblong, glumes 5 to 7-nerved, lower one subrotund and perfoliate; neuter floret with 2 paleæ. A very large Grass, clothing the margins of tanks throughout the Concan; anthers purple, long exserted. Supposed by Nees to be identical with P inundatum, Kunth.

Section FESTUCACEÆ, p 297.

21 A, ELYTROPHORUS, Beauv.

1. E ARTICULATUS, Beauv. Agr. *t.* 14, *fig.* 2.—Root fibrous; culms cespitose, simple, 3 to 8 inches high; leaves flat, elongated,

exceeding the culm ; inflorescence a green spike, from 1 to 4 inches long, sometimes interrupted here and there ; spikelets 3 to 7-flowered ; florets distichous, smooth ; glumes 2, membranaceous, keeled, subulate and awned at the apex, subequal and shorter than the spikelet ; stamen 1. Syn. Dactylis spicata, Willd ; Echinalysium strictum, Trinius. In rice-fields in the cold weather ; looks something like Setaria at a little distance.

Page 133, under N. balsamica, *read* “fruticose,” *instead of* “suffruticose.” This is a shrub, 6 to 7 feet high, as seen at Dowud, on the Sattara Road. Native name “Pirung.”

Page 148, under Cynanchum pauciflorum, *instead of* “anthers,” in 5th line, *read* “5 of the folds.”

Page 2,	line 3,	*for*	“crevato,”	*read*	“crenato.”
5,	,, 35,	,,	“hirsatum,”	,,	“hirsutum.”
6,	,, 8,	,,	“specie,”	,,	“species.”
6,	,, 16,	,,	“pellatum,”	,,	“peltatum, twice.”
8,	,, 30,	,,	“religioso,”	,,	“religiosa.”
9,	,, 20,	,,	“pedicles,”	,,	“pedicels.”
9,	,, 28,	erase “but.”			
10,	,, 14,	*for*	“pedicles,”	,,	“pedicels.”
11,	,, 29,	,,	Do.	,,	Do.
11,	,, 30,	,,	Do.	,,	Do.
12,	,, 9,	*cancel* “y” *after* “capense.”			
13,	,, 24,	*for*	“alac,”	*read*	“alæ.”
13,	,, 30,	,,	“pedicles,”	,,	“pedicels.”
13,	,, 34,	,,	“bipid,”	,,	“bifid.”
15,	line 3 from bottom,	*for*	“pedicles,”	,,	“pedicels.”
15,	,, 13,	*for*	Do.	,,	Do.
17,	,, 16,	,,	Do.	,,	Do.
17,	,, 22,	,,	Do.	,,	Do.
17,	,, 25,	,,	Do.	,,	Do.
18,	,, 18,	,,	Do.	,,	Do.
19,	,, 13,	,,	“Titiaceum,”	,,	“Tiliaceum.”
19,	,, 17,	,,	“tiliacens,”	,,	“tiliaceus.”
20,	,, 7,	,,	“pedicles,”	,,	“pedicels.”
20,	,, 34,	,,	“phœnicens,”	,,	“phœniceus.”
21,	,, 14,	*for*	“pedicles,”	*read*	“pedicels.”
24,	line 5 from bottom,	*for*	“Siliaceæ,”	,,	“Tiliaceæ.”
26,	Do.		“ulimfolia,”	,,	“ulmifolia.”
28,	line 24,	*for*	“pedicles,”	*read*	“pedicels.”
30,	,, 27,	,,	“Elentherandra,”	,,	“Eleutherandra.”
32,	,, 6,	,,	“Speurium,”	,,	“Spurium.”
33,	,, 6 from bottom,	*for*	“Sounnerat,”	,,	“Sonnerat.”

Page 33, line 2, *for* "Roxburghana," *read* "Roxburghiana."
35, ,, 5, ,, "Melicocea," ,, "Melicocca."
36, ,, 6 from top, *for* "Lukhmee," ,, "Zukhmee."
36, after line 18, *add* "Maratha name, Kapoor Bendy."
38, ,, Limbara ,, "Maratha name, Teesul."
41, ,, 10, *for* "cerriherous," *read* "cirrhiferous."
43, ,, line 8 from bottom, *for* "Balsamania," *read* "Balsaminia."

Page 47,—Celastrus rothiana is armed with long, straight, 1½ inch thorns, arising from the base of the petioles, particularly in the younger shoots. On the old branches these thicken with prominent warty knobs.

Page 48, *after* Elæodendron Roxburghii, *add*—

2. Elæodendron Glaucum.—A middle-sized tree, having opposite leaves quite smooth, and regularly serrate to within an inch of the petiole, which is channelled; fruit oblong, of the size and shape of that of Olea dioica, but remains green. Found growing in waste places and hills inland from the Ghauts; name "Bootkus." This tree is quite distinct in appearance and habit from E. Roxburghii, which is only found on the Ghauts, and even there rare.

Page 49, line 7, *for* "Lournef," *read* "Tournef."
49, ,, 24, ,, "Xylopyras," ,, "Xylopyrus."
50, ,, 2 from bottom, *for* "Rorar," ,, "Rora."
59, ,, 21, *for* "anymoxylon," ,, "animoxylon."
60, ,, 8 from bottom, *for* "tufolium," ,, "trifolium."
61, line 16, *for* "lancæfolia," ,, "lanceæfolia."
62, ,, 9, ,, "opinulosa," ,, "spinulosa."
65, ,, 2, ,, "graminium," ,, "gamineum."
65, ,, 18, ,, "Cylindracens," ,, "cylindraceus."
65, ,, 38, ,, "fruit," ,, "fruits."
67, after weather in Alhagi, *add* "Hindoostanee name, Jawasa."
70, line 18, *for* "may do," *read* "it does."
72, ,, 2 from bottom, *for* "Cajamus," *read* "Cajanus."

Page 77,—Brachypterum robustum is an introduction from Seharunpore seed, and is not found growing naturally in any part of Western India.

Page 81, line 10, from bottom, *for* "Aroul," *read* "Awul."

Page 86,—Mimosa tomentosa is not found in any part of the Deccan or Kandeish; but specimens were originally from two trees in the garden at Dapoorie, and these are said to have been raised from Nepal seed.

Page 88, bottom of the page, *after* "549," *write* "Maratha name, Oodul."
91, *after* "Bherda," *write* "also Yehela."
92, line 19, *for* "Keerijul," *write* "Keenjul."

Page 94, line 12, *expunge* " Jambool" *before* " streams."
98, " 17, *for* " Flosegina," *read* " Flos-Reginæ."
103, " 21, " " Colocynths," *read* " Colocynthis."
105, " 21, " " Colytedon," *read* " Cotyledon."
111, " 4 from bottom, *for* " Vaginnans," *read* " Vaginans."
112, " 2 from top *for* " Vaginnans," *read* " Vaginans."

Page 114,—Morinda. We have not had an opportunity of determining the species, which is grown so extensively in the north of Kandeish and Berar. It is allowed to remain 3 years in the grounds (*vide* As. Res. 4, p. 38). We doubt if J. Graham be correct in stating, as he does, that M citrifolia is the species (*vide* p 90, of list). It has not a tree habit.

Page 118, line 8 from bottom, *for* " swellon," *read* " swollen."
119, " 3 from bottom, *after* " South Concan," *add* " Ghaut Jungles," most common.
122, " 16, *for* " shall," *read* " small."
125, " 11, *cancel* " as."
132, " 5 from bottom, *for* " nerufolia," *read* " nereifolia.
148, " 8, *for* " Puchanani," *read* " Buchanani."
159, " 16, " " Karamba," " " Karambu."
163, " 12, " " Thuleria," " " Shuteria."
168, " 8 from bottom, *for* " Mark," *read* " Maratha."
196, " 8, *for* " aurculare," *read* " auriculare."

Page 199,—Tectona.—We have lately seen a striking instance of the effect of fresh Teak seeds applied to the Umbilicus in a case of infantile Suppression of Urine, therefore the statement of Endlicher is probably founded on sound observation.

Page 200, line 30, *for* " Mahul," *read* " Mawul."
201, " 9 from bottom, *for* " Altissmia," *read* " Altissima."
226, " 9, " " " " lacta," " " lactea."
230, " 14, " " " " uranda," " " urandra."
236, " 16 from top—Leaves are made into a soft paste with tobacco, and thus applied. The plant is very common in waste, uncultivated places.

Page 240, line 6 from bottom, *for* " terta," *read* " testa."

Page 241—Urostigma religiosum.—A peculiar variety, with pinnate drooping leaves, is to be seen at Sattara.

Page 247, line 15 from bottom, *for* " Bull-bearing," *read* " Bulb-bearing."
251, " 12 from top, *for* " Spring," *read* " Spreng."

INDEX TO No. I.

A

C

D

E

H

I

M

N

T

SUPPLEMENT,

EMBRACING TREES AND PLANTS INTRODUCED INTO WESTERN INDIA FROM FOREIGN COUNTRIES, AND THOSE CULTIVATED OR NATURALISED.

I.—RANUNCULACEÆ.

THE CROW-FOOT TRIBE.

SUB-TRIBE ANEMONEÆ, DC. *Prod.* 1, p 2.

I.—THALICTRUM, Polyandria Polyginia.

1. T FOLIOLOSUM, DC. *Prod.* 1, p 12.—Leaves quadripinnate; flowers yellow; raised at Dapoorie from seed received from Seharunpore. Native of Gosaen Khan, Himalaya.

2. ANEMONE JAPONICA. Native of Japan; introduced at Dapoorie.

SUB-TRIBE HELLEBOREÆ.

II.—DELPHINIUM, Polyandria Trigynia. From *delphine*, a dolphin, fancied resemblance in nectary.

3. D AJACIS, Southern Europe, W. and A. 12; DC. *Prod.* 1, p 342.—An annual, with purple flowers; common in gardens in the rainy or cold season. It is by no means so handsome as the native species.

III.—NIGELLA, Polyandria Pentagynia. From *nigh*, black, the colour of the seeds.

4. N SATIVA, Qu. Indica, Roxb. Fl. 2, p 646.—We have raised this from Italian seed, but have not seen it indigenous.

II.—ANONACEÆ, DC. *Prod.* 1, p 83.

THE CUSTARD-APPLE TRIBE, Lind. Nat. Syst., p 22.

IV.—ANONA, Polyandria Polyginia. Latin for *corn*. Name given by reason of the nutritive qualities of the fruit (?).

1. A SQUAMOSA.—Native of Central America. From thence it has spread all over India, where it grows wild, particularly about Moosulman burial-grounds. The bruized leaves have a peculiar fœtor, and are used for destroying worms bred in sores, a complication common in India.

2. A RETICULATA.—"Ramphul." America. Scarcer than the last, but often found in native gardens; fruit very luscious.

3. A MURICATA, DC. *syst.* p 467.—Soursop. Native of South America. A very handsome tree, with smooth, shining, dark-green leaves; now common in Bombay; fruit size of a citron, sour flavour.

4. A CHERIMOLIA, DC. *syst.* 1, p 473.—Cherimolia or soft-fruited Custard-apple; native of Peru; dark-purple fruit; introduced at Hewra by Colonel G. R. Jervis, through Messrs. Loddiges; flowers, but has not borne fruit.

5. HYALOSTEMMA, Roxb., Uvaria Diœcia, Wallich. Cat. No. 6434; Lind. Maut. 2nd ed., p 439.—Native of Eastern Bengal. A small shrub, with elegant alternate entire leaves. Garden at Dapoorie. This is the only diœcious plant in the family.

V.—ARTABOTRYS, Polyandria Polygynia. *Artao,* to suspend; and *botrys*, a bunch. The peduncle has a curious hook, which lays hold of any support near.

6. A ODORATISSIMA, W. and A. 33; Uvaria Odoratissima, Roxb. Fl 2, p 666.—"Kala Chumpa." Native of Eastern Islands; now not uncommon in gardens. The ripe flowers have a rich scent of apples; the shrub is scandent, with shining, smooth leaves; fruit size and shape of a myrobolan.

7. ANONA ODORATA.—China (?). A small tree, with narrow lanceolate leaves, and flower of three long yellow wings; fruit round; flower much more fragrant than the last, especially in moist weather, when it can be scented at a distance of eight or ten feet. U Discolor, described in 1st ed., p 3, No. 17, as at Dapoorie, introduced from China, must, we think, have been mistaken for the abovementioned tree; at all events, we have not seen it either at Dapoorie or elsewhere.

VI.—GUATTERIA, Polyandria Polygynia. Named from *Guatteri,* an Italian botanist.

8. G LONGIFOLIA, Southern Peninsula, DC. *syst.* 1, p 492.—"Asoca," "Asupala," Gujarati. A handsome, erect-growing tree, having waved long lanceolate shining leaves; often planted in Indian avenues; wood is good. The Lancewood of America belongs to this family.

9. G SUBEROSA, Roxb. Cor. Pl. 1, *t.* 34.—Native of Carnatic and Bengal. A beautiful small tree, with shining, smooth leaves, and fruit in umbellets along the branches on the underside. Garden at Hewra.

III.—MENISPERMACEÆ, DC. *Prod.* 1, p 95.

THE COCCULUS TRIBE, Lind. Nat. Syst. 31.

VII.—COCCULUS, Diœcia Hexandria. From *Coccus*, cochineal, the berries of some being of a scarlet colour.

1. C Palmatus, DC. *Prod.* 1, p 515.—Columba root; native of Mosambique; garden Hewra. Roots received from the late Furdonjee Murzbanjee Weyd, a very zealous promoter of the European materia medica, and author of a Gujarati work on domestic medicine, well known to most of his Parsee brethren; leaves large, tomentose, 5-lobate; flowers small; fruit size of a pea; has occasionally flowered and produced abortive seeds; in the dry season it withers, and in May the roots begin to shoot. This plant is much cultivated in the Mauritius, and is much valued in medicine for its tonic and antiseptic properties. The C Indicus, largely imported into England for adulterating beer, belongs to this family.

IV.—PAPAVERACEÆ, DC. *Prod.* 1, p 125.

THE POPPY TRIBE, Lind. Nat. Syst. 1, p 8.

VIII.—ARGEMONE, Polyandria Monogynia.

1. A Mexicana, W. and A. 59; Wight's Illust., part 2, *t.* 11; Bot. Mag. *t.* 243.—Yellow-flowering Mexican Thistle. *Fico del' inferno* of the Spaniards; native of Mexico. No plant has established itself in India more widely than this, and it is now found in all the tropical and sub-tropical parts of the world. In the Concan the poor people may be seen collecting the seeds for the extraction of oil. The yellow juice is used as an application to indolent ulcers, and for the removal of specks on the cornea. A white-flowered variety was introduced from Bengal, but it has died out.

IX.—PAPAVER, Polyandria Polygynia, Lam. *t.* 451; Gaert. *t.* 60.—Native of Asia Minor.

2. P Somniferum. "Afoo-ke-Thar.' Ainslie Mat. Ind. 1, p 326, and 2, p 339; Eng. Bot. *t.* 2145.—The Poppy, of which there are several varieties. It is extensively cultivated in Malwa, and in a few parts of Guzerat. Its cultivation in the British provinces of Western India is prohibited on fiscal grounds. The expressed juice of the seeds is a very useful remedy in infantile bowel-complaints. The seeds afford a bland oil, and are much used as an ingredient in the composition of curry-powder, under the name "Kuskus."

3. P Rheas, DC. *syst.* Veg. 2, p 76; Eng. Bot. *t.* 645.—Native of Southern Europe; a favourite flower in native gardens in Gujarat, where it is sown so as to give the appearance of a rich vegetable carpet of varied colours. The flowers are called "Lala."

V.—CRUCIFERÆ, DC. *Prod.* 1, p 131.

X.—BRASSICA, Tetradynamia Siliquosa. From *bresic,* Celtic for cabbage.

1. B Oleracea. "Kobee," DC. *Prod.* 1, p. 213.— Including Cabbages of various kinds, Nolcole, Brocoli, Cauliflower, and Turnips; commonly cultivated during the cold season. The first becomes unprolific when planted among, or near to, Cabbages.

XI.—RAPHANUS, Linn., Tetradynamia Siliquosa.—*Ra,* quickly; *phainomai,* to appear. The seeds vegetate quickly.

2. R Sativus. "Mohlee," Radish. DC. *Prod.* 1, p 228.—The red Radish of Europe; much cultivated in the rainy season. The white native Radish grows at all seasons. It is much larger and less delicate than the European plant.

3. R Caudatus, DC. *Prod.* 1, p 228.—Java Radish; has long tapering whip-like pods, which are eaten; is much cultivated in Gujarat.

Mathiola, in honour of Peter Andrew Matheoli, an Italian physician.

4. M Incana, Robt. Brown in Aiton Hort. Kew., 2nd ed., vol. 4, p 119.—An herbaceous plant, with lanceolate hoary leaves, and flowers scarlet or purple.

Bromton Stock—Annual, from Europe seed; gardens, common.

Iberis, Linn. Gen. No. 804; Gaert. Fr. 2279.—Candy Tuft. Herbaceous plant, having flowers sometimes white and oftener purple.

5. I Umbellata, Linn. sp. 906.—Purple, Candy Tuft.

6. I Odorata.—A fragrant variety.

XII.—NASTURTIUM, Tetradynamia Siliquosa, Smith Bot. *t.* 855. Common Water-cress, in gardens.

XIII.—LEPIDIUM, Tetradynamia Siliquosa. From *Lepis,* a scale. The pods resemble scales.

7. L Sativum, Smith Fl. Græca. *t.* 616; Wight Illust. 212.—"Halim," Persian Cress; much cultivated in Guzerat.

VI.—CAPPARIDEÆ, DC. *Prod.* 1, p. 237.

XIV.—CLEOME, Tetradynamia Siliquosa.

1. C SPECIOSISSIMA, Lind. Bot. Reg. 1312.—Herbaceous, unarmed; leaflets 5 to 7, lanceolate; flowers large, rose-coloured, with pink stamens; very showy. Native of Mexico, now common in gardens.

VII.—RESEDACEÆ, Don's Syst. 1, p 286.

XV.—RESEDA, Dodecandria Trigynia. Mignonette, Gaert. *t.* 75; Lam. *t.* 410.

1. R ODORATA.—Mignonette. Much cultivated in gardens; native of Southern Europe; seems to grow best far inland, as at Ahmednuggur, from whence the best seed is procured.

VIII.—FLACOURTIANEÆ, DC. *Prod.* 1, p 255.

XVI.—FLACOURTIA, W. and A., Diœcia Polyandra. From *Etienne de Flacourt,* once a Director of the French East India Company.

1. F JANGOMAS, DC. *Prod.* p 257.—Joagom, of Goa. In gardens at Salsette; rare; fruit edible. We have not seen this. *Gom,* Waree. Is not this identical with the indigenous P Cataphracta (*vide* 401, p 10)?

2. F RAMONLII, W. and A. 103; Wight Ic. 5, *t.* 85.—Panawla, the Mauritius Plumb. A small tree armed with straight thorns; leaves oval crenate.

IX.—BIXINEÆ, DC. *Prod.* 1, p 259.

THE ARNOTTO TRIBE, Lind. Nat. Syst. 1, p 152.

XVII.—BIXA, Linn., Polyandria Monogynia.—The American name adopted, Lam. *t.* 669; Gaert. *t.* 61. Native of S. America.

1. B ORELLANA, W. and A. 112; Rumph. Amb. 2, *t.* 19; Bot. Mag. *t.* 1456.—Native names "Kisree," "Sendree." Long naturalised in India, where it is valued for the colouring matter surrounding the seeds; this is used for colouring butter, and in the dyeing of clothes. The small tree, with its lilac flowers and red seed-vessels, is very ornamental. There is a white-flowered variety, which has no colouring matter.

X.—VIOLARIÆ, DC. *Prod.* 1, p 287.

THE VIOLET TRIBE, Lind. Nat. Syst. p 146.

XVIII.—VIOLA, Linn., Pentandria Monogynia.

1. V TRICOLOR, Don's *syst.* 1, p 332; Eng. Bot. *t.* 1287.—Heart's-Ease. "Pansey." Native of Europe; in gardens.

XI.—CARYOPHYLLACEÆ, DC. *Prod.* 1, p 351.

XIX.—DIANTHUS, Decandria Digynia.

1. D CHINENSIS.—Pink and clove-pink.

2. D CARYOPHYLLUS.—Pink; in gardens; cultivated with faint success, as compared to the more splendid varieties in Europe.

XX.—LYCHNIS, Decandria Pentagynia. From *Luchnos,* a link.

3. L CHALCEDONICA, Scarlet Lychnis.—A brilliant flower, now established in many gardens.

XII.—MALVACEÆ, DC. *Prod.* 1, p 429.

THE MALLOW TRIBE, Lind. Nat. Syst. p 33.

XXI.—MALVA, Monodelphia Polyandria; Lam. *t.* 582; Gaert. *t.* 136. Native of Southern Europe, Asia, and America.

1. ALTHEA ROSEA.—Common Hollyhock; in gardens.

2. M MAURITIANA, W. and A. 162.—Mauritius; annual, erect plant, with variegated light-purple flowers; found in gardens, Fakeer's stations, &c.

3. M POLYSTACHIA, Don's *syst.* 1, p 461; Cavanilles Dissert. 5, *t.* 138, *fig.* 3.—Native of Peru; Botanical Garden at Hewra, from Calcutta seed.

4. MALOPE TRIFIDA, Don's *syst.* 1, p 460.—Native of Southern Europe; leaves 3-nerved, trifid-toothed, glabrous; flowers large, purple. Dapoorie garden.

XXII.—ANODA, Monadelphia Polyandria. From *a,* privative; and *nodus,* a knot, because the pedicels are without the articulations of Sida.

5. A HASTATA, Cavanilles Dissert. 1, p 38; Sida Hastata, Don's *syst.* 1, p 489.—A small plant, with cordate acuminate leaves, and deep-blue flowers, erect, on long peduncles; in gardens; rare.

XXIII.—HIBISCUS, Linn., Monadelphia Polyandra. From *hibiscos,* the Greek name of the Mallow. Lam. *t.* 584; Gaert. *t.* 134.

6. H ROSA SINENSIS. Shoe-flower; "Jasood," Maratha. Linn. sp. 977; Don's *syst.* 1, p 478.—Very common in gardens;

leaves ovate-acuminate, smooth; flowers purple, also frequently yellow or fawn-coloured. A favourite offering at temples; juice uusd to blacken leather, hence the English name.

7. H ROSA MUTABILIS, Don's *syst.* 1, p 481.—Native of Eastern Islands. Leaves cordate-angular, acuminate-toothed; flowers white, changing to red, often double.

8. H LILIFLORUS, Malavinsus Puniceus, Cavanilles Diss. 3, p 154; Don's *syst.* 1, p 476.—Native of Bourbon, now common in gardens of Western India; flowers scarlet. A very ornamental plant.

9. H GIGANTEUS (?)—Flower not seen. Dapoorie Garden; seed from Bengal.

10. H PATERSONII (?) Australia; Dapoorie Garden; raised from seed given by the late Lord Elphinstone. Regarding this, as well as the last species, we await the further development of the plants before endeavouring to trace them.

11. H ERIOCARPUS, DC. *Prod.* 1, p 452.—A small tree with three-lobed five-nerved leaves; leaves of involucel oblong, slightly toothed; capsules oblate, very hispid, pricking the hand, like Cowage; flowers white, beautifully variegated with purple, and base of the corolla deep-purple. They are not yellow with a dark centre, as described by Don 1, p 482. Gardens at Dapoorie and Hewra.

12. H LINDLEYI.—Wall., P. A. Rarior. p 4, *t*, 4.—Native of Ava; now common in our gardens of Western India; leaves palmately 3 to 7-parted; flowers large, purple, with dark centre. A very ornamental species.

13. H SUBDARIFFA, DC. *Prod.* 1, p 453.—Native of the East Indies. Roselle; cultivated for the excellent jelly which the red, thickened, and very ornamental calyx affords.

XXIV.—ABELMOSCHUS, W. and A., Monadelphia Polyandra. From the Arabic *Kabb-el-Mish*, a grain of Musk.

14. A ESCULENTUS, Linn. sp. 980.—Native of the West and East Indies. "Bendy," Indian name; "Okra," West-Indian name. One of the vegetables the most widely cultivated in India, and a most excellent and safe one it is. The seed-vessels bruised form a good emollient poultice.

15. A MUSCATUS.—Eastern Islands; seed from Bengal; capsule like that of the last, but shorter and more obtuse. The species is remarkable only for the musky odour of the seeds.

16. H SYRIACUS, Roxb. Fl. 3, p 195.—Gardens (?) About this species there is a doubt. Information is solicited.

XXV.—PARITIUM, W. and A., Monadelphia Polyandra. The Malabar name latinised.

17. P TRICUSPIS, Hibiscus Tricuspis, W. and A. 190; Roxb. Fl. 3, p 202.—A tree; leaves long-petioled, three-lobed; flowers

bright yellow, with a purple base. Bombay Esplanade, near the Native Hospital; planted.

XXVI.—GOSSYPIUM, Linn., Monadelphia Polyandra. Name applied by Pliny to a shrub of Upper Egypt which bore cotton.

18. G HERBACEUM; G. Album. Roxb. Fl. p 181; Rheed. Mal. 1, *t.* 31; Wight Ic. 1, p 198.—Native of India. The common Indian cotton, "Kapusachejhar." A robust-spreading shrub in Gujarat, whereas in Dharwar and Eastern Deccan it is a single-stemmed plant, hardly rising above two feet. It is not found wild in India, but is supposed to be the cultivated offspring of G Obtusifolium, a climber found in hedges, and very common in Sind.

19. G RELIGIOSUM, G Vitifolium (?) Roxb. 3, p 186.—"Nurma Kuppas"; arboreous, slender, hardly having the habit of a tree; cultivated rather extensively in the north-west of Gujarat as a triennial (?) also in Sind. Derives its name "Deo Kupas" from it being most extensively used for the sacred thread of the Banians, "Moonj."

20. G ACUMINATUM, W. and A. 200.—The name "Religiosum" is employed in the former edition of this book (erroneously we think) to designate this species, which is the true Pernambuco cotton, a later introduction by the Portuguese from Peru or Brazil. It also is often found planted in the enclosures of Brahmins' houses, and is used for the "Moonj," as abovementioned. The use of the word "Moonj" affords one more argument as to the progress of the Brahminical caste from Upper India southward. The word is the Sanscrit name of a species of "Saccharum" common there, and which may have been originally used for the same purpose.

The cultivation of this Pernambuco plant has several times been attempted by Government and by individuals on a large scale in Western India, but uniformly without success, shelter and frequent watering being essential to its growth. In Graham's list, G Vaupellii (No. 115) as well as Religiosum (No. 114) refer to this species.

A gold medal was presented by the Agri. and Horticultural Society of Bombay to the late Mr. Vaupell, on his presentation of this species as a discovery!

21. The valuable species (?) or variety of G Herbaceum, named G Barbadeuse, which has failed in Gujarat and all the northern provinces of the Presidency, appears to be established as a successful growth in the Dharwar Collectorate; still the produce of cleaned cotton per acre appears even there to be very small.

All the other varieties of exotic cotton cultivated seem to be referable to one or other of the abovenamed species variously modified by soil and climate.

22. ABUTILON STRIATUM.—Mauritius; a shrubby species with serrate leaves and large roseate flowers, with white streaks. Dapoorie

M MALACHRA, Monadelphia Polyandria.

23. M Rotundifolia.—An annual, with orbicular leaves and small yellow flowers. A native of Brazil; introduced by the late Mr. Nimmo. It seems now to have over-run the cultivated portions of the Island of Bombay.

XIII.—BOMBACEÆ, DC. *Prod.* 1, p 475.

HELICTERES, Monadelphia Decandria. From *helix*, a screw.

1. H Hirsuta, Don's *syst.* 1, p 507.—A shrub, with oblong lanceolate serrate leaves; Parell Garden (?); has disappeared from Dapoorie. The fruit is straight, and covered with a thick coat of soft thistles.

2. H Purpurea.—This also has disappeared from Dapoorie; it was originally introduced from Bengal. Information is solicited as to whether it is now found in any garden of Western India.

ADANSONIA, Monadelphia Polyandria. Named from *Adanson*, a French botanist.

3. A Digitata, W. and A. 226; Roxb. Fl 3, p 164; Bot. Mag. *t.* 2791 and 2792.—"Gonik Chentz," Maratha; "Goruk Amla," Hindoostanee; Monkey-bread tree. Native of Africa, and from thence introduced by the Arabian traders; is now found at many places on our western coast, and at inland stations erst the seats of the Mussulman power, such as Baroda, Beejapore, Joonere, &c.

The quaint appearance of the tree, with its immense stem, will always render it a curious object to an European inquirer.

From Dr. Livingston's researches, it appears that the Adansonia is the Village-Tree, or Place of Assembly, in all the villages of the highlands of Eastern Africa; flowers in May and June. The large pendulous fruit is used as a float for fishing-nets on our western coast. The virtues of the subacid pulp of the fruit do not appear to be known to the natives of India. The bark affords cordage, and is also used as a febrifuge (*vide* DuChassaigne in Pharm. Jour. for 1845). The light, porous wood is often used as a float to support the fisherman in tanks.

BOMBAX, Monadelphia Polyandra. From *bombax*, Greek name for cotton or silk.

4. B Heterophyllum.—Seed from Calcutta. We insert this as a species of doubtful authenticity. It has not yet reached any size, but is left for future inquiry. Botanical gardens at Hewra and Dapoorie.

XIV.—BYTTERNACEÆ, DC. *Prod.* 1, p 481.

STERCULIA, Linn., Monœcia Monadelphia.

1. S ALATA, Roxb. Fl. 3, 152.—A very tall rumous tree; habitat North Canara; leaves cordate entire, 5 to 3-nerved; fruit size of a child's head; seeds winged.

There are two trees in the garden at Hewra, raised from seed brought from Koorsullie, on the Black River.

2. S PLATANIFOLIA, Linn. Fil. Supp. 423; Don's *syst.* 1, p 517. —The tree raised under this name from Bengal seed, and now growing in the garden at Hewra common, answers in its leaves rather to the description of S Populifolia, than to that of Platanifolia. As it has not yet flowered, the species remains doubtful. It is rather an ornamental tree, with regular horizontal branches, and branchlets dividing off at right angles.

3. S FÆTIDA, W. and A. 236; Roxb. Fl. 3, p 153; Rumph. Amb. 3, *t.* 107.—"Jungly Budam," Bastard Poon Tree; a stately tree with digitate leaves, deciduous in cold weather; flowers in March and April; smell of flowers very offensive; carpels large, kidney-shaped. Gardens in Southern Concan, Mahim, Dapoorie, &c.

4. ERIOCHLENA HOOKERI, W. and A. 259.—We have this tree growing at Hewra. The indigenous species of Western India, described in our former edition, will be found in our Indigenous Catalogue, under its true name. This has a capsule much more blunt, and the habit of the tree is different from that of ours.

KLEINHOVIA, Monadelphia Polyandria.

5. K HOSPITA, W. and A.; Roxb. Fl 3, p 141; Rumph. Amb. *t.* 113.—Eastern Islands; a tree, with alternate broad cordate leaves, small pink flowers, and pear-shaped inflated capsule. We have never seen nor heard of this tree in the Southern Concan.

THEOBROMA, Monadelphia Decandria. From *theos*, God; *broma* food; celestial food.

6. T CACOA, W. and A. 239. Native of South America. The Chocolate-nut tree; dies when planted at any distance from the coast. Gardens in Bombay.

ABROMA, Monadelphia Decandria. Not fit for food, in contradistinction to the last; *a*, privative.

7. A AUGUSTA.—Eastern Bengal (?); Devil's Cotton; a shrub, with soft velvetty branches, ovate oblong-acuminate leaves, and dark-red flowers; capsule 5-angled, containing the seeds in a very light cottony envelope, hence the name. In gardens; not common. The bark affords a strong fibre.

GUAZUMA, W. and A., Monadelphia Dodecandria. A Mexican name.

8. G TOMENTOSA.—Native of Brazil, now widely cultivated in Bombay; flowers yellow, rather showy; wood light and loose-grained, but is said to be fit for coach-pannels; juice of the bruised bark is used for clarifying sugar. It has been recommended in Elephantiasis or Leprosy.

PENTAPETES, Linn., Monadelphia Polyandria. From *pente*, five, in allusion to the 5-celled fruit.

9. P PHŒNICEA, Roxb. Fl. 3, p 157; Rheede Mal. 10, *t.* 56.—A common, rather showy, scarlet flower, in gardens; native of Bengal.

DOMBEYA, Monadelphia Polyandria. Named from *Dombey*, a French traveller in Peru.

10. D PALMATA, W. and A. 249; Wall. Pl. As. rar. 3, *t.* 235.—A shrub, native of Mauritius, having lobate subpalmate leaves, and showy flowers, at first white, changing to yellow, and finally rust-coloured. In a few gardens, Bombay. It was last introduced by Mr. Young, C. S., from Mauritius.

11. ASTRAPEA WALLICHII, DC. *Prod.* 1, p. 500.—Information is solicited regarding this showy shrub, which we have been unable to trace in gardens.

GLOSSOSPERMUM, Monadelphia Pentandria, Wallich's Catalogue.

12. G VELUTINUM.—A large tree, having dark-coloured bark, cordate-serrate, broad downy leaves on long petioles; each petiole has a broad lanceolate retrofacted bract, flowering along the branches and from the axils on a loose panicle. In the garden at Dapoorie, and also among Esplanade trees, Bombay. The wood is worthless.

XV.—TILIACEÆ, DC. *Prod.* 1, p 503.

GREWIA, Polyandria Monogynia. From *Grew*, an English Physician.

1. G ASIATICA, W. and A. 289; Roxb. Fl 2, p 586.—"Phulsee," Hindoostanee. We insert this here because it has hitherto been known only as a cultivated tree, whereas it is found truly wild in the Deccan. Common in gardens, Bombay and Surat. Fruit gratefully acid, and makes a sherbet well known in Gujarat.

BERRYA, Polyandria Monogynia. Named from *Dr. A. Berry*, a Malabar Surgeon and Botanist, a friend of Roxburgh's.

2. B AMONILLA, Roxb. Cor. Pl 3, p 59, *t.* 264; DC. *Prod.* 1, p 516.—Trincomalie Wood tree; native of Ceylon; leaves entire, ovate-acuminate, 7-nerved at base; capsule roundish, 6-winged,

3-celled, a rather handsome tree of robust habit. Gardens Dapoorie and Hewra.

3. TRIUMFETTA BARTRAMII, Linn. sp. 638.—We insert this as the produce of Calcutta seed. It now grows at Dapoorie, but is yet too immature to enable us to solve the doubt which continues to hang over this plant, viz. as to whether it be a Urena or a Triumfetta (*vide* Don's *syst.* 1, p 54).

XVI.—AURANTIACEÆ, DC. *Prod.* 1, p 535.

THE ORANGE TRIBE, Lind. Nat. Syst., p 123.

TRIPHASIA, W. and A., Hexandria Monogynia. From *triphasios*, in allusion to the tricleft calyx.

1. T TRIFOLIATA, W. and A. 323; Bot. Rep. *t.* 123; Citrus Parva Dulcis, Sonnerat It. *t.* 63.—An ornamental shining-leaved shrub, common in gardens. It is a native of China, and is not found in Southern Concan, as erroneously stated in the 1st edition.

MURRAYA, Decandria Monogynia. Called from *Murray*, Professor of Botany at Göttingen.

2. M EXOTICA, W. and A. 335.—"Koontee" (?). We have never heard this name. Wight Ic. No. 5, *t.* 96.

3. CAMUNIUM CHINENSE, Rumph. Amb. *t.* 18, *f.* 2.—A pretty shrub, with white fragrant flowers. Native of China. Dr. Royle remarked that it is found all along the jungly forest below the Himalayas.

COOKIA, Decandria Monogynia. Named from *Captain Cook*, the celebrated voyager.

4. C PUNCTATA, Rumph. Amb. 1, *t.* 55; W. and A. 338.—"Wampee," Chinese. Found in gardens, Bombay (?), also at Hewra and Dapoorie, Deccan. A Chinese tree; fruit the size of a marble; pleasantly acid for tarts and preserves.

CITRUS, Polydelphia Polyandria. Origin of name unknown, Lam. *t.* 639; Gaert. *t.* 121.

5. C DECUMANA, W. and A. 343; Rumph. Amb. 2, *t.* 24.—"Pamplenoose," Shaddock. Native of Eastern Islands; now most successfully cultivated in Bombay, at Goa, and in some of the Soonda Ghaut gardens south of it, as at Woolvee; rind of the fruit is so good a bitter, that by many druggists it is made to supply the place of the more expensive Gentian root for Tinct. Caveat Emptor!

6. C AURANTIUM, W. and A. 343.—This choice fruit is now found as a common article of cultivation in gardens at Poona, Ahmednuggur, Aurungabad, and Kunhur. The Kunhur Oranges bear the palm as to size, juiciness, and flavour; does not succeed

well in Bombay, which, however, receives large supplies of the delicious orange of Mosambique from thence.

The varieties of the Orange cultivated in Western India are:—

1st.—The Mosambique, as now naturalised in India.

2nd.—The Cintra, of Portuguese origin, as the name denotes.

3rd.—The China, or red, loose-skinned Orange.

4th.—The Cowla, inferior to the above three.

5th.—The small China, very delicate in frame, but dry.

7. C LIMETTA, Risso. Ann. Mus. 20, p 195; Don's *syst.* 1, p 589.—Sweet Lime. The original habitat of this it is difficult to trace, as it has been so long cultivated in India; is found in gardens from Shikarpore to Ceylon; insipid, but the young plants afford the best grafting or budding stocks.

8. C BERGAMIA.—Sour Lime; much cultivated as a sales-product in most native gardens. Eaten daily with salt as a remedy in Spleen diseases, it is of the utmost importance. This we state on repeated experience.

9. C MEDICA, Risso. Ann. Ser. 20, p 199.—The Citron; fruit coarse, but very valuable as an adjuvant to medical treatment in low fevers. In Yucatan, where, owing to the limestone soil, bad fevers are common, it is reckoned a specific. In Western India we have not the art of forming the fingered Citron so common in China.

10. C LIMONUM.—Portugal Lemon; cultivated at Dapoorie, where it yields fruit of a fair size, and good flavour. We have thus done our best to reduce into order and intelligibility this very difficult genus, as it appears in India. We have not been fortunate enough to meet with, or hear of, the Maloonga mentioned in p 25 of Graham's list, but information is solicited regarding it and any other exotic varieties of the tribe which we may have overlooked.

AGLAIA, Linn., Monadelphia Pentandria. The name of one of the *Graces* expressive of beauty.

11. A ODORATA; Opilia Odorata, Spr. p 936; Roxb. Fl.—A native of China; leaves ternate and pinnate; flowers in axillary racemes, very small, yellow. In gardens, Bombay.

XVII.—SAPINDACEÆ, DC. *Prod.* 1, p 601.

NEPHELIUM, Octandria Monogynia. Old name of *Burdock*, on account of the rough fruit.

1. N LITCHI, Roxb. Fl. 2, p 269.—Litchee Tree; native of China, now common in gardens in Bombay; dies off inland.

2. BLIGHIA SAPIDA, Octandria Monogynia.—Akee Tree; native of Africa; has pinnate shining leaves, bright-red pear-like indifferent fruit. Parell and Dapoorie gardens; fruit can only be eaten fried, and is insipid.

3. SAPINDUS RUBIGINOSUS, Roxb. Fl. 2, p 282 ; Roxb. Cor. p 1, *t.* 62.—Native of Bengal ; in the woods of Girgaum, but certainly planted.

XVIII.—CEDRELACEÆ, Don's *syst.* 1, p 686.

SWIETENIA, Monadelphia Octodecandria. Named from *Van Swieten*, the celebrated Vienna Physician, Commentator on Bœrhaaves Aphorisms.

1. S MAHOGANI, Linn. sp. 271 ; Hook. Bot. Mis. p 1, *t.* 16 and 17.—Native of South America ; long ago introduced into Bengal, and from thence to Botanical Gardens at Hewra and Dapoorie, from a living plant received from the late Colonel J. R. Jervis. There are now upwards of 30 trees of about 25 feet in height, and growing robustly ; they have not yet flowered.

KHAYA, Adrien de Juss. in Med. Mus. xix. 249, *t.* 21.

2. K SENEGALENSIS.—The tree received from Messrs. Loddiges, under the name Kye Apple of Senegal. As it has never flowered during the 21 years it has been in the gardens at Hewra, we remain in doubt as to the identity of the species ; the more so, as it has long, sharp thorns from the axils of the pinnate leaflets, a mark not alluded to in the description of Khaya by Jussicu. (*Vide* Endlicher Genera, p 1054.)

XIX.—GUTTIFERÆ, DC. 1, p 557.

GARCINIA MANGOSTANA, Roxb. Fl. 2, p 618 ; Rumph. Amb. 1, *t.* 43.

1. G AFFINIS, Roxb. ; G Zeylanica ; G Cowa, Wight Illust. 8, p 125.—Native of Malabar ; fruit furrowed. Some very large trees grow in a grove at Belgaum, Mr. Law.

MAMMEA, Polyandria Monogynia. Name in its native country.

2. M AMERICANA.—Leaves obovate, blunt, entire, having often pellucid dots ; flowers solitary, along the branches ; fruit large, round, few-seeded. This very ornamental tree is found in the Parell garden.

XX.—MALPIGHIACEÆ, DC. *Prod.* 1, p 677.

MALPIGHIA, Monadelphia Decandria.

1. M COCCIFERA, DC. *Prod.* 1, p 578 ; Bot. Reg. *t.* 568.—Barbadoes Cherry. Native country West Indies. With lobed spinous leaves, and bright-red fruit. In gardens ; an ornamental shrub.

XXI.—MELIACEÆ, DC. *Prod.* 1, p 619.

MELIA, Decandria Monogynia. The only one of this extensive Indian family which can be called an exotic is—

1. M Sempervirens.—Native of Persia (?), and generally called Persian Lilac. This specie is erroneously named M azedarach in the 1st edition of this Catalogue. St. Vincent, West Indies, Cuba, Lind. The tree looks always scraggy, as if the climate did not suit it.

XXII.—AMPELIDEÆ, DC. *Prod.* 1, p 627.

1. Vitis Vinifera, W. and A. p 429, Pentandria Monogynia.—The Vine, originally a native of Persia, has now spread to most parts of Europe, and is successfully cultivated in numerous places in India; grows luxuriantly above the Ghauts. In the Berar and Aurungabad Soobas the long black and the green Fakeera are the most excellent kinds; the former is also cultivated largely at Ahmednuggur, Poona, and Seroor. The common Grape sells in the eastern bazars, near Aurungabad, at about 32 lbs. per rupee, and they are largely exported to the Coast. The varieties (cultivated) of the Vine in India are too numerous to be inserted here. A vineyard in India requires a vast amount of manual labour in removing vermin, &c. The plant does not love the air of the lower country; the Grapes produced there have often an acid quality, which renders them dangerous.

XXIII.—GERANIACEÆ, DC. *Prod.* 1, p 637.

PELARGONIUM, Monadelphia Heptandria.—Of Geraniums the variety in gardens is too great for a list of them to be ventured on here. The chief of them are—

1. P Capitatum.—The rose-scented Pelargonium, DC. *Prod.* 1, 974; a native of the Cape.
2. P Inquinans, DC. *Prod.* p 659.—The rose-coloured Geranium, also from the Cape. The Lemon-scented and Oak-leaved Geranium, also choice species, not uncommon in gardens.

TROPÆOLUM, Octandria Monogynia.

3. T Majus, Linn. sp. 490.—Large-leaved Indian Cress; common in gardens, and conspicuous by its large red flowers, streaked with yellow.
4. T Pentaphyllum, Lam. Dict. 1, p 605; Illust. *t.* 277.—Canary Creeper; scandent, with deeply divided leaves, and delicate yellow flowers; in gardens; rare.

XXIV.—LINEÆ, DC. *Prod.* 1, p 423.

1. L Usitatissimum, Pentandria Pentagynia, W. and A. 441; Eng. Bot. *t.* 1359.—"Jowas," Maratha; "Ulsee," Hindoostanee. Said to be originally from Egypt, Don; has long been grown in India, and is very common as an edging-ridge to fields, because cattle do not eat it. Of late years the cultivation has been pushed to a very great extent in Berar, Kandeish, and Eastern Deccan. The unripe capsule is used by the natives as a base for chutnee. It is only cultivated for the sake of the seed, as it has been found, by repeated experiments made in India Proper, that it is too short, weak, and worthless as a fibre. The virtues of an infusion of the seed as an emollient in certain diseases are well known, as also its use as an emollient poultice.

2. L Rubrum (Grandiflora) Don's *syst.* 1, p 456.—A native of Agrigentum (Gergenti) in Sicily; has been raised at Dapoorie from Europe seed.

XXV.—OXALIDEÆ, DC. *Prod.* 1, p 689.

AVERHOA, Decandria Pentagynia.

1. A Carambola, W. and A. 464; Rumph. Amb. 1, *t.* 35; Rheede Mal. 3, *t.* 43 and 44.—"Kurmul." A common tree in Coast gardens, with close, thick-set, drooping branches; flowers lateral, on short racemes, white and purple variegated; fruit acutely angled.

2. A Bilimbi, W. and A. 465; Rheede Mal. 3, *t.* 45 and 46; Rumph. Amb. 1, *t.* 36.—"Dakta Anvula," Maratha, Small tree; fruit oblong, obtusely angled; grows on the trunk and branches. These trees take their name from *Averhoes*, an Arabian physician of Cordova. They are believed to be natives of the Eastern Islands. The acid they afford is used to clean silver and take spots out of linen; the fruit is sold in the bazar for preserves.

MELIANTHUS, Tetrandria Monogynia. Honey Flower. From *mel*, honey; *anthos*, flower.

3. M Comosa, Linn. sp. 892.—Shrub; native of the Cape; leaves villous, downy beneath; flowers alternate, in pendent clusters, yellowish; seed received from the Cape through the late Dr. Wallich. Fort Sewnere. M major, received at the same time, has since died off.

4. Oxalis.—A small annual, from English seed; common as a pot plant; flower small, white.

XXVI.—RUTACEÆ, DC. *Prod.* 1, p 709.

RUTA, Octandria Monogynia.

1. R. GRAVEOLENS, DC. *Prod.* 1, p 710; Ainslie Mat. Ind. i, p 351.—Rue; "Suntap," Maratha. Southern Europe; is now extensively cultivated below the Ghauts, being much used by the Concan people as a fumigation in infantile Cattarh. The Mussalman Weyds use it in Dyspepsia.

CYMINOSMA, Octandria Monogynia.

2. C PEDUNCULATA, Rheed. Mal. 5, *t.* 4 and 15; Vahl. Symb. *t.* 61.—An ornamental shrub, with shining entire leaves, and whitish-yellow flowers, fragrant; garden at Hewra. We have failed to find this tree in the Southern Concan. The present specimen is believed to have been received from the Royal Garden, Kew.

XXVII.—OCHNACEÆ, DC. *Prod.* 1, p 735.

LVIII.—OCHNA, Polyandria Monogynia.

1. O SQUARROSA, Roxb. Cor. *t.* 89; Fl. 2, 643.—A tree with oblong shining leaves, slightly serrated; flowers numerous, yellow, growing from the branches below the leaves; capsules several, placed in a circle round the base of the style. Parell Road, from Calcutta seed (?); also garden at Hewra. Respecting Gomphia, as given in the 1st edition of the book, we solicit information, as we have never been able to hear of it as existing in the Southern Concan.

XXVIII.—PITTOSPOREÆ, DC. *Prod.* 1, p 345.

PITTOSPORUM, Pentandria Monogynia. From *pitti,* resin; and *sporos,* seed; in allusion to the resinous pulp which surrounds the seed.

1. P SALICIFOLIUM. (?) P Tenuifolium of Don's *syst.* 2, p 374.—Native of Australia; gardens Dapoorie and Hewra; has not yet flowered with us; leaves long, willow-like, drooping; raised from Australian seed.

2. P FERRUGINEUM, Aiton Hort. Kew, 2nd ed, vol. 2, p 27.—Native of Africa; leaves elliptical, acuminated at both ends. Garden at Dapoorie; raised from seed furnished by the late Lord Elphinstone; has not yet flowered.

3. P TOBIRA, Sim's Bot. Mag. 1396.—A shrub, having obovate smooth shining leaves; garden at Dapoorie. As the shrub has not flowered, the name is given doubtfully, rather from a resemblance to the same tree as seen by us at Athens and Malta than from any certain marks.

XXIX.—RHAMNEÆ, DC. *Prod.* 2, p 19.

ZIZIPHUS, Pentandria Monogynia. From *zizouf*, a native of the Egyptian Lotus Tree. Gaert. *t.* 43; Lam. *t.* 185.

1. Z VULGARIS, Lam. Illust. 185, p. 1; Don's *syst.* 1, p 23.—"Bherber," Marathi, cultivated "Bher." Native of Arabia and Persia; has a fine-flavoured, long fruit; it is a favourite tree in Sind and in the Eastern Deccan, as Teesgaum, &c. From experiments made at Hewra, there seems reason to think that this cultivated species(?) degenerates into the common Bher of India.

2. Z BONARIENSIS.—Native of Buenos Ayres. Living plant received from Messrs. Loddiges through Colonel Jervis in 1841. A very distinct species, having thick branchlets angularly bent; leaves broad lanceolate, serrate, 3-nerved; flower as in the family; fruit red, round, size of a large pea, produces fertile seeds, from which many plants have been raised.

3. Z LOTUS, Lam. Dict. 3, p 317.—Native of Egypt. Low-growing shrub, having ovate, oblong, obtusely crenated, smooth leaves, and twin prickles, one recurved, the other straight. We had plants of this shrub at Dapoorie and Hewra, and it is believed it may be found in the Civil Engineer's ravelin in the fort of Bombay. It has not, to the best of our knowledge, fruited in Western India.

HOVENIA, Thunb., Pentandria Monogynia. From *Hoven*, a Dutch resident in Japan.

4. H DULCIS, Roxb. Fl. 1, p 630; Bot. Mag. *t* 2360.—A Chinese fruit tree, said to have been introduced by the late Mr. Nimmo in 1833. We cannot find any trace of this tree. Information as to its existence or otherwise in Bombay is desiderated.

XXX.—TEREBINTHACEÆ, Juss.

ANACARDIUM, Polygamia Diœcia. From *ana*, above; *kardia*, the heart; the heart-shaped Nut, contrary to the usual practice of nature, is borne on the outside of the fruit. Lam. *t.* 332; Gaert. *t.* 40.

1. A OCCIDENTALE, W. and A. 522; Roxb. Fl. 2, p 312; Rheed. Mal. 3, *t* 54.—"Hijulee-badam" or Cashew-nut. Native of Brazil; now common in Goa and the Warree Country, also in Southern Concan and Salsette. Is now quite naturalised, and affords rather a valuable resource as food. According to Garcias ab Horto, it was first planted at Santa Cruz (?) in Malabar, where only three trees existed in his time. The nuts are eaten roasted. A transparent gum exudes from incisions in the wood. The wood is much used in France for fine cabinet-work, under the name of Bois d'Acajou,

which name is also applied to Mahogany and some other trees, (*vide* Dictionaire de'l' Academie sub-verbo.)

RHUS, Pentandria Trigynia. From *ross*, red; in allusion to the colour of the leaves and fruit of some of the species. Lam. *t.* 207; Gaert. *t.* 44.

2. R PARVIFLORA, Roxb. Illust. Beng. p. 22.—Leaflets obovate crenate-toothed, velvetty; has not yet flowered with us; raised from Calcutta seed at Hewra and Dapoorie.

SPONDIAS, Decandria Pentagynia. Greek name for a *plumb*, which the fruit resembles. Lam. *t.* 384; Gaert. *t.* 104.

3. S MANGIFERA, W. and A. 553; Roxb. 2, p 451; Rheed. Mal. 1, *t.* 50; Rumph. Amb. 1, *t.* 61.—Is not uncommon in gardens; fruit like a small mango, indifferent in flavour. The tree has pinnate deciduous leaves, having a peculiar smell when bruized.

SCHINUS, Diœcia Decandria. From the Greek name for *mastich*, in allusion to the white resinous juice which exudes from the tree. Linn. Gen. No. 1130; Lam. Illust. *t.* 822.

4. S MULLI,—Linn. Gen. No. 1130; Miller Ic. *t.* 246; DC. *Prod.* 1, p 274.—Native of South America, where it is called Pepper tree; thrives well in India, and ripens fruit; many large trees in Hewra garden; leaves pinnate; leaflets linear; flowers small, white; berry size of a grain of pepper, rich pink colour, hanging in drooping racemes; the leaves and tender shoots have a pleasant aromatic flavour. The white aromatic gum which exudes from the tree is used in Peru for strengthening the gums. A vinous liquor is made from the fruit in Chili. The seed of this tree was received from Naples through the late Dr. C. Lush; it is now common in Southern Italy and Greece as an ornament to the public walks.

AMYRIS, Roxb., Octandria Monogynia. *A* and *myrrh*, as the juice of the tree has a strong aromatic odour.

5. A HEPTAPHYLLA, Roxb. Fl. 2, 248. "Karunphul."—A shrub with alternate pinnate leaves, and small yellowish flowers in terminal panicles; said to be found in Mr. Baxter's garden, Tardeo (?) Does it still exist there, or elsewhere in Bombay?

BALSAMODENDRON, Diœcia Octandria. From *balsamon*, balsam; and *dendron*, a tree. One of the species produces the Balsam of Mecca, DC. *Prod.* 2, p 76.

6. B MYRRHA.—Myrrh tree; native of Arabia; thorny, ternate, small serrate leaflets; garden at Dapoorie; is stunted in growth, and will probably never flower with us. A specimen was received from Aden through the late Captain Haines.

7. B ROXBURGHII, Syn. Amyris Commiphora; Roxb. Fl. Ind. 2, p 244.—A small tree, native of Berar and Kandeish; crooked; bark like the Birch, peeling off and leaving a green surface below;

branchlets generally spinous; leaves small, alternate ovate-serrate, having a smaller pair at the insertion of the petiole; flowers small, red, appearing in April. The whole plant aromatic, abounding in a viscid balsamic juice, which is exported in considerable quantities from Oomrawuttee. We have met one tree in the jungle between Salheir and Abhowna in Kandeish, no doubt others exist there. It is also found forming the enclosure of a temple at Pait, north of Poona, but evidently imported. Gardens at Hewra and Dapoorie. It does not bear fruit with us.

ICICA, Octodecandria Monogynia. *Icica* is the name of one of the species in Guiana. Aublet Guiana 1, p 337.

8. I INDICA, Juss. Gen. 370; DC. *Prod.* 2, p 77.—We accept the specific name of this, as received from Calcutta, with a doubt; leaves ternate, terminal one larger. This family belongs to South America; ornamental and useful trees, celebrated for their aromatic virtues. Gardens at Dapoorie and Hewra.

XXXI.—LEGUMINOSÆ, DC. *Prod.* 2, p 93.

SOPHORA, Linn., Decandria Monogynia. Said to be from the Arabic *sophero*. Lam. *t.* 325; Gaert. 2, *t.* 149.

1. S TOMENTOSA, W. and A. 548; Roxb. Fl. 2, p 316; Rumph. Amb. 4, *t.* 22.—A shrub, native of Brazil; pinnate leaves; yellow flowers in terminal racemes; necklace-shaped pod, each bead-like knot contains one seed. In gardens.

2. S JAPONICA, Linn. Maut. 68.—Native of Japan; shrub with pinnæ of 11 to 13 pair of leaflets, delicate, glabrous; raised from seed received from Professor Savi of Pisa; as yet has not flowered with us. Garden at Hewra.

VIRGILIA, Lam., Decandria Monogynia.

3. V AUREA, W. and A. 549; Lam. *t.* 326, fig. 1.—Native of Abyssinia; a small shrub with leaves impari-pinnate, ovate leaflets; 5-cleft calyx; petals equal; vexillum flat, as is also legume; flowers bright yellow. Garden at Hewra, from Calcutta seed.

4. V CAPENSIS FLORE ROSEO.—Of this we have met with no trace at Dapoorie.

5. V FLORÆ RUBIGINOSO VIOLACEO, Don's *syst.* 2, 112 (?).—In gardens at Sewree and Bombay, not in the Deccan; handsome blue flowers.

SPARTIUM, Monadelphia Decandria. From *sparton*, cordage, in allusion to the uses of the plants.

6. S JUNCEUM, DC. *Prod.* p 145.—Spanish Broom; native of Southern Europe. In Lanquedoc thread is made from the bark; the tops are a powerful diuretic. In gardens; not common. The leaves and stem afford a yellow dye.

MEDICAGO, Diadelphia Decandria, Gaert. *t.* 155 ; Lam. *t.* 612.

7. M SATIVA, DC. *Prod.* 2, 173 ; Eng. Bot. *t.* 1749.—Lucerne Grass ; now much cultivated in India for the food of horses ; it is not cultivated by natives for their cattle.

TRIGONELLA, Diadelphia Decandria. From *treis,* three ; and *gonos,* an angle ; in allusion to the shape of the flowers. Gaert. *t.* 152 ; Lam. *t.* 611.

8. T FENUGRECUM, W. and A. 610 ; Woodville Med. Bot. *t.* 158.—"Maitee-ke-Baji." Native of Southern Europe and Asia (?) ; is extensively cultivated in Indian gardens as a vegetable. The seeds form the base of a medicinal confection (Luddoo) extensively used by the natives. They also enter into the composition of an imitation of Carmine. The yellow decoction, used with Sulphate of Copper, produces a fine permanent green.

MELILOTUS, Tourn., Diadelphia Decandria. From *mellotus,* honey lotus, bees being fond of the flowers. Lam. *t.* 613 ; Tourn. *t.* 229.

9. M LEUCANTHA, W. and A. 612 ; Lam. *t.* 613 ; Tourn. *t.* 29.—White-flowered Melilot ; native of Europe (?) ; is found near the streams in garden-lands in India ; Islands of the Krushna, near Nalutwar, Mr. Law ; has a delicate fragrance.

10. M PARVIFLORA, W. and A. 613.—Annual, on pasture grounds, &c. ; appears in the cold season.

CYAMOPSIS, DC., Diadelphia Decandria.

11. C PSORALOIDES.—"Gouree." Cultivated as a vegetable ; has trifoliate leaves, and erect blue flowers.

INDIGOFERA, Diadelphia Decandria, Linn. Gen. 889 ; Lam. Illust. 626. Name derived from a corruption of *Indicum* and *fero,* to bring.

12. ATROPURPUREA, Hamilton in Horn. Hort. Africanus Add, 152.—A large shrub, having pinnate leaves ; 5 to 7 to 10 pair of oval mucronulate leaflets ; younger leaves pubescent, older glabrous ; flowers in axillary racemes, somewhat cernuous, large, dark-purple ; the plant is a native of Nepal. Gardens at Hewra and Dapoorie.

SESBANIA, Pers., Diadelphia Decandria. From *Sesban,* the Arabic name.

13. S ÆGYPTIACA, Æschynomene Sesban, Roxb. Flor. p 332 ; Rheed. Mal. 6, *t.* 27 ; Wight Ic. p. 2, *t.* 32.—Native of Arabia ; a small tree of very quick growth ; "Sewrie," Maratha ; flowers dark-purple, with yellow spots, in axillary pendulous racemes ; it is extensively cultivated in the plain parts of the Deccan as a substitute for the Bamboo for rafters. There is a Sind variety, with flowers much brighter and varied. The wood is said to afford the best charcoal for gunpowder.

AGATI, Adans, Diadelphia Decandria. The Native name adopted.

14. A GRANDIFLORA; Æschynomene Grandiflora.—" Augusta." Native of Eastern Islands; ornamental from its large white and red flowers; often seen as a hedge round native gardens. The leaves and tender pods are used in curries.

LOUREA, Neck., Diadelphia Decandria.

15. L VESPERTILIONIS; Hedysarum vespertilionis.—Native of Eastern Bengal (?); Bat-winged Lourea; seen occasionally in gardens.

CICER, Tourn., Diadelphia Decandria. The Roman family *Cicero* probably derived their name from it. Gaert. *t.* 121; Lam. *t.* 632.

16. C ARIETINUM, W. and A. 723.—" Hurbura," Maratha; " Chunna, " Hindoostanee. Native of Egypt; is now cultivated most extensively in India. The white variety has been introduced from Egypt or Eastern Italy. It is a more robust and productive plant than the others; but under an Indian sun, and in an Indian soil, it will gradually merge into the common species.

ERVUM, Linn., Diadelphia Decandria. Said to be derived from a Celtic word signifying *tilled land.*

17. E LENS, Cicer Lens, W. and A. 724; Roxb. Fl. 3, p 324; " Musoor," Maratha. Originally from Syria; is now extensively grown in the Ghaut and other districts; it affords a reddish grain. This, powdered along with Jowaree flour, forms the much-vaunted Revalanta Arabica Food.

PISUM, Diadelphia Decandria. From the Celtic for a *pea.*

18. P SATIVUM, DC. *Prod.* 2, 368.—Cultivated in Deccan gardens during the rains, and in Guzerat, Bombay, &c. in the cold season; the field variety is a smaller plant with a purple flower, and smaller and less succulent than that of the garden species; it is a common rotation Rubbee crop in the Deccan and Guzerat. The garden variety is now a common article of native cultivation for sale at European stations.

LATHYRUS, Diadelphia Decandria. From *Lathouros,* impetuous, in reference to the exciting quality of the seeds.

19. L SATIVUS, Don's *syst.* 2, p 355; Bot. Mag. *t* 115.—Chickling Vetch; " Lang, " Gujarati. A native of France, Italy, and Spain; it is commonly cultivated in Gujarat; the grain has an exciting property.

PHASEOLUS, Linn., Diadelphia Decandria. From *phaselus,* a little boat, in allusion to the shape of the corolla, Lam. *t.* 610; Gaert. *t.* 150.

20. P VULGARIS.—French Bean. Very commonly cultivated in many varieties; said to be a native of India, but who has seen it wild?

21. P Caracalla, DC. *Prod.* 2, p 390; Bot. Rep. *t.* 341.—The Snail plant. Native of South America; introduced by the Portuguese. Flowers large, purple and yellow. It is called "Caracalla," by reason of its hooded flower.

22. P Mungo, Roxb. Fl. 3, p 292. "Ooreed," "Moong." Cultivated extensively. It is the earliest crop of the season.

23. P Rostratus, W. and A. 750; Roxb. Fl. 3, p 287.—"Hullounda," "Hullowla." Much cultivated, being sown along with Bajri, and left to ripen afterwards; the flower is small. This appears a different plant to that noted in No. 397 of the 1st edition.

SOJA, Diadelphia Decandria. Name from the Chinese sauce *Soy*, prepared from the seeds.

24. S Hispida, W. and A. 762; Roxb. Fl. 3, p 314.—An annual, hairy plant; flowers small, of a reddish purple; this we have failed to find in gardens. Information is solicited.

25. P Aconitifolius, Roxb. Fl. 3, 299.—"Mut." Commonly cultivated with Bajri; good for horses.

DOLICHOS, Linn., Diadelphia Decandria.

26. D Uniflorus, W. and A. 766; Pluk *t.* 213, *fig.* 4.—"Kooltee." Commonly cultivated as food. When a spur or ergot grows on the seed, it is often very deleterious.

27. D Sinensis, W. and A. 771; Rumph Amb. 5, *t* 134.—"Chowlie." Of this there are two varieties, one white-seeded, one black. The seed is much used by the Parsees, who even import it from China.

JOHNIA CONJESTA, Dalz., D uniflorus; W and A. 766; Pluk. *t* 213, *fig.* 6; D biflorus, Roxb. Fl. 3, p 313.—"Kooltee." A grain commonly cultivated in the Deccan and Carnatic, especially in the latter; softened by boiling, it is given as a food for horses.

LABLAB, W. and A., Diadelphia Decandria.

28. L Vulgaris, W. and A. 772; Roxb. Fl. 3, p 305; Rumph. Amb. 5, *t* 136, 137, 141.—"Pauti." A bean much cultivated during the cold season, especially in the sloping lands on rivers.

PSOPHOCARPUS, Neck., Diadelphia Decandria.

29. P Tetragonolobus, W. and A. 776; Roxb. Fl. 3, p 105. "Chowdaree," Maratha; *Chevaux-de-Frize* Bean, so named from the pods having four membranous jagged wings; it is much cultivated at the Mauritius, *Pois Carrè*. It is not a delicate vegetable.

CANAVALLIA, W. and A., Diadelphia Decandria. *Canavali* is the name of one species in Malabar.

30. C Gladiata.—Patagonian Bean; commonly cultivated. There are varieties with red and white flowers; legume a foot long.

CAJANUS, Diadelphia Decandria. Amboina name *Catjang*. Lam. *t.* 618.

31. C Indicus, W. and A. 789; Roxb. Fl 3, p 325.—"Toor." Native of America and Asia (?); much cultivated, both in Gujarat and the Deccan; sown in rows amongst Bajri. Near Mhar, and in other alluvial limits of the Concan, as also in the hilly districts, it is sown by itself, when it reaches a much larger size, rising to the height of 5 and 6 feet. The Dall stalk is used as a charcoal for gunpowder in the Government works. It also affords a choice material for baskets, grain-bins, &c.

32. Lotus Jacobeus.—Very narrow-linear leaves; dark-brown flowers.

CLITORIA, Linn., Diadelphia Decandria, Gaert. *t.* 149; Lam. *t.* 609.

33. C Virginiana, C. Mexicana (?) or Mariana, Don's *syst.* 2, p 215.—To which of these species this small plant, introduced from Calcutta seed at Dapoorie, may belong, remains to be seen; it has not flowered. The ovate lanceolate leaves would seem to mark it as E Mariana.

ERYTHRINA, Linn., Diadelphia Decandria. From *erythros*, red; the flowers are of a very brilliant red, and hence the name.

34. E Superba.—Eastern Bengal (?) A low tree with the habit of the family; flowers large, very ornamental. Garden at Dapoorie; raised from Calcutta seed.

DALBERGIA, Linn., From *Dalbergh*, a Swedish botanist.

35. D Sissoo, Roxb. Fl 3, p 223; Wight and Arnott 813.—"Seesoo." Native of North-Western India. This, the real D Seesoo, and differing considerably, as in the pointed leaf, &c. from our "Sissoo" (D Latifolia), has been introduced into Southern India with success. It is of rapid growth, and the timber, though possibly inferior to that of D Latifolia, is nevertheless excellent for beams, wheels, and all agricultural purposes. The Esplanade at Mangalore is now bordered by young trees of this species.

36. D Robusta, Roxb. Hort. Beng. p 53; Don's *syst.* 2, 375. —Native of Lylhet. This tree has been raised at Dapoorie and Hewra from Seharunpore seed. A tall tree, with pinnate leaves; leaflets 13 to 21, ovate-mucronate; flowers small; legume small, leafy, marginated. With us it hardly merits the name Robusta, as it is smaller in size, and of slower growth than most of our indigenous species. Syn. Brachypterum robustum. This will be found noticed in our No. 1, p 77. The tree is not a native of Western India.

37. D Melanoxylon.—Native of Abyssinia. This species was raised from seed furnished by the late Nimmo, under the name "Sennaar Ebony." It is a small tree, with long diverging branch-

lets, pinnate leaves; leaflets obovate; bark white; flowers small, white; legume 1 to 2-seeded, leafy. Heart wood of the older stem a deep black. Gardens at Hewra and Dapoorie.

ROBINIA, Diadelphia Decandria. Named in honour of *Robin*, Herbalist to Henry IV. of France.

38. R CANDIDA.—Eastern Bengal. A shrub, having narrow-lanceolate leaflets, and drooping racemes of white flowers; raised from seed received from Calcutta. Garden at Hewra.

TEPHROSIA, Pers., Diadelphia Decandria.

39. T CANDIDA, T Anœna (?).—A shrubby plant with narrow tomentose leaves, and showy spikes of white flowers; seed received from Calcutta. Garden at Hewra.

MIMOSA, W. and A., Polygamia Monœcia. From *mimos*, a mimic, in allusion to the sensitive leaves.

40. M PUDICA, Roxb. Fl. 2, p 564.—"Lajaloo," Maratha. Sensitive plant; native of Brazil; now common in Indian gardens; root is said to be emetic.

INGA, Polygamia Monœcia. The South American name of one of the species.

41. I DULCIS, Roxb. Fl. 2, p 556; Roxb. Cor. *t*. 99.—Native of Eastern Islands. "Wilayutee Chintz," Maratha. A large and handsome tree with drooping branches, armed with short, straight thorns; pods curiously twisted, the seeds being imbedded in a sweet, firm, white pulp, of which parrots are very fond; gardens Bombay, Deccan, &c.

42. I BIGEMINA, Rheede Mal. 6, *t*. 12; Mimosa lucida.—Raised at Hewra from Bengal seed. We have not seen the tree in the Concan. A second species, received under the same name from Calcutta, shows linear leaflets, like Schotia, and is quite different from I bigemina at first received; as it has not flowered, it must be kept in view. Garden at Hewra.

43. I HÆMATOXYLON.—A small tree, raised from Calcutta seed; leaves pinnate, 12 to 15 pair, oblique; leaflets blunt, finally mucronate. Gardens at Dapoorie, Parell, and Sewree. This promises to be a very ornamental small tree.

PARKIA, Monadelphia Decandria. Named after *Mungo Park*, the celebrated traveller.

44. P BIGLANDULOSA, W. and A. 865.—"Chendoophul." Native of Africa; a very elegant tree, with drooping pinnated leaves; the flower-buds, dependent from long peduncles, are like balls of fawn-coloured velvet. Occasionally found in gardens, as at Kurmulla, Belgaum, &c. The numerous trees raised at Dapoorie and Hewra from Calcutta seed, marked P brunonis, do not appear to differ from this our older species.

ADENANTHERA, Decandria Monogynia. From *aden*, a gland; and *anther*. The anthers are tipped with deciduous glands.

45. A Pavonina, W. and A. 839; Roxb. Fl. 2, p 370; Rheede Mal. 6, *t.* 14; Rumph. Amb. 3, *t.* 109.—"Thorla Goonj," Maratha. Native of Southern India; common in gardens in Bombay and elsewhere; the wood is dark-red, like that of Plerocarpus santalinus. The large scarlet seeds are used as weights, and are worn as necklaces.

VACHELLIA, W. and A., Polygamia Monœcia. Named from the *Rev. G. H. Vachell*, residing in China.

46. V Farnesiana, W. and A. 841; Pluk. *t.* 73, *f.* 1; Roxb. Fl. 2, p 557.—"Eree Babool." A native of Southern Europe; shrub with bipinnate leaves and turgid legumes, now very common on the black soil nullas, &c. of the Deccan; flowers deep yellow, fragrant. In America it is indigenous, from New Orleans to Chili; some say it is also a native of Nubia.

ACACIA, W. and A., Polygamia Monœcia. From *akadzo*, to sharpen, in allusion to many of the species being armed with thorns.

47. A Leucocephala, A Glauca (?), Spr. *syst.* 3, p 139.—Found in every garden and a great pest, as, owing to its spreading roots, it is difficult to eradicate.

48. A Julibisrin, Forsk. Disc. 777; Lam. Dict. 7, p. 13.—Native of Levant; seeds received from Professor Savi, of Pisa; a tall unarmed shrub, having pinnæ of rather large leaflets; it has not flowered. Garden at Hewra.

49. A Longifolia.—Native of Australia; gardens at Hewra and Dapoorie, from seed imported by the late Dr. Griffith; has occasionally flowered and borne fruit here. This is the Wattle tree of Australia.

50. A —— (?).—Raised from Brazil seed; a fine arboreous species; very tall, unarmed; it is a very ornamental tree, and promises to be a valuable addition to our Indian timbers.

51. A Lenticularia.—Native of North-Western India; pinnate leaves; 10 to 15 pair of leaflets, rather blunt; inflorescence as in A catechu; spines binate, minute, strong, at base of petioles.

ENTADA, Polygamia Monœcia. The Malabar name, DC. Mem. Leg. 12.

52. E Madagascarensis.—Of this we can only say that it has been raised from Calcutta seed; that it appears to be scandent in habit; and that the leaflets are small-linear, as in Acacia intsia, &c.

ARACHIS, Diadelphia Decandria. Name from the fruit being produced under-ground.

53. A Hypogea, Roxb. Fl. 3, p 280.—" Bhooee-Moong," Ground-Nut. Originally a native of Africa; is now cultivated extensively in different parts of India and China as a food, and for the extraction of oil, which, in taste, is nearly equal to the Olive. Both the nut and the oil are extensively exported from India, the latter chiefly for the adulteration of Olive-oil. The nut is a favourite food on the fast-days of the Hindoos; the oil-cake is excellent for cattle. The oil contains but little stearine, therefore does not readily become rancid, and from the same cause it is well adapted for using in fine machinery, as Watches, &c.

GLEDITSHIA, DC, Decandria Monogynia. Named from *Gleditch*, a Berlin Professor.

54. G Triacanthos, Linn. sp. 1509.—Honey Locust. Tree of the Rocky Mountains; a rather tall tree with pinnate leaves, blunt, oblique leaflets, and long tri-compound robust thorns. Gardens at Dapoorie and Hewra; has occasionally seeded.

55. G Sinensis, Lam. Dict. 2, p 465.—Leaves ovate, elliptic-obtuse; spines simple. A much less robust tree than the last. Gardens at Dapoorie and Hewra.

CÆSALPINIA, Diadelphia Decandria. Named from *Cæsalpinus*, Physician to Pope Clement VIII. Lam. *t.* 335; Gaert. *t.* 144.

56. C Coriaria.—Libi-Dibi. Native of South America. A spreading, umbrageous tree, not high; leaflets minute; legumes very numerous, variously contorted; has been raised extensively at Hewra and Dapoorie from seed received through the late Dr. Wallich. This tree is likely to be of great importance, on account of the excellent tanning material which it affords.

57. C Tortuosa, Roxb. Hort. Bengal p 32.—As this has not yet reached any size, we note it here merely that it may be kept in view. The leaflets are nearly as minute as those of C mimosoides. Garden at Hewra.

58. C Sappan, Linn. sp. 544—We merely notice this as a variety received from Brazil per Steamer *Ajduha*. It seems different from our indigenous C sappan, from the darker colour of the bark, and less robust habit of the tree. It has been in the Hewra garden for 13 years, but has never yet flowered.

POINCIANA, Decandria Monogynia. Named from *Poincè*, once Governor of the Antilles.

59. P Pulcherrima, Linn. sp. 554.—" Goolmohr." Originally a native of Arabia and India; said to have emigrated westward to America and the West Indies. Common in all gardens, but never found in the forests; several subvarieties.

60. P Regia.—Royal Goolmohr. Introduced from the Mauritius; is now becoming rapidly naturalised, and is very ornamental.

61. P Gillesii, Hook. Bot. Misc. 1, p 129, *t.* 34; Don's *syst.* 2, p 433.—Native of Chili, near Mendosa. A smaller species, with sulphur-coloured flowers, and showy, long, red stamens, said by the common people of Chili to be injurious to the eyes, hence the name *Mul-de-Ozers*. We have not seen this beautiful species in other gardens than Hewra and Dapoorie.

62. P Elata, Linn. sp. 554; Swartz. Obs. 166.—This we hold to have migrated from Abyssinia; it is a large tree species, having white flowers, finally changing into yellow, and long, dark-purple filaments; leaflets inferiorly tomentose; it is chiefly found at Beejapore, and other places formerly the centre of Mussulman dominions. Gardens at Dapoorie and Hewra.

PARKINSONIA, Decandria Monogynia.

63. P Aculeata, DC. *Prod.* 2, p 485; Linn. Gen. 513.—Native of America and the West Indies; is now common everywhere in India in waste places, borders of fields, &c., but is never found in forests.

HÆMATOXYLON, Decandria Monogynia.

64. H Campechianum, Lam. Illustr. *t.* 340; DC. *Prod.* 2, p 485.—Logwood tree; native of Campeachy and Honduras, in Spanish America; has been reared with us from Calcutta seed; leaves abruptly pinnate; leaflets obovate; thick spikes of yellow flowers and small indehiscent leafy legume, containing 1 seed; makes an excellent hedge. The dye from the wood and bark is afforded in great abundance. As a medicinal tree for use in chronic bowel-complaints, chiefly in the form of extract, its virtues are well known. Attempts have been made to propagate this tree in the Concan, but as yet unsuccessfully.

65. Ceratonia Siliqua, Polygamia Decæcia. Lam. Illustr. *t.* 859; Linn. Gen. 1167.—Native of Levant. Carob tree; St. John's Bread; a stout tree, having the flowers thickly spread on the branches; leaflets oval or obovate, coriaceous; legume large, dark-red, woody, filled with a sweet pulp, which is used in Spain as a food, and also for fattening horses and cattle. It is believed that it is now imported into England for this purpose. Gardens at Hewra and Dapoorie.

TAMARINDUS, Monadelphia Enneandria.

66. T Occidentalis, Gaert. Fr. 2, p 310, *t.* 146.—West-Indian or Red Tamarind; differs from our indigenous species, chiefly in the shorter legumes and purple stamens of the flowers; is common at Ahmedabad, and found in other places where the Mussulman power has been, but not seen elsewhere. A pleasant sherbet is made from the juice, and the pulp is often preserved. Gardens at Hewra and Dapoorie, from seed sent by Captain Giberne, 16th Regiment Native Infantry.

CASSIA, Decandria Monogynia.

67. C LANCEOLATA, W. and A. 892; Lam. Illustr. *t.* 322, *fig.* 2.—Officinal Senna, "Sona Mukhee." Described as being indigenous in Gujarat, about Dholka. We doubt the accuracy of this observation. It certainly, however, grows wild in Sind. The narrow-lanceolate leaves, and peculiar broad falcate legume, at once distinguish it from our other Cassias, of which A obovata is the only one having a similar legume. Introduced at Hewra from seed furnished by Captain Haines from Aden; is now largely cultivated by ryots near the Hewra garden, from whence it is supplied to the Medical Stores, quite free from all admixture of other leaves.

68. C JAVANICA, Spr. *syst.* 2, p 333; Rheede Mal. 1, *t.* 22.—Java Cassia. A beautiful tree, having thick clusters of pale-lilac flowers; leaflets blunt, tomentose. Gardens at Dapoorie and Hewra.

69. C SUMATRANA, W. and A. 893; C florida, Roxb. Fl. 2, p 347.—"Kassod," Maratha. A handsome, robust tree, with large clusters of yellow flowers. It is very umbrageous, and the wood is strong and tough. This tree is well worthy of extensive propagation. Hewra, Dapoorie, Dharwar, &c.

70. C GRANDIS.—The tree raised from Calcutta seed under this name is a 10 feet shrub having a scandent tendency; leaves pinnate, on a long sulcated petiole swelled at insertion; leaflets opposite, blunt-ovate, not seen with a mucro; bractes of the common peduncle large, ear-shaped, stem-embracing; calyx 4 to 5 divided, having erect hyaline sepals; petals 5, equal, abortive; anthers from 3 to 4; legume half inch broad, containing 4 to 5 seeds, somewhat woody. Why it should have been called C grandis we are at a loss to discover!

71. C ALATA, W. and A. 890; Senna alata, Roxb. Fl. 2, p 349; Rumph. Amb. 7, *t.* 18; C herpetica.—A stunted shrub; with pinnate leaves, 7 to 10; leaflets large, rounded; legume ovate. In gardens. It does not appear to flourish on this side of India.

72. C BICAPSULARIS, W. and A. 888; Senna bicapsularis, Roxb. Fl. 2, p 342; Don's *syst.* 2, p 440.—A shrub, common in gardens; has flowers of a vivid yellow; may always be recognised by its roundish-curved legume, having a double row of seeds.

73. C HIRSUTA.—Received under this name from the late Mr. Nimmo; shrubby, 3 feet; stem quadrangular, sulcated hirsute; leaves impari-pinnated, 4 to 5 pair; leaflets opposite, in short petioles, 4 to 5 pair, all hirsute, broad-lanceolate entire, no glands; bractes double, awl-shaped, concave; peduncles from leaf axils, longer than the leaves, also terminal in a panicle; corolla patent, having 5 equal petals, and 3 abortive anthers; calycine leaves small, 3 in

number; legume much as in Cassia tora, 4 inches long, hirsute compressed; no corina. Garden at Hewra; has now run wild.

74. C —— (?).—Another shrubby species; stem covered with very long hairs; 8 to 10 pair of impari-pinnate ovate leaflets; an erect gland on the common petiole below the insertion of the first pair of leaflets; stem quadrangular sulcated; has not produced seed; springs up annually. Hewra.

75. C Glauca, Roxb. Fl. 2, p 345; Senna arborescens, Rheede Mal. 6, *t.* 9 and 10.—A tree common in gardens; flowers very numerous, in axillary racemes; bark of the root said to be diuretic.

76. Cynometra Cauliflora, W. and A. 906; Rumph. Amb. 1, *t.* 62.—A small tree with conjugate leaves and reddish flowers, growing in clusters from the trunk; legume thick, half orbicular; the tree is a native of the Eastern Islands. In gardens, Bombay (?). We have seen it at Randal Lodge only.

HYMENEA, Decandria Monogynia.

77. H Courbaril, DC. *Prod.* 2, p 511; Don's *syst.* 2, p 458.—Gum Animi tree; is at once recognisable by its divided leaf, having two broad ovate lobes. Gardens at Hewra, Dapoorie, from Calcutta. It is a native of Malabar.

78. Macrolobium Bijugum, Don's *syst.* 2, p 457; DC. *Prod.* 2, p 511; Colebrooke Linn. *t.* 12, p 359.—Native of Eastern Bengal. Outea bijuga. Hewra garden, from Calcutta seed.

79. Schotia Speciosa, Decandria Monogynia.—Native of the Cape; a straggling small tree with pinnate leaves, 10 to 15 pair, shining; leaflets small; flowers off from the branches, on short peduncles, of a bright-red and peculiar form. Garden Hewra.

BAUHINIA, Decandria Monogynia.

80. B Purpurea, W. and A. 915; Roxb. Fl. 2, 320; B triandria, Rheed. Mal. 1, *t.* 33.—Dewa-Kunchun. A tree with flowers of a deep rose-colour; native of India, but found only in gardens.

81. B Variegata, W. and A. 913; Roxb. Fl. 2, p 318; Rheed. Mal. 1, *t.* 32.—The flowers of this variety are of a deeper purple, streaked with white.

82. B Candida.—Native of Java. "Duola-Kunchun." This species is very distinct from the two last, having smooth sepals ending in a long taper point. In gardens.

83. B Richardiana, DC. *Prod.* 2, p 517; Don's *syst.* 2, p 463.—Leaves cordate, 5 to 7-nerved, acute, smooth; flowers beautifully maculated with red on a white ground; small tree. Native of Guiana.

84. B Acuminata, W. and A. 910; Roxb. Fl. 2, p 324; Rheede Mal. 1, *t.* 34.—A shrub, 8 feet high, with acuminate lobes of the demi-bifid leaves, and flowers white, fragrant.

85. B Tomentosa, W. and A. 911; Roxb. Fl. 2, p 323; Pluk. *t*. 34, p 6; Rheed. Mal. *t*. 35.—Petals pale-yellow, with a deep purple spot at the claw. Native of Malabar.

86. B Venusta.—The shrub produced from the Calcutta seed marked with this name, differs in no respect from the last, except in the want of the purple spot on the claw of the petals; both are very ornamental. Gardens at Hewra.

87. B Corymbosa, Roxb. Hort. Bengal 31; Burm. Fl. Ind. 94.—A very extensive climber, with beautiful large, white flowers. Our plant differs from that of Don 2, p 461, in having the leaflets cleft to the base. It gradually bears down the highest trees in its ascending course.

88. B (?) Abyssinicæ Affinis.—We have not been able to fix the species with certainty. An immense climber, with compressed, woody, furrowed stems, and terminal racemes of flowers small, whitish-yellow; laciniæ having crisped edges; stamens 3, length of laciniæ; calyx 3-divided, one division always revolute; peduncular bracts narrow-lanceolate, erect, persistent; length of laciniæ of petals three-fourths of an inch; legume 8 inches in length, broad, velvetty, containing 3 to 4 seeds. Raised at Hewra and Dapoorie from Calcutta seed.

XXXII.—ROSACEÆ, DC. *Prod*. 2, p 525.

FRAGARIA, Linn., Icosandria Polyginia, Gaert. *t*. 73; Lam. *t*. 442.

1. F Elatior, W. and A.; Don's *syst*. 2, 543.—Strawberry. This species is a native of N. America and the South of England (?). It is successfully cultivated in gardens above the Ghauts, and extensively by natives near Poona, for sale in Camp. The Strawberries of Kolapoor and its vicinity appear to be the best in the Deccan.

RUBUS, Icosandria Polygynia, Lam. *t*. 441; Gaert. *t*. 73. Name said to be derived from the Celtic for *red*.

2. R Idæus, Linn. sp. 706.—Common Raspberry of England; has been successfully cultivated at Phoonda Ghaut, south of Kolapoor. It probably would not succeed further inland.

ROSA, Icosandria Polyginia. From *rhos*, red; Greek, *rhodon*.

3. R Damascena, Don's *syst*. 2, p 571.—The Damask Rose; commonly cultivated.

4. R Microphylla, Don's *syst*. 2, p 581.—Smaller leaved Rose, pale-red. A native of China, common.

5. R Indica, R Semperflorens, Don's *syst*. 2, p 581.—China Rose, of which there are several varieties; in flower all the year.

6. R Glandulifera, Roxb. Fl. 2, p 515.—"Shewatee Goolab." Common in gardens.

7. R Rubiginosa, Don's *syst.* p 577; Eng. Bot. *t.* 991.—Sweet Briar, Eglantine. In gardens. The variety of Roses introduced into Western India within the last 20 years is so great that to enumerate them were out of place here. Suffice it to say, that it is only above the Ghauts that they receive anything like their normal development, and that in all the fragrance, when it does exist, is much inferior to that of the Roses of Europe. In the dry air of the Deccan, from November to the end of April, the perfume appears to vanish altogether.

8. Eriobotra Japonica.—Loquat, Mespilus Japonica, Icosandria Pentagynia, Roxb. Fl. 2, p 510; Pluk. Amb. *t.* 371, *f.* 2; Don's *syst.* 2, p 602.—A Chinese fruit tree; leaves broad, lanceolate, wrinkled, serrate, woolly beneath; flowers in terminal, compressed, woolly racemes; they have the smell of Hawthorn blossoms. Belgaum is the only place with us where the Loquat gives a fruit fully developed and of good flavour.

PYRUS, Icosandria Pentagynia. From the Celtic for a *pear*.

9. P Malus, Roxb. Fl. 2, p 511; Don's *syst.* 2, p 623.—Apple. Native of Europe; cultivated in gardens at Ahmednuggur, Poona, &c. The fruit appears only occasionally in particular seasons, and seldom has any size or flavour. The Baking Apple is produced at Dapoorie in greater perfection, and certainly superior flavour, to the American importations.

10. Amygdalus Communis, Roxb. Fl. 2, p 500.—Almond tree; occasionally found in gardens, but does not flourish.

11. A Persica, Roxb. Fl. 2, p 500; Don's *syst.* 1, p 483.—Peach tree; flourishes well in gardens at Dharwar, Belgaum, Ahmednuggur, &c. The air of the Concans does not suit it; the leaves, containing, as they do, Hydrocyanic Acid, are useful in dyspeptic complaints.

CRATEGUS, Icosandria Digynia. Himalaya White Thorn, Roxb. Fl. 2, p 509.

12. C Crenulata.—Native of Gosaen Khan, Himalaya; raised at Hewra and Dapoorie from seed received from the late Dr. Wallich. The shrub, as described by Roxburgh, is spinous, with narrow-elliptic, crenulate, polished leaves, with terminal small white flowers, and an oblate red berry.

13. Chrysobalanus Icaco, Don's *syst.* 2, p 477; Jaquin Amer. *t.* 94.—Coco Plum tree. Of this tree, said to be introduced by the late Mr. Nimmo, we can find no trace. Can any information be given regarding it?

PARINARIUM, Juss., Icosandria Monogynia. *Parinari*, the Guiana name. Lam. *t.* 429.

14. P Excelsum, Don's *syst.* 2, p 479.—A large tree; Goa, introduced by the Jesuits from Mosambique. "Matomba," the

Portuguese name. The fruit, which ripens in December and January, resembles a large, coarse, grey-skinned Plum. The tree is not found elsewhere in Western India. Can any of our readers supply information regarding it ?

XXXIII.—SALICARIÆ, DC. *Prod.* p 302.

THE LOOSE-STRIFE TRIBE, Lind. Nat. Syst. p 59.

LAGERSTRŒMIA, Icosandria Monogynia.

1. L INDICA, W. and A. 951; Roxb. Fl. 2, p 505; Rumph. Amb. 7, *t.* 28.—China "Mendie." An erect-growing shrub, with beautiful pink flowers in terminal panicles; flowers in July; does not seed. In gardens.

CUPHEA, Dodecandria Monogynia. Plants with entire leaves, and violaceous or rose-coloured flowers. Natives of South America.

2. C PLATYCENTRA, DC. *Prod.* 3, p 85.—A small demi-herbaceous shrub; corolla with long scarlet tube, not tomentose. Garden Parell, from English seeds.

3. C SELENOIDES.—Very tomentose, with a purple corolla. Garden Dapoorie.

4. C MINIATA.—Corolla of a bright crimson with burrat purple; hairy. Garden Parell. All these are beautiful annuals, of late introduction.

XXXIV.—COMBRETACEÆ, DC. *Prod.* 3, p 9.

THE MYROBOLAN TRIBE, Lind. Nat. Syst. p 67.

1. TERMINALIA CATAPPA, W. and A. 965; Roxb. Fl. 2, p 430; Rumph. Amb. 1, *t.* 68.—"Bengalee Badam," Hindoostanee. Bengal Almond. Native of the Malaccas; is now common in Indian gardens, where it may be recognised by its horizontal branches in table-like tiers, and its large, rather obovate, leaves. The fruit is very insipid as compared with the Almond.

2. T BENZOIN, T angustifolia, Jacquin Hort. Vind. 3, *t.* 100; Don's *syst.* 2.—Benzoin Tree. Leaves linear-lanceolate, attenuated at both ends; pubescent, or slightly pilose; branches horizontal, with terminal foliation; trunk slender; has not yet flowered with us; is a native of the Eastern Islands, where one description of Benzoin (there being several) is procured by incision of the trunk or branches. Garden Hewra. Does not flourish away from shelter.

QUISQUALIS, Rumph., Decandria Monogynia; Lam. *t.* 357.

3. Q INDICA, W. and A. 982; Roxb. Fl. 2, p 427; Rumph. Amb. 5, *t.* 38; Bot. Mag. 2023.—A scandent shrub with beautiful

and varying flowers, passing from white to orange and red. Common in gardens and on trellises. Though named Indica, it is nowhere found wild here; it belongs to the Eastern Islands.

4. Poivrea Coccinea, Roxb. Cor. Pl. *t.* 59.—An elegant climber, having opposite or alternate ovate smooth leaves, and a terminal secund revolute spike of vivid crimson flowers. Gardens at Dapoorie, Parell, and Sewree. Native of tropical America (?), also of Eastern Bengal.

XXXV.—MYRTACÆ, W. & A. *Prod.* 1, p 326.

PUNICA, Tourn., Icosandria Monogynia. P carthaginian; it is a native of the north of Africa.

1. P Granatum, W. and A. 1010; Roxb. Fl. 2, p 499; Ainslie Mat. Ind. 1, p 322; and 2, p 157.—Is now cultivated throughout the drier provinces of India. The Pomegranate gardens at Allundie, east of Poona, are extensive, and the fruit is exported to Bombay. The virtues of the root-bark in tape-worm are now well known, having first been brought into notice by the late Dr. Fleming, of Calcutta.

PSIDIUM, Icosandria Monogynia.

2. P Pyriferum, W. and A. 1012; P pomiferum, one species; Rheed. Mal. 3, *t.* 34; Rumph. Amb. 8, *t.* 37.—Guava. Native of the West Indies and South America; now extensively cultivated throughout India. The wood is excellent for carpentry, and the bark for tanning leather.

3. P Pumilum, Vahl. Symb. 2, p 56.—Native of Moluccas, Ceylon, and Java. A small shrub, with tetragonal branches and lanceolate leaves, glabrous above, and tomentose below; fruit globose; found cultivated only in gardens at Domus, near Surat.

MYRTUS, Icosandria Monogynia.

4. M Communis, Roxb. Fl. 2, p 496.—"Wiliatee Mendie," Myrtle. Native of Southern Europe; now common in Indian gardens.

5. M Acuminata.—This variety, having a sharply acuminate leaf; has been established at Hewra from seed received through the Marchese Ridolfi, of Florence.

6. Caryophyllus, Icosandria Monogynia. From the Arabic name of the *Clove.* Clove Tree, "Quarenphul," Gaert. *t.* 33; Lam. *t.* 417.—Is now successfully cultivated at Mosambique. Large trees may be seen at Parell and some other gardens at Bombay; leaves have a very aromatic flavour.

JAMBOSA, Icosandria Monogynia. Altered from *Sehambee,* the Malay name of one of the species.

7. J VULGARIS, W. and A. 1032; Roxb. Fl. 2, p 494; Rumph. Amb. 1, *t.* 39; Rheede Mal. 1, *t.* 17.—Eugenia jambos, Rose Apple; often cultivated in gardens, but the fruit is insipid. Some rather fine trees may be seen planted on the hill-fort of Pertabghur.

8. J MALACCENSIS, W. and A. 1035; Roxb. Fl. 2, p 483; Rheede Mal. 1, *t.* 18; Rumph. Amb. 1, *t.* 37 and 38, *f.* 1—Cultivated in Bombay, but rather for the sake of the flowers than the fruit. The flowers, of a deep crimson, are very ornamental.

MELALEUCA, Polydelphia Polyandria. From *melos*, black; *lenkos*, white; the trunk being black, and the branches white.

9. M GENISTIFOLIA, Smith Ex. Bot. 1, *t.* 55.—Broom-leaved Melaleuca. We have put down the species doubtfully, but neither the habit nor the leaves answer to M cajputi. M genistifolia is a native of New South Wales, where it is called White Tea Tree. There are several specimens in the gardens at Dapoorie and Hewra; they flower, but produce a fruit imperfectly developed.

FŒTIDIA, Com., Icosandria Monogynia. From *fæteo*, so named from the smell of the wood.

10. F MAURITIANA, Roxb. Fl. 2, p 489; Don's *syst.* 2, p 871.—A longish-stemmed, weakly tree, with veinless leaves, having the mid-rib of a reddish colour; flowers white. These we have not seen; Parell Garden, probably introduced from Mauritius, where it is indigenous, and is called *Bois Puant*,—stinking wood.

EUCALYPTUS, Linn., Icosandria Monogynia, DC. *Prod.* 3, p 216. Name derived from the Greek *eu*; and *kalypti*, to cover; in reference to the structure of the flower and its calyx.

11. E —— (?) sp.—Gum tree of Australia. Of these we have at least two species in the Botanical Gardens at Hewra and Dapoorie. Tall slender trees, having entire coriaceous alternate leaves. As they have never produced flowers, we remain uncertain as to the species to which they can be referred. They were raised from Australian seed received through the late Dr. Griffith.

XXXVI.—ONAGRARIÆ, W. & A. *Prod.* 1, p 335.

THE EVENING PRIMROSE TRIBE.

ŒNOTHERA, Octandria Monogynia.

1. O BIENNIS.—Common Evening Primrose, Belgaum. In gardens, Mr. Law.

2. O MOLISSIMA.—Native of South America. In gardens at Belgaum, Mr. Law. Besides these we might bring forward numerous other species or varieties raised in private gardens from seed, but these are of a character too evanescent to allow of their appearing in this list.

XXXVII.—CUCURBITACEÆ, W. & A. *Prod.* 1, p 340.

THE GOURD TRIBE, Lind. Nat. Syst. p 192.

LAGENARIA, Monadelphia Triandria. From *lagena*, a bottle, in allusion to the shape of the fruit.

1. L VULGARIS, W. and A. 1051; Don's *syst*. 3, p 4; Rumph. Amb. 5, *t*. 144; Roxb. Fl. 3, p 718; Rheede Mal. 8, *t*. 1, 4, and 5; Lam. Illustr. *t*. 795, *f*. 2.—Bottle Gourd. Native place uncertain; extensively grown, and is of all shapes, and used for many purposes. The fruit is most useful to the natives for toddy vessels, &c. The better variety, which is more tough in the rind, is extensively grown in the mountainous parts of the Deccan for floats used in crossing rivers. Four or five of them are strongly bound together with string or whip-cord, and thus support a man crossing a river with his head burden.

CUCUMIS, Monœcia Monadelphia. From *sikuos*, a cucumber; *sikueraton*, a garden of cucumbers. Is. ch. 1, v. 8; Gaert. *t*. 88; Lam. *t*. 795.

2. C MELO, W. and A. 1052; Roxb. Fl. 3, p 720.—Extensively cultivated, especially in the beds of rivers, in the hot season. Its cultivation is quite an art, and quantities of human manure (Poudrette) are employed by the Hindoo cultivators in raising this product; it forms a staff of life to the poorer classes in the hot season.

3. C SATIVUS, W. and A. 1054; Roxb. Fl. 3, p 720; Rheede Mal. 8, *t*. 6; Lam. Illustr. *t*. 795.—"Kakeree," common Cucumber; cultivated to a great extent by the natives.

4. C UTILISSIMUS, W. and A. 1056; Roxb. Fl. 3, p 721.—Field Cucumber, called also "Kakri"; cultivated much more commonly than the last.

5. C MOMORDICA.—This and the above two are all varieties of one species.

LUFFA, Tourn., Monœcia Pentandria, Cav. Ic. *t*. 9.

6. L PENTANDRIA, P acutangula, "Toorai Gosalee." W. and A. 1064-65; Roxb. Fl. 3, 712-13; Rheede Mal. 8, *t*. 7, 8; Rumph. Amb. 5, *t*. 147-49.—These two are also extensively cultivated as an article of diet.

BENINCASA, Savi, Monœcia Triandria. Named in honour of *Benincasa*, an Italian Nobleman.

7. B CERIFERA, W. and A. 1070; Roxb. Fl. 3, p 718.—"Pandree Chikee." Fruit subrotund, 12 or 15 inches in diameter; hairy when young, smooth, with a whitish bloom, when ripe; commonly cultivated in Bombay and the Deccan.

TRICHOSANTHES, Monœcia Monadelphia. From *thrix*, hair; and *anthos*, a flower; the flowers being beautifully fringed. Lam. *t.* 794; Don's *syst.* 3, p 38.

8. T ANGUINA, W. and A. 1093; Roxb. Fl. 3, p 701; Rumph. Amb. 5, *t.* 148; Ainslie Mat. Ind. 2, p 392; Lam. *t.* 794, *f* 1.—"Chikonda," Snake Gourd. Commonly cultivated about Bombay; fruit long, spindle-shaped, and often curiously twisted.

CUCURBITA, Linn., Monœcia Monadelphia. Gaert. 2, *t.* 88; Lam. *t.* 795.

9. C MAXIMA, W. and A. 1096; C melopepo, Roxb. Fl. 3, p 719; Rheede Mal. 8, *t.* 2; Rumph Amb. 5, *t.* 145.—Squash Gourd, or Pumpkin. Commonly cultivated.

10. C CITRULLUS, W. and A. 1098; Roxb. Fl. 3, p 719; Ainslie Mat. Ind. 1, p 217; Rumph. Amb. 5, *t.* 146; Moris. Hist. 1, *t.* 6; Pluk. *t.* 164, *f.* 1.—"Turbooza," Water Melon; extensively cultivated in the same localities, and with the same appliances, as C melo.

11. C OVIFERA, Don's *syst.* 3, p 41; DC. *Prod.* 3, p 317; Lob. Hist. 367, *f.* 2.—Vegetable Marrow. Commonly cultivated from Europe seed, but the cultivation requires considerable care, otherwise the fruit rots or drops off rapidly.

12. TELFAIRIA PEDATA, Ampelosicyos scandens, Bot. Mag. 2751-2 and 2681.—A large perennial plant, running over trees on the eastern coast of Africa, and bearing a fruit 2 or 3 feet long; full of seeds, which yield a oil equal to that of the finest Olives. In the 1st edition this plant is quoted as having been introduced by the late Mr. Nimmo (?) Is it still found in gardens in Bombay?

XXXVIII.—PAPAYACEÆ, W. & A. *Prod.* 1, p 351.

THE PAPAW TRIBE.

CARICA. From *Caria*, in Asia Minor, of which country it was erroneously supposed to be a native.

1. C PAPAYA, W. and A. 1099; Roxb. Fl. 3, p 824; Rumph. Amb. 1, *t.* 50; Bot. Reg. *t.* 459; Bot. Mag. *t.* 2898 and 2899.—Papai. Native of Brazil; now common in Indian gardens; generally said to be diœcious, but is often found with male and female flowers on one tree. The property which this tree has of making meat hung on its branches tender is well known in India.

XXXIX.—PASSIFLOREÆ, W. & A. *Prod.* 1, p 352.

THE PASSION-FLOWER TRIBE.

PASSIFLORA, Monadelphia Pentandria. Name given by the Jesuits, with relation to an incident in the Passion of our Saviour.

1. P LAURIFOLIA, DC. *Prod.* 328; Plum. Amer. *t.* 80; Cav. Dis. 10, 284; Pluk. Alm. *t.* 2, 11, *f.* 3.—Native of Brazil. It may easily be known by its ovate, oblong-entire, dark-green leaves.

2. P QUADRANGULARIS, Linn. sp. 1356.—Native of South America; leaves glabrous cordate, at base acuminate; branches quadrangular winged; flowers odoriferous, beautifully variegated. This is the species which produces the delicious Granadilla fruit; this has ripened at Dapoorie.

3. P ALATO-CŒRULEA, DC. *Prod.* 3, p 329; Bot. Reg. *t.* 848.—Leaves smooth, cordate, 3-lobed, lobes entire, ovate-lanceolate. This species is also very ornamental. Native of Brazil.

4. P FŒTIDIA, DC. *Prod.* 3, p 331; Cav. Dis. 10, *t.* 289; Bot. Mag. *t.* 2619; Bot. Cab. *t.* 138.—An annual hairy plant, with small flowers of little beauty. In gardens, mostly growing wild. A Native of Brazil.

5. P SERRULATA, DC. *Prod.* 3, p 329; Jaq. Obs. 2, *t.* 46, *f.* 2.—Perennial; leaves 3-lobed, middle lobe longer than the others, all slightly serrate. In gardens, common.

6. P MINIMA, DC. *Prod.* 3, p 325.—Leaves smooth, 5-nerved, 3-cleft; lobes ovate, flowers small, gardens.

7. MURUCUJA OCELLATA, Linn. Amœn. 1, *t.* 10, *f.* 10; Plum. Amer. *t.* 87.—Leaves emarginate at base; truncately lobed at the apex; flowers deep red, very beautiful berry, size of a pigeon's egg. Syrup and decoction of the plant used as a narcotic. Vulgar name in Jamaica, Dutchman's laudanum.

8. P KERMESINA.—A very ornamental species; petals bright-red, narrow. Garden Parell.

XL.—TURNERACEÆ, Don's Syst. 3, p 66.

TURNERA, Linn., Pentandria Trigynia. In memory of Dr. Turner, Prebendary of York, author of some botanical works.

1. T ULMIFOLIA, Don's *syst.* 3, p 67.—A very common herbaceous plant, with yellow cistus-like flowers, growing in the leaf-stalk; now grows as a weed in gardens. It is a native of South America.

XLI.—PORTULACEÆ, W. & A. *Prod.* 1, p 354.

PORTULACA, Decandria Monogynia. From *porto,* to carry; *lac,* milk; plants milky (?).

1. P SPENDENS, P gillesii, Hook. Bot. Mag. 3064.—An annual; native of Chili; with red stem, and splendid crimson flowers. Dapoorie.

2. TALINUM INDICUM, W. and A. 1112; Don's *syst.* 3, p 77.—An erect-growing plant, with flat fleshy wedge-shaped leaves; stem red; flowers reddish coloured. Native of Arabia.

3. PORTULACARIA AFRA, Pentandria Monogynia.—With cuneate, obovate, fleshy veinless leaves; stems red, succulent, rapidly tapering. Native of South America (?); has not been seen in flower. Common as a pot-plant about bungalows. (*Vide* Don *syst.* 3, p 80.)

XLII.—FICOIDEÆ, W. & A. *Prod.* 1, p 361.

MESEMBRYANTHEMUM, Icosandria Tetragynia, Gaert. *t.* 126; Lam. *t.* 438.

1. M CRYSTALLINUM.—The Ice plant, DC. *Prod.* 3, 448. Native of the Cape; common in gardens, and recognisable by the crystalline-like drops which stud the thick fleshy leaves.

2. TETRAGONIA EXPANSA, Icosandria Trigynia. New Zealand Spinach, DC. *Prod.* 3, p 452; Don's *syst.* 3, p 151.—Occasionally reared in gardens as a spinach; it does not succeed well.

XLIII.—CACTEÆ, DC. *Prod.* 3, p 457.

THE INDIAN FIG TRIBE, Lind. Nat. Syst. p 55.

CEREUS.—DC., Icosandria Monogynia. From *cereus*, pliant; in allusion to the pliant shoots of some of the species.

1. C PENTAGONUS, DC. *Prod.* 3, p 468.—An erect plant; stems jointed, 5-angled; flowers large, white. In gardens. Native of South America.

2. C GRANDIFLORUS, DC. *Prod.* 3, p 468; Don's *syst.* 3, 168; Bot. Mag. *t.* 3381.—Night-blowing Cereus; a climber, 5 or 6-angled; stems rooting at the joints; flowers large, white, with yellow stamens, very showy. Native of West Indies. In gardens.

3. C TRUNCATUS, DC. *Prod.* 3, p 470; Bot. Mag. *t.* 2562; Bot. Reg. *t.* 696. Epiphyllum truncatum, Don's *syst.* 3, p 171.—All of the above (natives of Brazil) have been introduced into the Botanical Gardens by cuttings, chiefly from Calcutta. Numerous other varieties of various forms and fantastic shapes are to be seen in the Botanical Gardens Dapoorie.

OPUNTIA, Tourn., Icosandria Monogynia. From the town *Opus*, where some species grow.

4. O DILLENII, W. and A. 1127; Roxb. Fl. 2, p 475; Bot. Reg. *t.* 255; Don's *syst.* 3, p 173.—Prickly Pear. Native of Brazil; now too common about most of the Deccan villages, where it forms a nidus for snakes, filth, and malaria of every description.

It were most advisable that Government should, as a measure of Sanitary Police, take for its eradication more energetic and continuous steps than those hitherto adopted. The health of the people ought to form a reason quite sufficient for the adoption of compulsory measures with respect to it. In the Grass Preserves of the Beema and Moota-Moola (whither it has been carried from the Poona City and Cantonment), many hundreds of rupees have been spent on rooting it out, as it smothers and destroys the crop of grass. The native tradition is that a few seeds of the plant were brought by a Sirdar (Dubharhè) in his palankin from Delhi, and verily his gift has been as noxious to the Deccan as was that of the poisonous Shirt to Hercules. It is hardly found in Gujarat; there we have only noticed it in Sidhpore, between Ahmedabad and Deesa. There is a variety, with numerous spines, often grown in gardens.

5. O Toonah, Mill. Dict. No. 3; Kunth. nov. Gen. America 6, p 69; Don's *syst.* 3, p 173.—This is a species on which, according to Humboldt and Bonpland, the Cochineal "Grana Fina" is fed; others say that the false Cochineal insect only feed on trees. We have had numerous experiments regarding the introduction of this product. In the new-production-fever years, ranging from 1833 to 1845, sundry attempts were made by the late M. Sundt and others, but after considerable expense incurred, and a heavy amount of correspondence, as usual in such cases, the whole ended in smoke.

6. O Rubescens Rosea (?), DC. Diss. *t.* 15.—This unarmed species is often seen in gardens at Bombay, Mahim, &c.; flowers flesh-coloured.

PERESKIA, Plum., Icosandria Monogynia. Named by Plumier after *Peiresk*, of Aix, in Provence.

7. P Aculeata, Cactus Pereskii, Spr. *syst.* 2, p 498; Pluk. *t.* 215, *f.* 6; Dill. Hort. *t.* 227, *f.* 294.—A scandent shrub with smooth elliptic leaves, and long thorns in their axils; flowers white; appears in the rains.

8. P Grandiflora.—Native of Mexico. A very distinct species, having long, broad, lanceolate leaves, and showy roseate flowers. In gardens; not common. The long roseate flowers, contrasted with the deep green of the stems and leaves, render it a choice plant for the Green-house.

XLIV.—SAXIFRAGACEÆ, DC. *Prod.* 4, p 4.

HYDRANGEA, Linn., Decandria Trigynia.

1. H Hortensia, Don's *syst.* 3, 233; Bot. Mag. *t.* 438.—Chinese Guelder Rose; a shrubby plant, with flowers of various

shades of rose colour. In gardens; native of China. Does not flower freely in this climate.

XLV.—UMBELLIFERÆ, DC. *Prod.* 4, p 55; Lind. Nat. Syst., p 4.

APIUM, Pentandria Digynia. From a Celtic name for *water*, in allusion to the place of growth.

1. A PETROSELINUM, Linn. sp. 379; Don's *syst.* 3, p 379.—Parsley; now generally cultivated in the gardens of Europeans in India, but seldom in those of natives, who do not appear to appreciate the value of this plant as a seasoning ingredient.

2. A GRAVEOLENS, W. and A. 1135.—Celery; in gardens.

3. A INVOLUCRATUM, Roxb. 2, p 97.—"Ajmood." Is much cultivated in Gujarat; it is the native substitute for Parsley; seeds medicinal.

PTYCHOTIS, W. and A., Pentandria Digynia.

4. P AJWAN, W. and A. 1137; Roxb. Fl 2, p 91.—"Owa," Hindoostanee and Maratha. Native of Persia (?); not found wild in India, Roxb. The warm, pungent, aromatic seeds are extensively used for culinary and medicinal purposes.

5. ANETHUM SOWA.—"Sowa"; is extensively cultivated for culinary and medicinal purposes.

FŒNICULUM, Pentandria Digynia.

6. F VULGARE, W. and A. 1145; Eng. Bot. *t.* 1208. Common in gardens.

PASTINACA, Pentandria Digynia. Latin name *Pustinum*, for a dibble, shape of root.

7. P SATIVA, Don's *syst.* 3, p 338.—Parsnip; native of Europe and America; cultivated in gardens.

CUMINUM, Pentandria Digynia, Gaert. *t.* 23; Roxb. Fl. 2, p 42; Lam. *t.* 194.

8. C CYMINUM, W. and A. 1153; Roxb. 2, 42.—"Jeera," Cuminum; cultivated in gardens for its aromatic, medicinal seeds. "Kalee Jeeree" is the seed of Vernonia anthelmintica.

DAUCUS, Pentandria Digynia.

9. D CAROTA, W. and A. 1154; Roxb. Fl. 2, 90.—"Gajir," Hindoostanee and Maratha. Carrot; said to be a native of Persia; is extensively cultivated in gardens, and also as a field crop in the Balaghat and Eastern Deccan, where it attains a size, and has a flavour, nearly equal to that of Europe. In those countries it forms, during the cold season, a staple food of the people far superior in salubrity to the Potatoe.

10. CORIANDRUM, Pentandria Digynia.—*Koris*, a bug; in allusion to the peculiar smell of the plant. Native of Southern

Europe; is extensively cultivated as a rainy season crop in India, especially in the Deccan; is never irrigated.

XLVI.—ARALIACEÆ, DC. *Prod.* 251.

THE ARALIA TRIBE, Lind. Nat. Syst., p 4.

PANAX, Polygamia Diœcia. *Pan*, all; *akos* (?), remedy; the celebrated universal remedy. Ginsing of the Chinese belongs to this family.

1. P COCHLEATUM, P Conchifolium, DC. *Prod.* 4, p 253; Roxb. Fl. 2, p 77; Rumph. Amb. 4, *t.* 31.—Shell-leaved Panax; native of Eastern Islands; in gardens. Native of Java and Moluccas.

2. P FRUTICOSUM, W. and A. 1157; Roxb. Fl. 2, 76; Rumph. Amb. 4, *t.* 33; Bot. Rep. *t.* 595.—A shrub, with large supra-decompound leaves; very common in gardens and pots about bungalows. Native of Eastern Islands. We have seen this plant perfect its flower and seed only at Dharwar.

3. P OBTUSUM, DC. *Prod.* 4, p 254; Don's *syst.* 3, p 386.—A shrub, in gardens, rare. Dapoorie and Hewra; leaves supra-decompound; leaflets obovate roundish.

4. P FRAGRANS, DC. *Prod.* 4, p 253.—Native of Nepaul. This shrub is not now traceable at Dapoorie. Do any specimens exist in gardens elsewhere?

5. HEDERA PALMATA.—There is a doubt as to the correctness of the specific name given here; scandent, leaves trilobate.

6. ARALIA PAPYRIFERA.—Chinese Rice-Paper Plant. (*Vide* Bot. Mag.)—An unarmed shrub, 5 or 6 feet high; stem filled with white pulp; leaves 5 to 7-lobed, 1 foot long; lobes acute and serrated with deep sinuses; leaves and inflorescence covered with thick down. Garden at Parell; native of Formosa.

PARATROPIA, Pentandria Pentagynia. *Paratrope*, bending; in allusion to the bent petioles.

7. P VENULOSA, Aralia digitata, W. and A. 1163; Rheede Mal. 7, *t.* 28; Roxb. Fl. 2, p 187.—Native of Southern India. A small tree with digitate leaves; in the late Colonel Hough's garden, Colaba; has now disappeared.

XLVII.—CAPRIFOLIACEÆ, DC. *Prod.* 4, p 321.

THE HONEY SUCKLE TRIBE, Lind. Nat. Syst., p 206.

LONICERA, Pentandria Monogynia. From *Lonicer*, a German Botanist of the 16th Century.

1. L SEMIPERVIRENS, DC. *Prod.* 4, p 432; Bot. Mag. *t.* 781, and 1753.—Evergreen or Trumpet Honeysuckle; flowers scarlet outside, yellow within; native of North America. In gardens, pretty common.

2. L LESCHENAULTII, W. and A. 1205; Wall. ed. of Roxb. Fl. p 2, 178.—Leschenault's Honeysuckle. A native of the Neilgherries; twining, villous; with flowers variegated red and purple.

3. L CHINENSIS, DC. *Prod.* 4, p 333; Bot. Cab. *t.* 1037; Bot. Reg. *t.* 712.—Leaves entire, opposite, broad-lanceolate, shining; flowers in the rains, of a light-yellow colour. Parell Garden. The elegant Linnea borealis found in Sweden and Scotland belongs to this tribe.

XLVIII.—RUBIACEÆ, DC. *Prod.* 4, p 341.

1. NAUCLEA CADAMBA, Roxb. Fl. 1, p 512; N purpurea, W. and A. 1209; Rheed. Mal. 3, *t.* 33; Rumph. Amb. 3, *f.* 19; As. Res. 4, p 257; Don's *syst.* 3, p 467.—" Nhew," Maratha. A spreading, umbrageous large tree, with cordate, broad-acuminate, cross-veined leaves, on long petioles; fruit the size of a small orange, yellow when ripe, and covered with innocuous bristles; is eaten, but is not very palatable. The tree is common near to villages in the Concan, but is never in as far as we have seen; found wild therefore is probably not a native of the Peninsula. (*Vide* remarks by Wight and Arnott as to its not being a native.) One tree may be seen in the compound of the Grant College, near to the Byculla Road.

Sub-Tribe 2nd.—GARDENIACEÆ.

GARDENIA, W. and A., Pentandria Monogynia. Named from *Dr. Garden*, of Charleston, a correspondent of Linnæus.

2. G —— (?) sp.—A 3-feet shrub, with narrow, shining opposite leaves, tapering from both ends, and considerably waved; flower very minute, white, with a tinge of lilac; as yet no fruit. This species should be kept in view, as we have not yet been able to trace it in books. Introduced by Mr. Young, C. S., from the Cape or Mauritius.

3. G FLORIDA.—Native of China; Cape Jessamine. "Gundaraja," Roxb. Fl. p 703; Rumph. Amb. 7, *t.* 14; Bot. Mag. *t.* 2627, 3349, 1842; Don's *syst.* 3, p 496.—A small unarmed shrub of slow growth. In gardens; flowers in the rains, pure white, and very fragrant.

Sub-Tribe 3rd.—COFFEACEÆ.

COFFEA, Pentandria Monogynia. *Caffee* a province of Africa, where it grows, Graham. We consider this derivation very doubtful. The Latin name is probably a transmutation of the Arabic one "Kawa."

4. C ARABICA, W. and A. 1339; Roxb. 1, p 539; Bot. Mag. *t.* 1303; Ainslie Mat. Ind. 1, p 81; Wight Ic., part 3, *t.* 53.—"Kawa," Hindoostanee; "Boon," Maratha. Native of Africa; is grown to some extent in the south-west part of Belgaum Collectorate, as at Jambotee, Khanapore, &c. The climate further north does not suit the plant, though it may be here and there seen in gardens reared as a pet production. Its introduction near Bombay, on a small scale, has been several times attempted, as at Poway, &c., but without any success. In Malabar, Wynaad, and Mysore, it is fast rising into importance as an export. Ceylon now produces annually 56 millions of pounds; Wynaad and Mysore about 11 millions. The cultivation of the tree by natives is, as may be seen in Malabar, very slovenly, as compared with that followed by the European planters; the fruit also is often picked by them in an unripe state.

5. IXORA STRICTA, W. and A. 1307, Roxb. Fl. 1, p 379; Bot. Mag *t.* 169; Rumph. Amb. 4, *t.* 47; Don's *syst.* 3 p 571.—An erect-growing shrub, in gardens, Bombay; flowers of an orange, scarlet colour, much crowded. Native of China.

6. I BARBATA, Roxb. Fl. 1, p 384; Rheede Mal. 2, *t.* 14; Bot. Mag. *t.* 2505.—A shrub, with pure white flowers, appearing in the rains; terminal panicles. Sir R. de Faria's garden, Mazagon.

SERISSA, Pentandria Monogynia, Lam. *t.* 151.

7. S FŒTIDA, W. and A. 1356; Roxb. Fl. 1, p 579; Bot. Mag. *t.* 361.—A small shrub, with shining acuminate myrtle-like leaves, which, as well as the small white flowers, are very fœtid on being bruised.

8. PENTAS CARNEA.—Native of Sierra Leone; demi-herbaceous, with spreading branches from the roots, and terminal heads of long-tubed, pink flowers.

HAMELIA, Jaq. Amer. p 71; Linn. Gen. p 232; Lam. Illustr. *t,* 155.—So-called in honour of *DuHamel*, the celebrated Vegetable Physiologist.

9. H PATENS, Jaq. Amer. p 72, *t.* 50; Pict. *t.* 72.—A six feet shrub, with ovate villous leaves, entire, markedly veined; flowers in lateral and terminal cymes; scarlet and yellow. Native of South America; Plant received from Royal Gardens, Kew. Hewra, Dapoorie, and Parell.

RONDELETIA, Plum. Gen. p 15, *t.* 12. Name given by Plumier, in honour of *Rondelet*, a Physician of Montpellier.

10. R ODORATA, Jaq. Amer. p 59, *t.* 42; Pict. *t.* 61; Don's *syst.* 3, p 516.—A shrub, with ovate, subcordate, scabrous leaves, and handsome scarlet and yellow fragrant flowers. Native of Cuba and Mexico; lately introduced into gardens in Western India. Gardens Hewra, Sewree, and Parell. The shrub appears to flourish better near the seathan inland. A delicate perfume is extracted from this plant.

11. CATESBEA, Tetrandria Monogynia. Named after *Catesby*, author of the History of Carolina.—Shrubby, with small oval leaves in fascicles; simple straight thorns from insertion of leaves; flowers whitish, elongated, drooping; native of Carolina. Society's garden, Sewrie.

XLIX.—COMPOSITÆ, DC. *Prod.* 5, p 1.

LACTUCA, Syngenesia Polygamia Æqualis. From *lac*, milk, as the plant abounds in milky juice.

1. L SATIVA, Roxb. Fl. 3, p 403; Black. *t.* 81.—Common garden Lettuce. Native of Southern Europe; the juice is narcotic. The varieties raised from Europe seed are numerous.

CICHORIUM, Syngenesia Polygamia Æqualis.

2. C ENDIVA.—This also is commonly cultivated, and, when blanched, is as delicate as Lettuce.

HIERACIUM, Syng. Polygymia Æqualis, Eng. Bot. 1469.

3. H AURANTIACUM.—Orange Hawk Weed; in gardens, Belgaum; Mr. Law.

CYNARA, Syngenesia Polygamia Æqualis.

4. C SCOLYMUS, Willd. 3, p 1691; Spr. *syst.* 3, p 369; Roxb. Fl. 3, p 409; Ainslie Mat. Ind. 1, p 22; Bot. Mag *t.* 2862, and 3241.—Kingin, Artichoke, and Var. Cardoon. Native of Southern Europe; cultivated, but seldom with full success, as it yields to the climate before the base of the involucre (the edible portion) leaves are fully developed.

CARTHAMUS, Syngenesia Polygamia Æqualis. Name said to be derived from the colouring matter afforded by the flowers.

5. C TINCTORIUS, Roxb. Fl. 3, p 409; Rumph. Amb. 5, *t.* 79; Bot. Reg. *t.* 170; Ainslie Mat. Ind. 2, p 364.—Kosoomba, Safflower. Cultivated in all the black-soil districts over India for the use of dyers, and for the oil obtained from the seeds. The variety which affords the colouring matter is much less spinose on the edges and extremities of the leaves than the other. The seeds are excellent for fattening poultry.

CENTAUREA, Syngenesia Polygamia Frustranea.

6. C MOSCHATA, Roxb. Fl. 3, p 444.—" Shah-pusund," Sweet-Sultan. In gardens, flourishes chiefly in the cold weather. We have not seen it.

7. C CYANUS, Willd. 3, p 2291 ; Eng. Bot. *t.* 277.—Blue bottle. In gardens, Belgaum, Mr. Law.

LAGASCA, Cav., Syngenesia Polygamia Segregata. In honour of Professor *La Gasca*, of Madrid.

8. L MOLLIS, DC. *Prod.* 5, p 91 ; Bot. Mag. *t.* 1804 ; Noccea mollis, Jacq. Frag. *t.* 113.—Native of West Indies and South America ; is now a most troublesome weed in gardens. The seeds carried down from the Dapoorie garden by the floods of the Moota-Moola, have established the plant in the Grass Preserves of Bheemthurree to such an extent, as in many places to interfere with the growth of the grass.

ASTEROMEA, Syngenesia Polygamia.

9. CATHOLIPHUS, Roxb. Fl. 3, p 433 ; Aster. Dill. Elth. *t.* 34.—The China Aster, common in gardens. Varieties are numerous.

EMILIA, Syngenesia Polygamia Æqualis.

10. E SAGITATA, DC. *Prod.* 6, p 301.—A plant, with stem-clasping byrate leaves, and showy red flowers in twos and threes.

11. CACALIA SEMPERVIRENS, Spr. *syst.* 3, p 428.—Forest shades of Arabia ; C cuneifolia. Native of the Cape of Good Hope ; herbaceous plant, with broad cuneate leaves, and yellowish inflorescence from a single stem ; common in pots about bungalows.

TAGETES, Syngenesia Polygamia Superflua.

12. T PATULA, Roxb. Fl. 3, p 434 ; Dill. Elth. *t.* 279, *f.* 361 ; Bot. Mag. *t.* 150.—" Gool-Jafree," French Marygold ; common in every garden. It is quite naturalised about Belgaum, growing on the borders of rice-fields.

ZINNIA, Syngenesia Polygamia Superflua. Named after *Zenn*, a German Botanist.

13. Z ELEGANS, DC. *Prod.* p 536 ; Jacq. It. rar. 3, *t.* 589 ; Bot. Reg. *t.* 55, and 1294.—Flowers deep red, merging into purple. This plant, with its several varieties (for they are no more) is now so completely naturalised, that in its unassisted growth it serves to point out " Where once a garden smiled."

BELLIS, Linn. Gen. No. 962 ; Gaert. 4, 419, *t.* 168.

14. B PERENNIS, Endlich., N. 2348.—The Daisy ; native of Europe and North America ; grows at Dharwar and Mahableshwur pretty freely.

XIMENESIA, Cav. Ic. 2, 60, *t.* 178.

15. X EUCELLOIDES, Ic. 2, 60, *t.* 178; DC. *Prod.* 5, 627.—Native of Mexico, annual, with showy yellow flowers, and ovate oblong, toothed leaves. Raised from seed received *viâ* Calcutta.

16. SANVITALIA PROCUMBENS, DC. *Prod.* 5, 628.—Annual; native of Mexico, with ovate, 3-nerved leaves, and small flowers having a dark centre, and bright yellow rays. Dapoorie, not common.

17. FLAVIERA CONTRAYERVA, Ex. *Prod.* 418, No. 2571.—Native of South America; annual, with 3-nerved leaves, having spinous edges, and midrib, dense heads of small yellow flowers; is medicinal; raised from seed received from Pisa. In garden Hewra, and runs wild on the adjacent slopes.

MELAMPODIUM, Linn. Gen. No. 989; DC. *Prod.* 5, 517.

18. M PALUDOSAM, Endlich. No. 402.—Annual; native of America, having opposite broad-lanceolate, serrate leaves, and small flowers on erect peduncles; flower of a deep yellow in the centre and rays.

EUPATORIUM, Tourn., Mit. 455; Vahl. Symb. 3, *t.* 72 and 73.

19. E AYAPANA, DC. *Prod.* 5, p 169.—Native of America and Asia Minor; a herbaceous plant, now common in Indian gardens; the leaves are a good bitter, according to Dr. Lush, and used as a substitute for Tea in the Isle of France; flowers of a slaty blue.

HELIANTHUS, Syngenesia Polygamia Frustranea. From *helios*, the sun; *anthos*, a flower. The common Sun Flower; frequent in gardens, both Native and European. Roxb. Fl. 3, p 443.

20. H. TUBEROSUS, Spr. *syst.* 3, p 616; Jacq. Vind. 2, *t.* 161.—"Jerusalem Artichoke." Commonly cultivated in gardens. The root is one of the best of vegetables.

DAHLIA, Cav., Syngenesia Polygamia Superflua. Named after *Dahl*, a Sweedish Botanist, and Pupil of Linnæus.

21. D VARIABILIS, DC. *Prod.* 5, p 494; Spr. *syst.* 3, p 610; Cav. Ic. 1, *t.* 80, and 3, *t.* 265.—The well-known Dahlia, the most beautiful flower in all the Compositæ. The varieties are numerous.

CALIOPSIS, DC., Syngenesia Polygamia Frustranea. From *kalos*, fair; *opsis*, sight; in allusion to the eye-like beauty to the flowers.

22. C TINCTORIA, DC. *Prod.* 5, 568.—A pretty annual, with flowers having long yellow rays, and purple capitula. C bicolor is a still more showy variety.

23. GAILLORDIA PICTA, Emargmala, and Drummondii, are all of them more recent introductions from America *viâ* Europe. They are among the most beautiful of the Compositæ. Garden Dapoorie.

CHRYSANTHEMUM, Syngenesia Polygamia Superflua. From *chrysos*, gold; *anthos*, a flower.

24. C INDICUM, Roxb. Fl. 3, p 436; Rheed. Mal. 10, *t.* 44; Rumph. Amb. 5, *t.* 91, *fig.* 1; Linn. Trans. 13, p 561; Bot. Mag. *t.* 327, 2042, and 2556.—"Gool-Daodee," Hindoostanee name. Native of Persia. There are several varieties with flowers of various colours, yellow, purple, &c. &c. The flowers make a tolerable substitute for Camomile medicinally.

PYRETHRUM, Syngenesia Polygamia Superflua.

25. P INDICUM, Roxb. Fl. 3, p 436; Spr. *syst.* 3, p 588; Bot. Mag. *t.* 15, 21.—Indian Feverfew; annual; leaves alternate, linear-pinnatifid, stem-clasping; flowers terminal, solitary, yellow, on long and smooth peduncles. The following omitted in their proper subdivisions are inserted here.

CALENDULA, Syngenesia Polygamia Necessaria, Gaert. 2, *t.* 168; Lam. *t.* 715.

26. C OFFICINALIS, C arragonensis, Spr. *syst.* 3, p 623.—The common Marygold. C arragonensis, a Spanish Marygold, has been raised from seed sent by the Marchese Ridolfi, of Florence.

COSMOS, Cav., Syngenesia Polygamia Frustranea.

27. C SULPHUREUS, Var. Roseus, DC. *Prod.* 5, p 606.—Coreopsis pinnatifida. Tall herbaceous plant, with minutely subdivided leaves, and showy pink or light-yellow flowers.

ACHILLEA, Syngenesia Polygamia Superflua.

28. A MILLEFOLIUM, Spr. *syst.* 2, p 600; Eng. Bot. *t.* 758.—Yarrow, Milfoil; native of Southern Europe. A common plant in gardens, readily known by its heads of broad white flowers.

29. CINERARIA (?) sp.—Flower whitish-yellow; garden Parell.

ARTEMISIA, Linn., Syngenesia Polygamia Superflua.

30. A ABROTANUM.—Native of Europe. Southern Wood. It always remains a sickly, poor plant in India.

LEONTODON, Linn. Gen. No. 912; Willd. sp. No. 1408.

31. L TARAXACUM.—Having radical, oblong obovate leaves, dentate-pinnatifid, and often runcinate, with a yellow flower; in gardens, not common. Is now cultivated in quantity at Dapoorie and Hewra for the sake of the roots, from which is made the extract now supplied in large quantity to the Medical Stores. The extract is made in the hot season, and at once powdered and enclosed in hermetically sealed boxes; any decomposition arising from fermentation is thus avoided.

L.—DIPSACEÆ, Don's Syst. 3, p 681.

THE SCABIOUS TRIBE, Lind. Nat. Syst. p 196.

SCABIOSA, Linn., Tetrandria Monogynia.

1. S ATROPURPUREA, Don's *syst.* 3, p 691; Bot. Mag. *t.* 247.—A sweet-scented, ornamental plant. Native of the Cape. Dapoorie.

LI.—LOBELIACÆ, Don's Syst. 3, p 697.

PRATIA, Don, Pentandria Monogynia. Named after *M. Prat*, Bernon, formerly of the French Navy.

1. P RADICANS, Don's *syst.* 3, p 700; L radicans.—An annual, creeping, glabrous plant; native of China; flowers of a pink colour. It spreads over the soil, rooting at every branch, and is well adapted for binding the earth in pots wherein shrubs are planted. Gardens; now rather common.

SIPHOCAMPYLUS, Tetrandria Monogynia, Pohl. Pl. Braz. 2, 104.

2. S BICOLOR, Chamisso in Linn. 7, p 202.—A showy herbaceous plant; native of Brazil, having narrow oblong leaves, and red flowers, beautifully variegated with yellow. Parell and Sewree gardens, also Dapoorie.

LOBELIA, Pentandria Monogynia. Named after *Lobel*, Physician to James I.

3. L ERINUS, Linn. sp. 1321; Cond. Bot. Mag. 901; Fl. 2, p 39.—A small plant with slender blue flowers, with stems often radical, and villous leaves; native of the Cape. Dapoorie.

4. L RAMOSA.—This we insert with a doubt as to the specific name, which is not traceable. It will be further remarked on hereafter. Garden Dapoorie (?). Native of Europe.

LII.—SAPOTACEÆ, Don's Syst. 4, p 27.

THE SAPODILLA TRIBE, Lind. Nat. Syst. p 180.

CHRYSOPHYLLUM, Pentandria Monogynia. From *chrysos*, gold; and *phyllon*, leaf. Jaq. Amer. 51; Schriber. Gen. 355.

1. C POMIFORME (?), Star Apple, Bert. Spr. *syst.* p 667.—Received through the late Colonel G. R. Jervis, from Messrs. Loddiges and Co., as C. acuminatum, or Jamaica Star Apple; with broad, somewhat obovate or rounded leaves; has once borne fruit of the size of a small apple; few seeded.

ACHRAS, Linn., Pentandria Monogynia. The Greek name of the wild Pear. Lam. *t.* 255.

2. A SAPOTA, Roxb. Fl. 2, p 181 ; Don's *syst.* 4, p 33 ; Sloanes Jamaïca 2, *t.* 230 ; Bot. Mag. 3111 and 3112 ; Gaert. 2, *t.* 104.—Sapota Plum ; native of South America. A small tree with dull white scentless flowers ; fruit size of a quincĉ, covered with a brown scabrous rind. Gardens Bombay and the Deccan. The fruit attains more complete maturity near to the sea.

INOCARPUS, Decandria Monogynia.

3. I EDULIS, Roxb. Fl. 2, p 416.—The Otaheite Chesnut, said to have been introduced by Nimmo in 1833. We have failed to trace it, but insert it here in the hope that the doing so may lead to a more successful search.

4. MIMUSOPS KANKI, Roxb. Fl. 2, p 238 ; Bot. Mag. *t.* 3157. Metrosideros macassierensis, Rumph. Amb. 3, *t.* 8 ; Don's *syst.* 4, p 35.—A tree with ovate and often obovate glabrous leaves, and a handsome straight stem ; has not yet flowered with us ; sent by Mr. Elphinston, C. S. There are some good specimens of this tree at the Monastery on the southern head of the Goa Harbour entrance. Garden Hewra. The tree is native of the Molucca Islands.

LIII.—OLEINÆ, Don's Syst. 4, p 43.

OLEA, Diandria Monogynia. From *elaia,* the Greek name of the Olive, sacred to Minerva.

1. O SATIVA, Don's *syst.* 4, p 46.—Native of Southern Europe. This tree in two more varieties, the broad-leafed, the box-leafed, and the redoutè, was introduced through the late Colonel G. R. Jervis in 1842. It is now well established at Hewra, Sewnere, and Dapoorie. Several of the trees have reached a height of 20 feet, and dispatches of young plants (rooted suckers) have been made to Calcutta and the Punjaub. On Sewnere Fort the growth of the trees are particularly robust and healthy, but they have yet shown no disposition to flower or form fruit. Propagation is easy, and effected by means of slices from the root-stock, or "novello."

2. O FRAGRANS, Roxb. Fl p 105 ; Osmanthus fragrans, Don's *syst.* 4, p 48 ; Lour. Cochin China ; Thunb. Japan *t.* 2 ; Bot. Mag. 1552.—A small tree, native of China ; elliptic-lanceolate leaves, and yellowish flowers, exquisitely sweet-scented. The flowers appear early in June, and again partially in September. Does not produce seed. In China the flowers are used to flavour the higher qualities of tea.

3. O FERRUGINEA, O. salicifolia (?), Wall. Cat. No. 6305.—Seed received from Calcutta under former name ; narrow salicine

leaves. There is about the plant nothing of a ferruginous character to account for the name. The plants are yet young, but have the habit of a robust and quick-growing tree; raised by seed from Calcutta. Gardens Hewra and Dapoorie. The tree is a native of Eastern Bengal.

4. O Robusta, Wall. Cat. No. 2822; Phillyrea robusta.—A young tree, native of Sythet, with ovate-oblong entire leaves. Of the two species of Syringa mentioned in the former edition of this Catalogue, we can find no trace. Information is solicited. Dapoorie; raised from Bengal seed.

LIV.—JASMINEACEÆ, Don's Syst. 4, p 59.

THE JASMINE TRIBE, Lind. Nat. Syst. p 222.

JASMINIUM, Diandria Monogynia. Said to be derived from the Arabic name. Lam. *t.* 7; Tourn. *t.* 368; Gaert. *t.* 242.

1. J Aureum.—Don. *Prod.* Fl. Nepaul, p 106.—Native of Nepaul and the Neilgherries. Yellow Jasmine; in gardens.

2. J Odoratissimum.—Native of Arabia and Madeira. Differs from the last in the alternate bluntish and often ternate and pinnate leaves; generally known by the name of Arabian Jasmine. The flowers have very little fragrance. In gardens, commoner than the last species.

NYCTANTHES, Linn., Diandria Monogynia. *Nyx*, night; *anthos*, a flower; in allusion to their blossoming at night, and falling off in the morning.

3. N Arbor-Tristis, Parut harsinaghar, Roxb. Fl. 1, p 86; Don's *syst.* 4, p 64; Rheed. Mal. 1, *t.* 21; Linn. Trans. 13, p 484; Gaert. Fr. 2, *t.* 128; As. Res. 4, p 244; Bot. Reg. *t.* 399.—A shrub or small tree, very common in Native gardens; branches 4, square; leaves scabrous, deciduous in the hot season; flowers delicate, white, with a deep orange tube, very fragrant. They are used in dyeing. Believed to be a native of Arabia, but, if we mistake not, it is mentioned in some of the most ancient books of the Hindoos. Since writing the above, we recollect to have seen it unmistakeably wild in the Satpoora Forests, near Arawud, in Kandeish. The rough leaves are used to polish wood.

LV.—APOCYNEÆ, Don's Syst. 4, p 69.

AGANOSME, Don, Pentandria Monogynia.

1. A Caryophyllata, Echites caryophyllata, Don's *syst.* 4, p 77; Roxb. Fl. 2, p 11; Rheed. Mal. 7, *t.* 55; and 9 *t.* 14; Bot.

Mag. 1919.—A large climbing shrub, with opposite leaves, the midrib of which is generally of a reddish colour, having terminal panicles of exquisitely fragrant flowers. Gardens Bombay and Hewra, from Calcutta seed.

BEAUMONTIA, Wall., Pentandria Monogynia. Named from *Mrs. Beaumont,* of Bretton Hall, Yorkshire.

2. B Grandiflora.—Native of Nepaul; a gigantic climber, with long showy white flowers, and brown thick seed-vessels, 7 to 8 inches in length. Gardens Hewra, Parell, Dapoorie.

NERIUM, Pentandria Monogynia. From *neros,* wet (?).

3. N Obesum.—Native of Arabia; leaves entire, cross-veined, deciduous and succeeded by a few large red flowers on the ends of the branchlets. This species is distinguishable by the immense size of the root, which appears half above ground. Gardens Parell, Sewree, Dapoorie; plant received from Aden.

STROPHANTHUS, R. Br., Pentandria Monogynia. From *stropho,* twisted; and *anthos,* a flower. The segments of the corolla are long and twisted.

4. S Dichotomus, Don's *syst.* 4, p 85; Nerium caudatum, Roxb. Fl. 2, p 9; Bot. Reg. *t.* 469; Burm. Ind. *t.* 26.—A climber of considerable extent, with long appendices to the laminæ of the corolla, red and white. Native of China.

5. S Laurifolius (?), DC., Disfontain's Ann. Mus. 1, p 410, *t.* 27.—A strong climber with opposite whorled, shining, ovate, blunt leaves and axillary flowers, red and white. Native of Sierra Leone. Garden Hewra.

6. Roupellia Grata, Strophanthus stanleyanus, Bot. Mag. 4466.—A climbing shrub, with large broad leaves, and a large rose-coloured flower, with ample tube surmounted by processes, as in Nerium. The appendices to the laciniæ of the corolla are very short. Gardens Hewra, Dapoorie, Parell, and Sewree.

7. Alstonia Venenata, Don's *syst.* 4, p 87.—Leaves oblong-lanceolate, cross-veined; flowers small, white; follicles slender. It is believed that this is the Spatulata noted under 873 of 1st edition of this book (*vide* R. Br. Mem. Soc. Wern. 1, p 751).

PLUMERIA, Pentandria Monogynia. Named after *Plumier,* a celebrated French Botanist.

8. P Acutifolia, P acuminata, Roxb. Fl. 2, p 20; Rumph. Amb. 4, *t.* 38; Bot. Reg. *t.* 114.—The "Khair Chumpa," of Forbes' Oriental Memoirs; having blunt truncate branches, and flowers white and yellow, delightfully fragrant. Abounds in viscid juice, which may afford an inferior caoutchouc. We have never seen this tree in seed; it is a native of the Eastern Islands.

CATHARANTHUS, Don, Pentandria Monogynia.

9. C Roseus, Don's *syst.* 4, p 95; Vinca rosea, Roxb. Fl. 2, p 1; Bot. Mag. *t.* 248.—Native of the Tropics, propably Madagascar, Don; flower pale rose-colour, variegated with white; does not produce seed in Western India.

CERBERA, Linn, Pentandria Monogynia.

10. C Odollam, Roxb. Fl. 1, p 692; Rheede Mal. 1, *t.* 39; Bot. Mag. *t.* 1845; Ainslie (?) Mat. Ind. 2, p 260; Gaert. 2, *t.* 124; Tanghinia odollam, Don's *syst.* 4, p 97.—A tree, native of salt swamps in Malabar, having a white fragrant flower, and fruit the size of an apple. Cerbera tanghin, of Bot. Mag. *t.* 2968, is the famous ordeal tree of Madagascar.

11. C Thevetia, Don's *syst.* 4, p 97; Bot. Mag. 2309; Pluk. Alm. *t.* 207, *f.* 3.—Native of South America and the West Indies; a large shrub, often a tree, with oleander-looking leaves, yellow flower, and fruit the size of a crab-apple. Often found in gardens, Bombay and elsewhere.

ALLAMANDA, Pentandria Monogynia. Named from *Allamand*, a Surgeon who travelled in Guiana.

12. A Aubletii, Don's *syst.* 4, p 103; A cathartica, Roem. and Schultz; Bot. Mag. 338; Ainslie Mat. Ind. 2, p 9.—A scandent, milky shrub, with large yellow flowers, which come out in succession throughout the year; common in gardens, probably introduced by the Portuguese from Brazil. It may be seen growing quasi wild about the Fort of Morgam, south of Goa; the flowers are very showy. It seems never to produce seed in India.

CARISSA, Pentandria Monogynia.

13. C Spinarum, Don's *syst.* 4, p 104; Rumph. Amb. 7, *t.* 19, *f.* 1; Bot. Cat. *t.* 162; Lam Illust. *t.* 118, *f.* 2.—A thick, bushy, thorny, shrub; looks very beautiful when covered with the bright-red fruit. In gardens, probably introduced from the Eastern Islands; the fruit makes good tarts.

14. C Arduina.—Cape of Good Hope, introduced by A. Shaw, Esq., C. S. This has not been traced by us. Can any information be given regarding it?

RAWOLFIA, Pentandria Monogynia. Named from *Rawolfi*, a German Physician and Botanist, who died in 1596.

15. R Canescens, Linn. *syst.* 250; Plum. Gen. G. Ic. 236, *f.* 2; Sloanes Jamaica, 173; Thwaites 2, p 107, p 188, *f* 1.—A small shrub with whorled, oblong-ovate, entire leaves, small white flowers, and dark-red drupes. Native of the West Indies; raised at Hewra and Dapoorie from Calcutta seed.

LVI.—ASCLEPIADEÆ, Don's Syst. 4, p 106.

STEPHANOTIS, Ceropegia stephanotis, Don, Poir. Encycl. 3, p 185. From *stephanos*, a crown.

1. S FLORIBUNDA.—Native of Madagascar; an extensive climber with marginated acuminate subcordate coriaceous leaves, and long flowers, greenish-white, very ornamental; gardens Parell and Sewree.

STAPELIA, Pentandria Digynia. Named by Linnæus in memory of *Stapel*, a Dutch Physician.

2. S BUFONIA, Spr. 1, p 838; Bot. Mag. *t.* 1676; Orbea bufonia, Don's *syst.* 4, p 120.—A strange-looking, stemless, plant, with fœtid flowers, spotted like a toad's back; corolla flat, with no tube; flowers in the rains. Native of the Cape; garden Dapoorie.

3. S LENTIGINOSA.—This second species, also a native of the Cape, is not at present traceable at Dapoorie. Is it found elsewhere?

HOYA, Pentandria Digynia. Named after *Mr. Hoy*, formerly Gardener to the Duke of Northumberland.

4. H CARNOSA, Don's *syst.* 4, p 126; Wight's Com. Ind. Bot. p 38; Lour. p 165; Bot. Mag. *t.* 788; Smith Ex. Bot. 4.—Wax Plant, common in gardens and on trellises about bungalows. The appearance of the full umbels of flowers is very beautiful.

PERGULARIA, Pentandria Digynia. Pergula, said to be used by Pliny for trellis-work, the plant being suitable for covering trellises, Lam. 1, *t.* 176.

5. P ODORATISSIMA, Don's *syst.* 4, p 132; Wight Cont. Ind. Bot. p 43; Asclepias odoratissima, Roxb. Fl. Ind. 2, p 46; Bot. Rep. *t.* 185; Bot. Mag. *t.* 755; Rumph. Amb. 7, *t.* 26, *f.* 1.—A climber, with membraneous leaves; flowers yellow, very fragrant.

ASCLEPIAS, R. Br., Pentandria Digynia.

6. A CURASSAVICA, Don's *syst.* 4, p 139; Bot. Cab. *t.* 349; Bot. Reg. *t.* 81; Dill. Elth. *t.* 30, *f.* 33.—Herbaceous, erect, with linear-lanceolated leaves, and terminal, reddish orange flowers. The juice and pounded plant are said to be an excellent styptic. The root is much used by the Negroes in the West Indies as a substitute for Ipecacuanha. The plant is a native of the West India Islands. We have seen it growing wild below the Neelcoond Ghaut, in Canara, but here it may have been as a relic of some former garden, though now in the jungle.

CRYPTOSTEGIA, R. Br., Pentandria Digynia. From *cryptos*, hidden; and *stege*, covering; in allusion to the corona being concealed within the tube of the corolla.

7. C GRANDIFLORA, Don's *syst.* 4, p 164; Wight's Cont. Ind. Bot. p 66; Nerium grandiflorum, Roxb. p 10; Bot. Reg.

t. 435.—A climbing shrub, running over the highest trees, having showy rose-coloured, bell-shaped, flowers, and triangular follicles. The whole plant abounds in a milky caoutchouc juice, which is like India Rubber, but hardly elastic.

VICARIA, Pentandria Digynia. Name given in honour of *Captain Vicary*, employed in Assam.

8. V Cristata, Wall. Cat. (?)—An extensive climber, with broad-acuminate, regularly veined, entire leaves, and thick follicles, deeply wrinkled; garden Hewra; seed received from late Dr. Wallich.

GOMPHOCARPUS, Pentandria Digynia. Name given from the club-like appearance of the seed-vessel.

9. G Arborescens, R. Br. in Mem. of West. Soc. p 37; Hort. Kew., 2nd ed., vol. 2, p 79.—A tall straight-growing shrub, with villous stem and glabrate leaves; white flowers; follicle terminal, having numerous spines; garden Dapoorie. From Cape seed.

LVII.—BIGNONIACEÆ, Don's Syst. 4, p 214.

THE TRUMPET-FLOWER TRIBE.

BIGNONIA. Named from the *Abbe Bignon*, Librarian to Louis XIV.

MILLINGTONIA, Linn., Didynamia Angiospermia; Linn. Supp. 291; Juss. Gen. 138; Willd. sp. 3, p 382; Bignonia suberosa, Roxb.

1. M Hortensis, Linn. Suppl. 291; Willd. sp. 3, p 382; Bignonia suberosa, Roxb. Fl. Ind. 3, p 111.—Leaves about 2 feet long, variously divided and subdivided; have much resemblance to the foliage of Melia; flowers long-tubed, pure white, fragrant. It is believed to be a native of Ajmere. It has never been seen to produce seed in this latitude, but plants are readily obtainable from the numerous root-shoots. It is a magnificent tree, tall and straight.

TECOMA, Juss. Gen. p 139; R. Br. *Prod.* 471; H. B. Kunth, nov. Gen. Amer. 3, p 142.

2. T Capensis.—A scandent shrub, with pinnate leaves, and 9 or 10 serrated shining leaflets; flowers red, with a darkish tint of orange. Native of the Cape; now common as a pot-plant and a shrub in Indian gardens.

3. T Stans.—A tall shrub with branches somewhat quadrate; pinnate leaves; leaflets in one variety deeply serrate, in another entire, showy, yellow flowers, streaked with red lines on the inside. Common in gardens, Bombay, Poona, &c.

4. T Radicans, Willd. 3, p 301; Spr. *syst.* 2, p 834; Don's *syst.* 4, 225; Bot. Mag. *t.* 485; Catesby carolina 1, *t.* 65.—The rooting

or Ash-leaved Bignonia. A very beautiful climber, with pinnate leaves; leaflets gashed; stems with rooting joints, by which it adheres to walls, &c. like Ivy; flowers in large bunches at the end of the shoots, of a scarlet orange-colour. Native of Florida. Gardens Parell and Dapoorie. We doubt whether this be not the true Bignonia venusta, which name has been wrongly given to another species. In this the tendrils merely cling to a support; they are not roots.

5. T Jasminoides.—Leaves impari-pinnate and often ternate, glabrous; flowers pale-blue; a climber, native of Moreton Bay, in New Holland; Dapoorie, &c. not common.

6. T Chrysotricha DC. v. 9, p 216.—Native of Brazil; the flowers appearing after the fall of the leaf, which is 3-divided; does produce seed not with us. Garden Hewra, from plant sent by Mr. Law.

7. Bignonia Unguis, Var. tenuis, Linn. sp. 869; Mill. Dict. No. 5; Tourn. Inst. 164.—A delicate extensive climber, rooting like Ivy to the trees on which it ascends; leaves ovate-acuminate, shining, somewhat corrugated; flowers vivid yellow; has not borne fruit. It is a native of Barbadoes, J. St. Domingo; plant sent by Mr. Law, C. S.

8. B Colei, Don's *syst.* 4, p 221; Colea candlelabra, Bot. Mag. *t.* 2817.—A small erect tree, with unequally pinnated leaves; flowers from the stem, red, veined with yellow; no fruit. Garden Parell. A very beautiful species, native of Madagascar.

9. B Gracilis (?).—A climber with narrow-lanceolate leaves and double tendrils. Garden Hewra; plant from Mr. Law.

10. B Venusta.—The climber which bears this name in the Bombay gardens, Parell, Sewree, &c., though in some respects similar to that described in Don's *syst.*, is altogether different in the form and colour of the flowers, which in B venusta are partially crimson; but as these scandent, exotic species with us seldom or never bear seed, there is necessarily much uncertainty in applying specific names to each, and hence a considerable margin must be left for possible error.

11. B Stipulata, Spathodea slip, Wall. Pl. Asiat. Res. 1, p 81, *t.* 95, 96.—A tall tree, impari-pinnate; leaves acuminate, entire; flowers large, outside dark yellow and inside purple; seed-vessel 20 inches long, flat, the seeds have long wings. Gardens Hewra and Dapoorie, from Calcutta seed.

12. B Adenophylla, Wall. Cat. No. 6503.—Leaves impari-pinnate, downy beneath; leaflets obovate-oblong, mucronate sessile; corolla large yellow, thickly tomentose outside; superior laciniæ much curled; pods variously contorted, tomentose. Native of Burmah; gardens Hewra and Dapoorie, from Calcutta seed.

13. SPATHODEA, (?)—Is to be seen in the Sewree gardens, marked Spathacea, but erroneously, as the leaves are much larger, and the leaflets acuminate; flower said to be white; pod about 2 feet long, variously twisted. We reserve this tree for further investigation.

14. PITHOCOCTENIUM MURICATUM.—An extensive woody climber; native of Brazil, having broad entire acuminate opposite leaves; tendrils bifid; and flowers in long erect panicles by threes from the axils; flowers white and fleshy, they are incurved so as to resemble a parrot's-beak, hence the name. This is by far the most robust of any of the scandent Bignonias which we have seen. Plant sent by Mr. Law, C. S.

15. B CHAMBERLAYNII, Sims Bot. Mag. 2148.—We have seen this beautiful climber in one locality, but cannot at present recollect where. Information is requested regarding it.

16. B —— (?) sp. yet undetermined.—Of this there is only one specimen in Bombay, being a tree at the south-west angle of the bungalow of S. Compton, Esq. It was sent by Messrs. Loddiges & Co. to the late Colonel G. R. Jervis, and it is said to have a very beautiful flower. We have not seen it either in flower or in fruit. To be kept in view for future description.

CRESCENTIA, Schrib. Gen. No. 1021; Juss. Gen. 127; Gaert. Fr. Supp. 1, p 229, *t.* 223; named by Linnæus from *Crecentio,* an Italian writer on Agriculture, in the 13th Century. Didynamia Angiospermia.

17. C CUJETE, Linn. sp. 873.—Calabash tree, Jacq. Amb. 175, *t.* 111; Plumb. Gen. 23, *t.* 109.—Leaves oblong cuneate, often obovate, entire, shining; flowers variegated with green purple, red and yellow; fruit large, gourd-shaped, from 2 inches to a foot in diameter. Much used in South America to boil water in, as the shells bear the fire well; pulp of the fruit is used as a Poultice in diseases of the chest. Botanical Gardens, Hewra.

18. C ALATA, H. B. et Kunth. nov. Gen. Amer. 3, p 157.—Native of Mexico, near Acapulco; leaves ternate or sometimes simple and obovate oblong; common petiole broadly winged. The tree grows robustly, but has not yet flowered. Raised at Hewra and Dapoorie from seed received from Calcutta.

LVIII.—PEDALINEÆ, Don's Syst. 4, p 233.

THE OIL-SEED TRIBE.

MARTYNIA, Didynamia Angiospermia. In honour of *Martyn,* once Professor of Botany at Cambridge. Lam. *t.* 337; Gaert. 2, *t.* 110.

2. M DIANDRA, Don's *syst.* 4, p 235; Bot. Mag. *t.* 1656; Gaert. Fr. 2, 110; Bot. Rep. *t.* 575.—Native of Mexico; springs up everywhere in waste places of gardens, &c. during the rains. The flower is very ornamental, and the quaint-shaped, beetle-like seed, with its two sharp anterior hooks, is often an object of curiosity.

3. M PROBOSCIDLA.—Has been raised by us from seed sent by the Marchese Ridolfi, of Florence; the hooks at the end of the seed-vessel are about 3 inches in length; flower pink; leaves broad, ovate, downy. It has for the present disappeared from the gardens.

LIX.—COBEACEÆ, D. Don. in Echn. (?) Phil. Jour. 1824, Vol. 10.

1. COBEA SCANDENS.—A climber, with leaves alternate, abruptly pinnate, branched tendrils; calyx 5-wingled; corolla long, having a deep purple throat, and the laciniæ spreading, ciliated. Native of South America. Garden Dapoorie.

LX.—POLEMONACEÆ, Juss. Gen. p 136.

This family contains some of the Californian annual plants, mostly of great beauty. They are, however, generally of too evanescent a character to merit a place here. We have at different times had in flowers, Gilia tricolor, Cantua coronopifolia, and Leptosiphon androsaceus. The only one which merits a place as an established annual, renewed from its own seed, is Phlox drummondii, which has ovate-lanceolate, half stem-clasping, entire leaves, and showy purple flowers, darker in the centre.

LXI.—CONVOLVULACEÆ, Don's Syst. 4, p 253.

THE BINDWEED TRIBE, Lind. Nat. Syst. p 218.

PHARBITIS, Choisy, Pentandria Monogynia.

1. P LEARII.—Native of Brazil; a very beautiful Convolvulus, with large, blue flowers tinged with streaks of purple; it is now a favourite ornament of verandas and trellises in Western India, throwing out many flowers in the rains. Is not this the Ipomea hookeri of Don's Catalogue, otherwise Ipomea rubo-cœrulea? We ask the question doubtingly; but there is evidently some uncertainty, as Don asks whether it be not a Rivea. In fact, there is great confusion in the more modern classification of the Convolvulaceæ.

2. P Hispida, Choisy. in Mem. Soc. Phys. 6, p 438.—This species varies much in the colours of the flower, the latter being often a mixture of white-purple and violet. It is a native of the Sandwich Islands, Ceylon, and South America; the leaves are cordate acuminate entire.

IPOMŒA, Pentandria Monogynia, Choisy. Mem. 6, p 444.

3. I Sinuata, Don's *syst.* 4, p 279.—Stems hairy; leaves smooth, 7-parted; segments sinuated; peduncles axilliary; flowers white, with a dash of pink. Native of the West Indian Islands.

4. I Tuberculata, I tuberosa, Don's *syst.* 4, p 281; Pluk. Alm. *t.* 2, 76, *f.* 6; Sloanes Hist. *t.* 96, *f.* 2; Bot. Reg. 768.—An immense climber, with leaves palmately 7-parted, and light-yellow flowers, appearing in October and November. It is in general use for covering old walls, trellises, &c.

PORANA, Pentandria Monogynia.

5. P Volubilis.—Native of Eastern Islands; leaves cordate-acuminate. This species is conspicuous from its huge branches of white flowers. Gardens Bombay.

6. Quamoclit Phœnicea, Don's *syst.* 4, p 258; Ipomœa phœnicia, Roxb. Fl. 1, p 502.—Crimson Quamoclit; leaves cordate, reniform, and flowers in the cold weather; tube long and slender. In waste places and in gardens, common. The plant is said to be originally a native of the Coromandel coast and Molucca Islands.

7. Q Vulgaris, Don's *syst.* 4, p 260; I quamoclit, Roxb. Fl. 1, p 503; Lam. Encycl. 3, p 567; Rumph. Amb. 5, *t.* 2; Rheed. Mal. 11, *t.* 60; Bot. Mag. *t.* 244.—Native of America and Brazil; commonly called China Creeper; may at once be recognised by its multifid, filiform leaves, and bright crimson flowers, appearing at early morn.

8. Ipomœa Pileata.—Received under this name from Java; seed furnished by the late Mr. Davis, C.S.; a stout, climbing species, having broad tomentose, heart-shaped leaves, cross-veined; flowers white; seeds covered with long, dark hair. Garden Hewra. The specific name we have been unable to trace, but leave it for future inquiry. In the foregoing enumeration of the Convolvulaceæ exotic, or presumed to be so, it is to be noted that the list can be by no means complete, seeing that many species raised from exotic seed are likely to be found in the gardens of private persons. It is hoped that a list of all such introductions as may be considered established will yet be furnished in time for a future edition of this work.

LXII.—BORAGINEÆ, Don's Syst. 4, p 306.

THE BORAGE TRIBE, Lind. Nat. Syst. p 241.

ECHIUM, Pentandria Monogynia. From *echis*, a viper, in allusion to a fancied resemblance of the inflorescence.

1. E VIOLACEUM, Don's *syst*. 332.—This and several other species or varieties are to be found in gardens. They are distinguishable by their secund repand spikes of blue or purple flowers. They can hardly be considered as established. They are natives of the Cape de Verde Islands.

2. NONEA ROSEA, Linn. Gen. No. 167.—A native of Siberia and the Caucasus; a very hispid plant, having a roseate and yellow flower; may often be seen in gardens.

HELIOTROPIUM.—From *helios*, the sun; and *trope*, turning; in allusion to the flowers said to turn towards the sun.

3. H PERUVIANUM, Bot. Mag. *t.* 141; Don's *syst*. 4, p 357.—A 2-feet plant, with sweet-scented lilac-coloured flowers in terminal spikes; was introduced into Western India by the late Earl of Clare (?). It is a Peruvian plant, as the name denotes.

LXIII.—CORDIACEÆ, Don's Syst. 4, p 374.

EHRETIA, Pentandria Monogynia. Named by Linnæus in honour of a French botanist.

1. E BUXIFOLIA.—A small shrub, with leaves tapering at both ends, serrate; flowers small, white; fruit size of a grain of pepper. From seed sent from Calcutta. Gardens Hewra.

LXIV.—SOLANACEÆ, Don's Syst. 4, p 397.

THE NIGHT-SHADE TRIBE, Lind. Nat. Syst. p 231.

SOLANUM, Pentandria Monogynia, Tourn. *t.* 62.

1. S TUBEROSUM, Don's *syst*. 4, p 400. "Batatta," Maratha. Blackwell *t.* 523.—"Aloo," Bengal name. This useful root is now spread over many provinces of India as a cultivated product. Of the most superior quality it is raised at Mahableshwur, and in the Joonere Sooba. From the latter, hundreds of carts may daily in the season be seen conveying Potatoes to Bombay, where, owing to the wants of the shipping and the dense population, the supply required is enormous. In cholera seasons the natives reckon it (and it is believed with reason) to be a very unsafe diet.

It has not been observed that any epidemic disease has attacked the Potatoe in India, as has been the case in Europe.

2. S MACROPHYLLUM, S acerifolium (?), Kunth. nov. Gen. Amer. 3, p 46.—Native of South America; seed received from the India House; a tree 12 to 15 feet in height, having flowers just like those of the Potatoe, and fruit the size of an apple; leaves about four inches long, with acuminated and laterally diverging lobes; was introduced in 1843; is now not uncommon in gardens, where, notwithstanding its woody habit, the strong family likeness may be at once recognised.

3. S MELONGENA.—Native place uncertain. Brinjal, "Bengun," Maratha. Egg. Plant, Eng. This plant has never been seen wild, but cultivated; it may be noticed as extending from Avignon to Ceylon. It is one of the best of our Indian vegetables, and in an Omelette, as prepared by the French, it is very superior.

4. S LYCOPERSICUM.—Tomato, "Wel-Wangee," Maratha. Roxb. Fl. 1, p 565. Pomum amoris, Rumph. Amb. 5, *t.* 154; Lour. Cochin China p 130.—Originally a native of South America; is now often cultivated in Indian gardens, and has run wild in many places remote from garden-lands, as in the Fort of Sewnere, &c. The fruit is excellent both as a salad and as the base of a sauce.

5. CAPSICUM FRUTESCENS, Don's *syst.;* Roxb. Fl. p 574; Rumph. Amb. 5, *t.* 88, *f.* 1.—"Lal Mirchee"; extensively cultivated throughout the Deccan and Gujarat; that grown above the Ghauts is superior in sharpness and flavour to the product of more level countries. It is valuable in medicine as the basis of a gargle, used in sore-throats of a malignant character.

6. C PENDULUM (?), Don's *syst.* v. 4, p 445.—Bird's-eye Pepper; native of Africa (?). When introduced into India does not appear; it is much more robust in habit than the last, and is perennial. This species (?) forms the best Cayenne Pepper.

7. C NEPALENSIS.—A yellow variety, first introduced by Dr. Owen, at Seroor; it is in flavour very superior to any of the other Peppers.

8. C GROSSUM, Linn. *syst.* 226.—Caffree Merich. Is of various shapes and hues, and varies in size from that of a cherry to an apple; it is much milder than any of the others, therefore preferred for a pickle.

PHYSALIS, Pentandria Monogynia. From *physa,* a bladder, in relation to the inflated calyx. Lam. *t.* 116; Tourn. *t.* 64.

9. P PERUVIANA, Don's *syst.* 4, p 449; Roxb. Fl. 1, p 562. "Phoptee," Maratha. Bot. Mag. *t.* 1068; Linn. Trans. 17, p 67.—Cape Gooseberry; native of Peru; annual and biennial, diffuse plant; much cultivated for the sake of its fruit, which is of an agreeable acid, and forms excellent preserves.

10. NICANDRA PHYSALOIDES. "Ran Popatee," Don's *syst.* 4, 457; Jaq. Obs. *t.* 98.—Native of Peru and Chili, but now grows wild in waste places in India.

NICOTIANA, Pentandria Monogynia. In honour of *Nicot*, once French Ambassador in Portugal. Gaert. *t.* 55; Tourn. *t.* 41; Lam. *t.* 113.

11. N TABACUM, Don's *syst.* 4, p 462; Blackwell *t.* 146.—Tobacco Plant; cultivated to a large extent in the Deccan and Gujarat. The crops are frequently injured by a parasite (Orobanche indica.) From Gujarat, especially from Neriad, much Tobacco is exported to Sind. The best Tobacco grown in the Presidency next to that of Bilsa, in Malwa, is that raised on the deep alluvial lands near the Krishna River. The varieties, N longifolia and N rustica, the Havannah and Persian, are sometimes grown for private use, and are certainly superior in flavour to the common kinds; but whether this superiority is to be permanently maintained, is a different question.

12. N GLAUCA.—Native of Buenos Ayres, Grah. in Bot. Mag. 2837.—A tall erect species, glabrous; leaves unequally cordate ovate with yellow flowers; is merely ornamental; garden Dapoorie. In the above enumeration we have included N longifolia and persica as one species with N tabacum. We feel doubtful, however, whether they (at least the last, N persica) should not have been separated. The Jibbel Tobacco is more like in habit and appearance to N longifolia than to N persica.

13. HYOSCIAMUS NIGER, Pentandria Monogynia. Herbaceous; the whole plant clothed with clammy villæ; leaves stem-clasping, grossly serrate; corolla lurid, purple variegated with white sessile on lateral and terminal spikes; seed-vessel round, obovate acuminate, containing many small seeds. This plant, a native of Europe, is successfully cultivated at Hewra and Dapoorie for supply of the Medical Stores. The favourite time for cultivation is the cold season, when it may be sown either broad-cast or in beds for transplantation, but the former is most easy and effective. It requires high manuring to produce leaves in quantity. We have seen bullocks die from feeding on the leaves. The seed imported from Cabul or Persia is sold by the native druggists in Bombay under the name of "Khorasany Ajwan." They are used as a narcotic medicine.

CESTRUM, Pentandria Monogynia. Linn. Gen. No. 261; Sch. Gen. No. 342; Gaert. Fr. 1, p 378, *t.* 77; Lam. Illust. *t.* 112.

14. C CONGLOMERATUM, (?) Ruiz. and Pavon. Fl. Per. 2, p 29.—A shrub with oblong-lanceolate leaves, and corolla of a greenish-yellow, having a longish tube, with segments of laciniæ erect acute. Garden Hewra. Native of Brazil; has not seeded.

15. PETUNIA, Pentandria Monogynia, Juss. in Ann. Mus. 2, p 215, *t.* 47 ; Persoon Ench. 1, p 218.—Of this herbaceous plant, which is a native of South America, many varieties, as to the colour of the flowers, are annually raised in garden flower-beds. To specify these would be a work of too much detail. The flowers vary from white to deep purple.

BROWALLIA, Didynamia Angiospermia.—These plants, natives of South America, have been raised from seed received from Professor Savi, of Pisa.

16. B DEMISSA.—Having leaves ovate-acuminate, oblique, and a corolla, like the Verbenaceæ, of a pale blue.

17. B ELONGATA.—Having broader leaves, and a pubescent stem ; flower like that of B demissa. Garden Dapoorie.

BRUGMANASIA, D. Don in Sweet. Fl. Gard. Nat. *syst.* 272 ; Roem. and Schultz *syst.* 4, p 23.

18. B CANDIDA.—Native of Peru ; not uncommon in our gardens ; the flower is long-lobed, plaited, crisped at edges of laciniæ, and altogether like a gigantic Datura.

LYCIUM, Pentandria Monogynia, Lam. Illust. *t.* 112.

19. L AFRUM.—Linn. *syst.* 228 ; Mant. p 47 ; Don's *syst.* 4, p 458.—The shrub did exist at Dapoorie ; having a number of fascicled spathulate leaves, rising from spinous processes along the branches. We are not sure that it still exists ; it never flowered.

The ornamental annuals Salpiglossis, &c. belong to this family, but as these are always renewed from foreign seed, they can hardly have a place here. Schizantus venusthus is one of the choicest of our annuals.

LXV.—VERBASCINEÆ, Don's Syst. 4, p 504.

1. VERBASCUM TOMENTOSUM.—This is a tall erect plant, having a thick round stem finally covered with sessile yellow flowers. We have raised it from seed received from Dr. Jameson, Seharunpore. Is it found in any garden at present (?) Ours has disappeared.

LXVI.—SCROPHULARINEÆ, Don's Syst. 4, p 504.

THE FIGWORT TRIBE.

MAURANDYA, Don, Didynamia Angiospermia. Named in honour of *Dr. Maurandy*, Botanical Professor at Carthagena.

1. M BARCLAYANA, Lind. Bot. Reg. *t.* 1108.—A climbing shrub, having cordate-acuminate, often hastate, leaves, and flowers of a violet purple colour. It is a native of Mexico ; gardens common.

2. M SEMPERFLORENS, Jacq. Hist. 3, p 20, *t.* 288; Curtis Bot. Mag. 460.—Very similar in habit and leaves to the foregoing; the corolla is of a roseate purple, streaked with white.

3. M ANTIRRHINIFOLIA.—Blue-flowered Maurandya, Bot. Mag. *t.* 1643; Don's *syst.* 4, p 533.—An elegant climber, like the last.

4. M ALBA.—We doubt if this be anything more than a variety, and the same remark may be deemed to apply to two out of the three species above enumerated.

LOPHOSPERMUM, Didynamia Angiospermia. Named from *lophos*, a crest; and *sperma*, a seed; in reference to the crest-like wing of the seed, Don. May be so, but with us it never ripens seed.

5. L SCANDENS, D. Don in Linn. Trans. 15, p 349.—Climber, native of Mexico, with serrate, villous, somewhat hastate, leaves, and showy flowers of a deep roseate colour.

ANTERRHINUM, Didynamia Angiospermia, G. Don's *syst.* 4, p 515.—Annual; native of Southern Europe. The great variety of these introduced annuals prevents the possibility of detail; colours varying from yellow to purple. In gardens, common.

RUSSELIA, Didynamia Angiospermia. Named after *Russel*, author of History of Aleppo, Schren. Gen. 1, 41; Jacq. Amer. p 1781.

6. R JUNCEA.—A showy demi-herbaceous plant; stems widely-spreading, with linear leaves, and rich scarlet flowers; native of Terra Caliente, of Mexico. In gardens, now common; was introduced about ten years ago.

7. R FLORIBUNDA, Kunth. nov. Gen. 2, p 359.—Herbaceous; stems spreading, erect, quadrangular; leaves opposite cordate, flowering in axillary corymbs, each having many showy red flowers. Less common than the last; gardens Dapoorie and Parell. Besides the above-named exotic Scrophularineæ, we have just met with two of great beauty, viz.:—

ANGELONIA, Humboldt and Bonpland Pl. Equinoct 2, p 92, *t.* 108. Didynamia Angiospermia.

8. A LOBANIFOLIA, A salicaræfolia, Humb. and Bonp. loc. cit. *t.* 108.—Corolla short-tubed, concave bottom, and a bilabiate limb. The whole of a rich purple hue; leaves opposite, narrow-lanceolate pilose, as is the whole plant; stem quadrangular. Native of Caraccus. Gardens Parel, received from Madras.

BRUNFELSIA, Didynamia Angiospermia. Called after *Brunpelsius*, a Physician of Metz.

9. B NITIDA, Bot. Mag. 4287; B undulata, Don's Dict. p 476.—An elegant shrub, with lanceolate ovate leaves, shining; corolla erect, with a long tube, containing the organs; laciniæ

short, fleshy, at first pale-yellow, finally white. Native of West Indies, Garden Sewree. Presented by Sir Cursetjee Jamsetjee.

10. Browallia Cervias Rowski.—A species raised from seed sent by Lawson and Sons; flower much larger than in the other Browallias, probably only a cultivated variety.

LXVII.—OROBANCHEÆ, Don's Syst. 4, p 629.

PENTESTEMON, Didynamia Angiospermia, Aiton Hort. Kew. 3, p 511.

1. P Gentianoides.—Native of Mexico; a beautiful, herbaceous plant, distinguishable by having one of the four filaments sterile; long-lanceolate entire leaves; a violet colour; downy corolla, flowering on several peduncles, but not rounded; the lower lip of the corolla trifid, and wants the down which covers the remainder. Garden Dapoorie.

LXVIII.—GESNERACEÆ, Don's Syst. 4, p 644.

GESNERIA, Didynamia Angiospermia. All these are very showy plants, natives of Brazil, and now partially naturalised in Indian gardens. Named by Plumier in honour of *Gesner*, a Botanist of Zurich.

1. G Douglasii, Lind. in Bot. Reg. *t.* 1110.—Pubescent with ovate acute, toothed leaves, and drooping, orange-coloured corolla, varied with darker stripes. We are of opinion that G bulbosa, mentioned in the 1st edition of the Catalogue, No. 1086, must have been intended for this plant.

2. G Zebrina.—Is so called from the varied colour of the leaves, which are from deep-green to dark-purple, and very beautiful; flower much as in G douglasii. Dapoorie.

GLOXINIA, Didynamia Angiospermia. Named in honour of *B. P. Gloxin*, a Botanist of Colmar.

3. G Speciosa.—Hispid with villous peduncles; ovate, crenate leaves, and corolla large, bluish-purple. Gardens, rare. Dapoorie.

Of the beautiful Achimenes which belong to this order, we may enumerate the following varieties:—Achimenes longiflora, A major, A grandiflora, A skinneri gigantea, A sp. Indet. These are all annual, appearing in full flower in August and September, and preserved as Dahlias are for next season, by burying the roots in sand.

LXIX.—LABIATÆ, Don's Syst. 4, p 665.

THE MINT TRIBE, Lind. Nat. Syst. p 239.

COLEUS, Don, Didynamia Angiospermia. From *koleos*, a sheath, in allusion to the filaments being connected at the base and sheathing the style.

1. C AROMATICUS, Don's *syst.* 4, p 682; Plectranthus aromaticus.—"Pathoor Choor," Maratha; Country Burrage. A native of Northern India, but with us found only in gardens; it forms an agreeable addition to the cooling drinks used in the hot season.

LAVANDULA, Don, Didynamia Gymnospermia. From *lavo*, to wash, from the use of the plants in baths.

2. L STŒCHAS (?), Don's *syst.* 4, p 709; Stœchas L purpurea, Tourn. Ins. *t.* 95.—A plant with very glaucous, linear leaves, having revolute margins; spike tetragonal; verticels 6 to 10-flowered; flowers dark-purple. In gardens Belgaum and Dharwar; said to have been introduced from the Cape of Good Hope, and commonly called Lavender, Mr. Law.

3. L SPICA, Don's *syst.* 4, p 710.—Spica, or broad-leaved Lavender. In gardens, Belgaum, Mr. Law. The flowers are used in the south of France for the distillation of what is called *Oil of Spike*, Don.

4. L VERA (?), Don's *syst.* 4, p 709; Woodville's Med. Bot. *t.* 55.—Long, narrow-linear leaves, covered with white tomentum; never flowers in this climate, and drags out a sickly existence as a pot-plant around bungalows.

POGOSTEMON, Don, Didynamia Angiospermia. From *pogon*, a beard; and *stemon*, a stamen; in allusion to the filaments being generally bearded.

5. P PATCHOWLI.—Native name "Pach." Native of Eastern Islands, as Java, &c. The peculiar perfume of this plant has been long known to the natives, and more lately to the European world. The leaves, strewed among woollen-cloths, are said to keep off insects. The plant has generally a purplish tinge.

MERIANDRA, Don, Diandria Monogynia. From *meris*, a part; and *aner*, a male; in allusion to the superior stamens being abortive.

6. M BENGHALENSIS, Don 4, p 722; Salvia benghalensis, Roxb. Fl. 1, p 145; Ainslie Mat. Ind. 1, p 359.—A tall, shrubby plant, leaves and branches canescent. Exhales a strong smell of camphor on rubbing the leaves; flowering in axillary terminal, thickly-set whorls.

SALVIA, Diandria Monogynia. From *salvo*, to save, in allusion to the healing qualities of Sage. Gaert. *t.* 66; Tourn. *t.* 83; Lam. *t.* 20.

7. S PSEUDO-COCCINEA, Don's *syst.* 4, p 749; Jaq. Ic. rar. 2, *t.* 209; Bot. Mag. *t.* 2864.—Native of tropical America; flowers of a beautiful scarlet.

8. S COCCINEA, Linn. Mant. p 88.—Erect and more robust than the last; leaves 2 inches, very soft; calyx purplish, corolla scarlet. Native of South America, and also of East Indies (?); found in gardens occasionally.

ROSMARINUS, Diandria Monogynia.

9. R OFFICINALIS, Smith's Fl. Græca. 1, *t.* 14; Woodv. Med. Bot. *t.* 87; Blackwell *t.* 159; Don's *syst.* 4, p 749.—Native of Europe; is now often found in Indian gardens; in those of the Deccan it flowers freely.

MARJORANA, Didynamia Gymnospermia.

10. M HORTENSIS, Don's *syst.* p 766.—Sweet Marjoram; annual; gardens, common.

THYMUS, Didynamia Gymnospermia.

11. T VULGARIS, Woodv. Med. Bot. *t.* 109.—English Thyme; common in gardens.

12. T —— (?) sp.—A plant belonging to this genus in gardens, Belgaum, Mr. Law. Was also at Dapoorie, but appears to have died out. Information is solicited as to the Belgaum plant.

LEONOTIS, Didynamia Gymnospermia. From *leo*, a lion; and *ous*, an ear; in allusion to the fancied likeness in the flowers.

13. L NEPETIFOLIA.—" Matee-Sool." A tall erect-growing plant, with globular whorls of orange-coloured flowers, and calyces spinous toothed. Native of Asia, Africa, and Brazil. With us, if not indigenous, it is often found in waste places near towns, in hill-forts, &c. wild.

14. L LEONURUS, Don's *syst.* 4, p 850; Bot. Mag. *t.* 478; Willd. sp. 3, p 127.—Flowers scarlet, much larger than the last, drooping. Gardens, Belgaum, Mr. Law; rare, climber.

15. S TARTARICA OR SIBERICA.—A species having whorls of rich pink flowers, variegated with white, raised from seed sent by Professor Savi, of Pisa. It grows in Dapoorie, Hewra, and Parell gardens. This is a very marked and beautiful species.

HOLMSKOLDIA, Didynamia Gymnospermia. In memory of *Holmskold*, a Danish botanist.

16. H SANGUINEA, Don's *syst.* 4, p 856; Haslingia coccinea, Roxb. 3, p 65; Smith Ex. Bot. *t.* 100; Bot. Reg. *t.* 792.—An elegant shrub, with bright-scarlet flowers, in a membranaceous, round-spread calyx of a dim red. Native of Sylhet. Gardens not uncommon.

17. MENTHA ARVENSIS is the common species found in Indian gardens under this name. "Pudeena," Hindoostanee. It is a native of Europe; but with us spreads readily in moist places.

LXX.—VERBENACEÆ, Br. *Prod.* 1, p 510.

THE VERVAIN TRIBE, Lind. Nat. Syst. p 238.

VERBENA, Spr., Didynamia Angiospermia.

1. V OFFICINALIS, Spr. *syst.* 2, p 570; Eng. Bot. *t.* 769.—Common Vervain. Of this there are numerous varieties in gardens having various colours, all of them ornamental and fitted for brilliant contrasts in flower-beds. Natives of South America.

STACHYTARPHETA, Vahl., Diandria Monogynia. From *stachys*, a spike; *tarpheios*, dense; in allusion to the flowers growing in dense spikes.

2. S URTICFOLIA, S jamaicensis, Spr. *syst.* 1, p 53; Jacq. Obs. 4, *t.* 85.—Jamaica Vervain; an annual, with blue flowers in terminal spikes. A decoction of this plant has been supposed to be useful as a diaphoretic in Fevers.

3. S MUTABILIS, Spr. *syst.* 1, p 53; Bot. Mag. *t.* 976; Willd. sp. 1, p 115; Jacq. Ic. Pl. rar. 2, *t.* 207.—Changeable-flowered Vervain; a shrubby plant, with scarlet and pink flowers variegated with white in terminal spikes.

ALOYSIA, Pers., Didynamia Angiospermia. Named after *Louisa*, Mother of Ferdinand 7th, of Spain.

4. A CITRIODORA.—Lemon-scented Aloysia; a shrub with linear-lanceolate, ternate leaves, and flowers in axillary and terminal sub-panicled spikes. Now common in gardens, and is much esteemed for its fragrance, particularly in the rainy season. This plant was introduced by the late Earl of Clare, who was a great Horticultural amateur. It is a native of Chili.

LANTANA, Didynamia Angiospermia. An ancient name of the Viburnum, to which this shrub bears some resemblance.

5. L MELISSÆFOLIA, Spr. *syst.* 2, p 761; Bot. Mag. *t.* 96; Pluk. Alm. *t.* 233, *f.* 5; Willd. sp. 3, p 320.—A straggling shrub, flowers orange-coloured. Common in gardens; native of West Indies.

6. L ACULEATA.—Scandent, with opposite ovate leaves, smelling of black currants, square prickly stems, and orange-coloured flowers. There are two other species or varieties,—one with lilac flowers, and the other of mixed red and orange; but as the whole of these exotic species are rapidly becoming wild, a separate enumeration here appears to be needless. The infusion of L. pseudo-thea is used in the Brazils as a substitute for Tea.

Capitaõ do Matto, Lindley. The foreign Lantanas may now be seen everywhere in Bombay climbing on hedges and walls.

CLERODENDRON, Didynamia Angiospermia, Gaert. Fr. 1, *t.* 57; Lam. 111, *t.* 544.

7. C SQUAMATUM.—Native of China or Japan; an herbaceous erect plant, having large, broad ovate-cordate leaves, and flowers of a bright scarlet.

8. C SIPHONANTHUS, Spr. *syst.* 2, p 760; Volkameria japonica, Roxb. Fl. Ind. 3, p 67; Lam. Illust. 79, *f.* 1; Burm. Ind. 3, *t.* 43, *f.* 1; Willd. 3, p 382.—A tall erect suffruticose plant, with linear leaves, and flowers having long, white fleshy tubes.

9. C FRAGRANS, Spr. *syst.* 2, p 760; Volkameria japonica, Bot. Mag. *t.* 1834.—Double variety, herbaceous, with large wrinkled or rather cochleate leaves, and flowers white, merging into dark purple. Native of China; and now common in gardens, Bombay, &c.

10. C ACULEATUM, Volkameria aculeata, Spr. *syst.* 2, p 760; Br. Jam. *t.* 20, *f.* 2; Pluk. Phyt. 1, 351, *fig.* 2; Jacq. Amer. *t.* 117; Sloane Jam. 2, *t.* 166, p 2 and 3.—A thick bushy shrub, somewhat armed; flowers white, fragrant, lateral and terminal corymbs. Native of the West Indies; in the garden of the Byculla Club main circle.

11. C NUTANS, Bot. Mag. *t.* 2925.—A shrub with dingy white flowers, in terminal drooping corymbs; very ornamental. Parell Gardens, introduced from the Mauritius; a native of Madagascar.

GMELINA, Linn., Didynamia Angiospermia. In honour of *Gmelin,* a German Naturalist and Traveller. Gaert. Fr. 1, *t.* 56; Lam. *t.* 542.

12. G VILLOSA.—Native of Penang; Arboreous, spinous; spines long and straight, bushy in habit; flowers bright-yellow, smaller than those of G asiatica; fruit size of a large cherry, finally yellow. Is now common in gardens and garden-lands.

13. G ASIATICA.—This is a shrub smaller than the last both as to habit and leaves; the latter are small, scolloped, and shining.

CONJEA, Roxb. Pl. Cor. 3, 90, *t.* 293; Ic. 106, *f.* 1; Roscoea, Roxb. Fl. Ind. 3, 54.

14. C AZUREA, Roscoea tomentosa, Jackson and Hook. Bot. Mag. 1, 283.—A stout woody climber; leaves opposite, cordate, entire villous; involucre 3-leaved, containing 6 to 9 flowers, of a beautiful pink-colour; border of the corol bilabiate; exterior lip very long and bifid; under of 3 equal segments. Native of Eastern Bengal, not common in gardens of Western India. At Dapoorie and Sewrie (?).

DURANTA, Linn. Gen. No. 186; Jacq. Amer. 186, *t.* 176.

15. D Ellisii, P. Br. Jam. *t.* 29, *f.* 1; Castirea Plum. Ic. 79.—Native of South America; leaves opposite, generally simple and terminal; panicle of bright blue flowers lighter in the throat of the corolla. Gardens, common.

16. D Plumieri.—The difference between this and the former is not easily detected, both are stout, subarboreous species, often armed with long thorns, and form a very ornamental hedge division in a garden. We have received a third (D spinosa) with white flowers, from Parell gardens, very thorny. The contrast of the green of the leaves, and the vivid yellow of the clusters of acuminated fruit, is very pleasing.

PETREA, Tetrandria Monogynia. Linn. Gen. No. 764; Jacq. Amer. *t.* 114.

17. P Volubilis.—A scandent shrubby plant, native of tropical America, having blunt-ovate shining leaves of 3 to 4 inches in length, and axillary peduncles bearing a few showy blue tubular flowers, and the laciniæ of the corol spreading; has not seeded with us. Gardens Parell, Hewra, and Dapoorie.

RIVINA, Tetraoctandria Monogynia.

18. R Madagascarensis.—Herbaceous, with shining entire alternate feather-nerved leaves, small flowers, and cernuous clusters of showy red fruit.

19. Pircunia Dioica, Olim Phytolacca arborea, Moq.—A tree with entire cross-nerved, long-petiolate leaves, and racemes of green flowers, distinguishable in the female by the many-lobed nectary. Introduced from Egypt to Bombay under the name "Bella Sombra." The tree is found in the Mediterranean Provinces, but is a native of America. One tree may be seen among those planted on the Esplanade, opposite the Marine Lines.

LXXI.—ACANTHACEÆ, Br. *Prod.* p 472.

THE JUSTICIA TRIBE, Lind. Nat. Syst. p 233.

THUNBERGIA, Didynamia Angiospermia. In honour of *Thunberg*, the Botanist.

1. T Grandiflora, Roxb. Fl. Ind. 3, No. 36; Bot. Reg. *t.* 493.—A perennial twining plant, with opposite cordate, often lobate, leaves; flowers large, of a light-blue colour; common in gardens, Bombay. Found in the rains often climbing over high trees. It is a choice plant for trellises. The plant is a native of Eastern Bengal.

2. T Alata.—Plant said to be a native of Zanzibar; leaves cordate sagittate; petiole a little winged; laciniæ of corol yellow, with a deep purple spot in base of the tube.

CROSSANDRA, Salisbury, Parud. 12.

3. C Coccinea, C Flava, Nees in Wall. Pl. As. rar. 3, 98.—Herbaceous, with whorled, entire leaves, and a quadrangular flower; spike of red or yellowish flowers. Native of Eastern Bengal (?). In gardens, common.

JUSTICIA. Named in honour of *Mr. Justice,* a Scotch Gardener and Botanist.

4. J Picta, Graptophyllum pictum, Nees.—Native of East Indies, Nepal (?); an erect shrub, often seen in pots and tubs at bungalows, conspicuous by its beautifully varied leaves and dark purple flowers. It bears no seed with us.

5. J Gendarussa, Roxb. Fl. 1, p 126; G vulgaris, Wall. Pl. As. rar. 3, p 104.—Is now very common in gardens, being a favourite plant for the edging of flower-beds. The plant is strong-scented, and of a purple hue.

6. Goldfussia, Nees in Wall. Pl. rar. 3, 87; Bot. Mag. *t.* 3404; Ruel. sp. Roxb. Hook. Exot. Fl. *t.* 191.—A demi-shrubby plant, with opposite, deeply-veined leaves, and inflorescence in long axillary panicles, and often also in terminal spikes; flowers drooping, of a rich purple. Native of north-east of Bengal; gardens Dapoorie and Sewrie.

7. Aphelandra, R. Br. *Prod.* 475.—Native of tropical America; erect, demi-shrubby plants, with opposite leaves and axillary and terminal peduncles finally ending in a long quadrangular, tapering, and finally cernuous spike of showy red flowers. In gardens Sewree and Dapoorie; not common. There may be two species of this elegant plant in our gardens, but we are not sure on this head. Information is solicited.

8. Ruellia Formosa.—A small perennial, native of South America; leaves entire, downy, nearly sessile; flower large, bright-red; upper laciniæ of corol erect revolute; lower much smaller; lateral laciniæ large revolute.

LXXII.—PLUMBAGINEÆ, Sweet. Hort. Brit. p 332.

PLUMBAGO, Pentandria Monogynia.

1. P Coccinea.—Native of Southern India and Eastern Islands. "Lal Chitra," Hindoostanee, Thunb. Roxb. Fl. 1, p 463; Rheede Mal. 12 to 9; Rumph. Amb. 5, *t.* 168; Bot. Mag. *t.* 230; As. Res. 11, p 175; Ainslie Mat. Ind. 2, p 379.—Herbaceous, erect, with vivid red flowers blooming throughout the year.

2. P Capensis, Spr. *syst.* 1, p 537; Bot. Mag. Reg. *t.* 417; Bot. Mag. 2110.—Blue-flowered Leadwort. Native of the Cape; common in gardens. All these Plumbagos have strong, acrid properties, and may be used in cases of necessity where immediate blistering is required.

LXXIII.—NYCTAGINEÆ, Sweet. Hort Brit. p 334.

MIRABILIS, Pentandria Monogynia, Lam. *t.* 105; Gaert. 2, *t.* 127.

1. M Jalapa, Spr. *syst.* 1, p 537; Rheed. Mal. 10, *t.* 75; Rumph. Amb. 5, *t.* 89; Blackwell *t.* 404; Bot. Mag. *t.* 371; Ainslie Mat. Ind. 2, p 284.—"Gool Abass," Marvel of Peru; common in evey garden.

2. Bougainvillea Spectabilis.—Native of Brazil; an extensive thorny climber, with broad-lanceolate pubescent leaves; having a few small yellow flowers enclosed in the large and showy pink involucre. This plant was introduced from Bengal by Sir E. Perry, late Chief Justice. It is now most common as a covering to trellises, archways, &c.

PISONIA, Heptandria Monogynia. Named by Plumier in honour of *Piso*, a Physician of Amsterdam.

3. P Morindifolia.—Native of the Eastern Islands. China Lettuce; a shrub, with long smooth leaves, and minute inconspicuous, olive-coloured flowers in terminal cymes. The leaves of this plant have the remarkable peculiarity of becoming darker in the shade unlike most other plants, which become pale under similar circumstances. As a pot plant around bungalows most common.

LXXIV.—AMARANTHACEÆ.

GOMPHRENA, Pentandria Monogynia, Gaert. 2, *t.* 128; Lam. *t.* 180.

1. G Globosa, Roxb. Fl. 2, p 63; Rumph. Amb. 5, *t.* 100, *f.* 2; Rheed. Mal. 10, *t.* 37; Bot. Mag. 2315.—Jafferee Goondee, Hindoostanee, Globe Amaranth. Annual, common in every garden. The flowers are in heads, and look much like Red Clover. The native women wear them in their hair. They are also used for decorating churches and the images in Hindoo temples.

LXXV.—CHENOPODEÆ, Sweet. Hort. Brit. p 338.

THE GOOSE-FOOT TRIBE, Lind. Nat. Syst. p 167.

BASELLA, Pentandria Trigynia. "Myal-ke-Bajee," Hindoostanee.

1. B Alba, Roxb. Fl. Ind. 2, p 104; B rubra (variety), Rheede Mal. 7, *t.* 24; B lucida and Cordifolia, Willd. sp. 1, p 514; Rumph. Amb. 5, p 417, *t.* 154, *f.* 2; Pluk. Alm. *t.* 63, *f.* 1.—Twining, succulent plants, with smooth fleshy leaves; they grow very rapidly, and are often cultivated as a Spinach. The purple juice of the red variety, if it could be fixed, might form a choice dye.

ATRIPLEX, Polygamia Monœcia.

2. A Hortensis, Spr. *syst.* 3, p 916; Blackwell *t.* 99 and 525.—Garden Orache, occasionally cultivated as a Spinach. There are several varieties tinged with red or purple.

BETA, Pentandria Digynia. From the Cetic *bet*, red. Lam. *t.* 182; Gaert. *t.* 75.—"Paluk," Maratha; "Chukunder," Hindoostanee. Is now a common article of cultivation in European gardens, the varieties being numerous, and all appear to succeed equally well. The Mangel Wurzel also grows freely enough, but from its size and coarseness is useless for the table, while as a sugar-producing plant, it can never compete in India with the Cane.

SPINACIA, Diœcia Pentandria. From *spina*, a prickle, in allusion to the prickles on the seeds. Gaert. *t.* 126.

3. S Oleracea, Spr. *syst.* 3, p 903.—Common Spinach (Paluck) cultivated in gardens. It succeeds best when sown on raised beds in June.

CHENOPODIUM, Pentandria Didynia, Gaert. *t.* 75; Lam. *t.* 181.

4. C Ambrosioides.—Native of South America and Algeria; herbaceous, with serrate lanceolate leaves, and numerous spikes of flowers, axillary and terminal. These, when bruised, exhale a strong camphoraceous small. Botanical Garden Hewra, from seed sent by Professor Savi, of Pisa. Is not this plant a native of Southern India?

AMBRINA, Triandria Monogynia, Roubieva Moq. Tand. in nov. Ann. Sc. Nat. 1, 293, *t.* 10, *f.* 6.—Chenopodium Payco molina, Chili 283; Chenop. multifidum, Linn.

5. A Botrys.—Herbaceous plant, with deeply serrate lobate leaves, and numerous axillary and terminal spikes of flowers. The whole plant is very fragrant. It is a native of South America. Our specimens were raised from seed from Pisa. Garden Hewra, where it annually re-appears as a weed.

BEGONIA, Sweet. Hort. Brit. 341.—Of this family, the only one which appears to be really exotic is—

6. B HYDROCTYLIFOLIA.—A beautiful, low-growing plant with cochleate entire humifuse leaves, round cordate, and variously tinged from dark-green to red and purple; small pink flowers, in long upright peduncles. That this beautiful Begonia belongs to the American Continent we believe there is little doubt, though it is said to have been found in Malabar.

LXXVI.—BERBERIDEÆ, Juss. Gen. 286.

THE BARBERRY TRIBE.

BERBERIS, Hexandria Monogynia. Barberry, Linn. Gen. No. 442. Of these we may state that—

1. B ARISTATA and Asiatica are to be found in the Botanical Gardens reared chiefly from Seharunpore seed, but they can hardly be considered as established trees, seeing that their growth is slow and stunted, and probably will never flower. The Barberry in its wild state is, we believe, found on the hills north and east of Aboo, beyond Danteewarra; but as no specimens have reached us, we leave the subject open for future inquirers. The power of the bark in the cure of fever is said to be considerable.

LXXVII.—POLYGONEÆ, Sweet. Hort. Brit. p 341.

THE BUCK-WHEAT TRIBE, Lind. Nat. Syst. p 169.

1. POLYGONUM TARTARICUM—Buck Wheat; native of Northern Asia; is occasionally seen as a cultivated product in the Deccan, the grain being eaten toasted as a fast-day food by the Hindoos. The broad cordate leaves, and the upright head of handsome white flowers, render it very conspicuous in a field. It is believed that the cultivation of this grain has originated long anterior to the settlement of Europeans in India.

LXXVIII.—LAURINEÆ, Sweet. Hort. Brit. p 344.

1. CINNAMOMUM AROMATICUM, Nees in Wall. Pl. As. rar. p 74; Wight Ic. *t.* 139.—The Ceylon Cinnamon tree, at once recognised by its regular 3-nerved coriaceous shining leaves, and the terminal panicles of flowers, the leaves exhaling the peculiar and pleasant cinnamon odour when bruised. The fruit does not ripen in the specimens which we have seen at Bombay and Tanna. In gardens Bombay, Parell, &c. The best specimen we have seen is a tree in a compound in Tanna, just north of the Adawlut.

PERSEA, Enneandria Monogynia.

2. P GRATISSIMA, Spr. *syst.* 2, p 268; Laurus persea, Willd. sp. 2, p 480; Pluk. Alm. *t.* 267, *f.* 1; Sloanes Jam. 2, *t.* 222, *f.* 2.—The Alligator or Avocado Pear of the West Indies. The fruit is of the size and shape of a large pear, and is esteemed in the West Indies; grows in gardens at Belgaum, but the specimens of the fruit as seen by us are by no means delicate.

LXXIX.—MYRISTICEÆ, Sweet. Hort. Brit. p 345.

THE NUTMEG TRIBE, Lind. Nat. Syst. p 23.

1. MYRISTICA, Diœcia Monadelphia. Native of the Eastern Islands; is said to have been successfully cultivated at Sion and Poway. Away from the sea air the tree immediately languishes.

2. LAURUS CAMPHORA, Roxb. Fl. Ind. 2, p 304.—In the first edition of this work it is stated that the Laurus camphora tree had been introduced by the late Mr. Nimmo. We have, however, been unable to trace it: information on the subject is solicited.

LXXX.—ARISTOLOCHIÆ, Brown's *Prod.* p 349.

THE BIRTH-WORT TRIBE, Lind. Nat. Syst. p 72.

ARISTOLOCHIA, Gynandria Hexandria. Of this family we can only as yet reckon as introduced one of the several very ornamental species found in tropical America. Some of these have flowers so large that they are used as coverings for the head, for which their coal-scuttle-like shape well adapts them. Ours is—

1. A RINGENS.—An extensive climber, with round, deeply cordate, leaves, and large 4-inch flowers of the usual yellow, mottled with purple. The plant has not seeded; it does not possess any of the bitterness of two of our Indian species—A indica and A bracteata, therefore we infer that it has none of the medicinal virtues which both of these are known to possess; the powdered seeds of A bracteata being in particular a powerful remedy in intermittent fever. For A ringens we are indebted, as in many other instances, to the kindness of J. S. Law, Esq., C.S. To this gentleman, as well as the late Colonel G. R. Jervis, we owe many valuable exotics to the garden.

LXXXI.—EUPHORBIACEÆ, Sw. Hort. Brit. p 355.

THE EUPHORBIUM TRIBE, Lind. Nat. Syst. p 102.

EUPHORBIA, Dodecandria Trigynia. Named after *Euphorbus,* Physician to Juba, King of Mauritiana.

1. E TITHYMALOIDES, Willd. 2, p 890; Jacq. Amer. *t.* 92; Pluk. Alm. *t.* 230, *f.* 2; Dill. Elth. *t.* 288, *f.* 372; Ainslie Mat. Ind. 2, p 99.—A small unarmed shrub, about 3 feet high, with fleshy leaves, deciduous in the cold weather, and small red flowers of a slipper-like shape. It is commonly used as a bordering for walks.

2. E SPLENDENS.—Native of Terra Caliente of South America; shrubby; stem variously twisted, obovate, often spathulate; leaves whorled; flowers of a vivid red. This ornamental plant was introduced within the last ten years.

3. E TIRUCALLI, Roxb. Fl. Ind. 2, p 470; Tirucalli, Rheed. Mal. *t.* 44; Ossifraga lactea, Rumph. Amb. 7, *t.* 29; Pluk. Phyt. *t.* 319, p 6.—The common smooth Milk-Bush; grows to the height of about 20 feet; it is much used as a hedge-plant, and, though unarmed, makes a good fence, as cattle avoid it from fear of the acrid juice. The older plants are often preserved for rafters, as the wood is strong, and not liable to attacks of worms.

4. POINSETTIA PULCHERRIMA.—This plant also has been introduced within the last 12 years, and is so easily propagated from cuttings, that it is to be found in every garden. The deep crimson of the terminal bracteas, as contrasted with the yellow flowers, and the bright green of the other parts of the plant, render it at once recognisable; leaves grossly serrate, regularly cross-veined.

ALEURITES, Monœcia Monadelphia.

5. A TRILOBA, Roxb. Fl. Ind. 3, p 629; Canurium, Rumph. Amb. 2, *t.* 58; C cordifolium, Gaert. Fr. 2, *t.* 25.—Japhal, Bengal Walnut. A large tree; leaves petioled, cordate-entire or scolloped, frequently 3 or 5-lobed, from 5 to 8 inches long, and nearly as broad; flowers small, white, in terminal panicles; fruit roundish, somewhat compressed, pointed, very hard, 2-celled, each cell containing a nut like a walnut, but much inferior in flavour. In gardens, Bombay; said to grow wild about Belgaum, but this we consider very doubtful; at all events it is found in gardens there. We have not seen it either flourish or produce fruit to the north of Belgaum.

HURA, Monœcia Monadelphia. The South American name, Lam. Illust. *t.* 793.

6. H CREPITANS, Spr. *syst.* 3, p 884; Lam. Illust. *t.* 793.—The Sand-Box tree; native of West Indies; a small armed tree, having a few prickles on the stem. The fruit is like a finely turned sand-box, round and oblate. When fully ripe, the numerous valves burst with a loud noise, hence the name. The sap of the leaves and bark are corrosive; flowers in red pyramidal aments in the retroverted calyx.

SAPIUM, Roxb., Monœcia Monadelphia. Said to be derived

from *sap*, the Celtic for fat, in allusion to the unctuous juice with which the plants abound.

7. S SEBIFERUM, Roxb. Fl. Ind. 3, 693; Stillingia sebifera, Willd. 4, p 588; Croton sebiferum, Linn. Pluk. Amal. *t*. 390, *f*. 3; Ainslie Nat. Ind. 2, p 433.—Willaittee Peepul; Talim Trag, China. A tree, with drooping branches; leaves rhomb-obovate, pendulous; flowers yellow, in terminal drooping racemes; fruit size of a small cherry, very hard; seeds covered with a vegetable tallow, which gives the name to the tree. In our climate this appears in too small quantity to be turned to any useful purpose. Gardens at Dapoorie and Hewra; not common.

XYLOPHYLLA, Tripentandria Trigynia, Linn. Gen. 1299; Bot. Reg. *t*. 373; Bot. Mag. *t*. 1021 and 2652. Name derived from the position of the flowers and fruit.

8. X FALCATA.—Native of the Bahama Islands; leaves linear lanceolate subfalcate; flowers fasciculated on the crenulæ of the leaves, unisexual. Gardens at Dapoorie, Hewra, and Sewree.

CROTON, Monœcia Monadelphia. Name derived from the Greek for a *tick*, which the seeds of some of the species resemble.

9. C VARIEGATUM, Roxb. Fl. Ind. 3, p 678; Rheede Mal. 6, *t*. 61; Rumph. Amb. 4, *t*. 25 and 26, *f*. 2; Bot. Mag. 3051; Bot. Cab. *t*. 870.—A very common, ornamental shrub, in gardens and flower-pots. It is easily raised from cuttings. There is a broad-leaved and a yellow-leaved variety, the latter conspicuous for the greater quantity of yellow colouring in its leaves.

JATROPHA, Monœcia Monadelphia. From *jatron*, a remedy; and *phago*, to eat; some of the species possessing medicinal properties, and others affording food. Tourn. Inst. *t*. 438; Gaert. Fr. *t*. 108; Lam. *t*. 791.

10. J CURCAS, Roxb. Fl. Ind. 3, p 686; Ainslie Mat. Ind. 2, p 45; As. Res. 11, p 169; Jacq. 3, *t*. 63.—A shrub, now very common over the country, though originally a native of Brazil; used as a hedge plant throughout the Concans. The nuts afford a good burning oil in some quantity, and it is this oil which, boiled with Oxyde of Iron, forms a varnish much used by the Chinese. The fresh juice of the stem when dried forms an elegant lac-like substance, which may be yet applied in the arts.

11. J MANIHOT, Willd. 5, p 563; Janipha manihot, Spr. *syst*. 3, 77; Pluk. Alm. p 205, *f*. 1; Sloanes Jam. 1, *t*. 85, *f*. 141; Ainslie Mat. Ind. 1, p 428; Bot. Mag. *t*. 3071.—The Tapioca, a native of Brazil, and Cassada plant, West Indies, has been introduced by the Portuguese *viâ* Goa, and from thence has spread into gardens, where it is now not uncommon. About 22 years ago attempts were made by the Agri. and Horticultural Society to extend its growth as a plant useful for food, but the experiment, as

might have been expected in a great bread-corn country like this, failed, as the produce is by no means equal in nutritive property to that of our numerous cereals.

12. J Gossypifolia.—Native of Brazil; shrubby plant, 5 feet in height, recognisable by its lobate, entire leaves, beautifully changing from reddish-brown to green, and its flowers of red and yellow. Common as a pot-plant about bungalows; has been introduced within the last 10 years.

RICINUS, Monœcia Monadelphia.

13. R Communis, Roxb. Fl. Ind. 3, p 689; Blackwell *t.* 148; Rheede Mal. 2, *t.* 32; Bot. Mag. *t.* 2209; Rumph. Amb. 4, *t.* 41.—The latter seems a variety, Ainslie Mat. Ind. 2, 472. "Erendi," Hindoostanee; said to be originally a native of Arabia, but is now exclusively cultivated in India, though never seen in a wild state; the taller species, a six feet shrub, is commonly grown as an edging to sugar-cane fields; the smaller, or "Teerkie," is grown extensively in Kandeish and Gujarat, in fields having a brownish-black soil, as a cold weather crop. This variety yields proportionally more oil than the other; it is much used as a lamp-oil in Gujarat. When cold-drawn, the oil is an excellent and safe cathartic. That extracted by heat is a little better than a poison, owing, it is supposed, to the action of heat on the embryo, which is very virulent, its after effects inducing the very symptoms for which it is often given as a remedy. Large supplies of the cold-drawn oil are made at Hewra by means of the hydraulic press, and supplied to the Medical Stores.

CICCA, Monœcia Triandria.

14. C Disticha, Willd. 4, p 332; Roxb. Fl. Ind. 3, No. 673; Rheede Mal. 3, *t.* 47 and 48; Rumph Amb. 7, *t.* 33, p 2; Jaq. Hort. 2, *t.* 194.—Country Gooseberry, Harparewree. A small tree with pinnate leaves, chiefly terminal, and 1 to 2 feet long; flowers racemed, small, of a reddish colour, growing from the branches; fruit oblate, size of a gooseberry, ribbed, of an agreeable acid flavour.

LXXXII.—URTICEÆ.

THE NETTLE TRIBE, Lind. Nat. Syst. p 93.

URTICA, Monœcia Tetrandria. From *uro*, to burn, in allusion to the stinging properties of many of the species.

1. U Tenacissima, Roxb. 3, 590.—Low shrub, with alternate broad-cordate grossly serrate leaves, the under surface covered with white tomentum; native of Sumatra. Many plants in Hewra garden, furnished by Mr. Law, C. S. The plant does not appear

to have any vigour in our Deccan climate. A strong twine is made from the bark.

2. U Nivea.—Dapoorie, from Bengal seed; as yet immature; may hereafter be reported on.

CANNABIS, Diœcia Tetrandria. Probably derived from the Arab name *quonab*. Gaert. 1, *t.* 75; Tourn. *t.* 308; Lam. *t.* 814.

3. C Sativa, Roxb. Fl. 3, p 772; Rumph. Amb. 5, *t.* 77; Rheede Mal. 10, *t.* 60 and 61; Ainslie Mat. Ind. 2, p 189.—Native of Northern India; is extensively cultivated in many parts of the Peninsula for the sake of the intoxicating material furnished by the leaves, stalks, and flowers, all of which furnish the well-known "Churrus" and "Bhang" used as a drink and in smoking. The use of these drugs is almost universal amongst our native population, and in moderate quantity they seem to be as little hurtful as wine. Thus in Poona a native beer, called "Bhoj," is brewed from Joowaree grain malted, and the Bhang is added as a substitute for hops; this is drunk in large quantities, and is said to be a refreshing and innocuous drink. Taken in excess Bhang gives rise to many diseases; as a medicinal agent it is of much importance, being used as an extract. The culture of the plant is a regular art, and Bhang doctors travel about to give their services in pruning the plants, or nipping off the superfluous buds. Culture is especially common in the districts east of Nuggur, the Balaghat, &c. The plant as grown within the Tropics has been tried for its fibre, but totally without success, a short, cottony material being the only result.

LXXXIII.—ARTOCARPEÆ.

THE BREAD-FRUIT TRIBE, Lind. Nat. Syst. p 95.

ARTOCARPUS, Monœcia Tetrandria, No. 93. From *artos*, bread; and *karpos*, fruit. Bread-fruit tree, first made known to Europe by Dampier and Anson, and the celebrated Captain Cook.

1. A Indica, Roxb. Fl. 3, p 528; Rumph. Amb. 1, *t.* 32 to 34; Bot. Mag. *t.* 2869 to 2871; Sonnerat's Voy. New Guinea, *t.* 57 to 60.—Parell Garden, Girgaum Woods, Fort, Colaba. Only 5 or 6 trees are to be found in the Island. They seem to be of slow growth, but to thrive well. Roxburgh says the winters in Bengal are too cold for the tree. It does not appear to be affected by them here. Most people have heard of the unfortunate Captain Bligh, who was sent to the South Sea Islands for the purpose of introducing the Bread-fruit into the West Indies. The tree dies when planted at any distance from the sea.

FICUS, Polygamia Monœcia.

2. F Elastica, Roxb. Fl. 3, 541.—Indian Rubber Tree;

in gardens about Bombay, Tanna, &c. The largest are to be found on or near to the Esplanade, Tanna. In our climate this tree appears to afford but a small supply of caoutchouc, as compared to that obtained from the same tree in Eastern Bengal. This is probably owing to the greater dryness of the air in Western India.

3. F CARICA, Roxb. Fl. Ind. 3, p 528. "Unjeer," Hindoostanee, Blackw. *t.* 125; Gaert. 2, *t.* 91, *f.* 7.—The common cultivated Fig. In gardens, but chiefly above the Ghauts, where it is cultivated extensively. The fruit is inferior in size and flavour to the Smyrna Fig. Does this arise from caprification not being practised in India? This process consists in drilling the half ripe Fig with a thorn or a needle, in imitation of the same process as done by an insect with its probosis. The scientific pruning of the Fig tree is well understood, especially by the Mussulman gardeners.

MORUS, Linn., Monœcia Tetrandria. Derived from *moria* or *moron*, a Greek name of the Mulberry (1st Maccabees 6, 34—"The blood of grapes and mulberries"); Gaert. 2, *t* 126; Tourn. *t.* 362; Lam. *t.* 762.—According to the elegant fable of Ovid, the Mulberry bore a snow-white fruit, till stained by the blood of Pyramus (*vide* Meta. Book 4, Fable 4.

4. M INDICA, Roxb. Fl. 3, p 596; Willd. sp. 4, p 370; Spr. *syst.* 1, p 492; Rumph. Amb. 7, *t.* 5.—Roxburgh says this is the species cultivated in Bengal for feeding silk-worms, and that it is usually cut down four times a year, and kept down as a bush. The system was tried in the Deccan by Dr. Graham at Ahmednuggur, but without success, as might have been anticipated, from difference in soil and climate. We may add that the tree system as tried by Signor Mutti and others at Poona, and many other places, proved equally abortive. After about 12 years of patient trial, during which the expenditure by Government must have been close upon two lacs of rupees, and extensive correspondence as to the relative value of the tree and bush Mulberry, it was finally determined, by a committee assembled in 1846, that both were in our climate equally worthless as regards the profitable production of silk. Medals, watches, and land had, in the progress of this experiment, been lavishly bestowed on candidates whose success was deemed to be undoubted, and the most brilliant anticipations had been indulged in as to the productive benefits of this cultivation (*vide* reports of the Chamber of Commerce of Bombay, and Transactions of Agri. and Horticultural Societies of Western India from 1836 to 1843).

5. M ALBA, Roxb. Fl. 3, p 594; Willd. sp. 4, p 368; M italica, Poir.—A tree; leaves cordate-serrate, entire or variously lobed; fruit rather small, white; in gardens. This, the Doppia foglia, formed the great staple tree for the tree cultivation. We doubt if

any trees of it are now to be found in gardens. It is a native of Italy.

6. M Atropurpurea, Roxb. Fl. 3, 595 ; M rubra, Lour. Cochin China.—Shahtoot. This is an undoubted introduction by the Mussulmans from the north. It reaches a large size, having cordate, coriaceous, and often lobate, serrate leaves, and dark-purple, cylindric fruit. It grows well in gardens, particularly when planted near watercourses.

7. M Nigra, Willd. sp. 4, p 369 ; Blackwell *t.* 126.—A tree, with leaves cordate-ovate, unequally toothed ; fruit black. Parell garden, in front of the house, Graham. This species we have not traced as still existing.

8. M Leptostachya, Wall.—Dapoorie, introduced from Bengal, Dr. Lush. This tree has a fine fruit 2½ inches long.

9. M Mauritiana.—The Phillippine Mulberry. A species introduced in 1837, having a bushy tendency, and large cochleate serrate leaves. We suspect this species must now be extinct, as we have not seen it for years. There were many trees of it in a garden at Parell kept by Mr. Ramos, who was one of the victims of the Mulberry speculations.

10. M Persica.—Regarding this tree there hangs a doubt. One or more are, or were, in the garden at Dapoorie, having an obovate sessile, smooth, entire, somewhat coriaceous, leaf, and a 1½ inch dependent fruit, similar to that of M leptostachya, but not, in as far as we remember, edible. The fruit of the Mulberry is very choice, from its mild acid qualities, which fit it well for preserves, and for a cooling drink in fevers.

11. Conocephalus Naucleiflora, Roxb.—A climber, introduced from Java, having ovate entire leaves, and umbellets of yellowish flowers, springing from the stem. They are very fragrant. The shrub is a native of Java.

LXXXIV.—SALICINEÆ, Lind. Nat. Syst. p 98.

SALIX, Diœcia Diandria.—Said to be derived from the Celtic *sal,* near ; *lis* water ; in allusion to the *habitat* of the Willow Tribe.

1. S Babylonica, Willd. sp. 4, p 671 ; Lour. Cochin China 2, p 609.—The Weeping Willow. Many specimens of this are to be seen in gardens in Bombay. Some imported direct from the banks of the Euphrates ; others by the more circuitous route of St. Helena, from the spring close to the tomb of the great Napoleon.

2. S Ægyptiaca.—Has leaves very narrow, almost linear, but not drooping, as in the former variety. The flower does not appear to differ from that of our indigenous species. Both may be seen growing in close apposition on the right hand side of the road from

Poona to Kandalla, just west of the Wurgaum bungalow. The difference of the habit and leaves of the two species is at once apparent. The bark of the indigenous species is of some account as a febrifuge. From both a very fine charcoal is obtained; it has been tried as a base for gunpowder, which is more free from various neutral salts than is that made from other charcoal, but on this account the strength of the powder is inferior, though considerably superior as regards long preservation without deterioration of quality.

LXXXV.—MYRICEÆ.

THE GALE TRIBE, Lind. Nat. Syst. p 100.

CASUARINA, Monœcia Monandria.—Name taken from Rumphius, who probably gave it in allusion to the resemblance the foliage bears to the plumage of the Cassowary.

1. C MURICATA.—The Casuarina tree. Tinian Pine, now common about Bombay. In sandy or river soil it grows rapidly, assuming a graceful appearance resembling the Fir, more especially in the mournful-like sound of the wind as it passes through the leaves. A very fine tree is to be seen at the Cooperage, Bombay. The Chinese prisoners have pointed out to us that in their country a decoction of the bark is used as an astringent in bowel-complaints, and from some trials we have made we think this assertion is most fully borne out.

2. C EQUISETIFOLIA, Rumph. Amb. 3, *t.* 57.—This species has linear leaves, much longer than the last, and altogether drooping, which gives it a much more striking appearance than C muricata. It is much less hardy, and often dies out, hence rare to be seen in gardens.

LXXXVI.—CONIFERÆ.

THE FIR TRIBE, Lind. Nat. Syst. p 247.

PODOCARPUS, L'Her, Monœcia Monadelphia. From *pous,* the foot; and *karpos,* fruit; in allusion to the stalk of the fruit.

1. P ELONGATUS, Spr. *syst.* 3, 889; Taxus elongata, Thunb.—A tall, erect-growing shrub, with subverticelled branches, and linear lanceolate leaves. Parell and Dapoorie gardens. Though many years in the gardens, it has not flowered. It is a native of the Cape.

THUJA, Linn., Monœcia Monadelphia.

2. T ORIENTALIS, Roxb. Fl. 3, 653; Chinese Arbor-Vitæ, Lam. Illust. *t.* 787, *f.* 2; Gaert. 2, *t.* 91, *f.* 2; Lour. Cochin China 2,

p 580.—A shrub, now common in gardens, at once recognisable by its spreading fan-like branches, and leaves like the Pine.

AGATHIS, Salisb., Monœcia Monadelphia.

3. A Australis, A loranthifolia, Lamb. Pin. 2, *t*. 6.—The New Zealand and Norfolk Island Pines; most stately trees. Those which existed at Dapoorie have died off, and we suspect that those in Bombay have shared the same fate.

JUNIPERUS, Linn. Gen. No. 1134.

4. J Virginiana.—A 15-feet tree, with wide-spreading, somewhat drooping, horizontal branches, with linear minute leaves, having all the appearance of those of the Cypress; has not flowered at Dapoorie, where there are two large trees planted 15 years ago, having been raised from seed obtained through the India House.

CUPRESSUS, Monœcia Monadelphia. Named from the *Island of Cypress*, where the tree grows abundantly. Lam. *t*. 787; Lour. *t*. 358.

5. C Glauca, Spr. *syst*. 3, p 889; C lusitanica, Willd. sp. 4, p 511; Pers. Syn. 2, p 580.—Now common in gardens, Native and European. It does not succeed below the Ghauts, and above only when the soil is rich and deep. When the tap root touches the rock below, the tree begins to die. Those planted at Koregaum and Phoolshuhur have long ago assumed an appearance denoting speedy extinction. Of those at Dapoorie, one or two of the largest die off every year. The healthiest appear to be those planted in front of Sir Jamsetjee's bungalow in Poona, but they are yet young, and have their trials to go through. At Dapoorie we have C horizontalis and another variety with drooping leaves, both received from the late H. Hart, Esq.

6. C Torulosa.—This tree, which from habit and the form of the fruit (?) may be reckoned a distinct species, has been exclusively grown at Dapoorie from seed received from Seharunpore. It is very ornamental, having long, drooping branches, and waving tops. It appears to succeed better in the Deccan than the Mediterranean tree; casualties have been fewer. C cashmeriana does not appear to differ from this.

LXXXVII.—CYCADEÆ.

CYCAS, Diœcia Polyandria.

1. C Circinalis, Roxb. Fl. 3, p 744; Olus calappoides, Rumph. Amb. 1, *t*. 22 and 23; Todda panna, Rheede Mal. 3, *t*. 13 to 21; C inermis, Lour. Cochin China 2, p 632; Bot. Mag. 2826.—A handsome tree, with long pinnæ diverging and finally drooping;

seed from the central spikes, each on a separate erect peduncle, round, size of a plumb. Gardens at Hewra, Parell, &c. Native of the Eastern Islands, also of Malabar. It is the common tree from Tellicherry to the foot of the Ghauts. The fructification of Manicaria saccifera, Lam. *t.* 774, and Gaert. *t.* 176, is somewhat similar. It is placed among the Palms. Does it connect that tribe with the Cycadeæ?

ZAMIA, Diœcia Polyandria. From *zemia,* loss or damage (?). In what language?

2. Z HORRIDA, Encephalartos allerstynii, Spr. *syst.* 3, p 998; Jaq. Frag. *t.* 27 and 28.—A strange-looking, low plant, with pinnate fronds; leaflets lanceolate, acute-pointed, glaucous, with strong double teeth on the outside. Native of the Cape. One plant has been 20 years at Hewra, and in that space of time has neither flowered nor grown two inches.

3. Z —— (?) sp.—Leaves much larger than the last, with long leaflets from the upper extremity, each armed with two terminal thorns, and from 1 to 3 on the sides of the leaflet. Sir Roger D'Faria's garden, Mazagon. Received from Mozambique.

LXXXVIII.—PIPERACEÆ, Sweet. Hort. Brit. p 380.

PIPER, Triandria Trigynia. From the Indian name. Lam. *t.* 23; Gaert. 2, *t.* 92.

1. P LONGUM, Roxb. Fl. 1, p 154; "Pepul," Latin Terpali. Rheede Mal. 7, *t.* 14; Peeplee Mool, Pluk. Alm. *t.* 104, *f.* 4.—Was cultivated at Poway, in Salsette, &c. (*vide* Graham's list, 1st edition, p 199). It does not appear, however, that it can be successfully grown at a distance from the air of the Ghauts. The roots "Peepula Mool" form rather an important article in the Hindoo Materia Medica, and do doubtless possess considerable medicinal powers.

2. P NIGRUM, Roxb. Fl. 1, p 150; Molaga-Kode, Rheede Mal. 7, *t.* 12; Bot. Mag. *t.* 3131; Pluk. Alm. *t.* 437, *f.* 1.—"Meeree," "Kala Meeree," Black Pepper. Is cultivated in Canara and Soonda, even to the limits of the Dharwar Zillah. North of these provinces it can be grown within the Ghaut line, but hardly with profit, as it is the case further to the south. These southern provinces have been famed for their Pepper gardens from the earliest times of which we have any record.

3. P BETLE, Roxb. Fl. 1, p 158; Rheede Mal. 7, *t.* 15; Bot. Mag. *t.* 3132; Rumph. Amb. 5, *t.* 116, *f.* 2; Burm. Zeyl. *t.* 82.—"Pawn," Betel leaf; Tamboolee, the name of the seller; cultivated chiefly above the Ghauts, from Kandeish limits to Soonda. The leaves are sold in every bazar, and the export from the Deccan

and Bombay to Kurrachee is now very large. The mode of laying out and cultivating a Pan garden is well worthy the attention of any person desiring to be acquainted with tropical horticulture. Everything is arranged so that the greatest possible amount of coolness, shade, and moisture shall be concentrated in the spot where the garden is. The cultivators usually are Brahmins bred to the work. Of P trioicum kakurwail we say nothing in this Supplement, as it is a plant found in abundance within our own Presidency (*vide* List No. 1).

LXXXIX.—ORCHIDEÆ, Sweet. Hort. Brit. p 381.

THE ORCHIS TRIBE, Lind. Nat. Syst. p 262.

The exotic species of this family we approach with much hesitation, because we so seldom find that they flower in our comparatively dry air. Intensified as this dryness is by the long prevalence of the north-west winds during the fair season, and these winds having blown over many thousand miles of mountain and desert ere they can reach us, this cause affects our production of exotic cottons not less than that of our exotic Orchideæ. Viewing these circumstances, it is not surprising that the exotic Orchideæ from the north of India, and from the Terra Caliente of America, should remain undeveloped, so that although we have been furnished with supplies of many and varied species through the late Colonel G. R. Jervis and His Excellency Sir George Clerk, when formerly Governor of Bombay, we have not been able to show more than an occasional and very evanescent flower. During the past season, Phyas alba, Calcutta importation, flowered, and formerly Zygopetalum makaii.

VANILLA, Linn.

1. V Aromatica, Fr. Bau. Orch. Gen. *t.* 10 and 11; Bl. Rumph. 1, 196, *t.* 67 and 68.—This choice climber was originally imported through the late Colonel G. R. Jervis, and presented to the Horticultural Society. It grows vigorously at Sewrie. In the Deccan gardens or at Dapoorie, the dry air renders it comparatively stunted.

XC.—SCITAMINEÆ.

THE GINGER TRIBE, Linn. Nat. Syst. p 265.

ALPINIA, Linn., Monandria Monogynia. In memory of *P. Alpinas*, a celebrated Medical Botanist.

1. A Nutans, Roxb. Fl. Ind. 1, p 65; Globba nutans, Pers.; Renealmia nutans, Bot. Rep. *t.* 360; Rumph. Amb. 6, *t.* 62 and

63; Bot. Mag. 1903; Roscoe in Linn. Trans. 8, p 346.—Poona Chumpa, Nag-Dumnee. A very gaudy plant, having flowers of a rich pink variegated with white, and long sheathing leaves. Native of the Eastern Islands, common in gardens.

2. A CARDAMOMUM, Roxb. Fl. Ind. p 70; Amomum repens, Roscoe, Willd., and Sonnerat; Ellettaria cardamomum, Mal. in Linn. Trans. 10, *t.* 4 and 5; Sonnerat 2, *t.* 136; Rheed. Mal. 11, *t.* 4 and 5; Roxb. Cor. 3, *t.* 226; Buch. Jour. 2, 336, 510, 538; and 3, 225; Thomson's Lond. Dist. p 437.—Elachee, Cardamum; is largely cultivated in the Bilghy and in Soonda, near the limits of the Bombay Presidency to the south; Ginger, Areca, Pepper, &c. are cultivated in those beautiful hill-gardens, often in alternate rows with the Cardamum, and not unfrequently the Pomaloe, Orange, and Nag-Chumpa diversify the picture. Nothing can be more beautiful than those hill-gardens in Soonda, and, planted as they always are by the large, roomy, and comfortable dwellings of the Brahmin renters, they give a high idea of the prosperity of that beautiful and healthy country, where the running streams are conducted even through the houses into the gardens. When one wanders from these favoured spots towards the village enclosures, and finds there a Rat'h, or movable temple, mounted on immense wooden wheels, and covered with carvings of the most obscene description, he may well say with Byron—

" All but the spirit of man is divine."

The Cardamum as grown in the jungles of Coorg and Wynaad is well described by Roxburgh:—" Gives a larger and coarser Cardamum, which has in common a value considerably below that of the smaller and more highly cultivated product."

3. HEDYCHIUM CORONARIUM, Roxb. Fl. 1, p 10; Rumph. Amb. 5, *t.* 69, *f.* 3; Linn. Trans. 8, p 342; Ex. Bot. *t.* 107; Bot. Mag. *t.* 708.

4. H FLAVUM, Roxb. Fl. 1, p 12; Roscoe Scit. Pl.; Bot. Mag. *t.* 3039; Bot. Cab. *t.* 604.—Son Tukha, Hema Chumpa. Flowers yellow, large, fragrant; native of Eastern Bengal. Of the remaining Hedychiums, other than our indigenous species, we have not any trace, but as it is probable that they are to be found in gardens and conservatories, we would solicit information regarding any others.

KÆMPFŒRIA, Monandria Monogynia. In honour of *Kempfœr*, a German Botanist.

5. K ROTUNDA, Roxb. Fl. Ind. 1, p 16; Malan-Kua, Rheede Mal. 1, *t.* 317; Bot. Mag. *t.* 920; As. Res. 3, p 242 and 327.—Bhooee Chumpa. Heart-curved snake-dragon, round-rooted Galangal; in gardens; flowers before the rains, when the plant is leafless, fragrant; flower of various shades of purple and white.

6. K PANDURATA, Roxb. Fl. Ind. 1, p 18; K ovata, Roscoe Linn. Trans. 11, p 274; Roxb. in As. Res. vol. 11; Bot. Reg. *t.* 73; Zerumbet claviculatum, Rumph. Amb. 5, *t.* 69, *f.* 1.—Manga Kua; native of Sumatra and Java; a very beautiful plant, with pale, pink-coloured flowers. Rumphius says it is cultivated for culinary and medicinal purposes. Rheedes notices its use in Dysentery. The above are all of the Kæmpfœrias which we have ventured to insert as not indigenous to Western India. K pandurata being described as found in South Concan by Nimmo, we beg on this head to solicit information, as we have been unable to trace it.

ZINZIBER, Gaert., Monandria Monogynia. Arabic *zinzeber*, hence Zinziber.

7. Z OFFICINALE, Roxb. Fl. Ind. 1, p 47; Jacq. Hort. Vind. 1, *t.* 75; Rumph. Amb. 5, *t.* 66, *f.* 1; Rheede Mal. 11, *t.* 2; Wartz. Obs. p 2; Pluk. Alm. *t.* 317; Lour. Coch. China 1, p 2; Ainslie. Mat. Ind. 1, p 152.—Name of fresh root, "Aleh"; Maratha name (dried) "Soont." Common Ginger, cultivated in garden villages in Deccan, Gujarat, Soonda, &c. In the Kaira Zillah it is planted in May, and the produce, which averages from 50 to 150 maunds per beega, gathered in the following February and March. In the green state it sells from 25 to 30 seers per rupee.

CURCUMA, Monandria Monogynia.

8. C LONGA, Roxb. Fl. Ind. 1, p 32; Amomum curcuma, Gmelin and Jacq. Hist. Vind. 3, *t.* 4; Blackw. *t.* 396; Bot. Reg. *t.* 886; Rumph. Amb. 5, *t.* 67; Rheede Mal. 11, *t.* 11; Ainslie Mat. Ind. 1, p 454.—"Huldee," Hindoostanee; "Ulud," Mussulman. This plant, conspicuous by its beautiful pink coma, is largely cultivated in those parts of the country where the garden-soil is of superior quality and water in abundance. Thus in Gujarat and in some parts of the Deccan it is a regular article for crop-rotation, and requires high manuring. In the Kaira Zillah it is planted in May, and yields from 60 to 300 maunds (of 26 lbs. each) per beega. Thus an average crop will give a return equal to sugar-cane, viz. Rupees 100 per beega. The root is roasted to dryness in ovens, and thereafter exported. It is in universal use for domestic and medicinal purposes. A powder, containing equal parts of Turmeric and of Peruvian Bark, is a sovereign remedy for sores infested with worms. We do not admit any of the other Curcumas in this Supplement, as they are not cultivated. Regarding the five Curcumas, and the three Globbas, stated to have been introduced by the late Mr. Nimmo, we shall be happy to receive any information. It is possible they may be scattered in different gardens in Bombay.

XCI.—MARANTACEÆ.

THE ARROWROOT TRIBE, Lind. Nat. Syst. p 267.

CANNA, Monandria Monogynia. From the Hebrew for a *reed* or *cane*.

1. C INDICA.—Native of the Eastern Islands, Roxb. Fl. 2, p 1; Bot. Mag. *t.* 454; Rheede Mal. 11, *t.* 43; Bot. Cab. *t.* 739; Rumph. Amb. 5, *t.* 71, *f.* 2.—In gardens, everywhere conspicuous by its bright-red flowers, and sheathing cauline leaves, and in flower all the year. The seeds black, and round like a Pea, yield a beautiful but evanescent purple dye.

2. C LUTEA.—Is a more rare species than the former, and shows leaves more lanceolate, with bright-yellow flowers. This affords the amylaceous food, called *Tous-les-mois*, of the West Indies.

3. C LATIFOLIA, C flaccida, and C speciosa, are not known to us as distinct species, but points of difference, if pointed out, will be carefully attended to.

4. C DISCOLOR.—This species, a native of Japan, does seem entitled to rank as a distinct one. It is much more robust in habit. The leaves are variously shaded from purple at the edges to green in the centre.

5. C NEPALENSIS, Wallich.—Said to be the most beautiful genus; introduced by the late Mr. Nimmo. We have failed to find any trace of it in gardens at Bombay or in the Deccan. Can any information be afforded regarding it?

MARANTA, Linn., Monandria Monogynia.

6. M ZEBRINA, M ramosissima—The latter, with long clavate tubers, much resembling the West India Arrowroot, was formerly cultivated in the Botanical Gardens, but has disappeared. The amylaceous product (Arrowroot) did not appear to be in any respect superior to that of our indigenous species.

XCII.—MUSACEÆ, Sweet. Hort. Brit. p 392.

THE BANANA TRIBE, Lind. Nat. Syst. p 268.

MUSA, Polygamia Monœcia.

1. M SAPIENTUM.—"Khela," Hindoostanee and Maratha. Roxb. Fl. 1, p 663; Rheede Mal. 1, *t.* 12 to 14; Rumph Amb. 5, *t.* 60 and 61; Pliny Nat. Hist. 13, 12; Hamilton in Linn. Trans. 13, p 376; Ainslie Nat. Ind. 1, p 316; Roxb. Cor. p 3 to 275.—The cultivated Plantains, of which there are many varieties. The most esteemed are the red (Banana), the Soneree (small Plantains), and

others, all of which are to be found at Bassein, the chief emporium in the Concan for the fruit; but they are so extensively cultivated in the Concan, the Deccan, Gujarat, Soonda, &c., as to be within the reach of the poorer classes. A plantation lasts from 4 to 5 years, according to soil, climate, &c. The young parts of the spadix are eaten cooked, and are a very delicate vegetable. The leaves form an excellent and cooling application to blistered surfaces, burns, &c. In fact, the Plantain is one of the greatest blessings of Providence to tropical climates.

URANIA, Hexandria Monogynia. The name of one of the Muses. "Descend from heaven, Urania, by that name, if rightly thou art called."

2. U Speciosa, Roxb. Milton. Fl. 2, p 114; Ravenalia madagascarensis, Sonnerat Voy. *t*. 124 to 126; Jaq. Schœnb. *t*. 93.—Plantain-leaved Urania. A very elegant tree, with leaves like the Plantain, and very long petioles sheathing the stem, which appears entirely composed of these; flowers large, white, sessile, alternate and imbricated, sitting in a curious cross-fashion on the upperside of the branches of the spadix. The tree is a native of Madagascar. Parell, Sewree. Does not grow away from the sea line; a very elegant tree.

HELICONIA, Pentandria Monogynia. From *Helicon*, Mountain of the Muses.

3. H Buccinata, Roxb. Fl. 1, p 670; Rumph. Amb. 5, *t*. 62, *f*. 2.—This we insert on the authority of the 1st edition of this book, but we have failed to trace it in gardens, Bombay. With a view to its recognition, we add this short description:—A stemless plant, with large lanceolate glossy leaves, from 2 to 4 feet long, and 1 broad, with sheathing petioles from 3 to 6 feet long. Native of Eastern Islands. Introduced by Nimmo in 1833.

STRELITZIA, Pentandria Monogynia. Named by Sir Joseph Banks in honour of the late Queen *Charlotte*.

4. S Reginæ, Spr. *syst*. 1, p 833. Redoute liliaceæ, *t*. 77 and 78; Hort. Kew. 1, p 285, *t*. 2.—A stemless plant, with thin, reddish-orange large flowers, and the habit of a Plantain. Parell Gardens, Dapoorie; rare.

XCIII.—IRIDEÆ, Loud. Hort. Brit. p 337.

IRIS, Triandria Monogynia. From *iris*, the rainbow, in allusion to the variety and brilliancy of the colours of this genus.

1. I Persica, Bot. Mag. *t*. 1. The Persian Iris, or *Flower-de-luce*. Introduced by the late Nimmo. Does any trace of this exist in gardens, Bombay? Information is solicited.

MARICA, Schreb. Triandria Monogynia.

2. M Northiana.—The same remark applies to this plant. We can find it nowhere.

PARDANTHUS, Ker, Triandria Monogynia. From *pardos*, a leopard; and *anthos*, a flower; the flower being spotted like a leopard. Gaert. 1, *t.* 13; Lam. Illust. 1, *t.* 31. Common in gardens; wild below the slopes of the Himalayas.

TIGRIDIA, Jacq., Monadelphia Triandria. From the petals being striped like a tiger.

3. T Pavonia, Bot. Mag. 532.—The Tiger Flower; an herbaceous plant, having a splendid large flower of reddish-orange, striped with yellow; in gardens, rare.

4. Anthalyza Æthiopica and Gladiolus namaquensis. Both of them appear in the 1st edition, but of these and of the Amaryllideæ we can trace few of the exotic species which are sufficiently permanent or established to merit a place here. Of the Jacobia Lily, Crinum mothuccanum, Coburghia fulva, Pancratium speciosum, P calathinum, Narcigus tuzetia, and N orientalis, all mentioned in the first edition as introduced by Dr. Lush and the late Mr. Nimmo, we cannot find any trace. It is, however, very possible that we may hear from others that some of these are established in Bombay, and, if so, we will be happy to give them a place in the next edition of this Catalogue.

5. Zephyranthes Candida, Bot. Mag. *t.* 2583.—Native of tropical America; in the Horticultural Society's garden, Sewree; having linear leaves, and showy white flowers.

XCIV.—HEMEROCALLIDEÆ, Loud. Hort. Brit. p 538.

LILIACEÆ.—The Lily Tribe.

Of Hemerocallis fulva, Funkia cordata, Agapanthus umbellatus, all of them mentioned in the former edition of this work, we have been unable to find any trace, and information is requested as to whether they are now in any gardens of this Presidency.

POLYANTHES, Hexandria Monogynia. From *polus*, many; and *anthos*, a flower; not from *polis*, a city, as erroneously stated by Mr. Graham.

1. P Tuberosa. Gool-Shubba, Tube-Rose, Bot. Mag. 1817; Rumph. Amb. 5, *t.* 98; Roxb. Fl. Ind. 2, p 166; Redoute liliaceæ *t.* 147.—Common in gardens; corolla white, with inside of tube yellow; powerful in fragrance.

2. Velthemmia Viridiflora, Bot. Mag. 501.—Cape of Good Hope; introduced at Dapoorie, Dr. Lush. No trace can now be found of it.

SANSEVIERA, Thunb., Hexandria Monogynia. From *Sansevier*, a Swedish botanist.

3. S ZEYLANICA, Roxb. Fl. Ind. 2, p 161; Hort. Mal. 11, *t.* 42; Cor. Pl. 2, 184; Bot. Reg. *t.* 160.—Bow-string Hemp; leaves from the root deeply canaliculated, striated, spotted; flowering scape central higher, finally a spike with numerous purple flowers. In gardens, not common; does not seed with us. In Malabar, of which country it is a native, it does produce seed. The twine made from the fibre, steeped and afterwards stripped, is very strong.

ALOE, Hexandria Monogynia. From *alloe* or *elia*, the Arabic name.

4. A SOCOTRINA, DC. Bot. Mag. 1474.—It seems doubtful whether this species is also not found wild with us; at least we think it has been observed in some villages in the Kheir Talooka, Zillah Poona. It may, however, have been introduced there. Is chiefly distinguishable from the yellow-flowered indigenous Aloe by its dark crimson spike of flowers.

5. A ZEBRINA.—A small species, having short thick leaves of a deep-green, variegated with white spots. Cultivated in gardens as an ornamental plant; has not been seen to flower. Dapoorie and Hewra. Native of the Cape.

6. A VARIEGATA.—Leaves long, green, variegated with yellow, especially towards the border; spines of the leaves strong and sharp. Native of Southern Europe; commonly found in Italy planted on the pillars of gates or terraces. Gardens Deccan and Bombay.

7. A BARBADENSIS.—In what does this differ from the first two species?

8. A STRIATULA, Kunth. Enum. vol. 4, p 529; Haworth. Phil. Mag. 1825, p 281.—Having a stem variously cut; leaves long, narrow, with cartilaginous teeth; sheaths of the leaves pale-coloured, striated, hence the name. Is found often suspended from the roofs of native apartments, as it is said to attract fleas, and keep away bandicoots. The use of the Socotrina and Barbadoes Aloes in medicine is too well known to need detail here. The leaves are a favourite native application to guinea-worm sores, but it cannot be averred that they have any specific action on the worm.

9. A PERFOLIATA.—In what does this differ from some of the species above-noted? Information is solicited.

XCV.—DIOSCORINÆ.

DIOSCOREA, Diœcia Hexandria. In memory of *Dioscorides*, a Greek Physician. Gaert. *t.* 17; Lam. Illust. *t.* 818. To what country can we refer the origin of these edible Dioscorea. The roots of our indigenous species are unsuitable as food, being generally acrid and unsafe in their properties. As the best developed specimens of the Yam are in the far east, we may safely assign the Eastern Islands as its original *habitat*.

1. D Sativa, Willd. 4, p 795; Hort. Mal. 8, *t.* 51.—This is the most common species cultivated. Native name "Godree."

2. D Globosa.—The White Yam, nearly as common as the last.

3. D Aculeata, Roxb. Fl. Ind. 3, p 800; Rumph. Amb. 5, *t.* 126; Rheede Hort. 7, *t.* 37.—Goa Potatoe; a very useful esculent; common in Bombay, but imported from Goa. It is the smallest of the cultivated species, but it is also the most delicate.

XCVI.—SMILACEÆ.

THE SMILAX TRIBE, Lind. Nat. Syst. p 277.

SMILAX, Diœcia Hexandria.

1. S Prolifera.—Native of Bengal, from Calcutta seed. Roxb. 3, p 795. A stout climber with prickly stem and branches; leaves oblong, 3-nerved; umbels proliferous, with globular long-peduncled umbellets. Gardens Hewra and Dapoorie.

2. S Deltoides.—Received under this name from Calcutta. It has a triangular deltoid-like leaf, hence the name.

XCVII.—ASPHODELEÆ, Lind. Nat. Syst. p 273.

ANTHERICUM, Hexandria Monogynia.

1. A —— (?) sp.—Seed from Seharunpore. A large robust species, having many narrow leaves about one foot long; scape one foot, flowers as in its congeners. Native of Gosaen Khan, Himalaya; Gardens Dapoorie and Hewra.

ALLIUM, Hexandria Monogynia.

2. A Cepa, Linn.—The common Onion; Bombay has long been celebrated for the cultivation of the White or Portugal Onion. The common Onion is cultivated most extensively throughout the Deccan and Gujarat as a cold season crop.

3. A Sativum, Roxb. Fl. Ind. 2, p 142.—"Lussun," Garlic; cultivated chiefly in irrigated lands of the Deccan and Southern Maratha Country. It is extensively exported to the Coast.

4. A Porrum, Roxb. Fl. Ind. 2, p 141; Blackw. 421.—The Leek, cultivated to a small extent, but grows well, and even produces seed.

DRACÆNA, Hexandria Monogynia. From *drakon*, a dragon, the inspissated juice being esteemed like dragon's blood.

5. D FERREA, Roxb. Fl. Ind. 2, p 156; Bot. Mag. 2053; Terminalis rubra, Rumph. Amb. 4, *t.* 34, *f.* 2.—The leaves of a deep ferruginous or copper hue; common in gardens. A native of the Eastern Islands.

6. D MAURITIANA.—A species with a bright-green, long, narrow, lanceolar leaves, and bright-blue seeds. This seems identical with a species which we have raised from seed obtained in the garden of Prince Demidoff, at St. Donato, near to Florence. Parell and Dapoorie.

7. D BRASILIENSIS.—A species, native of Brazil, having large, broad leaves. Parell garden.

8. ASPARAGUS OFFICINALIS.—Often cultivated in the gardens of Europeans in India, but requires careful treatment and high manuring for the shoots to attain a good size.

9. DIANELLA ENSIFOLIA.—Herbaceous; native of Eastern Islands; leaves ensiform striated; flowers whitish, succeeded by a blue-coloured fruit, containing several seeds. Garden Parell. This is the only specimen of this choice plant which we have yet seen in Western India.

XCVIII.—TULIPACEÆ.

THE TULIP TRIBE, Loud. Hort. Brit. p 539.

YUCCA, Linn., Hexandria Monogynia. The St. Domingo name; Gaert. Carp. 2, *t.* 85.

1. Y GLORIOSA.—Adam's Needle; native of West Indies, Bot. Mag. *t.* 1260.—In gardens, where it seems to be quite naturalised; flowers in the rains, when the large panicle has a very showy appearance, being covered with white blossoms; the leaves afford a good twine.

XCIX.—BROMELICEÆ.

THE PINE APPLE TRIBE, Loud. Hort. Brit. p 540.

1. AGAVE CANTULA, Aloe americana, Roxb. Fl. Ind. 2, 167.—A stately Aloe-looking plant. The central scape rising to the height of 15 or 20 feet; flowers in the rains. The broad ensiform leaves give material for rope or twine.

2. A VIVIPARA is the narrower-leaved plant; leaves flexuous and drooping, which may be seen growing in waste places, and is planted in situations where its roots may retain the earth when

washed down by the rains. In the Madras Presidency it is employed in this way to keep up the earth near to the parapets of bridges, a practice which might with advantage be followed on our side of India.

3. FURCROYA FŒTIDA, Vent. in Usteri Ann. 19, 54.—A plant, similar in habit to Agave cantula, but having thinner and more flaccid leaves, and green flowers. In gardens Bombay, rare. We have failed to find it in the Police Office compound, where it formerly existed.

BROMELIA, Hexandria Monogynia. Named in memory of *Bromela*, a Sweedish Naturalist. Tourn. Inst. *t.* 426 and 428; Gaert. Carp. 1, *t.* 11; Lam. Illust. *t.* 223.

4. B ANANAS, Roxb. Fl. Ind. 2, p 116. Pine Apple; Bot. Mag. *t.* 1554.—As Roxburgh truly observes, we have no warrant for believing the Pine Apple to be indigenous in India proper; we must look for its *habitat* in the islands from Penang eastward. It is extensively cultivated in Bombay, but the fruit is, in size and flavour, by no means equal to that of Penang.

C.—COMMELINEÆ, Lind. Nat. Syst. p 255.

TRADESCANTIA, Hexandria Monogynia. In memory of *Tradescant*, Gardener to Charles I., of England. Gaert. Carp. 1, *t.* 15; Lam. Illust. *t.* 226.

1. T DISCOLOR, Willd. 2, p 18; Smith Ic. *t.* 10; Bot. Mag. *t.* 1192.—A large American species of Spider-Wort, having broad, ensiform leaves, purple-coloured on the underside, and a large inflorescence deep in the axils of the leaves. Common in gardens and in pots about bungalows.

2. T ZEBRINA.—A humifuse species, native of America; creeping extensively, and distinguished by its narrow lanceolate leaves variously striped, hence the name.

CI.—PALMÆ.

THE PALM TRIBE, Lind. Nat. Syst. p 279 and 280.

Palms, the splendid offspring of Tellus and Phœbus, chiefly acknowledge as their native land those happy regions seated within the Tropics, where the beams of the sun for ever shine.—Von Martius.

CORYPHA, Hexandria Monogynia. Takes its name from *koryphe*, the summit, in allusion to the uppermost leaves or fronds, which form immense fans. Gaert. 1, *t.* 7; Lam. Illust. *t.* 899.

1. C UMBRACULIFERA, Roxb. Fl. Ind. 2, p 177; Rheede Mal. *t.* 1 to 12; Rumph. 1, *t.* 8.—The Talipot Palm of Ceylon,

distinguishable by its large, spreading leaves. Mart. Palm 231. After the white inflorescence on the top has been fully developed, the tree dies. In Bombay, not common. We have seen one in a garden in Nesbit Lane, Mazagon, north side. In the town of Nagam, in Angrias Colaba, it is often to be seen in the gardens attached to the houses, and more thinly scattered in some other parts of Colaba; the leaves are used for writing on with an iron style, and the Ooria-bearers or Hamals in Calcutta may often be seen keeping their own or their master's accounts on these leaves. Be it noted that with the Oorias or Oripa men, the art of writing seems to be as common as it is in the Southern Konkun.

TALIERA, Mart., Hexandria Monogynia. Its vernacular name in Bengal.

2. T Bengalensis, Spr., Roxb. Fl. Ind. 2, p 174; Cor. Pl. 3, *t.* 25 to 256.—This Palm has been introduced into the Hewra Garden by seed from Calcutta. It is yet too small for original description (?). Is it to be found in Bombay, we have as yet failed to trace it?

OREODOXA, Willd. Mem. Acad. Berolin 1804, p 34; Mart. Palm 166, *t.* 156 to 163. *Oros*, mountain; *doxa*, glory. The glory of the mountain. Diœcia Decandria.

3. O Regia.—Native of Organ Mountain, Brazil; also of the Barbadoes. A very splendid Palm, with polished, straight, often acuminated, stem with terminal pinnate sheathing fronds unequally bifid at the apex. One tree is in the Society's Garden at Sewree. We have seen it nowhere else, and it has not borne fruit.

HYPHÆNE, Gaert., Diœcia Hexandria. From *hyphaino*, to entwine, alluding to the fibres on the fruit.

4. H Coriacea, Spr. H crinita thebaica, Delile.—The Doom Palm of the upper Thebaid; several branches, spreading from the roots with the broad fan-like leaves; fruit size of an apple or large potatoe, irregular and sublobed in shape. To this we refer B dichotomus in p 226 of the 1st edition of this Catalogue. A tree, in the garden at Sewree; ripens its seeds, which have exactly the taste of Ginger-bread; the fruit is commonly sold in the market of Grand Cairo. A plate of the tree may be seen on referring to Lord Valentia's Travels, vol. 4.

ARECA, Monœcia Hexandria. *Soopara*, said to be in the Malabar or Malay name latinised.

5. A Catechu, Roxb. Fl. Ind. 3, p 615; Rheede Mal. 1, *t.* 5 to 8; Rumph. Amb. 1, *t.* 1 to 4; Roxb. Cor. Pl. 1, *t.* 75.—The Betelnut Palm, extensively cultivated in garden-land near the coast within and more inland in Canara and Soonda. The Sooparee is extensively exported to the interior of India from all the places where it is grown on the coast.

GOMUTUS, Rumph. Monœcia Polyandria.

6. G SACCHARIFER, Spr. 2, p 624; Saguerus rumphii, Roxb. Fl. Ind. 3, p 626.—"Bhirlee," Maratha. A very stately Palm, with the aspect of the Cocoanut tree, but with leaves considerably large. The pith affords Sago; the sap, Palm-wine and sugar; and the black, horse-hair-like fibres of the trunk are converted into excellent cordage. See Marsden's History of Sumatra, and Crawford's Indian Archipelago. Near Cowasjee Patel's tank, Bombay. We find this tree has disappeared.

7. G —— (?) sp.—A Palm in Parell Garden, with smooth stem and pinnate leaves. What, and whence introduced?

8. CHAMŒROPS HUMILIS, Mart. Palm. 247.—A small specimen in Garden Dapoorie.

ACORUS, Linn., Hexandria Monogynia, Lam. *t.* 252; Gaert. 2, *t.* 84.

9. A CALAMUS, Roxb. Fl. 2, p 169; Rheede Mal. *t.* 48; Rumph. Amb. 5, *t.* 72, *f.* 1; Eng. Bot. *t.* 356.—Calamus aromaticus of the shops; Calamus veras of Willd. "Yekund," Hindoostanee. The Sweet Flag; is much cultivated in gardens for the medicinal, subaromatic qualities of its root. It is used by the natives as a febrifuge, but is chiefly valuable for the property which the roots have of defending woollen and flannel clothing from the attacks of insects. The Cobra-de-capello snake is said never to approach it, but whether this be a tradition or a fact we cannot say. As a febrifuge it is mixed with the seeds of Cassia tora.

CII.—GRAMINEÆ.

THE GRASS TRIBE, Lind. Nat. Syst. p 292; Loud. Hort. Brit. p 542.

HORDEUM, Triandria Digynia. The Latin name of *Barley*.

1. H HEXASTYCHON, Linn., Roxb. Fl. Ind. 1, p 358; Moris. Hist. 3, 5, 8, *t.* 6, *f.* 3.—"Satoo," Maratha; "Jow," Hindoostanee. Is cultivated to a considerable extent in the Deccan, chiefly as an offering to gods. In the north of Gujarat it is a common food. The plant grows best in alluvial patches of river-soil; usual selling price about 64 lbs. the rupee; makes much better broth than that made with the Pearl Barley imported from Europe, inasmuch as it is always fresher. The brewing of beer from malted Barley has been tried at Mahableshwur, Poona, and Kurrachee, but uniformly without success; the mean temperature being too high during fermentation. As usual, a good deal of money has been spent, and extensive correspondence taken place, regarding these trials. The Nilgherry experiment gives promise of better success.

TRITICUM, Triandria Digynia.

2. T ÆSTIVUM, Roxb. Fl. Ind. 1, p 359; T aristatum, Blackw. *t.* 40, *f.* 4 and 5.—"Gehoon," Hindoostanee and Marathi. The bearded Wheat is the variety most commonly grown in the Deccan, Gujarat, and Kandeish. The stem is seldom two feet high, and the produce in a given area not above a quarter that of Europe. One variety of unbearded Wheat is often cultivated; another "Khuplè" is only grown in irrigated land. It contains much more gluten than the others: selling price of Wheat is generally from 60 to 70 lbs. to the rupee.

3. T PILOSUM.—Bukshee Wheat, having the calices covered with much soft tomentum. From this and other differences it may be ventured to be quoted as a distinct species. It is always raised in irrigated land, and reaches a height of from 3 to 3½ feet. The grain abounds in starch, and is much longer and fuller than that of the others; selling price is generally 5 to 10 lbs. less than that of the others. On the high table-lands of the Deccan, as Mahableshwur, &c., Wheat is a common corp, and here the grain has, in a given bulk, about one-fifth more weight than that raised in the plains. Below the Ghauts, Wheat does not grow, as neither the soil nor climate suit it.

AVENA, Linn. Gen. No. 91; Hort. Grah. 2, *t.* 50.

4. A SATIVA.—The common Oat; is now pretty extensively grown in some parts (chiefly northern) of India; likewise near to European stations further south, as at Hudupseer, near Poona. It can be purchased there at the rate of 65 to 70 lbs. per rupee. It is often used for the feeding of horses, but as the paleaceous material is much more predominant than is the case in the Oat of Europe, it often gives rise to chronic cough and huskiness. Hence many prefer the Cicer arietinum, or Gram, to the Oat as a horse's food.

PASPALUM, Triandia Digynia. From the Greek name *Willet.*

5. P SCROBICULATUM, var. P Kodroo-Kora, Roxb. Fl. Ind. 1, p 278 and 279.—A very common and cheap grain, but not very wholesome; grown in the hill-lands of the Konkun, especially the variety Hurreek, which often induces temporary insanity and spasms, &c. Large numbers of people may be occasionally seen thus affected.

ELEUSINE, Gaert., Triandria Digynia. From *Eleusis,* near Athens, where games were celebrated in honour of Ceres.

6. E CORACANA, Nachnee Naglee-Ragee, Roxb. Fl. Ind. 1, p 342; C ryriosurus, Pluk. Alm. *t.* 9, *f.* 5; Rheed. Mal. 12, *t.* 78; Rumph. Amb. 5, *t.* 76, *f.* 2; Schreb. Gram. 2, *t* 35; Gaert. Fr. 1, *t.* 1; Pluk. Phyt. *t.* 91, *f.* 2.—Extensively cultivated in the Ghaut hills, and in the plains to 20 miles inland. The return from it is

great in proportion to the area. It is transplanted like rice; is a very productive crop: selling price may be quoted as being from 80 to lbs. 100 per rupee.

ORYZA, Linn., Hexandria Didynamia. From the Arabic *eraz* (?)

7. O SATIVA, Linn. Roxb. Fl. Ind. 2, 200.—Much cultivated throughout the Concan and the Ghaut Districts of Gujarat. The "Kummode" of Gujarat, and the "Ambeh Mohr" of the Ghauts, are the best varieties. It is generally grown by transplantation, though from the remarks of Hove it would appear that this practice has not been known for above 100 years. In the southern rice-lands, from the top of the Ghauts towards Belgaum, it is sown broad-cast, and left to grow. In many parts of Canara and Malabar three crops are commonly raised from the same ground. Rice is distinguished among the Grasses by having double the number of stamens.

PANICUM, Linn., Triandria Digynia. From *panis*, bread, as most of them produce grain from which Bread is made. Lam. Illust. *t.* 43; Gaert. Fr. 1, 71.

8. OPLISMENUS FRUMENTACEUS, P frumentaceum, Roxb. Fl. Ind. p 301.—" Shamoola," commonly grown in and near the Ghaut Districts, species with head nodding, smooth.

9. P ITALICUM, Roxb. Fl. Ind. 1, p 302; Setaria italica, R. Brown; Rheede. Mal. 12, *t.* 79; Rumph. Amb. 6, *t.* 5, *f.* 2; Hort. Gr. 4, *t.* 14.—Kangnee Kora-Kang; a small grain, cultivated in the Ghaut Districts; spikes little different from those of P frumentaceum.

10. P MILIACEUM.—" Wuree Sawa." This is also a Ghaut grain, having spikes shorter than those of the last species.

11. P PILOSUM.—" Badlee." Echinochloa hispidula. Is cultivated more inland than the former three species, and distinguishable by the long hairy rough spikes clustering all round the rachis.

12. P —— (?) sp.—" Rale"; much less hairy than the last, probably only a variety. The grain is deemed very nutritious, and is a favourite food in cases of exhaustion. Is also cultivated inland.

13. P —— (?) sp.—" Danglee"; has a lax cernuous panicle of awnless flowers. This also is more cultivated inland than in the Ghauts. We have not yet succeeded in fixing it as belonging to any of the species enumerated by Roxburgh. Is it a Panicum at all? Pencillaria spicata.

14. P ALTISSIMUM, P (?) Maximum guianiense, Sloanes Jam. p 106; Duchesne Pl. Utiles, p 16.—Guinea Grass; extensively cultivated in the West Indies, but sparingly in India, where the dryness of the climate does not admit of its being raised, except with the aid of shade or of frequent watering. The great abundance of

the Millet and other artificially raised Grasses prevents the loss being felt. It is, however, an excellent food for cattle when in milk. In the West Indies it is planted on the sides of hills and Savanna streams.

HOLCUS, Linn., Triandria Digynia. From *helko*, to draw, in allusion to the emollient property it has as a poultice to indurated tumours.

15. H SPICATUS.—"Bajri." This cultivated grain is the staff of life in the Deccan, Kandeish, and Gujarat. It does not grow in the Concans, but is extensively imported there from the more inland districts, and used as a food instead of rice, which, under the high run of prices, is exported. Bajri is best grown in brownish soil; the deep black does not suit it.

16. H SORGHUM, Roxb. Fl. Ind. 1, p 269. "Johndla," Marathi; "Juwarree," Hindoostane. Great Millet, Gaert. Fr. 2, *t.* 80, *f.* 2. Andropogon sorghum, Rumph. Amb. 5, *t.* 75.—A common food, especially in the Carnatic, Berar, &c. It generally sells about one-third cheaper than Bajri, being at from 70 to 90 lbs. per rupee. The stalks of this grain often reach a height of 15 feet and upwards.

17. H CERNUUS.—Shalloo; having its head of fruit drooping; extensively cultivated as a cold weather crop in Eastern Deccan, Gujarat, &c. The stalk, as a forage for cattle, is unsurpassed. It contains a great deal of saccharine matter, and is thus very nutritive. In the Broach Collectorate this Shaloo is grown in the Dejbarra and other districts, under the name "Soondia."

18. H SACCHARATUS.—"Imphee"; native of the Cape and China. Introduced two years ago as a plant for the production of sugar.

ANDROPOGON, Triandria Digynia. From *aner*, a man; and *pogen*, beard; in allusion to the tuft of hair on the flowers.

19. A SCHÆNANTHUS, Roxb. Fl. Ind. 1, 274; Rumph. Amb. 5, *t.* 72, *f.* 2; Wall. Pl. Ainslie rar. 3, *t.* 280; Rheed. Hort. Mal. 12, *t.* 72; Mors. Hist. 3, *t.* 8, *f.* 9 and 25.—The well known Lemon Grass cultivated in gardens; native of Ceylon and Malabar. With us the Hindoostanee name is "Wuolee Châ." It is much grown in gardens on account of its aromatic flavour. An infusion of it as a fever drink has great effect in inducing a remission or intermission by bringing on sweat.

SACCHARUM, Triandria Digynia. From the Arabic *sakur*, which has its root in the Sanskrit.

20. S OFFICINARUM, Roxb. Fl. Ind. 1, p 237; Rumph. Amb. 5, *t.* 74; Sloanes Jam. 1, *t.* 66.—This plant, the glory of the

Tropics, is cultivated throughout Western India. The varieties are numerous :—

1st.—The large, yellow, or Mauritius Cane.

2nd.—The common red.

3rd.—The Bamunee, or striped red and white.

4th.—The small, white, or reed Cane.

5th.—The black Egyptian variety first introduced by the Horticultural Society about 1840, and now (it is believed) is found only about Hewra. It is quite equal to the Mauritius Cane in size and juiciness.

The Mauritius Cane was imported and extensively distributed by Government 25 years ago, but its growth has not been continued to any extent, as it is found to require more water, and to be more liable to be gnawed and eaten by Jackals and Porcupines than the others. It is still, however, grown pretty largely in the low-lying lands near the Ghauts, where it can be raised without irrigation, also at Bassein, &c., as a Cane for eating. It affords an extract much superior in colour and firmness to that of the common Cane. Sugar is annually made from this variety at Hewra, in the Deccan.

ZEA, Linn., Monœcia Triandria. The Greek name for corn; from *zao*, to live.

21. Z Mays, Roxb. Fl. Ind. 3, p 567; Lam. Illust. *t.* 749.—"Boota," Maratha; "Mucca," Hindoostanee; Indian Corn; extensively grown in the early part of the rains, especially near large towns, where it affords a choice food for all classes, being sold ready roasted. The plant is also sown in the beginning of the hot season (20th March) to afford a forage for cattle, called Kuddol. At this time it is sown only for the straw, therefore very close. The grain is seldom used in India as a flour. Several large varieties of Maize have, at different times, been imported from America, but these gradually degenerate to the size of the common country species.

ADDENDA ET CORRIGENDA

TO SUPPLEMENT.

THE FOLLOWING LIST OF PLANTS, SHRUBS, AND FERNS, NEW TO WESTERN INDIA, WAS RECEIVED TOO LATE TO ALLOW OF THEIR BEING INSERTED IN THE BODY OF THE WORKS IN THEIR PROPER PLACES; THEY ARE, THEREFORE, ADDED HERE.

List of BATAVIAN FLOWER SEEDS AND FERNS *introduced in the Government House Garden, Parell,* 1860.

Abroma fastuosa.
Anaxagorea Javanica.
Cassia marginata.
Calliandra hæmatocephala.
,, sancti pala.
Climændra obovata.
,, var. petiol. purp.
Cloranthus officinale.
,, hirsutus.
Combretum grandiflorum.
Eletharia speciosa.
Grewia umbellata.
Hydrolea spinosa.
Ipomea rubens.
Nepenthes gracilis.
,, lævis.
Ondemansia viscida.
Saraca dechinata.
Scævola lobelia.
Solanthum atroanthum.
Pterolhoma triquetrum.
,, alatum.
Pæderea lanceolata.
Thea Bohea.
,, Cochin Chinensis.
,, viridis.

FILICES.

Acrostichum inæquata, *Wild.*
,, speciosum, *Bl.*
,, comosa, *Walln.*
Alsophila contaminans, *Walln.*
,, glabra, *Hook.*
,, cumulata, *Br.*
Aspidium superbescens, *Bl.*
,, vastum, *Bl.*
Asplenium abscissum, *Bl.*
,, furcatum, *Thunb.*
,, phyllitides, *Wldmr.*
,, squamulatum, *Bl.*
Angiopteris ankalana, *De Vr.*
,, Angustata, *Miq.*
,, Hartingeana, *De Vr.*
,, hypoleuca, *Ac. Vr.*

Angiopteris longifolia, *G. Hosk.*
„ Miqueliana, *De Vr.*
„ paninosa, *Kunze.*
Anisogonium decussatum, *Presl.*
„ integrifolium, *Do.*
Balantium chrysotrichum, *Linn.*
Blechnium orientale, *Linn.*
Campium repandum, *Presl.*
Cyclodium menniscoides, *Do.*
Cibotium Assamicum, *Hook.*
Davallia polypodioides, *Don.*
„ tenuifolia, *Sw.*
Diplazium alternifolium, *Presl.*
Digrammaria ambigua, *Do.*
„ aspera, *T. & B.*
„ marginata, *T. & B.*
„ dilatata, *T. & B.*
„ polypodioides, *T.&B.*
Dictyopteris irregularis, *Presl.*
Didimochlæna sinuosa, *DC.*
Diplazium umbrosum, *Wild.*
Grammitis obtusata, *Presl.*
Gymnogrammachrysophylla, *Kf.*
Lastrea abrupta, *Presl.*
„ coryugata, *T. & B.*
„ patens, *Presl.*
Marginariasubauriculata, *Haskl.*
Mardtia sylvatica, *Bl.*
Meniscium cuspidatum, *Bl.*
Nephrodium callosum, *Hsskl.*
„ lineatum, *Do.*
„ longipes, *Do.*
„ obscurum, *Do.*
„ unitum, *Schott.*
Nephrolepis davallioides, *Presl.*
Osmunda Javanica, *Bl.*
Pleopeltis affinis, *Hsskl.*
„ nigrescens, *Do.*
Pleocnewia Leuceana, *Presl.*
Phymatodes musæfolia, *Hsskl.*
„ gigantea, *Do.*
Pæcilopteris diversifolia, *Presl.*
„ hetroclita, *Do.*
Polypodium asperum, *Lipp.*
„ commutatum, *Bl.*
„ irregulare, *Bl.*
„ nigripes, *Hsskl.*
„ pteropus, *Bl.*
Pteris crenata, *Linn.*
„ dimidiata, *Wildnw.*
„ normalis, *Don.*
„ subverticillata, *Sw.*
Stenosemia aurita, *Presl.*
Tænites blechnoides, *Wild.*

Page 1, Nigella. It is believed, however, to be cultivated in the north of Gujarat.

Page 2, Anona Squamosa, *add* "Custard Apple."

Page 4, *insert*—No. 8, Sinapis, Tetradynamia Siliquosa.—Several species or varieties are cultivated in India, particularly in Gujarat and Central India, where the oil is extensively used under the name "Sircial." Our most common variety has ovate lanceolate-toothed and often runcinate leaves, with the heads of yellow flowers common to the tribe. In the Deccan it is commonly grown along with Wheat, and seldom or never sown alone. The seed is now extensively exported from Malwa.

Page 5, line 20, *for* "Ramonlii," *read* "Ramontii."
5, „ 22, „ "oval" „ "ovate."
7, „ 3, „ "uusd" „ "used."
7, „ 7, „ "Malavinsus," *read* "Malaviscus."

Page 8, line 37, *for* "Barbadeuse," *read* "Barbadense."
9, „ 18, „ "Gonik" „ "Goruk."
10, „ 2, „ "rumous," „ "ramous."
10, Kleinhovia Hospita, *vide* remark in page 23, Part 1st, Gardens Dapoorie and Hewra.
12, line 5 from bottom, *for* "Tinct." *read* "Tincture."
20, „ 35, *for* "Floræ," *read* "Flore."
23, „ 19, *omit* "Dolichos Uniflorus," its place being supplied by Johnia Conjesta.
25, line 10, *for* "Anœna," *read* "Amœna."
26, „ 24, „ "Julibisrin," „ "Julibrissin."

LEGUMINOSÆ, p 24.

LOTUS, DC. *Prod.* 2, p 210.

(*Amended description.*)

Page 26. 32.—L Jacobeus. A suffruticose plant, native of the West Indies (?), having small linear mucronate leaves on short peduncles, with a handsome dark-purple flower and yellow vexillum. In gardens, rare. Our seeds were received from the Cape; legume narrow, subrotund, many-seeded.

Page 31, *insert*—No. 89, Bauhinia Porrecta. A small tree, lobes of the leaves deeply incised and very divergent; flower small, white, having the laciniæ of the corolla 5-lobed; style very long, curved; has not seeded. Garden Dapoorie from seed received from Calcutta.

ACACIA, p 26.

(*Add* the following.)

51 a. A Rugosæ Affinis.—Seed received from the late Dr. Wallich, under this name; legume 2 inches long, scabrous, prominent and rugose over the seeds, which are large and subrotund. The plant is a strong woody climber sparingly armed with recurved broad-based thorns; common petioles long, glandless; leaflets blunt, shining, about 18 pair, no medial glands; common petiole much swelled at insertion into the common stem. Has been 12 years in growth, but has never yet flowered. Garden Hewra.

Page 33, line 19, *for* "burrat," *read* "laciniæ bright purple."
33, „ 27, „ "Malaccas" *read* "Moluccas."
34, „ 7 from bottom, *add* "Aromaticus," *after* "Caryophyllus."
35, line 10, *for* "lenkos," *read* "leukos."

Page 35, in Onagrariæ, *add* as No. 3 the Fuschias as follows :—

FUCHSHIA, Octandria Monogynia, DC. C. Dolu *Prod.* 3, 36. Name given from *Fuchsh*, a German Botanist, who first introduced these beautiful plants from South America.

FUCHSHIA FULGEUS, F Globosa, F Villosa. These and several other species, conspicuous by their crimson and scarlet flowers, occasionally beautifully variegated with white and purple, are now not uncommonly found in conservatories in India. They are generally distinguishable by their opposite petiolated leaves mostly smooth, but sometimes villous or pilose, and by the lengthened lobes of the calyces, and the unique beauty of their flowers. We have not seen the plants produce seed in this climate.

Page 36, line 10 from the bottom, *for* "Pentandria," *read* "Pentandra."

38, line 13, *for* "fœtidia," *read* "fœtida."
38, „ 3 from bottom, *for* "Spendens," *read* "Splendens."
46, „ 20, *for* "Sagitata," *read* "Sagittata."
47, „ 15, „ "Paludosam," „ "Paludosum."
48, „ 1, „ "Emargmala," „ "Emarginata."
50, „ 26, „ "two," „ "three."
52, „ 33, „ "Disfontain's," „ "Desfontains."
57, „ 22, „ "Schrib," „ "Schreber."
58, „ 6, „ "Proboscidla," „ "Proboscidea."
58, „ 4 from bottom, *for* "rubo-cœrulea," *read* "rubro-cœrulea.

Page 63, in "Lycium Afrum," *add*—We have lately seen this shrub flower at Dapoorie; flowers long-tubed, of a rich purple, very ornamental.

Page 63, line 25, *for* "Schizantus venusthus," *read* "Schizanthus venustus."

Page 64, line 16, *for* "Anterrhinum," *read* "Antirrhinum."

Page 65, Browallia Cervias Rowski, *transfer* to p 63 as No. 17A, *after* Browallia Elongata.

Page 84, Zamia.—We have reason to believe now that the second species is in reality not different from the first, but merely more luxuriant and better developed, owing to climate and soil.

INDEX TO SUPPLEMENT.

M

N

O

P